Game Theory and the Environment

Game Theory and the Environment

Edited by
Nick Hanley

Professor of Natural Resource Economics, Institute of Ecology and Resource Management, University of Edinburgh, Scotland, UK

Henk Folmer

Professor of Economics, Wageningen Agricultural University, The Netherlands and Professor of Environmental Economics, Tilburg University, The Netherlands

Edward Elgar
Cheltenham, UK • Northampton, MA, USA

© N. Hanley and H. Folmer, 1998

All rights reserved. No part of this publication may be reproduced, stored in a retrieval system or transmitted in any form or by any means, electronic, mechanical or photocopying, recording, or otherwise without the prior permission of the publisher.

Published by
Edward Elgar Publishing Limited
8 Lansdown Place
Cheltenham
Glos GL50 2HU
UK

Edward Elgar Publishing Company, Inc.
6 Market Street
Northampton
Massachusetts 01060
USA

A catalogue record for this book is available from the British Library

Library of Congress Cataloguing in Publication Data
Game theory and the environment / edited by Nick Hanley, Henk Folmer.
  Includes index.
   1. Natural resources—Management. 2. Environmental economics.
  3. Game theory. I. Hanley, Nick. II. Folmer, Henk. 1945–   .
HC26.G35   1998
333.7—dc21   97–52041
                                                                              CIP

ISBN 1 85898 415 7

Printed and bound in Great Britain by
Biddles Limited, Guildford and King's Lynn

Contents

List of figures	vii
List of tables	viii
Contributors	xi
Foreword	xiv

1. Game-theoretic modelling of environmental and resource problems: an introduction 1
   Henk Folmer, Nick Hanley and Fanny Mißfeldt

2. Cooperation versus free-riding in international environmental affairs: two approaches 30
   Henry Tulkens

3. Dynamic resolution of inefficiency due to international environmental externalities 45
   Mark B. Cronshaw

4. Commitment and fairness in environmental games 65
   Tim Jeppesen and Per Andersen

5. Acid rain and international environmental aid: transboundary air pollution between Finland, Russia and Estonia 84
   Veijo Kaitala and Matti Pohjola

6. Nuclear power games 98
   Fanny Mißfeldt

7. Renegotiation-proof equilibria in a bargaining game over global emission reductions – does the instrumental framework matter? 135
   Alfred Endres and Michael Finus

8. Linking environmental and non-environmental problems in an international setting: the interconnected games approach 165
   Jardena Kroeze-Gil and Henk Folmer

9. Strategies for environmental negotiations: issue linkage with heterogenous countries 181
   Michele Botteon and Carlo Carraro

10. Environmental conflicts and interconnected games: an experimental note on institutional design 204
    Stephan Kroll, Charles F. Mason and Jason F. Shogren

11. Environmental conflicts with asymmetric information: theory and behaviour 219
    Terrance M. Hurley and Jason F. Shogren

12. International dynamic pollution control 237
    Art de Zeeuw

13. Learning about global warming 255
    Alistair Ulph

14. Migration and the environment 287
    Markus Haavio

15. Strategic international trade and transboundary pollution: a dynamic model 310
    Talitha Feenstra

16. Going green or going abroad? Environmental policy, firm location and green consumerism 341
    Michael Kuhn

17. A game-theoretic approach to the roundwood market with capital stock determination 392
    Erkki Koskela and Markku Ollikainen

Index 415

List of figures

1.1	Pollution abatement under full cooperation, Nash and business as usual (BAU)	10
3.1	Unidirectional externality – indifference curves	49
3.2	Unidirectional externality – utilities	51
3.3	Bilateral externality	54
3.4	Symmetric equilibria	57
4.1	The prisoners' dilemma in a global CO_2 agreement	67
4.2	Number of signatories out of 100 for various values of c and b, homogeneous countries	70
4.3	Environmental game for two agents	76
6.1	Ranking of solutions for the West	113
6.2	Ranking of solutions for the East	114
7.1	Aggregate equilibrium emission levels in the five regimes	149
7.2	Comparative analysis of aggregate welfare	151
11.1	Extensive form game	222
11.2	Actual and predicted experimental game dynamics	230
11.3	Proportions of the maximum obtainable rewards by session and period	232
13.1	First-period emissions with learning and no learning	262
13.2	Why expected marginal cost with learning is less than with no learning	262
13.3	Welfare for *ON*, *OL*, *CN*, *CL* as functions of correlation coefficient	275
17.1	Stable Nash equilibrium	399
17.2	Comparative statics of the Nash equilibrium	400

List of tables

1.1	Static game-theory concepts applied to international environmental problems	5
1.2	Rules for redistribution of gains	7
1.3	Reducing the incentive to free-ride	17
4.1	The size of an IEA, global abatement and global net benefits with homogeneous countries	71
4.2	Stability analysis, hypothetical example, homogeneous countries	73
4.3	Committed countries and the expanded coalitions	74
4.4	Global net benefits with fairness incorporated	79
5.1	Sulphur emissions and depositions in 1980 and 1987	86
5.2	Sulphur transportation matrix for the year 1987	87
5.3	Abatement cost function parameters	89
5.4	Marginal abatement (MC) and damage (MD) costs	91
5.5	The consequences of cooperation and its annual monetary benefits	93
5.6	Estonian damage costs and the benefits from cooperation	94
6.1	Proxies for economic bargaining power	109
6.2	Nash bargaining shares x (in %) in different scenarios	111
6.3	Scenario 0.0	117
6A.1	Risk abatement in absolute terms in the East	128
6A.2	Risk abatement in absolute terms in the East	128
6A.3	Risk abatement in absolute terms in the West	128
6A.4	Risk abatement in absolute terms in the West	129
6A.5	Total risk abatement in absolute terms	129
6A.6	Total risk abatement in absolute terms	129
6A.7	Utility derived by the East as percentage difference from what could be reached under Nash	130
6A.8	Utility derived by the West as percentage difference from what could be reached under Nash	130
6A.9	Total utility as percentage difference from what could be reached under Nash	130
6A.10	Utility derived by the East as percentage difference from what could be reached under Nash	131

List of tables ix

6A.11	Utility derived by the West as percentage difference from what could be reached under Nash	131
6A.12	Total utility as percentage difference from what could be reached under Nash	131
6A.13	Normal forms of the static game: scenario 1.1	132
6A.14	Normal forms of the static game: scenario 1.2	132
6A.15	Normal forms of the static game: scenario 1.3	132
6A.16	Normal forms of the static game: scenario 1.4	132
6A.17	Normal forms of the static game: scenario 1.5	132
6A.18	Normal forms of the static game: scenario 1.6	132
6A.19	Normal forms of the static game: scenario 1.7	133
6A.20	Normal forms of the static game: scenario 1.8	133
6A.21	Normal forms of the static game: scenario 2.1	133
6A.22	Normal forms of the static game: scenario 2.2	133
6A.23	Normal forms of the static game: scenario 2.3	133
6A.24	Normal forms of the static game: scenario 2.4	133
6A.25	Normal forms of the static game: scenario 2.5	134
6A.26	Normal forms of the static game: scenario 2.6	134
6A.27	Normal forms of the static game: scenario 2.7	134
6A.28	Normal forms of the static game: scenario 2.8	134
7A.1	Emission levels under the quota regime	158
7A.2	Emission levels under the tax regime	159
7A.3	Emission levels under the permit regime	160
7A.4	Comparative static analysis of aggregate emission levels with respect to the damage parameter	161
9.1	Countries' data set	191
9.2	Stable coalitions – Nash bargaining burden-sharing rule	193
9.3	Stable coalitions – Shapley value burden-sharing rule	193
9.4	Stable and optimal coalitions with 'issue linkage'	194
9.5	The effect of increasing asymmetries in R&D costs	197
9A.1	Internally stable coalition ranking (Nash bargaining)	202
9A.2	Internally stable coalition ranking (Shapley value)	202
9A.3	Internally stable coalition ranking (Nash bargaining)	202
9A.4	Internally stable coalition ranking (Shapley value)	202
9A.5	Internally stable coalition ranking (Nash bargaining)	203
10.1a	The trade game	206
10.1b	The pollution game	206
10.2	The joint institution	207
10.3a	Parallel games in the experiment	208
10.3b	Parallel games in the experiment	208
10.4	Joint game in the experiment	208
10.5a	Outcome frequencies in treatments without cheap talk	209

10.5b	Action frequencies in treatments without cheap talk	209
10.6a	Outcome frequencies in the binding stages of the treatments with parallel institutions	211
10.6b	Action frequencies in the binding stages of the treatments with parallel institutions	211
10.7a	Action frequencies in binding and cheap talk stages of the treatment with parallel institutions and cheap talk (all periods)	212
10.7b	Action frequencies in binding and cheap talk stages of the treatment with parallel institutions and cheap talk (periods 1–10)	213
10.8a	Outcome frequencies in the binding stages of the treatments with a joint institution (all periods)	214
10.8b	Outcome frequencies in the binding stages of the treatments with a joint institution (periods 11–20)	214
10.9	Outcome frequencies in the binding stages of treatments with cheap talk	215
11.1	Subject strategies by group and period	228
12.1	Bi-matrix games for three states in period 2	243
12.2	Bi-matrix game of periods without and with expected costs of period 2	243
12.3	Bi-matrix game for two periods at once	244
13.1	States of the world	269
13.2	Value of information	282
16.1	Strategic form representation of technology/location stage for $(r_A = r_B = 0)$	355
16.2	Strategic form representation of the technology/location stage for $(r_A = 1, r_B = 0)$	359
16.3	Strategic form representation of the policy stage of the game for the relocation case	364
16.4	Strategic form representation of the policy stage of the game for the non-relocation case	367
17.1	Comparative statics of the Nash equilibrium	401
17.2	FIML estimation results of the capital stock–timber price system	405
17.3	OLS estimation results of alternative timber demand equations	407

Contributors

Nick Hanley
Institute of Ecology and Resource Management
University of Edinburgh
Edinburgh
Scotland

Henk Folmer and Jardena Kroeze-Gil
Department of Economics
Wageningen Agricultural University
The Netherlands

Henry Tulkens
CORE
Louvain-la-Neuve
Belgium

Mark B. Cronshaw
Environment and Behavior Program
Economics Institute
Boulder, Colorado
USA

Tim Jeppesen and Per Andersen
Economics Department
University of Odense
Denmark

Veijo Kaitala and Matti Pohjola
Systems Analysis Laboratory
Helsinki University of Technology
Espoo
Finland

Fanny Mißfeldt
Energy and Environment Programme
Royal Institute of International Affairs
London
England

Alfred Endres and Michael Finus
Fachbereich Wirtschaftswissenschaft
Fern Universität
Germany

Carlo Carraro and Michele Botteon
Fondazione Eni Enrico Mattei
Milan
Italy

Stephan Kroll, Charles F. Mason and Jason F. Shogren
Department of Economics and Finance
University of Wyoming
USA

Terrance M. Hurley
Center for Agriculture and Rural Development
Department of Economics
Iowa State University
Des Moines
Iowa
USA

Art de Zeeuw
CENTER
Tilburg University
The Netherlands

Alistair Ulph
Economics Department
University of Southampton
England

Markus Haavio
Department of Economics
University of Helsinki
Finland

Talitha Feenstra
CENTER
Tiiburg University
The Netherlands

Michael Kuhn
Economics Department
University of Rostock
Germany

Erkki Koskela and Markku Ollikainen
Dept of Economics
University of Helsinki
Finland

Foreword

Game theory has become an indispensable part of the environmental and resource economist's tool box. Since Mäler's 'Acid Rain Game' the number of studies applying game theory in these fields has rapidly increased. Despite this increase no book exists which presents an overview of the possibilities that game theory offers in analysing environmental problems. The present volume aims to fill this niche.

This book is aimed at two audiences. First, at economists and students of economics who have no background or experience in environmental game theory and applications, but who would like to 'get into' the area. Second, for those currently working in environmental game theory the book provides a collection of state-of-the-art contributions in the area (although we do not pretend to have covered all aspects of the literature).

The chapters in this book have been written by some of the foremost authorities in game-theory applications in environmental economics, but also by some of the 'new generation' of post-doctoral researchers in Europe and the US who are just starting to make a name for themselves. In almost all cases, the contributions were specially written for this book. They cover many different aspects of the application of game theory to the environment.

The editors (Nick Hanley and Henk Folmer) would like to thank all the authors for their cooperation in putting the book together and their willingness to participate in the project. We would also like to thank Edward Elgar and Dymphna Evans for their patience. Thanks also to Yue Ma (University of Stirling) for comments on an earlier draft of parts of Chapter 1. Nick Hanley would like to thank Kerstin Schneider of the Economics Department, University of Dortmund for helping him get the project off the ground: this book is partly her fault, and so he would like to dedicate the book to her and to Sebastian. Finally, Henk Folmer would like to thank the Department of Energy, Environmental and Mineral Economics at Penn State University for the stimulating environment in which he carried out his work on this book.

Nick Hanley
Henk Folmer

1. Game-theoretic modelling of environmental and resource problems: an introduction

Henk Folmer, Nick Hanley and Fanny Mißfeldt

1. ABOUT THIS BOOK

Many of the major environmental problems facing the world today have one particular feature in common. This is that they involve strategic interactions and interdependencies between economic agents. For example, the problem of global warming is added to by all countries in the world, each contributing to this global externality. In order to achieve significant reductions in global warming, many countries will have to reduce their emissions of greenhouse gases such as carbon dioxide and methane. Yet the global public-good aspects of pollution reduction mean that each country has an incentive to free-ride on the actions of its neighbour. Putting together world agreements for cuts in greenhouse gas emissions has proved to be a difficult task. These strategic interdependencies can also exist in domestic environmental problems and policy, for example, in terms of the interaction between firms and regulators in the setting and enforcement of environmental standards, and interactions between firms in tradable pollution permit markets. *Game theory* has been developed as a powerful set of tools for analysing such problems, and is what this book is concerned with.

The book has been written for the attention of several audiences. First, it is aimed at economists and students of economics who have no background or experience in environmental game theory and applications, but who would like to 'get into' the area. Second, the book is aimed at those currently working in environmental games, as a collection of state-of-the-art contributions in the area (although we do not pretend to have covered all aspects of the literature). An important point to note is that we have not tried to explain the basic concepts of pure game theory in this book. This is for two reasons: (i) to do a good job, we would have to take up a lot of valuable space; and (ii) several excellent introductions to game theory already exist. The reader is directed, for instance, to Gibbons (1992), Binmore (1992) and Bierman and Fernandez (1995). For a more formal treatment, the best reference is probably still Fudenberg and Tirole (1991). Those looking for a historical perspective will be interested by Luce and Raiffa (1957) and Schelling (1960).

This volume consists of a set of contributions that reflect the 'state of the art' in the application of game theory to environmental economics. A major part of game-theoretic applications in environmental and resource economics is related to international environmental problems. This is reflected by the fact that 14 out of the 17 contributions included in this book deal with this topic. However, we have attempted to include work that not only elaborates upon the existing kinds of problems and applies well-established approaches, but which also deals with new areas or applies new notions and methods.

In the remainder of this introductory chapter, we first of all make some general comments about game-theory applications in environmental economics. Next, we present a brief but thorough overview of the literature on international environmental problems up to the present. Finally, we preview the contents of the rest of the book.

2. WHY GAME THEORY?

Game theory has become an indispensable tool in environmental and resource economics. Since Mäler's (1989) 'acid rain game', the number of publications applying game theory in this field has increased rapidly. The reason is that the typical features of many environmental problems can be most adequately handled by means of game-theoretic notions and models. These provide a comprehensive framework for the analysis of the fundamental cause of environmental problems: multi-actor decision making in situations characterized by the lack of property rights and the existence of externalities. Such situations occur both at the national and the international level, and at both levels game theory has been successfully applied.

Applications of game theory to environmental and resource problems can be broadly grouped into three categories:

- international environmental problems
- competition
- asymmetric information and principal–agent theory.

International Environmental Problems

This type of pollution problem, where more than one country is affected by pollution, and where many countries are responsible for emissions, is known as transboundary pollution, and constitutes the main area of study and application for game theory. The basic feature of this kind of problem is the absence of an institution with the international jurisdiction to enforce environmental policy. The key issue is the analysis of the gains associated with international cooperation, and ways of achieving this cooperation. Global warming, depletion of the ozone layer, acid deposition, river and marine pollution and risks from nuclear accidents are all examples of the kind of environmental problems considered in this area of the literature.

Competition

Like the previous area, this subfield is also characterized by the absence of an institution with the jurisdiction to enforce policy. Contrary to the former, however, where the emphasis is on cooperation, the emphasis here is on competition. A distinction can be made between competition among firms and competition between countries and regions. Whereas competition among firms traditionally took place in terms of price and quantity setting, recently environmental management has become an important element of competitive strategy. The key issue of competition among countries and regions is ecological dumping. This is based on the assumption that imperfectly competitive markets allow producers to earn rents, which provides incentives for governments to try to shift these rents in favour of their domestic producers.

Asymmetric Information and Principal–Agent Theory

Typically, this is concerned with an institution with the jurisdiction to implement and enforce environmental policy. Two subcategories can be distinguished, namely public and private environmental policy making. In the former case, the government is the institution with the jurisdiction to enforce environmental policy. It is the regulatory agency, as agent, which executes policies and supervises the regulative process. The regulatory agency in its turn is the principal for industry, consumers and other interest groups. The second subcategory relates to environmental policy making at the firm level. The key issue here is to analyse systems of corporate incentives and controls in order to promote a firm's environmental performance.

In addition, applications and theories can be classified according to whether they are concerned with static (one-shot) or dynamic (repeated) games, and by the number of players involved and what those players know about payoffs and actions.

3. A REVIEW OF THE LITERATURE ON APPLYING GAME THEORY TO ENVIRONMENTAL PROBLEMS

Since game-theory applications in environmental economics have largely focused on transboundary pollution problems, this section concentrates on this part of the literature. One of the first attempts to estimate actual spillovers from transboundary pollution was undertaken by Mäler (1989) for the case of acid rain in Europe.

An important distinction in the literature on international environmental problems is that between axiomatic, or cooperative, game theory and non-cooperative game theory. If it is possible for players to make binding agreements, a cooperative outcome can be implemented. In cooperative game theory, the focus of analysis is the coalition of players, its stability and its characteristic function (that is, the total of net benefits that the coalition can achieve for itself). In contrast, non-cooperative game theory focuses on the individual player who maximizes a net benefit function subject to the net benefit maximizing behaviour of the other players, and various technical and economic constraints. The main focus is thereby on the analysis of different strategies available to players with the help of which they may improve on their current state, always taking into account the strategic reaction of opponents or co-players. In reality, and especially in the inter-country context, cooperation is extremely difficult to bring about, because a free-rider problem occurs even if cooperative solutions exist. Consequently non-cooperative outcomes often result.

Cooperation, Coalitions and the Sharing of Gains

A *full-cooperative solution* is one which would result if a central planner was to optimize the welfare of all countries with respect to the control of transboundary pollution, whereby the total marginal damage over all countries equals each country's marginal cost. The technical conditions necessary for full cooperation to hold in a static context are stated in Table 1.1. The outcome of such action is 'full-cooperative' in the sense that it optimizes the overall situation. This is also known as the Samuelson (1954) condition for public goods. Taken together, all the countries involved are better off under full cooperation than under any other solution concept. However, individual countries might lose out in comparison with non-cooperation, unless the overall gains from cooperation are shared.

Full cooperation is purely a point of reference and by no means constitutes an equilibrium. This is so for two reasons. First, full cooperation does not imply that every country individually is better off. Some countries may lose out under cooperation unless the gains from cooperation are redistributed, through the use of side payments, for instance. Side payments are redistributions of income

Table 1.1 Static game-theory concepts applied to international environmental problems

Type of Analysis		Business as usual	Nash equilibrium	Full cooperation	Pareto dominance
Cost–benefit analysis	Payoff function	$\min_i (AC_i)$	$\max_i (D_i - AC_i)$	$\max_i \sum_{i=1}^{N}(D_i - AC_i)$	$\max_i \sum_{i=1}^{N}(D_i - AC_i)$ $U^p \geq U^n$
	Solution	$MAC_i = 0$	$MD_i = MAC_i$	$\sum_{i=1}^{N} MD_i = MAC_i$	$\sum_{i=1}^{N} MD_i = MAC_i$ $U^p \geq U^n$
Cost-efficiency	Payoff function	$\min_i (AC_i)$	$\min_i (AC_i)$ subject to a pollution constraint	$\min_i \sum_{i=1}^{N} AC_i$ subject to a pollution constraint	$\min_i \sum_{i=1}^{N} AC_i$ subject to a pollution constraint, and $U^p \geq U^n$
	Solution	$MAC_i = 0$	$MAC_i = \lambda$ which fulfils a pollution constraint	$\sum_{i=1}^{N} MAC_i = \lambda$ which fulfils a pollution constraint	$\sum_{i=1}^{N} MAC_i = \lambda$ which fulfils a pollution constraint, and $U^p \geq U^n$

Notes: The subscripts i stand for country i and N for the total number of countries. The superscripts p and n stand for the type of solution concept: p denoting Pareto dominance, and n the Nash outcome. MAC denotes marginal abatement costs and MD marginal damage. U is the payoff or utility function across all players while U_i stands for the payoff of player i alone. P stands for the pollution-flow in the time considered, D denotes damage and AC abatement costs. λ is the shadow value of the abatement constraint.

from countries which gain under an agreement to countries that lose out. Second, all countries have a free-rider incentive, because they would in general still be better off by not cooperating: while they would incur lower or zero abatement costs, they would at the same time enjoy the pollution abatement brought about by the cooperating countries. Free-riding refers, in this context, to situations where countries take advantage of other countries' abatement efforts. For example, if one country free-rides on the greenhouse gas abatement efforts of other countries, this implies that this country will benefit fully from the others' efforts, but will at the same time not incur any additional costs. However, it should be noted that not all transboundary pollution problems are pure public goods: acid rain, for example, is rival in consumption. Therefore there exists some 'selfish' interest in pollution abatement in a country suffering from acid rain.

Besides the full-cooperative solution, 'Pareto-dominant' outcomes have been evaluated by, for example, Mäler (1989). Folmer and Musu (1992) also refer to the 'Pareto-dominant' outcome as the 'constrained social optimum'. According to this concept the objective function is optimized under the constraint that no country should be worse off with than without cooperation. Hence, such a solution would make all countries at least as well off as they were before. Like full cooperation – and for the same reasons – the Pareto-dominant outcome does not constitute an equilibrium. Furthermore, the gains from a Pareto-dominant outcome are lower than the gains from full cooperation.

Another way of guaranteeing that all parties are at least as well off as before cooperation is to redistribute the additional gain from (full) cooperation via side payments. With the help of negotiations, a procedure for reallocation can be selected that is acceptable to all parties. The basis defined by such negotiations is the section on the full-cooperation hyperplane where all parties are at least as well off as at the *Nash equilibrium*. The Nash equilibrium results when countries choose their (optimal) abatement strategies in reaction to the choice of abatement strategies of all other countries. It is the best state that a country can reach in the absence of cooperation, in maximizing its own self-interest. The Nash equilibrium is sometimes referred to as a 'threat point': if cooperation cannot be agreed upon, the Nash situation will result.

Several allocative mechanisms of gain sharing have been put forward, and an overview of them is given in Table 1.2. These mechanisms can be compared on the basis of various properties, such as individual rationality, group rationality, and Pareto optimality, which they may or may not fulfil. Individual rationality means that a single party cannot be better off by using a given strategy. Group rationality implies that no coalition or subgroup of countries can be better off by taking some alternative action, whilst Pareto optimality means that the biggest efficiency gain is achieved.

Table 1.2 Rules for redistribution of gains

Rules	Individual rationality	Group rationality	Pareto optimality
Equity-based rule	No	No	No
Shapley value	Yes	Yes	Yes
Nash bargaining solution	No	No	Yes
Chander–Tulkens cost-sharing rule	Yes	Yes	Yes
Kalai–Smorodinsky solution	Yes	No	No
Stable coalition	Yes	No	Possible

In actual negotiations of international environmental agreements allocative rules which take account of equity considerations are very popular. Barrett (1992a) proposes three types of equity-based rules: uniform percentage reduction, uniform per capita allocation and uniform per Gross National Product (GNP) allocation. In practice, uniform percentage abatement with respect to a specified base year has been used most, for example within the Montreal Protocol and within the Climate Change Convention. Equity-based rules are generally inefficient.

The notion of a 'stable coalition', as developed in this framework by Carraro and Siniscalco (1993), also targets the redistribution of gains from cooperation with the strategic aim of enlarging a nucleus of already cooperating countries. A stable coalition is one where, for all parties in the coalition, there is no incentive to defect from the coalition and, for all parties outside the coalition, no incentive to join. Such a group of countries may be thought of as a group of environmental 'forerunners' if they are the first to develop a given environmental policy. Carraro and Siniscalco (1993) show that such coalitions exist in the global pollution context, and that they involve a small fraction of negotiating countries. However, no economic justification for the formation of such a coalition is given. The authors show that the gains from partial cooperation of this subgroup can be used to expand the coalition. If countries are not identical, side payments can be found to increase the stable coalition so as to make even full cooperation among all players 'stable' (Botteon and Carraro, 1995). The stable coalition is always individually rational, albeit not group-rational. This is the case because if individuals not part of the coalition join the coalition, the enlarged group can be better off. The outcome is only Pareto-optimal if all parties are in cooperation, thus forming the 'grand coalition'. Tulkens (Chapter 2, this volume) gives indications about the size of the transfer required to enlarge the stable coalition.

Hoel and Schneider (1995) analyse a scheme which incorporates the idea of social norms. They find that while a coalition may be increased through side payments, the prospect of receiving a transfer for reducing emissions of non-cooperating countries may create an incentive for them initially to stay out of cooperation (see also Folmer, van Mouche and Ragland, 1993). What is more, total emissions may be higher if such a scheme is implemented. Petrakis and Xepapadeas (1994) use a similar framework. They go on to analyse the situation when it is not possible, or very costly, to measure each country's contribution to global pollution, as is the case for climate change. This creates a supplementary enforcement problem to which the authors suggest a theoretically possible solution. Along more practical lines, joint implementation can be thought of as a tool to extend abatement efforts, as it is, for example, in the Kyoto Protocol to the Climate Change Convention.

Other rules suport the idea that countries should receive payments in proportion to their contribution to the full-cooperative outcome. They reward each country for coordination according to its contribution to the net gain. An example of such rules, which have been applied to the analysis of transboundary pollution, is the Shapley value. It attributes to every player in the game a payoff which corresponds to that player's contribution to the (potential) gain from full cooperation. The Shapley value fulfils group rationality and a number of other properties such as symmetry and additivity. Barrett (1992a) evaluates Shapley values for the case of climate change. However, he rejects the use of the Shapley value on the basis that it is in practice very difficult to evaluate.

The Chander–Tulkens (1991) cost-sharing rule was developed especially for the context of international negotiations on transboundary pollution. Technically speaking, it is based on the game-theoretic concept of a 'core' on to which a dynamic process has been attached. While the Shapley value was only used in a static framework, the Chander–Tulkens rule applies over time. The Chander–Tulkens cost-sharing rule is based on literature about dynamic processes for public goods and aims at devising a trajectory of feasible allocations that converge to a Pareto optimum. Their rule implies that at every stage in time the process of pollution abatement is locally strategically stable. This means in this context that no coalition of players can generate for itself a larger payoff along the path to the Pareto optimum. This property is also called 'time consistency'. Application of the Chander–Tulkens rule, however, requires (as in the case of the Shapley value) information about each country's willingness to pay for a marginal improvement in environmental quality as well as knowledge about marginal abatement costs. Both types of information are certainly not readily available, mainly because of difficulty in evaluation and unwillingness by players to reveal the truth.

The Nash bargaining solution has been put forward to determine the distribution of gains among countries, for example by Bartsch (1992), Escapa and Gutierrez (1995), Heister (1993) and Kuhl (1987). The rule distributes the gains from cooperation minus the conflict payoffs to players in equitable shares. The Nash bargaining solution fulfils a series of desirable properties: it is Pareto-optimal, independent of the units in which it is accounted for, independent of irrelevant alternatives, and symmetric. Symmetry here means that the solution is not affected by who the player is (Rasmussen, 1989). Unlike the core and the Shapley value, which may be 'empty' or alternatively yield a wealth of solutions, the Nash bargaining solution generates a unique outcome. Although it is a static concept, its outcome has been shown to correspond to the solution of a bargaining process as described by Zeuthen (Harsanyi, 1977, p.152). It usually requires further specification of asymmetries in preferences, disagreement points and players' beliefs about the environment in the construction of relevant threat points. Asymmetries in players' time preferences can also be incorporated. A shortcoming of the Nash bargaining solution is that its evaluation becomes quickly quite complex when more than two players are involved.

Finally, the Kalai–Smorodinsky solution has been evaluated by Escapa and Gutierrez (1995). Instead of using full cooperation as a point of reference, this uses the best outcome for each country that is consistent with individual rationality. The solution concept is based on the Nash bargaining solution, but here the outcome is individually rational. However, this property is traded off against Pareto optimality. The solution is still better (or at least equally good) as a non-cooperative outcome. Unfortunately, as is the case for the Nash bargaining solution, group rationality is not achieved.

Mechanisms or instruments to implement allocative rules, such as the Chander–Tulkens rule and the Shapley value, could be an international tax, an international tradable permit scheme or mechanisms based on the ability to pay of the countries involved. Transfers need not be made in monetary terms. Folmer, van Mouche and Ragland (1993) and Cesar (1994), for instance, analyse the scope of technology transfers. When talking about side payments, one should, however, keep in mind that side payments seem to endorse a victim pays principle (VPP), since they generally entail polluting countries being bribed to reduce their emissions. Officially, however, the polluter pays principle is the legal basis for international agreements within the OECD. It is not easy to assess what the net consequences of an explicit switch to the VPP would be, because it may create an incentive to maintain or increase pollution in anticipation of side payments (Folmer, van Mouche and Ragland, 1993).

The Possible Gains from Cooperation and the Base Case

Full cooperation certainly constitutes the first-best solution, and thus the upper limit of what is achievable in terms of international negotiations. But is there also a lower limit which could serve as a point of reference for comparison? Some environmental economists (Mäler, 1989; Barrett, 1992a) take it to be the Nash equilibrium. Given the emissions of all other countries, each country maximizes its net benefit and chooses the abatement level so that the marginal damage equals its marginal cost. But this implies that the public is aware of transboundary pollution, and that each country has fully internalized domestic externalities (an unlikely situation). In order to evaluate how far the actual situation is located from Pareto-efficient or full-cooperative solutions, a 'business as usual' (BAU) bottom reference can be evaluated. BAU assumes welfare optimization under the assumption that there are no emission controls at all, because agents do not yet perceive the pollutant as being risky or harmful.

This is the approach followed by Fankhauser and Kverndokk (1992). In the light of this analysis, the Nash equilibrium turns out to be an improvement on the situation under BAU. Barrett (1995, p.15) warns that it is incorrect to assume that the BAU would result if no pollution agreement were reached: even in the absence of an agreement countries ought to abate for the sake of economic efficiency, so that marginal costs equal marginal benefits of abatement. Given the public-good character of pollution at the national levels, the actual situation in terms of pollution might lie somewhere between the BAU and the Nash levels.

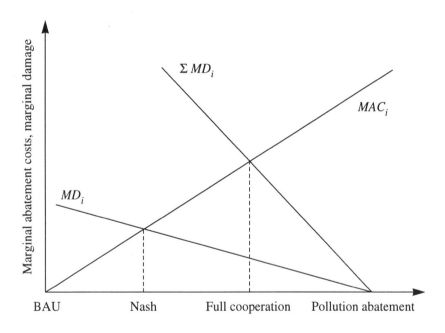

Figure 1.1 Pollution abatement under full cooperation, Nash and business as usual (BAU). For notations see notes of table 1.1

While we have so far argued purely in terms of utility gains, it is also important to note that an equivalent ranking of solution outcomes results when the amount of pollution abatement undertaken is considered. Figure 1.1 illustrates the problem in terms of cost–benefit analysis, for the case of linear marginal damage and cost functions. Full cooperation implies that every country abates so that its individual marginal abatement costs equate to *total* marginal damage costs (see also Table 1.1), while the Nash equilibrium only requires them to equate to *individual* marginal damage costs. Given common assumptions of functional forms, the pollution abatement under full cooperation is higher for each country than under the Nash equilibrium. The situation under BAU is even more drastic because no (further) pollution abatement is undertaken, given that individual marginal abatement costs equal zero in this case.

Cost-effectiveness Analysis

Rather than maximizing the net benefit from pollution abatement, a cost-effectiveness approach can be taken instead. This involves estimating abatement costs and choosing an abatement constraint, and has the advantage of avoiding the specification of a damage–emissions relationship in the form of a damage function. Uncertainty and lack of information about such functions is generally considerable; and appropriate modelling would require the function in most cases to exhibit high non-linearities. Taking a cost-effectiveness approach, then, has considerable attractions.

Kaitala, Pohjola and Tahvonen (1993) examine cost-efficiency of a Finnish–Russian SO_2 agreement. Abatement cost functions are minimized with respect to emission constraints, and a Nash equilibrium as well as a full-cooperative outcome are evaluated. In the cost-efficiency context the first-order conditions look different, as illustrated in Table 1.1. While for the full-cooperative outcome the sum of the marginal costs of all countries should equal the shadow value of the constraint, λ, the Nash equilibrium prescribes that the marginal costs of each country has to equal λ. The conclusion of the paper is that Finland should make side payments to induce the former Soviet Union to cooperate. The amount of these side payments coincides with the payments agreed upon by Finland in an actual agreement between both countries. More recently, Kaitala and Pohjola (Chapter 5, this volume) have revised earlier cost–benefit papers to cover three independent decision makers: Estonia, Russia and Finland. This leads to slightly modified conclusions in that Finland should only pay Estonia to cooperate.

Kverndokk (1993) examines the implications of a global CO_2 agreement from a cost-effectiveness perspective. In his paper, abatement costs are specified for five different world regions. He finds that under such an agreement, the industrialized nations would be responsible for the entire level of abatement, whilst the developing countries would be allowed to increase their emissions compared to the 1990 levels. But Kverndokk points out that 'if we take into consideration the high potential growth rates in CO_2 emissions for the developing countries, these countries will face considerable future reductions in emissions compared to BAU emissions under a cost-effective agreement' (Kverndokk, 1993, p.110).

As with a full-cooperative solution, a cost-efficient solution imposes different burdens on the countries involved. To share them, one can consider the use of cost-sharing schemes similar to the rules for redistribution of gains as discussed above. Alternatively, tradable permits constitute a powerful and efficient tool to reach the cost-effective outcome. The main advantage of tradable permits is that no cost analysis has to be carried out before the scheme is introduced: ideally the market for permits will establish an equilibrium price which generates a least-cost solution. Provisions for trading have in practice been made under the Montreal Protocol where countries can trade their obligations *vis-à-vis* the controlled substances against obligations of other countries. An approach related to tradable permits is *joint implementation*, which allows actors for whom it is costly at the margin to abate in their own country to transfer projects to other countries where marginal abatement costs are lower. An example would be power companies in the US paying for forestry projects in South America to cover their obligations to reduce CO_2 emissions, if theirs is a lower-cost option for them (since growing forests sequester CO_2). This results in a transfer of money and know-how from the country which would like to keep its emissions high to the country which has accepted to undertake more abatement. The net effect is thus similar to a tradable permit scheme between two countries.

Despite the advantage of not having to specify a damage function under cost-efficiency, Barrett (1992a) points out that it remains important to model benefits directly in terms of foregone damage. Taking European Union (EU) negotiations on behalf of climate change as an example, he shows that incentives for cooperation might only be revealed if benefit considerations are introduced.

The main conclusion from the static game papers on transboundary pollution are that full cooperation outperforms non-cooperation and leads to lower levels of pollution. One of the problems with full cooperation is, however, that individual countries may lose out. Cost-sharing rules can remedy this problem. In the future it may be desirable to focus on rules which are more readily evaluated, and thus easier to implement in a political negotiation framework, even if this is at the expense of reaching a Pareto-efficient solution. In the static framework it appears nevertheless particularly difficult to deter players from free-riding, even if equitable cost-sharing rules are applied.

Dynamic Games[1]

When countries are allowed to act in a sequence over time, the game is called dynamic. Dynamic game-theory models are developed in both discrete and continuous time. The first category encompasses both 'repeated games' and 'difference games', while the term 'differential games' applies to the second case. Repeated games are strategic gaming situations in which players make repeatedly the same decision under the same circumstances for a limited or infinite time span.[2] Such strategies may be particularly useful in reducing the free-rider problem. One of the big advantages of difference and differential games is that they can take into account the fact that most pollutants exhibit some form of structural time dependence. This means that not only the flow of pollution is important for the level of damage, but also the pollution stock or concentration. The latter is taken to be a 'state variable' of the dynamic game, and can be thought of as, for example, the atmospheric concentration of greenhouse gases or the acidification of soils through acid rain. The players exercise 'control variables', that is, instruments with which they can influence the level of pollution. Such instruments can be thought of as simply the emitted amount of pollution, the level of fossil fuel used, investment in abatement technologies, and taxes. The aim of this type of game is to find the (intertemporal) optimal level of such instruments in response to the choice of all other players. In order to take account of this aspect of pollution, transboundary pollution dynamic games incorporate a 'motion equation' which depicts the changes of the pollutant over time.

In Cesar (1994), an overview of natural resource models is given which includes a discussion of possible pollution constraints. In particular the issue of the specification of the assimilation function is taken up. From environmental studies, it is clear that assimilation of pollutants in the case of greenhouse gases can hardly be approximated by a linear function, although this is common practice. Cesar shows that the choice of assimilation function influences the results from such a model quite dramatically in that small changes in the choice of parameters in the assimilation function lead to big changes in terms of location of the steady state. Non-linear specifications, moreover, lead to an entirely different outcome with the possibility of multiple equilibria. Cesar and de Zeeuw (1994) therefore conclude that their results imply 'a strong warning to researchers in environmental economics who use deterministic optimal control models for policy purposes when there is incomplete knowledge about complex ecosystem interaction' (Cesar and de Zeeuw, 1994, p. 17).

In order to take account of the complex relationships between, for example, the greenhouse effect and the accumulation of CO_2, various approaches have been adopted. Tahvonen (1993) chooses to use an interconnected system of two state variables: the change of temperature and the carbon concentration above the industrial level. A two-step framework is used in Kaitala, Pohjola and Tahvonen (1992c) for the case of acid rain between Finland and the former Soviet Union. In a first step the transport of sulphur dioxide emissions is depicted. The motion equation of the model in turn shows how the quality of the soil is affected by acidification, i.e. by the deposition of the emissions as described in the sulphur transport equation. The state variable of the motion equation is defined in terms of the fraction of base cations in the soil, and hence is also referred to as 'base saturation'. Mäler and de Zeeuw (1995) incorporate critical loads in their differential acid rain game between Great Britain and Ireland. They find that in the steady state in both the feedback Nash equilibrium and the full-cooperative outcome depositions will be equal to the critical loads. However, the stocks of pollutants accumulated in the steady state differ. Stocks in the steady state of the feedback Nash equilibrium[3] turn out to be particularly high, so much so that there might be a greater chance of irreversible damage. Their finding for Great Britain and Ireland is that emission abatement to the optimal level in Britain alone yields deposition levels in Ireland below the critical loads. Unless Ireland prefers even further emissions reductions, it thus need not compensate Britain for its environmental gains because it is in the self-interest of Britain to abate.

Capital accumulation and population growth, as well as accumulation of human capital, may also be taken account of in dynamic gaming models. Furthermore, impacts of various types of pollution reduction measures, such as abatement in the sense of 'end-of-pipe' technology, recycling and process-integrated changes can be considered.

The game-theory concepts which are evaluated in the dynamic context differ from the concepts which are examined in the static framework mainly because the game structure allows for various information features. Economists typically analyse three different types of concepts: the open-loop Nash equilibrium, the feedback Nash equilibrium and the Pareto-optimal solution(s). In fact there is an infinite number of Pareto optimal solutions, depending on which weights have been attached to the countries when maximizing the overall welfare function. While the notion of the Pareto solution is comparable to the notion used in the static framework, the two types of Nash equilibria have to be explained. Even though the general idea is the same as in the static case, the resulting choice of emission paths depends additionally on the type of information which is available to the players over the entire time span of the game. In the open-loop case, the players only know the initial value of the state variable (for instance the concentration of pollution in the atmosphere). Along the time path, no changes in response to new information can be made because players cannot observe the current state. In some respects, this corresponds to a type of pre-commitment in the first period. Given that choices (for example in the energy sector) are often irreversible, such a type of Nash equilibrium appears nevertheless realistic. Under the feedback Nash equilibrium it is assumed that only the current state is known but the players cannot be committed to any action. The idea behind this is that as players see the value of the state variable evolve, they might adapt their policy instruments to these changes. The feedback Nash equilibrium is often also referred to as subgame-perfect Nash equilibrium, because of its 'strong time consistency' or 'subgame perfectness' (Cesar, 1994). The latter implies that the solution will be reached not only from any point on the time path towards equilibrium, but also from any point which is not on this time path.

Typically a ranking of the various Nash and the Pareto-optimal solutions in terms of the state variable can be established. The general result is that the stock or the concentration of the pollutant is lowest under cooperation, and that with the open-loop Nash equilibrium, the pollution concentration is lower than in the feedback solution. Such results come about for instance in the analyses of Hoel (1993), van der Ploeg and de Zeeuw (1992), Cesar (1994), Kaitala et al. (1992b), and Xepapadeas (1994), each in a slightly different framework. Xepapadeas (1994) gives the following intuitive explanation for the difference between open-loop and feedback Nash equilibrium in the case of climate change. Under the feedback Nash equilibrium

> a country expects other countries to reduce their emissions when CO_2 concentration increases ... . Thus it has an incentive to increase emissions and reduce abatement contributions since it realises that the effects of its action will be partly offset by the rest of the countries' reduced emissions ... . Since all countries follow the same policy, total emissions are increased. (Xepapadeas, 1994, p.16).

Also the interaction among countries as such can be modelled in a more realistic way than in a static framework: the set of strategies available to the countries is bigger. The free-rider incentive can, for example, be reduced by using trigger strategies or renegotiation-proof strategies. Trigger strategies imply that as soon as one country deviates, all other countries will play their threat strategy for ever. The threat consists of playing the non-cooperative strategy forever after the deviation. The 'folk theorem' for repeated games states that by playing these trigger strategies any feasible, individually rational payoff can be sustained in a (subgame-perfect) Nash equilibrium as long as each player has a payoff at least as large as what that player can guarantee for him/herself and as long as the players are sufficiently patient. Renegotiation-proof strategies take up the criticism that the punishing player would be better off if continuation of cooperation could be achieved. Both strategies are considered in more length in the section on free-riding.

Unlike repeated games, with differential/difference games the question of whether cooperative outcomes can be sustained by non-cooperative strategies has been largely unresolved. A generally valid 'folk theorem' has not yet been developed for this type of games (de Zeeuw, 1997; Cesar, 1994). There are mainly two problems that render the derivation of a folk theorem for differential games difficult. First, in differential games the state evolves over time in response to players' actions and the state itself, and 'it may happen that cooperation breaks down in the course of the game when a previously sustainable policy becomes unsustainable' (Kaitala and Pohjola, 1990, p.423). The second problem relates to the fact that differential games are continuous in time. Punishment in the 'next period' lasts therefore for an infinitesimal length only, and artificial time intervals have to be introduced. An attempt to derive a folk theorem for differential games was made by Dockner and van Long (1993) who show that the cooperative outcome can be approximated by non-linear feedback Nash equilibria. But strategies become very complex, and it is questionable whether they have practical relevance. Cesar (1994) shows how the simpler trigger strategies can be used to make cooperation sustainable in a differential game. By considering outcomes on the Pareto frontier only, he proves that the folk theorem holds for a particular type of differential game.

The instrument considered in the differential/difference game context to implement the full-cooperative outcome is, apart from side payments, a tax. Hoel (1993) and Martin, Patrick and Tolwinski (1993) look at the impact of imposing a carbon tax. An international tax requires (as in the static framework) an international agency in order to be implemented or administered. It is then up to the countries to decide how to implement the tax rate(s) at the national level. Hoel also looks at a tradable permit scheme which is shown to achieve the same result as an international tax. Martin, Patrick and Tolwinski look at a highly asymmetric constellation of players: one player has a net benefit from polluting and the other player is a net loser or victim. Their numerical simulations indicate that the optimal strategies of players *vis-à-vis* a tax differ substantially.

With differential games, it is also possible to incorporate capital accumulation and R&D accumulation processes. For example, the possibility of investing in new abatement technologies was looked into by Cesar (1994), who introduces the possibility that each country on its own can build up some energy-related stock of capital. In the steady state, the level of capital then turns out to be highest under cooperation, and the pollution level is lowest. Xepapadeas's analysis is wider since it considers not only the possibility that all countries together build up an R&D 'stock' (under full cooperation), but also how technology differentials might occur among countries (Xepapadeas, 1994). He finds, among other things, that the CO_2 concentrations are smaller and the level of technology is higher under the Pareto optimum than under both types of Nash equilibrium. Another finding is that rich countries[4] may not have an incentive to commit themselves in a worldwide R&D agreement if technology differentials generate substantial benefits. This holds even though their failure to do so brings about a higher global concentration of CO_2.

Free-riding

While it is possible to redistribute gains from international cooperation on pollution control so that every single country benefits from an agreement, for example by means of side payments, this does not deter countries from free-riding. It appears almost as an unavoidable phenomenon given that contracts to limit emissions are not credibly enforceable at the international level: every country on its own is still better off by not complying with abatement measures because it can benefit from the efforts of other countries while not incurring any costs (due to the public-good nature of the environmental improvements). What is more, as noted above, side payments may give the wrong signals in terms of incentives. The anticipation of side payments, for example, may induce countries initially to minimize their environmental policy below the non-cooperative level (Folmer, van Mouche and Ragland, 1993). Furthermore, the offer of side payments may lead to a loss of reputation and thus to a weakened negotiation position. In order to circumvent these problems, a range of propositions has been suggested. Table 1.3 gives an overview of strategies and concepts which have been referred to as remedying the free-rider problem in this context.

Table 1.3 Reducing the incentive to free-ride

Strategy	Limitation of free-riding	Discussed by:
Issue linkage	Yes	Whalley (1991), Barrett (1992a), Folmer–van Mouche–Ragland (1993), Cesar (1994).
Legal enforcement	Not modelled	Barrett (1992a)
Matching	Yes	Barrett (1995)
Self-enforcement	Yes	Barrett (1994b), Endres and Finus (1997)
Social norms	Yes	Hoel and Schneider (1995)
Tit-for-tat	Yes	Cesar (1994)
Trigger strategy	Yes	Barrett (1994a), Cesar (1994)
Unilateral action	No	Hoel (1992), Barrett (1995)

In the previous section it was mentioned that repeated non-cooperative games may lead to a cooperative outcome. The famous folk theorem says that this outcome can be sustained in an infinitely repeated game if the discount rate is low enough. This solution is based on players using *trigger strategies*, as explained above. They yield an equilibrium for which outside enforcement is not needed, and which holds as long as cooperation is individually rational.

To be sustainable, the threat has to be credible in order to be renegotiation-proof. The threat in the trigger strategy to play non-cooperation for ever in response to another player's deviation may not be credible, because full cooperation is still more profitable for all players. The agreement may thus be renegotiated. The term 'renegotiation-proofness' implies that the punishing players resist the temptation to renegotiate, and thus to 'forgive' their opponent. Barrett (1994a) evaluates a renegotiation-proof strategy in a biodiversity supergame. He finds that making a self-enforcing agreement renegotiation-proof, on the basis of trigger strategies, may only be possible at the expense of reduced welfare gains. Put differently, he finds the improvement compared with non-cooperation in a renegotiation-proof situation to be very small. Barrett (1994a) and Zaccour (1993) also use renegotiation-proof strategies in a transboundary pollution context.

Cesar (1994) points out that a trigger strategy is not necessarily renegotiation-proof. Instead, he suggest the application of *tit-for-tat*. If under tit-for-tat one of the players chooses to deviate, s/he will be punished until s/he cooperates again. In the period following his/her cooperation, all players will go back to the cooperation strategies. Like trigger strategies, tit-for-tat reduces free-riding. The benefit of tit-for-tat in a more general context has been shown by Axelrod (1991) in a computer tournament where 'tit-for-tat' overcame all other strategies which were entered in the competition.

Whalley (1991) and others propose to *link negotiations* on transboundary pollution with other issues such as free access to trade. They suggest that this could reduce the need for monetary side payments if interests in interlinked topics are complementary. While linkage with trade could have negative repercussions in view of the liberalization of international trade within the General Agreement on Tariffs and Trade (GATT),[5] linkage with other complementary environmental problems is conceivable. Barrett (1992a) proposes the joint bargaining of CO_2 reductions and biodiversity preservation. As a practical example one can refer to the Rio Conference in 1992, where the Climate Convention, which was in the interest of the OECD countries, was agreed on only in exchange for guaranteeing an international desertification convention – one of the biggest concerns of the developing countries at that point in time. The examples given so far can be referred to as 'mutual linkage' (Stein, 1980). Similarly issue linkage may also relate to 'coerced' or 'threat-induced' issue linkage. The threat of sanctions, such as the trade sanctions incorporated in the Montreal Protocol, may be taken as an example. 'Coerced' or 'threat-induced' issue linkage can, in contrast to 'mutual' issue linkage, entail supplementary problems such as credibility of action. Heister (1993) shows in a simple one-shot game structure that the threat of sanctions is only credible if the country imposing the sanctions is itself not hurt by them, and if it prefers sanctions to a non-cooperative outcome regardless of what other players are doing. These results change in a repeated-game framework.

Folmer, van Mouche and Ragland (1993), Folmer and van Mouche (1993) and Kroeze-Gil and Folmer (1997) have formalized the idea of linkage in their articles on interconnected games. The notion of 'interconnected games' incorporates the view that countries can condition their actions in the environmental area to outcomes previously observed in, say, the trade area and vice versa. In their analysis of tensor and direct-sum games they show that linking or interconnecting games yields supplementary Nash equilibria. Therefore, the set of possible as well as feasible outcomes is increased. Thus, interconnection may be a means to overcome a prisoner's dilemma type situation and to induce a Pareto improvement.

Barrett (1995) suggests that a *matching* mechanism could reduce the incentives of countries to free-ride on other countries' efforts. Although he advocates this mechanism in relation to donations to an environmental fund for the Third World, the concept can easily be adapted to the case of actual pollution abatement. The idea of matching implies that emission abatement is offered if it is matched by abatement on the part of other parties. Guttman (1978) and Guttman (1987) have shown that such a mechanism yields an improvement *vis-à-vis* non-cooperation and, in the case of identical players, may result in a Pareto-efficient outcome.

The literature has also examined whether *unilateral action* by one country or by a coalition of countries can induce other countries to undertake abatement themselves. The idea behind this is that these countries' behaviour would be an example to other parties, and has mainly been put forward by green non-governmental organizations. Victor (1991) for instance writes in this context that 'Cooperation will be easier if there is a leader, but the largest contributors to climate change ... are moving slowly' (p.451). However, Hoel (1992) shows that this is not necessarily the case. The argument is as follows: Country A chooses unselfishly a lower emission level than that which follows from its own response function. Country B, which maximizes its welfare by taking the pollution of A as given, is now faced with a lower ambient pollution level. Consequently, it is beneficial for B to increase its own emissions. However, Hoel (1992) analyses the situation within a purely static-game framework, and the result might not be quite the same when a longer time span is taken into consideration. Indeed, time is an important factor in this context.

Barrett (1992a) suggests that a certain degree of enforceability of a climate change convention could also be achieved through *legislation*. He argues that the introduction of a third party to arbitrate conflicts between two member parties of a convention could prevent conflicts from occurring in the first place. Finally, Hoel and Schneider (1995) introduce the idea that *social norms* may affect behaviour of countries in a transfrontier pollution context. The argument is that governments may feel uncomfortable to free-ride on the other governments' efforts by breaking the agreement, even if this yields a benefit in economic terms.

In their analysis this term is portrayed via a cost function that is increasing in the number of cooperating countries. Their analysis shows that strong social norms increase the likelihood of countries cooperating in a coalition. The concept of social norms appears something of an artefact. Factors that are likely to have a stronger impact on countries' behaviours, at least among industrialized countries, are, for example, non-governmental organizations or simply social pressure.

Further Issues

The problems with cooperation on international environmental problems are not confined to gain sharing and free-riding. There is a range of issues relating mainly to informational aspects that generally have not yet been formally dealt with in transfrontier game-theoretic analysis. The three aspects that are looked at in this section are transaction costs, information and the motivation of players.

For most cooperative solutions, *transaction costs* will be high: an agreement must expend resources not only to reach, but also to enforce, a bargained outcome. Depending on the choice of mechanism of enforcement, costs can vary substantially. Barrett (1995) gives an example for the first two joint implementation projects undertaken under the Climate Change Convention:

> the budget of the two projects is $4.5 million, of which $400,000 is for administrative costs. For comparison, one offset trade in the United States involved a project which cost $16 million to carry out, but which also cost $50,000 in direct outlays to search for trading candidates and negotiate an agreement, and $70,000 to prepare an environmental impact report. While the transactions costs are substantially lower for this United States offset as compared with the Norwegian joint implementation project, these costs were nonetheless perceived as being a major impediment to trading. (Barrett, 1995, p.19)

This leads Barrett (1995) to state that although the game-theoretic model he developed showed that joint implementation would be preferable to a tradable permit scheme, high transaction costs could reverse the situation. Since these costs were not modelled explicitly, no conclusion is possible about when this would be the case.

Another issue that could be dealt with more explicitly in the future in the models discussed above is the role of *information*: information is not freely available to all parties equally. A step towards dealing with these issues was made by Pethig (1991). He gives an example of transboundary pollution in a two-country model with principal–agent features. He looks in particular at the 'enforcement deficit' arising when governments who decide on pollution

An introduction 21

abatement incur costs from monitoring the agencies in charge of implementing these measures.[6]

The literature finally assumes, in terms of *motivation* of the acting governments, not only that countries represented by their governments act as rational players, but also that they pursue the interests of their constituencies. More realistic modelling, however, would suggest that they should be modelled as agents that want to be re-elected in only a few years' time. Such governments may thus have a very short time horizon, which in turn has repercussions on the choice of their environmental policy.

4. A PREVIEW OF THE REST OF THIS BOOK

As discussed in the previous sections, international environmental problems (IEP) usually require cooperation among countries on issues of transfrontier pollution for efficacy and efficiency reasons. The nature of and incentives for cooperation on international environmental problems are the main themes of many chapters in this volume. In Chapter 2 Henry Tulkens discusses a pessimistic and optimistic view on the feasibility of cooperation. According to the former, only small subsets of the countries involved can sign a treaty; according to the latter, there exists a grand stable coalition in the sense that the grand treaty will be signed by all countries involved, without regret. The difference between the two is based on two assumptions. First, the existence of a grand coalition postulates the possibility of making transfers to the countries with negative net benefits which are linked to the amounts of emissions abated. Second, it assumes a rational threat of not forming as a coalition but playing Nash, against the free-riding coalition. Whether the pessimistic or optimistic view prevails in practice is still a matter of further theoretical and empirical investigation.

Chapter 3, by Mark Cronshaw, elaborates on the use of future punishments in order to remedy economic inefficiency due to environmental externalities. It characterizes all Pareto-efficient outcomes in two-country infinitely repeated games into either unilateral or bilateral externalities. It provides an n-country example with an efficient equilibrium even for high interest rates. The worst symmetric punishment in the example has only one bad period followed by the best symmetric continuation equilibrium. Such a punishment is more severe than infinite Nash reversion, and more credible. The chapter also reviews the literature on efficient equilibria in differential games, some of which are also enforced by threats. This suggests that the main problem of international environmental externalities is not inefficiency, but rather obtaining agreement on an equitable outcome.

Tim Jeppesen and Per Andersen introduce Rabin's concept of fairness in Chapter 4 and show that under this condition the countries involved in an IEP not only maximize their own welfare but are affected by the welfare of others as well. They show how fairness may thus induce full cooperation. The authors also show that a simple form of commitment may easily expand the stable agreement and, in the end, induce full cooperation.

Some of the ideas found in Chapters 2 and 3, in particular efficient cooperation, and in chapter 4, notably fairness, can be found in Chapter 5. Veijo Kaitala and Matti Pohjola show that efficient cooperation in reducing transboundary air pollution in the border region between Finland, Russia and Estonia requires substantial sulphur emission cuts in Estonia and in the Kola peninsula. Pareto optimality may also entail financial transfers from Finland to Estonia because it is an important source of sulphur deposited in Southern Finland, because sulphur abatement costs are much lower in Estonia, and because Estonia lacks the financial resources for investments in abatement. The analysis is based on the European Monitoring and Evaluation Programme (EMEP) transportation model of sulphur dioxide across Europe, on estimated regional abatement cost functions, and on the revealed preference approach to estimating the damage costs from pollution.

Chapter 6, by Fanny Mißfeldt, is along the same lines. A static two-player game is introduced in order to analyse the expected damage in the event of a nuclear accident in a power station. The two players are thought of as Eastern Europe and Western Europe. Given the higher accident risk in the East, the author looks at the Nash, Stackelberg and cooperative solutions. She finds that if the West acts as a Stackelberg leader, it will do less abatement than with all other strategies discussed (although the East could also take this role). Most abatement will be done under cooperation, both at the aggregate and the country level. Simulation also indicates that the gains from cooperation may be substantial, although large data limitations are apparent here. Cooperation is not readily achievable, given the free-rider incentive for both areas. However, this incentive is not as high as with other transfrontier pollution problems such as greenhouse gases, whilst a number of potential control organizations already exist. Moreover, abatement control is technically straightforward in the case of nuclear power.

In Chapter 7 Alfred Endres and Michael Finus address the self-enforcing nature of an international agreement on global emission reductions. In particular they investigate how the instrumental framework affects the bargaining outcome over pollution control. They focus on three policy frameworks: emission reduction quotas, effluent taxes and tradable emission permits. The analysis is confined to a two-country model in which no transfer payments take place. The countries differ in terms of abatement costs and environmental preferences. The model framework is a three-stage game. In the first stage the bargaining equilibria of the three policy frameworks are determined. In the second stage the focus is on the incentives of a country to overfulfil the terms of a treaty and in the last stage on the stability of the bargaining equilibria of the first two stages in a dynamic setting. Stability is defined as renegotiation-proofness. The authors show that except for the globally optimal solution, all equilibrium levels considered can be backed by credible retaliation strategies in a dynamic supergame, provided the discount factor is close to one. Another interesting finding is that in a second-best world with political restrictions the well-known result that taxes and permits are superior to command and control instruments has to be qualified.

In the next three chapters an alternative to side payments as an instrument to induce countries to cooperate, namely issue linkage, is discussed. In Folmer, van Mouche and Ragland (1993) several objections to side payments are discussed. The anticipation of side payments may induce countries initially to minimize policy even below the Nash equilibrium in order to extract larger side payments. Moreover, countries that offer side payments may weaken their negotiation position by raising expectations with negotiation partners that it will be prepared to make such payments in other cases as well. Finally, side payments signify application of a victim pays principle.

In Chapter 8 Jardena Kroeze-Gil and Henk Folmer discuss several types of issue linkage. Moreover, they model issue linkage by means of cooperative game theory and show that the interconnected cooperative game (linking, for example, an environmental game and a trade game) may have a solution whilst not each of the underlying isolated games (that is, the environmental game) can be solved.

Michele Botteon and Carlo Carraro continue the discussion of this theme in Chapter 9, where they present an empirical analysis of the formation of emission abatement coalitions in the case of five asymmetric world regions. The analysis is carried out using the Nash bargaining solution and the Shapley value as burden-sharing rules, and assesses the effects on the stability of environmental coalitions. The authors also test issue linkage as a strategy with respect to the profitability and stability of international environmental coalitions. They find that the stable coalition is usually larger when countries negotiate on two linked issues. However, they also find that the stable coalition may not be optimal and conclude that much further theoretical and empirical research on issue linkage and institutions such as burden-sharing rules on the achievement of agreements with many signatories is required.

In Chapter 10, Stephan Kroll, Charles Mason and Jason Shogren test some issues in the interconnected games literature using an experimental approach. They explore the difference between linking games through a parallel (informal) institution and linking games through a joint (formal) institution, in a laboratory setting. Although the two institutions are theoretically equivalent, the authors find that efficient outcomes are far more common in the joint institution case. Another important finding is that 'cheap talk' did not add to efficiency. This observation can be seen as a challenge to the common view that a summit where binding contracts are signed has to be prepared with many preliminary meetings.

Rather than facilitate efficient outcomes, such meetings could result in attempts at strategic manipulation.

Although cooperation has been dealt with most extensively in the literature, attention also needs to be given to conflicts on environmental and resource problems. Fishery conflicts have, for example, occurred between Spain and Canada. Conflicts may also arise with respect to global warming policy and preservation of natural resources, such as tropical rainforests, between industrialized and developing countries. Terrance Hurley and Jason Shogren take up the issue of environmental and resource conflicts in Chapter 11 and argue that asymmetries in ability and valuation are critical factors driving the combatants' effort levels. In particular, they consider information asymmetry in the sense that tangible market prices strongly signal development values whilst intangible non-market preferences weakly signal preservation values. They apply these notions to a tropical rainforest and consider a developed northern country that accounts for both the economic and ecosystem value and a southern country that considers mainly the economic value of development. They explore the nature of the perfect Bayesian equilibrium for both countries. The analytical results suggest that the informed North tries to take advantage of the information gap by persuading the uninformed South to undercommit effort in the conflict. If the South does not fight as hard as it would if it knew the true North value, the North has a greater chance of preserving the forest. The theoretical results are broadly consistent with behavioural patterns observed in an experimental application.

Dynamic game theory offers many new analytical possibilities in the consideration of environmental conflicts and strategies. In Chapter 12 Aart de Zeeuw considers damages caused by accumulated pollutants such as the stock of greenhouse gases. Moreover, he argues that adapting to sustainable pollution levels takes time. Both of these *dynamic* features require an analytical framework which can handle intertemporal objective functionals with dynamical constraints, such as optimal control theory. The author also focuses on transboundary pollution problems and argues that this type of problem can most adequately be handled by means of game theory. The combination of an optimal control problem and a game leads to a so-called differential game. The author presents an introduction to some of the main concepts and techniques of differential game theory and to applications to dynamic international pollution problems. Finally, some important unsolved issues, in particular with respect to self-enforcement of agreements on dynamic international pollution problems, are discussed.

In Chapter 13 Alistair Ulph combines two of the central policy questions that arise in the climate change debate: how to secure cooperation to reduce emissions and how to respond to the considerable uncertainty about both the extent of any possible climate change and the resulting damages in different parts of the world. With respect to the latter, the possibility that better scientific information in the future will reduce uncertainty leads to the suggestion that actions to curb emissions be delayed; whilst concern about the possible irreversible nature of accumulation and damages leads to the suggestion that such delay could be costly. Ulph shows that by combining the two literatures (that is, dynamic game theory and uncertainty/irreversibility), some of the results from the separate literatures are not robust. Specifically, the conclusions about the differences in emissions and stocks of pollution between cooperative and non-cooperative equilibrium carry over to a world of uncertainty and learning, as do the conclusions about the benefits from cooperation. However, the conclusions from the literature on uncertainty, irreversibility and learning for a single decision maker do not generalize to a world of many countries acting non-cooperatively: in a non-cooperative equilibrium better information could make all countries worse off. This possibility of information having a negative value arises when global warming has very different implications in terms of costs and benefits for different countries.

Dynamic game theory is applied to the issue of migration by Markus Haavio in Chapter 14. There are many links between population movements and environmental quality: for example, in the role of shifting cultivation on forest loss, or migration and desertification. Haavio looks at the interplay between migration and environmental policy coordination. A two-period game is used to analyse two specific questions: first, if imperfectly mobile households can be a substitute for environmental policy coordination, and second, to consider whether predictions from previous static analyses carry over into a dynamic setting. Haavio finds that the forward-looking nature of household behaviour (on the part of migrants) can offset incentives for strategic environmental policy making on the part of national governments, and induce implicit cooperation. The extent to which governments can make credible commitments on environmental policy turns out to be crucial in terms of welfare effects.

The next two chapters deal with environmental policy, international trade and firm location. In Chapter 15 Talitha Feenstra uses a differential game model of an international duopoly to describe environmental policy setting by a national government that seeks to balance environmental targets and domestic competitiveness. She shows that the national regulators distort policy instruments (taxes and standards) from their Pigouvian levels to increase the profits of the home firm and to improve the environment at home at the cost of foreign profits. All these distortions lead to suboptimal policy levels, seen from the point of view of an overall welfare maximizer. She also shows that if a regulator cannot commit to his policy, s/he turns out to have no direct influence on the firm's investment in abatement technology with either taxes or standards. In that case the regulator will set policy solely based on temporary firm profits and environmental effects.

In Chapter 16 Michael Kuhn analyses endogenous firm location in a discrete two-region, two-firm model of product differentiation. In a non-cooperative game, the two regional governments first decide on the imposition of domestic production standards; firms then choose technology (clean or polluting), location and price. Equilibrium quality and location structure are determined analytically. The existence of consumers' willingness to pay in the form of a premium on clean production methods, and the possibility of inter-firm pollution alleviate the tendency of firms to move into regions with weaker regulation. This implies that a 'race to the bottom' is less likely.

Use of game theory in the context of the specification of econometric models related to environmental and resource problems is scarce. This scarcity has often been used to criticize the application of game theory in this field. Chapter 17, by Erkki Koskela and Markku Ollikainen, shows that this criticism is not valid and that game theory can play a major role in empirical applications. The chapter provides a framework to approach price and quantity determination in the roundwood market. In the spirit of the trade union literature, a model of timber-price determination is formulated according to which the forest owners' association determines timber prices and then forest firms unilaterally decide upon the timber to be used. The novelty here is to incorporate investment decisions of firms as a strategic factor into the model. The structure of the model is the following. The game is played in two stages. First, the forest owners' association and the firms in the forest industry decide on timber prices and capital stock, respectively. In the second stage, the firms determine timber demand conditional on the timber price–capital stock game, so that the equilibrium concept is the subgame-perfect Nash equilibrium. This game-theoretic model is applied to the annual data from the Finnish paper and pulp industry over the period 1960–92. Estimation and testing results concerning the price and quantity determination of timber as well as capital-stock determination are generally favourable for the hypotheses presented. In particular, diagnostics and various test procedures indicate that these equations outperform conventional specifications derived from the theory of the demand for factors of production.

NOTES

1. For a more complete introduction to dynamic games, see de Zeeuw's chapter in this volume (Chapter 12).
2. The distinction between finite and infinite time horizon has a strong influence on the outcome of a repeated game. While with a finite horizon a non-cooperative equilibrium results, the prospect of an infinite horizon may offer strategic possibilities that lead to an improvement of the non-cooperative outcome.
3. The term 'feedback Nash equilibrium' is explained further below.

4. Whether a country is 'rich' or 'poor' in this context depends on the country's initial value of primary input and on its growth rate.
5. Since 1995, the Agreement comes within the framework of the World Trade Organization.
6. See also the contribution by Hurley and Shogren in this volume (Chapter 11).

REFERENCES

Axelrod, R. (1991), The Evolution of Co-operation, London: Penguin Books.
Barrett, S. (1992), *Convention on Climate Change – Economic Aspects of Negotiations*, Paris: OECD.
Barrett, S. (1994a), 'The Biodiversity Supergame', *Environmental and Resource Economics*, **4**, 111–22.
Barrett, S. (1994b), 'Self-Enforcing International Environmental Agreements', *Oxford Economic Papers*, **46**, 878–94.
Barrett, S. (1995), 'The Strategy of Joint Implementation in the Framework Convention on Climate Change', UNCTAD/GID/10.
Bartsch, E. (1992), 'Grenzüberschreitende Umweltprobleme am Beispiel der Schwefeldioxidemissionen in Europa', *Kieler Arbeitspapier*, no. 538, Kiel.
Bierman, H.S. and L. Fernandez (1995), *Game Theory with Economic Applications*, Reading, UK: Addison-Wesley.
Binmore, K. (1992), *Fun and Games: a text on game theory*, Lexington, MA: D.C. Heath.
Botteon, M. and C. Carraro (1995), 'Burden sharing and coalition stability in environmental negotiations with asymmetric countries', paper presented at the second meeting of the HCM network 'Designing economic policy for management of natural resources and the environment', Venice, May 1995. FEEM Nota di Lavoro no. 78.95 (November).
Carraro, C. and D. Siniscalco (1993), 'Strategies for the International Protection of the Environment', *Journal of Public Economics*, **52**, 309–28.
Cesar, H.S.J. (1994), *Control and Game Models of the Greenhouse Effect*, Lecture Notes in Economics and Mathematical Systems, **146**, Springer-Verlag.
Cesar, H.S.J. and de Zeeuw, A. (1994), 'Sustainability and the Greenhouse Effect: Robustness Analysis of the Assimilation Function', paper presented at the fifth annual meeting of the EAERE, Dublin, 22–4 June.
Chander, P. and H. Tulkens (1991), 'Strategically Stable Cost Sharing in an Economic–Ecological Negotiation Process', CORE Discussion Paper, no. 9135, revised 1992, Louvain.
Dockner, E. and N. van Long (1993), 'International Pollution Control: Cooperative versus Noncooperative Strategies', *Journal of Environmental Economics and Management*, **24**, 13–29.
Escapa, M. and M.J. Gutierrez (1995), 'Distribution of Potential Gains from International Environmental Agreements: The case of the greenhouse effect', Southern European Economics Discussion Series (SEEDS), D.P.144.
Fankhauser, S. and S. Kverndokk (1992), 'The Global Warming Game – Simulations of a CO_2 Reduction Agreement', Memorandum no. 13 from the Department of Economics, University of Oslo, and GEC WP92-10, CSERGE, University College London and University of East Anglia.
Folmer, H. and I. Musu (1992), 'Transboundary Pollution Problems, Environmental Policy and International Cooperation: An Introduction', *Environmental and Resource Economics*, **2**, 107–16.

Folmer, H., P. van Mouche and S. Ragland (1993), 'Interconnected Games and International Environmental Problems', *Environmental and Resource Economics*, **3**, 313–35.

Folmer, H. and P. van Mouche (1993), 'Interconnected games and International Environmental Problems II', Landbouwuniversiteit Wageningen.

Fudenberg, D. and J. Tirole (1991), *Game Theory*, Cambridge, MA: MIT Press.

Gibbons, R. (1992), *A Primer in Game Theory*, Hemel Hempstead: Harvester Wheatsheaf.

Guttman, J.M. (1978), 'Understanding collective action: matching behaviour', *American Economic Review*, **68**, 251–5.

Guttman, J.M. (1987), 'A non-Cournot model of voluntary collective action', *Economica*, **54**, 1–19.

Harsanyi, J. (1977), *Rational behaviour and bargaining equilibrium in Games and social situations*, Cambridge: Cambridge University Press.

Heister, J. (1993), 'Who will win the Ozone Game?' Kiel Working Paper no. 579, Institute of World Economics, Kiel.

Hoel, M. (1992), 'International Environmental Conventions: the Case of Uniform Reductions of Emissions', *Environmental and Resource Economics*, **2**, 141–59.

Hoel, M. (1993), 'Intertemporal properties of an international carbon tax', *Resource and Energy Economics*, **15**, 51–70.

Hoel, M. and K. Schneider (1995), 'Incentives to participate in an international environmental agreement', paper presented at the EAERE conference in Umeå, Sweden.

Kaitala, V. and M. Pohjola (1990), 'Economic Development and Agreeable Redistribution in Capitalism: Efficient Game Equilibria in a Two-Class Neo-Classical Growth Model', *International Economic Review*, **32**, 421–38.

Kaitala, V., K.-G. Mäler and H. Tulkens (1992a), 'The Acid Rain Game as a Resource Allocation Process with an Application to the Cooperation among Finland, Russia, and Estonia', CORE Discussion Paper 9242, revised June 1993, Université Catholique de Louvain.

Kaitala, V., M. Pohjola and O. Tahvonen (1992b), 'An Economic Analysis of Transboundary Air Pollution between Finland and the Former Soviet Union', *Scandinavian Journal of Economics*, **94** (3), 409–23.

Kaitala, V., M. Pohjola and O. Tahvonen (1992c), 'Transboundary Air Pollution and Soil Acidification: a Dynamic Analysis of an Acid Rain Game between Finland and the USSR', *Environmental and Resource Economics*, **2**, 141–81.

Kaitala, V., M. Pohjola and O. Tahvonen (1993), 'A Finnish–Soviet Acid Rain Game: Noncooperative Equilibria, Cost Efficiency, and Sulfur Agreements', *Journal of Environmental Economics and Management*, **24**, 87–100.

Kuhl, H. (1987), *Umweltressourcen als Gegenstand internationaler Verhandlungen: eine theoretische Transaktionskostenanalyse*, Frankfurt am Main: Verlag Peter Lang.

Kverndokk, S. (1993), 'Global CO_2 Agreements: a Cost-Effective Approach', *The Energy Journal*, **14** (2), 91–112.

Luce, D. and H. Raiffa (1957), *Games and Decisions*, New York: Wiley.

Mäler, K.-G. (1989), 'The acid rain game', in H. Folmer and E. van Ierland (eds), *Valuation Methods and Policy Making in Environmental Economics*, Amsterdam: Elsevier.

Mäler, K.-G. and A. de Zeeuw (1995), 'Critical Loads in Games of Transboundary Pollution Control', FEEM Nota di Lavoro no. 7.95.

Martin, W.E., R.H. Patrick and B. Tolwinski (1993), 'A Dynamic Game of a Transboundary Pollutant with Asymmetric Players', *Journal of Environmental Economics and Management*, **24**, 1–12.

Pethig, R. (1991), 'International Environmental Policy and Enforcement Deficits', in H. Siebert (ed.), *Environmental Scarcity*, Kiel: Institute for World Economics.

Petrakis, E. and A. Xepapadeas (1994), 'Environmental Consciousness and Moral Hazard in International Agreements to Protect the Environment', Economics Department, University of Crete, research paper, 34.

Rasmussen, E. (1989), *Games and Information – an introduction to game theory*, Oxford: Blackwell.

Samuelson, P.A. (1954), 'The Pure Theory of Public Expenditure', *The Review of Economics and Statistics*, **36**, 387–9.

Schelling, T. (1960), *The Strategy of Conflict*, Harvard: Harvard University Press.

Stein, O. (1980), 'The politics of linkage', *World Politics*, **32**, 62–81.

Tahvonen, O. (1993), 'Carbon Dioxide Abatement as a Differential Game', University of Oulu, Finland.

Van der Ploeg, F. and A.J. de Zeeuw (1992), 'International Aspects of Pollution Control', *Environmental and Resource Economics*, **3**, 117–39.

Victor, D.G. (1991), 'How to slow global warming', *Nature*, **349**, 451–6.

Whalley, J. (1991), 'The Interface between Environmental and Trade Policies', *The Economic Journal*, **101** (March), 180–9.

Xepapadeas, A. (1994), 'Induced technical change and international agreements under greenhouse warming', *Resource and Energy Economics*, **16**, 1–16.

Zaccour, G. (1993), 'Side Payments in a Dynamic Game of Environmental Policy Coordination', GERARD and Ecole des Hautes Etudes Commerciales, Montreal.

2. Cooperation versus free-riding in international environmental affairs: two approaches[1]

Henry Tulkens

1. INTRODUCTION

This chapter is about a controversy regarding the feasibility, and as a consequence the likelihood, of cooperation among countries on issues of transfrontier pollution. I want to contrast two theses, a pessimistic one and an optimistic one. Both of them are based on concepts rooted in economic analysis, and both of them claim additional support from game theory. Nevertheless they reach opposing conclusions. It is thus a challenging task to try to disentangle the arguments used on each side, in order to see whether the two theses can be reconciled or are intrinsically antagonistic.

The structure of the chapter is as follows. Before entering into the dispute, I think it is important to remind the reader, in Section 2, of how economic analysis shows that cooperation raises a severe problem in international environmental affairs, and what the logical structure of that problem is. Section 3 then contains a summary presentation of the two theses. Section 4 (which is the heart of the chapter) is devoted to a systematic comparison of their respective characteristics, and to a search for a conceptual framework for reconciling the two approaches. Section 5 concludes with considerations on the two basically different notions of 'stability' for coalitions that are at stake.

2. THE UNDERLYING ECONOMIC–ECOLOGICAL MODEL AND THE QUESTIONS RAISED

I briefly[2] remind the reader of the structure of the economic model, which is common to the two theses. A set N of countries, indexed by $i = 1, 2, ..., n$, share a common environmental resource. For each country, the function $u_i(x_i, z)$ describes national preferences over the consumption of some private good

($x_i \geq 0$) and of some environmental good ($z \leq 0$).[3] The function is assumed to be of the quasilinear form $u_i(\cdot) = x_i + v_i(z)$, with v_i concave and increasing. Define $\pi_i = (\partial u_i/\partial z/\partial u_i/\partial x_i) \geq 0$ as country i's marginal willingness to pay (in commodity x) for the environmental good. Furthermore, let $y_i = g_i(p_i)$ be country i's production function, linking[4] its output $y_i \geq 0$ of the private good with its emissions $p_i \geq 0$ of pollutant in the environment, and assume $\gamma_i = dy_i/dp_i > 0$ up to some maximum value p_i^o, and zero above it. The derivative γ_i is then naturally interpreted, when taken to the left, as the country's marginal cost (in y_i) of abating its emissions.

The 'transfer function' $z = -\Sigma p_i$ specifies how the pollutant emissions of all countries are diffused and transformed by ecological processes into the ambient quantity z. And finally, the private good is assumed to be transferable[5] between the countries, in amounts denoted as T_i (< 0 if given away by country i, > 0 if received by it).

For the *economic–ecological* system so described, we have:

Definition 1: A *feasible state* is a vector

$$(x, y, p, z, T) \equiv (x_1, ..., x_n; y_1, ..., y_n; p_1, ..., p_n; z; T_1, ..., T_n)$$

such that:

$$\forall i, \quad x_i = y_i + T_i$$
$$y_i = g_i(p_i)$$
$$\Sigma x_i = \Sigma y_i$$
$$z = -\Sigma p_i.$$

Notice that the first three constraints imply $\Sigma T_i = 0$.

Definition 2: A *non-cooperative equilibrium* in the sense of Nash is a feasible state $(\bar{x}, \bar{y}, \bar{p}, \bar{z}, \bar{T})$ such that:

$$\forall i, (\bar{x}_i, \bar{p}_i) \text{ maximizes } x_i + v_i(z)$$
$$\text{s.t.} \quad y_i = g_i(p_i)$$
$$p_i + z = -\sum_{j \neq i} \bar{p}_j,$$

letting $\bar{T}_i = 0 \; \forall_i$.

Definition 3: An *internationally efficient state* (or, for short, an *international optimum*) is a feasible state $(x^*, y^*, p^*, z^*, T^*)$ that maximizes

$$\sum_{i \in N}[x_i + v_i(z)].$$

The well-known fact – readily established from first order conditions – that the non-cooperative equilibrium is not an international optimum suggests that environmental efficiency at the world level can only be achieved through some form of cooperation among the countries involved. This is the source of the economists' motivation for interpreting and/or designing international treaties as instruments towards world efficiency.

But what should be the contents for such a treaty? and which countries the signatories? If all countries are convinced of the need to cooperate, an 'efficient' treaty would naturally specify the joint abatement policy corresponding to the internationally optimal emissions vector $(p_1^*, ..., p_n^*)$ derived above.[6] For some countries, however, the emission policy p_i^* may be so costly that it makes them worse off at the optimum compared with the non-cooperative equilibrium (i.e. the situation prevailing without a treaty). To keep such countries convinced of the desirability of cooperating, the treaty might in addition provide for private-good transfers compensating for that cost. It is by now well known[7] that such transfers can be designed, and conceivably managed by an international agency,[8] ensuring that the condition $x_i^* + v_i(z^*) \geq \bar{x}_i + v_i(\bar{z})$ be met for each potential signatory, taken individually.

Subgroups of countries – henceforth called 'coalitions' – should also be considered, because for various reasons they may wish to act jointly instead of in cooperation with the full set N of the countries involved in the transfrontier problem. But acting in this way would mean designing treaties for themselves, involving abatement policies most likely different from $(p_1^*, ..., p_n^*)$ – thus suboptimal at the world level. Is this inevitable, or can it be avoided? This is exactly the point on which the controversy arises that is to be discussed presently.

Two alternative theses exist: on the one hand there is what I call the 'small stable coalitions' (SSC) thesis, according to which only small subsets of the n countries can ever emerge and sign a treaty; there is on the other hand the 'grand stable coalition' (GSC) thesis, presenting the contents of a feasible treaty which is shown to be in the interest not only of all members individually but also of all subgroups of N. These two views are developed in the next section.

3. THE TWO THESES: A SUMMARY PRESENTATION

The 'Small Stable Coalitions' (SSC) Thesis

This thesis has been formulated prominently by Carraro and Siniscalco (1993) and Barrett (1994). It is based on a concept of coalitions stability (due to d'Aspremont and Gabszewicz, 1986) borrowed from the industrial organization literature on cartels. I follow here – and limit myself to – the first authors' presentation in Carraro and Siniscalco (1995) (hereafter CS).

Let $S \subseteq N$ be a 'coalition', i.e. a set of countries that are willing to cooperate and to sign among themselves a treaty to that end. Using in this subsection the authors' notation, let $P_i(S)$ denote the utility of country i if i is a member of S, and $Q_i(S)$ denote the utility[9] of i if i is *not* a member of S.

Definition 4: The coalition $S \subset N$ is called *stable* if it satisfies the following two conditions:

(i) *internal stability*: $\forall_i \in S, P_i(S) \geq Q_i(S \setminus \{i\})$ and
(ii) *external stability*: $\forall_j \notin S, P_j(S \cup \{j\}) \leq Q_j(S)$.

For the coalition $S = N$, only internal stability applies.

For the proponents of the SSC thesis, treaties are only likely to be signed by subsets of countries that meet these two conditions. As to the likelihood of worldwide environmental treaties on worldwide pollution problems (typically climate change, where N is the set of all countries in the world), these authors are led to pessimism because of the following result (henceforth, I denote by S^* a stable coalition):

Proposition CS: *If all countries are assumed to be identical,*

(a) *the existence of stable coalitions can be established;*
(b) *the size of stable conditions is always small, in the sense that $\forall S^*, |S^*| << |N|$;*
(c) *introducing private-good transfers between countries does not increase the size of stable coalitions.*

A second result,[10] due to Botteon and Carraro (1995 – BC hereafter), mitigates the pessimism of the one just quoted. It is also based on the more realistic premise of non-identical countries. But it rests on a numerical example only:

Proposition BC: *When countries are not identical, a numerical example with five countries shows*

(a) the existence of stable coalitions;
(b) that, without transfers, stable coalitions are always small;
(c) that private-good transfers can be found that increase the size of stable coalitions, all the way to making stable even the grand coalition N.

As for transfers, it should be pointed out that those considered by these authors are not linked with the countries' emissions: they are all formulated as lump-sum transfers.

The 'Grand Stable Coalition' (GSC) Thesis

This thesis has been formulated and defended in the two papers Chander and Tulkens (1995, 1997) (CT hereafter; we use here mainly the model of the latter). It is based on the cooperative game-theoretic concept of the γ-core,[11] and can be summarized in the following two steps:

Assumption 'γ': If a coalition $S \subset N$ forms, the highest aggregate utility it can achieve for its members is given by the function

$$w^\gamma(S) = \underset{\{(x_i, p_i)_{i \in S}\}}{Max} \sum_{i \in S}[x_i + v_i(z)]$$

subject to

$$\sum_{i \in S} x_i \leq \sum_{i \in S} g_i(p_i)$$

and

$$\sum_{i \in S} p_i + z = -\sum_{j \in N \setminus S} p_j,$$

where $\forall j \in N \setminus S$, (x_j, p_j) maximizes $x_j + v_j(z)$
subject to

$$x_j \leq g_j(p_j)$$

and

$$p_j + z = -\sum_{\substack{i \in N \\ i \neq j}} p_i.$$

If coalition N forms, the highest aggregate utility it can achieve for its members is given by

$$w^\gamma(N) = \sum_{i \in N}\left[x_i^* + v_i(z^*)\right],$$

where x^*, z^* are values given by an international optimum $(x^*, y^*, p^*, z^*, T^*)$.

Proposition CT: *Given the vector of optimal emissions* $(p_1^*, \ldots, p_n^*)$, *private-good transfers of the form*[12]

$$T_i^* = -\left[g_i(p_i^*) - g_i(\bar{p}_i)\right] + \frac{\pi_i(z^*)}{\pi_N(z^*)}\left[\sum_{i \in N} g_i(p_i^*) - \sum_{i \in N} g_i(\bar{p})\right], \quad i \in N \quad (1)$$

induce a feasible state $(x^*, y^*, p^*, z^*, T^*)$ *of the economic–ecological system which is such that, for every coalition* $S \subset N$,

$$\sum_{i \in S}\left[x_i^* + v_i(z^*)\right] > w^\gamma(S).$$

The proposition asserts that with transfers defined as in (1), the feasible state $(x^*, y^*, p^*, z^*, T^*)$ cannot be improved upon to the benefit of its members by any coalition $S \subset N$. Technically, the feasible state $(x^*, y^*, p^*, z^*, T^*)$ is a strategy that belongs to the core of a cooperative game associated with the economic–ecological system, $w^\gamma(S)$ being the characteristic function of that game.

The assumption yielding the function $w^\gamma(S)$, on which the proposition's statement rests, specifies that if S forms, its members choose the actions that are the most beneficial for themselves as a group, while the other players (countries) act to the best of their individual interests, 'playing Nash' against S and the other countries. The outcome of these behaviours is a state of the economic–ecological system that the authors call a 'Partial Agreement Nash Equilibrium with respect to S' (denoted henceforth as P.A.N.E. w.r.t.(S)). The core property of the state $(x^*, y^*, p^*, z^*, T^*)$ is thus that if a treaty is proposed to N that induces this state, no subset S of countries can hope to gain from inducing instead a P.A.N.E. w.r.t. itself. Therefore the 'grand treaty' should be signed by all, without regret.

Let me briefly recall the structure of the transfers formula (1). Each individual transfer consists of two parts: a payment *to* each country i that covers its increase in cost between the Nash equilibrium and the optimum (first squared bracket), and a payment *by* each country i of a proportion $\pi_i(z^*)/\pi_N(z^*)$ of the total of these differences across all countries (second squared bracket). In other words, each country's abatement cost is covered and each country's contribution is determined by the relative intensity of its preferences for the public-good component (z^*) of the problem. Notice that the sum of these transfers is equal to zero: they break even.[13]

Most important for our present purposes is also to note that the transfers are linked to the emissions – actually to the level of their abatement cost.

4. DIFFERENCES AND SIMILARITIES

As the preceding summary has already made clear, a theory of stable coalitions is here opposed to the theory of the core of a cooperative game. We consider here four aspects of this opposition.

On Coalitions, Coalition Formation, and the Final Outcome of the Games

Let us remind ourselves first that the theory of the core of a cooperative game, on which the GSC thesis rests, is basically *not* a theory of the formation of coalitions. Its scope is in fact more limited. It does indeed focus on arguments to support the view that only the so-called 'grand coalition'[14] of all players will form, and that the other coalitions will not form.

By contrast to this, the SSC approach claims to be able to identify some specific subsets of N for which it asserts that they will form as 'coalitions' because they are stable (in the specific SSC sense), and other subsets that will not form in this way. The justification for the assertion of stability is provided by comparing, for each conceivable subset, the payoffs of each individual player when s/he belongs to the coalition and when s/he stays out.

It thus appears that the term 'coalition' is not used in the same way by the two groups of authors. In the language of the SSC view held by the latter group, a coalition denotes a set of 'good' guys, who do cooperate among themselves,[15] and intend to sign a treaty together – while those who stay outside of the coalition are the 'bad' guys, who act in isolation. Note that, in this parlance, any coalition must comprise at least two players (here, countries): singletons are meaningless as 'coalitions'.

In the GSC (core-theoretic) way of reasoning, things are reversed: the strategy in the core (that is, the contents of a treaty for N) is supposed to be first proposed to all players; and then the term 'coalition' is used to denote people who might possibly object to it. Coalitions are thus here a set of 'bad guys', who put in question the fact of cooperating within N, and refuse to sign the grand treaty proposed to them; they instead consider doing something else – specifically, achieving what was specified above as a P.A.N.E. w.r.t.(S). Note that here a singleton *is* meaningful as a 'coalition', because the essence of a coalition is not the fact that its members cooperate, as is the case above; it is instead the fact that the coalition does (or envisages to do) something different from what is being proposed to N.

With this clarification of the vocabulary in mind, as well as of the behaviours this vocabulary is intended to describe, one can perhaps better see the central difference between the two theses, which lies in the final outcome of the transfrontier pollution game that they each envisage:

- For the SSC literature, the final outcome is a twofold situation consisting of, on the one hand, the formation of some small coalition of countries whose members do sign an abatement treaty and, on the other hand, the other countries who decline to join in signing (and enjoy a free ride from the signatories' clean-up: more on this below). Note that this outcome is in fact exactly what CT have dubbed a P.A.N.E. with respect to some coalition.
- In the GSC literature, the final outcome is a joint strategy for all players – the grand treaty, which is better for any coalition S than the P.A.N.E. this S might achieve.

In terms of the cooperative game theoretic literature on 'stable coalitions structures',[16] where a coalition structure is defined as a partition of the all-players' set, one can restate the above as follows: the SSC literature predicts an outcome with a coalition structure of the form $\{S, \{j\}_{j \in N \setminus S}\}$, where the sets $\{j\}$ are singletons, whereas the GSC literature predicts an outcome with a coalition structure of the form $\{N\}$, with no singletons. Neither of the two views under study here refers to the concept of stable coalitions structures. But it obviously applies very well to what we are dealing with.

On Free-riding and Threats

Just as with 'coalition' the expression 'free-riding' is also used with different meanings in the two strands of literature under review.

In the SSC approach, the free-riding that is dealt with is one that occurs when – in the words of its authors – 'a country lets other countries sign a cooperative agreement, and thereby enjoys a cleaner environment at no cost' (Carraro and Siniscalco, 1995, pp. 264–5). This prompts two remarks:

(i) It refers to *individual* free-riding only. Of course, one may rephrase the definition and speak of countries instead of just one. This is indeed the case with the SSC final outcome I have just recalled. But the set of such free-riders then amounts to a collection of singletons, not a set of cooperating players.

(ii) Suppose a (for example upstream) country is a major polluter, but does not care at all for the quality of the (downstream) environment, for objective reasons. As it pollutes a lot, it should be brought into the treaty, since its actions are determinant ones for achieving a full international optimum. If it stays out nevertheless, is it to be considered as a free-rider? In fact, the above definition of free-riding does not apply very well to such a case.

Turning to the GSC view, I immediately see two elements emanating from the core concept that are relevant to free-riding:

(i) Free-riding is considered for *any* subset S of N, that is, for singletons but also for larger subsets of N. We have thus explicitly the possibility of *coalitional* free-riding.
(ii) It is supposed that free-riders do cooperate among themselves: they indeed are assumed to achieve $w^\gamma(S)$, as defined in Assumption γ.

Much more importantly, however, the GSC view adds another ingredient in describing free-riding behaviour, namely a reaction of the other, non-free-riding countries. This reaction is not intended to punish the free-riders in an irrational way; it is simply not to form as a coalition, and to just play Nash against the free-riding coalition S. This is a threat element that I like to call an individually reasonable threat.

Threats against free-riders[17] are absent from the SSC analysis; but the constructive results yielded by the GSC analysis, using some form of threat, make one wonder whether this is not precisely an important source of the difficulty, for the former, in finding grounds for cooperative agreements.

Characteristic Functions: A Common Tool for Further Analysis

We have observed above that the final outcome of the SSC approach is nothing else than a P.A.N.E. w.r.t.(S) where some S is found to be stable. On the other hand, that same concept is used by the GSC approach to formulate the characteristic function $w^\gamma(S)$ whereby a coalitionally stable strategy is claimed to be found for N.

This rapprochement suggests that while the SSC thesis does not use the tool of a characteristic function, one could nevertheless ask whether there is not some characteristic function underlying, or hidden within, the SSC approach. I want to argue here that this is indeed the case, after having made two preliminary remarks on the characteristic function $w^\gamma(S)$.

Let me observe, first, that with the characteristic function $w^\gamma(S)$, in the special case where $S = \{i\}$ is a singleton, the resulting P.A.N.E. w.r.t. $(\{i\})$ is nothing else than the Nash equilibrium of the problem. Any individual free-riding, in the GCS framework of thought, entails absence of any cooperation at all. This is the extreme form of the threat I described above.

Second, there is also something to be learned from considering, still with the characteristic function $w^\gamma(S)$, the other extreme case where $S = N\backslash\{i\}$, and the final outcome is the P.A.N.E. w.r.t.$(N\backslash\{i\})$. Here, $N\backslash\{i\}$ are cooperating (thus, they are 'coalitional' free-riders), and $\{i\}$ is left alone. Compared with the previous case, things are reversed. The 'free-rider' expression is perhaps not too appropriate a vocabulary any more, since the outcome may be more naturally seen as what occurs when the full players' group N throws out the singleton $\{i\}$.

What do we learn from considering this case? Essentially that the core strategy for N is to be understood as one that deters $N\backslash\{i\}$ to act that way. This is relevant for the case mentioned above, namely when i is a strong polluter, careless of the environment, and neglecting to cooperate with N: the core strategy is one such that for the members of $N\backslash\{i\}$, it is not in their interest to leave $\{i\}$ out.

My main point in this subsection is a different one, however. In the definition of the characteristic function $w^\gamma(S)$, it is assumed that, given S, the players not in S play Nash against this coalition, and $w^\gamma(S)$ then denotes the payoff for the members of S, given that assumption.

Now, why not change this assumption, and consider what the SSC literature denotes as the magnitude $Q_i(S)$, that is, the payoff of player i when he is not a member of S, *and S is formed*.[18] Let us, in particular, consider this magnitude for $S = N \setminus i$, that is, $Q_i(N \setminus i)$. Using now the variables of the underlying economic–ecological model, let us exhibit the strategies of all players that induce such a payoff. In the notation used earlier, we have:

$$Q_i(N \setminus i) \equiv \text{Max } u_i = x_i + v_i(z)$$

$$\text{s.t. } x_i \leq g_i(p_i)$$

$$p_i + z = -\sum_{j \neq i} p_j$$

where the vector $(p_j)_{j \in N\backslash i}$ maximizes

$$\sum_{j \in N\backslash i} u_j = \sum_{j \in N\backslash i} \left[x_j + v_j(z) \right]$$

$$\text{s.t.} \sum_{j \in N \setminus i} x_j \leq \sum_{j \in N \setminus i} g_j(p_j)$$

$$\sum_{j \in N \setminus i} p_j + z = -p_i.$$

To harmonize notation, let me now substitute[19] $w^\delta(\{i\})$ for the value of $Q_i(N \setminus i)$ so defined. Let me further define this value $w^\delta(\{i\})$ for all singletons of N, and write for N itself $w^\delta(N) = w^\gamma(N)$ as defined in Assumption γ.

I thus define a function $w^\delta(\cdot)$ that associates with all singletons of N, and N itself, a real number. In cooperative game-theoretic parlance, this is of the nature of a characteristic function, with the peculiarity that its domain is restricted to only some subsets of N. Nevertheless, we have a cooperative game, defined by the pair $[N, w^\delta(\cdot)]$.

If for this game a core imputation exists, then N is a stable coalition *in the SSC sense*, and we have a reconciliation of the two theses. If the core is empty, then N is not a stable coalition in that sense, in spite of Proposition CT: the two concepts cannot be reconciled, in general.

This is what Proposition CS establishes, using the case of identical players: the core of the game $[N, w^\delta(\cdot)]$ is thus empty, in general. However, Botteon and Carraro (1995) showed, with an example, that with non-identical players and transfers, the core of that game may not be empty: reconciliation is thus not a hopeless task. It only remains to find out how strong, and realistic, general conditions can be under which non-emptiness holds. I have not done that work, but I am convinced that it would be worth doing, if only because the economic–ecological world we are dealing with is essentially and immensely diversified, and transfer of resources across countries is evidently a tool of international economic policy.

With the construct just presented, I have attempted to reformulate the stable coalitions theory in terms of the theory of cooperative games. The scope of that attempt is of course limited to the issue of the stability of the grand coalition *vis-à-vis individual*[20] free-riding, and its interest essentially rests in delineating the conditions of reconciliation[21] between the two theories.

On Transfers and 'Side Payments'

A final dissimilarity lies in the formulation of transfers. As pointed out in Section 3, they are of the lump-sum form in the SSC models, whereas in Formula (1) of the GSC approach they appear as linked with the amounts of emissions abatement. While in the former case they are just 'side payments' between countries, they can be given in the latter case an interpretation in terms of a formula[22] for sharing, between the countries, the aggregate abatement costs.

Introducing this second kind of transfer in the characteristic function apparatus I have just outlined would definitely be relevant. While such transfers would not change the negative result obtained by CS with identical countries, they might reinforce the positive result of Botteon and Carraro with non-identical countries.

5. CONCLUSION

What is essentially at stake in this controversy is the stability of the grand coalition: are all countries likely to sign treaties in matters of worldwide transfrontier pollution problems? The above comparative exercise suggests an answer in the form of a further question: what kind of stability does one have in mind: (1) a *passive* stability with respect to *singletons only*, with 'passive' meaning stability without threat against defecting singletons? – this is the SSC view; or (2) an *active* stability with respect to *all conceivable coalitions*, with 'active' meaning stability with the threat of playing Nash against defecting coalitions? – this is the GSC view.

From a positive economics point of view, both concepts are defensible, and it remains to the analyst to find out which one is more often observed, and therefore more realistic. From a normative point of view, in which I would include the discourse of policy advisers, I cannot help thinking that the active stability perspective has stronger merits for two reasons: it embodies the reality of threats in a richer way; and it has shown that it lends itself to formulating explicit emissions and transfers policies that are both implementable and computable.

Yet there is, of course, a long way, a very long way indeed, between what our modest models allow us to assert, and the immensely complex reality we are facing. But I cannot help being happy with theoretical thinking that gives some ground for optimism, because in this way it becomes possible that our intellectual and scientific activity contributes positively to the endeavours of negotiators and decision makers who are in charge of those matters. When theory can help them in a constructive way, I submit we do our job best.

NOTES

1. Invited keynote speech at the Sixth Meeting of the European Association of Environmental and Resource Economists, Umeå, Sweden, 22 June 1995. The research reported here was part of the activities carried out under support of the European Union, within the project 'Environmental Policy, International Agreements and International Trade' coordinated by Professor Alistair Ulph, as well as within the HCM Network 'Designing economic policy for

management of natural resources and the environment' (CHRX CT93-0228) coordinated by Professor Anastasios Xepapadeas. It originated much earlier, however, during stimulating and valuable discussions with Carlo Carraro and Domenico Siniscalco that started at the Cambridge 1991 meeting of the European Economic Association and were pursued at several other occasions, in particular at the Harvard 1994 Congress of the International Institute of Public Finance and at the CORE–FEEM workshop 'Coalitions in environmental games and other economic applications' held at the Center for Operations Research and Econometrics (CORE), Louvain-la-Neuve in March 1995. For the completion of the chapter the author also benefited from the comments of Claude d'Aspremont and the editors of this volume, as well as from the hospitality and support of the Fondazione ENI Enrico Mattei (FEEM), which he gratefully acknowledges.

2. More detailed presentations, with some discussion of the main assumptions can be found in Section 2 of Chander and Tulkens (1992).
3. The absence of a subscript attached to this variable reflects its public-good character; and with the convention of measuring the ambient characteristic in non-positive amounts, our assumption $\partial u_i/\partial z \geq 0$ implies that z is felt by the consumers as a public bad. Notice also that z is treated in this chapter as a flow only. Extensions to stock pollutants have been made recently for the GSC thesis (expounded below) in Germain, Toint and Tulkens (1996) as well as in Germain, Tulkens and de Zeeuw (1996). Another limitation of all models discussed here is that they deal with scalar-measured pollutants only.
4. Labour, capital and the other inputs are taken as constant and subsumed in the functional symbol g.
5. With some abuse of language, these transfers will often be called 'financial' in what follows.
6. Close analysis of the economic model reveals that, just as in reality, there are many optima in general – optima that may differ either in terms of the emissions vector $(p_1^*, ..., p_n^*)$, or in terms of the consumption levels $(x_1^*, ..., x_n^*)$, or both. The quasi-linearity assumption simplifies the reasoning in this respect because it implies that the emissions vector $(p_1^*, ..., p_n^*)$ is the same at all international optima (for a proof, see Proposition 1 in Chander and Tulkens, 1995b).
7. As amply elaborated upon in Chander and Tulkens (1991 and 1992). For a more sceptical review, see, however, Folmer, Mouche and Ragland (1993, pp. 314–15).
8. As suggested in Tulkens (1979, p. 206).
9. These utilities could also be written in the notation of the previous section, but I shall turn to that later.
10. I shall leave aside the otherwise interesting results of CS concerning the implications of possible *commitments* to cooperate, because the issue here is only the explanation of cooperation.
11. As distinct from those of α- and β-cores. The Greek letters used refer to alternative specifications of the assumption just about to be stated. The references cited contain a discussion of these alternative assumptions.
12. Notation: $\pi_i = dv_i/dz$ and $\pi_N = \Sigma_{i \in N} \pi_i$
13. Several further comments and properties are given in Chander and Tulkens (1995, pp. 289–91).
14. As will appear below, it may be expositionally convenient to keep the term 'coalition' for *proper* subsets of players only and avoid using it for denoting the full players' set. As an additional justification for this terminological convention, one may remember that a coalition is usually conceived of as a group opposing itself *against* some other people. Clearly there are no such other people when the 'coalition' is the full players' set.
15. In both theories, 'to cooperate' means the same thing, namely: for any set of players whose cardinal number is at least two, to do together something different from what each of the cooperating players would do alone.
16. A concept used and studied by Aumann and Drèze (1974), as well as Hart and Kurz (1983).
17. Threats are of course not to be confused with the 'reaction functions' analysed with much detail in section 3.2 of CS. On reaction functions, however, it is interesting to note that while stability in the SSC sense is shown by CS to be weakened by non-orthogonal functions, the P.A.N.E.(S) on which stability of N in the GSC sense is established do imply non-orthogonal reaction functions (see assertion (*iii*) in Proposition 4 of Chander and Tulkens, 1997).

18. This proviso was not explicitly mentioned earlier; but it is unquestionably present, albeit implicitly, in the SSC theory.
19. The superscript δ is used to point out to the once more different assumption made here on the behaviour of players that do *not* belong to the coalition S under consideration. Writing this δ case in a more explicit way as $w^\delta(\{i\} \mid N \setminus \{i\})$, one could also imagine still further cases suggested by the expression $w^\varepsilon(\{i\} \mid S, \{j\}_{j \neq i, j \notin S})$ Examining these is beyond the scope of the present discussion.
20. Thus, not coalitional free-riding.
21. When the core is empty, one may consider as a substitute the nucleolus.
22. The details of this are given in section 6 of Chander and Tulkens (1995).

REFERENCES

Aumann, R.J. and J. Drèze (1974), 'Cooperative games with coalition structures', *International Journal of Game Theory*, **3**, 217–37.

Barrett, S. (1994), 'Self-enforcing international environmental agreements', *Oxford Economic Papers*, **46**, 878–94.

Botteon, M. and C. Carraro (1995), 'Burden sharing and coalition stability in environmental negotiations with asymmetric countries', paper presented at the 2nd meeting of the HCM network, 'Designing economic policy for management of natural resources and the environment', Venice, May 1995. FEEM Nota di Lavoro no. 78.95 (November).

Carraro, C. and D. Siniscalco (1993), 'Strategies for the international protection of the environment', *Journal of Public Economics*, **52**, 309–28.

Carraro, C. and D. Siniscalco (1995), 'International coordination of environmental policies and stability of global environmental agreements', chap. 13 in L. Bovenberg and S. Cnossen (eds), *Public economics and the environment in an imperfect world*, Boston, London, Dordrecht: Kluwer Academic Publishers.

Chander, P. and H. Tulkens (1991), 'Strategically Stable Cost Sharing in an Economic–Ecological Negotiation Process', CORE Discussion Paper no. 9135, June 1991 (revised October 1992); to appear in K.G. Mäler (ed.), *International Environmental Problems*, a volume sponsored by the European Science Foundation, Boston and Dordrecht: Kluwer.

Chander, P. and H. Tulkens (1992), 'Theoretical foundations of negotiations and cost sharing in transfrontier pollution problems', *European Economic Review*, **36** (2/3), 288–99.

Chander, P. and H. Tulkens (1995), 'A core-theoretic solution for the design of cooperative agreements on transfrontier pollution', *International Tax and Public Finance*, **2** (2), 279–94.

Chander, P. and H. Tulkens (1997), 'The Core Of An Economy With Multilateral Environmental Externalities', *International Journal of Game Theory*, **26**, 379–401.

d'Aspremont, C. and J. Jaskold Gabszewicz (1986), 'On the stability of collusion', chapter 8 (pp. 243–64) of J.E. Stiglitz and G.F. Mathewson (eds), *New developments in the analysis of market structure*, Cambridge, MA: MIT Press.

Folmer, H., P. van Mouche and S. Ragland (1993), 'Interconnected games and international environmental problems', *Environmental and Resource Economics*, **3**(4), 313–36.

Germain, M., P. Toint and H. Tulkens (1996), 'Financial transfers to ensure cooperative international optimality in stock pollutant abatement', CORE Discussion Paper no. 9701, Center for Operations Research and Econometrics (CORE), Université

Catholique de Louvain, Louvain la Neuve; to appear in F. Duchin, S. Faucheux, J. Gowdy and I. Nicolaï (eds), *Sustainability and Firms: Technological Change and the Changing Regulatory Environment*, Cheltenham: Edward Elgar.

Germain, M., H. Tulkens and A. de Zeeuw (1996), 'Stabilité stratégique et pollution-stock transnationale: le cas linéaire', IRES Discussion Paper no. 9701, Université Catholique de Louvain, Louvain-la-Neuve, forthcoming in *Revue Economique*, 1998.

Hart, S. and M. Kurz (1983), 'Endogenous formation of coalitions', *Econometrica*, **51** (4), 1047–65.

Tulkens, H. (1979), 'An Economic Model of International Negotiations Relating to Transfrontier Pollution', chapter 16 (pp. 199–212) in K. Krippendorff (ed.), *Communication and Control in Society*, New York: Gordon and Breach Science Publishers.

3. Dynamic resolution of inefficiency due to international environmental externalities

Mark B. Cronshaw*

1. INTRODUCTION

It is well known that economic externalities can lead to outcomes which are not Pareto-efficient.[1] Pollution is a negative externality, since the emissions of one country have an adverse effect on the well-being of others. In the absence of any corrective measures, each country will tend to pollute too much, since it does not internalize the cost that such pollution imposes on other countries. Corrective measures include command and control, taxes or tradable permits. Command and control or permits directly limit emissions, while the additional cost imposed by taxes causes reductions in emissions.

There is another approach which can potentially correct the inefficiency, when one recognizes that there is a time dimension to real economies. A country can be threatened with a future punishment if its emissions are too high. The threat can overcome a country's temptation to emit at a level which is inefficient, providing that the punishment is sufficiently severe. A punishment is severe if it has a low actual payoff, and if countries do not discount the future too heavily, which is commonly referred to as being patient. If there is too much discounting, then the severity of the low future payoff is mitigated. There are two assumptions implicit in such a solution. First, it must be possible to monitor the actions of each country. Of course such monitoring is also required in order to implement the other corrective measures mentioned above. Second, the threatened punishment must be credible, that is, it must itself be an equilibrium of the game.

The Folk theorem, which applies to infinitely repeated games, addresses the issue of credibility. Friedman (1971) showed that a threat of a static Nash equilibrium forever after any deviation from an equilibrium path gives players

---

* I am grateful to the editors for very careful and helpful comments, and also to Henk Folmer for suggesting the topic.

an incentive to cooperate and thereby achieve Pareto-efficient outcomes, if they do not discount the future too heavily. The Nash threat is credible since it involves each player choosing a best response to the other. McMillan (1979) used this idea to show that an efficient amount of a public good could be provided in an infinitely repeated game. Pollution abatement is a public good. Mäler (1993) and Barrett (1994) discuss such a supergame solution for international environmental externalities.

Barrett suggests that Nash threats may not be credible since countries would have an incentive to renegotiate away from such an inefficient punishment outcome, if they were actually called upon to enforce it. This is an important possibility. Unfortunately, there is not a consensus amongst game theorists concerning a notion of renegotiation-proofness. Different notions have been proposed by Farrell and Maskin (1989) and Pearce (1987). Farrell and Maskin's notion of weak renegotiation-proofness requires that the continuation payoffs after any histories in the game cannot be Pareto-ranked. Pearce calls an equilibrium renegotiation-proof if its lowest continuation payoff (after any history) is required in order to provide incentives to conform with the equilibrium or, in other words, if a less severe punishment would not be sufficient to support the equilibrium.

Renegotiation is a delicate issue. In an efficient equilibrium of a deterministic game, the players would not actually have to carry out the punishment. They merely need to believe that the punishment would be carried out if they were to deviate. It is in their interests to believe this, since it is the threat that gives them an incentive to cooperate.

The Folk theorem was strengthened by Fudenberg and Maskin (1986 and 1991), who showed that there are more severe threats than reversion to Nash for ever. Abreu (1986) gave a nice characterization of the worst symmetric punishment for oligopoly games in terms of a 'stick and carrot'. That is, there is one bad period followed by a good future. The prospect of a good future gives the players an incentive to go along with the single punishment period. A punishment with only a single bad period is somewhat more credible than one that is infinitely long. It is also more severe than Nash in oligopoly games. The reason for this is that the 'stick and carrot' punishment allows for different behaviour depending on whether players accept their punishment. The Nash punishment does not permit such flexibility.

However, the worst punishment in other games may not have the 'stick and carrot' structure. For example, the worst punishment in a prisoners' dilemma game is the static Nash equilibrium for ever. It is of interest to know the structure of the worst punishment in games with environmental externalities. Section 4 gives an example of such a game where the worst symmetric equilibrium does have the 'stick and carrot' structure. It also shows that countries do not have to be very patient in order for a Pareto-efficient outcome to be an equilibrium.

Sections 2 and 3 discuss the folk theorem for repeated environmental games with two countries. Section 2 is concerned with a unidirectional externality; Section 3 with bidirectional externalities. These sections emphasize that the main issue concerning international environmental externalities need not be efficiency, but rather equity. No taxes or permits are required in order to achieve an efficient outcome. What is required instead is good monitoring of emissions, and a meeting of all affected parties, such as the Montreal Protocol, to agree on one of the many efficient equilibria which is equitable. The debate at such meetings must of necessity be intense, since in matters of equity, any gain for one country is at the expense of another.

There is an obvious deficiency in repeated game models of environmental externalities, namely that most pollutants accumulate over time. Thus it is not the same game that is repeated. In addition, a stock of abatement capital may accumulate and/or preferences and technology may change over time. Section 5 contains a review of dynamic environmental game models. There are some exciting recent developments, which show that efficient equilibria exist in certain games. Some of these equilibria rely on threats similar to those in repeated games. Thus it is useful first to understand the simpler class of repeated games.

2. UNIDIRECTIONAL EXTERNALITY

This section considers a simple infinitely repeated game with two countries. In each period the upwind (or upstream) country chooses its level of emissions. The downwind (or downstream) country is adversely affected by the emissions. Emissions do not accumulate over time. We consider two models. In the first, it is not possible for the downwind country to make any monetary transfers to the upwind country. Although unrealistic, this simple model shows that an externality need not lead to inefficiency. The second model adds realism by allowing for monetary transfers between the two countries. We shall show that the static Nash equilibrium in the game with money transfers is not efficient, and discuss the many efficient outcomes. Any of these can be realized as a subgame-perfect equilibrium of an infinitely repeated game if the countries can monitor each other while they maximize their present value payoffs, providing that they are sufficiently patient. This shows that the main problem when there is a unidirectional externality in a repeated game is not inefficiency, but rather the establishment of an agreement concerning which of the many efficient outcomes is equitable.

Without Monetary Transfers

This model is deliberately simple and naïve. However, it illustrates the efficiency and equity aspects of international externalities quite clearly. Suppose that the utility of the upwind country when it chooses a level of emissions x is $u(x)$. Suppose also that $u(x)$ achieves a maximum for some unique level of emissions x^*. The emissions affect the downwind country. This country may have mitigation measures available to reduce the impact of the emissions. Let $v(x)$ be the utility of the downwind country when it applies these mitigation measures optimally. Assume that v is strictly decreasing in x.

In a static (and rather degenerate) game the upwind country chooses its level of emissions, and the downwind country receives them. In equilibrium, the upwind country will choose the level of emissions x^*. Notice that this outcome is Pareto-efficient! Any other level of emissions will make the upwind country worse off.

Of course, there are also other Pareto-efficient outcomes in which the upwind country emits less than x^*. Whether any of these other outcomes is more desirable is a matter of equity, and not of efficiency. Unfortunately, any discussion of equity is inevitably controversial, since it involves trading off the well-being of one country for that of the other.

We mention briefly that none of these other Pareto-efficient outcomes can be achieved by a subgame-perfect equilibrium of a supergame, even if the countries are patient. According to the folk theorem, any feasible outcome which is individually rational, that is, at least as good as the security level,[2] can be achieved by a subgame perfect equilibrium if the players are sufficiently patient. In this unrealistically simple model the security level of the upwind country is $u(x^*)$, since the downwind country cannot affect the utility of the upwind country. Thus there is a unique feasible and individually rational outcome, with emissions of x^*.

Clearly the restrictive assumptions of this model lead to an unrealistic conclusion that there is no inefficiency when there is a unidirectional externality. We now turn to a more realistic model in which the downwind country can compensate the upwind country for reducing its emissions. In this case, the static equilibrium is not efficient.

With Monetary Transfers

Consider almost the same model as before, but with one change. Suppose that each country also gets utility from some other good, which we will call money. Let M be the aggregate amount of money, and let ω_1 and ω_2 be the money endowments of the upwind and downwind countries respectively. The utility functions of the two countries are now $u(x, m_1)$ and $v(x, m_2)$, where m_i is the amount of money for country $i = 1, 2$. Assume that

(i) both u and v are strictly increasing in money,
(ii) v is strictly decreasing in x,
(iii) for any given m_1 there is a unique best level of emissions for the upwind country $x^*(m_1)$,
(iv) the utility functions of each country are strictly concave, and
(v) there is a maximum possible level of emissions, X.

In a static game, the upwind country decides on its level of emissions, and simultaneously each country decides how much money to give to the other.[3] There is a unique Nash equilibrium, in which neither country makes any transfers to the other, and the upwind country chooses a level of emissions $x^*(\omega_1)$.

This outcome is not Pareto-efficient, since both countries could be better off if the downwind country compensated the upwind country for reducing its emissions. This is illustrated in Figure 3.1. The horizontal axis represents money, with m_1 measured from the left axis. The width of the axis is M. Thus m_2 is measured from the right axis. The point labelled ω represents the money endowment of each country. Emissions are measured on the vertical axis. The figure shows indifference curves for each country. The indifference curves for

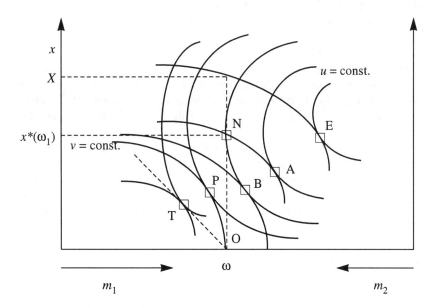

Figure 3.1 Unidirectional externality – indifference curves

the upwind country are shaped like the letter 'C', since for any fixed amount of money its utility at first rises as emissions increase from zero, but then falls as emissions exceed the optimal level. The utility of the upwind country increases to the right. The other indifference curves are for the downwind country, whose utility increases to the southwest. These indifference curves always slope down, since utility is assumed to be strictly increasing in money and strictly decreasing in emissions.

At the static Nash equilibrium, labelled N, the upwind country chooses its level of emissions to maximize its utility given its monetary endowment ω_1. This outcome is not efficient because the upwind country's indifference curve is vertical at this point, whereas that of the downwind country is not. Point A shows a Pareto-superior outcome at which the downwind country pays the upwind country to reduce its emissions. The downwind country is just as well off at A as at the Nash equilibrium, while the upwind country is better off. Point B shows another Pareto-efficient outcome in which the upwind country is again compensated for reducing its emissions, but all gains accrue to the downwind country.

Notice that the downwind country is worse off at A, B or N compared to the situation with no emissions (point O). The outcome with no emissions is itself not efficient. The point P corresponds to an efficient outcome in which the downwind country is compensated by the upwind country for accepting some pollution. At point P the upwind country is worse off than at the static Nash equilibrium, reflecting the fact that it pays for the right to pollute. Point P is consistent with the polluter pays principle, since the downwind country is just as well off at P as at O.

Point T is another efficient outcome that satisfies the polluter pays principle. It is the outcome that would be achieved by an efficient Pigouvian tax, with proceeds going to the downwind country. The figure is drawn with a lower level of emissions under the tax than at point P. This need not be the case, but the downwind country will always be at least as well off if it receives the proceeds of the tax as at P. That is, among all efficient points which satisfy the polluter pays principle, point P is the worst for the downwind country.

Figure 3.2 shows the utilities of the two countries for these same outcomes. The static Nash equilibrium is in the interior of the utility possibility set, since it is not Pareto-efficient. Points A and B are both Pareto-superior to the static Nash equilibrium. Points P and T are also efficient, but give the upwind country a lower utility than it gets in the Nash equilibrium. Point M is the minmax point. The upwind country's minmax utility is its Nash equilibrium utility, since the worst action that the downwind country can impose on the upwind country is not to give it any money. However, the minmax utility of the downwind country is below its Nash utility, since the upwind country can 'punish' the downwind country by emitting its maximum level of emissions, X.

According to the Folk theorem, any outcome[4] in the region BME can be achieved by a subgame-perfect equilibrium, if the countries are sufficiently patient. Thus any of the efficient outcomes on the frontier BE can be achieved by an equilibrium. The inefficient static Nash outcome is also an equilibrium in the supergame. However, if the countries can meet to coordinate on an equilibrium, then there is no reason why they would choose such an inefficient one. The negotiations at such a meeting will not be trivial, since they will be over equity. However, it is important to note that the environmental externality need not lead to any inefficiency.

It is worth commenting on the structure of an efficient agreement. Given that the utility functions are strictly concave, the utility possibility frontier is strictly convex (see Appendix, Result 2). Thus any outcome on the frontier BE must be stationary, that is, the same in every period. Each country will have an incentive to deviate from this stationary outcome. The upwind country can increase its utility by emitting more (see Figure 3.1), and the downwind country can increase its utility by paying the upwind country a smaller amount (possibly zero). However, if either of the countries deviates from the efficient outcome, then there is a credible (subgame-perfect) punishment which will be imposed. The threat of this punishment deters a country from deviating.

Such a threat is an elegant way of correcting for the potential inefficiency due to an environmental externality. In this deterministic model, the threat need never

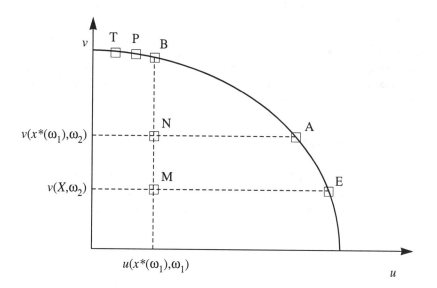

Figure 3.2   Unidirectional externality – utilities

be carried out, because the countries will not deviate. Efficiency is achieved without taxes or permits! There is a need for perfect monitoring of the country's actions, so that any deviation would be detected. The set of equilibria is smaller if monitoring is less effective (Kandori, 1992). However, the monitoring requirements are no more stringent than they would be under a system of taxes or permits. Both tax and permit schemes also require monitoring of the actual emissions.

There is an equity issue which cannot be addressed by a threat of punishment. The highest utility which can be achieved by the downwind country in a subgame-perfect equilibrium is at point B, which is lower than its utility if there is no pollution (point P, which gives the downwind country the same utility as point O; see Figure 3.1). Thus implicitly the upwind country has the right to pollute by virtue of geographical and/or meteorological conditions. Naturally this will seem quite reasonable to the upwind country, but less so to the downwind one!

Some of the equilibria seem particularly inequitable, for example, point E. In this equilibrium the upwind country receives a large payment from the downwind country (see Figure 3.1). This extortion is supported by the threat of a large emission if the downwind country does not make the payment. In effect, the ability to pollute at a high level allows the upwind country to extract resources from the downwind country. Although this outcome is Pareto-efficient, it seems to violate notions of morality. It illustrates the fact that although Pareto-efficiency may be a necessary condition for a desirable outcome, it is by no means sufficient.

There are two remaining issues concerning these supergame equilibria: (i) how patient do the countries have to be for efficient outcomes to be an equilibrium, and (ii) would they carry out the punishments if called upon to do so? These are reasonable concerns, which will be addressed in Section 4. We first consider the case of bilateral externalities.

3. BILATERAL EXTERNALITIES

Consider now an economy with two countries, each of which chooses its own level of emissions. The emissions of each country impose a negative externality on the other. Let x and y be the emissions of the two countries, and let $u(x, y)$ be the utility of the country which emits x and $v(x, y)$ the utility of the country which emits y. Assume that:

(i) Both u and v are strictly concave in (x, y),
(ii) u is strictly decreasing in y, and v is strictly decreasing in x, that is, $u_y < 0$ and $v_x < 0$, where subscripts denote partial derivatives,

(iii) marginal utility is decreasing in the other country's emissions, that is, for all (x, y), $u_{xy} \leq 0$ and $v_{xy} \leq 0$,
(iv) the maximal emissions of the two countries are X and Y respectively.

In a static Nash equilibrium, each country chooses its emissions simultaneously. The equilibrium is a pair of emissions (x^N, y^N), such that[5]

$$x^N = \underset{0 \leq x \leq X}{\operatorname{argmax}}\, u(x, y^N)$$

and

$$y^N = \underset{0 \leq y \leq Y}{\operatorname{argmax}}\, v(x^N, y).$$

Assume that the maximal emissions are greater than the Nash equilibrium quantities. The Nash equilibrium is not Pareto-efficient due to the externalities, as we shall now show.

Pareto-efficient Outcomes

One can find Pareto-efficient outcomes by choosing a level of utility $\underline{u}$ for the first country and maximizing the utility of the other. Let $V(\underline{u})$ be the maximal utility of the other country. It is given by:

$$V(\underline{u}) = \max_{x,y} v(x, y)$$

$$\text{s.t. } u(x, y) \geq \underline{u}$$

The Pareto frontier is the set of utility pairs $\{(\underline{u}, V(\underline{u}))\}$. The first-order necessary and sufficient conditions for an interior point on the frontier are:

$$v_x(x, y) + \lambda u_x(x, y) = 0$$
$$v_y(x, y) + \lambda u_y(x, y) = 0$$

together with feasibility and complementary slackness, where $\lambda \geq 0$ is the Lagrange multiplier on the constraint. Notice that $\lambda > 0$ at all points on the frontier, since $v_x < 0$ by Assumption (ii).

The Nash equilibrium quantities are not Pareto-efficient. They satisfy $u_x(x^N, y^N) = v_y(x^N, y^N) = 0$, which is not consistent with the efficiency first-order conditions, since both v_x and u_y are non-zero by Assumption (ii).

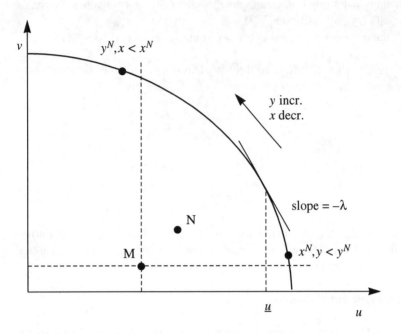

Figure 3.3 Bilateral externality

It is interesting to characterize the Pareto frontier, which is shown in Figure 3.3. The Appendix (Result 2) shows that the frontier is strictly convex given the assumptions. Furthermore, by the envelope theorem, the slope of the frontier is $V'(\underline{u}) = -\lambda$. Thus λ is a convenient parameter for characterizing the frontier.

One can examine how the pair of emission quantities varies along the frontier by totally differentiating the efficiency first-order conditions with respect to λ and rearranging to get

$$\begin{bmatrix} \dfrac{dx}{d\lambda} \\ \dfrac{dy}{d\lambda} \end{bmatrix} = -[\nabla^2 v + \lambda \nabla^2 u]^{-1} \begin{bmatrix} u_x \\ u_y \end{bmatrix}$$

where ∇^2 denotes the Hessian. At any point on the Pareto frontier,

$$u_x = -v_x / \lambda > 0, \text{ and}$$
$$u_y < 0.$$

Straightforward matrix algebra leads to the result that x is increasing and y is decreasing in λ. That is, as one would expect, efficient points with a high utility for the first country (high λ) allow it to emit large amounts, while the emissions of the other country are restricted, and vice versa.

Figure 3.3 also shows the point on the Pareto frontier at which the second country emits at its Nash equilibrium level. At this efficient point the emissions of the first country are lower than its static Nash level. This is because $u_x > 0$ according to the first-order condition for efficiency.

Since $u_x(x^N, y^N) = 0$, and u is assumed to be strictly concave, it follows that the first country emits less than x^N. This in turn means that the utility of the second country is above its static Nash level (since v is strictly decreasing in x), and that of the first country is below its Nash level (since it does not choose a best response to y^N).

Similar arguments hold for the point on the Pareto frontier at which the first country emits at its static Nash level. It follows that both countries emit less than their Nash levels at points on the frontier which Pareto-dominate the static Nash equilibrium. However, there are efficient outcomes in which one of the countries emits at a higher level than its Nash amount.

The figure also shows the minmax point, labelled M. The minmax utility for a country is achieved when the other one emits at its maximal level and it chooses a best response to this maximal level. The mimnax utility will always be below the Nash utility, since a country's highest possible utility is decreasing in the emissions of the other country (see Appendix, Result 1). However, it may or may not be below the efficient point at which the other country emits at its Nash level, depending on the maximal emissions of the other country.

According to the Folk theorem, any utility pair above the minmax point can be achieved by a subgame-perfect equilibrium if the countries are sufficiently patient. Thus one would expect the countries to coordinate on one of the efficient outcomes. The selection of a particular outcome is again a matter of equity, and will doubtless be controversial. However, it seems important to recognize that the debate about international environmental externalities should not be about efficiency, but rather equity.

4. PATIENCE AND THE WORST PUNISHMENT

This section considers the issues of (i) how patient the countries must be for the results of the Folk theorem to apply, and (ii) the nature of the worst punishment, that is, the subgame-perfect equilibrium with the lowest payoff. These must be considered together since the deterrence which is provided by the threat of a future punishment depends both on the severity of the punishment and on the countries' rates of time preference. It would be desirable to present results for general games.

However, there are no known general results. This section uses the well-developed theory for symmetric equilibria of games with identical players (Cronshaw and Luenberger, 1994, hereafter CL). In a symmetric equilibrium each player receives the same payoff. In fact, a stronger notion of symmetry is used, namely that each player uses the same action both on and off the equilibrium path. This is referred to as a strongly symmetric equilibrium (SSE).

Consider an example of a symmetric economy with n identical countries, each of which imposes an externality on all of the others. This example will show that (i) a Pareto-efficient outcome can occur in equilibrium even when the countries are not at all patient, and (ii) the worst symmetric punishment has a 'carrot and stick' form, namely, it involves only one bad period followed by the best possible symmetric future. This latter result has important implications for the credibility of the punishment. The threat to punish with the static Nash equilibrium for ever may not be credible; countries will have an incentive to renegotiate and avoid the punishment. However, even though the worst symmetric punishment gives a lower overall payoff than the static Nash, it is more robust against renegotiation since it involves only one bad period. Clearly one must exercise caution in extrapolating the results from one example to other cases, but the results presented here are quite suggestive.

Let $x_i \geq 0$ be the emissions of country $i = 1, 2, ..., n$. Suppose that the utility of country i is

$$U_i = x_i - \frac{1}{2}\left(\sum_{j=1}^{n} x_j\right)^2.$$

This section uses the procedure given in CL to find the set of all strongly symmetric subgame perfect equilibria, SSE. The utility of each country when each one emits x is $u(x) = x - n^2x^2/2$, and the highest utility that a country can achieve if each of the other countries emits x is

$$u^*(x) = \max_{x_i} x_i - \frac{1}{2}(x_i + (n-1)x)^2 = \frac{1}{2} - (n-1)x.$$

The temptation for a country to cheat is $\Delta(x) = u^*(x) - u(x) = (1 - nx)^2/2$. The static Nash equilibrium is the level of emissions, x^N, for which there is no temptation to cheat. Solving $\Delta(x^N) = 0$ gives this level as $x^N = 1/n$. The corresponding utility is $u^N = u(x^N) = \frac{1}{n} - \frac{1}{2}$. The symmetric efficient level of emissions, x^E, is that level which maximizes $u(x)$, namely, $x^E = 1/n^2$. Let $\bar{u} = u(x^E) = 1/2n^2$ be the utility of each country given the efficient emissions. Note that the Nash emissions are higher than the efficient level, and that correspondingly the Nash utility is lower than the efficient level because of the externality.

Dynamic resolution of inefficiency

Let $\beta \geq 0$ be a scalar which represents the maximal deterrence, that is, the difference between the best and worst SSE payoffs. One finds the set of SSE payoffs by defining two functions:

$$f(\beta) = \max_x u(x) \quad \text{s.t.} \quad \Delta(x) \leq \beta$$

$$g(\beta) = \min_x u^*(x) \quad \text{s.t.} \quad \Delta(x) \leq \beta$$

CL show that $f(\beta)$ is the best SSE payoff and $g(\beta)$ is the worst SSE payoff for an appropriate value of β. The solution for f and g is illustrated graphically in Figure 3.4. The figure shows the graphs of the functions u, u^* and Δ, all as functions of x. Suppose that the maximal deterrence is β, as shown on the vertical axis of the figure. The set of emissions which satisfies the constraint $\Delta(x) \leq \beta$ in the definitions of f and g is the interval $[x_-(\beta), x_+(\beta)]$, where $x_-(\beta)$ and $x_+(\beta)$ are the two roots of $\Delta(x) = \beta$. That is, x_- and x_+ are the solutions of $(1-nx)^2/2 = \beta$. These solutions are $x_-(\beta) = (1-\sqrt{2\beta})/n$ and $x_+(\beta) = (1+\sqrt{2\beta})/n$.

The solution for $g(\beta)$ is straightforward. Since u^* is strictly decreasing in x, and $g(\beta)$ is the lowest value of $u^*(x)$ among all values of x that satisfy $\Delta(x) \leq \beta$, it follows that

$$g(\beta) = u^*(x_+(\beta)).$$

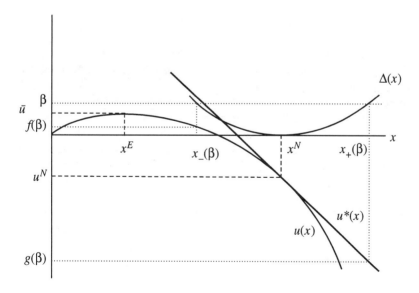

Figure 3.4 Symmetric equilibria

The value of $f(\beta)$ is the largest value of $u(x)$ among all values of x that satisfy $\Delta(x) \leq \beta$. Since $u(x)$ is non-monotonic, the solution for $f(\beta)$ depends on whether $x_-(\beta)$ is above or below x^E, or equivalently whether β is below or above $\Delta(x^E)$. For low values of β it is the case that $x_-(\beta)$ is above x^E as shown in the figure, and then $f(\beta) = u(x_-(\beta))$. However, for large values of β, $x_-(\beta)$ is below x^E, and then x^E, the level of emissions that maximizes $u(x)$, satisfies the constraint $\Delta(x) \leq \beta$, so that $f(\beta) = u(x^E) = \bar{u}$. The critical value of β that distinguishes the two cases is

$$\beta = \beta^E := \Delta(x^E) = \tfrac{1}{2}(1 - \tfrac{1}{n})^2.$$

It follows that

$$f(\beta) = \begin{cases} u(x_-(\beta)) & \text{for } \beta \leq \beta^E \\ \bar{u} & \text{for } \beta \geq \beta^E \end{cases}$$

The next step in the solution is to find the level of deterrence which can be achieved with a given interest rate. CL show that for any interest rate r, the maximal deterrence is the largest value of β that solves the so-called deterrence equation:

$$r\beta = f(\beta) - g(\beta)$$

Let β_r be the largest solution. Then the set of SSE payoffs is the interval $[g(\beta_r), f(\beta_r)]$. So $f(\beta_r)$ is the best SSE payoff and $g(\beta_r)$ is the worst SSE payoff given an interest rate r.

A minor rearrangement of the deterrence equation reveals some simple intuition: $\beta_r = (f(\beta_r) - g(\beta_r))/r$. The term $f(\beta_r)/r$ is the present value of the average discounted payoff $f(\beta_r)$, i.e., the present value of the best SSE. Similarly, $g(\beta_r)/r$ is the present value of the worst SSE. Thus the rearranged deterrence equation simply states that the maximal deterrence is the difference between the best and worst SSE payoffs.

The efficient outcome, $\bar{u}$, is an equilibrium providing that the maximal deterrence satisfies $\beta_r \geq \beta^E$. The lowest value of the deterrence for which the efficient outcome is an equilibrium occurs when $\beta_r = \beta^E$. The interest rate that corresponds to this level of deterrence is found by solving the deterrence equation for r. Substitution into the deterrence equation shows that the corresponding interest rate is

$$r^E = [f(\beta^E) - g(\beta^E)]/\beta^E = [\bar{u} - u^*(x_+(\beta^E))]/\beta^E = 300\%$$

for any number of countries. Thus the countries do not have to be at all patient for an efficient outcome to be an equilibrium.

CL show that the maximal deterrence is decreasing in r. That is, the maximal deterrence is larger when countries are more patient (lower r). Hence for interest rates below 300 per cent the maximal deterrence is above β^E, and the efficient outcome is also an equilibrium.

It is clear from Figure 3.4 that the worst symmetric equilibrium payoff, $g(\beta)$, is substantially lower than the static Nash equilibrium payoff. It is interesting to explore the nature of this worst SSE. Let $\delta = 1/(1 + r)$ be the discount factor. Then the average discounted payoff for any time sequence of symmetric actions $\{x(t)\}_{t=1}^{\infty}$ is

$$\frac{\sum_{t=1}^{\infty} \delta^t u(x(t))}{\sum_{t=1}^{\infty} \delta^t} = (1-\delta)u(x(1)) + \delta w,$$

where $w = \sum_{t=1}^{\infty} \delta^t u(x(t+1)) / \sum_{t=1}^{\infty} \delta^t$ is the average discounted continuation payoff. CL show that the action in the first period of the worst SSE is $x_+(\beta_r)$, and that the continuation payoff is $\hat{w}$, where $\hat{w}$ is defined by

$$g(\beta_r) = u^*(x_+(\beta_r)) = (1-\delta)u(x_+(\beta_r)) + \delta\hat{w}.$$

It is straightforward to show that the continuation payoff $\hat{w}$ is the *best* SSE utility, $f(\beta_r)$. Subtracting $\delta u^*(x_+(\beta_r)) = \delta g(\beta_r)$ from the second of the two equalities above gives $(1-\delta)u^*(x_+(\beta_r)) = (1-\delta)u(x_+(\beta_r)) + \delta(\hat{w} - g(\beta_r))$. Rearranging gives

$$\hat{w} - g(\beta_r) = \frac{1-\delta}{\delta}\left(u^*(x_+(\beta_r)) - u(x_+(\beta_r))\right) = \frac{1-\delta}{\delta}\Delta(x_+(\beta_r)) = \frac{1-\delta}{\delta}\beta_r = f(\beta_r) - g(\beta_r),$$

where the last equality follows from the deterrence equation, since $r = (1-\delta)/\delta$. Hence $\hat{w} = f(\beta_r)$.

The high continuation payoff $\hat{w}$ provides the countries with an incentive to go along with the first bad period of the punishment. This is the 'carrot' described by Abreu in his analysis of oligopoly supergames. If a country attempts to avoid the low utility in the first period of the punishment, then it will be punished again in the next period. Overall it will be worse off by doing so, and therefore it accepts the one bad period as a punishment.

In summary, we have presented an example in which the countries do not have to be at all patient for an efficient outcome to be an equilibrium. Furthermore, we have shown that the worst symmetric punishment in this example has the structure of a 'stick and carrot': there is one bad period followed by the best symmetric equilibrium thereafter.

This discussion has only considered symmetric equilibria. There are also asymmetric equilibria in which the countries are not required to emit the same amount as each other. This may enable more severe punishments to be imposed than the worst strongly symmetric equilibrium. If so, then efficiency can be achieved in equilibrium for even higher interest rates. Depending on the interest rate, some of the asymmetric efficient outcomes will also be equilibria. One could analyse what degree of patience is required for such outcomes to be equilibria, when supported by the worst symmetric punishment. This would be a conservative estimate, since the more severe punishments afforded by asymmetric equilibria make it easier to enforce efficiency.

5. CONCLUSIONS

This chapter has considered several environmental games with complete information and infinitely lived countries. If it is possible to detect deviations from an equilibrium path, then there is a multiplicity of non-cooperative equilibria in these and other infinitely repeated environmental games. Some of the equilibria are Pareto-efficient if the countries are sufficiently patient. Thus international environmental externalities need not lead to any inefficiency.

However, it is important to recognize that there is not a single efficient outcome. The problem with international environmental externalities is not efficiency, but rather equity. Unfortunately, addressing the issue of equity is more challenging than addressing that of efficiency. Perhaps this chapter will stimulate more research and solutions on how to establish an equitable outcome.

This strong conclusion relies heavily on the assumptions that countries have no private information, play an infinitely repeated game, and maximize the present value of their utility. There has been some work to relax these assumptions. Bac (1996) considers a supergame with private information. Becker (1982) considers a dynamic single-agent problem with a minmax objective, that is, to maximize the lowest instantaneous utility over time.

More realistic models would allow for the accumulation of pollution and/or abatement capital over time. Such models are no longer repeated games, but rather dynamic or differential games.

It is traditional in the literature on differential games to consider Nash equilibria in open- or closed-loop strategies. Fershtman and Nitzan (1991), Kaitala, Pohjola and Tahvonen (1992), van der Ploeg and de Zeeuw (1992), Martin, Patrick and Tolwinski (1993), and Tolwinski and Martin (1995) each present such equilibria for environmental games. However, there are more general classes of strategies, some of which are described in Basar and Olsder (1990). These more general strategies allow players to condition their actions on previous play in the game.

Tolwinski, Haurie and Leitmann (1986) introduce the concept of a δ strategy (not related to the discount factor). Such a strategy allows players to choose different actions depending on the actions taken previously in the game. Such strategies include feedback strategies. They point out that this class of strategies leads to a multiplicity of equilibria. Haurie and Pohjola (1987) use such strategies to find efficient equilibria in a game between workers and capitalists in which capital is accumulated. Kaitala and Pohjola (1988) use them to construct efficient equilibria in a two-player fishery game.

Benhabib and Radner (1992) also consider a two-player fishery game. They show that an inefficient Markov Nash equilibrium (MNE) exists, and that it can be used as a threat to enforce an efficient outcome, when defection can only be detected with some delay. They point out that any outcome which Pareto-dominates the MNE can occur in equilibrium if defection can be detected immediately. The reason is that there can be no benefit to defection, if it is detected instantaneously.

Dockner and van Long (1993) consider a two-player game in which emissions contribute to a stock of pollution. They show that the equilibria in open-loop strategies and in linear Markov-perfect strategies are not Pareto-efficient. However, they show that there are many equilibria with non-linear Markov-perfect strategies, one of which has the efficient steady-state level of pollution, if the countries are sufficiently patient.

There are other types of dynamic model which also warrant consideration, including overlapping generations models, and evolutionary models, such as Sethi and Somanathan (1996), a fishery model in which evolutionary pressure can lead to efficient outcomes.

We conclude that it is possible for countries to coordinate on a Pareto-efficient outcome when there are environmental externalities without taxes or permits, providing that there is complete information. Threats of future punishment are sufficient to overcome short-term incentives to over pollute, if countries are reasonably patient. One must temper this optimistic conclusion with the observation that the real economy is beset with asymmetric information. Important next research steps are to incorporate such uncertainty, and to continue work on environmental games with state variables.

NOTES

1. On the other hand, some writers argue that bargaining or creation of property rights will ensure efficiency. In contrast, this chapter assumes non-cooperative behaviour.

2. The security level is the minmax payoff, that is, the lowest payoff which a player can be held down to given that it chooses its own action optimally.
3. The same outcome would occur in a subgame perfect equilibrium of a static game with sequential moves.
4. Payoffs in the supergame are average discounted payoffs, for example,

$$\frac{\sum_{t=1}^{\infty} \delta^t u(x(t), m_1(t))}{\sum_{t=1}^{\infty} \delta^t}$$

5. Each country has a unique best response, since the utility functions are strictly concave by assumption.

REFERENCES

Abreu, D. (1986), 'Extremal Equilibria of Oligopolistic Supergames', *Journal of Economic Theory*, **39**, 191–228.

Bac, M. (1996), 'Incomplete Information and Incentives to Free Ride on International Environmental Resources', *Journal of Environmental Economics and Management*, **30**, 301–15.

Barrett, S. (1994), 'Self-Enforcing International Environmental Agreements', *Oxford Economic Papers*, **46**, 878–94.

Basar, T. and G.J. Olsder (1990), *Dynamic Noncooperative Game Theory*, 2nd edition, London: Academic Press.

Becker, R.A. (1982), 'Intergenerational Equity: The Capital–Environment Trade-Off', *Journal of Environmental Economics and Management*, **9**, 165–85.

Benhabib, J. and R. Radner (1992), 'The Joint Exploitation of a Productive Asset: A Game-Theoretic Approach', *Economic Theory*, **2**, 155–90.

Cronshaw, M.B. and D.G. Luenberger (1994), 'Strongly Symmetric Subgame Perfect Equilibria in Infinitely Repeated Games with Perfect Monitoring and Discounting', *Games and Economic Behavior*, **6**, 220–37.

Dockner, E.J. and N. van Long (1993), 'International Pollution Control: Cooperative versus Noncooperative Strategies', *Journal of Environmental Economics and Management*, **24**, 13–29.

Farrell, J. and E. Maskin (1989), 'Renegotiation in Repeated Games', *Games and Economic Behavior*, **1**, 327–60.

Fershtman, C. and S. Nitzan (1991), 'Dynamic Voluntary Provision of Public Goods', *European Economic Review*, **35**, 1057–67.

Friedman, J. (1971), 'A Noncooperative Equilibrium for Supergames', *Review of Economic Studies*, **28**, 1–12.

Fudenberg, D. and E. Maskin (1986), 'The Folk Theorem in Repeated Games with Discounting or with Incomplete Information', *Econometrica*, **54**(3), 533–54.

Fudenberg, D. and E. Maskin (1991), 'On the Dispensability of Public Randomizations in Discounted Repeated Games', *Journal of Economic Theory*, **53**, 428–38.

Haurie, A. and M. Pohjola (1987), 'Efficient Equilibria in a Differential Game of Capitalism', *Journal of Economic Dynamics and Control*, **11**, 65–78.

Kaitala, V. and M. Pohjola (1988), 'Optimal Recovery of a Shared Resource Stock: A Differential Game Model with Efficient Memory Equilibria', *Natural Resource Modeling*, **3**(1), 91–119.

Kaitala, V., M. Pohjola and O. Tahvonen (1992), 'Transboundary Air Pollution and Soil Acidification: A Dynamic Analysis of an Acid Rain Game between Finland and the USSR', *Environmental and Resource Economics*, **2**, 161–81.

Kandori, M. (1992), 'The Use of Information in Repeated Games with Imperfect Monitoring', *Review of Economic Studies*, **59**(3), 581–93.

Mäler, K.G. (1993), 'The Acid Rain Game II', Beijer Discussion Paper Series no. 32, Stockholm.

Martin, W.E., R.H. Patrick and B. Tolwinski (1993), 'A Dynamic Game of a Transboundary Pollutant with Asymmetric Players', *Journal of Environmental Economics and Management*, **24**, 1–12.

McMillan, J. (1979), 'Individual Incentives in the Supply of Public Inputs', *Journal of Public Economics*, **12**, 87–98.

Pearce, D. (1987), 'Renegotiation-Proof Equilibria: Collective Rationality and Intertemporal Cooperation', Yale Cowles Foundation Discussion Paper.

Sethi, R. and E. Somanathan (1996), 'The Evolution of Social Norms in Common Property Resource Use', *American Economic Review*, **86** (4), 766–88.

Tolwinski, B., A. Haurie and G. Leitmann (1986), 'Cooperative Equilibria in Differential Games', *Journal of Mathematical Analysis and Applications*, **119**, 182–202.

Tolwinski, B. and W. Martin (1995), 'International Negotiations on Carbon Dioxide Reductions: A Dynamic Game Model', *Group Decision and Negotiation*, **4**, 9–26.

Van der Ploeg, F. and A.J. de Zeeuw (1992), 'International Aspects of Pollution Control', *Environmental and Resource Economics*, **2**, 117–39.

APPENDIX

This appendix contains a couple of technical results.

Result 1: Suppose that x and y are scalars and that $u(x, y)$ is decreasing in y. If $\max_x u(x, y)$ exists, then it is decreasing in y.

Proof: Let $y' > y$, and let x be optimal given y, and x' be optimal given y'. Then since u is decreasing in y, $u(x', y') \leq u(x', y)$. Also, by the definition of optimality, $u(x', y) \leq u(x, y)$.

Result 2: Let $\mathbf{z}$ be a vector, and a be a scalar. Let v be a strictly concave function which satisfies local non-satiation, and u be a concave function. Suppose that $V(a) = \max_{\mathbf{z}} \{ v(\mathbf{z}) \text{ s.t. } u(\mathbf{z}) \geq a \}$ exists for all a. Then V is a strictly concave and strictly decreasing function.

Proof: Let $a' > a$, and let $\mathbf{z}$ be optimal given a, and $\mathbf{z}'$ be optimal given a'. Note that $\mathbf{z}' \neq \mathbf{z}$. This is because $u(\mathbf{z}') \geq a' > a$, so there is a neighbourhood of $\mathbf{z}'$ which satisfies $u(\tilde{\mathbf{z}}) > a$. Since v satisfies local nonsatiation there is some value $\tilde{\mathbf{z}}$ in this neighbourhood for which $v(\tilde{\mathbf{z}}) > v(\mathbf{z}')$. Also, $V(a) = v(\mathbf{z}) \geq v(\tilde{\mathbf{z}})$ by the definition of optimality. So $v(\mathbf{z}) > v(\mathbf{z}')$ and hence $\mathbf{z}' \neq \mathbf{z}$. Note also that $V(a) = v(\mathbf{z}) > v(\mathbf{z}') = V(a')$ so that V is strictly decreasing.

Since u is concave, $u(t\mathbf{z} + (1-t)\mathbf{z}') \geq tu(\mathbf{z}) + (1-t)u(\mathbf{z}') \geq ta + (1-t)a'$ for all $t \in [0, 1]$. Therefore for all $t \in (0, 1)$ it is the case that

$$V(ta + (1-t)a) \geq v(t\mathbf{z} + (1-t)\mathbf{z}') > tv(\mathbf{z}) + (1-t)v(\mathbf{z}') = tV(a) + (1-t)V(a').$$

The first inequality is due to optimality; the second holds because v is strictly concave by assumption.

4. Commitment and fairness in environmental games*

Tim Jeppesen and Per Andersen

1. INTRODUCTION

In 1990, one could read that the topics of environmental and resource economics were now very cold as topics for analytical investigation, and dead as research problems (Dasgupta, 1990). Dasgupta's somewhat provocative statement implies that not much new could be developed as regards the analytical foundation of, for instance, environmental taxes. Embedded in Dasgupta's article is, however, also the fact that environmental economics in the neoclassical approach has in many ways failed to explain even the basic problems of environmental economics. Dasgupta's statement was mainly directed to the partial analysis of economic instruments in environmental policy, and the statement does not include a distinction between *local* and *international* environmental problems. If this distinction is made, it may be that Dasgupta's statement is a bit harsh. The statement may be valid for local environmental problems, but international environmental problems are surely not 'dead' as a research problem. This is evident if one takes even a brief view of the research topics in environmental economics in the first half of the 1990s.

There are two properties that distinguish international environmental problems from local environmental problems:

- *Global aggregate emissions.* In the case of international environmental problems, global aggregate emissions are at the heart of the matter. This generates a kind of contradiction: what one country emits is diminishing compared to the total emission, but at the same time the emissions from one country affect all the other countries. The countries are thus highly interdependent, which is not the case with local environmental problems.

---

* This chapter is based on a paper written during Tim Jeppesen's stay at The Beijer International Institute of Ecological Economics, The Royal Swedish Academy of Sciences, autumn 1995. The authors would like to thank Karl-Göran Mäler, The Beijer International Institute of Ecological Economics, and Peter Bohm, Department of Economics, Stockholm University, for fruitful discussions and their comments and suggestions.

66   *Game theory and the environment*

> For example, two obvious cases with a high degree of interdependence are global warming due to emissions of CO_2 and the rarefaction of the ozone layer due to emission of CFC gases.
>
> - *Absence of a supranational institution.* Environmental taxes or pollution permits must be set by some kind of institution, for instance a government. In the case of international environmental problems, such an institution does not exist.[1] Environmental problems are instead managed by voluntary agreements among a group of countries. Thus, environmental economics must deal with such important questions as: Under what conditions are these agreements signed? How can agreements be induced? How can they be made stable?

These two circumstances have shifted the focus in environmental economics from government interventions to negotiations and coordination. These issues and problems are neither 'cold' nor 'dead' as Dasgupta stated; they are 'hot' and 'alive and kicking'.

International environmental problems have the same properties as a communally owned good. In the absence of specified property rights, there is an incentive for each individual to overuse the good in order to maximize individual welfare. This is the well-known 'tragedy of the commons' and contains one of the core issues in this chapter: it is in the common interest to agree to cooperate and reduce the consumption of common resources. Cooperative agreements are not stable, however, because every country will profit even more by free-riding. For instance, it will be in Denmark's interest to have an international agreement on reducing the world's emission of CO_2 by introducing a tax on CO_2 emissions. But it will be even better for Denmark to withdraw from the agreement and not introduce an emission tax. In this way, Denmark will still benefit from improved environmental quality due to the actions taken by the other countries, but Denmark would obtain these benefits at a lower cost than the cooperating countries. In the parlance of game theory, this can be described as the classic prisoners' dilemma, where we, for simplicity, illustrate the problem in a two-country context.

Figure 4.1 illustrates the incentives in the prisoners' dilemma in a global CO_2 agreement: If both A and B initially cooperate in a CO_2 agreement, country A will prefer to drop out, earning profits of 5 instead of 4. However, country B decides that if country A defects, B will not cooperate either, earning 1 instead of 0. This is exactly the key point in the prisoners' dilemma: each country will prefer to defect, whatever the other country does. Thus the solution (1,1) is an equilibrium strategy for both countries. The paradox is that both countries would be better off if both chose to cooperate. Put in a simple way, the prisoners' dilemma shows that an international CO_2 agreement will either not be reached in the first place, or, if it is reached, it will inevitably be undermined by free-rider behaviour. This free-riding behaviour is the origin of the instability of international environmental agreements (IEAs).

		Country B	
		Cooperates in a CO_2 agreement	Defects from the CO_2 agreement
Country A	Cooperates in a CO_2 agreement	4,4	0,5
	Defects from the CO_2 agreement	5,0	1,1

Figure 4.1   The prisoners' dilemma in a global CO_2 agreement

The solutions to this rather unfortunate conclusion are few and not easy to implement in practice. Despite this, however, more than 140 IEAs exist today (Barrett, 1991) with the Montreal Protocol for phasing out ozone depleting substances as one of the most prominent. The Montreal Protocol was first signed in 1987 by 24 countries, but by 1995, about 140 countries had ratified the protocol. Thus, even though the prisoners' dilemma leads to non-cooperation, countries *do* cooperate in reality. In order to induce cooperative behaviour, the key issue is to build *incentives* into voluntary environmental agreements. These incentives should induce cooperative behaviour and make the coalition stable. In order to identify the incentives, it is first of all helpful to distinguish the static one-shot game from dynamic games where negotiation takes place continuously. The incentives in these two groups may be different depending upon the type of the game. Second, it is important which type of regulation the game is about, for example, eco-taxes, standards, emission targets and so on (Barrett, 1992a; Hoel, 1991a). Third, it can be shown that it is of major importance for international agreements whether or not the environmental issue is linked to some other policy issues (see for example Folmer and Kroeze Gil in Chapter 8 of this book; Carraro and Siniscalco, 1993; Cesar and de Zeeuw, 1994). This third issue is, however, not dealt with in this paper. Neither do we deal with dynamic games, and we do not discuss issues concerning different economic instruments.

Instead we concentrate on static games. Our point of departure is the work done by Scott Barrett (Barrett, 1990, 1992a, 1992b, 1993, 1994a). A somewhat rigid conclusion from this work is that IEAs are unavoidably undermined by free-riding and thus become very small. However, IEAs do exist, and the purpose of this chapter is to elaborate on why reality contradicts (economic) theory. We do this by introducing two factors into Barrett's model which enhance the possibilities of reaching and maintaining an IEA. These two factors are commitment and fairness.

The chapter is structured as follows: In Section 2, we present Barrett's (1994a) model on which we base our work. In Section 3, we introduce one kind of commitment and illustrate how it affects the size of an IEA. In Section 4, we present the concept of fairness in environmental policy, inspired by Rabin (1993). In Section 5, we incorporate fairness into the model and again illustrate how this may actually enlarge the IEA. The concluding remarks are presented in Section 6.

We should initially emphasize that our work so far is only indicative. We work with a simple version of commitment, and we have specified a very simple form of fairness. Our purpose in this chapter is to focus on the policy issues rather than the technicalities. The aim is to identify some preliminary suggestions on how game theory can be improved and become more applicable as a policy-oriented tool.

2. BARRETT'S MODEL

The tradition of looking at IEAs from a prisoners' dilemma point of view gives a rather pessimistic outlook on the possibility of creating and maintaining IEAs.

The purpose of this section is to review briefly the conclusions from the literature on static environmental games. The model we present here is from Barrett (1994a), but work by Mäler (1989), Hoel (1993a, b, c, and 1994a, b, c) and Carraro also provides some valuable insights into static environmental games. In the remaining part of this chapter, we use the Barrett (1994a) model as a point of departure for discussing the importance of commitment and fairness in IEAs.

First, it is assumed that there are N identical countries (that is, identical size and identical benefit and cost functions connected to the emission reduction). Further, assume that the benefit function can be specified as

$$B_i(Q) = b\left(aQ - \frac{Q^2}{2}\right)/N \qquad (1)$$

where i is the $1, ..., N$ countries, Q is the global emission abatement ($Q = \Sigma q_i$), and a and b are parameters, where b is the slope of the global marginal benefit function.

Country i's abatement cost function can be specified as:

$$C_i(q_i) = cq_i^2/2 \qquad (2)$$

where c is the slope of each country's marginal abatement cost curve.

The choice of the functional forms makes it possible[2] to identify global emission abatement in the cooperative solution

$$Q_c = \frac{a \cdot N}{N + \gamma} \qquad (3)$$

where $\gamma = c/b$. If the countries maximize their own net benefits, the global emission reduction in the non-cooperative Nash solution[3] will be obtained, where

$$Q_0 = \frac{a}{N(1+\gamma)}. \qquad (4)$$

Further, the global net benefit under full cooperation and non-cooperation is denoted Π_c and Π_o, respectively.

With this starting-point, the question arises whether or not it is possible to obtain some degree of cooperation between many countries. To answer this question, it is necessary to specify how the agreement is entered. It is assumed that the countries which enter into the agreement maximize their combined net benefits under the assumption that the other countries adapt their emission abatement. It is necessary to require that the gains of being a member of an IEA are larger than being outside. When this is the case, the IEA is said to be stable and self-enforcing. The equilibrium fraction of signatories is denoted α^* where $0 \leq \alpha^* \leq 1$ (where $\alpha = 0$ is the non-cooperative solution, and $\alpha = 1$ is the full-cooperative solution). In this framework, Barrett (1994a) analyses the possibilities for signing an IEA and the gains from cooperation. Figure 4.2 shows the size of the stable IEA for various values of c and b. It is clear that the result can be categorized as:

- $\gamma \geq 1$: the IEA consists of no more than three countries
- $\gamma < 1$: the IEA consists of more than three countries.

The intuitive explanation for the results in the first category is that if one has an environmental problem where one additional unit of abatement is very expensive and the benefits low, the countries would be unwilling to form an IEA. This is caused by a strong incentive to free-ride due to the relatively high abatement costs. In the second category, with very high benefits accruing from

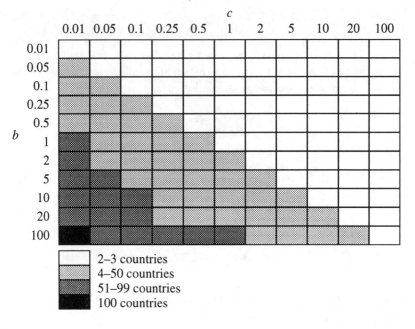

Source: Barrett (1994a), p. 885.

Figure 4.2 Number of signatories out of 100 for various values of c *and* b, *homogeneous countries*

one additional unit of abatement and very small costs, the countries would be very willing to form an IEA because there is a weak incentive to free-ride.

The next step is to show what happens with the global effects when the relative size of b and c is changed. Table 4.1 shows the outcomes under full cooperation (Π_c), non-cooperation (Π_o), and the outcome when an equilibrium number of countries has signed ($\Pi_{\alpha*}$). As in Figure 4.2, Table 4.1 illustrates that an IEA cannot consist of more than three countries when γ is large, and notice that when γ is large the difference between the full-cooperative and the non-cooperative outcome is quite significant. On the other hand, when a large IEA is possible, the IEA does not contribute to the global net benefits. The paradox here is obvious: *when cooperation is possible, it does not matter, and when it does matter, cooperation is not possible.*

The most interesting case is when both c and b are large. In this case, the difference between the cooperative and the non-cooperative outcome is actually quite significant, but, as noted before, when $\gamma \approx 1$ the IEA comprises no more than three countries. However, here we are on a border-line, and with a declining c, the size of the IEA will rise, and the global benefits will fall. Nevertheless, it is in this case that the most promising possibilities exist for a relatively large IEA, and relatively large global net benefits.

Table 4.1   *The size of an IEA, global abatement and global net benefits with homogeneous countries*

	Number of signatories out of 100 countries	Global abatement	Global net benefits
$\gamma = c/b = 100/0.01$		$Q_o = 0.1$	$\Pi_o = 1$
$= 10000$	2	$Q_{\alpha*} = 0.1$	$\Pi_{\alpha*} = 1$
		$Q_c = 9.9$	$\Pi_c = 50$
$\gamma = c/b =$		$Q_o = 500.0$	$\Pi_o = 373750$
$1/1 = 1$	2	$Q_{\alpha*} = 503.9$	$\Pi_{\alpha*} = 375659$
		$Q_c = 990.1$	$\Pi_c = 495050$
$\gamma = c/b =$		$Q_o = 990.1$	$\Pi_o = 499902$
$0.01/1 = 0.01$	51	$Q_{\alpha*} = 990.2$	$\Pi_{\alpha*} = 499903$
		$Q_c = 999.9$	$\Pi_c = 499950$
$\gamma = c/b = 0.01/100$		$Q_o = 999.9$	$\Pi_o = 49999949$
$= 0.0001$	100	$Q_{\alpha*} = 1000.0$	$\Pi_{\alpha*} = 49999950$
		$Q_c = 1000.0$	$\Pi_c = 49999950$

Source: Barrett (1994a), pp. 885–6.

Barrett (1993) extends his analysis to the more realistic case where the countries differ with respect to the cost and benefit parameters. However, the conclusions remain the same: it is the exception rather than the rule that the IEA consists of more than three countries. Thus the conclusion for the case with heterogeneous countries is identical to the case with homogeneous countries: *where the relative gains from cooperation are largest, cooperation is absent, and where cooperation takes place, the absolute gain to cooperation is negligible.*

As noted earlier, more than 140 IEAs exist, which at a first glance seems to contradict (economic) theory. It should be noted, however, that many of the IEAs are ineffective, because it is the non-affected parties which have joined the agreement, or because the agreement is not effectively enforced. What remains is, however, that the agreements are signed and established. It would therefore be of great interest to see why the theoretical conclusions above are not the whole truth. Something is missing.

In the remaining part of this chapter we include two aspects which both increase the probabilities of signing IEAs. As noted earlier, there are a number of other aspects which also point in the same direction, where the most promising aspect is to link environmental policy to other policy areas. Here we only deal with commitment and fairness, which are taken from a large array of relevant aspects.

3. COMMITMENT

The preceding results were based on the idea that IEA must be self-enforcing, and clearly, the first results are discouraging, independent of whether the countries are homogeneous or heterogeneous. Stable coalitions consist of a small number of signatories compared to the potential number of potential signatories. An instrument for obtaining larger IEAs is if some countries are *committed* to environmental politics. It can then be shown that the committed countries can give additional countries an incentive to sign the agreement.

It is an empirical fact that some countries are focusing more on environmental issues than other countries (see for instance Andersen, 1994 for a discussion about the differences in the EU), and it is well known that some countries have taken unilateral actions to reduce emissions. This could be modelled by assuming that some countries are committed to environmental cooperation. In other words: if ten countries agree to cooperate to reduce their emissions, regardless of what other countries do, these ten countries are said to be committed. This definition of commitment is equivalent to the definition in Hoel (1991b), where he discusses the consequences of a country's 'setting a good example'. In the case of global warming, the EU countries seem to be committed to some extent, but the US doesn't appear to be, and certainly not China, India, and so on. Of course, this commitment could take several forms. Carraro and Siniscalco (1991) use the Nash bargaining solution for emission setting among the cooperating countries, whereas Barrett (1994a) uses maximization of net abatement benefit among cooperators. Barrett (1994a) does not consider the possibility for commitment and is in fact critical about it:

> The snag in this proposal [about the existence of a number of committed countries] ... is that the commitment is not credible; the expanded agreement is not self-enforcing. If commitment could be made credible, then the full cooperative outcome would be easy to sustain: every country would simply commit to choose the full cooperative abatement level (q_c). (Barrett, 1994a, p. 883)

We do not agree with Barrett's statement that commitment is not credible. In fact, it is our suggestion that one of the explanations of why more than 140 IEAs exist today is that commitment exists and certainly is credible. It would be nice to have a theory about conditions for commitment. However, we do not try to provide such a theory; we simply take commitment for granted.

In order to illustrate the consequences of credible commitments, we continue with Barrett's (1994a) model. Table 4.2 illustrates the stability of a coalition consisting of four signatories. In Table 4.2 α is the fraction of signatories, q_s is the abatement level of any individual signatory, q_n is the abatement level of any individual non-signatory, π_s is the net benefit of any individual signatory, and π_n is the net benefit of any individual non-signatory. Q and Π denote, as mentioned above, global abatement and global net benefits. The signatories are assumed to choose q_s in order to maximize their collective net benefits, whereas non-signatories maximize their individual net benefits. The signatories are assumed to have a Stackelberg leader role, and the other countries are followers.

Table 4.2 Stability analysis, hypothetical example, homogeneous countries

α	q_s	q_n	π_s	π_n	Q	Π
0.0	–	8.0	–	472.0	80.0	4720.0
0.1	1.9	8.5	476.8	468.1	78.7	4690.0
0.2	4.2	8.7	474.0	466.6	78.2	4681.2
0.3	6.7	8.4	472.3	468.9	78.9	4699.4
0.4*	8.9*	7.6*	472.2*	474.9*	81.1*	4738.1*
0.5	10.5	6.3	473.7	482.5	84.2	4781.2
0.6	11.3	4.9	476.4	489.4	87.7	4816.0
0.7	11.5	3.6	479.5	494.3	91.0	4839.8
0.8	11.1	2.5	482.7	497.3	93.8	4855.9
0.9	10.5	1.6	485.4	498.8	95.9	4867.8
1.0	9.8	–	487.8	–	97.6	4878.0

Note: $N = 10, a = 100, b = 1, c = 0.25$

Source: Barrett (1994a), table 1.

The equilibrium fraction of signatories ($\alpha^* = 0.4$) can be found by starting at $\alpha = 1.0$. Here $\Pi_s(\alpha = 1.0) = 487.8$, but any country could do better by withdrawing from the agreement. According to the stability definition above, a country compares the profit from taking part in the agreement with the profit from withdrawing from the agreement. Starting from a point where all countries are signatories, they obtain a profit of $\Pi_s(\alpha = 1.0) = 487.8$. However, if any single country leaves the agreement, it obtains a profit of $\Pi_n(\alpha = 0.9) = 498.8$. Clearly there is an incentive to leave the agreement. This means that an agreement consisting of ten countries is unstable. Next, by comparing the profit of $\Pi_s(\alpha = 0.9) = 485.4$ with $\Pi_n(\alpha = 0.8) = 497.3$, we see again that the agreement is unstable. Following this line of argument, we end up with a stable agreement consisting of four countries. Note that none of these four countries has an incentive to leave the agreement since $\Pi_s(\alpha = 0.4) = 472.2$ is greater than $\Pi_n(\alpha = 0.3) = 468.9$.

Suppose now that only one country is committed in the sense that it would choose the value of q_s corresponding to the number of signatories, and that the country would willingly use the increase in net gain to 'bribe' the non-cooperating countries to participate.[4] At first sight, Table 4.3 seems to indicate that it is unnatural to have an agreement with one member. The reason is that the member is assumed to have the leader role in a Stackelberg game, whereas the other countries are followers. Note that the committed country would lose by trying to expand the coalition to less than seven members, because $\Pi_s(\alpha = 0.1) = 476.8$ is greater than $\Pi_s(\alpha = 0.6) = 476.4$. Thus the committed country would not earn a net profit if the agreement were expanded up to six countries. Further, the committed country would be unable to finance larger coalitions. If it tried to use its net gain to maintain a coalition of, say, nine members, its own net gain from the expansion ($\Pi_s(\alpha = 0.9) = 485.4 - \Pi_s(\alpha = 0.1) = 476.8$) should be distributed so that each of the other eight countries prefers to stay in the coalition rather than dropping out. However, if we have a coalition of nine members, each country could earn a profit of $\Pi_s(\alpha = 0.9) = 485.4 - \Pi_s(\alpha = 0.8) = 497.3$. The net gain from the enlarged coalition is obviously too small to bribe the uncommitted countries. In this sense, unilateral actions are not necessarily welfare-increasing.

Next, consider a stable coalition (i.e. with four members) where all members are committed. They would gain in total from full cooperation $4(\Pi_s(\alpha = 1.0) = 487.8 - \Pi_s(\alpha^* = 0.4) = 472.2) = 62.4$, but to compensate each new member for not leaving the agreement, it must pay the new member ($\Pi_n(\alpha = 0.9) = 498.8 - \Pi_s(\alpha = 1.0) = 487.8) = 11$, i.e. in total $6*11 = 66$ which is greater than 62.4. Hence it is not possible to establish full cooperation but, using the same argument, it is possible to establish a coalition of six members, since $4(\Pi_s(\alpha = 0.6) = 476.4 - \Pi_s(\alpha^* = 0.4) = 472.2) = 16.8 > 2(\Pi_n(\alpha = 0.5) = 482.5 - \Pi_s(\alpha = 0.6) = 476.4) = 12.2$.

Table 4.3 Committed countries and the expanded coalitions

Committed countries	1	2	3	4	5	6	7	8	9	10
Size of expanded coalition	1	2	3	6	10	10	10	10	10	10

Note: The table draws on the specific example in Table 4.2.

Using the same technique, we have calculated the maximum probable size of a coalition as a function of the number of committed countries in Table 4.3. We see that five committed countries are necessary for full cooperation, but we also see that with less than four committed countries, it is impossible to expand the coalition.

Table 4.3 illustrates the possibilities for obtaining full cooperation in the specific case of Barrett's (1994a) model. Carraro and Siniscalco (1991) use slightly different specifications of the cost and benefit functions, and they conclude that the slope of the reaction functions is of critical importance. If the reaction functions are orthogonal, or near-orthogonal, a fraction of committed countries is sufficient for expanding the coalition to full cooperation, but if the reaction functions are sufficiently sloped, then attempts to cooperate are undermined by incentives to free-ride.

4. FAIRNESS IN ENVIRONMENTAL POLITICS

The partial success of commitment has its limitations as in itself it does not explain where commitment comes from. It is obvious that the committed countries can leave the agreement with advantage. This leads to a possible criticism of models based on countries which solely take care of their own interests. Empirical results from negotiation games indicate that agents even in static games make choices which contradict self-interest alone. This is documented in the extensive literature on public-good provision (see for example Marwell and Ames, 1981), and in the literature on ultimatum games (see for example Thaler, 1988).

One possible specification could be that one or more countries has global gains as an argument in its welfare function. Another insight is achieved by introducing the concept of 'fairness equilibria', where the individual countries in their investments want to sacrifice their own profit in order to benefit others or to sacrifice their own profit to hurt others. In relation to environmental agreements, the emission abatement in country i depends positively on the emission abatement in country j. Countries will hereafter do their part of the job, if enough of the others do theirs as well. In such a game, various Nash equilibria may occur. In a cooperative equilibrium, countries may forego profit-increasing moves if that would hurt others who 'behave well'.

In Rabin (1993), a model is set up where the individual agents take care of things other than their own material interests. A simple version is a model where the agents have altruistic preferences, that is, they are worried about payoffs to others. The problem is that individual agents are typically not altruists in general. Altruism is more complex; many agents want to be altruistic towards others who treat them well, but will be motivated to hurt those who try to hurt them.

Rabin constructs a game in which two players, beyond the material payoffs, worry about how the other player acts depending on that other player's motives. In the following, the model will be used in an economy where there are two agents who can enter into an environmental agreement (and observe it), or not. As the profits of an environmental agreement are collective and the costs individual, conventional game theory suggests that this will end up in a prisoners' dilemma situation (unless the collective profits are very large in relation to the individual costs), that is, a payoff matrix with the structure as shown in Figure 4.3. In Figure 4.3, x represents a scale variable for material payoff. A change in x changes the scale of payoffs without changing the structure of the game.

		Player 2	
		Cooperate in an agreement	No agreement
Player 1	Cooperate in an agreement	$4x, 4x$	$0, 5x$
	No agreement	$5x, 0$	x, x

Figure 4.3 *Environmental game for two agents*

Following Rabin, two expectations are crucial here:

- what player 1 expects player 2 to choose;
- what player 1 expects that player 2 expects player 1 to choose.

If we assume that player 1 expects that player 2 chooses 'no agreement', and that player 1 thinks that player 2 thinks that 1 plays 'no agreement', then player 2, by having chosen agreement, could have benefited player 1 considerably. As player 2 is not expected to do that, player 1 has no particular reason to be nice to player 2, that is, there is every reason to believe that the result will be the usual prisoners' dilemma solution ('no agreement', 'no agreement').

If we alternatively assume that player 1 expects that player 2 chooses agreement, and that player 1 thinks that player 2 thinks that player 1 chooses agreement, then player 2 is nice to player 1, as player 2 relinquishes $1x$ so that player 1 can win $4x$.

It is natural to believe that player 1 would consider rewarding player 2's kindness by giving up the materially dominating strategy and instead use the materially dominated strategy. Rabin gives a specific definition of the concept of kindness and uses this as an argument in the utility function of the individuals. In Rabin's specification, the immaterial aspects will dominate by small material payoffs (small values of x in Figure 4.3), while the immaterial aspects are dominated, if the material payoffs are sufficiently large (large values of x in Figure 4.3).

Notice the central role of expectations: player 1's payoffs do not depend simply on the actions taken, but also on player 1's beliefs in player 2's motives. Rabin shows that it is impossible to model these emotions (immaterial payoffs) by transforming immaterial payoffs to material payoffs.

The force of Rabin's model is that it makes several various equilibria possible, which appears to be a good description of the reality.[5] Sometimes the game ends up in a negative equilibrium, where the material payoff is low, and where the agents get their negative expectations to the counterpart confirmed. Other times the game ends more satisfactorily, that is, the players realize a high material payoff and enjoy the reciprocity of kindness.

In most IEAs there are many participants and, due to the public-good character of environmental externalities, it is not possible to be nice to someone and less nice to others, so that countries are either nice to everybody, or to nobody (unless environmental political instruments are supplemented with other instruments). It is natural to assume that a country will join an agreement if it expects that sufficient other countries are joining the agreement.

We assume that a country expects $\tilde{n}$ countries to enter into and observe the agreement, and where $B(\tilde{n})$ is the material profit without participation and $B(\tilde{n}) - A$ is the material profit with participation, where A is the loss in net benefits by entering the agreement.

Assume now that there is a loss, f, by not signing, when $\tilde{n}$ is large (and a profit, when $\tilde{n}$ is small), that is:

$$f(0) > 0, f(n) < 0, f^i(\tilde{n}) < 0$$

This means that a country experiences a loss by staying inside the agreement if it expects many other countries to participate. This loss presents the stigma of not being a part of a generally accepted agreement. In the same way, the country experiences a profit if it stays out of an agreement which very few countries sign. If $|f(\tilde{n})| > A$, the country will sign the agreement, if it expects that $\tilde{n}$ countries will do so. If it is assumed that all countries are identical, they will all sign.

In more realistic conditions, the countries are different in several respects. It cannot therefore be expected that all countries will necessarily sign. This has the derivative effect that one might fear that some of the countries which would have signed, if other countries had signed, now withdraw, which further undermines the accession to the agreement (for example, nuclear testings). In such situations, a diversified treatment of diversified countries will not only impel the individual countries to sign, but will also prevent derivative effects from the fact that some withdraw.

Above it is assumed that the possibilities of action are two-sided. It is more realistic to look at the possibilities as continuous (degrees of an environmental improvement). In future work, it will undoubtedly be fruitful to combine Rabin's approach (adequately modified) with Barrett's excellent analyses of IEAs.

5. INCORPORATING FAIRNESS INTO BARRETT'S MODEL

How would Barrett's rather pessimistic results be affected if we incorporated fairness into the model?

When analysing this, we use Table 4.2 above, where a coalition consisting of four countries is self-enforcing. In addition to the material payoffs, countries are concerned about their behaviour relative to others.

Barrett (1990) touches upon this issue in his discussion about morality in non-cooperative environmental games. As an illustration, Barrett refers to the considerations made by the House of Commons Environment Committee (1984), recommending that the UK join the Thirty Per Cent Club:

> As our inquiry has progressed, the stance of the United Kingdom has become increasingly isolated by its refusal to legislate to reduce SO_2 and NO_x emissions. ... The other European nations are reducing their emissions, so we should, too (Barrett, 1990, pp. 73–4).

The argument seems to be a moral one, unrelated to material payoffs. It is the committee's opinion that the UK *ought* to reduce its emissions. This argument captures exactly Rabin's idea of fairness.

In order to incorporate this into Barrett's model, we assume that this concern about other countries' behaviour is captured in the f function, where two alternative specifications are used:

$$f_1(n) = 10 - 2n, \quad f_2(n) = 20 - 4n$$

The f function is the loss from not joining an agreement and should be added to the Π_s column in Table 4.2. This gives Table 4.4. Hence Π_n^1 now denotes the non-cooperative global net benefit when fairness is incorporated ($\Pi_n^1 = \Pi_n + f_1(n)$, and $\Pi_n^2 = \Pi_n + f_2(n)$). $F(n)$ is increasing in n, that is, the more countries who sign the agreement, the larger the loss from not joining the agreement.

Consider the case with $f_1(n)$ and consider the coalition with four countries. Since $\Pi_n^1 > \Pi_s$ (472.9 > 472.2), it is no longer stable. In fact, it is seen that no coalition is stable with the new payoff structure. For example, a full coalition is not stable, since $\Pi_n(\alpha = 0.9) = 490.8 > \Pi_s(\alpha = 1.0) = 487.8$.

On the other hand, if the non-material part has a higher weight, as in $f_2(n)$, it is seen that full cooperation is a stable coalition, since $\Pi_s(\alpha = 1.0) = 487.8 >$

$\Pi_n(\alpha = 0.9) = 482.8$, that is, if a country expects all others to be signatories, it will join the agreement.

Table 4.4 Global net benefits with fairness incorporated

α	Π_s	Π_n^1	Π_n^2
0.0	–	482.0	492.0
0.1	476.8	486.1	474.1
0.2	474.0	472.6	478.6
0.3	472.3	472.9	476.9
0.4	472.2	476.9	478.9
0.5	473.7	482.5	482.5
0.6	476.4	487.4	485.4
0.7	479.5	490.3	486.3
0.8	482.7	491.3	485.3
0.9	485.4	490.8	482.8
1.0	487.8	–	–

Note: The table is based on the specific example in Table 4.3.

If a country expects all others not to sign an agreement, it will choose to act non-cooperatively. In that sense, it is possible to have two equilibria and, as Rabin notes, sometimes cooperation is obtained, and sometimes it fails. This seems to describe IEAs very well. In some cases IEAs are seen as codification of what the countries would have done anyway, but the agreements may also be seen as an attempt to end up in the cooperative equilibrium by ensuring support from all important countries. In fact, many treaties are contingent on a certain number of countries signing the treaty.

The model including fairness allows for multiple equilibria without any explanation of which equilibrium is realized. This can be considered a weakness, but also a challenge, since it would be nice to identify factors increasing the probability of successful cooperation. Happily, recent research addresses these questions in relation to common-pool resources (Ostrom, Gardner and Walker, 1994). They study how individuals have been able to overcome the 'tragedy of the commons'. They conclude that players both in experimental designs and field studies are able to develop stocks of social capital, such as trust and norms of reciprocity, that tend to be self-enforcing and cumulative, especially when the players are able to communicate, and when they have relatively symmetric interests. On the other hand absence of these trusts is also self-enforcing. In Sethi and Somanathan (1996) it is shown that cooperation can be stable against invasion by narrowly self-interested behaviour. With respect to IEAs there are no serious problems with communication, but different countries have very different interests due to differences in income levels, location and availability of natural resources. These differences lead to different criteria for reductions in CO_2 emissions which could serve as focal points for negotiations, ranging from emissions allocated according to the population size or according to GNP. This complicates the use of the fairness concept, since signing one type of agreement might be considered more or less fair than signing another agreement. A rich country could sign an agreement with associated net costs relative to staying outside the agreement, without being considered fair, if the agreement is based on emission entitlements related to GNP.

In many models, as for instance Carraro and Siniscalco's (1991) and Barrett's (1994a), a self-enforcing coalition consists of two or three countries. Do these results have a counterpart in real-life IEAs? Probably not. An explanation could be that two or three countries do not like to help other countries even though it is in their own (self-)interest. As an old proverb reads:

Next to own fortune, the misfortune of others is not to be despised.

6. CONCLUSION

This chapter gives an introduction to a subset of the literature on international environmental policy. Common to the literature used here is the extensive use of game theory. Game theory is strong as an analytical and theoretical tool when it comes to analysing the dynamic in strategic interactions when countries are forming IEAs. However, we think that when it comes to real negotiations and cooperation, there are so many factors that influence the games that it seems evident that game theory is unable to describe more than small parts of the process. Additionally, game theory still suffers from the paradigm that it uses archetypical games such as the prisoners' dilemma, the battle of the sexes, or the chicken game. Like game theory in general, these games serve very well as analytical and theoretical instruments, but are very distant from reality. Much work still has to be done in applying the game structure in a more realistic way.

It is well known from the literature that commitment enhances the success of IEAs. This we have illustrated here by introducing a very simple form of commitment into one of Barrett's models. This shows how an increasing number of committed countries increases the size of the IEA and finally is able to establish full cooperation. However, commitment does not just come out of thin air, and future research will have to examine how different forms of commitment affect the IEAs.

Further, we have tried to apply Rabin's (1993) ideas of fairness into environmental games. This application turns the focus away from the rather simple Nash equilibria to the more realistic fairness equilibria where countries are rewarding the 'good ones' and punishing the 'bad ones'. The work so far is, however, very preliminary but it seems promising to combine Barrett's and Hoel's work with Rabin's ideas. We have introduced a very simple form of fairness into Barrett's model and show that if the countries are highly concerned about the welfare of other countries, full cooperation may be established.

In short, we argue here that fairness is a new aspect which has to be added to the list of different aspects, such as commitment and issue-linkage which all increase the size and stability of IEAs.

NOTES

1. The United Nations does not have a mandate to introduce environmental taxes, and the European Union is limited to only 15 countries.
2. The derivations of (3) and (4) are given in the Appendix.
3. Barrett (1994a) denotes this 'the open access solution'; this is the reason for the 'o' subscript.
4. This is equivalent to the idea of side payments.
5. Depending on viewpoint, this lack of predictability could be seen as a weakness.

REFERENCES

Andersen, Mikael Skou (1994), 'From Narvik to Naples: Environmental Policy in an Enlarged European Union', paper presented at the conference 'Governing Our Environment', Copenhagen, 17–18 November 1994.
Barrett, Scott (1990), 'The Problem of Global Environmental Protection', *Oxford Review of Economic Policy*, **6** (1), 68–79.
Barrett, Scott (1991), 'Economic Analysis of International Environmental Agreements: Lessons for a Global Warming Treaty', in OECD, *Climate Change: Selected Economic Topics,* Paris: OECD.
Barrett, Scott (1992a), 'Free-rider Deterrence in a Global Warming Convention', in OECD, *Convention on Climate Change. Economic Aspects of Negotiations*, Paris: OECD.
Barrett, Scott (1992b), 'International Environmental Agreements as Games', in Rüdiger Pethig, *Conflicts and Cooperation in Managing Environmental Resources*, Berlin: Springer-Verlag.
Barrett, Scott (1993), 'Heterogeneous International Environmental Agreements', CSERGE Working Paper, University of East Anglia and University College London.
Barrett, Scott (1994a), 'Self-Enforcing International Environmental Agreements', *Oxford Economic Papers*, **46**.
Barrett, Scott (1994b), 'Strategic Environmental Policy and International Trade', CSERGE Working Paper, University of East Anglia and University College London.
Carraro, Carlo and Domenico Siniscalco (1991), 'Strategies for the International Protection of the Environment', CEPR Working Paper no. 568.
Carraro, Carlo and Domenico Siniscalco (1993), 'Policy Coordination for Sustainability: Commitments, Transfers, and Linked Negotiations', FEEM Nota Di Lavoro no. 63.93.

Cesar, Herman and Art de Zeeuw (1994), 'Issue Linkage in Global Environmental Problems', FEEM Nota Di Lavoro no. 56.94.
Dasgupta, Partha (1990), 'The Environment as a Commodity', *Oxford Review of Economic Policy*, **6**(1), 51–67.
Hoel, Michael (1991a), 'Efficient International Agreements for Reducing Emissions of CO_2', *The Energy Journal*, **12**(2), 93–107.
Hoel, Michael (1991b), 'Global Environmental Problems: The Effects of Unilateral Actions Taken by One Country', *Journal of Environmental Economics and Management*, **20**, 55–70.
Hoel, Michael (1993a), 'Harmonization of Carbon Taxes in International Climate Agreements', *Environmental and Resource Economics*, **3**, 221–31.
Hoel, Michael (1993b), 'Cost-effective and Efficient International Environmental Agreements', Reprint Series no. 441, University of Oslo.
Hoel, Michael (1993c), 'Stabilizing CO_2-Emissions in Europe: Individual Stabilization versus Harmonization of Carbon Taxes', in Carlo Carraro and Domenico Siniscalco (eds), *The European Carbon Tax: An Economic Assessment*, Amsterdam: Kluwer.
Hoel, Michael (1994a), 'Efficient Climate Policy in the Presence of Free Riders', *Journal of Environmental Economics and Management*, **27**, 259–74.
Hoel, Michael (1994b), 'Environmental Policy as a game between Governments when Plant Locations are endogenous', unpublished paper, University of Oslo.
Hoel, Michael (1994c), 'International Coordination of Environmental Taxes', unpublished paper, University of Oslo.
Mäler, Karl-Göran (1989), 'The Acid Rain Game', in H. Folmer and E. van Ierland (eds), *Valuation methods and Policy Making in Environmental Economics*, Amsterdam: Elsevier.
Marwell, Gerald and Ruth Ames (1981), 'Economists Free Ride, Does Anyone Else?: Experiments on the Provision of Public Goods, IV', *Journal of Public Economics*, **15**, 295–310.
Ostrom, Elinor, Ray Gardner and James Walker (1994), *Rules, Games and Common-Pool Resources*, Ann Arbor, MI: The University of Michigan Press.
Rabin, Mathew (1993), 'Incorporating Fairness into Game Theory and Economics', *American Economic Review*, **83**(5), 1281–302.
Sethi, Rajiv and E. Somanathan (1996), 'The Evolution of Social Norms in Common Property Resource Use', *American Economic Review*, **86**(4), 766–88.
Thaler, Richard H. (1988), 'Anomalies: The Ultimatum Game', *Journal of Economic Perspectives*, **2**, 195–207.

APPENDIX

Derivation of Global Emission Abatement in the Cooperative Solution (3)

Since the N countries are assumed to be identical, we can write the global optimization problem as:

$$\text{Max}_{q_i} b\left(aQ - \frac{Q^2}{2}\right) - Nc\frac{q_i^2}{2}. \tag{1A}$$

The first-order conditions are:

$$ba - bQ - Ncq_i = 0 \quad i = 1, ..., N. \tag{2A}$$

Solving these equations, we obtain:

$$Q = \frac{aN}{N + \gamma} \tag{3A}$$

where $\gamma = c/b$.

Derivation of Global Emission Abatement in the Non-cooperative Solution (4)

The non-cooperative solution can be computed by assuming that each country chooses its abatement level given the abatement levels of all other countries, i.e. each country solves the following problem:

$$\operatorname{Max}_{q_i} \frac{b\left(aQ - \frac{Q^2}{2}\right)}{N} - c\frac{q_i^2}{2} \quad i = 1, ..., N. \tag{4A}$$

The first-order conditions are:

$$\frac{b(a - Q)}{N} - Cq_i = 0 \quad i = 1, ..., N. \tag{5A}$$

Solving the equations, we obtain:

$$Q_0 = \frac{a}{N(1 + \gamma)} \tag{6A}$$

5. Acid rain and international environmental aid: transboundary air pollution between Finland, Russia and Estonia*

Veijo Kaitala and Matti Pohjola

1. INTRODUCTION

In the autumn of 1989 the governments of Finland and the Union of Soviet Socialist Republics signed an action plan for the purpose of limiting and reducing the deposition and harmful effects of air pollutants emanating from areas near their common border (Action Programme, 1989). The areas included the whole territory of Finland and the following regions in the Soviet Union: Kola, Karelia, Leningrad and Estonia. The parties agreed that, in addition to active participation in international cooperation, they would reduce total annual sulphur emissions by 50 per cent in these areas as soon as possible but by the end of 1995 at the latest. The reductions would be calculated on the basis of the 1980 levels. It was agreed to reduce nitrogen emissions in such a way that after 1994 they would not exceed 1987 levels. It was further decided that the parties would meet in 1993 to make a new agreement, the goal being not to exceed the critical loads, i.e. the amounts which do not significantly affect the environment.

The recent political events in Eastern Europe have made this agreement obsolete. Finland has responded to the change in the international environment by seeking cooperation with the new independent nations. An agreement with Estonia was signed in November 1991. It sets the guidelines under which bilateral cooperation will be pursued. A joint commission was also established and its first duty is to draw up an agreement on reducing emissions of air

---

* This chapter is part of Task Force 3 of the European Science Foundation Programme on Environment, Science and Society. We are grateful to Henk Folmer and Nick Hanley for helping us to improve the manuscript. We thank Ilkka Savolainen and Markus Tähtinen for providing us with unpublished data on sulphur abatement costs and to the Yrjö Jahnsson Foundation for financial support.

pollutants. Estonia, unlike Russia, does not recognize the agreements signed by the former Soviet Union.

The government of Finland has also recently decided on a programme of environmental aid to Eastern Europe. The plan is to support environmental investments in areas which are sources of transboundary air pollutants deposited in Finland. Financial aid can be given for up to 80 per cent of the total costs of such projects on the condition that Finnish technology or expertise is applied. The government allocated 42 and 67 million Finnish marks for this purpose in its 1991 and 1992 budgets, respectively.

This chapter sets out to evaluate the net benefits to Finland, Russia and Estonia of trilateral environmental cooperation as well as the possible need for financial transfers in achieving efficient abatement programmes. Because of data problems, the analysis reported here is confined to sulphur emissions. At present, sulphur accounts for 50–70 per cent of aggregate acidification in Southern Finland. Our analysis is based on a restrictive set of assumptions, but it has been qualified in a number of respects in some of our other work. In Tahvonen, Kaitala and Pohjola (1993) we have replaced the damage cost functions by upper limits on sulphur depositions and assumed joint minimization of abatement costs. In Kaitala, Pohjola and Tahvonen (1992) we have investigated the long-run aspects of acidification in a dynamic game framework. These generalizations do not, however, change the qualitative results of the present chapter concerning emissions cuts and side payments. In addition, Kaitala, Mäler and Tulkens (1995) have shown that international environmental cooperation can be implemented under incomplete information on marginal emission abatement costs and damage costs.

The next section presents emission data, and a model describing the transportation of sulphur between the regions as well as abatement costs. Section 3 contains an analysis of the optimal form of cooperation and an evaluation of the need for side payments. The current chapter extends our previous paper (Kaitala, Pohjola and Tahvonen, 1991) by generalizing the analysis to cover three independent decision makers.

2. THE DATA AND THE MODEL

In 1988 the Finnish–Soviet Commission for Environmental Protection established a joint programme for estimating the flux of air pollutants emitted close to the border between the two countries. It consists of the estimation of emissions, model calculations of the transboundary transport of pollutants, analysis of observational results from measurement stations and conclusions for emissions reductions. The emissions inventory includes sulphur, nitrogen and heavy metals.

Table 5.1 gives information on the depositions and emissions of sulphur in the relevant regions in the years 1980 and 1987. Depositions were calculated by Tuovinen, Kangas and Nordlund (1990) by applying the latest version of the long-range transport model for sulphur developed at the Western Meteorological Centre of the European Monitoring and Evaluation Programme (EMEP). Emission data approved by both the Finnish and Soviet parties were used as inputs to the model calculations. Finland is here divided into three subregions: Northern, Central and Southern Finland. To align the analysis to the current political environment, the areas close to the eastern border of Finland are divided into two independent units: Russia and Estonia. The Russian areas are further split into three: the Kola peninsula, Karelia and the St Petersburg region.

Table 5.1 Sulphur emissions and depositions in 1980 and 1987 (1000 tons per year)

	Emission E		Deposition Q			
	1980	1987	1980		1987	
Northern Finland	18	5	50	(27)	46	(26)
Central Finland	107	60	124	(66)	98	(59)
Southern Finland	167	97	89	(38)	66	(35)
Finland total	**292**	**162**	**263**	**(131)**	**210**	**(121)**
Kola	362	350	156	(36)	131	(27)
Karelia	85	85	118	(65)	95	(50)
St Petersburg	125	112	108	(57)	88	(46)
Russia total	**572**	**547**	**382**	**(158)**	**314**	**(123)**
Estonia	**120**	**104**	**71**	**(38)**	**60**	**(32)**

Source: Tuovinen, Kangas and Nordlund (1990).

Both components of pollution (depositions and emissions) are much higher in the Russian areas than in either Finland or Estonia. In 1987 the total emissions from the nearby Russian regions were about three times larger than those of Finland. However, the trends are declining in all areas. In making comparisons between the regions it should be kept in mind that this Russian territory is about 25 per cent larger than Finland and that Estonia is about the same size as Southern Finland. The annual sulphur deposition per square metre ranges from 0.5–0.6 grams in Northern and Central Finland as well as in Karelia to 1.2–1.3 grams in Southern Finland and Estonia.

The numbers in parentheses in Table 5.1 denote exogenous deposition, that is, deposition originating from emissions coming from outside the regions under consideration, as well as deposition coming from unidentified (both natural and man-made) sources. About half of the total sulphur problem can thus be covered by the trilateral analysis.

Tuovinen, Kangas and Nordlund (1990) have also estimated an annual sulphur budget between these seven regions for the year 1987. It can be used to formulate a sulphur transportation matrix indicating how emissions in one area are transported in the atmosphere for deposition in another. The columns of Table 5.2 specify the deposition distribution between the regions of one unit of sulphur emitted in each area. The bold numbers on the diagonal show how important own sources of pollution are for each region. The column and row sums are not equal to unity because all areas both emit sulphur to and receive it from the rest of the world.

Table 5.2 Sulphur transportation matrix for the year 1987

	Emitting region:						
	NFin	CFin	SFin	Kol	Kar	StP	Est
Receiving region							
Northern Finland	**.200**	.017	.010	.046	.012	.000	.000
Central Finland	.000	**.300**	.062	.011	.047	.036	.029
Southern Finland	.000	.017	**.227**	.003	.000	.027	.038
Kola	.000	.017	.000	**.286**	.023	.009	.000
Karelia	.000	.033	.031	.017	**.318**	.045	.019
St Petersburg	.000	.017	.031	.003	.012	**.268**	.058
Estonia	.000	.000	.031	.000	.000	.018	**.221**

Source: Tuovinen, Kangas and Nordlund (1990).

The asymmetry of the Finnish–Russian pollution problem can be seen by combining the information in Tables 5.1 and 5.2. In 1987 about 16 per cent of sulphur deposited in Finland originated from the nearby Russian areas whereas only 3 per cent of their deposition came from Finland. The main reason for this does not lie in the behaviour of the emissions in the atmosphere (Table 5.2) but is to be found in the asymmetry of the emissions: in 1987 the emissions of the nearby Russian areas were 3.4 times higher than Finnish emissions. The two other sulphur budgets, namely those between Estonia and Finland and between Estonia and Russia, were approximately in balance. For example, about 3 per cent of the Estonian deposition came from the Russian areas, whereas 2.5 per cent of their deposition originated from Estonia.

A sulphur transportation model can now be constructed on the basis of Tables 5.1 and 5.2. Let E_i and Q_i denote the annual emission and deposition of sulphur, respectively, in region i, and let A stand for the matrix of Table 5.2 and B for the vector of exogenous deposition in 1987 as specified in the last column of Table 5.1. The model can then be expressed in vector notation as

$$Q = AE + B. \tag{1}$$

For further analysis it is useful to partition the vectors according to the countries: $Q = (Q_F, Q_R, Q_E)$, $E = (E_F, E_R, E_E)$, $B = (B_F, B_R, B_E)$, where the subscript F refers to Finland, R to the nearby areas of Russia and E to Estonia. Matrix A can then be written as

$$A = \begin{pmatrix} A^{FF} & A^{FR} & A^{FE} \\ A^{RF} & A^{RR} & A^{RE} \\ A^{EF} & A^{ER} & A^{EE} \end{pmatrix}. \tag{2}$$

The dimensions and contents of each submatrix are easily seen from Table 5.2. The (i, j) component of, say, A^{FF} is denoted by a_{ij}^{FF}.

Given the sulphur transportation model, let us next consider the costs of air pollution. Following Mäler (1990), these can be thought of as having two components: the first is the cost of abating sulphur emissions in region i, $C_i(E_i)$, and the second the damage, measured in monetary units, that sulphur deposition causes to the environment, $D_i(Q_i)$. The total costs to Finland, Russia and Estonia can then be written as

$$J_F(E_F, E_R, E_E) = \sum_{i=1}^{3} \{C_{Fi}(E_{Fi}) + D_{Fi}(Q_{Fi})\}, \tag{3}$$

$$J_R(E_F, E_R, E_E) = \sum_{i=1}^{3} \{C_{Ri}(E_{Ri}) + D_{Ri}(Q_{Ri})\}, \tag{4}$$

$$J_E(E_F, E_R, E_E) = C_E(E_E) + D_E(Q_E), \tag{5}$$

respectively. The regions have here been indexed so that $F1$, $F2$ and $F3$ denote Northern, Central and Southern Finland, and R1–R3 denote Kola, Karelia and St Petersburg, respectively.

Both cost components are assumed to be continuous, convex functions of their arguments. It is reasonable to regard $C_i(E_i)$ as decreasing in E_i, and $D_i(Q_i)$ as increasing in Q_i.

The cost function $C_i(E_i)$ is defined as the minimal cost envelope encompassing the entire range of sulphur abatement options for region i in a given time period. Here we use the data provided by the Finnish Integrated Acidification Assessment (HAKOMA) project at the Technical Research Centre of Finland and described in more detail in Johansson, Tähtinen and Amann (1991). The original data are in piecewise linear form but here we use quadratic approximations with the assumption that only the parts decreasing in E_i are relevant for the analysis. The quadratic approximations enable us to estimate damage costs in the indirect way as suggested by Mäler (1990, see below). Let

$$C_i(E_i) = \alpha_i(\bar{E}_i - E_i) + \beta_i(\bar{E}_i - E_i)^2 + \gamma_i, \qquad (6)$$

where $\bar{E}_i$ denotes the actual emissions of region i in the base year, that is, in 1987. The parameter α_i has been chosen to be equal to the observed marginal costs at $\bar{E}_i$ and γ_i to be equal to the respective total cost. β^i is estimated by the ordinary least squares technique.

Table 5.3 *Abatement cost function parameters (standard deviations in parentheses)*

	α	β	γ
Northern Finland	10.0	2.093 (1.181)	5.9
Central Finland	3.8	0.172 (0.012)	33.0
Southern Finland	4.6	0.068 (0.006)	53.6
Kola			
– for $98 < E_{R1} \leq 350$:	1.0	0.0	0.0
– for $0 < E_{R1} \leq 98$:	1.0	0.077 (0.005)	252.0
Karelia	4.0	0.045 (0.004)	0.0
St Petersburg	6.0	0.051 (0.003)	0.0
Estonia			
– for $60 < E_E \leq 104$:	2.0	0.0	0.0
– for $0 < E_E \leq 60$:	2.0	0.191 (0.009)	88.0

Table 5.3 presents the parameters of (6) for the seven regions. Because the quadratic function approximates rather poorly the sulphur abatement costs in Kola and Estonia, their cost functions are here adjusted by making them consist of two components: first, of a linear segment describing the abatement costs for initial reductions of emissions from the 1987 level and, second, of a quadratic segment.

It is much harder to obtain information about the damage functions $D^i(Q^i)$. Instead of direct measurements we here apply an indirect way, suggested by Mäler (1990). It is assumed that actual sulphur emissions are the results of rational choices by nations acting in isolation and, therefore, reveal to an outside observer the implicit cost resulting from sulphur deposition.

More specifically, suppose that the policy authorities of Finland, Russia and Estonia act independently of each other in carrying out their environmental policies. Then, acting rationally, it is optimal for each country to allow sulphur emissions up to the amount at which the marginal abatement cost in each region equals the marginal damage to the whole nation from further deposition in the specific region.

The problem here is that our data are from the period in which Estonia was part of the Soviet Union and was not able to pursue its own environmental policies. We deal with this by assuming first that Estonia is a member state of the Soviet Union and then by making a sensitivity analysis for the estimated damage costs.

Consequently, suppose that the emission levels in Finland are chosen in such a way that

$$-C'_{Fi}(E_{Fi}) = \sum_{j=1}^{3} a_{ji}^{FF} D'_{Fj}(Q_{Fj}) \qquad (7)$$

for $i = 1, 2$ and 3 and in the Soviet Union so that

$$-C'_{Si}(E_{Si}) = \sum_{j=1}^{4} a_{ji}^{SS} D'_{Sj}(Q_{Sj}) \qquad (8)$$

for $i = 1, 2, 3$ and 4. Here A^{SS} is the submatrix of A containing the Russian and Estonian transportation coefficient and $S4$ stands for Estonia. These emission levels minimize in each country – Finland and the Soviet Union – the national cost function ((3) or the sum of (4) and (5)) subject to the constraints given by the transportation model (1) and the fixed emissions of the neighbouring nation. Acting in isolation, each country pays attention to the deposition of sulphur in its own area only. The externalities between the regions are internalized within but not between the countries.

The estimation of the damage functions can be completed easily if – again following Mäler (1990) – we make the simplifying assumption that these functions are linear, i.e.

$$D_i(Q_i) = \pi_i Q_i, \qquad (9)$$

where π_i is positive. Knowing the marginal abatement costs (the αs of Table 5.3) and the transportation coefficients (matrix A in Table 5.2), the first-order conditions (7) and (8) then immediately provide estimates for the π^is if the observed emission vector $(\bar{E}_F, \bar{E}_S) = (\bar{E}_F, (\bar{E}_R, \bar{E}_E))$ in 1987 is assumed to be the Nash equilibrium of this acid rain game:

$$\pi_F = (A^{FF})^{-1}\alpha_F, \qquad (10)$$

$$\pi_S = (A^{SS})^{-1}\alpha_S. \qquad (11)$$

The numerical values of these marginal damage vectors are given in Table 5.4, which for comparison also displays the marginal abatement costs.

Table 5.4 Marginal abatement (MC) and damage (MD) costs (Finnish marks/kilogram of sulphur)

	MC α	MD π
Northern Finland	10.0	50.0
Central Finland	3.8	8.9
Southern Finland	4.6	15.6
Kola	1.0	2.6
Karelia	4.0	11.6
St Petersburg	6.0	20.2
Estonia	2.0	2.8

Sulphur abatement costs are the lowest in Kola and Estonia – 1 and 2 Finnish marks per kilogram of sulphur, respectively – and the highest in Finnish Lapland – 10 marks per kilo. The marginal damage cost is the highest in Northern Finland – 50 marks per kilogram of sulphur deposited – and the lowest in Kola and Estonia – about 3 marks per kilo. This approach reveals that the Soviet decision makers regarded additional sulphur deposition to be about eight times more harmful in the Leningrad, that is St Petersburg, area than in Kola or Estonia.

Armed with the damage costs, we can now turn to consider the potential benefits of environmental cooperation between the countries as well as to assess its optimal form. Here we return to our original assumption that Estonia and Russia are now independent decision makers and can thus pursue their own policies.

3. OPTIMAL COOPERATION AND ENVIRONMENTAL AID

A full-cooperative sulphur abatement contract between the countries can be derived by minimizing the joint costs

$$J(E_F, E_R, E_E) = J_F(E_F, E_R, E_E) + J_R(E_F, E_R, E_E) + J_E(E_F, E_R, E_E) \quad (12)$$

with respect to the emissions in the Finnish areas (vector E_F), in the Russian regions (vector E_R) and in Estonia (E_E) under the constraints set by the transportation model (1). The optimal emission vector (E_F^*, E_R^*, E_E^*) is obtained by solving the first-order conditions

$$-C'_{Fi}(E_{Fi}) = \sum_{j=1}^{3} a_{ji}^{FF} \pi_{Fj} + \sum_{j=1}^{3} a_{ji}^{RF} \pi_{Rj} + a_i^{EF} \pi_E, \quad i = 1, 2, 3 \quad (13)$$

$$-C'_{Ri}(E_{Ri}) = \sum_{j=1}^{3} a_{ji}^{FR} \pi_{Fj} + \sum_{j=1}^{3} a_{ji}^{RR} \pi_{Rj} + a_i^{ER} \pi_E, \quad i = 1, 2, 3 \quad (14)$$

$$-C'_E(E_E) = \sum_{j=1}^{3} a_j^{FE} \pi_{Fj} + \sum_{j=1}^{3} a_j^{RE} \pi_{Rj} + a^{EE} \pi_E, \quad (15)$$

where the costs functions C_i are given in (6).

Table 5.5 displays the optimal emissions, the resulting depositions in all areas as well as the monetary benefits from cooperation to the three countries. The exogenous deposition (vector B) is assumed to remain at the 1987 level. It does not affect the optimal emission levels but has an impact on the depositions and the total costs. The monetary benefit has been calculated for each country by subtracting the optimal cost from the non-cooperative cost: benefit to country I equals $J_I(\bar{E}_F, \bar{E}_R, \bar{E}_E) - J_I(E_F^*, E_R^*, E_E^*)$, $I = F, R, E$.

Table 5.5 *The consequences of cooperation and its annual monetary benefits*

	Emissions (10^3 tons) E^*	Emission reduction (%)	Depositions (10^3 tons) Q^*	Deposition reduction (%)	Benefit (10^6 FIM) $\bar{J} - J^*$
Northern Finland	5	0.0	34	26.1	
Central Finland	58	3.3	92	6.1	
Southern Finland	89	8.2	61	7.6	
Finland	**152**	**6.2**	**187**	**10.9**	**700**
Kola	82	76.6	54	58.8	
Karelia	74	12.9	85	10.5	
St Petersburg	104	7.1	82	6.8	
Nearby Russia	**260**	**52.5**	**221**	**29.6**	**42**
Estonia	**58**	**44.2**	**49**	**18.3**	**−64**

The joint cost minimization requires Russia to cut her sulphur emissions by more than 50 per cent from the 1987 level in the areas near the Finnish border. The greatest reductions should be carried out in the Kola peninsula. Two nickel smelters are the main sources of sulphur there. Emissions should also be cut by about 45 per cent in Estonia where oil-shale-based electricity production is the principal source of sulphur. The abatement activities should be concentrated on these regions for two reasons: first, their sulphur abatement costs are rather low and, second, their emissions contribute significant amounts to deposition in Northern and Southern Finland as well as in the St Petersburg area where the marginal damage of pollution is rather high. The Finnish emissions were quite close to the optimal level in 1987 – they should have been 8 per cent lower in the southern area and 3 per cent lower in the central part of the country. This asymmetry in the abatement requirements between the countries can be explained by the asymmetries in marginal abatement costs (Table 5.3) and in observed emission levels (Table 5.1).

Table 5.5 also reveals that both Finland and Russia benefit from the cooperation, but that Estonia loses. The Finnish benefit is quite large, at 700 million Finnish marks a year, and comes from the sizeable reductions in sulphur damage costs. The greatest gain accrues to Northern Finland. The Russian benefit is more modest – only 42 million marks a year. All its areas benefit roughly equally from the reduction in sulphur depositions but Kola bears the greatest burden of the abatement costs. Estonia's net loss follows from the rather large abatement requirement and from the fact that our estimate for the marginal damage cost is quite low.

As no sovereign state can be forced into cooperation, it is reasonable to expect that in order to sign such an agreement Estonia should be compensated for its loss, that is 64 million marks a year. Finland is the obvious candidate for the party which finances the required side payment as Russia's net gain does not even equal Estonia's loss. It is interesting that the government of Finland has initiated an environmental aid programme covering Eastern Europe. The amounts allocated in the 1991 and 1992 budgets were 42 and 67 million marks, respectively. It should be kept in mind, however, that besides air pollution abatement this aid is also meant for other environmental investments and targeted to other areas besides Estonia.

The side payment should be even larger and given to Russia as well if sharing the net benefit from cooperation is regarded as fair. Assuming that the net gain – 678 million marks – is split equally between the countries, Finland should pay Estonia 290 million and Russia 184 million Finnish marks a year.

As was mentioned earlier, the estimated sulphur damage cost for Estonia may not reflect the true preferences of the decision makers of this new-born state. We therefore conduct a sensitivity analysis in Table 5.6 to find out how robust the qualitative conclusions concerning the need for Finnish transfer payments are. The Estonian net benefit from environmental cooperation increases as π_E is increased from its estimated value. For $\pi_E = 9.3$ the net benefit equals zero. No side payments are needed to induce Estonia to cooperate if the value of marginal damage is higher than this. If sulphur deposition were regarded to be as harmful as in Southern Finland, the net annual benefit to Estonia would be 68 million Finnish marks. Here the benefits from reduced sulphur deposition outweigh the costs of the large emission reductions required by cooperation.

Table 5.6 Estonian damage costs and the benefits from cooperation

Marginal damage in Estonia (FIM/kg)	Emission reduction in Estonia (%)	Net gain from cooperation (10^6 FIM)		
		Finland	Russia	Estonia
2.8	44.2	700	42	−64
6.0	46.2	702	45	−33
9.3	48.1	703	48	0
12.0	49.6	704	50	28
15.6	51.6	705	54	68

But if the Estonian damage coefficient were so high that its net benefit from cooperation were positive, then we should observe considerable cuts in Estonian sulphur emissions even without any international cooperation. For $\pi_E = 9.3$ the non-cooperative emission level should be 42.5 per cent lower than it was in the year 1987. Nothing indicates that measures as drastic as this are currently planned, and we may thus be fairly confident about the robustness of our qualitative results concerning the need for side payments.

Finally, we can check the robustness of our conclusions by reducing the number of countries. Let us leave Russia out of the analysis and consider cooperation between Finland and Estonia only. This is a relevant case to analyse as an agreement on air pollutants is being negotiated between the two countries. By repeating the calculations of Sections 2 and 3, we obtain the conclusion that, given existing Russian emissions, optimal bilateral cooperation requires Estonian sulphur emissions to be cut by approximately the same amount as given in Table 5.5. Finnish emissions are almost optimal – only small reductions are needed in Southern Finland. The net benefit from cooperation is, however, much smaller now. Finland benefits by 39 million marks annually whereas Estonia loses by 3 million marks. The minimum annual side payment Finland should offer her neighbour is thus 3 million marks. The exclusion of Russia explains the low gain from cooperation. The size of the side payment is also affected by the fact that the bilateral analysis gives a much higher estimate than the trilateral one for the Estonian damage coefficient.

On the basis of this sensitivity analysis we may speculate what the consequences are of increasing the number of countries. Poland and Sweden are the relevant new players. Poland is an important source of sulphur deposited in both Sweden and Finland. Sweden is also affected by sulphur emitted in Kola. The gains from international cooperation are now likely to increase as a greater part of the acidification problem is covered. Further, we may expect Sweden to join the donors and Poland the receivers of international environmental aid.

4. CONCLUSIONS

We have conducted a case study of optimal cooperation on transboundary air pollution abatement between Finland, Russia and Estonia. Acid rain is an example of a regional reciprocal externality in which countries are both sources and victims of an environmental problem. The economics of such cases was pioneered by, among others, d'Arge (1974), Scott (1972) and Walter (1975). More recent work can be found, for example, in the survey papers of Mäler (1990) and Newbery (1990).

Our approach was practical, the aim being to demonstrate how the basic concepts of game theory, namely, Nash equilibrium and Pareto optimum, can be used to devise optimal sulphur abatement programmes. It was shown that it is rational to abate sulphur to a greater extent in the Russian and Estonian territories than in Finland simply because it is much less expensive there. This is because considerable emission reductions were carried out in Finland in the 1970s and the 1980s, whereas not much happened in this respect in the Soviet Union. Finland is thus further into the region of increasing marginal cost for pollution reduction.

Optimal programmes may, however, entail transfer payments from Finland to Estonia because the former benefits whilst the latter loses from cooperation. Transboundary air pollution is a game in which those who potentially gain have to devise incentives for those who potentially lose to ensure their participation. Despite the fact that there may be problems inherent in side payments (see Folmer, van Mouche and Ragland, 1993), agreements may not be enforceable without side payments as there is no supranational authority with the power to enforce them. The case for transfer payments is even more relevant when – as is the case here – the polluting parties are rather poor and lack the financial resources for investments in abatement technology.

REFERENCES

Action Programme (1989), 'Action programme agreed between the Republic of Finland and the Union of Soviet Socialist Republics for the purpose of limiting and reducing the deposition and harmful effects of air pollutants emanating from areas near their common border', unofficial translation, 7 November 1989, Ministry of the Environment, Helsinki.

D'Arge, R.C. (1974), 'Observations on the economics of transnational environmental externalities', in *Problems in Transfrontier Pollution*, Paris: OECD, pp. 147–65.

Folmer, H., P. van Mouche and S. Ragland (1993), 'Interconnected games and international environmental problems', *Environmental and Resource Economics*, **3**, 313–35.

Johansson, M., M. Tähtinen and M. Amann (1991), 'Optimal strategies to achieve critical loads in Finland', in *Proceedings of the 1991 International Symposium on Energy and Environment*, Espoo.

Kaitala, V., K.-G. Mäler and H. Tulkens (1995), 'The acid rain game as a resource allocation process with an application to the international cooperation among Finland, Russia, and Estonia', *Scandinavian Journal of Economics*, **97**(2), 325–43.

Kaitala, V., M. Pohjola and O. Tahvonen (1991), 'An analysis of SO_2 negotiations between Finland and the Soviet Union', *Finnish Economic Papers*, **4**, 104–12.

Kaitala, V., M. Pohjola and O. Tahvonen (1992), 'Transboundary air pollution and soil acidification: A dynamic analysis of an acid rain game between Finland and the USSR', *Environmental and Resource Economics*, **2**, 161–81.

Mäler, K.-G. (1990), 'International environmental problems', *Oxford Review of Economic Policy*, **6**, 80–108.

Newbery, D. (1990), 'Acid rain', *Economic Policy*, **11**, 288–346.

Scott, A.D. (1972), 'The economics of international transmission of pollution', in *Problems of Environmental Economics*, Paris: OECD, pp. 255–73.

Tahvonen, O., V. Kaitala and M. Pohjola (1993), 'A Finnish–Soviet acid rain game: cooperative equilibria, cost efficiency and sulphur agreements', *Journal of Environmental Economics and Management*, **24**, 87–100.

Tuovinen, J.-P., L. Kangas and G. Nordlund (1990), 'Model calculations of sulphur and nitrogen depositions in Finland', in P. Kauppi, P. Anttila and K. Kenttämies (eds), *Acidification in Finland*, Berlin: Springer-Verlag, pp. 167–97.

Walter, I. (1975), *International Economics of Pollution*, London: Macmillan.

6. Nuclear power games
Fanny Mißfeldt[*]

1. INTRODUCTION

Since the nuclear accident in Chernobyl, the public has become increasingly aware of the fact that a nuclear accident cannot be confined to a limited area of some 30 or 40 km around the nuclear power plant. In 1986 radioactive fall-out travelled as far as Japan (Wheeler, 1988). Even today, the Chernobyl accident still imposes real costs on European countries. The public feels uneasy in particular about the safety of nuclear reactors in Central and Eastern Europe and the former Soviet Union (henceforward referred to as CEE/CIS) where mainly Soviet-designed power plants are in operation. Even though substantial work has been done to improve the safety of nuclear reactors[1] in the East since the breakdown of the communist system, there is still much to be done until Western safety standards are reached.[2] But within Europe nuclear safety is not simply a one-sided problem, in particular given that there are many more nuclear reactors in the West than in the East, even though the situation remains asymmetric.

The aim of this chapter is to formalize the problem of nuclear accident risk with Western Europe and EE/CIS as the main actors. These 'players' can also be thought of as two representative countries such as Germany for the West, and Slovakia for the East. Here, a game-theory approach is chosen in order to analyse the safety spillovers in terms of transboundary pollution. The analysis follows, approaches taken in the recent literature on acid rain and global warming, such as Mäler (1989) and Barrett (1991).

The safety spillover can give rise to bargaining among the countries concerned in order to reduce the accident risk. Such bargaining could be advantageous for the East European countries, which today have neither sufficient financial resources for improving the state of their nuclear industry nor other sufficiently large energy sources so that nuclear power could be abandoned in the medium run. On the other hand, Western countries might possibly take advantage of coop-

---

[*] I would like in particular to thank Henk Folmer, Alistair Munro, Felix Ritchie and Aart de Zeeuw for their valuable comments. I am grateful to my supervisors Yue Ma and Nick Hanley for their help. The usual disclaimer applies. This chapter was made possible through the funding of my PhD by the EC Human Capital and Mobility Programme, for which I am very grateful.

eration as well. An argument behind this is that the reduction of the nuclear accident risk is less costly in CEE/CIS than in Western Europe, because safety measures in the former have not been taken as extensively as in the West. Although cooperation in the nuclear energy sector appears to be fairly high, countries do not yet seem to be able to appreciate the advantages that a more comprehensive form of cooperation could entail. Therefore, an empirical analysis on safety spillovers should be undertaken. However, theoretical considerations already indicate which strategies might be favourable for East, E, and West, W, and under which conditions. Here, a theoretical path is pursued which is supplemented by a simulation exercise.

Following these general remarks, a safety variable is introduced, and safety payoff functions are presented. Subsequently, optimization of safety also *vis-à-vis* spillovers is analysed under different assumptions. The following solution concepts are evaluated and compared: a Nash equilibrium, a Stackelberg solution, and the full-cooperative solution. We shall consider in which circumstances countries are better off through leadership and through cooperation when comparing the situation with the Nash equilibrium. Finally, proxies for actual bargaining power are used to evaluate the Nash bargaining solution in order to see how far actual bargaining influences a 'fair' share. The Nash bargaining solution exhibits various favourable features, such as uniqueness, Pareto optimality, independence of the units of account, independence of irrelevant alternatives, and symmetry. By choosing the Nash equilibrium as point of reference, the Nash bargaining solution evaluated here also exhibits individual rationality. Although a static concept at heart, it has been shown to be the outcome of a bargaining process as described by Zeuthen (Harsanyi, 1977, p. 152).

Both players of the game are countries or regions which have nuclear power programmes. As mentioned above, a particular country can be thought of as either representing the Western European countries or the CEE/CIS countries. Each aims at optimizing its nuclear safety payoff function. The safety function indicates whether it is profitable to install (further) safety equipment in either country when safety spillovers from other countries are taken into account. Such additional safety equipment can be thought of, for example, as secondary containment, emergency shutdown devices, or secondary valve circuits. Alternatively, protection measures against radioactivity in the event of an accident can be taken outside the nuclear power plant. Such emergency preparations may involve the distribution of iodine to the population or emergency exercises.[3]

To capture the impact of safety equipment, the safety payoff function consists of a benefit part which expresses the foregone expected damage through implementation of safety measures, as well as a cost part relating to the abatement cost incurred when safety measures are implemented. Questions about the profitability of nuclear reactors as such will be neglected. Issues such as waste management, plutonium smuggling and decommissioning are not dealt with, even though all these aspects can be considered as part of the nuclear power transboundary pollution problem.[4] It is assumed that the players have complete information.[5] In the light of regular inspections regarding nuclear safety, at least in Eastern Europe, by the International Atomic Energy Agency (IAEA), this does not appear to be too restrictive an assumption.

A 'safety variable', P^E for the East and P^W for the West, is given by the expected nuclear risk reduction in each region and describes the risk of an accident. It is defined here as the difference between the actual value of expected nuclear risk in the East, P^E_c, or the West, P^W_c, and the desired value of expected nuclear risk in the East, P^E_d, and the West, P^W_d.

$$P^i = P^i_c - P^i_d \quad \forall i \in \{E, W\}. \qquad (1)$$

P^E and P^W thus represent the risk reduction required in East and West to reach the desired risk level. P^i will generally be positive, because it is not credible that a country would willingly reduce the safety of its own territory: most of the damage in the event of an accident would still be caused in the country itself. The situation may, however, be different if economic pressures are too high; the economic upheaval in CEE/CIS, for example, has in places led to active deployment of safety equipment. P^E_d and P^W_d would ideally be zero. However, this would require all nuclear power plants to be shut down since risk is inherent in the production of nuclear energy. As in this static framework it is assumed that the electricity produced cannot be replaced otherwise, P^W_d would assume the lowest risk level that can be reached in a cost–benefit framework, as it is laid out here. P^E_c, P^E_d, P^W_c and P^W_d can be imagined as 'aggregate measures' of risk at the country level. As such, they reflect the number of plants in one of the regions, the probability of a major nuclear accident in each nuclear reactor,[6] and the emissions set free in the event of an accident at the plant source. These are the three main features which give a rough idea about the riskiness of the nuclear industry in either region. Current expected emissions in East and West can on this basis be formalized as the sum of expected emissions from all nuclear reactors J^E or J^W in East or West. J^E or J^W stand for the total number of nuclear reactors in East and West respectively. Current expected emissions from a nuclear reactor j in the East E or the West W can in turn be defined as the amount of emissions, E^E_j or E^W_j, released in the event of an accident times the probability p^E_j or p^W_j of the accident in nuclear reactor j. The emissions E^E_j or E^W_j are the emissions occurring during a major accident in the immediate vicinity of a nuclear reactor. The amount of emissions set free, as well as their emission mix, may vary significantly depending on the reactor design. The issue of emission transport is taken up further below. A similar aggregate measure can be defined for the level of desired aggregate risk reduction.[7]

$$P_c^i = \sum_{j=1}^{J} E_{jc}^i p_{jc}^i \quad \forall j = 1, 2, .., J; \quad i \in \{E, W\} \tag{2}$$

$$P_d^i = \sum_{j=1}^{J} E_{jd}^i p_{jd}^i \quad \forall j = 1, 2, .., J; \quad i \in \{E, W\} \tag{3}$$

The specification of risk as given in (2) and (3) has the advantage that it is not necessary to use aggregate accident probabilities. Whilst the overall level of safety improvement can be evaluated in this context, the question of the optimal mix of accident likelihood reduction, emissions reduction and number of power plants requires investigations which are beyond the scope of this chapter. Traditionally, the principle of reducing the probability of an accident is to the fore in risk analysis for nuclear power plants. The ideology behind this becomes to construct nuclear reactors so that an accident becomes extremely unlikely. However, experience from the Three-Mile Island accident indicates that safety policy should also focus on another aspect: the reduction of emissions to be expected in the event of a major accident. In the aftermath of the Three-Mile Island accident hardly any more radioactivity than during usual operation was released. This shows that it is worthwhile to focus on reducing emissions in the event of an accident. A rule of thumb could be: construct a nuclear reactor so that even the worst accident will not damage anyone's health.

While it would seem appropriate to assign a probability distribution over a range of accident types, here, it will be focused only on one particular and severe type of accident, a core meltdown. For the purpose of simplification, probabilistic safety assessment (PSA) for nuclear reactors has traditionally focused on this particular kind of accident, so that estimations of core meltdown probabilities exist. In the case of transboundary pollution, it does not seem to be too simplifying an assumption to concentrate only on core meltdown accidents, because it is unlikely that other 'undesired events'[8] entail major transboundary spillovers. The amount of radioactive emissions in the event of an accident is evaluated by considering mainly the state of the containment. For CEE/CIS countries, the expected emissions E_j^E can expected to be very high given that in most cases those nuclear reactors do not have any containment.

Having defined the 'safety variable' P^i, the specifications of the functions will now be considered in more depth. The *safety-payoff functions* consist of a benefit part D^i for country i and an abatement cost part C^i for country i. The countries weigh the benefits of reduced expected damage from a nuclear accident, D^i, against the cost, C^i, incurred through implementing further safety equipment. The superscripts indicate to which country the functions relate. E

refers to the representative Eastern European country, and W to the representative Western European country. The value of the (foregone) damage function varies with the efforts in both countries to increase safety. The increase in safety is expressed by the variables P^E and P^W. The damage to be expected from an accident in the other country will be taken account of by means of transfer coefficients. These coefficients reflect the extent to which the radioactive release will be transported from one country to the other. The abatement costs depend on P^E in country E and P^W in country W. Hence, the general specification of the safety functions looks as follows:

$$S^E = D^E (P^E, P^W) - C^E (P^E)$$
$$S^W = D^W (P^E, P^W) - C^W (P^W). \quad (4)$$

The damage functions D^E and D^W stand for the expected damage in countries E and W which is avoided by means of abatement policies. Put another way, they reflect the benefits from risk abatement. The abatement cost functions C^W and C^E stand for the cost which arises from risk abatement. The general set-up in terms of damage reduction follows the structure of Mäler's (1989) static version of the acid rain game.

In the following, the specific damage and abatement cost functions used below are discussed in more detail.

2. THE DAMAGE FUNCTION: BENEFIT VIA RISK ABATEMENT

As noted above, the damage function reflects foregone expected damage: it depicts how much less expected damage from a nuclear accident is incurred when risk abatement strategies are undertaken. The expected damage that country E incurs depends not only on the state of the nuclear power programme in E but also, due to the spillovers from transboundary pollution, on the state of the nuclear power programme in W as reflected by P^E and P^W. In order to be able to solve explicitly for solution concepts, assumptions about the specific shape of the benefit function have to be made. Here, a benefit function with a linear as well as a quadratic part is chosen:

$$d^E (P^E, P^W) = \eta_1 P^E + \eta_2 P^W - \gamma(\eta_1 P^E + \eta_2 P^W)^2$$
$$d^W (P^E, P^W) = \eta_3 P^E + \eta_4 P^W - \varepsilon(\eta_3 P^E + \eta_4 P^W)^2 \quad (5)$$

where γ, ε as well as $\eta_1, \eta_2, \eta_3, \eta_4 \geq 0$. Both parts of the benefit function are weighted with parameter γ for country E, and ε for country W. Furthermore, it is realistic to assume that $\varepsilon > \gamma$. This implies that further installation of safety equipment yields a higher benefit in the East than in the West. Benefits are zero when no risk abatement is undertaken, because only changes concerning risk abatement are taken into account. In order to take account of all damage caused by radioactivity from nuclear reactors, a constant term could be introduced in the damage function to represent low-level radiation emitted during ordinary operation of the plants. This, however, does not change the quality of the results given below.

The (negative) quadratic part of the function takes into account that, as efforts to augment safety increase, the benefit derived will not increase to the same extent. Thus, the benefit function incorporates the idea of diminishing returns from increasing safety. In order to avoid the problem that – given this functional form – at some point the benefit from risk abatement will finally decrease, a set of restrictions has to be imposed on both damage functions.[9] Similar functional specifications for transboundary pollution have been chosen for example by Barrett (1992) and by Stähler (1992). It is a mathematically convenient specification, but approximates the effective increased expected benefit only in a rather crude way. Damage caused by the release of radioactive isotopes is very difficult to evaluate. It entails not only the problem of accumulation of radioactivity in certain areas ('hot spots'), but also of evaluating long-term effects. The latter include, among others, aspects of morbidity, mortality, hereditary damage, economic loss (e.g. reduction in tourism) and environmental damage.

In order fully to specify the expected damage reduction function it is finally necessary to consider two more aspects. The first relates to the question of how to take into account how much radioactivity actually falls on E and W. The second aspect deals with the problem of how radioactive emissions can be translated into monetary terms: how much damage is caused by the fallout following a nuclear accident? First, emissions have to be transformed into depositions of radioactivity, i.e. radioactive fallout. This can be done with the help of a simple transfer coefficient matrix for countries E and W. In such a matrix, the parameter α_{EW} expresses how much radioactivity from an accident in W will be deposited in country E.[10] All the transfer coefficients can be scaled so that $0 \leq \alpha_{EE}, \alpha_{EW}, \alpha_{WE}, \alpha_{WW} \leq 1$. Consequently, every parameter reflects the percentage of expected damage which will fall out in either E or W. Multiplying the expected emissions with the transfer coefficient yields the expected deposition in the respective country. In order to obtain the monetary value of radioactive deposition, the deposition of radioactive fallout is multiplied by a factor μ. In the past, a couple of propositions have been put forward for evaluating such a parameter.[11] For simplicity, the transfer coefficients and the value of transboundary radiation exposure, μ, are multiplied by one another, and the resulting values replaced as follows:

$$\mu \begin{bmatrix} \alpha_{EE} & \alpha_{WE} \\ \alpha_{EW} & \alpha_{WW} \end{bmatrix} = \begin{bmatrix} \eta_1 & \eta_3 \\ \eta_2 & \eta_4 \end{bmatrix}. \tag{6}$$

It is also possible to think that the valuation of spillovers differs between East and West. In this case (6) could be reformulated as follows:

$$\begin{bmatrix} \alpha_{EE} & \alpha_{WE} \\ \alpha_{EW} & \alpha_{WW} \end{bmatrix} \begin{bmatrix} \mu_E \\ \mu_W \end{bmatrix} = \begin{bmatrix} \eta_1 & \eta_3 \\ \eta_2 & \eta_4 \end{bmatrix}. \tag{7}$$

Substituting these coefficients into the general benefit function yields the expressions as given in Equation (5).

3. THE ABATEMENT COST FUNCTION

The level of risk abatement costs of each country depends on the risk abatement instruments P^E and P^W. Increasing P^E and P^W implies that abatement costs increase as well. If the cost function is specified in terms of a quadratic function, the idea is supported that reducing the accident probability and/or expected release of emissions becomes progressively costly, and hence reflects the technical law of diminishing returns. Even though this might be true in principle, the assumption of a smooth function can be erroneous in practice. Lochard and Pages (1984) approximate, in the framework of a cost-effectiveness analysis of risk reduction at nuclear reactors, a piecewise linear function for a 1.3GW(e) pressurized water reactor. The graph can, however, be approximated by a quadratic function. With the help of parameters c^E and c^W it becomes possible to value the risk reduction in terms of costs:

$$\begin{aligned} c(P^E) &= c^E P^{E^2} \\ c(P^W) &= c^W P^{W^2}. \end{aligned} \tag{8}$$

The overall safety functions for both countries thus become

$$\begin{aligned} s^E &= (\eta_1 P^E + \eta_2 P^W) - \gamma(\eta_1 P^E + \eta_2 P^W)^2 - c^E P^{E^2} \\ s^W &= (\eta_3 P^E + \eta_4 P^W) - \varepsilon(\eta_3 P^E + \eta_4 P^W)^2 - c^W P^{W^2}. \end{aligned} \tag{9}$$

Having set out the basic structure of the model, it is now possible to proceed to further analysis.

4. TWO NON-COOPERATIVE SOLUTION CONCEPTS: NASH AND STACKELBERG

Mainly due to Chernobyl, transboundary radioactive fallout from accidents in nuclear reactors is recognized, and detailed monitoring of its deposition takes place.[12] When deciding on implementing safety equipment, spillovers from other countries have also to be taken into account. In response to the accident in Chernobyl, new safety investigations and analyses have been undertaken by many European countries (IAEA, 1988). A wide range of countries have changed their own safety strategy in response to the accident in the former Soviet Union. In what follows, radioactive spillovers are incorporated in the analysis by using the formulation of safety payoff functions as given in (5), which include η_2 and η_3. From there, reaction functions can be derived via first-order conditions of the safety functions which indicate to each country how it should optimally react to the actions taken by another country. They serve as the basis for both the calculation of the Nash and the Stackelberg solution:

$$P_R^E = \frac{1}{2} \frac{\eta_1(1 - 2\gamma\eta_2 P^W)}{\gamma\eta_1^2 + c^E}$$

$$P_R^W = \frac{1}{2} \frac{\eta_4(1 - 2\varepsilon\eta_3 P^E)}{\varepsilon\eta_4^2 + c^W}. \qquad (10)$$

The derivation of the reaction functions is given in appendix 2. Both functions are negatively sloped, with respect to P^W in the case of P_R^E, and P^E in the case of P_R^W, which implies that safety abatement strategies in both countries are substitutes for both regions. The higher the degree of safety in the West, the less important safety appears to be in the East. For example, if the valuation of spillover from country E increases, i.e. η_3 increases, the reaction curve of W will have a steeper slope. Hence, even if E decides to do only a little abatement, W will have an incentive to engage in relatively more abatement.

The effect of transboundary fallout in the event of an accident is certainly dominated by the fact that in such an accident most of the fallout will still go down in the country which has the accident.[13] For country E the spillover is represented by the parameter η_1. Changes in η_1 can occur when the valuation as represented by μ changes. The impact of an increase in η_1 on the slope of the reaction function of the East is ambiguous. From the slope of the reaction function, however, the following can be derived: if $\gamma\eta_1^2 < c^E$ holds, the slope of the reaction function will be steeper, as before, and thus the reactivity towards the action of the other player will increase. The following condition has to hold for the West: $\varepsilon\eta_4^2 < c^W$. The derivation of this condition is given in appendix 3. Whether the change in η_1 will increase the reactivity of E towards the actions of W depends therefore entirely on the economic conditions in the country itself: as can be expected, an increase in its own marginal costs $2c^E P^E$ via an increase in c^E decreases a country's reactivity regarding spillovers from abroad.

In a static game-theory context, various strategic possibilities can be considered. Among the non-cooperative concepts are the Nash equilibrium and the Stackelberg leadership. Both require that the players are either not willing to collaborate or that it is not possible for them to coordinate their actions. Similarly, no country can impose its wishes on the other country. The period just before the breakdown of the communist system could be thought of as a Nash-type situation: the possibility of radioactivity fallout was recognized by then as a consequence of the Chernobyl accident, but real collusion was still virtually impossible because of the (political) block structure of the East and the West. In these circumstances, the East had to choose its level of supplementary safety equipment by considering the reaction of the other player. The Nash equilibrium assumes that both players choose their action simultaneously. The resulting Nash point is the intersection of both reaction functions:

$$P_N^E = \frac{1}{2} \frac{\eta_1\left(\varepsilon\eta_4^2 + c^W - \gamma_2\eta_4\right)}{\left(\gamma_1^2\varepsilon\eta_4^2 + \gamma_1^2 c^W + c^E\varepsilon\eta_4^2 + c^W c^E - \gamma_1\eta_2\eta_3\eta_4\varepsilon\right)}$$

$$P_N^W = \frac{1}{2} \frac{\eta_4\left(\gamma_1^2 + c^E - \varepsilon\eta_1\eta_3\right)}{\left(\gamma_1^2\varepsilon\eta_4^2 + \gamma_1^2 c^W + c^E\varepsilon\eta_4^2 + c^W c^E - \gamma_1\eta_2\eta_3\eta_4\varepsilon\right)}. \quad (11)$$

The second-order conditions for the non-cooperative solutions are presented in appendix 4. The restrictions imposed on the damage function (see note 9) make it possible to attribute a positive sign to the numerators of (11). The denominators are positive as well, given that all transfer coefficients are smaller than one. A derivation of how the positive signs can be attributed is set out in appendix 5. Consequently risk under the Nash solution has to be positive. Impacts of changes in the coefficient regarding transboundary transfer of radioactivity and changes regarding the cost coefficients can also be attributed a sign. The higher the fallout transferred to the West, that is, the higher η_3, the higher are the efforts of risk abatement in the Nash equilibrium, that is, P_N^W is larger. The equivalent argument holds for the East with respect to changes in η_2. Any increase in the cost coefficients of both countries has the opposite effect by reducing the amount of safety equipment installed.

In this framework it is also conceivable that the West may be able to take the role of a leader in the Stackelberg sense, given its economic strength, by choosing P_S^W as a point on the reaction function of E that maximizes its safety payoff. In order to do so, the West has to be able to commit itself credibly to the type of policy which will guarantee leadership. Calculating the Stackelberg solution yields the following, unique solution for the West and the East:

$$P_S^W = \frac{1}{2} \frac{\eta_4\left(\gamma\eta_1^2 + c^E\right)^2 - \gamma^2\eta_1^3\eta_2\eta_3 - \gamma\eta_1\eta_2\eta_3 c^E + \gamma\epsilon\eta_1^2\eta_3^2\eta_2 - \gamma\epsilon\eta_1^3\eta_3\eta_4 - \epsilon\eta_1\eta_3\eta_4 c^E}{\left(\epsilon\eta_4^2 + c^W\right)\left(\gamma\eta_1^2 + c^E\right)^2 + \gamma\epsilon\eta_1\eta_2\eta_3\left(\gamma\eta_1\eta_2\eta_3 - 2\eta_4\left(\gamma\eta_1^2 + c^E\right)\right)}$$

$$P_S^E = \frac{1}{2}\frac{\eta_1\left(1 - 2P_S^W\gamma\eta_2\right)}{\left(\gamma\eta_1^2 + c^E\right)}.$$

(12)

A derivation of the Stackelberg solution is presented in appendix 6. It is not very clear-cut how changes in the parameters of the Stackelberg solution affect the choice of P_S^W and P_S^E. From the first-order conditions for the Nash and for the Stackelberg solution it follows that risk abatement is lower in the West, if it acts as leader. The table in appendix 9 shows why: the interesting term here is the third expression on the left. It turns out to be negative for the following reasons: η_3 is positive for obvious reasons, and $\partial P^E/\partial P^W$ is negative. The latter follows from the reaction function, the specification of which implies that both abatement measures are substitutes (see also appendix 3 on the slope of the reaction function). The last expression in brackets is also positive by the restriction imposed on the damage function. As a result, the left-hand side of the equation is smaller than in the Nash equilibrium. Therefore the equation can only hold if risk abatement is lower as well.

The decrease in risk abatement in the Stackelberg equilibrium will be responded to by an increase in safety measures undertaken in the East. The latter follows from the Eastern European reaction function, where in response to the relatively lower risk abatement in the West, a higher level in the East is chosen. It is difficult to judge what the net effect in terms of the total risk looks like without actual numerical values. Hoel's (1989) paper may give an indication. He shows[14] that the total risk reduction $(P^W + P^E)$[15] will be higher with the Nash solution than with the Stackelberg solution. Further indications about the relation of the Nash solution and the Stackelberg solution can be drawn from simulation. As is discussed further below, total reduction is lower under Stackelberg in all scenarios considered in the simulations.

5. FULL COOPERATION

Instead of making the assumption that no cooperation is possible, it also seems attractive to look at what gains can be made from cooperation, especially given the particular regulatory environment of nuclear power. In order to do so, the evaluation of a contract curve can give 'the set of efficient "contracts" or allocations' (Varian, 1992, p.325) feasible over the entire range of possible combinations of bargaining power. By attributing to country E a bargaining power h, and to country W a bargaining power $(1-h)$, a communal optimization problem can be set up. In what follows, h is defined for $h \in [0, 1]$. In the literature on international policy coordination it is common to regard h as an exogenously given parameter. However, in much of the cooperative game-theory literature, h is considered as an endogenous variable which, if suitably attributed, leads to an outcome which exhibits certain predefined qualities. These may only hold by accident if the bargaining power is assumed to be 'non-negotiable'. The objective function is defined below as the sum of the safety functions of both countries, weighted by their respective bargaining power:

$$s_{total} = hs^E + (1-h)s^W. \tag{13}$$

Maximizing (13) with respect to P^E and P^W and setting $h = 1/2$, that is, both countries have the same bargaining power, yields the full-cooperative outcome. The expression is as shown below:[16]

$$P^E_{full} = \frac{1}{2} \frac{\eta_1\left(c^W + \eta_4(\varepsilon\eta_4 - \gamma\eta_2)\right) + \eta_3\left(c^W + \eta_2(\gamma\eta_2 - \varepsilon\eta_4)\right)}{\left(c^E c^W + \varepsilon\eta_3^2 c^W + \gamma\eta_2^2 c^E + \varepsilon\eta_4^2 c^E + \gamma\eta_1^2 c^W + \gamma\varepsilon(\eta_2\eta_3 - \eta_1\eta_4)^2\right)}$$

$$P^W_{full} = \frac{1}{2} \frac{\eta_4\left(c^E + \eta_1(\gamma\eta_1 - \varepsilon\eta_3)\right) + \eta_2\left(c^E + \eta_3(\varepsilon\eta_3 - \gamma\eta_1)\right)}{\left(c^E c^W + \varepsilon\eta_3^2 c^W + \gamma\eta_2^2 c^E + \varepsilon\eta_4^2 c^E + \gamma\eta_1^2 c^W + \gamma\varepsilon(\eta_2\eta_3 - \eta_1\eta_4)^2\right)}. \tag{14}$$

As for the Nash equilibrium above, increasing costs at the margin, that is, higher c^W and c^E, lead to lower risk abatement, that is, P^w_{full} and P^E_{full} are lower. This can be demonstrated by taking the partial derivative of both expressions in (14) with respect to c^E and c^W. A derivation is given in appendix 8. The full-cooperative solution might not yield individually rational results for each of the players on their own. Put differently, E or W may not individually be better off by fully cooperating even though both countries taken together will always be at least as well off as under the Nash equilibrium.

However, in static game theory it was shown that in total and for all players, the overall outcome from full cooperation will be at least as beneficial as the Nash equilibrium.[17] As a result, it could be attractive for a player who is better off than under the non-cooperative regime to offer side payments which make the other player at least as well off as under the non-cooperative outcome. With the Nash bargaining solution a redistribution of gains can be evaluated, which makes both parties at least as well off as under the Nash equilibrium, if the Nash equilibrium is chosen as point of reference. Put differently, under these conditions the Nash bargaining solution fulfils individual rationality.

At the 'bliss' points, where either W or E has all bargaining power, the country with total bargaining power will not undertake any safety measures, and imposes the implementation of safety equipment in its entirety on the other country. While it appears conceivable that the West imposes, or has imposed, its strategies with respect to nuclear energy on some East European countries, the reverse is difficult to imagine. Table 6.1 gives some indication of actual bargaining powers of Central and Eastern Europe versus the European Union, and of Germany versus the Czech Republic and the Slovak Republic. The proxies used for bargaining power are GDP and a risk ranking of countries. Both numbers indicate that the economic position of Central and Eastern European countries in negotiations is in fact extremely low. This is particularly true for the comparison of GDP. As a proxy for actual power, country risk ranking is less indicative, but possibly gives the upper limit of bargaining power in the East.

Table 6.1 Proxies for economic bargaining power

Possible actors	GDP (in million US$)	Bargaining power (%)	Average country risk ranking	Bargaining power (%)
Germany	2 045 991	98.3	96.15	59.8
Czech Republic	36 024	1.7	64.69	40.2
EU	7 312 533	96.4	90.38	70.0
CEE	269 792	3.6	44.72	30.0
EU and USA	13 960 546	94.5	90.85	72.0
CEE and FSU	819 330	5.5	35.27	28.0

Notes: The risk ranking is based on various indicators including political risk and is scaled from 1 to 100 with 100 being the best outcome. The GDP figures for the European Union do not include Luxembourg.

Sources: Risk ranking data taken from *Euromoney* (1995). The GDP data are taken from World Bank (1996) for the year 1994.

It is worthwhile to compare the values in Table 6.1 with values of bargaining power that a Nash bargaining solution would require. The Nash bargaining solution of the problem above offers a distribution of gains from cooperation that fulfils a number of strategically desirable properties. Apart from being Pareto-efficient, as any cooperative outcome, it delivers a unique outcome and exhibits the properties of independence of irrelevant alternatives, irrelevance of utility calibrations and symmetry.[18] As the point of reference here is the Nash equilibrium, the solution is also individually rational. If side payments are possible, this solution may be the relevant concept for predicting the distribution of total gains from cooperation (Heister, 1993, p. 13). A parameter, x, for a Nash bargaining type distribution of gains is derived by maximizing the gains from cooperation as compared with the threat point, the Nash equilibrium. The Nash bargaining solution thereby evaluates x as the fair share for the West and $(1-x)$ as the fair share for the East of the total safety payoff $s^* = s^W_{full} + s^E_{full}$. In the problem set-up both parties' contribution to the full-cooperative solution is weighted by a proxy for political bargaining power: H for the west and $(1-H)$ for the East. Table 6.1 shows that a proxy of 96 per cent for the West is realistic. In order to derive x, the following function has to be maximized with respect to x:

$$\max_x \left(xs^* - s^W_N \right)^H \left((1-x)s^* - s^E_N \right)^{(1-H)}$$
$$s^* = s^W_{full} + s^E_{full}$$
$$x \in [0,1] \tag{15}$$

where s^W_N and s^E_N stand for the safety payoffs under the Nash equilibrium, and s^W_{full} and s^E_{full} represent the payoffs when countries fully cooperate. The set-up presented here assumes full transferability of payoffs. Equation (15) represents the maximum gains that countries can achieve jointly. It corresponds to the result of a maximized s_{total} as portrayed in (13) where $h = 0.5$. The full-cooperative solution is discussed at more length below. The solution for x, which stands for the optimal share of the West, is the following:

$$x = \frac{s^W_N}{s^*} + H \left(1 - \frac{s^E_N + s^W_N}{s^*} \right). \tag{16}$$

The first part of the expression says that the West should at a minimum receive as much as under the Nash equilibrium. The second part of (16) says that the share of the gain from cooperating, which the West is getting is proportional to the West's bargaining power H. The actual contribution of the players to the gain is only important in so far as it contributes to the total gain. Using a range of 16 different scenarios, which cover various possible constellations of spillovers and marginal abatement costs in E and W, hypothetical values for x were evaluated using MapleV-3. An overview of the scenarios is given in appendix

7. They are introduced more thoroughly in the section entitled 'simulation'. The results of the values for x are summarized in Table 6.2. The sensitivity of the size of share H to changes is analysed, again using the value $H = 0.5$.

Table 6.2 Nash bargaining shares x (in %) in different scenarios

Scenario	x (in %), $H = 0.96$	x (in %), $H = 0.50$
1.1	49.4	48.3
1.2	31.5	27.7
1.3	73.9	70.9
1.4	48.3	44.6
1.5	44.9	43.6
1.6	27.5	25.0
1.7	73.0	68.3
1.8	48.4	44.7
2.1	50.9	50.0
2.2	31.5	28.6
2.3	74.4	71.4
2.4	48.5	45.2
2.5	46.1	44.9
2.6	27.5	25.2
2.7	73.4	68.6
2.8	48.6	45.1

While the values for x range quite widely across scenarios, the use of differing levels of bargaining power does not greatly affect the share of s^* that West and East are attributed through the Nash bargaining solution. Also the differences in valuation of benefits of risk abatement do not yield differences in shares that exceed 2 per cent among otherwise equal scenarios. Differing abatement costs affect the shares to a greater extent with up to 5.1 per cent difference among otherwise equal scenarios. The most important factor, however, is the transfer parameters. Depending on which assumptions have been made, shares differ up to 45.9 per cent. This would imply that even if the West were 'generous' and offered a 50 per cent share to the East, it would not lose greatly.

The Nash bargaining solution shows a distribution of gains that is individually rational. It was suggested that the transfer of gain be undertaken via side payments. However, side payments cannot be readily enforced at an international level. Additionally, knowledge that such payments are available may lead to strategic behaviour, and countries may find it attractive to 'hoard' risk over time in order to elicit payments.[19]

Regarding the problem of enforcement of side payments, it might be expected that this problem is easier to overcome in the nuclear energy context than in the context of acid rain or global warming: a potential framework for such payments does already exist with a number of international organizations such as the IAEA, the Nuclear Energy Agency (NEA) or the Organization for Economic Cooperation and Development (OECD), and the World Association of Nuclear Operators (WANO). Additionally, it may be easier to monitor such an agreement since the installation of safety-related capital is straightforward once access to the nuclear reactors has been given. As a reaction to the G7 summit in Munich where 46 per cent of the reactors in the CEE/CIS were declared unsafe, a coordination structure for nuclear aid programmes was put into place, the Nuclear Safety Assistance Coordination (NUSAC), which is based in Brussels. Its purpose is to help to coordinate the various assistance programmes, and it has set up a G-24 database to collect details on all programmes. Furthermore, in 1993 a multilateral mechanism, the Nuclear Safety Account (NSA), was established at the European Bank for Reconstruction and Development (EBRD) that receives funding from Western donors. Its purpose is to enable the closing down of nuclear reactors in the East which cannot be brought up to Western safety standards. The allocation of resources is generally made conditional upon the agreement of the recipient countries to close down particularly unsafe power stations. Also a promising framework for coordinated action could have been the 'International Convention on Nuclear Safety' which entered into force in October 1996. However, it does not consider the potential for side payments, and as a whole is not a very strong piece of international legislation.

As mentioned above, a number of side payments are made on behalf of nuclear safety. According to the G-24 database, total funds available so far from Western donors constitute about US$ 1.2 billion as of June 1996 (NUSAC News, 1996/10, p. 8). It has been suggested that US$ 4.8 billion would be required to restructure the nuclear sector in Russia alone (Konoplyanik and Nechaev, 1994). But it is questionable whether these payments correspond to what would be economically desirable in the light of the above analysis. If one takes the German example, where safety externalities were internalized in the aftermath of German reunification, then one is led to suspect that much has still to be done: all nuclear reactors in East Germany were shut down after the fall of the Berlin Wall.

6. RISK ABATEMENT UNDER THE DIFFERENT SOLUTION CONCEPTS

From the first-order conditions we can derive how levels of risk abatement vary in both regions under different types of strategies. The table in appendix 9 depicts the first-order conditions for the East and the West. In order to be able to compare risk abatement, the first-order conditions for the various solution concepts were solved for the terms $2c^E P^E$ and $2c^W P^W$, which represents the marginal abatement costs of the respective region. Risk abatement under each solution concept is undertaken where marginal abatement costs equal marginal benefits. Since the location of the marginal cost curve remains the same across all solution concepts, it can be used as a measure of location of marginal benefit curves, as Figures 6.1 and 6.2 illustrate. The derivation of the ranking that results from the comparison of Stackelberg and Nash equilibrium has already been presented above and needs no repetition here. To sum up: if the West chooses to be a (Stackelberg) leader, it will abate even less than under the Nash strategy. Consequently the East will be forced to do more abatement. In practice it is, however, doubtful whether the East is currently able to react in terms of a Stackelberg strategy, given its economic constraints. Total abatement will, however, still be lower when choosing a Stackelberg strategy.

The table in Appendix 9 shows that under cooperation for both East and West marginal benefits from risk abatement are higher than under the Nash equilib-

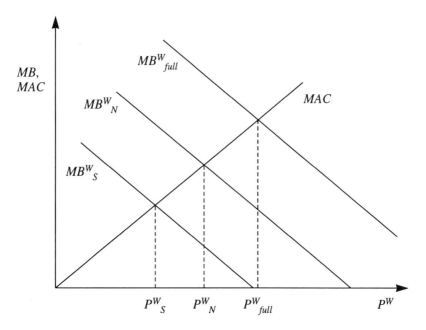

Notes: *MAC* means marginal abatement costs, *MB* stands for marginal benefit. The superscripts *W* and *E* are abbreviations for West and East. Subscripts *S*, *N* and *full* represent Stackelberg, Nash and full cooperation. *P* is the safety variable.

Figure 6.1   Ranking of solutions for the West

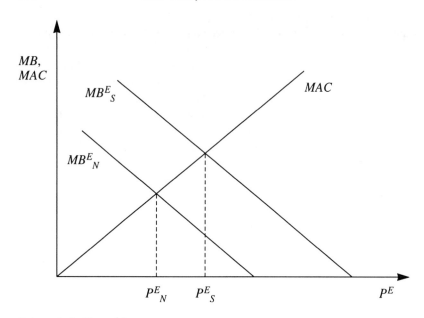

Notes: As for Figure 6.1.

Figure 6.2 Ranking of solutions for the East

rium. This holds because the supplementary terms $\eta_3 ((1 - h)/h) (1 - 2\varepsilon (\eta_3 P^E + \eta_4 P^W))$ for the East and $\eta_2 ((1 - h)/h) (1 - 2\gamma (\eta_1 P^E + \eta_2 P^W))$ for the West in the expression reflecting marginal benefits are positive due to restrictions imposed on the functional form to guarantee non-decreasing benefits. Consequently, risk abatement under cooperation for each region must be higher as well. What is more, this holds for each player on its own, and not only when aggregating over both players. The ranking of risk abatement can be summarized as follows:

$$P_S^W < P_N^W < P_{full}^W$$
$$P_N^E < P_S^E ; P_N^E < P_{full}^E. \qquad (17)$$

7. SIMULATION

The theoretical analysis showed how risk abatement strategies change under different types of solutions. While clear indications about risk abatement could be given, it was not possible to relate utility considerations under different solution concepts. In this section a simulation of these concepts is undertaken with fictitious numbers. Here, 16 different scenarios are used in order to analyse the potential gains which, due to the lack of appropriate data, may be regarded more in terms of sensitivity analysis than as a reflection of actual potential monetary gains. There are two sets of scenarios: scenarios 2.1 to 2.8 assume that both countries attach the same weight to their benefit function, here $\gamma = \varepsilon = 0.5$. Scenarios 1.1 through to 1.8 assume that the benefit functions differ, that is, $\gamma = 0.3$ and $\varepsilon = 0.5$. This difference may reflect that the immediate benefits from risk reduction are higher in the East because the initial risk level is also higher. Furthermore, scenarios 1.1 to 1.4 and 2.1 to 2.4 assume that the coefficient of marginal abatement costs is the same in East and West, while in scenarios 1.5 to 1.8 and 2.5 to 2.8 abatement in the West is assumed to be twice as costly as in the East. The parameter choices for the scenarios are summarized in Appendix 7. The results are shown in tables in Appendix 11.

As mentioned above, η_2 and η_3 reflect the transboundary component of the potential emissions whereby η_2 portrays the transfer of emissions from the West to the East, and η_3 the transfer of emissions from the East to the West. Scenarios 1.1–1.5 and 2.1–2.5 assume that spillovers are symmetric and moderate. Scenarios 1.2–1.6, 2.2–2.6 and 1.4–1.8, 2.4–2.8 are based on the general meteorological observation that in the northern hemisphere, with prevailing westerly winds, emissions are more likely to be transferred to the East than to the West. Scenarios 1.3–1.7 and 2.3–2.7 are a mirror image of 1.2–1.6 and 2.2–2.6. They assume that more emissions are transferred from the East to the West than in the other direction. This serves as a 'test' scenario, but also covers the case of Chernobyl where, due to unusual meteorological circumstances, more emissions were deposited in the West than in the East in the immediate aftermath of the accident. For simplicity, the transfer coefficients from any one country add up to one, that is, $\eta_1 + \eta_2 = 1$ and $\eta_3 + \eta_4 = 1$. This implies that the figures of the valued transfer coefficients in Table 6.2 can be interpreted as percentages of radioactive fallout being transported. A procedure to evaluate Nash, Stackelberg and full cooperation with the help of these scenarios was written using MapleV-3.

Before turning to consider how the different scenarios perform in welfare terms, the choices of various levels of risk abatement are analysed. The first observation is that the predictions of the theoretical model are found to be confirmed. Most risk abatement is undertaken if both countries cooperate, this is true for each country taken individually and both countries taken together. The West is, under Stackelberg, able to commit itself first. Consequently it can choose its optimal level of risk abatement more freely. Simulation confirms the theoretical result that the abatement under Stackelberg for the West is lower than under Nash. In response to that, the East has to undertake more risk abatement than under Nash. But under none of the scenarios is the East's abatement under

Stackelberg higher than under full cooperation. The simulation also permits us to draw conclusions on total risk abatement. It turns out that Hoel's (1989) findings are confirmed in that total abatement is lowest under the Stackelberg solution. Total abatement under cooperation is substantially higher than abatement under the non-cooperative concepts.

Although this would indicate that the Stackelberg solution is not very efficient in terms of risk abatement, it may still be a useful strategy. To see why, it should be recalled that the static model laid out here is defined on the basis of risk differentials, and not the total current risk of both regions. If it is considered that the actual 'starting-points', i.e. the initial risk levels, in both East and West differ quite substantially, then it may be relatively beneficial if the East is induced to undertake comparatively more risk abatement. This may be an interesting feature, particularly in a situation where cooperation is infeasible.

Looking at the welfare gains, the Nash equilibrium is taken as the 'point of departure' for the analysis: the utility under Stackelberg and cooperation is expressed as a percentage of the Nash outcome. Under the Stackelberg solution, the West gains in comparison with the Nash equilibrium. But the gains are very low. Under none of the scenarios do the gains exceed 0.11 per cent of the Nash equilibrium. The East loses out as the follower in the Stackelberg set-up. While the losses are not high when compared with Nash, they slightly exceed the gains of the West. Consequently, total welfare is only lower by a small percentage under Stackelberg than under Nash. In comparison, the total gains from cooperation are high. They range from 2.08 per cent to 11.39 per cent. Only a few scenarios yield outcomes under cooperation that are individually rational[20] for both countries when compared with Nash. They are scenarios 1.1, 1.5, 1.8, 2.1, 2.4 and 2.8. These scenarios have in common that they are based on fairly balanced parameter values for both regions. In scenario 2.1, where both countries are identical as far as their safety functions are concerned, they also have identical gains. The other scenarios are 'balanced' in that, for example, in scenario 2.8 the higher marginal costs in the safety payoff of the West are balanced by a higher share of spillovers in the benefit part in the East. Scenarios with substantial transboundary spillovers, that is, the scenarios 1.2, 1.6, 1.3, 1.7, 2.2, 2.6, 2.3 and 2.7, bring about situations where under full cooperation one or both parties incurs substantial losses. If the share of radioactivity transported from the West to the East is high, as in 1.2, 2.2, 1.6 and 2.6, the West has to undertake more abatement under full cooperation than under Nash. Similarly, the east is able to transfer a substantial part of its potential emissions to the West in scenarios 1.3–2.3 and 1.7–2.7, and thus free-ride on the abatement efforts of the West. Under full cooperation, burden sharing requires the East to undertake abatement such that it loses out in comparison with the Nash equilibrium. Heavy transboundary pollution may thus give rise to side payments if a full-cooperative outcome is to be reached. An overview of how such burden sharing may be undertaken is given in Mißfeldt (1995).

Even if full-cooperative outcomes are individually rational for all actors involved, they may not be strategically stable and lead to free-riding behaviour. In Appendix 6, Tables 6A.13 to 6A.28, the gains from defecting from full cooperation are evaluated for all scenarios. The Stackelberg solution is disregarded here, and the Nash equilibrium adopted as 'threat point'. In theory there are two possible strategic constellations in this two-person, two-strategies set-up: a prisoners' dilemma, which implies strictly dominated strategies for both players, or strictly dominated strategies only for one player. Strictly dominated strategies imply that for at least one player one strategy is better regardless of the choice of the other player. According to Axelrod (1991), a prisoners' dilemma is characterized by the following ranking of payoffs (Axelrod, 1991, p. 8):

$$T \geq R \geq P \geq S \tag{18}$$

where the consonants T, R, P, and S stand for the payoffs as portrayed in Table 6.3. The strategic outcome of a prisoners' dilemma is the Nash equilibrium. The Nash equilibrium is by no means a 'negative' outcome, because it indicates that potential gains from cooperation are to be made. However, the gains from defecting – if the other player cooperates – are even higher. This is quite a different problem, as individual rationality also needs to be overcome if a cooperative outcome is to result. An overview of possible strategies that may be used is given in Mißfeldt (1995). Axelrod (1991) finds that if a game is played over time the 'tit-for-tat' strategy is a particular powerful instrument.

Table 6.3 Scenario 0.0

West/East	Nash	Cooperation
Nash	*P/P*	*T/S*
Cooperation	*S/T*	*R/R*

Indeed, all 16 cases considered here constitute a prisoners' dilemma, whereby cooperation is a strictly dominated strategy for both players. Gains from defecting are particularly high if transboundary spillovers are high. For example, the East may gain around 30 per cent in terms of the Nash outcome if it defects from cooperation in scenarios 1.7–2.7.[21] This follows, because under cooperation the East has to face up to the high spillovers it imposes on the West. As was observed above, when radioactive spillovers are high, cooperation is not even individually rational. Put differently, it appears that if cooperation is individually rational, the gains from defecting from the full-cooperative solution are not so high. In situations where there are additional costs to defecting, such as loss of credibility or transaction costs, which have not been quantified here, cooperation may be a more stable outcome, as these simulations indicate.

To sum up, simulation shows that the Stackelberg solution is only interesting if the nuclear industry in the East is initially substantially riskier than in the West, and safety is very high in the West. Then leadership from the West may induce the East to undertake more abatement than under the Nash equilibrium. However, total welfare and total abatement are lower than under the Nash equilibrium, although only slightly so.

As predicted by the theoretical model, abatement is highest under full cooperation; and total welfare is highest under full cooperation. But all 16 scenarios constitute prisoner's dilemmas, where cooperation is strictly dominated for both East and West. When there are strong transboundary spillovers, cooperation is particularly difficult to reach because it is not individually rational for either of the two parties. What is more, gains from defecting from full cooperation are particularly high. High transboundary spillovers thus call for side payments to guarantee individual rationality and to dampen the free-rider incentive.

8. CONCLUDING REMARKS

In this chapter a framework of a two-player static game was set out in order to analyse the transboundary spillovers inflicted from the accident risk arising from operation of nuclear power. Crucial parameters of the 'safety functions' are η_2 and η_3 which represent the transboundary fallout. Their magnitude determines the extent to which gains are to be made from cooperation. This chapter looked at the concepts of Nash, Stackelberg and (full) cooperation. The analysis reveals that if the West acts as a (Stackelberg) leader, it will do less abatement than by using any of the other strategies discussed here. Most abatement will be done under cooperation, not only at the aggregate level, but also at the country level. What is more, utility gains from cooperation may be quite attractive, as a simulation exercise showed, ranging from 2–11 per cent for both countries as compared with the Nash equilibrium. Cooperation, however, is not readily achievable given the free-rider incentive for both countries. But it can be argued that the latter is not as high as with other transboundary pollution problems (for example, greenhouse gases), and a number of potential control organizations already exist. Cooperation can be made attractive through side payments. As mentioned above, some side payments are made by the West, for example by the European Union. Comparing bargaining powers derived from a Nash bargaining solution and proxies for actual bargaining power suggests that it may be advantageous for the West to redistribute a higher share to the East than its natural power would necessitate. While these considerations are valid in a static framework, it is, however, doubtful whether continued side payments over time yield an incentive-compatible outcome.

Unfortunately it is neither easy to compare the different solution concepts in terms of the total safety payoff evaluated above in purely theoretical terms, nor to say under which circumstances safety payoffs under one solution might be superior to safety payoffs under another solution. But as long as the abatement costs are not too high compared with potential benefits from abatement, the ranking of solution concepts as indicated by the amount of risk abatement will prevail. Further insights were gained from simulation or actual empirical analysis: it was shown that Stackelberg led to a Pareto-inferior outcome when compared with the Nash equilibrium. Simulation also indicated that when transboundary spillovers are very high, defecting from cooperation is particularly beneficial. If gains from cooperation can be redistributed so as to make the outcome individually rational for both actors, then the free-rider incentive may also be dampened. However, additional measures need to be taken to prevent free-riding.

The analysis at hand is somehow partial with respect to the dimension of time. Any restructuring undertaken in the energy sector, however, requires long-term planning (for example, with respect to future energy demand). Aspects such as radioactive waste transport and low-level radiation have been so far precluded from the analysis. The analysis is also confined to the expected damage from nuclear accidents. No comparison is made between the riskiness of nuclear power and other energy sources. However, this chapter has outlined that there are other examples of transboundary pollution in addition to the emission of sulphur dioxide and greenhouse gases which lead to transboundary spillovers. The expected spillovers from nuclear power should be considered before advocating nuclear energy as a remedy for acid rain or global warming.

NOTES

1. According to the G-24 database, the total sum of funds made available for safety assistance until 1995/96 amounts to 782.65 million ECU (bilateral help and Nuclear Safety Fund) as of May 1995. In the framework of the PHARE and TACIS aid programmes, implemented by the CEC in 1990 and 1991, a proportion of the help is confined to the problem of nuclear safety. Within those programmes alone 340 million ECU have been made available. Beginning in 1993, the 'Nuclear Safety Fund' was established under the auspices of the G7 Nuclear Safety Working Group. Its purpose is to finance technical assistance for limited continuation of operation of nuclear reactors, which cannot be brought up to Western safety standards. The allocation of resources is conditional upon the agreement of the recipient countries to close down particularly unsafe power stations. The total volume of available funds as of August 1994 was 151 million ECU. According to a study undertaken by Konoplyanik and Nechaev (1994), however, around US$4.8 billion (i.e. about 3.7 billion ECU with the exchange rate of 1 May 1995) are required to restructure the nuclear sector in Russia alone. (Bundesministerium für Umwelt, Naturschutz und Reaktorsicherheit, 1994; Konoplyanik and Nechaev (1994)).
2. One might think, for instance, of the nuclear reactor in Chernobyl which is still active in early 1998.

3. In this context it may be worth noting that in 1995 an emergency exercise with international participation took place in Russia, organized by the Department of Humanitarian Aid (DHA) of the United Nations (DHA, 1995).
4. Note, however, that trade in nuclear waste and plutonium smuggling do not constitute (transboundary) externalities. If nuclear waste is traded, the recipient country will receive a payment in exchange. It is another matter whether such payment turns out to be sufficient to cover the costs of waste storage. Plutonium smuggling is a criminal offence and can be brought to court.
5. This implies that each player knows the other player, knows about all actions available to the other player and knows all potential outcomes to both players. See Friedman (1986) for further details.
6. Considering that most East European nuclear reactors have no containment, the expected release of radioactivity in the event of an accident in the East will generally be higher than in the West. According to information given by the IAEA, it is expected that any core meltdown in such a nuclear reactor would entail a substantial release of radioactivity into the environment.
7. The magnitudes of $E_{jd}^{\ i}$ and $p_{jd}^{\ i}$ can be determined at the country level once P^i is chosen at the international level. The relationship of the parameters is not predetermined by the choice of P^i, and depends purely on the countries' own choices.
8. In the literature on probabilistic safety analysis (PSA), an 'undesired event' describes the failure of a system in a nuclear reactor, for example of the emergency and heat removal system; see for example Gesellschaft für Reaktorsicherheit (1990).
9. These restrictions turn out to be $\gamma < 1/(2(\eta_1 P^E + \eta_2 P^W))$ for the East and $\varepsilon < 1/(2(\eta_3 P^E + \eta_4 P^W))$ for the West. They are derived from the first-order derivative of the damage function, and ensure that the functions are not negatively sloped. It can be argued that a point of decreasing damage will not be reached, because of abatement costs becoming prohibitively high from a certain point onwards. A derivation of this condition is given in Appendix 1.
10. Instead of thinking of the transfer coefficients as a single parameter, it is also possible to perceive them as a vector of transport parameters for various radioactive isotopes.
11. See for example IAEA (1985).
12. For example by the Norwegian Meteorological Institute in Oslo with its 'Civil Nuclear Accident Programme' (CNAP).
13. However, this does not necessarily hold. In the case of Chernobyl, for example, most of the radiation fell on Belorussia, and not on the Ukraine where the damaged nuclear reactor is actually situated; Chernobyl is situated very close to the Belorussian border.
14. The functions chosen in his paper exhibit the same properties as the functions in this chapter. His argument is based on the slopes of the reaction functions.
15. In our case, risk abatement within both countries, E and W, is defined by $(\eta_1 + \eta_3)P^W + (\eta_2 + \eta_4)P^E$.
16. For the sake of completeness the general solutions for both P^E and P^W in terms of h are included in Appendix 10.
17. For a proof see Wang, Jianhua (1988), p. 94.
18. For a thorough discussion of these properties see Friedman (1986).
19. An overview of the problems inherent in the use of side payments and alternative solutions is presented in Folmer, van Mouche and Ragland (1993).
20. Individual rationality means here that a country on its own is better off by choosing to cooperate than by playing Nash.
21. Particular gains from defecting also accrue to the East under 1.3–2.3. The West is particularly keen on defecting under scenarios 1.2–2.2 and 1.4–2.4.

REFERENCES

Axelrod, R. (1991), *The Evolution of Cooperation*, London: Penguin Books.
Barrett, S. (1991), 'The Paradox of Environmental Agreements', London Business School.

Barrett, S. (1992), *Convention on Climate Change – Economic Aspects of Negotiations*, Paris: OECD.
Bundesministerium für Umwelt, Naturschutz und Reaktorsicherheit (1994), *Die westliche Unterstützung zur Verbesserung der Sicherheit von Kernkraftwerken sowjetischer Bauart*, Bonn, August.
Department of Humanitarian Aid (DHA) (1995), Exercise 'Northern Light – 95', Apatity, Kola Peninsula, Russian Federation.
Folmer, H., P. van Mouche and S. Ragland (1993), 'Interconnected Games and International Environmental Problems', *Environmental and Resource Economics*, **3**, 313–35.
Friedman, J. (1986), *Game Theory with Applications to Economics*, 2nd edition (1991), New York and Oxford: Oxford University Press.
Gesellschaft für Reaktorsicherheit (GRS) (1990), *German Risk Study, Nuclear Power Plants*, Phase B, Köln.
Harsanyi, J. (1977), *Rational behaviour and bargaining equilibrium in Games and social situations*, Cambridge: Cambridge University Press.
Heister, J. (1993), 'Who will win the Ozone Game?', *Kiel working paper* no. 579, Institute of World Economics, Kiel.
Hoel, M. (1989), 'Global Environmental Problems: The Effects of Unilateral Actions Taken by one Country', Memorandum from the Department of Economics, University of Oslo.
IAEA (1985), 'Assigning a Value to Transboundary Radiation Exposure', *Safety Series*, **67**, Vienna.
IAEA (1988), *Nuclear Power Performance and Safety*, **3**, Vienna.
Konoplyanik, A. and V. Nechaev (1994), 'Russia's nuclear power safety – an alternative proposal', *Energy Policy*, **22**(12), 1002–4.
Lochard, J. and P. Pages (1984), 'Cost-Effectiveness Analysis of Risk Reduction at Nuclear Power Plants', in *Risks and Benefits of Energy Systems, Proceedings of a Symposium in Jülich*, IAEA, Vienna.
Mäler, K.-G. (1989), 'The Acid Rain Game', in H. Folmer and E. Van Ierland (eds), *Valuation Methods and Policy Making in Environmental Economics*, Amsterdam: Elsevier.
Mißfeldt, F.K. (1995), 'Modelling Transboundary Pollution', Discussion Paper in Ecological Economics, EERG, Stirling University, 95/3.
NUSAC News (1996/10, p.8).
Stähler, F. (1992), 'Managing Global Pollution Problems by Reduction and Adaptation Policies', Kiel Working Paper no. 542, Kiel Institute of World Economics.
Varian, H. (1992), *Microeconomic Analysis*, 3rd edition, New York: W.W. Norton.
Wang, Jianhua (1988), *The Theory of Games*, Beijing: Tsinghua University Press.
Wheeler, D. (1988), 'Atmospheric Dispersal and Deposition of Radioactive Material from Chernobyl', *Atmospheric Environment*, **22**(5), 853–63.
World Bank (1996), *World Development Report*, New York: Oxford University Press.

APPENDICES

1. The Damage Function Conditions

The conditions to guarantee increasing benefit as risk is reduced are derived from the first-order conditions of the benefit part of the safety payoff function.

These conditions must remain positive. Looking at the damage part of the East, the first-order derivatives must satisfy the following conditions:

$$\frac{\partial d^E}{\partial P^E} = \eta_1 - 2\gamma \eta_1 \left(\eta_1 P^E + \eta_2 P^W\right) > 0$$

$$\frac{\partial d^E}{\partial P^W} = \eta_2 - 2\gamma \eta_2 \left(\eta_1 P^E + \eta_2 P^W\right) > 0.$$

Since the transfer coefficients assume a strictly positive value, these conditions can be reduced to the one below:

$$1 - 2\gamma \left(\eta_1 P^E + \eta_2 P^W\right) > 0.$$

Solving for γ yields

$$\gamma < \frac{1}{2\left(\eta_1 P^E + \eta_2 P^W\right)}.$$

The condition for the damage part of the West is found in a similar way.

2. The Derivation of the Reaction Functions

The reaction functions are solved for by deriving the first-order conditions of the safety function and setting them equal to zero. Subsequently, the equation is solved for P^E or P^W. For the case of the East, E, the derivation is as follows:

$$\frac{\partial s^E}{\partial P^E} = \eta_1 - 2\gamma \eta_1 \left(\eta_1 P^E + \eta_2 P^W\right) - 2c^E P^E = 0$$

$$\Leftrightarrow \eta_1 \left(1 - 2\gamma \eta_2 P^W\right) = 2\left(\gamma \eta_1^2 + c^E\right) P^E$$

$$\Leftrightarrow P^E = \frac{\eta_1 \left(1 - 2\gamma \eta_2 P^W\right)}{2\left(\gamma \eta_1^2 + c^E\right)}$$

3. Condition from the Slope of the Reaction Function

$$\frac{\partial P_R^E}{\partial P^W} = -\frac{\gamma \eta_1 \eta_2}{\gamma \eta_1^2 + c^E}$$

$$\frac{\partial \frac{\partial P_R^E}{\partial P^W}}{\partial \eta_1} = \frac{-\gamma \eta_2}{\left(\gamma \eta_1^2 + c^E\right)} + \frac{\gamma \eta_1 \eta_2 (2\gamma \eta_1)}{\left(\gamma \eta_1^2 + c^E\right)^2} < 0 \Leftrightarrow 2\gamma \eta_1^2 < \left(\gamma \eta_1^2 + c^E\right)$$

$$\gamma \eta_1^2 < c^E$$

A similar argument holds for the West.

4. Second-order Condition for Non-cooperative Solutions (Nash, Stackelberg)

$$\frac{\partial^2 s^E}{\partial P^{E^2}} = -2\gamma \eta_1^2 - 2c^E < 0 \quad \frac{\partial^2 s^E}{\partial P^{W^2}} = -2\gamma \eta_2^2 < 0 \quad \frac{\partial^2 s^E}{\partial P^W \partial P^E} = -2\gamma \eta_1 \eta_2 \neq 0$$

$$\frac{\partial^2 s^W}{\partial P^{W^2}} = -2\epsilon \eta_4^2 - 2c^W < 0 \quad \frac{\partial^2 s^W}{\partial P^{W^2}} = -2\epsilon \eta_3^2 < 0 \quad \frac{\partial^2 s^W}{\partial P^W \partial P^E} = -2\epsilon \eta_3 \eta_4 \neq 0$$

5. Derivation of the Sign of the Level of Nuclear risk P^E and P^W in the Nash Equilibrium

The numerator

The sign of the numerator can be derived from the conditions imposed on the benefit function by substituting in the values of the Nash equilibrium for P^E and P^W. The condition is

$$\gamma < \frac{1}{2\left(\eta_1 P^E + \eta_2 P^W\right)},$$

but if this holds, then the following inequality must hold as well:

$$\gamma < \frac{1}{\left(\eta_1 P^E + \eta_2 P^W\right)}.$$

This condition has to hold also under the Nash equilibrium. Plugging in the solutions for the Nash levels of P^E and P^W and some rearranging thus yields

$$\gamma < \frac{\gamma\varepsilon\eta_1^2\eta_4^2 + \gamma\eta_1^2 c^W + \varepsilon\eta_4^2 c^E + c^W c^E - \gamma\varepsilon\eta_1\eta_2\eta_3\eta_4}{\eta_1^2\left(\varepsilon\eta_4^2 + c^W - \gamma\eta_2\eta_4\right) + \eta_2\eta_4\left(\gamma\eta_1^2 + c^E - \varepsilon\eta_1\eta_3\right)}.$$

Multiplying by the denominator and simplifying the expression then produces the following:

$$\gamma\eta_2\eta_4 < \varepsilon\eta_4^2 + c^W$$

which implies that the numerator of P_N^E is positive. Similarly, plugging the Nash equilibrium choices for P^E and P^W into the other condition of the West's benefit function, namely into

$$\varepsilon < \frac{1}{2\left(\eta_3 P^E + \eta_4 P^W\right)},$$

and following through the same procedure as laid out above, it is possible to find

$$\varepsilon\eta_1\eta_3 < \gamma\eta_1^2 + c^E,$$

which implies that also the numerator of $P^W{}_N$ is positive.

The denominator
The denominator of both P_N^W and P_N^E is also positive. This can be shown by rearranging it slightly. First note that the denominators for both values are the same. The expression of the denominator as given in the text is

$$\gamma\eta_1^2\varepsilon\eta_4^2 + \gamma\eta_1^2 c^W + \varepsilon\eta_4^2 c^E + c^W c^E - \gamma\eta_1\eta_2\eta_3\eta_4\varepsilon.$$

Rearranging brings about the following expression:

$$\gamma\eta_1^2 c^W + \varepsilon\eta_4^2 c^E + c^W c^E + \gamma\eta_1\varepsilon\eta_4(\eta_1\eta_4 - \eta_2\eta_3).$$

The last expression in parentheses is positive as for the transfer parameters the following holds: $\eta_1 > \eta_3$ and $\eta_4 > \eta_2$. This is so because the share of radiation transported outside the country of origin is lower than the share of radiation that remains within the country borders in the event of an accident.

6. Derivation of the Stackelberg Solution

The West maximizes its welfare subject to what it thinks is the best response of the East, given the East's reaction function. To solve for the choice P_S^W of the West, the reaction function for the East is substituted in the safety payoff function of the West:

$$s^W = \left(\eta_3 \frac{\eta_1(1-2\gamma\eta_2 P^W)}{2(\gamma\eta_1^2 + c^E)} + \eta_4 P^W\right) - \varepsilon\left(\eta_3 \frac{\eta_1(1-2\gamma\eta_2 P^W)}{2(\gamma\eta_1^2 + c^E)} + \eta_4 P^W\right)^2 - c^W P^{W^2}.$$

Deriving this expression with respect to P^W and setting it equal to zero yields the necessary conditions for a maximum wealth:

$$\frac{\partial s^W}{\partial P^W} = \left(-\frac{\eta_1\eta_2\eta_3\gamma}{(\gamma\eta_1^2 + c^E)} + \eta_4\right)$$

$$-2\varepsilon\left(\eta_3\frac{\eta_1(1-2\gamma\eta_2 P^W)}{2(\gamma\eta_1^2 + c^E)} + \eta_4 P^W\right)\left(-\frac{\eta_1\eta_2\eta_3\gamma}{(\gamma\eta_1^2 + c^E)} + \eta_4\right) - 2c^W P^W = 0.$$

Some rearranging yields

$$\left(1 - \frac{\varepsilon\eta_1\eta_3}{\gamma\eta_1^2 + c^E}\right) = \left(\frac{2c^W(\gamma\eta_1^2 + c^E)}{\eta_4(\gamma\eta_1^2 + c^E) - \eta_1\eta_2\eta_3\gamma} - \frac{2\gamma\varepsilon\eta_1\eta_2\eta_3 - 2\varepsilon\eta_4(\gamma\eta_1^2 + c^E)}{(\gamma\eta_1^2 + c^E)}\right)P^W,$$

which can be solved for P^W as follows:

$$P^W = \frac{(\gamma\eta_1^2 + c^E - \varepsilon\eta_1\eta_3)(\eta_4(\gamma\eta_1^2 + c^E) - \eta_1\eta_2\eta_3\gamma)}{2c^W(\gamma\eta_1^2 + c^E)^2 - (\eta_1\eta_2\eta_3^2\gamma\varepsilon - 2\varepsilon\eta_4(\gamma\eta_1^2 + c^E))(\eta_4(\gamma\eta_1^2 + c^E) - \eta_1\eta_2\eta_3\gamma)}.$$

Multiplying out brackets and rearranging yields the expression as given in the text. The abatement of risk when the West is a Stackelberg leader can be solved for when plugging the choice of risk abatement into the West, P_S^W, in the reaction function of the East:

$$P_S^E = \frac{\eta_1\left(1 - 2P_S^W \gamma \eta_2\right)}{\left(\gamma \eta_1^2 + c^E\right)}.$$

Plugging in P_S^W yields the following expression:

$$P_S^E = \eta_1 \left((\varepsilon\eta_4^2 + c^W)(\gamma\eta_1^2 + c^E)^2 + \gamma\varepsilon\eta_1\eta_2\eta_3(\gamma\eta_1\eta_2\eta_3 - 2\eta_4(\gamma\eta_1^2 + c^E)\right.$$
$$\left. - \gamma\eta_2((\gamma\eta_1^2 + c^E)(\eta_4(\gamma\eta_1^2 + c^E) - (\eta_2\gamma + \eta_4\varepsilon)\eta_1\eta_3) + \eta_1^2\eta_2\eta_3^2\varepsilon\gamma))\right)/$$
$$(2(\gamma\eta_1^2 + c^E)((\varepsilon\eta_4^2 + c^W)(\gamma\eta_1^2 + c^E)^2 + \gamma\varepsilon\eta_1\eta_2\eta_3(\gamma\eta_1\eta_2\eta_3 - 2\eta_4(\gamma\eta_1^2 + c^E)))).$$

After some simplification, the expression can be rewritten as

$$P_S^E = \frac{\eta_1\left(\eta_1\eta_3(\gamma\eta_1 - \varepsilon\eta_4) + \left(\gamma\eta_1 + c^E\right)\left(\eta_4(\varepsilon\eta_4 - \gamma\eta_2) + c^W\right)\right)}{2\left(\left(\varepsilon\eta_4^2 + c^W\right)\left(\gamma\eta_1^2 + c^E\right)^2 + \gamma\varepsilon\eta_1\eta_2\eta_3\left(\gamma\eta_1\eta_2\eta_3 - 2\eta_4\left(\gamma\eta_1^2 + c^E\right)\right)\right)}.$$

7. The Scenarios from Simulation

Scenario	X.1	X.2	X.3	X.4	$c^E = c^W = 1$
	X.5	X.6	X.7	X.8	$c^E = 1; c^W = 2$
η_1	0.8	0.9	0.5	0.7	
η_2	0.2	0.5	0.1	0.4	
η_3	0.2	0.1	0.5	0.3	
η_4	0.8	0.5	0.9	0.6	

Notes: Scenarios 1.X with $\gamma = 0.3$ and $\varepsilon = 0.5$, and scenarios 2.X with $\gamma = 0.5$ and $\varepsilon = 0.5$.

8. The Partial Derivative of the Full-cooperative Outcome with Respect to a Change in c^E and c^W

Taking the risk abatement in the East under full cooperation as an example, the response of P^E with respect to changes of c^E can be found by taking a first-order derivative of P_{full}^E with respect to c^E. This results in the following expression:

$$\frac{\partial P_{full}^{E}}{\partial c^{E}} = -\frac{\left[\eta_1\left(c^W + \eta_4(\epsilon\eta_4 - \gamma\eta_2)\right) + \eta_3\left(c^W + \eta_2(\gamma\eta_2 - \epsilon\eta_4)\right)\right]\left(c^W + \gamma\eta_2^2 + \epsilon\eta_4^2\right)}{4\left(c^E c^W + \epsilon\eta_3^2 c^W + \gamma\eta_2^2 c^E + \epsilon\eta_4^2 c^E + \gamma\eta_1^2 c^W + \gamma\epsilon(\eta_2\eta_3 - \eta_1\eta_4)^2\right)^2} < 0.$$

The expression above is negative because the denominator is positive, as it is squared. The numerator is positive for reasons derived in Appendix 4. The response of P_{full}^{W} with respect to changes of c^W can be found accordingly.

9. First-order Conditions (FOC) under the Different Solutions

	FOC East	FOC West
Nash	$\eta_1 - 2\gamma\eta_1(\eta_1 P^E + \eta_2 P^W) = 2c^E P^E$	$\eta_4 - 2\epsilon\eta_4(\eta_3 P^E + \eta_4 P^W)$ $= 2c^W P^W$
Stackelberg	$\eta_1 - 2\gamma\eta_1(\eta_1 P^E + \eta_2 P_S^W) = 2c^E P^E$	$\eta_4 - 2\epsilon\eta_4(\eta_3 P^E + \eta_4 P^W)$ $+ \eta_3\,(\partial P^E/\partial P^W)\,(1 - \epsilon\,(\eta_3 P^E$ $+ \eta_4 P^W)) = 2c^W P^W$
Cooperation	$(\eta_1 - 2\gamma\eta_1(\eta_1 P^E + \eta_2 P^W)$ $+ \eta 3\,((1{-}h)/h)\,(1 - 2\epsilon\,(\eta_3 P^E + \eta_4 P^W))$ $= 2c^E P^E$	$(\eta_4 - 2\epsilon\eta_4(\eta_3 P^E + \eta_4 P^W)$ $+ \eta_2\,((1{-}h)/h)\,(1 - 2\gamma\,(\eta_1 P^E$ $+ \eta_2 P^W))$ $= 2c^W P^W$

10. General Solution for the Values of P^E and P^W along the Contract Curve

$P_{Contract}^{E} = \tfrac{1}{2}\,(-\eta_1\eta_2\eta_4\gamma h^2 + \eta_1\eta_2\eta_4\gamma h + \eta_1 c^W h^2 - \eta_1\eta_4^2\epsilon h - \eta_1 c^W h$
$+ \eta_1\eta_4^2\epsilon h^2 + \eta_2^2\eta_3\gamma h^2 - \eta_2^2\,\eta_3\gamma h - \eta_2\eta_3\eta_4\,\epsilon h^2 - \eta_3 c^W h^2$
$+ 2\eta_3 c^W h + \eta_2\eta_3\eta_4\epsilon h - \eta_3 c^W)\,/\,(-c^W c^E h - \eta_3^2\epsilon c^W + c^W c^E h^2$
$+ 2\eta_1\eta_2\eta_3\eta_4\gamma\epsilon h - 2\eta_1\eta_2\eta_3\eta_4\gamma\epsilon h^2 - \eta_2^2\gamma c^E h^2 - \eta_2^2\eta_3^2\gamma\epsilon h$
$+ \eta_2^2\eta_3^2\gamma\epsilon h^2 - \eta_1^2\eta_4^2\gamma\epsilon h - \eta_4^2\epsilon c^E h - \eta_1^2 c^W h + 2\eta_3^2\epsilon c^W h$
$+ \eta_1^2\eta_4^2\gamma\epsilon h^2 + \eta_4^2\epsilon c^E h^2 + \eta_1^2 c^W h^2 - \eta_3^2\epsilon c^W h^2)$

$P_{Contract}^{W} = \tfrac{1}{2}\,h\,(-\eta_2 c^E h - \eta_2\eta_3^2\epsilon + \eta_2\eta_3^2\epsilon h + \eta_1\eta_2\eta_3\gamma - \eta_1\eta_2\eta_3\gamma h$
$- \eta_1^2\eta_4\gamma - \eta_4 c^E + \eta_1\eta_3\eta_4\epsilon + \eta_1^2\eta_4\gamma h + \eta_4 c^E h$
$- \eta_1\eta_3\eta_4\epsilon h)\,/\,(-c^W c^E h - \eta_3^2\epsilon c^W + c^W c^E h^2 + 2\eta_1\eta_2\eta_3\eta_4\gamma\epsilon h$
$- 2\eta_1\eta_2\eta_3\eta_4\gamma\epsilon h^2 - \eta_2^2\gamma c^E h^2 - \eta_2^2\eta_3^2\gamma\epsilon h + \eta_2^2\eta_3^2\gamma\epsilon h^2$
$- \eta_1^2\eta_4^2\gamma\epsilon h - \eta_4^2\epsilon c^E h - \eta_1^2\gamma c^W h + 2\eta_3^2\epsilon c^W h + \eta_1^2\eta_4^2\gamma\epsilon h^2$
$+ \eta_4^2\epsilon c^E h^2 + \eta_1^2\gamma c^W h^2 - \eta_3^2\epsilon c^W h^2)$

11. Simulation Tables

Tables 6A.1–6A.6 Risk abatement under Nash, Stackelberg and Full cooperation

Table 6A.1 Risk abatement in absolute terms in the East

Scenario	Nash	Stackelberg	Cooperation
1.1	0.32416	0.32425	0.37672
1.2	0.33871	0.33916	0.35326
1.3	0.22860	0.22862	0.35784
1.4	0.28813	0.28867	0.36763
1.5	0.32908	0.32914	0.39217
1.6	0.34970	0.34995	0.37500
1.7	0.23025	0.23026	0.38277
1.8	0.29596	0.29627	0.39116

Table 6A.2 Risk abatement in absolute terms in the East

Scenario	Nash	Stackelberg	Cooperation
2.1	0.28571	0.28591	0.33333
2.2	0.28571	0.28671	0.29412
2.3	0.21587	0.21593	0.34118
2.4	0.25472	0.25600	0.32750
2.5	0.29319	0.29332	0.35048
2.6	0.30201	0.30257	0.32154
2.7	0.21852	0.21856	0.36610
2.8	0.26689	0.26763	0.35459

Table 6A.3 Risk abatement in absolute terms in the West

Scenario	Nash	Stackelberg	Cooperation
1.1	0.28338	0.28121	0.33917
1.2	0.21470	0.21053	0.36957
1.3	0.28368	0.28210	0.29412
1.4	0.23226	0.22497	0.35507
1.5	0.16107	0.15966	0.19288
1.6	0.11353	0.11121	0.20000
1.7	0.16557	0.16450	0.16949
1.8	0.12540	0.12116	0.19387

Table 6A.4 Risk abatement in absolute terms in the West

Scenario	Nash	Stackelberg	Cooperation
2.1	0.28571	0.28241	0.33333
2.2	0.21587	0.20968	0.34118
2.3	0.28571	0.28319	0.29412
2.4	0.23481	0.22343	0.33704
2.5	0.16230	0.16017	0.18971
2.6	0.11409	0.11064	0.18658
2.7	0.16667	0.16495	0.16949
2.8	0.12660	0.12001	0.18515

Table 6A.5 Total risk abatement in absolute terms

Scenario	Nash	Stackelberg	Cooperation
1.1	0.60754	0.60546	0.71589
1.2	0.55340	0.54969	0.72283
1.3	0.51228	0.51073	0.65196
1.4	0.52040	0.51364	0.72271
1.5	0.49015	0.48881	0.58505
1.6	0.46323	0.46116	0.57500
1.7	0.39582	0.39476	0.55226
1.8	0.42136	0.41743	0.58503

Table 6A.6 Total risk abatement in absolute terms

Scenario	Nash	Stackelberg	Cooperation
2.1	0.57143	0.56833	0.66667
2.2	0.50159	0.49639	0.63530
2.3	0.50159	0.49912	0.63530
2.4	0.48953	0.47943	0.66454
2.5	0.45550	0.45350	0.54019
2.6	0.41611	0.41321	0.50804
2.7	0.38519	0.38351	0.53559
2.8	0.39349	0.38764	0.53973

Tables 6A.7–6A.12   All outcomes scaled in percent of the Nash equilibrium

Table 6A.7   Utility derived by the East as percentage difference from what could be reached under Nash

Scenario	Stackelberg	Cooperation
1.1	99.81	103.00
1.2	99.36	122.56
1.3	99.83	79.78
1.4	98.71	116.62
1.5	99.86	100.18
1.6	99.56	115.23
1.7	99.87	66.43
1.8	99.04	107.64

Table 6A.8   Utility derived by the West as percentage difference from what could be reached under Nash

Scenario	Stackelberg	Cooperation
1.1	100.00	101.67
1.2	100.02	69.65
1.3	100.00	117.16
1.4	100.04	99.06
1.5	100.00	105.99
1.6	100.02	77.81
1.7	100.00	130.33
1.8	100.03	110.14

Table 6A.9   Total utility as percentage difference from what could be reached under Nash

Scenario	Stackelberg	Cooperation
1.1	99.90	102.36
1.2	99.53	108.98
1.3	99.95	106.83
1.4	99.29	108.87
1.5	99.92	102.70
1.6	99.67	106.66
1.7	99.96	111.39
1.8	99.48	108.74

Table 6A.10 Utility derived by the East as percentage difference from what could be reached under Nash

Scenario	Stackelberg	Cooperation
2.1	99.71	102.08
2.2	99.09	117.18
2.3	99.73	78.92
2.4	98.05	111.89
2.5	99.79	99.60
2.6	99.37	112.24
2.7	99.79	65.44
2.8	98.54	104.76

Table 6A.11 Utility derived by the West as percentage difference from what could be reached under Nash

Scenario	Stackelberg	Cooperation
2.1	100.01	102.08
2.2	100.05	78.92
2.3	100.00	117.18
2.4	100.11	102.29
2.5	100.01	106.13
2.6	100.04	83.58
2.7	100.00	130.41
2.8	100.08	112.04

Table 6A.12 Total utility as percentage difference from what could be reached under Nash

Scenario	Stackelberg	Cooperation
2.1	99.86	102.08
2.2	99.35	106.81
2.3	99.93	106.81
2.4	98.97	107.58
2.5	99.89	102.53
2.6	99.53	105.41
2.7	99.94	111.42
2.8	99.23	108.02

Normal forms of the static game

Table 6A.13   Scenario 1.1

West/East	Nash	Cooperation
Nash	100/100	104.38/98.18
Cooperation	97.57/104.97	101.67/103.00

Table 6A.14   Scenario 1.2

West/East	Nash	Cooperation
Nash	100/100	101.47/99.89
Cooperation	68.31/122.92	69.65/122.56

Table 6A.15   Scenario 1.3

West/East	Nash	Cooperation
Nash	100/100	117.50/78.70
Cooperation	99.93/101.13	117.16/79.78

Table 6A.16   Scenario 1.4

West/East	Nash	Cooperation
Nash	100/100	112.42/96.09
Cooperation	87.84/121.41	99.06/116.62

Table 6A.17   Scenario 1.5

West/East	Nash	Cooperation
Nash	100/100	108.14/97.05
Cooperation	98.10/103.24	105.99/100.18

Table 6A.18   Scenario 1.6

West/East	Nash	Cooperation
Nash	100/100	103.72/99.62
Cooperation	74.27/115.90	77.81/115.23

Table 6A.19   Scenario 1.7

West/East	Nash	Cooperation
Nash	100/100	130.51/65.96
Cooperation	99.98/100.49	130.33/66.43

Table 6A.20   Scenario 1.8

West/East	Nash	Cooperation
Nash	100/100	119.70/93.06
Cooperation	91.42/115.30	110.13/107.64

Table 6A.21   Scenario 2.1

West/East	Nash	Cooperation
Nash	100/100	104.14/98.17
Cooperation	98.17/104.14	102.08/102.08

Table 6A.22   Scenario 2.2

West/East	Nash	Cooperation
Nash	100/100	100.90/99.95
Cooperation	78.08/117.44	78.92/117.18

Table 6A.23   Scenario 2.3

West/East	Nash	Cooperation
Nash	100/100	117.44/78.08
Cooperation	99.95/100.90	117.18/78.92

Table 6A.24   Scenario 2.4

West/East	Nash	Cooperation
Nash	100/100	112.16/96.13
Cooperation	91.10/116.99	102.29/111.89

Table 6A.25 Scenario 2.5

West/East	Nash	Cooperation
Nash	100/100	107.82/97.02
Cooperation	98.52/102.75	106.13/99.60

Table 6A.26 Scenario 2.6

West/East	Nash	Cooperation
Nash	100/100	103.10/99.71
Cooperation	80.60/112.88	83.58/112.24

Table 6A.27 Scenario 2.7

West/East	Nash	Cooperation
Nash	100/100	130.53/65.12
Cooperation	99.99/100.35	130.41/65.44

Table 6A.28 Scenario 2.8

West/East	Nash	Cooperation
Nash	100/100	119.55/93.06
Cooperation	93.34/112.74	112.04/104.76

7. Renegotiation-proof equilibria in a bargaining game over global emission reductions – does the instrumental framework matter?

Alfred Endres and Michael Finus*

1. INTRODUCTION

An important prerequisite for international environmental agreements (IEAs) to be successful is that they are self-enforcing. Since there exists no 'world government', agreements on the terms, accession to and adherence to an IEA by every individual country must be voluntary. Thus, there are some difficult hurdles to be taken before progress can be made in international pollution control. In particular, stability of an agreement poses major problems to an IEA because of the free-rider incentive.

The purpose of this chapter is to investigate how the instrumental (that is, policy) framework affects the bargaining outcome over pollution control. We focus on three (out of many other possible) policy frameworks (also policy regimes in what follows): emission reduction quotas, effluent taxes and tradable emission permits. This choice is motivated by the fact that the first instrument is frequently part of IEAs,[1] whereas the last two are often recommended by economists as efficient means to tackle global pollutants. For simplicity, the analysis is confined to a two-country model.

To narrow the analysis further, we assume four specifics often associated with the bargaining process on the way to the ratification and enforcement of a typical IEA (Endres, 1996). First, we focus on uniform solutions. These imply that each country agrees to reduce emissions by the same percentage compared to some base level. Regarding the emission tax, we assume that the negotiated tax rate will be imposed in both countries uniformly. Where countries negotiate

---

* The authors gratefully acknowledge the receipt of grant number II 69 982 by the Volkswagen Foundation, Germany. The authors are indebted to Bianca Rundshagen for her research assistance and would like to thank Henk Folmer and Nick Hanley for helpful comments on an earlier draft.

the total amount of permits to be distributed, it is assumed that both countries receive half of this total.[2]

Second, we assume no transfer payments within an IEA. This we do because following the record of most IEAs up to now, transfers have either hardly been observed or else they constitute only a small fraction of total abatement cost.[3] In particular, for the tax regime this implies that we assume tax receipts remain in the country of origin. For the permit regime it implies that apart from the trade in permits no money or any in kind transfer takes place with the aim of inducing a country to endorse a more ambitious emission reduction target.

Third, we assume that during the bargaining process countries settle on the 'smallest common denominator'. This implies that they agree on the least ambitious abatement proposal which has been put forward by each country (for example, the smaller tax rate under a tax regime).[4]

Fourth, we assume a game of incomplete information. In particular we assume that a country knows, apart from its own payoff, only abatement cost in the other country, but not its environmental preference (damage cost).

In order to evaluate the bargaining equilibria of three policy frameworks we have first to investigate each stage of a three-stage game.

In the *first stage* the bargaining equilibria of the three policy frameworks are determined according to the specifics outlined above. In addition, to have a benchmark for the final evaluation, we also derive the Nash equilibrium and the social optimum of the emission game.

In the second and third stage the incentives to modify the abatement allocation agreed upon are analysed. In the *second stage* the focus is on the incentives of a country to 'overfulfil' the terms of a treaty. As will be argued below, in specific circumstances it is rational for a country to reduce more emissions than the target laid down in a treaty. Since this is also beneficial to the other party, this kind of individual adjustment behaviour is not considered to be a breach of contract.

In the *third stage* we check whether the bargaining equilibria of the first two stages are stable in a dynamic setting. Since most IEAs are of an 'open-ended character' in that they do not specify the termination of the contract, we treat the emission game as a supergame. Stability is checked by applying the concept of renegotiation-proofness.

In what follows we shall first present the fundamental functions of our model and derive the socially optimal emission levels and Nash equilibrium emissions (Section 2.1). Subsequently, we derive the outcome for the three bargaining regimes, namely quotas (Section 2.2), taxes (Section 2.3) and permits (Section 2.4). The analysis in these sections will also cover independent adjustment behaviour in stage two of the game. In the subsequent Section 3 we analyse stability. Section 4 then compares the three regimes with the fully cooperative and with the non-cooperative solution regarding emission and welfare levels. Section 5 concludes the analysis.

2. NEGOTIATING EMISSION REDUCTIONS

2.1 The Globally Optimal Solution and the Nash Equilibrium

Assume two countries negotiate emission reductions of a global pollutant, E, uniformly distributed in the atmosphere. Each country emits E_i; hence, total pollution is given by $E_1 + E_2 = E$.

Total cost, TC_i, of countries 1 and 2 is assumed to be

$$TC_1 = \frac{\alpha}{2}(E_1 + E_2)^2 + \frac{b}{2}\left(\frac{a}{b} - E_1\right)^2, \quad (1)$$

$$TC_2 = \Theta\frac{\alpha}{2}(E_1 + E_2)^2 + \frac{b}{4}\left(\frac{a}{b} - E_2\right)^2, \quad (2)$$

where α, a, b and Θ are constant parameters.[5] The first term in (1) and (2) represents the environmental damage caused by the global pollutant, for example, CO_2. A possible difference between both countries' environmental damage is represented by the parameter Θ. The functional form of damage costs has been chosen to depict increasing environmental damages if aggregate emissions increase. Moreover, damages increase at an increasing rate.

The second term portrays abatement cost. At $E_1^* = E_2^* = a/b$ abatement costs are zero. Hence, $E_1^* = E_2^* = a/b$ can be interpreted as the emission level when both countries do not abate any emissions at all. With respect to (1) and (2), this situation would materialize if both countries were not to recognize environmental damage at all (for example, $\alpha = 0$), and minimize these functions with respect to emissions. We assume this to be the reference point of the bargaining process from which negotiations commence.[6] $E_i \in [0, a/b]$ therefore defines the strategy space of the emission game. Thus, reducing emissions from $E_i^* = a/b$ increases abatement costs at an increasing rate. It is assumed that country 2 exhibits half of country 1's abatement cost. This difference might be due to the fact that country 2 is less dependent on CO_2 – intensive raw materials used in energy production.

From (1) and (2) it follows that marginal damage cost in country i, MDC_i, and marginal abatement cost (with respect to emission reductions), MAC_i, are given by

$$MDC_1 = \alpha E;\ MDC_2 = \Theta\alpha E;\ MAC_1 = a - bE_1;\ MAC_2 = \tfrac{1}{2}(a - bE_2). \quad (3)$$

Minimizing (1) and (2) from a social point of view ($MAC_1 = \Sigma MDC_i$ and $MAC_2 = \Sigma MDC_i$ hold in the optimum), we obtain

$$E_1^C = \frac{a(b+\alpha+\alpha\Theta)}{b(b+3\alpha+3\alpha\Theta)}; \quad E_2^C = \frac{a(b-\alpha-\alpha\Theta)}{b(b+3\alpha+3\alpha\Theta)}; \quad E^C = \frac{2a}{b+3\alpha+3\alpha\Theta}, \quad (4)$$

where E_1^C and E_2^C are the globally optimal emission rates in country 1 and 2 respectively, and $E^C = E_1^C + E_2^C$. The superscript 'C' indicates the 'fully cooperative solution' (also called fully cooperative regime); the subscripts 1 and 2 refer to the countries. To guarantee $E_i^C \geq 0$, we impose the non-negativity constraint $NNC_1: b \geq \alpha(1+\Theta)$.

For the Nash equilibrium ($MAC_i = MDC_i$ holds in equilibrium) we find

$$E_1^N = \frac{a(b-\alpha+2\alpha\Theta)}{b(b+\alpha+2\alpha\Theta)}; \quad E_2^N = \frac{a(b+\alpha-2\alpha\Theta)}{b(b+\alpha+2\alpha\Theta)}; \quad E^N = \frac{2a}{b+\alpha+2\alpha\Theta}. \quad (5)$$

The superscript N stands for *Nash* (also called non-cooperative regime). Moreover, $E_1^N + E_2^N = E^N$. Again, to ensure positive emission rates, we require $NNC2_i: b \geq \alpha(1-2\Theta)$ and $NNC_2: b \geq \alpha(2\Theta-1)$. Since NNC_1 is a stronger requirement than NNC_{2i}, we can drop NNC_{2i}. We refer to NNC_1 and NNC_2 as 'weak' non-negativity conditions and use them in the later analysis whenever they are sufficient. However, if we assume that Θ can take on any positive value (infinity at the extreme), NNC_1 and NNC_2 collapse to one 'strong' non-negativity condition, $NNCS: b \geq c\alpha$, where c can take on any positive value. We will make use of $NNCS$ in only a few cases in the later analysis.[7]

Casual inspection of (4) and (5) already reveals a familiar result: $E^N > E^C$, so that aggregate emissions in the globally optimal solution are lower than in the Nash equilibrium.

2.2 The Quota Scheme

As explained in the Introduction, we assume the bargaining process to be constrained by the assumption that equal percentage reductions are negotiated. If $E_1^* = E_2^* = a/b$ before negotiations commence, an equal percentage reduction implies the same absolute emission reduction in both countries. By this it follows that, after the agreement has been signed, equilibrium emissions in both countries are equal, $E_1^Q = E_2^Q = E^Q/2$. In other words, delegates of both countries know that under a uniform quota regime each unit of emission reduction their country 'contributes' to the agreement will be accompanied by a one-unit cut in the neighbour country (a buy one – get one free arrangement; see Endres,

1996, 1997). Hence, it is straightforward to calculate each country's proposal, $E_i^{Q(1)}$ and $E_i^{Q(2)}$ (the superscript refers to the country which makes the proposal), based only on its own total cost function.[8] We find

$$E_i^{Q(1)} = \frac{a}{4\alpha + b}; \quad E_i^{Q(2)} = \frac{a}{8\alpha\Theta + b}. \quad (6)$$

Comparing the two proposals it is obvious that for $0 < \Theta < 1/2$, $E_i^{Q(1)} < E_i^{Q(2)}$, for $1/2 < \Theta$, $E_i^{Q(1)} > E_i^{Q(2)}$, and for $\Theta = 1/2$, $E_i^{Q(1)} = E_i^{Q(2)}$ hold. According to the smallest common denominator argument, this implies that for $\Theta < 1/2$ the suggestion of country 2 (which happens to be the bottleneck[9] in this range), $E_i^{Q(2)}$, is laid down in the treaty. For $\Theta > 1/2$ the role of the bottleneck is taken over by country 1, and therefore $E_i^{Q(1)}$ is the emission quota ratified in the agreement.[10] Thus, stage 1 of the game has been solved. In order to check what happens in stage 2, we define an incentive index $D_i = MAC_i - MDC_i$, where it may be recalled that MAC_i denotes marginal abatement cost and MDC_i marginal damage cost in country i (Endres, 1996, 1997). If D_i is positive within a parameter range, this indicates an incentive to free-ride. In a static setting, therefore, one would expect a breach of contract. If $D_i = 0$, the conditions in the Nash equilibrium are met and by definition this is a stable bargaining outcome from country i's point of view. In contrast, if D_i is negative, this implies that it would be rational for country i to abate more than agreed upon in stage 1 (and obviously rational for country j not to object). Computing D_i for all possible parameter constellations one finds: $0 \leq \Theta < 1/4$: $D_1 < 0$ and $D_2 > 0$; $1/4 \leq \Theta < 1/2$: $D_1 \geq 0$ and $D_2 > 0$; $1/2 \leq \Theta < 1$: $D_1 > 0$, $D_2 > 0$ and $1 \leq \Theta$: $D_1 > 0$, $D_2 \leq 0$.

It seems plausible that if 'adjustment' takes place this is conducted according to country i's best response function, $RF_i(E_j)$:[11]

$$RF_1(E_2) = E_1 = \frac{a - \alpha E_2}{b + \alpha}; \quad RF_2(E_1) = E_2 \frac{a - 2\alpha\Theta E_1}{b + 2\alpha\Theta}. \quad (7)$$

Thus if $D_i < 0$ holds within a parameter range, emissions are adjusted downward, using (7), until $D_i = 0$. For $D_i \geq 0$ emissions are given by (6). Taken together, combining stage 1 and 2 of the emission game allows us to calculate individual and aggregate emission levels which materialize after the agreement has been put into practice. The results are provided in Table 7A.1 in Appendix 1. Clearly, they only hold under the provision of stability for which we check in Section 3, below.

2.3 The Tax Scheme

In this subsection we assume that each country makes a proposal regarding a uniform tax rate, t, meeting its interests best. In order to make such a proposal both groups of delegates must form expectations about how their own industry and the foreign industry will adjust to a given tax rate. For this, delegates of a country must assess the neighbour country's marginal abatement cost function. Assume for simplicity that this information is available to each country. This is an information requirement higher than in the quota regime but is still less stringent than an assumption of a game of complete information.

An efficient adjustment to a given tax rate, t, is defined by $MAC_i = t$, which implies $E_1^T = a - t/b$ and $E_2^T = a - t/(2b)$ in equilibrium (the superscript 'T' stands for tax regime). Thus, country 2 abates twice as much as does country 1 for each given tax rate t. Put differently, the tax scheme is of the 'buy one – get two free' type from country 1's perspective and of the 'buy two – get one free' type from country 2's perspective. Using the equilibrium conditions stated above, we find the proposals of both countries to be[12]

$$t^{(1)} = \frac{6a\alpha}{9\alpha + b}; \quad t^{(2)} = \frac{6a\alpha}{9\alpha + 2\dfrac{b}{\Theta}}. \tag{8}$$

Again, the superscripts in brackets denote which country is submitting the respective proposal. From (8) it is apparent that for $0 \leq \Theta < 2$, $t^{(1)} > t^{(2)}$, for $2 < \Theta$, $t^{(1)} < t^{(2)}$, and for $\Theta = 2$, $t^{(1)} = t^{(2)}$ hold. Thus, country 2 is the bottleneck in the range $0 \leq \Theta < 2$, and for $2 < \Theta$, country 1 takes over this role. For $\Theta = 2$, both countries make a perfect match, submitting identical proposals (see note 9).

Using (8), equilibrium emissions in stage 1 can be calculated which are then used to determine the sign of the incentive index D_i. After stage 1 we find: $0 \leq \Theta < 2/3: D_1 < 0, D_2 > 0; 0 \leq \Theta < 2: D_1 \geq 0, D_2 > 0; 2 \leq \Theta < 3: D_1 > 0, D_2 > 0; 3 \leq \Theta: D_1 \geq 0$. Thus, accordingly, whenever $D_i < 0$ we have to calculate adjusted emission rates. The procedure is the same as already outlined above for the quota regime. Equilibrium emission rates after stage 2 of the emission game are displayed in Table 7A.2 in Appendix 1.

2.4 The Transferable Discharge Permit Scheme

Under this regime it is assumed that each country receives an equal amount of emission permits. In contrast to the quota regime, some flexibility is introduced by allowing for trade in 'reduction burdens' between the countries. Again, as in the tax regime, it turns out that the information requirement for forwarding a proposal is higher than under the quota regime. In particular, it is necessary that each country has information on the abatement cost function of its neighbour country, which we assumed to be the case. Thus, after the permits have been distributed and trade has taken place, the equilibrium conditions in the permit market are given by $MAC_1 = MAC_2 = P$ and $2M = E_1 + E_2$ where M stands for the amount of emission permits each country receives and P for the permit price. In order to compute the proposal of each country's delegation we have to modify (1) and (2) slightly to accommodate the revenue effects associated with the trade in permits.

$$TC_1 = \frac{\alpha}{2}(2M)^2 + \frac{b}{2}\left(\frac{a}{b} - E_1\right)^2 + (a - bE_1)(E_1 - M) \quad (9)$$

$$TC_2 = \Theta\frac{\alpha}{2}(2M)^2 + \frac{b}{4}\left(\frac{a}{b} - E_2\right)^2 + \frac{1}{2}(a - bE_2)(E_2 - M). \quad (10)$$

The additional third term compared to (1) and (2) represents the expenditures from the purchase of permits (for $E_i - M > 0$), or revenues from the sale of permits (for $E_i - M < 0$). The first bracket in the third term is the price, which is equal to the marginal abatement cost in equilibrium. The second bracket is the amount of permits bought and sold respectively.

Using the market equilibrium conditions stated above, we derive the proposals of both delegations (after some basic algebraic manipulations):

$$M^{(1)} = \frac{2a}{9\alpha + 2b} \text{ and } M^{(2)} = \frac{2a}{18\alpha\Theta + 2b}. \quad (11)$$

Comparing $M^{(1)}$ and $M^{(2)}$ we find $M^{(1)} > M^{(2)}$ for $\Theta > 1/2$, $M^{(1)} < M^{(2)}$ for $\Theta < 1/2$ and $M^{(1)} = M^{(2)}$ for $\Theta = 1/2$. This implies that for $\Theta < 1/2$, country 2 is the bottleneck, for $\Theta > 1/2$, country 1 takes over this role (see note 7).

Knowing the amount of permits distributed within the two ranges of Θ ($0 < \Theta < 1/2$; $1/2 < \Theta$), it is straightforward to calculate the associated emission rates of stage 1 (see Appendix II). For the incentive index D_i we find: $0 \leq \Theta < 1/3$: $D_1 < 0, D_2 > 0$; $1/3 \leq \Theta < 1/2$: $D_1 \geq 0, D_2 > 0$; $1/2 \leq \Theta < 3/2$: $D_1 > 0, D_2 > 0$ and for $3/2 \leq \Theta$: $D_1 > 0, D_2 \leq 0$. Again, computing adjusted emission rates if $D_i < 0$ according to (7), gives equilibrium emissions after stage 2 of the game as given in Table 7A.3 in Appendix I.

3. STABILITY ANALYSIS OF EMISSION EQUILIBRIA

3.1 Preliminaries

So far stages 1 and 2 of the game have been dealt with. The first step included the negotiation between the two groups of delegates. In the second step individual adjustment behaviour to overfulfil the agreement has been discussed.

Now, in stage 3 of the analysis, we are concerned with problems of non-compliance. In a one-shot game, this issue is quite clear-cut: if after stage 2 $D_i = MAC_i - MDC_i > 0$ holds, then there is an incentive for country i to pollute more than agreed upon. Thus, for large ranges of Θ we would have to expect that the agreement is unstable.[13] However, as argued in the Introduction, negotiations are not conducted and treaties are not signed in a static world and therefore our emission game is approximated as a supergame. From game theory it is well known that in an infinite dynamic setting such a free-riding situation might be overcome (1) if agents are 'patient enough' to forego an immediate gain from cheating in favour of long-term higher gains from cooperation, and (2) if 'appropriate' punishment strategies are available to deter free-riding. Before defining what we mean by 'appropriate', it is worthwhile pointing out that in our simple emission game a threat strategy basically amounts to choosing a higher emission level than has been contracted for in the agreement. Put differently, the choice of the emission level is the only action a country can take to influence the payoffs in the emission game. In a richer game one could extend the strategy space, for instance, to include trade sanctions (see Barrett, 1997) or restrictions to benefit from positive spillovers of cooperation in R&D (see Carraro and Siniscalco, 1997). In a dynamic context, however, this would complicate the analysis substantially and therefore is left for future research.

By 'appropriate' punishment we mean that, on the one hand, the threat must be harsh enough to be a sufficient deterrent; but on the other hand, it must also be credible. Credibility can be defined in many ways. According to the concept of subgame-perfectness credibility requires that if defection occurs the threat must really be carried out. This will only be the case if the threat strategy constitutes a Nash equilibrium of the remaining game at each stage when defection might occur (Selten, 1965). Requiring threat strategies to be subgame-perfect Fudenberg and Maskin (1986) show that in a two-player game each individually rational outcome (giving every player more than his/her minimax payoff) can be sustained in the long run provided the players are sufficiently patient (that is, have a discount factor close to one). Recently, Farrell (1983) and Bernheim and Ray (1985) independently came up with a new concept called renegotiation-proofness, which defines credibility in a more restrictive way, narrowing the set of stable solutions.[14] Additionally, the concept requires that a threat strategy, if actually conducted, must generate a continuation payoff to the punisher at least as high as when both players comply with the treaty.[15] Otherwise, if defection were to occur, the potential punisher would be tempted to propose to the defector to treat bygones as bygones, and to resume cooperation. But then the threat loses its credibility and hence its power to enforce cooperation in a non-cooperative game. This temptation prevails basically in all games where some form of communication is possible during the game (which does not imply that the game is a cooperative one in the sense of game theory).

Therefore, it seems to be sensible in our emission game to require that an IEA is only called to be stable if it is renegotiation-proof. In the following we assume the discount factor of both countries to be close to one, as is common practice in the theoretical and applied literature. Clearly, this assumption is somewhat restrictive when confronted with reality where politicians frequently strive for short-term success and therefore impatience must be expected. However, due to lack of space we make this simplifying assumption.[16]

To achieve our task efficiently we split the stability check into three parts. First, we determine the lower and upper bounds of individually rational payoff vectors in our emission game (Section 3.2). Second, we derive the conditions for renegotiation-proofness (Section 3.3). Third we check whether the equilibria we derived in Section 2 lie within the individually rational payoff space and fulfil the conditions of renegotiation-proofness (Section 3.4).

3.2 Determination of the Individually Rational Payoff Space

Interestingly, in the present emission game it is not so straightforward to compute the minimax payoffs, the lower bounds of the individually rational payoff space. In a game of duopolistic competition zero profits are the natural candidates for the minimax payoffs (see for example Driffill and Schultz, 1995). Obviously, in the duopoly game if one firm produces nothing it receives no profits, and cannot be made worse off than this. In our emission game, however, a country can theoretically emit any amount from zero to infinity, and therefore, could cause total costs in its neighbour country to approach infinity at the extreme. However, such an 'artificial inflation of emissions' does not seem to be very convincing in the light of the credibility of strategies. The country choosing such high emissions would also harm itself. Therefore, a 'natural' upper bound for emissions seems to be given by those equilibrium emission levels, $E_i^* = a/b$, which prevail if both countries do not reduce emissions at all, which is also the upper bound of strategy space we defined in Section 2.1.

To facilitate welfare comparisons, we define country i's welfare, v_i, to be the negative of this country's total cost, that is, $v_i = -TC_i$. Computing the minimax payoffs of both countries, which may formally be written as $\min(E_j)\max(E_i)$: $v_i(E_i, E_j)$, we get[17]

$$v_1^M = \begin{cases} \dfrac{-2\alpha a^2}{b(b+\alpha)} & \text{with } E_1 > 0, \text{ for } \alpha < b, \\ \dfrac{-(\alpha+b)a^2}{2b^2} & \text{with } E_1 = 0, \text{ for } \alpha \geq b; \end{cases}$$

$$v_2^M = \begin{cases} \dfrac{-2\Theta\alpha a^2}{b(2\Theta\alpha + b)} & \text{with } E_1 > 0, \text{ for } 2\Theta\alpha < b, \\ \dfrac{-(b+2\Theta\alpha)a^2}{4b^2} & \text{with } E_2 = 0, \text{ for } 2\Theta\alpha \geq b. \end{cases} \quad (12)$$

v_i^M denotes the minimax payoff, where the superscript M stands for minimax. From (11) it is evident that the relevant minimax payoff depends on the parameter assumptions. For country 1, however, we can ignore the second case ($E_1 = 0$) because the non-negativity conditions NNC_1 and/or NNC_2 rule out $\alpha > b$. For country 2 things are more complicated: neither NNC_1 nor NNC_2 guarantee in its 'weak version' $2\Theta\alpha < b$ to hold. This requires its 'strong version', $NNCS$ (see Section 2.1). In order not to contemplate too many parameter constellations, we assume $NNCS$ to hold, hence $2\Theta\alpha \leq b$. Thus, the first term in each bracket is taken to be the relevant minimax payoff.

With regard to the maximax payoffs, the upper bounds in our emission game, calculations are straightforward (see Appendix 2). This is done by maximizing each country's payoff in a Nash fashion, setting the other country's emissions at zero. We get:

$$v_1^U = \frac{-\alpha a^2}{2b(b+\alpha)}; \quad v_2^U = \frac{-\alpha\Theta a^2}{2b(b+2\Theta\alpha)}. \quad (13)$$

The superscript U stands here for *upper bound*.

3.3 Conditions for Renegotiation-proofness

In this section we formulate the conditions which characterize the renegotiation-proof payoff space for our model. We thereby apply the weakly renegotiation-proof equilibrium strategy concept of Farrell and Maskin (1989). Due to the assumption of a discount factor close to one, two conditions, I and II, are sufficient for this characterization.[18]

$$\text{I}: v_1^D = \max_{E_1^D} -\frac{\alpha}{2}\left(E_1^D + E_2^P\right)^2 - \frac{b}{2}\left(\frac{a}{b} - E_1^D\right)^2 < (\leq) v_1^k \text{ if } E_1^k \notin RF_1 \left(\text{if } E_1^k \in RF_1\right); \quad (14)$$

$$\text{II}: v_2^P = -\frac{\alpha\Theta}{2}\left(E_1^R + E_2^P\right)^2 - \frac{b}{4}\left(\frac{a}{b} - E_2^P\right)^2 \geq v_2^k, \quad (15)$$

where the superscript D stands for defection, R for repentance and P for punishment. The payoffs have to be interpreted as average payoffs of the infinite game. v_1^k (E_1^k, E_2^k) is the payoff when both countries comply with the treaty, and $k \in \{N, C, Q, T, P\}$, where the variables denote the regime as previously introduced. For the interpretation of Condition (I) consider a situation where country 2 complies with the agreement and country 1 does not. The opposite case will be considered below. (I) requires that country 2 is able to choose a 'punishment emission level', E_2^P, such that the welfare level of the defecting country 1, v_1^D, is lower than when both comply, v_1^k. The second condition, (II), requires that the punishment emission level, E_2^P, at the same time generates more welfare to country 2 than in the normal phase. Whether a strategy is available which fulfils both conditions simultaneously might be checked as follows. From (7) we know country 1's maximization behaviour and may insert this into (I) to get

$$v_1^D = \frac{-\alpha\left(a + bE_2^P\right)^2}{2b(b+\alpha)} \leq v_1^k. \tag{14'}$$

Since $\partial v_2^R / \partial E_1 < 0$, we set $E_1^R = 0$ in (15). Thus, we assume that country 1 accepts the harshest possible punishment. This extreme assumption allows us to determine the outer boundaries in the payoff space which can be backed by renegotiation-proof strategies. Then (15) becomes

$$v_2^P = \frac{-\alpha\Theta\left(E_2^P\right)^2}{2} - \frac{b}{4}\left(\frac{a}{b} - E_2^P\right)^2 \geq v_2^k. \tag{15'}$$

Solving (15') for E_2^P gives

$$E_2^P \in \left\{ \frac{a - \sqrt{\frac{-4v_2^k b^2 + 2\Theta\alpha a^2 + 8\Theta\alpha b v_2^k}{b}}}{b + 2\Theta\alpha}, \frac{a + \sqrt{\frac{-4v_2^k b^2 + 2\Theta\alpha a^2 + 8\Theta\alpha b v_2^k}{b}}}{b + 2\Theta\alpha} \right\}.$$

(15'')

First, note that the root is always positive if $v_2^k \leq v_2^U$, which obviously holds by the definition of the upper bounds of the individually rational payoff space (see Section 3.2). Second, note that because $\partial v_1^D / \partial E_2^P < 0$ according to (14'), we should choose E_2^P as big as possible. However, E_2^P is restricted, due to our definition of the emission space, to $E_2^P \in [0, a/b]$ (see Section 2.1). Whether the right-hand-side expression in (15") or a/b is bigger depends on the specific parameter values. Thus, we take E_2^P to be

$$E_2^P = \min\left\{\frac{a}{b}, \frac{a+\sqrt{\frac{-4v_2^k b^2 + 2\Theta\alpha a^2 + 8\Theta\alpha b v_2^k}{b}}}{b+2\Theta\alpha}\right\}. \quad (16)$$

Assume first that the second term in (16) is bigger than the first one and hence $E_2^P = a/b$. In order to check for renegotiation-proofness, we substitute $E_2^P = a/b$ into (14') to find the first condition for stability, denoted L_1:

$$L_1: v_1^k > (\geq) v_1^M. \quad (17)$$

Hence, all individually rational payoffs from country 1's view point can be sustained using $E_2^P = a/b$ as a punishment. ((15') is fulfilled in any case since for country 2 $E_2^P = a/b$ generates a higher payoff than applying the punishment level given by the right-hand-side expression in (16).)

Condition L_1 is equal to the condition for subgame-perfectness for a discount factor close to one.

Now consider the second possibility, namely that the second term in (16) is smaller than a/b. Again, we simply check for renegotiation-proofness by inserting the second expression in (16) into (14') for E_2^P. This leads to the second necessary condition, C_1, for a welfare tuple $v^{k*} = \{v_1^k, v_2^k\}$[19] to be a weakly renegotiation-proof equilibrium, abbreviated WRPE.

$$C_1: v_1^k > \left\{\frac{\alpha\left(2ab + 2a\Theta\alpha + b\sqrt{\frac{-4v_2^k b^2 + 2\Theta\alpha a^2 + 8\Theta\alpha b v_2^k}{b}}\right)^2}{-2(b+2\Theta\alpha)^2 b(b+\alpha)}\right\} \quad (18)$$

Obviously, it is not sufficient to show that country 2 can credibly punish country 1 in case this country defects. We also have to formulate the conditions in the opposite case. Since the computation is basically the same as outlined above, we only present the final result:

$$L_2: v_2^k > (\geq) v_2^M, \qquad (19)$$

$$C_2: v_2^k > \left\{ \frac{\alpha\Theta\left(2ab + a\alpha + b\sqrt{-\frac{2v_1^k b^2 + \alpha a^2 + 2\alpha b v_1^k}{b}}\right)^2}{-2(b+\alpha)^2 b(b+2\Theta\alpha)} \right\}. \qquad (20)$$

Only if (17), (18), (19) and (20) hold for an equilibrium payoff tuple v^{k*} resulting from negotiations between the two countries (in the case of the three policy regimes, e.g. quota, tax and permit) or any other optimization procedure (for example, Nash or fully cooperative solution) can this payoff be backed by renegotiation-proof strategies.

3.4 Check for Renegotiation-proofness

We are now prepared to check whether the payoff tuples, v^{k*}, generated by the emission equilibria derived in Section 2, are renegotiation-proof for a discount factor close to one.[20] If v^{k*} is renegotiation-proof it must, first, be an element of the individually rational payoff space (condition L_1 and L_2) and, second, fulfil C_1 and C_2 derived above. Using condition NNCS, one can show that all three policy regime equilibria (for the Nash regime this follows by definition) fulfil these four conditions regardless of the parameter values, and are therefore renegotiation-proof. Since we assume a discount factor close to one, this implies that all three bargaining equilibria are also subgame-perfect.[21] For the fully cooperative solution we find that the conditions might not hold for $\Theta < -1/2 + 1/2\sqrt{5} \approx 0.618$ and $\Theta > 2 + 2\sqrt{2} \approx 4.828$. These results have an immediate interpretation.

In the three bargaining regimes negotiations are conducted in a cooperative spirit, but with the restriction of settling on the smallest common denominator. Therefore, within these three regimes a 'natural limit' is included, ensuring that no country receives an extremely low payoff. For the fully cooperative solution, however, the conditions mentioned above do not hold for 'extreme' values of Θ, either very high or very low. Extreme values of Θ imply relatively large differences in environmental preferences in the two countries. For example, high values of Θ indicate that country 2 suffers substantially more from emissions than country 1. Country 2 therefore prefers rather low emission levels. The opposite holds for country 1 in such circumstances. It prefers relatively high emission levels. The cooperative solution, however, requires that country 1 chooses a rather low emission level. Thus, even though such a low emission level would be advisable from a global point of view, it allocates the reduction burdens too asymmetrically so that country 1's incentive to defect cannot be overcome even in a dynamic setting. By the same token, low values of Θ ($\Theta <$ 0.618) require country 2 to carry an abatement burden which produces such a low payoff that free-riding becomes attractive.

Admittedly, stability could be jeopardized in the three bargaining regimes if we were to allow the discount factor to take on low values; however, this issue is treated elsewhere (see Finus and Rundshagen, 1998a and 1998b).

4. EVALUATING THE POLICY INSTRUMENTS

Since we have now considered all three stages of the emission game, we are now in a position to evaluate the three policy instruments. In particular, we focus on two issues in this section.

First, we want to find out which of the three bargaining regimes produces the lowest emissions worldwide. This is important from an ecological perspective. Second, we shall look at the welfare-economic implications of the bargaining regimes. Here we are interested in a comparison regarding the worldwide welfare generated under the three bargaining regimes. In the light of possibly high opportunity costs of abatement from the reduction of global pollutants (greenhouse gases) (Nordhaus, 1993; Kverndokk, 1993), it seems to be important to have information on this point.

Let us start by discussing the 'ecological part' of the problem. To facilitate a comparison of the five regimes in terms of aggregate emissions, the results are summarized in Table 7A.4 in Appendix 1 and graphically illustrated in Figure 7.1.

From Figure 7.1 it is apparent that aggregate emissions in the Nash equilibrium of the stage game are always the highest, and those of the fully cooperative solution the lowest of the five regimes. Emission levels of the three bargaining regimes, quota, tax and permits, lie between the fully and non-cooperative solution. This conforms to intuition: on the one hand, negotiations under the three bargaining regimes are conducted in a 'cooperative spirit' – both countries jointly want to improve the environmental situation. On the other hand, *institutional constraints* in the three bargaining regimes cause higher emission levels than required from a global perspective. In particular, we considered two political constraints, paying tribute to conditions frequently encountered in real politics: (1) uniform solutions; and (2) agreement on the smallest common denominator. In contrast, a socially optimal solution maximizes joint welfare without any restrictions at all. The first restriction causes an efficiency loss only in the

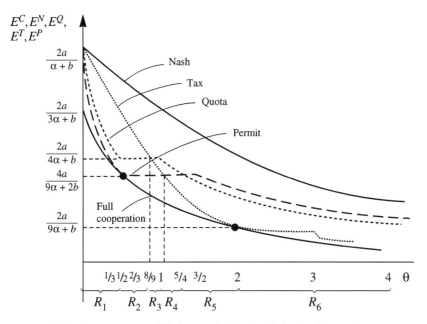

Figure 7.1   Aggregate equilibrium emission levels in the five regimes

quota regime because it means that marginal abatement costs in the two countries are *never* equalized (Welsch, 1995).

The second institutional restriction, however, is binding in all three bargaining regimes and causes a divergence of emission levels compared to what would be required in the social optimum.

Thus, observing Figure 7.1, we are not surprised to find that under the quota regime emission levels are *always* higher than under the fully cooperative regime. However, from Figure 7.1 we also see that for specific values of Θ the tax regime ($\Theta = 2$) and the permit regime ($\Theta = 1/2$) produce the same low emissions as the fully cooperative solution. This is so because for these specific values of Θ restriction number 2 is not binding. In other words, the suggestions of both groups of delegates make a perfect match. Thus, under those conditions the restriction to agree on the smallest common denominator does not cause an efficiency loss.

Comparing the three bargaining regimes among each other it is evident from Figure 7.1 that for $0 \leq \Theta < 1$, which corresponds to the ranges denoted with R_1, R_2 and R_3, the permit regime produces the lowest aggregate emissions. For $1 \leq \Theta$, including the ranges denoted R_4, R_5 and R_6, the tax regime does this. It is interesting that in the ranges R_1 and R_2 ($0 \leq \Theta < 8/9$) the quota regime produces lower emissions than the tax regime; in the ranges R_5 and R_6 ($5/4 < \Theta$) the quota regime is ecologically superior to the permit regime. To understand the result it is helpful to compare the policy regimes pairwise.

For a comparison between the quota and the tax regime recall that the former is of the 'buy one – get one free', the latter of the 'buy one – get two free' type from country 1's perspective. By symmetry, from country 2's perspective the tax is a 'buy two – get one free' arrangement. Further, note that in the range R_1 country 2 is the bottleneck in both regimes, whereas in the range R_6 this is country 1. Thus, since in R_1 the quota regime provides more favourable terms for country 2, it agrees on a higher aggregate emission reduction target (lower aggregate emissions) than under a tax regime. The mirror image of this argument holds in R_6, which explains lower aggregate emissions in this range. In the ranges R_2, R_3, R_4 and R_5 country 1 is the bottleneck under the quota regime and country 2 under the tax regime. Thus, several effects work in opposite directions and one has to rely on an algebraic comparison.

Comparing the tax with the permit regime we have to be aware that in R_1 country 2 is the bottleneck under both regimes, and in R_6 this is country 1. Due to $\omega < 1$, country 2 reduces more emissions than country 1. However, under the permit regime this country gets 'compensated' to some extent by selling permits to country 1. Thus, if country 2 determines the terms of the agreement in R_1, it is obvious that it proposes a higher abatement target under the permit regime than under the tax regime. By the same token, country 1 prefers the tax regime, because for a given amount of emission reduction it receives an 'abatement contribution' from country 2 for free, whereas under the permit regime it must pay for this to some extent.

Again, in the three mid-regions, R_2, R_3, R_4 and R_5, several effects are at work and one has to rely on calculations.

Finally, for a comparison between the permit and the quota regime, we may recall that the ranges where a country is the bottleneck are identical in both regimes. Thus, in R_1 country 2 is the bottleneck; in the other ranges this is country 1. Since each country can voluntarily decide whether to purchase or sell permits, each country must benefit from such a transaction. Hence, one would at first expect that under a permit regime a country is more likely to agree to lower aggregate emissions than under a quota regime. This is indeed the case under both regimes for $1/3 \leq \Theta \leq 1$, where no adjustment by any country after the treaty has been signed takes place. However, there are two more aspects to the problem. First, we could show in the previous section that an adjustment must be expected by country i if the terms of the agreement determined by country j (the bottleneck country) differ too much from country i's proposal ($D_i < 0$). Second, we assumed a game of incomplete information (see the Introduction and note 10). In particular, we assumed that a country has no information on environmental preferences in the neighbour country. Thus, country i, when putting forward its proposal, does not anticipate possible adjustment reactions by country j. However, it is this very adjustment reaction which generates the result that in the ranges R_5 and R_6 the quota regime is ecologically superior to the permit regime. For example, for $1 \leq \Theta \leq 3/2$ country 1 is the bottleneck and country 2 adjusts under the quota regime, but not under the permit regime. The reason is that due to $\omega < 1$ country 2 sells permits to country 1, and therefore in equilibrium its marginal abatement costs are higher under the permit than under the quota regime. Since, however, the incentive to adjust for country 2 is defined as $D_2 = MAC_2 - MDC_2$ (with $D_2 < 0$ indicating adjustment), country 2 already adjusts under a quota regime for smaller values of Θ than under the permit regime. Taken together, this implies that for $1 \leq \Theta \leq 5/4$ the 'adjustment effect' is smaller than the effect of a more ambitious abatement target proposal under the permit regime compared to the quota regime. For $5/4 \leq \Theta \leq 3/2$, however, the former effect is stronger than the latter, which causes aggregate emissions under the quota regime to be lower than under the permit regime. The latter relation holds also for values of Θ above $3/2$, where adjustment takes place in both regimes. This is confirmed by computing $|D_2^Q| - |D_2^P|$ with $D_2^Q = MAC_2(E_2^{Q(1)}) - MDC_2(E^{Q(1)})$ and $D_2^P = MAC_2(E_2^{P(1)}) - MDC_2(E^{P(1)})$ (for the notation see the Appendix), which reveals that this difference is always positive (and in fact increases with increasing Θ) in the ranges R_2 to R_6. This implies that the incentive to adjust under the quota regime is always higher for country 2 (the non-bottleneck country) than under the permit regime. In contrast, computing $|D_1^Q| - |D_1^P|$ in the range R_1, where country 1 adjusts for low values of Θ, reveals that the incentive to adjust is higher under the permit than under quota regime. Thus, the 'adjustment effect' and the 'abatement target effect' work in the same direction, leading to lower aggregate emissions under the permit than under the quota regime. Overall, the result stresses the role of information. Again, we have the interesting result that incomplete information might have a positive effect on the outcome of a game (see note 10).

We now turn to the welfare-economic implications of the emission reduction game. The comparison between the five regimes is depicted in Figure 7.2.

Again, the results are clear-cut regarding the regions of the parameter Θ. Basically, we find the same ranking as we did for aggregate emissions. Only

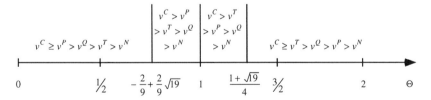

* The notation of superscripts is as explained in the text.

Figure 7.2 Comparative analysis of aggregate welfare*

the 'turning-points', where a regime is superior to another, have somewhat moved. For example, whereas for the quota and the tax regime the turning-point was 8/9 for aggregate emissions (for $\Theta < 8/9$, $E^Q < E^T$ and for $\Theta > 8/9$, $E^Q > E^T$) it is now $-2/9 + (2/9)\sqrt{19} \approx 0.746$ (for $\Theta < 0.746$, $V^Q > V^T$ and for $\Theta > 0.746$, $V^Q < V^T$). The turning-point of the tax and permit regime has moved from 5/4 for emissions somewhat right on the Θ-scale to $(1 + \sqrt{19})/4 \approx 1.339$. The turning-point of the tax and permit regime, however, has not changed. Thus, we may conjecture that the level of aggregate emissions has a great influence on aggregate welfare. For most values of Θ it holds that the closer a bargaining regime comes to the fully cooperative solution regarding aggregate emissions, the closer it comes to the social optimum in welfare terms. Therefore, it does not come as a surprise that for $\Theta = 1/2$ the permit regime produces the same welfare as the fully cooperative solution; for $\Theta = 2$ this occurs with the tax regime. However, for some values of Θ a comparison of emission levels and welfare levels produces different results (for example $a = 10$, $b = 10$, $\alpha = 1$ and $\Theta = 3/4$). The results suggest two important policy implications.

First, there is no bargaining regime which is superior to all others, neither according to the ecological criterion nor to the economic criterion. In fact, there is a range where the efficient[22] policy instrument of an emission tax is inferior to an emission reduction quota ($\Theta < 8/9$ regarding emissions and $\Theta < 0.746$ regarding welfare), a command and control instrument (see also Endres, 1997). The same phenomenon is found for the relationship between the efficient policy instrument transferable permits and the quota regime. Here, the quota is superior for high values of Θ ($\Theta > 5/4$ regarding emissions and $\Theta > 1.339$ regarding welfare). Thus, the results derived from our model challenge the 'fundamental folk theorem of environmental economics' claiming the general superiority of taxes and transferable permits over command and control instruments.

The second result conforms more to environmental economic intuition. Regardless of the value of Θ, the less efficient policy instrument, the quota, is never superior to both market-oriented instruments at the same time. Put differently, the quota regime never ranks first among the three bargaining regimes (second with respect to all five regimes). Thus, the general preference of environmental economists for market-based instruments for tackling environmental problems is not challenged. However, and this seems to be important, a policy recommendation must pay tribute to real-world conditions. In particular, there exist conditions where a tax is more advisable ($\Theta > 1.339$ from a welfare-economic perspective and $\Theta > 5/4$ from an ecological perspective) and conditions where a permit regime should be recommended by welfare economists ($\Theta < 1.339$) and ecologists ($\Theta < 5/4$) respectively. Obviously, a general recommendation to use any of the two market-based instruments instead of the emission quota is not sufficient, and in fact may be misleading. It may cause welfare losses (for example recommending the tax regime for $\Theta < 0.746$).

Admittedly, the results are stylized facts deduced from our specific model. Nevertheless, the message is clear: in a world where institutional restrictions exist, and hence, where we face a 'politically distorted medium' within which environmental policy is to be conducted, policy recommendations become more difficult and have to be based on a detailed analysis of the conditions associated with the problem.[23]

5. SUMMARY AND CONCLUSIONS

Two countries, different with respect to abatement costs and environmental preferences, negotiating emission reductions were considered. Negotiations were assumed to be on an emission reduction quota, an emission tax and transferable discharge permits, alternatively. With reference to phenomena frequently encountered in international politics, we assumed for the three bargaining regimes that both countries would settle for the smallest common denominator in negotiations and prefer 'uniform solutions', often associated in common parlance with the notion of a 'just' agreement.

In the first stage of a three-stage game, bargaining equilibria were determined. In the second stage, individual adjustment behaviour to overfulfil the terms of a treaty under specific circumstances was analysed. In the third stage, stability was checked according to the concept of renegotiation-proofness. To have benchmarks for a later comparison, we also derived equilibrium emissions for a globally optimal solution and the Nash equilibrium of the stage game. Applying the concept of renegotiation-proof equilibrium strategies, we could show that, except for the globally optimal solution, all equilibrium emission levels considered in the chapter could be backed by credible punishment strategies in a dynamic supergame, provided the discount factor is close to one.

A final comparison between all regimes revealed that in a second-best world with political restrictions the fundamental 'folk theorem' of environmental economics, which maintains that taxes and permits are superior to command and control instruments, e.g., emission quotas, has to be qualified.

One of the caveats which have to be mentioned when interpreting our model is that it is rather specific regarding the functions representing the interests of the two countries. However, the main results derived here do not vanish in a more general setting, as we show in Endres and Finus (1996b). Another extension of our model could be to expand the bargaining process to N countries. Whereas the determination of bargaining equilibria poses no problem, stability tests in the spirit of renegotiation-proofness become quite difficult. For example, coalition-proof equilibrium strategies must be analysed (see for example, Bernheim, Peleg and Whinston, 1987, Bernheim and Whinston, 1987, Moreno and Wooders, 1993). Because this inflates mathematical complexity substantially and therefore demands space, this issue has been left to another paper (see Finus and Rundshagen, 1998a).[24]

Another extension of our model could be to allow for discount factors smaller than one in order to capture more (impatient) real-world situations. Again, such an extension increases the complexity of the analysis and has therefore been treated elsewhere (see Finus and Rundshagen, 1998a).

Moreover, the choice of the policy instrument could be made an endogenous part of the emission game. Thus, both countries would not only have to agree on the allocation of emission reduction burdens in a given regime, but also the choice of the regime itself must be agreed upon (see comments in note 22).

Last, but not least, the strategy space could be extended to include other actions besides the choice of emission levels (see comments in Section 3.1).

NOTES

1. For example, the Montreal Protocol specifies a 20 per cent reduction of CFCs from 1989 levels by 1998 or the Helsinki Protocol, which suggests a 30 per cent reduction of long-range transboundary air pollutants from 1980 levels by 1993.
2. The prominence of uniform solutions in international politics is not readily explained. Barrett (1992) and Hoel (1992) suggest that they constitute some kind of focal point that countries find relatively easy to accept. Moreover, some notion of 'justice' is often believed to be associated with this kind of solution (see for example, Welsch, 1992, 1995). In addition, the transaction costs of negotiating uniform schemes may be lower than for differentiated ones.
3. Examples of those agreements which have no provision for transfers include the 'Convention Relative to The Preservation of Fauna and Flora in Their Natural State' (1933), 'International Convention for the Regulation of Whaling' (1946) and the 'Convention of the High Seas' (1958). Other agreements mention technical assistance for developing countries like the 'Convention of the Law of the Sea'. Most agreements are very unspecific regarding transfer obligations. They either contain only general statements or suggest voluntary contributions by their member states. Typical examples are the 'International Tropical Timber Agreement' (1983), the 'Basel Convention on the Control of Transboundary Movements of Hazardous Wastes and Their Disposal' (1989). In contrast, the number of agreements which have a provision for transfer and which have actually been conducted is rather small. An example is the financial fund within the Montreal Protocol.
4. We make this assumption (even though it does not possess axiomatic properties, as does the Nash bargaining solution or the Shapley value) because it seems to be a typical feature of most international negotiations. It particularly occurs if there is no long tradition of mutual cooperation on the particular issue under consideration. From a non-cooperative game-theory point of view the assumption reflects the voluntary character of agreements. Moreover, in an emission game with incomplete information (which we assume), the smallest common denominator decision rule has the interesting property that there is no incentive for a country to put forward a 'strategically manipulated' proposal. In Endres and Finus (1996b) it is shown that 'truth telling' is a dominant strategy.
5. For the sake of simplicity and to make fast progress in the analysis, differences in the two countries are modelled in a somewhat restrictive way. Nevertheless, this will be sufficient to point to the existence of certain problems associated with global environmental negotiations. These problems do not vanish in a more general setting (see Endres and Finus, 1996b and Finus and Rundshagen, 1998a for a more general approach).

Renegotiation-proof equilibria 155

6. Of course, one can think of other starting-points, for example, the Nash equilibrium. See, for instance, Mäler (1989).
7. If we were not to assume *NNCS* to hold, we would have to deal with some 'very small' undetermined ranges of the damage parameter Θ in Sections 3 and 4, below.
8. The derivation of (6) is given in Appendix 2. Note that to derive the proposals we only require that each country knows its own total cost function. It is in fact not necessary that a country knows its neighbour's abatement cost function. This will, however, be necessary in the tax and permit scheme discussed below.
9. That is, the country which prevents more ambitious joint abatement targets can be contracted for.
10. For an interpretation of this result see Endres and Finus (1996a).
11. Of course, country j might be tempted to adjust to country i's additional emission reduction by expanding its own emissions. However, by this activity country j would violate the agreement. The analysis of such a possible breach of contract is deferred until section 3, below. Moreover, note that due to our assumption of a game of incomplete information a country cannot anticipate its neighbour country's possible adjustment. In a game of complete information this could be possible, and would give rise to strategically manipulated proposals. Thus, lack of information might be seen to have a positive effect on the bargaining outcome. (In fact, one can show in the case of the quota regime that with 'strategically manipulated' proposals the bargaining outcome would imply higher aggregate emissions.)
12. The derivation is given in Appendix 2.
13. Under the quota regime a breach of contract would have to be expected by country 1 for $1 < \Theta$, by country 2 for $0 \leq \Theta < 1/4$, and by both countries for $1/4 < \Theta < 1$. In the tax regime a breach must be reckoned with by country 1 for $3 < \Theta$, by country 2 for $0 \leq \Theta < 2/3$, and by both countries for $2/3 < \Theta < 3$. In the permit regime this would most likely occur by country 1 for $3/2 < \Theta$, by country 2 for $0 \leq \Theta < 1/3$, and by both countries for $1/3 < \Theta < 3/2$.
14. For an extensive exposition of the concept see for example, Farrell and Maskin (1989) and Van Damme (1989). In the context of international environmental problems see Barrett (1994), Endres and Finus (1996a) and Finus and Rundshagen (1998a).
15. By continuation payoff of a punishment strategy we mean the discounted payoff at the time the punishment is conducted until perpetuity. It comprises the payoff during the punishment and the payoff when both countries return to the cooperative stage of the game after some time. The continuation payoff of cooperation (compliance) is the discounted payoff of infinite cooperation. See Finus and Rundshagen (1989) for details.
16. For a treatment of more impatient players see Finus and Rundshagen (1998a, 1998b). From their analysis it turns out that, most generally, (a) with impatient players stability requirements under the various policy regimes are different (in fact, in most cases they are lower under the quota regime than under the tax regime), and (b) stability requirements increase with the number of countries suffering from a global externality.
17. The details are given in Appendix 2.
18. For an extensive treatment on the number and type of conditions necessary to determine the renegotiation-proof payoff space in the context of a global emission game under various assumptions, see Finus and Rundshagen (1998a).
19. The asterisk denotes the welfare tuple. In contrast, v^k, which we shall use later, stands for aggregate welfare, where $v^k = v_1^k + v_2^k$.
20. We do not display the results regarding welfare levels as we do for emissions in Appendix 1, Tables 7A.1 to 7A.3. This is for two reasons. First, comparing the five regimes (that is, the three policy regimes, the Nash equilibrium and the social optimum) regarding welfare levels does not reveal results much different from a comparison of aggregate emissions, as conducted below in Section 4. Second, calculating total costs for the various regimes and parameter constellations of Θ produces huge terms which have no immediate interpretation. However, the interested reader may receive detailed calculations upon request from the authors.
21. This implies that for the particular bargaining equilibria we consider in this chapter renegotiation-proofness does not single out equilibria as unstable which are subgame-perfect. Generally, however, one can show that (a) renegotiation-proofness restricts the payoff space compared to subgame-perfectness (see Finus and Rundshagen, 1998a) and (b) other bargaining

equilibria might fail the renegotiation-proofness test but pass the test for subgame-perfectness (see Finus and Rundshagen, 1998a).
22. By 'efficient' we mean that *any* abatement target specified in a treaty is obtained at minimal aggregate cost (marginal abatement costs are equalized in any bargaining equilibria). A uniform tax or a uniform allocation of permits is always efficient if emissions are of the *pure* public-bad type, as has been assumed in the chapter. Note that in the case of transboundary fluxes (for example, SO_2) the efficiency condition could be violated by both instruments in their uniform specifications.
23. In the analysis we have treated the policy regime as exogenously given. One could imagine that the choice of the policy regime itself is an issue in the negotiations. Since we have treated this issue elsewhere, we refer to Endres (1997) and Finus and Rundshagen (1998a) in the case of two countries and to Finus and Rundshagen (1998b) in the case of N countries. In the two-country case a comparison of individual welfare is not so clear-cut as for aggregate welfare. As a tendency it turns out (for the specific setting) that for most parameter values the interests of the two countries regarding the most preferred policy regime are quite different. Thus, one should expect that an agreement with respect to this issue will be extremely difficult. In an N-country world, with the choice between a tax and a quota regime, Finus and Rundshagen (1997) show that in most cases the quota regime will emerge from the bargaining process when a coalition among some countries is formed.
24. For an alternative stability concept of coalitions see Tulkens, Chapter 2 in this volume.

REFERENCES

Barrett, S. (1992), 'International Environmental Agreements as Games', in R. Pethig (ed.), *Conflicts and Cooperation in Managing Environmental Resources. Microeconomics Studies*, Berlin: Springer-Verlag, chap. 1, pp. 11–37.

Barrett, S. (1994), 'Self-Enforcing International Environmental Agreements', *Oxford Economic Papers*, **46**, 878–94. 'The Strategy of Trade Sanctions in International Environmental Agreements', *Resource and Energy Economics*, **19**, 345–61.

Barrett, S. (1997), 'Strategic Multilateral Environmental Policy and Trade in Segmented Markets', mimeo, London Business School.

Bernheim, D., B. Peleg and M.D. Whinston (1987), 'Coalition-Proof Nash Equilibria. I. Concepts', *Journal of Economic Theory*, **42**, 1–12.

Bernheim, D. and D. Ray (1985), 'Pareto-Perfect Nash Equilibria', mimeo, Stanford University.

Bernheim, D. and M.D. Whinston (1987), 'Coalition-Proof Nash Equilibria. II. Applications', *Journal of Economic Theory*, **42**, 13–29.

Carraro, C. and D. Siniscalco (1995), 'R&D Cooperation and the Stability of International Environmental Agreements', in C. Carraro (ed.), *International Environmental Negotiations: Strategic Policy Issues*, Cheltenham: Edward Elgar, pp. 71–96.

Driffill, J. and C. Schultz (1995), 'Renegotiation in a Repeated Cournot Duopoly', *Economic Letters*, **47**, 143–8.

Endres, A. (1996), 'Designing a Greenhouse Treaty: Some Economic Problems', in E. Eide and R. van den Bergh (eds), *Law and Economics of the Environment*, Oslo: Juridisk Førlag, pp. 201–24.

Endres, A. (1997), 'Negotiating a Climate Convention – The Role of Prices and Quantities', forthcoming in *International Journal of Law and Economics*, **17**, 147–56.

Endres, A. and M. Finus (1996a), 'A Convention on Greenhouse Gases – The Impact of Instrumental Choice on the Success of Negotiations', Discussion Paper no. 224, University of Hagen.

Endres, A. and M. Finus (1996b), 'International Environmental Agreements: How the Policy Instrument Affects Equilibrium Emissions and Welfare', Discussion Paper no. 231 (revised version), University of Hagen.

Farrell, J. (1983), 'Credible Repeated Game Equilibrium', unpublished manuscript.

Farrell, J. and E. Maskin (1989), 'Renegotiation in Repeated Games', *Games and Economic Behavior*, **1**, 327–60.

Finus, M. and B. Rundshagen (1998a), 'Renegotiation-Proof Equilibria in a Global Emission Game When Players Are Impatient', forthcoming in *Environmental and Resource Economics*.

Finus, M. and B. Rundshagen (1998b), 'Toward a Positive Theory of Coalition Formation and Endogenous Instrumental Choice in Global Pollution Control', forthcoming in *Public Choice*.

Fudenberg, D. and E. Maskin (1986), 'The Folk Theorem in Repeated Games with Discounting or with Incomplete Information', *Econometrica*, **54**, 533–54.

Hoel, M. (1992), 'International Environment Conventions: The Case of Uniform Reductions of Emissions', *Environmental and Resource Economics*, **2**, 141–59.

Kverndokk, S. (1993), 'Global CO_2 Agreements: A Cost-Effective Approach', *Energy Journal*, **14**, 91–112.

Mäler, K.-G. (1989), 'The Acid Rain Game', in H. Folmer and E. van Ierland (eds), *Valuation Methods and Policy Making in Environmental Economics*, Amsterdam: Elsevier, chap. 12, pp. 231–52.

Moreno, D. and J. Wooders (1993), 'Coalition-Proof Equilibrium', Discussion Paper 93-7, Department of Economics, University of Arizona, Tucson, Arizona.

Nordhaus, W.D. (1993), 'Rolling the "DICE": An Optimal Transition Path for Controlling Greenhouse Gases', *Resource and Energy Economics*, **15**, 27–50.

Selten, R. (1965), 'Spieltheoretische Behandlung eines Oligopolmodells mit Nachfrageträgheit', *Zeitschrift für die gesamte Staatswissenschaften*, **12**, 301–24.

Van Damme, E. (1989), 'Renegotiation-Proof Equilibria in Repeated Prisoners' Dilemma', *Journal of Economic Theory*, **47**, 206–17.

Welsch, H. (1992), 'Inequality Aspects of Alternative CO_2 Agreement Designs', *OPEC Review*, **16**, 23–36.

Welsch, H. (1995), 'Incentives for Forty-Five Countries to Join Various Forms of Carbon Reduction Agreements', *Resource and Energy Economics*, **17**, 213–37.

APPENDIX 1: TABLES

Table 7A.1 Emission levels under the quota regime*

Emission levels\Range of Θ	$0 < \Theta \leq 1/4$	$1/4 \leq \Theta \leq 1/2$	$1/2 \leq \Theta \leq 1$	$1 \leq \Theta$
E_1^Q	$E_{1a}^{Q(2)} = \dfrac{a(b+8\Theta\alpha-\alpha)}{(b+8\Theta\alpha)(\alpha+b)}$	$E_1^{Q(2)} = \dfrac{a}{b+8\Theta\alpha}$	$E_1^{Q(1)} = \dfrac{a}{b+4\alpha}$	$E_1^{Q(1)} = \dfrac{a}{b+4\alpha}$
E_2^Q	$E_2^{Q(2)} = \dfrac{a}{b+8\Theta\alpha}$	$E_2^{Q(2)} = \dfrac{a}{b+8\Theta\alpha}$	$E_2^{Q(1)} = \dfrac{a}{b+4\alpha}$	$E_{2a}^{Q(1)} = \dfrac{a(b+4\alpha-2\Theta\alpha)}{(b+4\alpha)(b+2\Theta\alpha)}$
E^Q	$E_a^{Q(2)} = \dfrac{2a(b+4\Theta\alpha)}{(b+8\Theta\alpha)(\alpha+b)}$	$E^{Q(2)} = \dfrac{2a}{b+8\Theta\alpha}$	$E^{Q(1)} = \dfrac{2a}{b+4\alpha}$	$E_a^{Q(1)} = \dfrac{2a(b+2\alpha)}{(b+4\alpha)(b+2\Theta\alpha)}$

* Non-negativity is guaranteed by condition NNC_1 and NNC_2 derived in the text. The subscripts 1 and 2 refer to the country; a denotes that the emission level is individually adjusted after the agreement by the non-bottleneck country. The superscripts Q, T and P stand for quota, tax and permit regime. The superscript in brackets indicates which country's suggestion is put into practice, that is, which country is the bottleneck.

Table 7A.2 Emission levels under the tax regime*

Emission levels\Range of Θ	$0 < \Theta \leq 2/3$	$2/3 \leq \Theta \leq 2$	$2 \leq \Theta \leq 3$	$3 \leq \Theta$
E_1^T	$E_{1a}^{T(2)} = \dfrac{a(9\Theta\alpha b + 2b^2 - 2b\alpha + 3\Theta\alpha^2)}{b(9\Theta\alpha + 2b)(\alpha + b)}$	$E_1^{T(2)} = \dfrac{a(2b + 3\Theta\alpha)}{b(9\Theta\alpha + 2b)}$	$E_1^{T(1)} = \dfrac{a(b + 3\alpha)}{b(9\alpha + b)}$	$E_1^{T(1)} = \dfrac{a(b + 3\alpha)}{b(9\alpha + b)}$
E_2^T	$E_2^{T(2)} = \dfrac{a(2b - 3\Theta\alpha)}{b(9\Theta\alpha + 2b)}$	$E_2^{T(2)} = \dfrac{a(2b - 3\Theta\alpha)}{b(9\Theta\alpha + 2b)}$	$E_2^{T(1)} = \dfrac{a(b - 3\alpha)}{b(9\alpha + b)}$	$E_{2a}^{T(1)} = \dfrac{a(9\alpha b + b^2 - 2\Theta\alpha b - 6\Theta\alpha^2)}{b(9\alpha + b)(b + 2\Theta\alpha)}$
E^T	$E_a^{T(2)} = \dfrac{2a(2b + 3\Theta\alpha)}{(9\Theta\alpha + 2b)(\alpha + b)}$	$E^{T(2)} = \dfrac{4a}{(9\Theta\alpha + 2b)}$	$E^{T(1)} = \dfrac{2a}{(9\alpha + b)}$	$E_a^{T(1)} = \dfrac{2a(b + 6\alpha)}{(9\alpha + b)(b + 2\Theta\alpha)}$

* See Table 7A.1.

Table 7A.3 Emission levels under the permit regime*

Emission levels\Range of Θ	$0 < \Theta \leq 1/3$	$1/3 \leq \Theta \leq 1/2$	$1/2 \leq \Theta \leq 3/2$	$3/2 \leq \Theta$
E_1^P	$E_{1a}^{P(2)} = \dfrac{a(9b\Theta\alpha + b^2 - \alpha b + 3\Theta\alpha^2)}{b(9\Theta\alpha + b)(\alpha + b)}$	$E_1^{P(2)} = \dfrac{a(b + 3\Theta\alpha)}{b(9\Theta\alpha + 2b)}$	$E_1^{P(1)} = \dfrac{a(2b + 3\alpha)}{b(9\alpha + 2b)}$	$E_1^{P(1)} = \dfrac{a(2b + 3\alpha)}{b(9\alpha + 2b)}$
E_2^P	$E_2^{P(2)} = \dfrac{a(b - 3\Theta\alpha)}{b(9\Theta\alpha + b)}$	$E_2^{P(2)} = \dfrac{a(b - 3\Theta\alpha)}{b(9\Theta\alpha + b)}$	$E_2^{P(1)} = \dfrac{a(2b - 3\alpha)}{b(9\alpha + 2b)}$	$E_{2a}^{P(1)} = \dfrac{a(9\alpha b + 2b^2 - 4b\Theta\alpha - 6\Theta\alpha^2)}{b(9\alpha + 2b)(2\Theta\alpha + b)}$
E^P	$E_a^{P(2)} = \dfrac{2a(b + 3\Theta\alpha)}{(9\Theta\alpha + b)(\alpha + b)}$	$E^{P(2)} = \dfrac{2a}{(9\Theta\alpha + b)}$	$E^{P(1)} = \dfrac{4a}{(9\alpha + 2b)}$	$E_a^{P(1)} = \dfrac{4a(3\alpha + b)}{(9\alpha + 2b)(2\Theta\alpha + b)}$

* See Table 7A.1.

Table 7A.4 *Comparative static analysis of aggregate emission levels with respect to the damage parameter**

Range	Ranking
$0 \leq \Theta \leq 1/4$	$E^C < E^P < E^Q < E^T < E^N$
$1/4 \leq \Theta \leq 1/3$	$E^C < E^P < E^Q < E^T < E^N$
$1/3 \leq \Theta \leq 1/2$	$E^C \leq E^P < E^Q < E^T < E^N$; with $E^C = E^P$ for $\Theta = 1/2$
$1/2 \leq \Theta \leq 2/3$	$E^C < E^P \leq E^Q < E^T < E^N$; with $E^C = E^P$ for $\Theta = 1/2$
$2/3 \leq \Theta \leq 8/9$	$E^C < E^P < E^Q \leq E^T < E^N$; with $E^Q = E^T$ for $\Theta = 8/9$
$8/9 \leq \Theta \leq 1$	$E^C < E^P \leq E^T \leq E^Q < E^N$; with $E^Q = E^T$ for $\Theta = 8/9$ and $E^P = E^T$ for $\Theta = 1$
$1 \leq \Theta \leq 3/2$	$E^C < E^T \leq E^P \gtreqless E^Q < E^N$; with $E^P = E^T$ for $\Theta = 1$, $E^P < E^Q$ for $1 \leq \Theta < 5/4$ and $E^P > E^Q$ for $5/4 \leq \Theta \leq 3/2$
$3/2 \leq \Theta \leq 2$	$E^C \leq E^T < E^Q < E^P < E^N$; with $E^C = E^T$ for $\Theta = 2$
$2 \leq \Theta \leq 3$	$E^C \leq E^T < E^Q < E^P < E^N$; with $E^C = E^T$ for $\Theta = 2$
$3 \leq \Theta$	$E^C < E^T < E^Q < E^P < E^N$

* The notations of superscripts are as given in the text. The results have been established invoking NNC_1, NNC_2 and $NNCS$.

APPENDIX 2 ELABORATIONS

The Quota Scheme

An equal percentage emission reduction in each country from $E_1^* = E_2^* = a/b$ implies that after reductions have been conducted $E_1 = E_2 = E_i^{Q(i)}$ holds (the superscript Q stands for quota scheme and the superscript in brackets denotes the country which puts forward the proposal). To derive a country's proposal, we insert this information in (1) and (2) to give

$$TC_1 = \frac{\alpha}{2}\left(2E_i^{Q(1)}\right)^2 + \frac{b}{2}\left(\frac{a}{b} - E_i^{Q(1)}\right)^2, \quad (A1)$$

$$TC_2 = \Theta\frac{\alpha}{2}\left(E_i^{Q(2)}\right)^2 + \frac{b}{4}\left(\frac{a}{b} - E_i^{Q(2)}\right)^2. \quad (A2)$$

Differentiating (A1) and (A2) with respect to $E_i^{Q(1)}$ or $E_i^{Q(2)}$ respectively, and solving for this variable, gives (6) in the text. Whenever $D_i < 0$ we have to compute adjusted emission rates using (7).

The Tax Scheme

An equal tax rate, t, applied in both countries, leads to $MAC_i = t$ in equilibrium – each country reduces emission until marginal abatement costs in both countries are equal. With respect to (3) (or (1) and (2)) we have $t = a - bE_1^T = (a - bE_1^T)/2$ or, alternatively, $E_1^T = a - t/b$ and $E_2^T = a - t/(2b)$ (the superscript T stands for tax regime). Substituting this information into (1) and (2) ($E_1 = E_1^T$, $E_2 = E_2^T$), and denoting $t^{(1)}$ and $t^{(2)}$ the optimal tax rate from country 1 and 2's perspective respectively, we get:

$$TC_1 = \frac{\alpha}{2}\left(a - \frac{t^{(1)}}{b} + a - \frac{t^{(1)}}{2b}\right)^2 + \frac{b}{2}\left(\frac{a}{b} - \left(a - \frac{t^{(1)}}{b}\right)\right)^2, \quad (A3)$$

$$TC_2 = \Theta\frac{\alpha}{2}\left(a - \frac{t^{(2)}}{b} + a - \frac{t^{(2)}}{2b}\right)^2 + \frac{b}{4}\left(\frac{a}{b} - \left(a - \frac{t^{(2)}}{2b}\right)\right)^2. \quad (A4)$$

Differentiating (A3) and (A4) with respect to $t^{(1)}$ and $t^{(2)}$ respectively, and solving for this variable, gives (8). Substituting (8) into $E_1^T = a - t^{(i)}/b$ and $E_2^T = a - t^{(i)}/(2b)$ ($t^{(1)}$ if $\Theta \geq 2$ and $t^{(2)}$ if $\Theta \leq 2$), we derive non-adjusted emission rates as given in Table 7A.2. Adjusted emission rates are computed whenever $D_i < 0$ using (7).

The Permit Scheme

As in the tax regime, we know that in equilibrium, after trade in permits has taken place, marginal abatement costs are equal in both countries and equal to the price of permits, P, that is, $MAC_1 = MAC_2 = P$. With respect to (1) and (2) this implies

$$a - bE_1^P = \frac{1}{2}\left(a - bE_2^P\right) = P. \quad (A5)$$

Solving for E_1^P and E_2^P respectively, gives

$$E_1^P = \frac{1}{2}\left(\frac{a}{b} + E_2^P\right) \quad (A6)$$

and

$$E_2^P = 2E_1^P - \frac{a}{2b} \quad (A7)$$

where the superscript P stands for permit regime. Since we have $E_1^* = E_2^* = a/b$ in the initial situation, an equal percentage emission reduction (this implies that permits are 'grandfathered') implies that each country receives an equal amount of permits M and the total amount of permits is $2M$. Therefore, the allocation of emission rights, (E_1^P, E_2^P), attainable in the permit market, is constrained by

$$2M = E_1^P + E_2^P. \tag{A8}$$

Inserting (A7) in (A8) and solving for E_1^P yields

$$E_1^P = \frac{1}{3}\left(2M + \frac{a}{b}\right). \tag{A9}$$

Inserting (A6) in (A8) and solving for E_2^P reveals

$$E_2^P = \frac{1}{3}\left(4M - \frac{a}{b}\right). \tag{A10}$$

Substituting (A9) and (A10) into (9) and (10) in the text (see section 2.4; of course $E_1 = E_1^P$ and $E_2 = E_2^P$), and denoting $M^{(1)}$ and $M^{(2)}$ the amount of permits each country should receive according to country 1 and 2 respectively, we get

$$TC_1 = \frac{\alpha}{2}\left(2M^{(1)}\right)^2 + \frac{b}{2}\left(\frac{a}{b} - \frac{1}{3}\left(2M^{(1)} + \frac{a}{b}\right)\right)^2 + \left(a - b\frac{1}{3}\left(2M^{(1)} + \frac{a}{b}\right)\right)\left(\frac{1}{3}\left(2M^{(1)} + \frac{a}{b}\right) - M^{(1)}\right)$$

$$\tag{A11}$$

$$TC_2 = \Theta\frac{\alpha}{2}\left(2M^{(1)}\right)^2 + \frac{b}{4}\left(\frac{a}{b} - \frac{1}{3}\left(4M^{(2)} - \frac{a}{b}\right)\right)^2 + \frac{1}{2}\left(a - b\frac{1}{3}\left(4M^{(2)} - \frac{a}{b}\right)\right)\left(\frac{1}{3}\left(4M^{(2)} - \frac{a}{b}\right) - M^{(2)}\right)$$

$$\tag{A12}$$

Differentiating (A11) and (A12) with respect to $M^{(1)}$ and $M^{(2)}$ respectively, and solving for this variable, gives (11) in the text. Substituting (11) into (A9) and (A10) ($M^{(1)}$ if $\Theta \geq 1/2$ and $M^{(2)}$ if $\Theta \leq 1/2$) gives non-adjusted emission rates as given in Table 7A.3. For adjusted emission rates we use (7) whenever $D_i < 0$.

Computation of Minimax Payoffs

In Section 3.2 we determine the minimax payoffs. Below, a more extensive derivation is presented. Recall the strategy space is given by $E_i \in [0, a/b]$. Country 1's welfare, v_1 ($v_1 = -TC_1$), is given by

$$v_1(E_1, E_2) = -\frac{\alpha}{2}(E_1 + E_2)^2 - \frac{b}{2}\left(\frac{a}{b} - E_1\right)^2. \tag{A13}$$

The minimax payoff of country 1 is defined by $v_1^M = \min_{E_2} \max_{E_1} v_1(E_1, E_2)$. Note that

$$\frac{\partial v_1}{\partial E_1} = b\left(\frac{a}{b} - E_1\right) - \alpha(E_1 + E_2) = 0, \tag{A14}$$

$$\frac{\partial^2 v_1}{\partial E_1^2} = -b - \alpha < 0 \tag{A15}$$

$$\frac{\partial v_1}{\partial E_2} = -\alpha < 0 \tag{A16}$$

hold. The solution to (A14) is

$$E_1 = \frac{a - \alpha E_2}{\alpha + b} < \frac{a}{b}. \tag{A17}$$

Thus, we conclude that E_1 is a maximum and v_1 decreases in E_2. Thus, country 2 will choose $E_2 = a/b$ to minimize v_1. From (A17), however, it is clear that $E_1 < 0$ if $\alpha < b$. Because $E_1 < 0$ does not make sense, we have to set $E_1 = 0$ for $\alpha < b$. For $\alpha \geq b$, however, country 1 will choose E_1 according to (A17). Thus, for $\alpha < b$, we have $E_1 = 0$ and $E_2 = a/b$ and for $\alpha \geq b$ we have $E_1 = (a - \alpha E_2)/(\alpha + b)$ and $E_2 = a/b$. Substituting these emissions into (A13) gives us (12) in the text.

Since the derivation of country 2's payoff proceeds along the same lines we do not reproduce it here.

Computation of Maximax Payoffs

From (A16) we know that country 1's payoff is negatively affected by emissions in country 2. Hence, the most favourable situation for country 1 is $E_2 = 0$. Then it follows from (A17) that country 1's best reply is $E_1 = a/(\alpha + b)$. Substituting these emissions into (A13) gives us v_1^U in (12) in the text. By the same token, v_2^U is computed using country 2's best reply function, assuming $E_1 = 0$.

8. Linking environmental and non-environmental problems in an international setting: the interconnected games approach

Jardena Kroeze-Gil and Henk Folmer[*]

1. INTRODUCTION

By their very nature, international environmental problems are characterized by the fact that their impacts cannot be confined to the country of origin.[1] This relates not only to physical environmental problems where pollutants actually move across borders, as in the case of global warming and acid rain, but also to non-physical problems. The latter kind of problems are related to international trade and trade policies which, through altering the location and volume of production, have impacts on the environment (see among others Anderson and Blackhurst, 1992; Walley, 1991). International environmental problems can also be a consequence of domestic environmental policy, such as the termination of certain imports for reasons of environmental protection or the concern about the lack of environmental protection, as in the case of nuclear policy in certain countries. International environmental problems have occupied a major place in environmental and resource economics. Not only do these problems often have (expected) consequences which largely exceed those of most domestic problems; they also require economic theories and methodologies which are basically different from those related to the latter. This follows from the fact that in the case of domestic problems, national or local governments can introduce and enforce environmental policies, whilst in the international context no such institutions exist.

The absence of such institutions implies that an international environmental agreement must be voluntary and multilateral.[2] These features have several consequences for international cooperation and the conclusion of optimal agreements.

---

[*] The authors acknowledge the useful comments by Pierre van Mouche and Nick Hanley. The usual disclaimer applies.

In particular, there is a risk that cooperation may be foiled because of free-riding behaviour, whilst existing agreements may be undermined by defection.

Free-riding may influence the effectiveness of environmental policy because such policies often require the involvement of a minimum set of countries. For instance, a global warming abatement policy without the involvement of the developing countries would be futile (Folmer, van Mouche and Ragland, 1993). Countries will opt for free-riding behaviour if cooperation implies net welfare losses. Also, even if the net benefits of cooperation are positive (so that the country has an incentive to cooperate), a country can sometimes reap the same benefits without paying its share in the costs by staying out of the agreement.[3] Finally, the willingness to pay for environmental quality is different in countries of different income levels or physical or social circumstances.

The problem of international cooperation and of concluding optimal agreements with respect to international environmental problems has been in the limelight in the environmental economics literature for some years now. In order to induce countries to cooperate, Mäler (1989), among others, has suggested that those countries whose net benefits from cooperation would be negative should be compensated by those who gain. However, there is a good deal of resistance to the implementation of side payments. The anticipation of side payments may induce countries initially to minimize environmental policy below even non-cooperative levels (that is, the Nash equilibrium), thereby extracting larger side payments. Moreover, countries that offer side payments may incur a loss of reputation and may weaken their negotiation positions in the sense that such action raises expectation with their negotiation partners, so that they will be prepared to give in under other circumstances as well, both in the environmental arena and in other international affairs (Mäler, 1990). Finally, side payments signify application of a victim pays principle rather than a polluter pays principle.

In Folmer, van Mouche and Ragland (1993) and Folmer and van Mouche (1994) linking of different negotiated issues was proposed as an alternative to side payments. Moreover, Mäler (1989) suggested that side payments are rarely seen in practice since the countries in question are typically engaged in several areas of negotiation.

By linking several issues, the fact that countries are typically engaged in several areas of negotiation can be used as a means to reach agreement without side payments. In Stein (1980) three types of linkage in a two-player, two-issue case were introduced: coerced linkage, threat-induced linkage and mutual linkage.

In coerced linkage the aggrieved player deviates from his strategy in one issue, thereby forcing the other player to change course on the other issue. An example is the US attempt to persuade Britain to withdraw its forces from the Suez Canal in 1956. The US wanted the British to pull out of the Canal zone, but also wanted to continue its support of the British currency, regardless of Britain's Middle East policy. The British were reliant on the continuation of American support.

The US withdrew its support of the British pound, thereby forcing the British to change their policy in the Middle East. Thus the US used coerced linkage to achieve its second-best outcome, instead of its third-best outcome, the equilibrium outcome (the US supporting the British currency and the British staying in the Canal zone). The first-best outcome for the US, namely having the British pull out of the Canal zone whilst supporting the British currency, was not achievable, given the preferences of the British.

In threat-induced linkage the aggrieved player threatens to do what is not in his own interest in one issue and promises not to do so if the other player changes his course in the other issue. An example is a kidnapper with a hostage. The kidnapper wants to release the hostage (his dominant strategy), while the police meet his demands. He prefers not to kill the hostage, whether the police meet his demands or not, because with a dead hostage he will only incur a loss. The police, in turn, prefer not to meet the demands (their dominant strategy), whether the kidnapper kills the hostage or not. The equilibrium outcome (combining the dominant strategies) would be that the kidnapper releases the hostage without the police meeting the demands. This leaves the kidnapper aggrieved. The kidnapper can threaten to kill the hostage, hoping that the police will meet his demands, thereby reaching the linkage outcome of a released hostage and a satisfied kidnapper.

In mutual linkage either player introduces linkage by promising to do what is not in his own interest on one issue if the other agrees to do so on the other issue. One situation in which both countries can introduce mutual linkage is the case of two prisoners' dilemma games relating to two issues. Each player has a dominant strategy, that is, to defect, and both want the other player to do the opposite, namely to cooperate. Moreover, each player prefers to deviate from his dominant strategy and have the other cooperate. Obtaining the mutually desired outcome remains difficult. No player has any assurance that the other will also cooperate if he himself does, and both know that they will be exploited if the other does not cooperate. The linkage in this case is that one player in one game promises to cooperate rather than to play his dominant strategy in exchange for cooperation by the other player in the other game (and that player would also rather play his dominant strategy).

Our interest in this chapter lies mainly in the more general case of multi-player, multi-issue mutual linkage. Players represent countries and the issues concern environmental and non-environmental problems.

There are several reasons for (mutually) linking environmental problems to non-environmental problems in the process of reaching agreement in an international context. One reason is that side payments are not made directly but indirectly, which makes it possible to circumvent the disadvantages of financial side payments, in particular acquiring a reputation of a weak negotiator and extracting excessively large side payments (see above). One dispute is used as a leverage to another and concessions in the different areas of negotiation can be exchanged. Thus the different countries can use their superiority in one area of negotiation to make up for their relative inferiority in another area. Another reason for linking is the possibility of threats of retaliation. Lack of cooperation *during* the decision-making process by one country can be discouraged by a threat by other countries not to reach agreement in an area of negotiation that is of great interest to the non-cooperating country. Thus the problem of free-riding is avoided. Finally, defection from an agreement *after* the decision-making process can be discouraged by a threat of defection in another area.

Linking can be done provided that countries have well-defined interests in the outcome of the negotiation process and that these interests are reversed. The degree of reversedness depends heavily on the relative power of negotiation in the different areas of negotiation.

In Folmer, van Mouche and Ragland (1993) and Folmer and van Mouche (1994) linking was modelled by means of interconnected games. The analysis, however, was restricted to two special cases, that is, when each constituting isolated game is a game in strategic form (called a 'direct-sum game') and, more generally, when each constituting isolated game is a repeated game (called a 'tensor game').

In this chapter we shall further develop the concept of interconnected games. In particular, we shall consider cooperative games and show that the interconnected cooperative game may have a solution whilst not each of the underlying isolated games can be solved (Section 3). In Section 2 the main results for non-cooperative games will be summarized. Conclusions follow in Section 4.

2. NON-COOPERATIVE INTERCONNECTED GAMES

Consider a game in strategic form made up of non-empty strategy sets S^j ($1 \leq j \leq N$) and of payoff functions $f^j: S^1 \times \ldots \times S^N \to \mathbb{R}$ ($1 \leq j \leq N$). Such a game will be denoted by[4]

$$\Gamma = < S^1, \ldots, S^N; f^1, \ldots, f^N >$$

The convention of representing cartesian products and vectors (referring to all N players together) by bold type will be used here. For example **s** stands for the (row) vector $(s^1, \ldots, s^N)$ where $s^j \in S^j$ is player i's strategy, and **S** stands for $S^1 \times \ldots \times S^N$. We shall refer to elements of $\mathbf{S} = \Pi_{j=1}^{N} S^j$ as multi-strategies.

Direct-sum games will be constructed out of M given games in strategic form with the same N players in each game. The assumption that the same N players appear in all games does not hold in general. However, because of the growing interdependences between countries, especially in (co-)federations like the EU, it is likely that the generality is increasing (Folmer and Howe, 1991).[5]

We introduce a linear function $\alpha: \mathbb{R}^M \to \mathbb{R}$ that is strictly increasing in each of its M variables. α will be called a weight.[6] If α^j is a weight of player j for all j, then we call $\boldsymbol{\alpha} := (\alpha^1, \ldots, \alpha^N)$ a multi-weight. When α^j is a weight, there (uniquely) exist positive $_k\alpha^j$ ($1 \leq k \leq M$) such that $\alpha^j(w_1, \ldots, w_M) = \sum_{k=1}^{M} {_k\alpha^j} w_k$.

We define the trade-off direct-sum game ($\oplus \Gamma$) as the game in strategic form

$$\left\langle \prod_{k=1}^{M} {_k}S^1, \ldots, \prod_{k=1}^{M} {_k}S^N; f_{\alpha^1}^1, \ldots, f_{\alpha^N}^N \right\rangle$$

where the payoff $f_{\alpha^i}^i$ is defined as

$$f_{\alpha^i}^i \left(\begin{pmatrix} {_1}S^1 \\ \vdots \\ {_M}S^1 \end{pmatrix}, \ldots, \begin{pmatrix} {_1}S^W \\ \vdots \\ {_M}S^1 \end{pmatrix} \right) := \sum_{k=1}^{M} {_k\alpha^i} {_k}f^i \left({_k}S^1, \ldots, {_k}S^N \right).$$

We call $_1\Gamma, \ldots, {_M}\Gamma$ the constituting isolated games of $\oplus\Gamma$.

We now consider tensor games. A tensor game is constructed out of a given collection of repeated games. As shown by, among others, Friedman (1991), a repeated game is made up of a game in strategic form Γ called the stage game, a number T (positive or negative) representing the number of repetitions and $\delta \in [0, 1]$ a (player-independent) discount factor. Given a repeated game, the strategy set $[\mathbf{S}^i]$ equals the collection of sequences of mappings[7] $\sigma^i = (\sigma_t^i)_{0 \leq t < T}$ with $\sigma_t^i: \Pi_{\tau=0}^{t-1} \Pi_{j=1}^{N} \mathbf{S}^j \to \mathbf{S}^i$ and the payoff function $[f^i]$ is defined as

$$[f^i](\sigma) := \sum_{t=0}^{T-1} \delta^t f^i(\mathbf{a}_t(\sigma)),$$

with the outcome path $a_t^j(\sigma) \in \mathbf{S}^j$ ($0 \leq t < T$) inductively defined by $a_0^j(\sigma) := a_0^j$ and $a_t^j(\sigma) := \sigma_t^j(\mathbf{a}_0(\sigma), \mathbf{a}_1(\sigma), \ldots, \mathbf{a}_{t-1}(\sigma))$ ($1 \leq t < T$). When $T = \infty$ we always suppose, to avoid convergence problems that $\delta < 1$.

The (trade-off) tensor game $(\otimes_{k=1}^{M} {_k}\Gamma; T; \delta>)_\alpha$ is defined as the repeated game

$$\left\langle \left(\oplus_{k=1}^{M} {_k}\Gamma \right)_\alpha; T; \delta \right\rangle.$$

We also use the simpler notation $\otimes \Gamma$. We call $<{}_1\Gamma; T; \delta>, \ldots, <{}_M\Gamma; T; \delta>$ the constituting isolated games of $\oplus \Gamma$.

The direct-sum game $(\oplus_{k=1}^{M}{}_k\Gamma)_\alpha$ serves as the stage game for the tensor game $\otimes \Gamma$. Hence, the strategy set for player i in $\otimes \Gamma$ equals $[\Pi_{k=1}^{M}{}_kS^i]$ and his payoff function in this game is denoted by $[f^i_{\alpha^i}]$ and is given by (denoting multi-strategies of the tensor game by Σ)

$$[f^i_{\alpha^i}](\Sigma) = \sum_{t=0}^{T-1} \delta^t f^i_{\alpha^i,t}\left(A^1_t(\Sigma), \ldots, A^N_t(\Sigma)\right) \qquad (1)$$

where $A^j_t(\Sigma)$ ($0 \le t < T$) denotes now the outcome path for player j in the tensor game. More explicitly (denoting components referring to the objectives by a pre-subscript):

$$[f^i_{\alpha^i}](\Sigma) = \sum_{t=0}^{T-1} \delta^t \sum_{k=1}^{M} {}_k\alpha^i {}_kf^i\left({}_k\left(A^1_t(S)\right), \ldots, {}_k\left(A^N_t(S)\right)\right).$$

In the case where α^i is completely additive, that is, $\alpha^i(w_1, \ldots, w_M) = \Sigma_{k=1}^{M} w_k$, (1) becomes

$$[f^i_{\alpha^i}](\Sigma) = \sum_{t=0}^{T-1} \delta^t \sum_{k=1}^{M} {}_kf^i\left({}_k\left(A^1_t(S)\right), \ldots, {}_k\left(A^N_t(S)\right)\right).$$

Roughly speaking, a strategy for a player in $\otimes \Gamma$ consists of rules for each period t that determine what he will play in period t as a function of the history of the game, i.e. all previous actions.

Folmer, van Mouche and Ragland (1993) showed that for each Nash equilibrium of the direct sum game there exist corresponding Nash equilibria of the constituting isolated games and vice versa. In other words, in a static context interconnection does not lead to a 'new' Nash equilibrium. This means that in a static context, linking environmental problems and non-environmental problems does not lead to more cooperation; nor does it facilitate the conclusion of international agreements.[8]

The situation for tensor games is quite different. In order to show this we first introduce the notion of Friedman trigger strategies. Given a repeated game $<\Gamma; T; \delta>$, we call $\sigma^i = (\sigma^i_t)_{0 < t < T} \in [S^i]$ a trigger strategy for player i if there exists $\mathbf{p} \in S$ and $n^i \in S^i$, such that $\sigma^i_0 = p^i$, $\sigma^i_t(\mathbf{p}, \ldots, \mathbf{p}) = p^i$ and $\sigma^i_t(s_0, \ldots, s_{t-1}) = n^i$ if $(s_0, \ldots, s_{t-1}) \ne (\mathbf{p}, \ldots, \mathbf{p})$ $(1 \le t < T)$. We also denote such a σ^i by «$\mathbf{p}, n^i$».

Moreover, if « **p**, n^j » is a trigger strategy for player j ($1 \leq j \leq N$), then we denote the corresponding multi-strategy by « **p, n** ». We shall call a trigger multi-strategy « **p, n** » where **n** is a Nash equilibrium of Γ and $f^j(\mathbf{p}) > f^j(\mathbf{n})$ ($1 \leq j \leq N$) a Friedman trigger multi-strategy. Hence, in the case of a tensor game, « **P, N** » is a Friedman trigger multi-strategy means that $\mathbf{P, N} \in \Pi_{k=1}^{M} {}_k\mathbf{S}^1 \times \ldots \times \Pi_{k=1}^{M} {}_k\mathbf{S}^N$, **N** is a Nash equilibrium of $\otimes \Gamma$ and $f^j_{\alpha j}(\mathbf{P}) > f^j_{\alpha j}((\mathbf{N}))$ ($1 \leq j \leq N$).

In Folmer, van Mouche and Ragland (1993) it was shown that for $T \geq 2$ and $M \geq 2$ a tensor game contains Friedman trigger multi-strategies that allow players to achieve 'cooperative outcomes' in games that are non-cooperative, as the players' strategies contain possibilities to punish players who are observed to deviate. However, tensor games not only contain provisions to punish in the same (constituting isolated) game, as in the case of repeated games, but also in different constituting isolated games. This is the major distinguishing feature of tensor games.

Some other important results relating to tensor games were obtained in Folmer and van Mouche (1994). There it was shown that the sum over the constituting isolated games of the sets of payoff vectors larger than or equal to the minimax payoff vector is a subset of the corresponding set of payoff vectors of the trade-off tensor game. In particular, strict inclusion is possible. It was also shown that the maximum total Nash equilibrium payoff for the trade-off tensor game is at least as large as the weighted sum over the constituting isolated games of maximum total Nash equilibria payoffs. In particular, strict inequality is possible.

This implies that, in a dynamic setting, linking environmental and non-environmental problems may sustain cooperation. In particular, defection on an international agreement with respect to the environment could be discouraged by retaliation with respect to a non-environmental issue. A prerequisite is the existence of reversed interests. That is, the countries that are inclined to defect with respect to the environmental issue enjoy positive net benefit from cooperation with regard to the non-environmental problem.

3. INTERCONNECTION OF GAMES IN CHARACTERISTIC FUNCTION FORM

In this section the interconnection of games in characteristic function form is defined. We include a function that represents the 'preferences' of each player across the constituting games and a function that represents the power each player has.

Let $\mathcal{N} = \{1, \ldots, N\}$ be the set of players and let $\Gamma = <\mathbf{S}^1, \ldots, \mathbf{S}^N; f^1, \ldots, f^N>$ be a game in strategic form. A strategy $s \in \mathbf{S} := \Pi_{i=1}^{N} \mathbf{S}^i$ is sometimes denoted as $s = (s^K, s^{\tilde{K}}) \in \mathbf{S}^K \times \mathbf{S}^{\tilde{K}}$, where $\mathbf{S}^K$ is the strategy space of the coalition $K \subseteq \mathcal{N}$ and $\tilde{K} = \mathcal{N} \setminus K$. Let $(\mathcal{N}, {}_k v)$, $1 \leq k \leq M$, be a game in characteristic function form. The number ${}_k v^K$ is interpreted as the maximum payoff to members of coalition K that the coalition can guarantee itself. Let $\eta^i = ({}_1\eta^i, \ldots, {}_M\eta^i)$ be player i's linear weight and let $g = (g^1, \ldots, g^N) \in \mathbb{R}^N$ be power weights of the players. The weight ${}_k\eta^i$ represents the importance of game k to player i, thus reflecting his preference. Weight g represents the power of the different players. For notational convenience we define player i's adjusted linear weight function θ^i, that equals the linear weight function η^i, multiplied by player i's power weight g^i: $\theta^i = g^i \cdot \eta^i$.

Before defining interconnection for games in characteristic function form, we first give a definition of the characteristic function, which incorporates the adjusted linear weight function.

Definition 3.1 *The adjusted characteristic function ${}_k u: 2^{\mathcal{N}} \to \mathbb{R}$ for game k its defined as*

$$ {}_k u(K) := \max_{{}_k s^K \in \mathbf{S}^K} \min_{{}_k s^{\tilde{K}} \in \mathbf{S}^{\tilde{K}}} \sum_{i \in K} {}_k \theta^i \cdot {}_k f^i\left({}_k s^K, {}_k s^{\tilde{K}}\right). $$

By the assumption that all payoffs are continuous and bounded on S, we ensure that the maximin value of the game exists. The definition of interconnection for games in characteristic function form is as follows.

Definition 3.2 *Given M games in strategic form and their corresponding adjusted characteristic function form games $(\mathcal{N}, {}_k u)$, $1 \leq k \leq M$; the interconnected game in characteristic function form is defined as*

$$ \Gamma = (\mathcal{N}, w), \quad \text{with} $$

$$ w(K) = \sum_{k=1}^{M} {}_k u(K) \quad \forall K \subseteq \mathcal{N}. \tag{2} $$

Next the cores of an interconnected game in characteristic function form and of its constituting isolated characteristic function form games are compared. The total payoff in the core is used as the criterion to compare the cores. First a specific way to construct payoff vectors in the core is given. Then we give a condition under which it is possible to have a non-empty core of the interconnected game, even when some of the constituting isolated games have empty cores.

The interconnected games approach

The core consists of payoff vectors that give each possible coalition a total payoff no lower than any payoff the coalition can achieve for itself. Hence a strategy in the core cannot be blocked by any coalition, because the coalitions have no advantage in doing so. Following, among others, Friedman (1991), the core is defined as follows.

Definition 3.3 *The core of the game ($\mathcal{N}$, v), denoted C($\mathcal{N}$, v), is the subset of $\mathbb{R}^N$, defined by*

$$x \in C(\mathcal{N}, v) \Leftrightarrow \begin{cases} \sum_{i \in K} x^i \geq v(K) & \forall K \subset \mathcal{N} \\ \sum_{i \in \mathcal{N}} x^i = v(\mathcal{N}). \end{cases}$$

It is also shown that it is possible to determine if a game has a non-empty core by solving the following linear programming problem, which always has a solution:

$$\min \sum_{i \in \mathcal{N}} x^i \quad \text{s.t.} \sum_{i \in K} x^i \geq v(K) \quad \forall K \subset \mathcal{N}. \tag{3}$$

Moreover if $X \in \mathbb{R}$ is the solution of the linear programming problem (3), then:

$$C(\mathcal{N}, v) \neq \emptyset \Leftrightarrow X \leq v(\mathcal{N}). \tag{4}$$

A minimum payoff of a game in characteristic function form is defined as a payoff for which the minimum of the linear programming problem (3) is reached.

Definition 3.4 *Given ($\mathcal{N}$, v) and let X be the solution of the linear programming problem (3). Then a minimum payoff vector x^* of the game is defined as*

$$\sum_{i \in K} x^{*i} \geq v(K) \quad \forall K \subset \mathcal{N}$$
$$\sum_{i \in \mathcal{N}} x^{*i} = X.$$

Definition 3.5 *Given ($\mathcal{N}$, v) and X. The minimum game ($\mathcal{N}$, v^*) is defined as*

$$v^*(K) := v(K) \quad K \subset \mathcal{N}$$
$$v^*(\mathcal{N}) := X.$$

From Definitions 3.4 and 3.5 it is clear that the minimum payoff vectors of a game (N, v) are exactly the elements of the core $C(N, v^*)$ of the minimum game.

If the core is non-empty, a payoff vector in the core can also be constructed as a sum of two vectors: the minimum payoff vector and a payoff vector in the core of the excess game. The excess game is derived from the original game by use of Definitions 3.6 to 3.8.

Definition 3.6 *Given (N, v) and X. The excess of the game is defined as*

$$\Delta := v(N) - X.$$

From (4) it follows that

$$C(N, v) \neq \emptyset \Leftrightarrow \Delta \geq 0.$$

To define the excess game, we first need the notion of the zero-d-game. It is defined as follows.

Definition 3.7 *Given (N, v). For $d \in \mathbb{R}$ the zero-d-game (N, v^d) of (N, v) is defined as*

$$v^d(K) = 0 \quad \forall K \subset N$$
$$v^d(N) = |d|.$$

Lemma 3.1 *The core $C(N, v^d)$ of the zero-d-game is non-empty.*

Proof: Evident.

Definition 3.8 *Given (N, v) and Δ. The excess game (N, v^Δ) of (N, v) is the zero-d-game with $d = \Delta$.*

On this basis, a payoff in the core is constructed as the sum of a minimum payoff vector and a payoff vector in the core of the excess game.

Theorem 3.1 *Let (N, v) have non-empty core, i.e. $\Delta \geq 0$. Then*

$$C(N, v^*) + C(N, v^\Delta) \subseteq C(N, v).$$

Proof: Let $x^* \in C(N, v^*)$ and $x^\Delta \in C(N, v^\Delta)$. Set $x := x^* + x^\Delta$. We need to check whether $\Sigma_{i \in K} x^i \geq v(K) \; \forall K \subset N$ and whether $\Sigma_{i \in N} x^i = v(N)$. With Definitions 3.4 to 3.8, we find

$$\sum_{i \in K} x^i = \sum_{i \in K} x^{*i} + \sum_{i \in K} x^{\Delta,i} \geq v^*(K) + v^\Delta(K) = v(K) \quad \forall K \subset \mathcal{N},$$

$$\sum_{i \in \mathcal{N}} x^i = \sum_{i \in \mathcal{N}} x^{*i} + \sum_{i \in \mathcal{N}} x^{\Delta i} = X + \Delta = v(\mathcal{N}).$$

It must be noted that the other inclusion in Theorem 3.1 is not true in general. Thus it is not true that every payoff vector in the core of a game can be written as a sum of a minimum payoff vector and a payoff vector in the core of the excess game.

To be able to formulate a condition under which the core of an interconnected game is non-empty, we need the notion of negative core.

Definition 3.9 *For $\Delta < 0$ the negative core of the excess game is defined as*

$$C^-(\mathcal{N}, v^\Delta) := -C(\mathcal{N}, v^{|\Delta|}).$$

For $\Delta < 0$ it holds that

$$x^\Delta \in C^-(\mathcal{N}, v^\Delta) \Leftrightarrow -x^\Delta \in C(\mathcal{N}, v^\Delta) \Leftrightarrow \sum_{i \in \mathcal{N}} x^{\Delta i} = \Delta.$$

The condition under which the core of an interconnected game is non-empty is now given.

Theorem 3.2 *Let $(\mathcal{N}, {}_k u)$, $1 \leq k \leq M$, be M adjusted characteristic function form games and let ${}_k x^*$ and ${}_k \Delta$ be corresponding minimum payoff vectors and excesses. Let $x^{k\Delta}$ be such that*

$$\begin{aligned} {}_k x^\Delta &\in C(\mathcal{N}, {}_k u^{k\Delta}) \quad \text{if } {}_k\Delta \geq 0 \\ {}_k x^\Delta &\in C^-(\mathcal{N}, {}_k u^{k\Delta}) \quad \text{if } {}_k\Delta < 0. \end{aligned}$$

Let $(\mathcal{N}, w)$ be the interconnected characteristic function form game. Then

$$\sum_{k=1}^M {}_k \Delta \geq 0 \Rightarrow C(\mathcal{N}, w) \neq \emptyset.$$

Proof: Define $\Delta := \sum_{k=1}^{M} {}_k\Delta$, $z^* := \sum_{k=1}^{M} {}_kx^*$, $z^\Delta := \sum_{k=1}^{M} {}_kx^\Delta$, and $Z := \sum_{k=1}^{M} {}_kX$. Z is the solution to the linear problem (3) for w. We first show that $z^* \in C(\mathcal{N}, w^*)$ and $z^\Delta \in C(\mathcal{N}, w^\Delta)$:

$$\sum_{i \in K} z^{*i} = \sum_{i \in K} \sum_{k=1}^{M} {}_kx^{*i} \geq \sum_{k=1}^{M} {}_kv(K) = w(K) \quad \forall K \subset \mathcal{N},$$

$$\sum_{i \in \mathcal{N}} z^{*i} = \sum_{i \in \mathcal{N}} \sum_{k=1}^{M} {}_kx^{*i} = \sum_{k=1}^{M} {}_kX = Z,$$

$$\sum_{i \in K} z^{\Delta i} = \sum_{i \in K} \sum_{k=1}^{M} {}_kx^{\Delta i} \geq \sum_{k=1}^{M} 0 = 0 \quad \forall K \subset \mathcal{N},$$

$$\sum_{i \in \mathcal{N}} z^{\Delta i} = \sum_{i \in \mathcal{N}} \sum_{k=1}^{M} {}_kx^{\Delta i} = \sum_{k=1}^{M} {}_k\Delta = \Delta.$$

Let $z := z^* + z^\Delta$. Since $\Delta \geq 0$, it follows from Theorem 3.1 that $z \in C(\mathcal{N}, w)$, thus $C(\mathcal{N}, w) \neq \emptyset$.

The total of a payoff in the core is now used as the criterion to compare the cores. The totals of the payoffs in the cores equal

$$T_{{}_ku} := \begin{cases} 0 & \text{if } C(\mathcal{N}, {}_ku) = \emptyset \\ {}_ku(\mathcal{N}) & \text{if } C(\mathcal{N}, {}_ku) \neq \emptyset, \end{cases} \quad 1 \leq k \leq M$$

$$T_w := \begin{cases} 0 & \text{if } C(\mathcal{N}, w) = \emptyset \\ w(\mathcal{N}) & \text{if } C(\mathcal{N}, w) \neq \emptyset, \end{cases}$$

Define $P := \{k \mid {}_k\Delta \geq 0\}$. Set P is the collection of games with non-empty core. Suppose $C(\mathcal{N}, w) \neq \emptyset$. Then

$$T_w = w(\mathcal{N}) = \sum_{k=1}^{M} {}_ku(\mathcal{N}) \geq \sum_{k \in P} {}_ku(\mathcal{N}) = \sum_{k \in P} T_{{}_ku}.$$

Thus if the core of the interconnected characteristic function form game $(\mathcal{N}, w)$ is not empty, then the total of the payoffs in its core is at least as large as the sum of the totals of the payoffs in the cores of the constituting games.

We now give an example of interconnection, in which the core of one of the constituting games is empty, whereas the core of the interconnected game is not empty.

Let $\mathcal{N} = \{1, 2, 3\}$, $_1S^1 = {_2}S^1 = \{A, B\}$, $_1S^2 = {_2}S^2 = \{C, D\}$, $_1S^3 = {_2}S^3 = \{a, b\}$ and let the two constituting games in strategic form be given by

Game 1:

$$\begin{array}{cc} \text{Player 3's strategy} = a & \text{Player 3's strategy} = b \\ \begin{pmatrix} 25,0,0 & 0,50,50 \\ 10,10,0 & 0,40,60 \end{pmatrix} & \begin{pmatrix} 20,20,0 & 10,0,0 \\ 10,0,60 & 20,0,20 \end{pmatrix} \end{array}$$

Game 2:

$$\begin{array}{cc} \text{Player 3's strategy} = a & \text{Player 3's strategy} = b \\ \begin{pmatrix} 0,50,0 & 10,25,10 \\ 10,50,10 & 0,0,20 \end{pmatrix} & \begin{pmatrix} 20,50,20 & 10,10,25 \\ 0,0,20 & 10,10,0 \end{pmatrix} \end{array}$$

Let the weight of the players be $g = (1, 2, 2)$ and the preferences of the players be $\eta^1 = (8\ 2)$, $\eta^2 = (1\ 2)$ and $\eta^3 = (1\ 4)$. The adjusted linear weight functions then equal $\theta^1 = (8\ 2)$, $\theta^2 = (2\ 4)$ and $\theta^3 = (2\ 8)$. The characteristic function form games are given by

$$_1u(\{1\}) = \max_{s^1 \in S^1} \min_{(s^2, s^3) \in S^2 \times S^3} {_1}\theta^1 \cdot f^1(s^1, s^2, s^3)$$

$$= \max \{0, 0\} = 0$$

$$_1u(\{2\}) = \max \{0, 0\} = 0$$

$$_1u(\{3\}) = \max \{0, 0\} = 0$$

$$_1u(\{1, 2\}) = \max \{200, 80, 80, 80\} = 200$$

$$_1u(\{1, 3\}) = \max \{100, 80, 80, 200\} = 200$$

$$_1u(\{2, 3\}) = \max \{0, 40, 200, 0\} = 200$$

$$_1u(\mathcal{N}) = \max \{200, 200, 100, 200, 200, 80, 200, 200\} = 200$$

and

$$_2u(\{1\}) = \max_{s^1 \in S^1} \min_{(s^2, s^3) \in S^2 \times S^3} {_2}\theta^1 \cdot f^1(s^1, s^2, s^3)$$

$$= \max \{0, 0\} = 0$$

$$_2u(\{2\}) = \max \{0, 0\} = 0$$

$$_2u(\{3\}) = \max \{0, 0\} = 0$$

$$_2u(\{1, 2\}) = \max \{200, 60, 0, 0\} = 200$$

$$_2u(\{1, 3\}) = \max \{0, 200, 100, 20\} = 200$$

$$_2u(\{2, 3\}) = \max \{200, 160, 160, 40\} = 200$$

$$_2u(\mathcal{N}) = \max \{200, 200, 300, 160, 400, 260, 160, 60\} = 400.$$

The solution to the linear program problem (3) is $_1X = 300$ for game 1, with $_1\mathbf{x}^* = (100\ 100\ 100)$. The excess of game 1 equals $_1\Delta = 200 - 300 = -100$. Thus $C(\mathcal{N}, _1u) = \emptyset$. For game 2 the solution is $_2X = 300$ with $_2\mathbf{x}^* = (100\ 100\ 100)$. The excess of the game equals $_2\Delta = 400 - 300 = 100$. Thus $C(\mathcal{N}, _2u) \neq \emptyset$.

The interconnected game $(\mathcal{N}, w)$ is given by

$$w(\{i\}) = 0 \quad i = 1, 2, 3,$$

$$w(\{i, j\}) = 400 \quad i, j = 1, 2, 3, i \neq j,$$

$$w(\mathcal{N}) = 600.$$

The solution to the linear program problem (3) is $Z = 600$ with $\mathbf{z}^* = (200\ 200\ 200) = {}_1\mathbf{x}^* + {}_2\mathbf{x}^*$. The excess of the game equals $\Delta = 600 - 600 = 0$.

Comparing the cores of games 1 and 2 and of the interconnected game yields $P = \{2\}$ and

$$\sum_{k \in P} S_{k^u} = {}_2u(\mathcal{N}) = 400,$$

$$S_w = w(\mathcal{N}) = 600.$$

Through interconnection the positive excess $_2\Delta$ of game $(\mathcal{N}, _2u)$ is used to compensate the negative excess $_1\Delta$ of game $(\mathcal{N}, _1u)$. Although the core of game $(\mathcal{N}, _1u)$ is empty, the available payoff in game $(\mathcal{N}, _1u)$ can be added to the total payoff.

4. CONCLUSIONS

We have shown in this chapter that linking environmental and non-environmental issues may lead to international cooperation in cases where it otherwise would not be achieved. In particular, in a dynamic setting linking may sustain cooperation once it has been achieved. This means that linking enriches the set of instruments to achieve and sustain cooperation.

It should be observed that this is a two-way relationship. Not only may a non-environmental issue be instrumental in achieving and sustaining cooperation with respect to an environmental problem, but it may also be the other way around.

In economic research the notion of linking can not only be used as an instrument to achieve and sustain international cooperation; it may also be instrumental in explaining seemingly irrational behaviour. At the domestic level interconnection occurs in the context of coalition governments, where social, economic, cultural and ethical issues are frequently linked. Moreover, it also plays a role in collusion behaviour (Bernheim and Whinston, 1990). Examples in the environmental arena are the Columbia River Treaty between Canada and the US and the Colorado River Treaty between Mexico and the US which required the US to incur large costs, while Canada and Mexico enjoyed resulting benefits. Traditional modelling approaches that exclude the possibility of linking would not have predicted such an outcome.

The possibilities for linking have strongly increased because of growing interdependence between countries. This not only applies to environmental problems but also to non-environmental problems such as trade and defence.

We have also shown in this chapter that linking can be conveniently modelled by means of game theory. Both cooperative and non-cooperative game-theoretic approaches are relevant.

NOTES

1. International environmental problems can be bilateral or multilateral. The former frequently occur with, for example, water abstraction rights.
2. It should be observed that these features even hold in the case of co-federal systems, such as the European Union, under unanimous decision making. In the European Union decisions are taken by the Council of Ministers after consultation of the European Parliament and the Committee of Permanent Representatives (Coreper). The Coreper prepares the process of reaching agreement in the Council of Ministers by appointing working groups and consulting several institutions. It then submits its opinion to the Council of Ministers. Since decisions are ultimately concluded by the Council of Ministers, there is a possibility of defection.
3. So, in this case it is not so much the avoidance of a net welfare loss, as in the previous case, but rather the increase of the already positive net benefits that is under discussion.
4. No topological assumptions will be made for the strategy sets S^j and no smoothness and geometric assumptions will be made for the payoff functions f^j. However, to avoid some technicalities later on we shall always assume that each f^j is a bounded function.

5. Analysis of partly overlapping players is a major area of future research.
6. Strictly speaking we are dealing with linear strict weights.
7. In this definition σ_0^i should be interpreted as an element of $\mathbf{S}^i$.
8. It should be observed that in the context of bargaining, linkage can lead to a breakthrough (Peters, 1986).

REFERENCES

Anderson, D. and R. Blackhurst (1992), *The Greening of World Trade Issue*, Hemel Hempstead: Harvester Wheatsheaf.

Bernheim, B.D. and M.D. Whinston (1990), 'Multimarket Contact and Collusive Behavior', *Rand Journal of Economics*, **21** (1), 1–26.

Folmer, H. and C. Howe (1991), 'Environmental Problems and Policy in the Single European Market', *Environmental and Resource Economics*, **1**(1), 17–42.

Folmer, H., P.H.M. van Mouche and S. Ragland (1993), 'Interconnected Games and Environmental Problems', *Environmental and Resource Economics*, **3**, 313–35.

Folmer, H. and P.H.M. van Mouche (1994), 'Interconnected Games and International Environmental Problems II', *Annals of Operations Research*, **54**, 97–117.

Friedman, J. (1991), *Game Theory with Applications to Economics*, Oxford: Oxford University Press.

Mäler, K.G. (1990), 'International Environmental Problems', *Oxford Review of Economic Policy*, **6**(1), 80–108.

Peters, H. (1986), 'Simultaneity of Issues and Additivity in Bargaining', *Econometrica*, **54**, 153–69.

Stein, A. (1980), 'The Politics of Linkage', *World Politics*, **32**, 62–81.

Walley, J. (1991), 'The Interface between Environmental and Trade Policies', *Economic Journal*, **101**, 180–89.

9. Strategies for environmental negotiations: issue linkage with heterogeneous countries

Michele Botteon and Carlo Carraro[*]

1. INTRODUCTION

The atmosphere and international waters are currently managed as global common-property goods because there is no institution which possesses powers to regulate their use by means of supranational legislation, economic instruments, or by imposing a system of global property rights. As a consequence, environmental agreements among sovereign countries have been widely advocated in the last few years, following the Montreal Protocol on chlorofluorocarbons (CFCs), and the UN Conference on the Environment and Development organized in Rio de Janeiro in 1992.

In the recent history of international agreements to protect the global environment, one can observe different attempts to achieve cooperation among countries. The first attempt has been to design worldwide agreements to cut emissions by bargaining solely on emissions. The result has usually been frustrating. The conventions, whenever they are signed by a great number of countries, are rather empty in terms of quantitative targets and/or deadlines. Precise commitments, on the other hand, are signed by small groups of 'like-minded' countries. Examples are provided by the Climate Change Convention, which is widely signed but notoriously empty, and by the EC countries' commitment on CO_2 emissions, which is quite binding and precise, but confined to a small number of countries. The early outcome of the Montreal Protocol provides another example of a small group of signatories, *vis-à-vis* a global phenomenon, with many other countries in a position of free-riders.

The dissatisfaction with such an outcome, and in particular with small coalitions, has been followed by attempts at expanding the agreements by bribing reluctant countries by means of transfers (as in the follow-up of the

---

[*] The authors are grateful to the editors of this volume and to participants at seminars at the Universities of Venice and Aix-en-Provence, the NBER, and the Mattei Foundation for many useful comments on a previous version of this chapter.

Montreal Protocol, or in the plans for financial implementation of the Agenda XXI), again undermined by problems of free-riding and instability.[1]

Finally, recent negotiating experiences are trying to link environmental protection to other international agreements: on technological cooperation (as in the case of the Climate Change Convention) and trade (as in the environmental clause in GATT). This last evolution of negotiation strategies, usually named 'issue linkage', was recently analysed in the theoretical environmental literature (see Folmer, van Mouche and Ragland, 1993; Folmer and van Mouche, 1994; Cesar and de Zeeuw, 1996; Barrett, 1994; Carraro and Siniscalco, 1995), where it is shown under what conditions it can actually lead to the formation of large, and therefore effective, self-enforcing environmental agreements.

There are probably two reasons which explain the difficulty of achieving self-enforcing agreements with a large number of signatories. The first one is the large economic and environmental asymmetries across world regions. Less-developed countries, for example, are quite reluctant to adopt measures to control global pollution because this could slow down their growth, with high economic costs which are evaluated as larger than the environmental benefits provided by the emission reduction. In other words, signing an environmental agreement may not be profitable for all countries involved in the negotiation process. This is what we call the 'profitability problem'.

The second problem is the intrinsic instability of environmental agreements. Some countries may prefer to free-ride, i.e. to profit from the emission reduction achieved by the signatory countries (because the environmental benefit is not excludable). This phenomenon is not related to the presence of asymmetries, even if asymmetries can strengthen it, and it occurs even if countries are identical. Therefore, even when all countries are conscious that gains from environmental cooperation are above the economic costs of abating pollution, that is, that cooperation is profitable, most of them may not sign the environmental agreement because of the possibility to achieve the environmental benefit without paying the costs (that is, cooperation is unstable). This is the 'stability problem'.

These two problems usually characterize the modelling framework which is used to describe the decision process leading to the agreement. Some recent literature on environmental negotiations (for example, Hoel, 1991; Barrett, 1994, Carraro and Siniscalco, 1993; Heal, 1994) focuses on the second problem (stability) by assuming symmetry and by modelling the decision process through which countries decide to join an environmental coalition as a non-cooperative game. The goal is to determine the so called 'self-enforcing agreements', that is, agreements which are not based on the countries' commitment to cooperation. Other contributions (for example Chander and Tulkens, 1994) deal with the first problem (profitability) by designing mechanisms that guarantee the profitability of the agreement to all countries involved in the negotiation.

The two problems must also be accounted for when analysing the existing literature on the role of 'issue linkage' in international environmental negotiations. In the 'issue linkage' model proposed by Cesar and de Zeeuw (1996), the idea is that some countries gain on a given issue, whereas other countries gain on a second one. By 'linking' the two issues it may be possible that the agreement in which the countries decide to cooperate on both issues is profitable for all of them. Hence, 'issue linkage' is designed to address the profitability problem by focusing on countries' asymmetries. This also true in Folmer, van Mouche and Ragland (1993) where a repeated game framework enables the authors also to address the stability problem. In the present chapter, we prefer to focus on the stability of environmental agreements within a one-shot framework for two reasons. First, because all recent game-theoretic literature on the non-cooperative formation of stable coalitions analyses one-shot games, where the essence of the stability problem can be defined more easily.[2] Second, because from an economic viewpoint the one-shot game in which countries decide whether or not to sign the agreement can be thought of as the initial stage of a dynamic process in which implementation and monitoring are also crucial issues.[3]

The stability of 'issue-linked' environmental agreements was also studied by Barrett (1994) and Carraro and Siniscalco (1995), again within a one-shot game framework, but assuming symmetric countries. This chapter aims at analysing both profitability and stability of linked negotiations by assuming asymmetric countries. Notice that when dealing with heterogeneous countries a further problem arises. Countries which join the coalition have to decide in which way to cooperate, i.e. the burden-sharing rule to be adopted. This further problem may lead to non-robustness of the results because the formation of a coalition and its size depend on the burden-sharing rule which is chosen. For example, if cooperating countries decide to divide the net cost of reducing emissions (or the net environmental benefit) by using the Nash bargaining rule, the outcome (in terms of the existence and size of the coalition) generally differs from the one which can be obtained by assuming the Shapley value, or the core, as burden-sharing concepts. This chapter also addresses this problem (neglected in previous analyses of 'issue linkage') by focusing on both Nash and Shapley rules.[4]

From the above discussion it is easy to understand why 'issue linkage' can solve the profitability problem. The loss arising from signing the environmental agreement may be offset by the gain from signing another agreement (for example on trade). It is less clear what is the mechanism that leads 'issue linkage' to solve the stability problem. The mechanism can be explained through the following example. Suppose the environmental negotiation is linked to a negotiation on R&D cooperation, which involves an excludable positive externality and increases the joint coalition welfare. In this way, the incentive to free-ride on the benefit of a cleaner environment (which is a public good fully appropriable by all players) is offset by the incentive to appropriate the benefit stemming from the positive R&D externality (which is a partially excludable club good and therefore fully appropriable only by the signatory countries). The latter incentive can stabilize the joint agreement, thus increasing its profitability because countries can reap both the R&D cooperation and the environmental benefit (this second benefit would be lost without the linkage). This mechanism will be further analysed in the subsequent sections of this chapter.

A final important remark is necessary. Even if it would be interesting to provide a game-theoretic analysis of the formation of environmental coalitions with asymmetric countries, the implied mathematical problem quickly becomes very cumbersome. It is therefore necessary to use numerical simulations to discuss the issues raised by countries' asymmetry (see Barrett, 1997a). Instead of assuming hypothetical countries whose characteristics are often unrealistic, in this chapter we propose to analyse the problem of environmental coalition formation by focusing on a few countries with explicit and measurable environmental features.

To this end, we have used the statistical information provided by Musgrave (1994) to calibrate the payoff function of five world regions that are assumed to be formed by countries whose interests are homogeneous and which can therefore be aggregated. These five countries or regions are: (1) Japan; (2) the US and Canada; (3) the European Union; (4) Eastern Europe and Russia; and (5) India and China. Then, using a standard formulation of the environmental game that can be found in Carraro and Siniscalco (1992), Barrett (1994), Chander and Tulkens (1994), we have computed the payoff achieved by all possible coalitions among the five groups of countries, the incentives to free-ride (i.e. to exit the coalition) and the incentives to broaden a stable coalition. These results have been derived both in the case in which the burden-sharing rule is based on the Nash bargaining concept and in the case in which it is based on the Shapley value concept.[5] Finally, using the theoretical model developed in Carraro and Siniscalco (1997), we have analysed the effect of an 'issue linkage' strategy in which the benefits of environmental cooperation are linked to those of R&D cooperation.

The conclusions are very interesting and add further insights to the analysis of environmental coalitions. Our results confirm the main theoretical conclusion derived for the symmetric case, i.e. that the linkage of environmental issues to other economic issues (for example R&D cooperation) may be useful not only to reduce the constraints that asymmetries impose on the emergence of stable environmental agreements (for example some countries may not sign because they lose from the agreement), but also to increase the number of signatories in the stable coalition. However, there may be a conflict between individually optimal and stable coalitions that in the case of asymmetric countries may cause the stable equilibrium to collapse. For example, a given country i may prefer some countries, say j and h, as partners in the cooperating group, but these countries may want to sign the agreement with country k, rather than with i. And k may prefer i and h rather than j. In this case, an equilibrium may not exist, i.e. a stable international environmental agreement may not be signed.[6]

These remarks lead to the conclusion that issue linkage may *damage* environmental protection rather than benefit it. This is the case whenever the incentives to exclude some countries from the linked agreement or the possible political-economy problem that undermines the emergence of an equilibrium dominates the benefits of linking two synergetic (in terms of profitability and stability) issues.

The structure of the chapter is as follows: in the next section we introduce the basic theoretical concept, the model which will be used to describe the negotiation process and the data used to calibrate the countries' payoff functions. In Section 3, we present the results of our numerical simulations, and we discuss the impact on the existence and size of stable coalitions of the two burden-sharing rules. Moreover, we show how 'issue linkage' can be used to broaden the originally stable coalition. Finally, some concluding remarks are contained in Section 4.

2. AN ECONOMIC MODEL OF COOPERATION IN R&D AND CO_2 EMISSION REDUCTION

Consider n countries ($n \geq 2$) that interact in a common environment and bargain over emission control of a specific pollutant. Let $W_i(e_1, ..., e_n)$ be a country's welfare function, where e_i, $i = 1, 2, ..., n$, denotes a vector containing country i's emissions and all other economic variables affecting abatement costs and the environmental damage perceived in each country. The function $W_i(\cdot)$, $i = 1, 2, ..., n$, captures countries' interaction in a global environment, as welfare depends on all countries' emissions as well as on other transnational variables (for example trade policy variables). Let $P_i(s)$ denote the value of country i's welfare when it decides to join the coalition s, whereas $Q_i(s)$ is the value of its welfare when country i does not join the coalition s.

As the focus of this section is to analyse the formation of coalition, the only argument of the value of the welfare function is the identity and number of cooperating countries. As shown below, all other variables, including emissions and policy decisions in other countries, enter country i's welfare function, but have already been set at their optimal level (conditional on the coalition structure). Hence, the last decision to be taken concerns whether or not to cooperate (taking into account the consequences on the other economic variables). Let $P_i(\emptyset) = Q_i(\emptyset)$, $i = 1, 2, ..., n$ be a country's non-cooperative payoff (the non-cooperative Nash equilibrium payoff), whereas $P_i(S)$ is country i's payoff when all countries decide to cooperate (the grand coalition is formed).

Two conditions must be met for an environmental coalition to be self-enforcing (see Carraro and Siniscalco, 1993; Barrett, 1994). First, the coalition must be profitable, that is, each country $i \in s$ gains from joining the coalition, with respect to its position when no countries cooperate. Formally, a coalition s is *profitable* if $P_i(s) \geq P_i(\emptyset)$, $\forall i \in s$. Second, no country must have an incentive to free-ride, i.e. the coalition s must be *stable*. More precisely, a country i chooses the cooperative strategy if $P_i(s)$, the country's payoff for belonging to the coalition s, is larger than $Q_i(s\backslash i)$, the country's payoff when it exits the coalition, and lets the other countries sign the cooperative agreement. Hence, $Q_i(s\backslash i) - P_i(s)$, $i \in s$, is a country's incentive to defect from a coalition s, whereas $P_i(s \cup i) - Q_i(s)$, $i \in s$, is the incentive for a non-cooperating country to join the coalition s. Thus, a coalition s is stable iff: (i) there is no incentive to free-ride, that is, $Q_i(s\backslash i) - P_i(s) < 0$ for each country i belonging to s; (ii) there is no incentive to broaden the coalition, i.e. $P_i(s \cup i) - Q_i(s) < 0$ for each country i which does not belong to s.[7]

It has been shown that under fairly general conditions stable coalitions exist (see Donsimoni, Economides and Polemarchakis, 1986). However, this does not satisfactorily address the problem of protecting international commons, because, as has been demonstrated both in the oligopoly and in the environmental literature (see, for example, d'Aspremont and Gabszewicz, 1986; Hoel, 1991; Barrett, 1994; Carraro and Siniscalco, 1992, 1993), stable coalitions are generally formed by $j \leq n$ players, where j is a small number, regardless of n.[8] If stable coalitions are small, and countries are symmetric, the impact of their emission reduction on total emissions is likely to be negligible. However, the above-mentioned results concern models in which countries are supposed to be symmetric, that is, they share the same welfare function. One of the goals of this chapter is therefore to verify whether these results also hold in the case of asymmetric countries.

To this end, asymmetries have to be made explicit. Two problems arise. First, in order to achieve clear results, a specific functional form for the welfare function has to be chosen. Second, its parameters have to be calibrated for numerical simulations to provide information on the identity of countries which non-cooperatively decide to join a coalition.[9] Let us therefore consider the following formulation of the environmental game which introduces 'issue linkage' into the standard model that can be found in Carraro and Siniscalco (1992), Barrett (1994), and Chander and Tulkens (1994).

The model that we are going to present explicitly considers the interactions between the government and domestic firms in one country, and among governments in different countries. Firms maximize profit; countries maximize their own welfare, which includes profits, consumer surplus and environmental quality.

Consider an industry with n firms facing an inverse demand function $p(Y)$, where $Y = y_1 + y_2 + \ldots + y_n$ is the total quantity produced. Each firm has a cost of production $C_i(y_i, x_i, x_{-i})$, which is a function of its own production y_i, of the amount of research x_i that it undertakes, and the amount $x_{-i} = (x_1, x_2, \ldots x_{i-1}, x_{i+1}, \ldots, x_n)$ that its rivals undertake. For simplicity's sake, both $p(\cdot)$ and $C(\cdot)$ are assumed linear:

$$p(Y) = a - bY \qquad \text{with } a, b > 0 \qquad (1)$$

and

$$C_i(y_i, x_i, x_{-i}) = (c_i - x_i - \sigma_i \Sigma_j x_j) y_i \qquad i = 1, 2, \ldots, n \qquad (2)$$

where p is the price of the homogeneous good and $a > c_i > 0$, $1 > \sigma_i > 0$, $i = 1, 2 \ldots, n$, and $Y \leq a/b$. Notice that both own research and other firms' research help to reduce firm i's production costs. In particular, positive R&D externalities or spillovers σ_i imply that some benefits of each firm's R&D flow without payment to other firms. In our specification, the external effect of firm j's R&D is to lower firm i's unit production cost. One interpretation is that successful innovations of rivals can be imitated, and that imitation is cheaper than innovation. The cost of R&D is assumed to be quadratic, reflecting the existence of diminishing returns of R&D expenditures (see Equations 3a and 3b). Firms' strategies consist of a level of R&D and production. These two variables are set simultaneously and non-cooperatively by the n firms.

Each firm is assumed to be located in a different country and subject to a country-specific environmental legislation. The n firms are supposed to sell to a single global market. For simplicity, neither transportation nor other additional costs of selling the good abroad are considered. Each government can use, either cooperatively or non-cooperatively, two strategic variables: the abatement level q_i which is imposed on firms (for example an emission standard), and the degree of spillovers occurring in the production of innovations. Countries, in other words, can allow or push greater technological spillovers by means of appropriate instruments (say, technological cooperation). In particular, we assume that:

- there are just two degrees of spillovers, σ_{1i} and σ_{2i} (where $\sigma_{1i} < \sigma_{2i}$), $i = 1, 2, \ldots, n$.
- technological cooperation affects the level of technological spillovers in the following way: if countries cooperate on technological development and diffusion, the degree of spillovers is σ_{2i}; otherwise it is all, σ_{1i}, $i = 1, 2, \ldots n$.

Possible explanations are: (i) cooperating countries allow for patents agreements that provide the other countries in the coalition with a larger share of their own innovative technology; (ii) cooperating countries sign agreements on technology transfers and/or joint R&D projects that make the degree of innovation spillovers in the coalition larger than outside the coalition.

As previously stated, countries can also cooperate to protect the environment. Negotiations on environmental policies can take place independently of those on technological cooperation. In this case, technological spillovers are independent of the optimal cooperative abatement level. However, if the two negotiations are linked, we assume the following: if a government chooses to join the coalition, that is, to sign an international agreement on environmental and technological cooperation, the effect is twofold: the abatement level imposed on domestic firms is higher; and its policy towards technology transfers is differentiated. A government joining the coalitions makes possible larger R&D spillovers with the other members of the coalitions than with countries which do not sign the cooperative agreement. Vice versa, if a government does not join the coalition, both the abatement level imposed on the domestic firm and the degree of technological spillovers are lower. More formally, *if negotiations on environmental and technological cooperation are linked, the degree of innovation spillovers is larger among countries which cooperate than among countries which do not cooperate.*

This amounts to saying that the knowledge produced by firm i which spills over a firm j is larger when country i and country j choose cooperatively their environmental and technology policy than when they do not cooperate. Following the literature on R&D cooperation,[10] we define σ_{2i} as the 'information exchange' parameter, and σ_{1i} as the 'technological leakage' parameter. For simplicity's sake, we normalize σ_{1i} to zero, and we define $\sigma_{2i} = \beta_i > 0$. Hence, β_i (<1) is the 'differential technological leakage' or the 'coalition information exchange'.

Notice that the above assumptions define the benefit of linking the negotiation on the environment with that on technological cooperation. More cooperation is achieved, that is, a higher innovation spillover is allowed for, only among those countries which also cooperate to reduce emissions. Through this linkage, countries belonging to an environmental coalition can induce other countries to cooperate, because technological cooperation, if linked to environmental cooperation, provides an extra incentive to join the agreement.

Firm i's profit function can be defined as follows:

$$\pi_i(Y, x_i, x_{-i}, q_i) = [(a - bY) - (c_i - x_i - \beta_i \Sigma_j x_j)] y_i$$
$$- 1/2 g_i x_i^2 - 1/2 \Phi_i q_i^2 \qquad \text{if } i, j \in s \quad (3a)$$

$$\pi_i(Y, x_i, q_i) = [(a - bY) - (c_i - x_i)] y_i$$
$$- 1/2 g_i x_i^2 - 1/2 \Phi_i q_i^2 \qquad \text{if } i \in s \quad (3b)$$

where $\tfrac{1}{2}g_i x_i^2$ denotes the cost of R&D investments, whereas $\tfrac{1}{2}\Phi_i q_i^2$ is the cost of abating a level q_i of emissions. The quadratic abatement cost function reflects the existence of diminishing marginal returns in the abatement technology.

The environmental problem arises because the production activity of the n firms produces polluting emissions, which also damage all foreign countries (a global externality). Let v_i be the emission–output ratio of the ith firm, $i = 1, \ldots, n$. The level of emissions in country i is:

$$e_i = v_i y_i - q_i \geq 0 \qquad i = 1, \ldots, n \qquad (4)$$

In plain words, emissions are proportional to the output level, but can be reduced by the abatement activity imposed by the government and carried out by the firm. We assume that the firm's innovation effort affects only the economic but not the environmental features of the production technology. Hence, the firm's R&D does not affect the parameter v_i.[11]

The environmental damage depends on the emissions produced by all firms. The damage function can thus be written as:

$$D_i(E) = m_i(e_1 + e_2 \ldots + e_n) \qquad i = 1, \ldots, n \qquad (5)$$

where $E = e_1 + e_2 \ldots + e_n \geq 0$ are total global emissions and m_i, the marginal damage, parametrizes the level of perceived damage from pollution. By substituting Equation (4) into (5), we get:

$$D_i(Y, q) = m_i[(v_1 y_1 - q_1) + \ldots + (v_n y_n - q_n)] \geq 0 \qquad (6)$$

where $q = (q_1, \ldots, q_n)$.

In each country the government, or a regulatory agency, takes two decisions. The first one is whether or not to join the coalition. The government joining the coalition knows that it will obtain benefits both from environmental and technological cooperation, as the two issues are linked. The decision about cooperation is taken by anticipating that all countries which do not cooperate cannot profit from the coalition innovation leakage. The second decision concerns the environmental standard, i.e. the abatement level to be imposed on the firms. Both decisions are taken by maximizing a social welfare function defined as the sum of the domestic firm's profits, the domestic consumers' surplus, minus the environmental damage borne by the country:[12]

$$W_i(Y, x, q) = \pi_i(Y, x, q_i) + CS_i(Y) - D_i(Y, x, q) \qquad i = 1, \ldots, n \qquad (7)$$

Given the linearity of the inverse demand function, it is easy to show that $CS_i(Y) = \frac{1}{2}by_i^2$. The government sets the abatement (emission) levels by maximizing the welfare function $W(Y, E, q)$.

The firm's decisions are taken by maximizing the profit function (3a) or (3b). The firm's first-order conditions are:

$$h_i - bY + (k_i - b)y_i + \beta_i \Sigma_{j \neq i} k_j y_j = 0 \quad i, j \in s \tag{8a}$$

$$h_i - bY + (k_i - b)y_i = 0 \quad i \notin s \tag{8b}$$

where $h_i = a - c_i$, $k_i = 1/g_i$, $i = 1, 2, ..., n$.[13] We assume $k_i < b$ for firms' reaction functions to be negatively sloped. Moreover, we assume that no firm finds it profitable to exit the market, whatever the size of the environmental coalition. The reason is that we want to guarantee that the environmental game is played by n governments (that is, n firms).

One interesting feature of the model is that when governments bargain solely on emissions, the payoff function $P_i(s)$ coincides with the function representing countries' payoffs in Carraro and Siniscalco (1992), Barrett (1994) and Chander and Tulkens (1994). When countries negotiate on both R&D and environmental cooperation, the payoff function $P_i(s)$ is the sum of two components: the environmental one, resulting from negotiation on emissions only, and the economic one, which quantifies the benefits from R&D cooperation as a function of the number of cooperators. The additivity of the two components simplifies the analysis. For example, if $P_{1i}(s)$ is the payoff of country i when it joins coalition s on issue 1, and $P_{2i}(s)$ denotes country i's payoff when it joins the same coalition on issue 2, we have that the idea of 'issue linkage' solves the profitability problem if $P_{1i}(s) + P_{2i}(s) \geq P_{1i}(\emptyset) + P_{2i}(\emptyset)$ for all $i \in s$, where for some $i \in s$ we may have $P_{1i}(s) \leq P_{1i}(\emptyset)$ or $P_{2i}(s) \leq P_{2i}(\emptyset)$.[14] Similarly, there is no incentive to leave the linked coalition (that is, the coalition is internally stable) if $P_{1i}(s) + P_{2i}(s) \geq Q_{1i}(s\backslash i) + Q_{2i}(s\backslash i)$ for all $i \in s$, where for some $i \in s$ we may have $P_{1i}(s) \leq Q_{1i}(s\backslash i)$ or $P_{2i}(s) \leq Q_{2i}(s\backslash i)$.

The model described above has been calibrated using the set of data provided by Musgrave (1994). The profit and damage functions are calibrated for five groups of countries or regions: (1) Japan; (2) the US and Canada; (3) the European Union; (4) Eastern Europe and Russia; and (5) India and China. To abbreviate, in what follows each of the five groups will be referred to as a 'country'. Table 9.1 offers some relevant information on the environmental and economic features of the five countries. These data are derived from Musgrave (1994). Let us assume that the emission level (the third row of Table 9.1) corresponds to optimal emissions when no environmental damage is perceived and no abatement is carried out. This is used to calibrate the parameter v_i, given the value of the representative firm's output which is obtained as follows. In the oligopoly model described above we have that profits are equal to by_i^2. Hence, from the available data on aggregate profits in each region and assuming $b = 0.1$, we can obtain the value of y_i. Moreover, the last two rows provide the damage per unit of emission (the parameter m_i), and the slope of the marginal abatement cost function (the parameter Φ_i), respectively.

Table 9.1 Countries' data set

	Countries				
	1 Japan	2 US and Canada	3 European Union	4 Eastern Europe and Russia	5 China and India
GDP(billion US dollars)	2779	4920	5141	2800	557
Population (millions)	122	270	373	360	1862
GDP per cap. (US dollars)	22779	18222	13783	7778	299
CO_2 Emissions (million tons) (v_iy_i)	238	1320	815	1263	722
Emissions per cap. (tons)	1.951	4.889	2.185	3.508	0.388
Emissions per unit of GDP (tons per million US dollars)	85.64	268.29	158.53	451.07	1296.23
Domestic damage (as no. of deaths per million tons of emissions – the assumed increase of mortality rate is 0.2 per million people)	24.4	54	74.6	72	372.4
Domestic damage (US dollars per ton of emissions - the assumed average value of life is $349 000) ($m_i$)	8.51	18.83	26.01	25.10	129.84
Slope of marginal abatement cost function (ϕ_i)	4.89	0.54	1.02	0.44	0.62

Source: Musgrave (1994)

Following Musgrave (1994), damages are measured in terms of an increase in mortality rates.[15] Hence, this value has been computed using statistical information on the number of deaths per millions of emissions, based on the aggregate country population and on mortality rates in the different countries. In order to achieve a monetary evaluation of environmental damages, the value of life has been assumed to be a function of average per capita income. However, in order to avoid discrimination across countries, Musgrave assumes the same value of life in all five countries ($349 000). As a consequence, countries with high population (for example China and India) are characterized by a large marginal emission damage.

The marginal abatement cost Φ_i reflects the loss of consumer surplus due to reduced output of the damage-generating activity as well as the loss of surplus in the consumption of substitute products, the price of which rises. Musgrave (1994) assumes this marginal cost to be inversely related to emissions per unit of GDP.

The parameter h_i has been calibrated in such a way that the first-order conditions for profit maximization in the non-cooperative case are met in all countries. This guarantees that calibrated parameters reproduce the firms' optimal choice in the base year.[16] Finally, k_i ($< b$) was chosen to reproduce the amount of R&D carried out in each country as a share of GDP. Different degrees of R&D spillovers (the parameter β_j) were considered in the simulation experiments.

Even if the values chosen for these crucial parameters are largely an approximation of the real values, they are consistent with available information and may be found fairly reasonable. For example, the largest marginal abatement cost has been computed for Japan, whereas low values refer to Russia and Eastern Europe and to India and China. Notice that this parameter is also low for North America. On the other side, the marginal environmental damage is very low in Japan, whereas it achieves very large values in India and China, given the assumption of equal value of life across countries and the expected impact of global warming on mortality rates.

Given the above values of the model parameters, it is possible to compute the equilibrium values for total costs and emissions when some countries form a coalition, i.e. sign an environmental agreement, whereas other countries decide to free-ride. Given the payoff for each country and for all possible coalitions, it is possible to single out the stable coalitions, where stability has been previously defined.

This calculation has been performed both in the case in which the coalition members use the Nash bargaining equilibrium concept to share the cost of reducing emissions, and in the case in which they use the Shapley value. The results are presented in the next section.

3. ISSUE LINKAGE WITH HETEROGENEOUS COUNTRIES UNDER DIFFERENT BURDEN-SHARING RULES

Let us start by assuming that countries negotiate on emissions only and let us compute the stable coalitions resulting from the adoption of two different burden-sharing rules: Nash bargaining and the Shapley value. Countries outside the coalition minimize their own cost function with respect to their own emissions, given the strategy of the cooperating countries.

Definitions provided in Section 2 imply that a coalition is stable when there is neither an incentive to exit, nor an incentive to enter the coalition. This is the case for only two coalitions: the one formed by countries 1, 3 and 5 and the one formed by countries 1, 4 and 5. Table 9.2 summarizes these results by showing both the coalitions in which cooperating countries have no incentive to free-ride, but there is an incentive to broaden the coalition, and those which are stable.

Table 9.2 Stable coalitions – Nash bargaining burden-sharing rule

Coalitions without incentive to free-ride	Stable coalitions (no incentive to free-ride or to broaden the coalition
All two-country coalitions	
{1, 2, 5}	
{1, 3, 5}	{1, 3, 5}
{1, 4, 5}	{1, 4, 5}

Notice that all coalitions formed by four countries and the grand coalitions are unstable. This confirms the conclusions arrived at in the case of symmetric countries by Carraro and Siniscalco (1992, 1993).

A similar analysis using the Shapley value as the burden-sharing rule leads to the results shown in Table 9.3: the only stable coalition is formed by countries 2, 4 and 5. Again this confirms the theoretical result contained in Barrett (1997a) where it is shown, using the same model of negotiations on emissions only, that coalitions formed by four and five players are unstable.

Table 9.3 Stable coalitions – Shapley value burden-sharing rule

Coalitions without incentive to free-ride	Stable coalitions (no incentive to free-ride or to broaden the coalition)
All two-country coalitions	
{1, 3, 5}	
{2, 3, 5}	
{3, 4, 5}	
{2, 4, 5}	{2, 4, 5}

We have therefore reached two conclusions: first, consistent with previous theoretical findings in the symmetric case, at most three countries decide to sign the environmental agreement; second, the identity of the three signatories, which is crucial to assess the emission abatement power of the coalition in the asymmetric case, depends on the chosen burden-sharing rule. Only country 5 belongs to all stable coalitions that have been singled out. Notice that country 5 is the one with the highest environmental damage, that is, the one receiving the highest benefit from environmental cooperation.[17]

Let us now consider the case in which countries negotiate on both R&D and environmental cooperation. Table 9.4 shows the stable coalitions for increasing values of β, the amount of R&D spillovers, and for the two burden-sharing rules considered in this chapter.

Table 9.4 Stable and optimal coalitions with 'issue linkage'

β	Nash bargaining		Shapley value	
	Stable coalition	Optimal coalition	Stable coalition	Optimal coalition
No linkage (environmental coalition only)	{1, 2, 5} {1, 3, 5} {1, 4, 5}	{1, 2, 3, 4, 5}	{2, 4, 5}	{1, 2, 3, 4, 5}
0.0005	{1, 2, 3, 4} {1, 2, 3, 5}	Voting game (Table 9A.1)	{2, 4, 5}	Voting game (Table 9A.2)
0.0008	{1, 2, 3, 4} {1, 2, 3, 5} {1, 2, 4, 5} {1, 3, 4, 5}	Voting game (Table 9A.3)	{1, 2, 4, 5}	Voting game (Table 9A.4)
0.001	{1, 2, 3, 4}	Voting game (Table 9A.5)	{1, 2, 3, 4, 5}	{1, 2, 3, 4, 5}
0.01	{1, 2, 3, 4, 5}	{2, 3, 4}	{1, 2, 3, 4, 5}	{2, 3, 4, 5}
0.05	{1, 2, 3, 4, 5}	{2, 3, 4}	{1, 2, 3, 4, 5}	{2, 3, 4}
0.1	{1, 2, 3, 4, 5}	{2, 3, 4}	{1, 2, 3, 4, 5}	{2, 3, 4}
0.15	{1, 2, 3, 4, 5}	{2, 3, 4}	{1, 2, 3, 4, 5}	{2, 3, 4}

Let us look first at the column showing the stable coalitions. It is easy to see that issue linkage increases the size of the stable coalitions because at least a fourth country decides to belong to it. This result was previously anticipated because the linkage of R&D and environmental cooperation is designed to join two agreements with complementary features. Whereas benefits on R&D cooperation can be restricted only to members of the coalition (if spillovers are low), when countries cooperate on environmental protection their action benefits all countries, including the free-riders. Therefore, the linkage of the two negotiations extends the stability features of the R&D agreement to the joint R&D and environmental agreement. At the same time, the environmental benefits which would be lost because of the instability problem, and which might be relevant, are added to the benefits from R&D cooperation.

The second remark concerns the effects of an increase of the parameter β. When R&D spillovers increase, the size of the stable coalition tends to be larger (all countries join it). This is explained by the fact that when β increases, the gain from R&D cooperation increases whereas the loss from being excluded from the coalition increases. Hence the differential benefits from R&D cooperation becomes larger and larger (consistently with the prediction in d'Aspremont and Jacquemin, 1988). This implies that the incentive to defect from the linked coalitions decreases when β increases because the gain from free-riding on the environment is offset by the loss of being excluded from the gains yielded by R&D cooperation.

A third result is related to the comparison between the two burden-sharing rules. First of all notice that the Shapley value burden-sharing rule reduces the indeterminacy on the equilibrium outcome. Contrary to the Nash bargaining rule, the Shapley value guarantees a unique equilibrium stable coalition for all values of the R&D spillovers. Moreover, for small values of β the stable coalition coincides with the one which forms without linkage. Then country 1 enters the coalition and finally, for larger values of the R&D spillovers, country 3 joins the coalition. According to this result, the European Union (country 3) would be the most reluctant to sign the linked agreement. This apparent paradox is explained by contrasting stability and optimality of a coalition.

The optimal coalition for country i is defined as the coalition which maximizes country i's payoff. It is therefore generally different from the stable one. In particular, in the case in which R&D and environmental cooperation are linked, the optimal coalition is smaller than the stable coalition (see the third and fifth column of Table 9.4). Moreover, there may be no consensus among the countries on which coalition is actually optimal. For example, country i may prefer some countries, say j and h, as partners in the cooperating group, but these countries may want to sign the agreement with country k, rather than with i. And k may prefer i and h rather than j and k. In this case, shown in the first three rows of Table 9.4, a voting game must be analysed. This game may not possess an equilibrium, that is, no stable agreement would be signed even when at least one stable coalition exists.

Let us further explain these two conclusions by starting from the first one. Why is the optimal coalition smaller than the stable one? In the game analysed in this chapter, the environmental benefit increases with the number of countries in the coalition (more abatement is carried out). Hence the largest environmental benefit is achieved when all countries sign the agreement. This is not the case for R&D cooperation. Countries which join the R&D coalition share two benefits. First they have at their disposal a more efficient technology (production costs are lowered by R&D cooperation). Second, they share a competitive advantage *vis-à-vis* those countries which do not belong to the R&D cooperation. In a Cournot oligopoly this implies that countries in the coalition have larger market share and profits. This second benefit is lost as soon as all countries enter the R&D coalition. Therefore, there is an incentive for some countries to exclude other ones from the coalition. When 'issue linkage' takes place, the incentive to exclude some countries may still arise if the relative weight of benefits from R&D cooperation is sufficiently large.

This is what actually happens in our simulation experiments. Consider values of β above 0.05. Whatever the adopted burden-sharing rule (Nash bargaining or Shapley value), the stable coalition is formed by all countries, whereas the optimal one includes only countries 2, 3 and 4. In other words, these latter countries would like to exclude countries 1 and 5 from the optimal linked coalition.

Why is there consensus on the optimal coalition? The reason is that countries 2, 3, and 4 achieve their maximum payoff when they join the same coalition and this coalition is internally stable (no country has an incentive to exit). Hence, they agree to exclude countries 1 and 5 from the coalition. The intuition is that Europe and North America prefer to achieve the high environmental benefit provided by environmental cooperation with Eastern Europe rather than the technological benefits provided by R&D cooperation with Japan. This also solves the apparent paradox previously singled out (Europe would be the last to cooperate). When the optimality of the coalition and the incentive to exclude some countries are both accounted for, Europe belongs to all optimal (and internally stable) coalitions.

The conclusion that the optimal coalition is formed by countries 2, 3 and 4 may be modified when the R&D costs become very large in the two less developed countries. This is shown in Table 9.5 which reports the results of a simulation with an artificially higher value for R&D costs in China and India and in Eastern Europe. In this case, the optimal coalition is formed by countries 1, 2 and 3 because the loss from giving away technological cooperation with Japan becomes larger than the environmental benefit provided by environmental cooperation with Eastern Europe. Notice that the stable coalition is still formed by all countries.

The lesson to be derived from these results is therefore that a careful assessment of the relative weight of the benefits provided by the two agreements must be carried out in order to understand each country's incentive to join a given coalition (whenever it is not optimal to join the stable coalition).

When the parameter β is low, there is no consensus among countries on the optimal coalition. In order to explain this situation, consider the case in which $\beta = 0.0005$ and the burden-sharing rule is Nash bargaining. Table 9A.1 in the

Appendix shows the preferences of the five countries with respect to the internally stable coalitions (the ones from which no player wants to exit but from which some players can be excluded). Notice that countries 2, 3, 4 and 5 prefer the coalition which they do not belong to, that is, they prefer to free-ride on the other countries' cooperative abatement effort. Only country 1 belongs to the coalition that it considers as optimal. Therefore, even if stable coalitions exist, almost all countries are better off when free-riding. Moreover, no country considers the grand coalition (that is, the linked agreement signed by all countries) as optimal. Similar remarks also hold when considering the second-best coalition for all countries. Therefore, for reasonable rules of the voting game among the five countries, it would be difficult for an equilibrium to emerge.

Table 9.5 The effect of increasing asymmetries in R&D costs

β	$k_i (= 1/g_i)$	Nash bargaining		Shapley value	
		Stable coalition	Optimal coalition	Stable coalition	Optimal coalition
No linkage (environmental coalition only)		{1, 2, 5} {1, 3, 5} {1, 4, 5}	{1, 2, 3, 4, 5}	{2, 4, 5}	{1, 2, 3, 4, 5}
0.1	As in Table 9.4	{1, 2, 3, 4, 5}	{2, 3, 4}	{1, 2, 3, 4, 5}	{2, 3, 4}
0.1	k_i is 3/5 of the one in Table 9.4 for countries 4 and 5	{1, 2, 3, 4, 5}	{1, 2, 3}	{1, 2, 3, 4, 5}	{1, 2, 3}
0.1	k_i is 1/2 of the one in Table 9.4 for countries 4 and 5	{1, 2, 3, 4, 5}	{1, 2, 3}	{1, 2, 3, 4, 5}	{1, 2, 3}

The situation is different if the Shapley value is the burden-sharing rule (see Table 9A.2). In this case, countries 1, 3 and 4 prefer the coalition (2,4,5) which is also the second best for country 2. Therefore a small transfer to country 5 would be sufficient to induce this country to vote for the coalition (2, 4, 5). The transfer could be provided both by countries 2 and 4 and by countries 1 and 3 even if they do not sign the agreement (the latter is called external commitment transfer in Carraro and Siniscalco, 1993). The hint that the Shapley value rule is more likely to lead to an equilibrium outcome is also confirmed by Table 9A.4, where countries 1, 2, 3 and 4 prefer the coalition (1, 2, 4, 5) but country 5 prefers the coalition (1, 2, 3, 4), where it free-rides. Again a transfer from the first four countries to country 5 would lead the coalition (1, 2, 4, 5) to emerge as an equilibrium.

The other cases in which the voting game does not provide a clear equilibrium outcome are summarized in Tables 9A.3 and 9A.5 which show some inconsistencies in countries' preferences for the coalition they would like to take place.

4. CONCLUSIONS

In this chapter we have presented an empirical analysis of the formation of emission abatement coalitions in the case of five asymmetric world regions. The analysis has been carried out using two different burden-sharing rules (Nash bargaining and Shapley value) in order to assess the effects of these rules on the stability of environmental coalitions. The main goal was to verify the intuition that 'issue linkage' could constitute a useful strategy to guarantee the profitability (as argued in Cesar and de Zeeuw, 1996; Folmer, van Mouche and Ragland, 1993) and the stability (as argued, for example, by Folmer and van Mouche, 1994; Barrett, 1997b; Carraro and Siniscalco, 1997) of international environmental coalitions.

Our results provide only a partial support to the above intuition. It is true that the stable coalition is usually larger (more countries sign the agreement) when countries negotiate on two linked issues. However, this is not sufficient to conclude that the stable coalition would emerge at the equilibrium. We have indeed shown that the stable coalition may not be optimal. More precisely, in the case in which R&D and environmental cooperation are linked, the optimal coalition is smaller than the stable one. Furthermore, countries may disagree on the coalition that they find as optimal. In this case, countries' choices may be conflicting and no equilibrium may exist.

Therefore, one must be cautious when proposing 'issue linkage' as a way of solving the problems often arising in international environmental negotiations. Even when the usual profitability and stability problems can be solved, the conflict between optimality and stability of coalitions may be such that 'issue linkage' reduces, rather than increases, the number of signatories to the international environmental agreement. In some cases, there may not even exist any equilibrium coalition.

The above conclusions are just the beginning of a research programme that should assess the impact of institutions, such as burden-sharing rules or negotiating rules, on the achievement of environmental agreements with many signatories. With respect to this objective, the environmental model proposed in this chapter is the most favourable to the emergence of stable coalitions, as it assumes that environmental reaction functions are orthogonal (no leakage). Further work will therefore be devoted to assess the effects of marginal increases of leakage on the coalition stability. Moreover, in the model no uncertainty is introduced. As a consequence, the validity of the results should be checked against the presence of economic and scientific uncertainty, the related risk parameters, and the learning process that might take place.

Finally, more reliable results could be achieved whenever the numerical analysis of this chapter could be replaced by an explicit theoretical analysis of the optimality and stability of linked negotiations when countries are asymmetric. Moreover, the effects on the conclusions of alternative definitions of coalition stability should be considered (for example, the ones proposed in Bloch, 1994; Chew, 1994, Ecchia and Mariotti, 1997; or in Yi and Shin, 1994).

NOTES

1. On the role of transfers and the problems related to the use of this instrument, see Carraro and Siniscalco (1993).
2. See Bloch's (1997) excellent survey.
3. The impact that imperfect monitoring may have on the structure of the agreement and on the number of signatories is analysed in Petrakis and Xepapadeas (1996).
4. The problem of analysing the impacts of different burden-sharing rules on the outcome of environmental negotiations has already been addressed by Barrett (1997a) and Botteon and Carraro (1997). However, these papers do not consider the possibility of 'issue linkage'.
5. Numerical simulations which assess the existence of stable coalitions when the burden-sharing rule is based on the Shapley value concept can also be found in Barrett (1997a).
6. This problem is directly related to the fact that 'issue linkage' may transform the monotonic payoff function of environmental benefits into a non-monotonic function.
7. This definition corresponds to that of cartel stability presented in the oligopoly literature (see d'Aspremont and Gabszewicz, 1986). A similar definition is also used in Barrett (1994). A similar definition is also proposed by Yi and Shin (1994) under the name 'open membership stability'. Notice that the second part of the definition of stability may not be necessary. If not included, we have the notion of 'closed membership stability' used in Yi and Shin (1994) and in Carraro and Soubeyran (1995).
8. More satisfactory results are presented in Heal (1994), where a fixed cost of forming the coalition is introduced, and in Bauer (1993), which considers the possibility that a bloc of countries bargains with other blocs of countries. However, the results in this latter paper are based on a conjectural variations equilibrium concept which does not coincide with the fix-point defined by the best-reply mapping (that is, it is not a Nash equilibrium).
9. As previously mentioned, an explicit analytical derivation of the equilibrium coalition structures with asymmetric countries would be quite complex even with simple functional forms.
10. Pioneering works in this field are those by Katz (1986), and d'Aspremont and Jacquemin (1988). A good survey is Katz and Ordover (1990). Recent developments can be found in Wu and de Bondt (1991) and Motta (1993).

11. This assumption is relaxed in Carraro and Siniscalco (1997). The conclusions of the present chapter do not depend on this assumption.
12. Notice that the index i refers both to the firm and to the country, because one representative firm is assumed in each country.
13. It is easy to see that, at the equilibrium, $x_i = k_i y_i$, $i = 1, 2, ..., n$.
14. In this chapter the payoffs on the two issues are additive. More generally, it should be $P_{iu}(s) \geq P_{iu}(\emptyset)$ for all $i \in s$, where $P_{iu}(\cdot)$ denotes country i's payoff when the two issues are linked (see Carraro and Siniscalco, 1995, 1996).
15. This assumption is very restrictive. However, given the uncertainty on the assessment of damages from climate change (see chapter 6 of the last IPCC Report) and the fact that the main objective is the analysis of coalition structures rather than an assessment of benefits from environmental cooperation, we preferred to use Musgrave's work which provides a consistent data set.
16. In reality, Musgrave's data do not refer to a specific year but to an average of recent years designed to reproduce the distinctive features of each country/region.
17. The fact that country 5 corresponds to China and India should not lead to the conclusion that the model predicts that China and India will belong to any environmental coalition. In this chapter, we use a measure of environmental damage that may largely differ from the actual damage perceived in each country.

REFERENCES

Barrett, S. (1994), 'Self-Enforcing International Environmental Agreements', *Oxford Economic Papers*, **46**, 878–94.

Barrett, S. (1997a), 'Heterogeneous International Environmental Agreements', in C. Carraro (ed.), *International Environmental Agreements: Strategic Policy Issues*, Cheltenham: Edward Elgar.

Barrett, S. (1997b), 'Towards a Theory of International Cooperation', in C. Carraro and D. Siniscalco (eds), *New Directions in the Economic Theory of the Environment*, Cambridge: Cambridge University Press.

Bauer, A. (1993), 'International Cooperation over Environmental Goods', paper presented at the Oslo seminar on Environmental Economics, 15–17 September 1993.

Bloch, F. (1994), 'Sequential Formation of Coalitions in Games with Externalities and Fixed Payoff Division', presented at the CORE–FEEM Conference on Non-Cooperative Coalition Formation, Louvain, 27–21.8.2, 1995.

Bloch, F. (1997), 'Non-Cooperative Models of Coalition Formation in Games with Spillovers', in C. Carraro and D. Siniscalco (eds), *New Directions in the Economic Theory of the Environment*, Cambridge: Cambridge University Press.

Botteon, M. and C. Carraro (1997), 'Burden-Sharing and Coalition Stability in Environmental Negotiations with Asymmetric Countries', in C. Carraro (ed.), *International Environmental Agreements: Strategic Policy Issues*, Cheltenham: Edward Elgar.

Carraro, C. and D. Siniscalco (1992), 'Transfers and Commitments in International Environmental Negotiations', forthcoming in K.G. Mäler (ed.), *International Environmental Problems: an Economic Perspective*, Dordrecht: Kluwer Academic Publishers.

Carraro, C. and D. Siniscalco (1993), 'Strategies for the International Protection of the Environment', *Journal of Public Economics*, **52**, 309–28.

Carraro, C. and D. Siniscalco (1995), 'Policy Coordination for Sustainability: Commitments, Transfers, and Linked Negotiations', in I. Goldin and A. Winters (eds), *The Economics of Sustainable Development*, Cambridge: Cambridge University Press.

Carraro, C. and D. Siniscalco (1996), 'International Coordination of Environmental Policies and Stability of Global Environmental Agreements', in L. Bovenberg and S. Cnossen (eds), *Public Economics and the Environment in an Imperfect World*, Boston, London and Dordrecht: Kluwer Academic Publishers.

Carraro, C. and D. Siniscalco (1997), 'R&D Cooperation and the Stability of International Environmental Agreements', in C. Carraro (ed.), *International Environmental Agreements: Strategic Policy Issues*, Cheltenham: Edward Elgar.

Carraro, C. and A. Soubeyran (1995), 'R&D Cooperation, Innovation Spillovers and Firms' Location in a Model of Environmental Policy', forthcoming in E. Petrakis, E.S. Sartzetakis and A. Xepapadeas (eds), *Environmental Reputation and Market Structure*, Cheltenham: Edward Elgar.

Cesar, H. and A. de Zeeuw (1996), 'Issue Linkage in Global Environmental Problems', in A. Xepapadeas (ed.), *Economic Instruments for the Protection of Natural Resources and the Environment*, Cheltenham: Edward Elgar.

Chander, P. and H. Tulkens (1994), 'A Core-Theoretical Solution for the Design of Cooperative Agreements on Trans-frontier Pollution', paper presented at the 50th IIPF Congress, Harvard, 22–25 August 1994.

Chew, M.S. (1994), 'Farsighted Coalitional Stability', Department of Economics, University of Chicago.

d'Aspremont, C.A. and J.J. Gabszewicz (1986), 'On the Stability of Collusion', in G.F. Matthewson and J.E. Stiglitz (eds), *New Developments in the Analysis of Market Structure*, New York: Macmillan Press, pp. 243–64.

d'Aspremont, C. and A. Jacquemin (1988), 'Cooperative and Non-cooperative R&D in Duopoly with Spillovers', *American Economic Review*, December, 1133–7.

Donsimoni, M.P., N.S. Economides and H.M. Polemarchakis (1986), 'Stable Cartels', *International Economic Review*, **27**, 317–27.

Ecchia, G. and M. Mariotti (1997), 'The Stability of International Environmental Coalitions with Farsighted Countries: Some Theoretical Observations', in C. Carraro (ed.), *International Environmental Agreements: Strategic Policy Issues*, Cheltenham: Edward Elgar.

Folmer, H., P. van Mouche and S. Ragland (1993), 'Interconnected Games and International Environmental Problems', *Environmental Resource Economics*, **3**, 313–35.

Folmer, H. and P. van Mouche (1994), 'Interconnected Games and International Environmental Problems, II', *Annals of Operations Research*, **54**, 97–117.

Heal, G. (1994), 'The Formation of Environmental Coalition', in C. Carraro (ed.), *Trade, Innovation, Environment*, Dordrecht: Kluwer Academic Publishers.

Hoel, M. (1991), 'Global Environmental Problems: The Effects of Unilateral Actions Taken by One Country', *Journal of Environmental Economics and Management*, **20**(1), 55–70.

Katz, M.L. (1986), 'An Analysis of Cooperative Research and Development', *Rand Journal of Economics*, **17**(4), 527–43.

Katz, M.L. and J.A. Ordover (1990), 'R&D Cooperation and Competition', *Brookings Papers on Economic Activity*, special issue on Microeconomics, 1990, 137–91.

Motta, M. (1993), 'Cooperative R&D and Vertical Product Differentiation', *International Journal of Industrial Organisation*, **10**, 643–61.

Musgrave, P. (1994), 'Pure Global Externalities: International Efficiency and Equity', paper presented at the 50th IIPF Conference, Harvard, 22–26 August 1994.

Petrakis, E. and A. Xepapadeas (1996) 'Environmental Consciousness and Moral Hazard in International Agreements to Protect the Environment', *Journal of Public Economics*, **60**, 95–110.,

Yi, S. and H. Shin (1994), 'Endogenous Formation of Coalitions in Oligopoly: I. Theory', Dartmouth College, Working Paper 94–18.

Wu, C. and R. de Bondt (1991), 'On the Stability of R&D Cooperation', DTEW, Katholieke Universiteit Leuven.

APPENDIX

Table 9A.1 Internally stable coalition ranking (Nash bargaining)

β = 0.0005 Nash bargaining	Countries				
	1	2	3	4	5
1°	{1, 2, 4, 5}	{1, 3, 4, 5}	{1, 2, 4, 5}	{1, 2, 3, 5}	{1, 2, 3, 4}
2°	{1, 3, 4, 5}	{3, 4, 5}	{2, 4, 5}	{2, 3, 5}	{2, 3, 4}
3°	{1, 2, 3, 5}	{1, 2, 4, 5}	{1, 3, 4, 5}	{1, 2, 4, 5}	{1, 2, 4, 5}
4°	{2, 4, 5}	{2, 4, 5}	{1, 4, 5}	{2, 4, 5}	{2, 4, 5}

Table 9A.2 Internally stable coalition ranking (Shapley value)

β = 0.0005 Shapley value	Countries				
	1	2	3	4	5
1°	{2, 4, 5}	{1, 2, 3, 5}	{2, 4, 5}	{2, 4, 5}	{1, 2, 3, 4}
2°	{3, 4, 5}	{2, 4, 5}	{1, 2, 3, 5}	{3, 4, 5}	{2, 3, 4}
3°	{2, 3, 4, 5}	{2, 3, 5}	{1, 2, 3, 4}	{1, 4, 5}	{2, 4, 5}

Table 9A.3 Internally stable coalition ranking (Nash bargaining)

β = 0.0008 Nash bargaining	Countries				
	1	2	3	4	5
1°	{1, 2, 4, 5}	{3, 4, 5}	{1, 2, 4, 5}	{1, 2, 3, 5}	{1, 2, 3, 4}
2°	{1, 3, 4, 5}	{1, 3, 4, 5}	{2, 4, 5}	{2, 3, 5}	{2, 3, 4}
3°	{1, 2, 3, 5}	{1, 2, 4, 5}	{1, 3, 4, 5}	{1, 2, 4, 5}	{1, 2, 4, 5}
4°	{1, 2, 3, 4}	{2, 4, 5}	{3, 4, 5}	{2, 4, 5}	{2, 4, 5}

Table 9A.4 Internally stable coalition ranking (Shapley value)

β = 0.0008 Shapley value	Countries				
	1	2	3	4	5
1°	{1, 2, 4, 5}	{1, 2, 4, 5}	{1, 2, 4, 5}	{1, 2, 4, 5}	{1, 2, 3, 4}
2°	{1, 3, 4, 5}	{1, 2, 3, 5}	{2, 4, 5}	{1, 3, 4, 5}	{2, 3, 4}
3°	{2, 4, 5}	{2, 4, 5}	{1, 3, 4, 5}	{2, 4, 5}	{1, 2, 4, 5}
4°	{1, 2, 3, 5}	{2, 3, 5}	{1, 2, 3, 5}	{3, 4, 5}	{2, 4, 5}

Table 9A.5   Internally stable coalition ranking (Nash bargaining)

$\beta = 0.001$ Nash bargaining	\multicolumn{5}{c}{Countries}				
	1	2	3	4	5
1°	{1, 2, 4, 5}	{3, 4, 5}	{2, 4, 5}	{1, 2, 3, 5}	{1, 2, 3, 4}
2°	{1, 3, 4, 5}	{1, 2, 4, 5}	{1, 2, 4, 5}	{2, 3, 5}	{2, 3, 4}
3°	{1, 2, 3, 5}	{2, 4, 5}	{1, 3, 4, 5}	{1, 2, 4, 5}	{1, 2, 4, 5}
4°	{1, 2, 3, 4}	{1, 3, 4, 5}	{3, 4, 5}	{2, 4, 5}	{2, 4, 5}

10. Environmental conflicts and interconnected games: an experimental note on institutional design

Stephan Kroll, Charles F. Mason and Jason F. Shogren[1]

1. INTRODUCTION

Conflicts over environmental resources involve the strategic interactions of many nations. Such conflicts are often resolved by contracts that appear disadvantageous to some countries. Why would a country willingly agree to an outcome that makes it worse off? One possible explanation is that these nations interact in several distinct games at once, with the disadvantages of one contact offset by advantages of another, for example, more trade for less transboundary pollution (Folmer, van Mouche and Ragland, 1993, Folmer and van Mouche, 1994; Cesar, 1994). When these games are interconnected, the aggregate outcome can differ from the sum of outcomes of the single games, especially in repeated play where one nation can punish the other for non-cooperative behaviour. Linking two or more issues can generate greater payoffs by allowing countries (a) to exchange concessions across games, that is, quid pro quo, or (b) to use more flexible punishment strategies.

Nations have a choice – they can adapt an existing institution, like the World Trade Organization (WTO), to address environmental problems, or they can create a parallel environmental institution, that is, a GEO (global environmental organization). Most environmental conflicts commonly employ a parallel frame, for example the Montreal Protocol or the Rio conference. Separating trade from the environment 'would relieve pressure from GATT to be an environmental body as well as the cornerstone of the international trading system' (Esty, 1994, p. 80). The International Labour Organization (ILO) or the World Intellectual Property Organization (WIPO) might be better models than GATT for a GEO (see Esty, 1994).

This chapter explores how two elements of institutional design affect gaming behaviour in the lab – (1) explicit or implicit linkages between the two games,[2] and (2) the existence of pre-play communication or 'cheap talk'. An explicit link requires one joint institutional frame that integrates distinct actions into a single payoff before any decisions on how to play; an implicit link only requires two parallel institutions where the players make the connections themselves during play. The advantages of explicit links are that payoffs are more transparent, outcomes are less susceptible to rent-seeking (Petersmann, 1991), and that cooperation is less 'brittle'.[3] Disadvantages include institutional inertia and high transaction costs (Esty, 1994). Political passions could be excited by linkage (Fox, 1995; Krueger, 1995). Concessions in one issue might hurt the interests of domestic groups that are not concerned at all about the other issue, which could have unpleasant future repercussions for the empowered party.

While there is no reason in principle for outcomes to differ between the joint institution and parallel institution designs, in practice there are reasons to expect some efficiency loss in a parallel institution. When the games are connected, both players must figure out the implicit payoff structure before they can coordinate on two seemingly asymmetric actions. And not only must each agent make such calculations, each must believe that the other agent will also make the requisite calculations. By contrast, the joint institution design does not require agents to coordinate on asymmetric actions, and so may be simpler to discover and it may be easier for agents to anticipate that the rival will likewise make this discovery. Our experimental results support these expectations – payoffs are significantly lower in the parallel frame. We then alter the institutional design to test whether players could mitigate these efficiency losses through non-binding commitments, that is, cheap talk.[4] The results show that cheap talk did not recapture efficiency losses. Non-binding commitments do not necessarily compensate for the lack of an explicit link between distinct actions and joint payoffs.

2. AN EXAMPLE

As a motivating example, consider two nations linked by concurrent and repeated trade and environmental games (Folmer, van Mouche and Ragland, 1993). Country 1 restricts imports from country 2, an action country 2 would like to see end. Country 2 exports pollution to country 1, an action country 1 would like to see end. Tables 10.1a and 10.1b show the two games in normal form. In the trade game, the nations choose between low (LI) or high (HI) import restrictions; in the environmental game, they choose between low (LP) and high (HP) pollution emissions.

Table 10.1a The trade game

A:	LI_2	HI_2
LI_1	2,1	–3,2
HI_1	5,–1	0,0

Table 10.1b The pollution game

B:	LP_2	HP_2
LP_1	1,2	–1,5
HP_1	2,–3	0,0

Suppose two separate negotiations emerge. If player 1 and 2's discount rates exceed 0.6, such that the Folk theorem is fulfilled, (LI_1, LI_2): (2,1) can be supported as an equilibrium outcome in each period of the trade game, and (LP_1, LP_2):(1,2) can be supported in the environmental game.[5] Other outcomes cannot be supported, even in an infinitely repeated game, because they violate the minimax criterion. This eliminates the actions that yield the highest joint payoffs [(HI_1,LI_2): (5,–1), (LP_1, HP_2): (–1,5)].[6]

By linking the two games, basing negotiations on an exchange of concessions across the two issues, nations can obtain the highest joint payoffs. Country 1 increases imports from country 2; in exchange, 2 reduces the pollution exported to 1. For example in NAFTA, Mexico increases imports from the US, and the US reduces pollution export into Mexico. Concession exchange can be implicit or explicit depending on whether the nations use two parallel institutions or one joint institution. Their choice of institutional frame can affect efficiency.

In a parallel frame (again Table 10.1), the nations must implicitly link actions and joint payoffs as they exchange concessions across games. If they make this link successfully, the efficient action can be supported as an equilibrium in each game given that discount rates exceed 0.2 for each player. Joint payoffs are maximized when country 1 chooses high import restrictions and low pollution, and country 2 chooses low import restrictions and high pollution.[7] These actions imply (HI_1, LI_2):(5,–1) in the trade game and (LP_1, HP_2):(–1,5) in the environmental game, yielding a joint payoff of (4,4). Country 1 is willing to impose low import restrictions in exchange for country 2 selecting a low pollution level.

The joint institution explicitly links the two games before any choice of action, thereby transforming the two 2 × 2 games into one 4 × 4 game (Table 10.2). Each country now makes only one decision, choosing either LIP_i, $LIHP_i$, $HILP_i$, or HIP_i. For example, under LIP_1 country 1 chooses the action of low import restrictions and pollution; similarly, under $LIHP_1$ country 1 selects low import restrictions and high pollution. The action pair that maximizes joint payoffs, $(HILP_1, LIHP_2)$, is transparent because the links are explicit. As in the parallel frame, this outcome is also an equilibrium given that both players' discount rates exceed 0.2.[8]

Ideally, both institutional frames will generate actions that maximize joint payoffs. But the joint frame is likely to work because the symmetric outcome

(4,4) stands out among the others and is an obvious focal point. In contrast, the efficient outcome is not immediately obvious in the parallel frame. Both countries need to figure out the implicit joint payoff structure while they play before they can coordinate the two seemingly asymmetric actions; moreover, it must be common knowledge that such determinations have been made. This opens the door for more mistakes and less efficiency.

Table 10.2 The joint institution

	LIP_2	$HILP_2$	$LIHP_2$	HIP_2
LIP_1	3,3	–2,4	1,6	–4,7
$LIHP_1$	4,–2	–1,–1	2,1	–3,2
$HILP_1$	6,1	1,2	4,4	–1,5
HIP_1	7,–4	3,–4	5,–1	0,0

When the joint game is impossible due to political or pragmatic reasons, nations might be able to generate greater payoffs in the parallel frame by using non-binding communication or 'cheap talk'. Cheap talk is costless and non-binding communication, which can convey information and aid in coordination.[9] It can help players reach an equilibrium with higher joint payoffs but does not reduce the number of equilibria.[10] This is because the outcome of any equilibrium in the game without cheap talk can be matched by a babbling equilibrium. In the babbling equilibrium, agents send uninformative messages in the non-binding stage, and then play actions corresponding to an equilibrium in the game without cheap talk.

3. EXPERIMENTAL DESIGN

We designed four treatments to compare the parallel and joint institutions with and without cheap talk. All design features were identical across treatments except for the institution and cheap talk features. We denote the design for a parallel institution without cheap talk as treatment PI, and the design for a joint institution without cheap talk as treatment JI. Each subject was paired up with an unknown participant for the entire session of a treatment.[11] In the PI treatment, each dyad played the two 2 × 2 tables presented in Tables 10.3a and 10.3b simultaneously, where the numbers represented the amount of tokens both subjects could earn (150 tokens = $1). In each period, one subject of each dyad chose a row in both tables and the other subject chose columns. To capture the infinitely repeated game in the lab, we used a random end-game procedure. Twenty periods were played in each treatment. At the end of each period $t \geq 20$ one subject drew a chip from a bag containing seven white chips and one red chip. The experiment continued to period $t + 1$ if a white chip was drawn, and terminated if the red chip was drawn. Thus, the continuation probability was 7/8. Treatment PI had 29 periods, JI 20 periods, PI–CT 31 periods, and JI–CT 26 periods (defined below). The treatments lasted between 1 and 2 hours, and the subjects earned between $15 and $30.

Table 10.3a Parallel games in the experiment

A:	C1	C2
R1	60,50	10,60
R2	100,30	40,40

Table 10.3b Parallel games in the experiment

B:	C1	C2
R1	50,60	30,100
R2	60,10	40,40

Treatment JI was identical to treatment PI except that it used a joint institution, where subjects played a 4×4 table (Table 10.4). Here both subjects chose one row in each period. Treatments PI–CT and JI–CT were identical to PI and JI, respectively, with the addition of cheap talk. Each period of the cheap talk treatments had two stages. In stage 1, each subject announced to the other what he or she intended to play, in stage 2 he or she made a binding row or column choice. The binding choice did not have to be consistent with the non-binding commitment.

Table 10.4 Joint game in the experiment

	C1	C2	C3	C4
R1	110,110	60,120	90,150	40,160
R2	120,60	70,70	100,90	50,100
R3	150,90	90,100	130,130	70,140
R4	160,40	100,50	140,70	80,80

Each treatment was run in a computer lab with 14 subjects recruited at the University of Wyoming. At the beginning of each treatment the instructions were read aloud, followed by a practice session that used a sample 3×3 table. After all relevant questions had been addressed, a treatment began.

4. RESULTS: PARALLEL VERSUS JOINT INSTITUTIONS

We start by testing whether the institutional frame affects efficiency. Table 10.5a presents the frequency of outcomes in the treatments without cheap talk.

Outcome (R3,C3) is the Pareto-efficient combination. This is realized in the PI treatment when subject 1 chooses row 2 in game A and row 1 in game B and subject 2 chooses column 1 in game A and column 2 in game B. In the JI treatment this outcome is realized when subject 1 plays row 3 and subject 2 plays column 3. The payoffs are (130,130). Outcome (R4,C4) is the Nash equilibrium of the one-shot game. This obtains in the PI treatment when subject 1 chooses row 2, and subject 2 chooses column 2, in each game, or when subject 1 plays row 4 and subject 2 plays column 4 in the JI treatment. The payoffs are (80,80). Finally, 'others' includes any other combinations.

Table 10.5a Outcome frequencies in treatments without cheap talk

	PI	JI	Total
(R3, C3)	47	80	127
	(75.2)	(51.8)	
(R4, C4)	37	21	58
	(34.3)	(23.7)	
Others	119	39	158
	(93.5)	(64.5)	
Total	203	140	

Table 10.5b Action frequencies in treatments without cheap talk

	PI	JI	Total
R3	178	190	368
	(217.8)	(150.2)	
R4	168	70	238
	(140.9)	(97.1)	
Others	60	20	80
	(47.4)	(32.7)	
Total	406	280	

We observe that subjects in the JI treatment were more likely to play the Pareto-efficient combination than subjects in the PI treatment.[12] There were nearly twice as many observations of the Pareto-efficient combination in the JI treatment as in the PI treatment (80 versus 47), despite the fact that the PI treatment had about 30 per cent fewer total observations (140 versus 203). Indeed, had the 127 Pareto-efficient outcomes been identically distributed across the two treatments, we would have anticipated 51.8 observations in the PI treatment and 75.2 observations in the JI treatment.[13]

Clearly, the observed pattern of play differs between the two treatments. But is this disparity significant? To investigate this issue, we regard observations as having been generated by two multinomial distributions, and test for equality of these distributions. That is, we ask if the observed pattern of play, regarded as two distinct samples, can be considered as drawn from the same population (Mood, Graybill and Boes, 1974). Under the null hypothesis of identical distributions, the test statistic is distributed as a chi-squared variate with $k-1$ degrees of freedom, where k is the number of events in the multinomial distribution. Considering the distribution of play over the outcomes (R3, C3), (R4, C4), and others, so that $k=3$, we obtain a test statistic of 43.39. Compared to a chi-squared variate with two degrees of freedom this is significant at better than the 1 per cent level. Focusing on the distribution of the Pareto-efficient outcome, regarding all other observations as 'other', where $k=2$, we procure a test statistic of 41.06. Compared to a chi-squared variate with one degree of freedom this is again significant at better than the 1 per cent level.

We therefore conclude that behaviour in the two treatments was not drawn from the same population. Subjects in the joint institution were significantly more likely to select the Pareto-efficient outcome than those in the parallel institution.

While there is a significant difference between the distributions of outcomes under the two treatments, this does not imply a corresponding difference between individual play. Perhaps, by chance, a large frequency of individuals played their part of the Pareto-efficient combination in the PI treatment, but were matched with someone who played, say, the one-shot Nash action. To see if the differences documented above persist at the individual level, Table 10.5b presents the distribution of play, at the individual level, for the PI and JI treatments. The test statistic of equal distributions based on these data is calculated as 38.91, again strongly significant. Evidently there is a pronounced difference in the way individuals play these two games.

5. RESULTS: DOES CHEAP TALK HELP?

One plausible explanation for the relatively poorer efficiency in the parallel institution is that subjects had a harder time identifying the Pareto-efficient outcome as it entailed two asymmetric actions. A closely related hypothesis is that subjects were not sure that their rival had identified the optimal arrangement. In either event we should observe a greater frequency of Pareto-efficient play in sessions that allow subjects to communicate through non-binding messages before actual play. Specifically, the distribution of play in our parallel institutions with cheap talk (hereafter, PI–CT) treatment should be noticeably different from the distribution of play in the original parallel institutions treatment.

This hypothesis may be tested using the data in Table 10.6a, where the distributions of the three outcomes under the PI and PI–CT treatments are compared. Again, under the null hypothesis of identical distributions the test statistic is a chi-squared with two degrees of freedom. In this case the test statistic is 7.51, which is significant at the 5 per cent level. But if we focus specifically on the frequency of Pareto-efficient play, comparing the distribution based on (R3, C3) and 'other', we obtain a test statistic of 2.44. While cheap talk may appear to reduce the tendency for subjects to select the Pareto-efficient outcome, this effect is not statistically significant. We conclude that differences in play between the PI treatment and the PI–CT treatment are largely due to the larger tendency to play the one-shot Nash equilibrium in the cheap talk treatment. By contrast, there is no apparent difference in the tendency to play the Pareto-efficient combination.

Table 10.6a Outcome frequencies in the binding stages of the treatments with parallel institutions

	PI	PI–CT bind	Total
(R3, C3)	47	37	84
	(40.6)	(43.4)	
(R4, C4)	37	63	100
	(48.3)	(51.7)	
Others	119	117	236
	(114.1)	(121.9)	
Total	203	217	

Table 10.6b Action frequencies in the binding stages of the treatments with parallel institutions

	PI	PI–CT bind	Total
R3	178	156	334
	(161.4)	(172.6)	
R4	168	206	374
	(180.8)	(193.2)	
Others	60	72	132
	(63.8)	(68.2)	
Total	406	434	

212 Game theory and the environment

This similarity between distributions in the PI treatment with and without cheap talk remains in force when we look at patterns of individual play (see Table 10.6b). Here again the test statistic is not significant at conventional levels, and so we fail to reject the null hypothesis of identically distributed *individual* play between the PI and PI–CT treatments.

The inability of cheap talk to promote increased efficiency is somewhat surprising, in light of our remarks above. Perhaps this is due to a lack of information in the cheap talk – subjects babble. To analyse the validity of this explanation we compare the distribution of promised actions (those from stage 1, the cheap talk stage) with the distribution of binding actions (those from stage 2, actual play), for individuals (see Table 10.7a). The test statistic we obtain is 79.28, which is highly significant. This indicates that there is a pronounced difference between the actions subjects said they would take and the actions subjects actually played. Cason (1995) suggests that subjects' messages may influence play in the early rounds of a repeated game, but that they gravitate towards babbling in later stages (with later messages ignored). This suggests the hypothesis that the significant difference between non-binding and binding actions we found in the context of Table 10.7a may be largely due to differences in later rounds of the experiment. If so, a comparison of non-binding and binding actions based on earlier rounds, for example, the first ten rounds, would reveal no significant differences. Table 10.7b provides the relevant data for this test. The test statistic here is 13.32, which is reduced relative to the value calculated based on all observations. None the less, it remains significant at the 1 per cent level. In contrast to Cason's results, we conclude that the cheap talk stage in the parallel institution treatment contained little useful information, even in the early rounds.

Table 10.7a *Action frequencies in binding and cheap talk stages of the treatment with parallel institutions and cheap talk (all periods)*

	PI–CT bind	PI–CT cheap	Total
R3	156	147	303
	(151.5)	(151.5)	
R4	206	106	312
	(156.0)	(156.0)	
Others	72	181	253
	(126.5)	(126.5)	
Total	434	434	

Table 10.7b Action frequencies in binding and cheap talk stages of the treatment with parallel institutions and cheap talk (periods 1–10)

	PI–CT bind	PI–CT cheap	Total
R3	50	48	98
	(49.0)	(49.0)	
R4	65	42	107
	(53.5)	(53.5)	
Others	25	50	75
	(37.5)	(37.5)	
Total	140	140	

While cheap talk did not enhance efficiency in the PI treatments, the reader may wonder if it would be efficiency-enhancing in the joint institution treatment. To examine this possibility, we compare the distribution of outcomes in stage 2, where actions are binding, of the JI–CT treatment against the initial JI treatment. Table 10.8 presents the relevant data for this comparison. Part a uses all observations from the two treatments; part b focuses on the second half (periods 11–20). The test statistic for the entire set of observations is 15.00, which is significant at the 1 per cent level. The statistic from the second half of the treatments, however, is smaller, and insignificant at conventional levels. We conclude that play differed early on, but that these differences dissipated towards the end of the experiment. More specifically, focusing on the distribution of Pareto-efficient play, we procure a test statistic of 13.18 for all observations, again significant at better than the 1 per cent confidence level. This can be attributed to a significantly smaller frequency of Pareto-efficient play under the PI–CT treatment. Looking at the observations in periods 11 through 20, the test statistic drops to 4.24, which is not significant at the 1 per cent level for the second half of observations.

While cheap talk appears to hinder efficiency in the joint institution treatments, the JI–CT framework is still more efficient than the PI–CT framework. Table 10.9 contains the distribution of actual outcomes for these two treatments (that is, actions from stage 2, the binding stage). We obtain a higher proportion of Pareto-efficient play in the JI–CT treatment. Further, the test statistic for the hypothesis of identical distributions is 23.53, strongly significant. This inference is reinforced by the test based just on the distribution of Pareto-efficient versus 'other' play, where the test statistic is 20.06, again significant at better than the 1 per cent level.

Table 10.8a Outcome frequencies in the binding stages of the treatments with a joint institution (all periods)

	JI–CT bind	JI	Total
(R3, C3)	67	80	147
	(83.1)	(63.9)	
(R4, C4)	53	21	74
	(41.8)	(32.2)	
Others	62	39	101
	(57.1)	(43.9)	
Total	182	140	

Table 10.8b Outcome frequencies in the binding stages of the treatments with a joint institution (periods 11–20)

	JI–CT bind in periods 11-20	JI in periods 11–20	Total
(R3, C3)	35	47	82
	(41.0)	(41.0)	
(R4, C4)	16	10	26
	(13.0)	(13.0)	
Others	19	13	32
	(16.0)	(16.0)	
Total	70	70	

The literature is mixed on how non-binding commitments affect behaviour. Effects depend not only on the kind of game, but also on the method of communication. Our results are partially in contrast to Cason and Davis (1995), Cason (1995), and Palfrey and Rosenthal (1991), which all state that communication affects behaviour in systematic ways, at least for a while.[14] Despite the potential for cheap talk to affect behaviour, Cason and Davis (1995) note that 'the way that communications affect performance is unclear'. Similarly, Palfrey and Rosenthal (1991) observe a correspondence between the contributions and the theoretically predicted equilibrium in a public-goods provision setting, but they are unable to support the hypothesis that this improvement of efficiency is based on the inclusion of cheap talk. The results of Ostrom, Gardner and Walker (1994) and Hackett, Schlager and Walker (1994) are more optimistic regarding the effects of communication. Both works notice that face-to-face communication helps substantially to resolve the tragedy of the commons. Hackett, Schlager and Walker (1994), however, explicitly point to the difference between face-to-face communication and cheap talk.[15]

Table 10.9 Outcome frequencies in the binding stages of treatments with cheap talk

	PI–CT bind	JI–CT bind	Total
(R3, C3)	37 (56.6)	67 (47.4)	104
(R4, C4)	63 (63.1)	53 (52.9)	116
Others	117 (97.4)	62 (81.7)	179
Total	217	182	

When using non-face-to-face communication, one has to ask whether the sequence in which messages are transmitted matters. Cooper et al. (1989, 1992) observed that one-way communication was a more effective way than two-way communication to solve the coordination problem in a battle of the sexes game. Thus, it is possible that we would have observed a greater tendency towards Pareto–efficient play had we allowed only one subject to send messages. Of course, it is not clear what one-way communication would mean in environmental negotiations – unless one envisions a scenario where one country dictates actions to all other players.

6. CONCLUSION

Game theory is useful to examine international environmental conflicts between independent countries. Because countries interact on many issues, linking interconnected games can improve efficiency in an environmental conflict (Folmer, van Mouche and Ragland, 1993; Folmer and van Mouche, 1994). The manifestation of this linkage, however, is important.

In this chapter, we have explored the difference between linking games through a parallel institution and linking games through a joint institution in a laboratory setting. Our experiments reveal two main results of interest not only for environmental or international economists but also for experimental economists. First, we observe an important framing effect. Although the joint and parallel institutions are theoretically equivalent, efficient outcomes are far more common in the joint institution. This result suggests that explicit links between different games, for example by placing one agent in charge of negotiations in many arenas, may enhance efficiency. The question remains open whether the costs of creating a joint frame exceed the benefits of removing the slippage across games.

Second, our results also indicate that cheap talk did not add to efficiency. Rather, little correlation existed between what subjects said they would do and the actions they took. This observation can be seen as a challenge to the common view that a summit where binding contracts are signed has to be prepared with many preliminary meetings. Instead of facilitating efficient outcomes, such meetings might result in attempts at strategic manipulation. For example, our results suggest that the outcome of the climate change conference in Kyoto in December 1997 will not match promises implicit in the non-binding agreements that resulted from the 1992 Rio summit.

Our experiments are among the first that examine interconnected games combined with communication in an experimental setting. Further laboratory research in this area should include more than two players, two issues and two options. It might also be interesting to explore the effect of a one-way communication as opposed to the two-way communication we used. Finally, researchers should test whether our results are sensitive to the payoff structures.

NOTES

1. This chapter is based on the Master thesis of the first author. All views remain our own.
2. In their seminal piece, Tollison and Willett (1979) raise the question of the appropriate institutional setting for issue linkages in the international context.
3. McGinnis (1986) uses 'brittleness' to describe how attempts to delete or include issues may shatter the existing basis of cooperation.
4. Since the 1992 Earth summit in Rio de Janeiro, international global climate change policy, for instance, has used non-binding commitment of actions as nations work up to the binding treaty to be signed in Kyoto in December 1997.
5. Notice that the one-shot game is a prisoners' dilemma. The strategy HI (respectively, HP) is dominant in the trade (respectively, pollution) game. Thus, the outcome (0, 0) would obtain in each game, and these outcomes are Pareto-dominated by the upper left outcomes.
6. Subjects could find a way to agree on these outcomes if side payments were allowed.
7. This corresponds to the quid pro quo strategy in McGinnis (1986).
8. In a one-period game there would be no difference between this game and the isolated games since (HIP, HIP) is the only pure Nash equilibrium and dominates collusive action pairs even though they yield higher payoffs.
9. Farrell (1987, 1995) summarizes some ideas on cheap talk; Farrell and Gibbons (1989), Matthews, Okuno-Fujiwara and Postlewaite (1991) and Rabin (1994) present the analytics of cheap talk; Stein (1989), Matthews (1989), and Conlon (1993) present political applications. Dockner and van Long (1993) note that '[a] noncooperative Nash equilibrium may be interpreted as the outcome of international negotiations, whereby negotiators select self-

10. Cheap talk does not help in either zero-sum games or in one-shot prisoners' dilemma games. This changes, however, when we look at repeated prisoners' dilemmas where several equilibria exist that can be ranked. This situation is similar to a coordination game, so cheap talk might help agents reach an agreement.
11. The instructions are available from the authors upon request.
12. While less successful than the JI treatment in generating efficient outcomes, the PI treatment did outperform the identical games played in isolation. Kroll (1996) shows that subjects in isolated games were significantly less likely to find the joint maximum (100,30) relative to the subjects in the PI treatment (14 per cent versus 45 per cent). This confirms the basic intuition underlying Folmer, van Mouche and Ragland's (1993) model of interconnected games.
13. The expected number of an outcome i in a treatment j is $N_{\bullet i}(N_{j\bullet}/\Sigma N_{k\bullet})$, where $N_{\bullet i}$ is the total number of observations of outcome i, $N_{j\bullet}$ is the total number of observations in treatment j, and the summation is taken over the number of treatments. We refer to the numbers calculated in this fashion as the 'expected frequencies' in the tables that follow; they are presented in parentheses. In the applications discussed in the text, there are 127 total observations of Pareto-efficient play, 203 observations in the PI treatment, and 140 observations in the JI treatment, so that $127 \bullet 203 \div (140 + 203)$ instances of Pareto-efficient play would be expected in the PI treatment if the two distributions were equal.
14. Cason and Davis (1995) and Cason (1995) do not present their experiments in matrix form as we do, or as Phillips and Mason (1992, 1996) do. The latter also look at cooperation in multi-markets, but their interconnected games do not have more equilibria than the single games, and they do not include communication.
15. One of the first influential experimental studies with communication, Friedman (1967), also observes significant effects of face-to-face communication on cooperation.

REFERENCES

Cason, T.N. (1995), 'Cheap Talk Price Signaling in Laboratory Markets', *Information Economics and Policy*, **7**, 183–204.

Cason, T.N. and D.D. Davis (1995), 'Price Communications in a Multi-Market Context: An Experimental Investigation', *Review of Industrial Organization*, **10**, 1–19.

Cesar, H.S.J. (1994), *Control and Game Models of the Greenhouse Effect*, Berlin: Springer-Verlag.

Conlon, J.R. (1993), 'Can the Government Talk Cheap? Communication, Announcements, and Cheap Talk', *Southern Economic Journal*, **60**, 418–29.

Cooper, R., D.V. DeJong, R. Forsythe and T.W. Ross (1989), 'Communication in the Battle of the Sexes Game: Some Experimental Results', *RAND Journal of Economics*, **20**, 568–87.

Cooper, R., D.V. DeJong, R. Forsythe and T.W. Ross (1992), 'Communication in Coordination Games', *Quarterly Journal of Economics*, **107**, 739–71.

Dockner, E.J. and N. van Long (1993), 'International Pollution Control: Cooperative versus Noncooperative Strategies', *Journal of Environmental Economics and Management*, **24**, 13–29.

Esty, D. (1994), *Greening the GATT: Trade, Environment, and the Future*, Institute for International Economics, Washington, DC.

Farrell, J. (1987), 'Cheap Talk, Coordination, and Entry', *RAND Journal of Economics*, **18**, 34–9.

Farrell, J. (1995), 'Talk is Cheap', *American Economic Review*, **85**, 186–90.

Farrell, J. and R. Gibbons (1989), 'Cheap Talk Can Matter in Bargaining', *Journal of Economic Theory*, **48**, 221–37.

Folmer, H., P. van Mouche and S. Ragland (1993), 'Interconnected Games and International Environmental Problems', *Environmental and Resource Economics*, **3**, 313–35.

Folmer, H., and P. van Mouche (1994), 'Interconnected Games and International Environmental Problems, II', *Annals of Operations Research*, **54**, 97–117.

Fox, A.B. (1995), 'Environment and Trade: The NAFTA Case', *Political Science Quarterly*, **110**, 49–68.

Friedman, J.W. (1967), 'An Experimental Study of Cooperative Duopoly', *Econometrica*, **35**, 379–97.

Hackett, S., E. Schlager and J. Walker (1994), 'The Role of Communication in Resolving Commons Dilemmas: Experimental Evidence with Heterogeneous Appropriators', *Journal of Environmental Economics and Management*, **27**, 99–126.

Kroll, S. (1996), 'Interconnected Games in Experiments', Master thesis, University of Wyoming.

Krueger, A. (1995), *Trade Policies and Developing Nations*, The Brookings Institution, Washington, DC.

Matthews, S.A. (1989), 'Veto Threats in a Bargaining Game', *Quarterly Journal of Economics*, **104**, 347–69.

Matthews, S.A., M. Okuno-Fujiwara and A. Postlewaite (1991), 'Refining Cheap-Talk Equilibria', *Journal of Economic Theory*, **55**, 247–73.

McGinnis, M.D. (1986), 'Issue Linkage and the Evolution of International Cooperation', *Journal of Conflict Resolution*, **30**, 141–70.

Mood, A.M., F.A. Graybill and D.C. Boes (1974), *Introduction to the Theory of Statistics*, New York: McGraw-Hill.

Ostrom, E., R. Gardner and J. Walker (1994), *Rules, Games, and Common-Pool Resources*, Ann Arbor, MI: University of Michigan Press.

Palfrey, T.R. and H. Rosenthal (1991), 'Testing for Effects of Cheap Talk in a Public Goods Game with Private Information', *Games and Economic Behavior*, **3**, 183–220.

Petersmann, E.-U. (1991), 'Trade Policy, Environmental Policy and the GATT: Why Trade Rules and Environmental Rules Should be Mutually Consistent', *Aussenwirtschaft*, **46**, 192–221.

Phillips, O.R. and C.F. Mason (1992), 'Mutual Forbearance in Experimental Conglomerate Markets', *RAND Journal of Economics*, **23**, 395–414.

Phillips, O.R. and C.F. Mason (1996), 'Market Regulation and Multimarket Rivalry', *RAND Journal of Economics*, **27**, 596–617.

Rabin, M. (1994), 'A Model of Pre-Game Communication', *Journal of Economic Theory*, **63**, 370–91.

Stein, J.C. (1989), 'Cheap Talk and the Fed: A Theory of Imprecise Policy Announcements', *American Economic Review*, **79**, 32–42.

Tollison, R.D. and T.D. Willett (1979), 'An Economic Theory Of Mutually Advantageous Issue Linkages in International Negotiations', *International Organization*, **33**, 425–49.

11. Environmental conflicts with asymmetric information: theory and behaviour

Terrance M. Hurley and Jason F. Shogren*

1. INTRODUCTION

Environmental conflicts range from legal confrontations over the location of toxic waste storage to violent struggles over access conditions to private or common-property resources. The economic theory of environmental conflict demonstrates that asymmetries in ability – the marginal productivity of effort used to influence the outcome of the conflict – and valuation – the opportunity cost of losing the conflict – are key factors driving the players' effort when fighting over an environmental asset (Dixit, 1987; Baik and Shogren, 1992, 1994). Generally, the more lopsided the conflict, the more probably the players will expend less effort and waste fewer resources fighting over the environmental prize (Shogren, Baik and Crocker, 1991; Hurley and Shogren, 1997). Both players realize that the weaker one has relatively less to gain or is less effective at influencing the outcome of the conflict or both; therefore, the weak uses less effort, which encourages the strong to respond in kind. Both players are better off and so is society, since wasted resources are minimized.

One asymmetry that has not been sufficiently explored in the theory of environmental conflicts is information. An environmental asset generates an informational asymmetry in that tangible market prices strongly signal the value of development, whereas intangible non-market preferences weakly signal the value of preservation. A developer may be unaware of how his or her decision to fragment a forest affects the decline of migratory songbirds and the associated non-market value to bird watchers and others (Askins, 1995). A recreationist may not know or care about the nonmarket value of preserving the habitat of the Abert squirrel when fighting over four-wheeler access rights on Mount Graham, Arizona (Rhodes and Wilson, 1995). A Southern country might concentrate mainly on the market value of timber products from its tropical forest, but a Northern country may account for both the market and non-market value of local biodiversity (see Lutz and Daly, 1991; Myers, 1992).

* Thanks to the editors for their useful comments. All views remain our own.

This chapter examines the theory and behaviour of an environmental conflict with one-sided asymmetric information. We explore the nature of the equilibrium in a conflict between a Northern and Southern country battling over the preservation or development of a Southern resource. We presume the North knows the South's market value of development, but the South does not know the North's non-market value of preservation. The analytical results show that inefficient equilibria can be eliminated at the expense of increasingly subtle refinements on the South's beliefs about the North's value of preservation. Behaviour observed in an experimental application is mixed – some player types understand the refinement quickly, other types do not – which suggests an interdependent learning curve.

2. THEORY

Countries have long held conflicting views over the conservation or development of resources such as the open sea. But conflicts are not limited to how best to use international resources; they also include one country's attempt to sway how another country uses its sovereign land, such as the United States Agency for International Development funding foreign non-governmental organizations (NGOs) to promote the preservation of a Madagascar forest known for its biodiversity. While sovereignty is respected, valuable resources are still expended, attempting to influence global public opinion and local policy makers over the best social use of this forest. Nature's lack of respect for political boundaries can induce a country to challenge another country's sovereign but potentially non-sustainable use and misuse of resources such as soil, vegetation, water and air. Whether the meddling country is ultimately successful is not our focus; rather we examine the real resources spent in the conflict over how to use the resource.

As a motivating example, consider a North–South conflict about the preservation or development of a biodiversity-rich, old-growth forest located in the South. The North wants to preserve the forest for its diversity, while the South wants to develop the forest to increase the per capita income of the local residents. Madagascar, for example, is one of the ecologically richest and economically poorest countries in the world – 150000 of the 200000 species are unique to the island, while the per capita annual income of its 12 million inhabitants is about US$200. Many in Madagascar see development of the forests as a path to greater prosperity and well-being, while many outsiders see preservation as the key to maintaining local and global ecological stability.

Suppose the North and South both expend irreversible effort to influence the likelihood that policies will be enacted to serve their ends (see for example Deacon, 1995). We presume that the North has an informational advantage in that it knows both its own preservation value and the South's development value; the South knows only its development value and not the North's preservation value. The informational asymmetry arises because the South's profit comes from an observable market price, whereas the North's preferences for preservation can only be elicited through non-market valuation techniques such as surveys or indirect market prices. The well-documented imprecision in non-market valuation suggests that the South's data about the North's preferences will be less accurate than the North's data on the South's profits.

The North reveals its hidden preferences to the South in one of two ways: a strategic commitment of observable and irreversible effort in a Stackelberg contest that reveals its concern explicitly, or a complaint to the appropriate official to signal its concern implicitly. The South reveals its willingness to fight for development, but only after the North chooses its signal of discontent.

Analytical Framework

Figure 11.1 illustrates the simple analytics of the conflict. Suppose the South believes it has even odds that the North has a *High* versus *Low* preservation value. If the South's development value exceeds the North's preservation value, the South is the *favourite* – the country with more than a 50 per cent chance of victory in a complete information Nash contest (Dixit, 1987). If the South's development value is less than the North's preservation value, the South is the *underdog*. We transform this incomplete information game into an imperfect information game by assuming that play begins with a third player, Nature, randomly choosing the North's value, *High* or *Low*, with equal probabilities, $P = 0.5$ and $(1 - P) = 0.5$. Nature's choice is revealed only to the North.[1]

Once Nature has chosen the North's preservation value, the North can either signal its willingness to challenge the South without revealing effort, *Taunt*, or explicitly reveal its level of effort by leading in a Stackelberg contest, *Confront*. Let π_H represent the High North's expected payoff given *Confront*, which is derived from a Stackelberg contest; the South's expected payoff in this contest is 45.[2] Let π_L represent the Low North's expected payoff given *Confront*, which is similarly derived from a Stackelberg contest; the South's expected payoff is 50. We consider different levels of the North's expected payoff when choosing *Confront* to show how the reward structure affects equilibrium behaviour.

If the North decides to signal with *Taunt*, the South knows the North will fight, but it does not know how hard the North will fight.[3] Given the South's uncertainty, *Taunt* can convey useful information if the South can deduce from the North's expected payoffs whether a High North is more likely to *Taunt* than a Low North. Let Q and $(1 - Q)$ represent the South's updated probabilities that Nature chose *High* or *Low* given the North chooses *Taunt*.

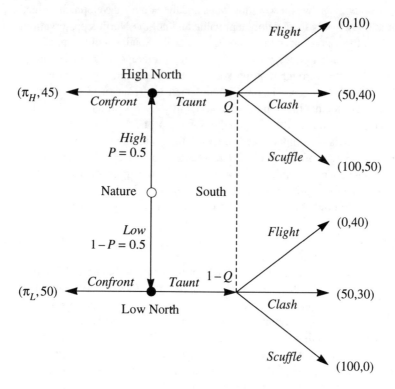

(North's expected payoff, South's expected payoff)

Figure 11.1 Extensive form game

Given *Taunt*, the South strategically commits one of three levels of effort in a Stackelberg contest given its updated beliefs: *Fight*, *Clash* or *Scuffle*. Effort expended is ranked: *Fight* > *Clash* > *Scuffle*. If the South thinks it faces a Low North, it prefers to *Fight* – investing greater effort to guarantee a high probability of victory. If the South thinks it faces a High North, it prefers *Scuffle* – investing minimal resources to encourage the High North to act similarly. But if the South is relatively uncertain as to relative preferences, the South prefers *Clash* – hedging its bets by overinvesting effort against a High North and underinvesting against a Low North. The South's expected payoffs reflect these incentives.

Regardless of whether it has a high or low value, the North prefers *Scuffle* to *Clash* and *Clash* to *Fight*, and thereby wants the South to invest as few resources as possible. The North's expected payoffs are 100, 50, or 0 depending on whether the South chooses *Scuffle*, *Clash* or *Fight*. The North benefits if it can convince the South to minimize effort because the North will have a better chance of preserving the forest.

Equilibria and Refinements

We begin by solving the game in Figure 11.1 using the perfect Bayesian equilibrium concept.[4] First, consider the South's best response to *Taunt* given its updated belief, Q. The South's expected payoff from choosing *Fight*, *Clash* or *Scuffle* is $10Q + 40(1 - Q)$, $40Q + 30(1 - Q)$, or $0Q + 50(1 - Q)$. Therefore, the South's best response to *Taunt* is

$$\beta_S(Q) = \begin{cases} \text{Fight} & \text{for } Q < 0.25 \\ \text{Fight or Clash} & \text{for } Q = 0.25 \\ \text{Clash} & \text{for } 0.75 > Q > 0.25 \\ \text{Clash or Scuffle} & \text{for } Q = 0.75 \\ \text{Scuffle} & \text{for } Q > 0.75 \end{cases}$$

Now consider the High and Low North's best responses, assuming the South chooses *Fight*, *Clash* and *Scuffle* with probability α_F, α_C, and α_S such that $\alpha_F + \alpha_C + \alpha_S = 1$. The North's best response is

$$\beta^i_N(\alpha_C, \alpha_S) = \begin{cases} \text{Confront} & \text{for } \pi_i > 50\alpha_C + 100\alpha_S \\ \text{Confront or Taunt} & \text{for } \pi_i = 50\alpha_C + 100\alpha_S \\ \text{Taunt} & \text{for } \pi_i < 50\alpha_C + 100\alpha_S, \end{cases}$$

where $i = H$ for the High North and $i = L$ for the Low North.

Define σ_H and σ_L as the probabilities the High North or Low North will *Taunt*. The South's equilibrium beliefs are $Q(\sigma_H, \sigma_L)$ and $1 - Q(\sigma_H, \sigma_L)$. If either the High or Low North chooses *Taunt* with some positive probability, the South's belief is determined by Bayes rule, $Q(\sigma_H, \sigma_L) = (\sigma_H^P)/(\sigma_H^P + \sigma_L(1 - P))$. If neither the High nor Low North ever chooses *Taunt*, $\sigma_H = 0$ and $\sigma_L = 0$, the South's equilibrium belief is said to be off the equilibrium path, and Bayes rule cannot be used to update the South's beliefs. Now the perfect Bayesian equilibrium requires that $Q(0,0) = \Omega$ ($0 \leq \Omega \leq 1$) such that the North's expected payoff is greater given *Confront* rather than *Taunt*, $\beta^i_N(\alpha_C, \alpha_S) = $ *Confront* for $i = H$ and L. The perfect Bayesian equilibrium is a combination of σ_H, σ_L, α_C and α_S, and belief Q such that $\beta_S(Q)$, $\beta^H_N(\alpha_C, \alpha_S)$, $\beta^L_N(\alpha_C, \alpha_S)$, and $Q(\sigma_H, \sigma_L)$ are jointly satisfied.

Consider four scenarios to illustrate how the North's relative payoffs affect the nature of the equilibrium in this environmental conflict.

(i) Weak North

Let $\pi_H = \pi_L = 105$, which is the case when the South's development value exceeds both the High and Low North's preservation values such that the South is always the favourite. $\beta_N^i(\alpha_C, \alpha_S)$ implies both the High and Low North prefer *Confront*, $\sigma_H = 0$ and $\sigma_L = 0$, regardless of the probabilities that the South chooses *Fight*, *Clash* or *Scuffle*. Therefore, $Q(0,0) = \Omega$, and the South must choose its best response given Ω, $\beta_S(\Omega)$. Technically, there is an infinite set of pooling perfect Bayesian equilibria, one for each possible belief, Ω, on the unit interval.[5] Both North types commit effort to reveal their strength to the South, thereby preventing it from overcommitting effort. By showing its hand to temper the South's response, the underdog North increases its expected payoff.

(ii) Weak North underdog

Let $\pi_H = 60$ and $\pi_L = 105$, which is the case when the High North is a favourite because its value exceeds the South and the Low North is a weak underdog because its value is substantially lower than the South's. This yields multiple equilibria with two distinct behaviours – a unique partially separating equilibrium (UPSE): $\sigma_H = 1$, $\sigma_L = 0$, $\alpha_F = 0$ and $\alpha_S = 1$, and belief $Q(1,0) = 1$; and multiple pooling equilibria (MPE), one for each $\Omega \leq 0.75$: $\sigma_H = 0$, $\sigma_L = 0$, $\beta_S(\Omega)$, and belief $Q(0,0) = \Omega$ such that $\Omega \leq 0.75$ and $\beta_S(\Omega) \neq$ *Scuffle*. The perfect Bayesian equilibrium reduces the set of possible outcomes under these parameters, but it does not yield a unique prediction.

While a prediction that consists of a set of equilibria may be sufficient in some instances, a unique prediction is usually preferred. The conditions for a perfect Bayesian equilibrium can be refined by sequentially adding intuitively appealing but increasingly subtle restrictions until a unique equilibrium survives. Perfect Bayesian equilibrium refinements such as the intuitive equilibrium (Cho and Kreps, 1987), and the divine and universally divine equilibria (Banks and Sobel, 1987) derive a unique equilibrium by arguing that the South should concentrate its off-the-equilibrium-path beliefs on types of opponents that are most likely to deviate from their equilibrium actions.[6] The opponent type most likely to deviate is established by identifying the 'deviation set' – the set of the South's best responses that would cause the High or Low North to prefer *Taunt* instead of *Confront*. If the High (Low) North's deviation set is empty, the South's posterior beliefs should place no probability weight on the High (Low) North given *Taunt*. If the High (Low) North's deviation set contains, but does not equal, the Low (High) North's deviation set, the South's posterior beliefs should increase its prior belief that its opponent is a High (Low) North, given *Taunt*. That is, if the Low North's deviation set is a subset of the High North's deviation set, and if the Low North chooses to *Taunt*, the High North will most certainly want to *Taunt* too; the reverse need not be true, however. The South's off-the-equilibrium-path belief should then increase its prior that its opponent is a High North such that $\Omega > P = 0.5$.

We use Cho and Kreps's (1987) intuitive refinement to eliminate the equilibria (MPE). The High North's deviation set includes $\beta_S(\Omega)$ such that $\alpha_S = 1.0$ for $\Omega > 0.75$; and $\beta_S(\Omega)$ such that $\alpha_S > 0.2$ and $\alpha_F = 0$ for $\Omega = 0.75$. The Low North's deviation set is empty because its equilibrium payoff, 105, exceeds any possible payoff from deviating by choosing *Taunt*: 0, 50 or 100. Therefore, the South should suspect that a deviation came from a High North, not Low North. If this line of reasoning is correct, the South should update its priors such that $\Omega = 1$. For $\Omega = 1$, the South chooses *Scuffle*, and *Confront* is no longer a best response for the High North. The equilibria defined by (MPE) are thus eliminated. The remaining unique equilibrium defined by (UPSE) is equivalent to an intuitive equilibrium.

The implication is that the High North, a favourite, will signal its willingness to fight by choosing *Taunt*, while the Low North, an underdog, will immediately reveal its strength by choosing *Confront*. The Low North reveals its type to eliminate any misperception that would cause the South to overinvest effort. If the South thinks the Low North is stronger than it really is, the South will try too hard and will reduce the Low North's expected payoff. The Low North avoids this by revealing its effort. The High North will not be hurt because the South should realize that a *Taunt* comes from a High North and therefore has no reason to hedge its effort.

(iii) North underdog

Let $\pi_H = 25$ and $\pi_L = 75$, which is the case when the High North is a favourite because its value exceeds the South and the Low North is an underdog because its value is lower than the South's. Again separating and pooling equilibria exist: (UPSE') $\sigma_H = 1$, $\sigma_L = 1/3$, $\alpha_C = 0.5$ and $\alpha_S = 0.5$, and belief $Q = 0.75$;[7] and (MPE') $\sigma_H = 0$, $\sigma_L = 0$, $\beta_S(\Omega)$, and belief $Q = \Omega$ such that $\Omega \le 0.25$ and $\beta_S(\Omega) = Fight$. We use the divine refinement to eliminate the pooling equilibria (MPE') (Banks and Sobel, 1987). The High North's deviation set includes $\beta_S(\Omega)$ such that $\alpha_S = 1$ for $\Omega > 0.75$; $\beta_S(\Omega)$ such that $0 < \alpha_S < 1$ and $\alpha_F = 0$ for $\Omega = 0.75$; $\beta_S(\Omega)$ such that $\alpha_C = 1$ for $0.25 < \Omega < 0.75$; and $\beta_S(\Omega)$ such that $0.5 < \alpha_C < 1$ and $\alpha_S = 0$ for $\Omega = 0.25$. The Low North's deviation set includes $\beta_S(\Omega)$ such that $\alpha_S = 1$ for $\Omega > 0.75$; and $\beta_S(\Omega)$ such that $\alpha_S > 0.5$ and $\alpha_F = 0$ for $\Omega = 0.75$. Since the High North's deviation set contains, but is not equal to, the Low North's deviation set, the South should expect that deviations are more likely from the High North such that $\Omega > P = 0.5$. For $\Omega > 0.5$, the South chooses *Clash* or *Scuffle*, and *Confront* is no longer a best response for the North favourite because it earns a greater expected payoff from choosing *Taunt*. The equilibria defined by (MPE') are again eliminated. The remaining unique equilibrium defined by (UPSE') is equivalent to a divine equilibrium.

The High North, a favourite, always signals its willingness to fight by choosing *Taunt*, while the Low North, an underdog, signals its willingness to fight by choosing *Taunt* one-third of the time, and immediately reveals its strength by choosing *Confront* two-thirds of the time. The Low North sends these occasional *Taunt* signals in an attempt to exploit the South's lack of information. But if the Low North signals too often, the South will overcommit effort because it will start to believe that the North is weaker on average. The conflict intensity can be minimized where all are better off if they can maintain the delicate balance of all-High and 1/3-Low *Taunts*. The divinity restriction supports this result by stating that the South should perceive better than 50/50 odds that *Taunts* come from a High North.

(iv) Strong North underdog
Let $\pi_H = 60$ and $\pi_L = 75$, which is the case when the High North is a favourite and the Low North is a strong underdog because its value is only slightly lower than the South's. The equilibrium behaviours are: (UPSE") $\sigma_H = 1$, $\sigma_L = 1/3$, $\alpha_C = 0.5$ and $\alpha_S = 0.5$, and belief $Q = 0.75$; and (MPE") $\sigma_H = 0$, $\sigma_L = 0$, $\beta_S(\Omega)$, and belief $Q = \Omega$ such that $\Omega \leq 0.75$ and $\beta_S(\Omega) \neq$ *Scuffle*. Consider the equilibria defined by (MPE"). The High North's deviation set now includes $\beta_S(\Omega)$ such that $\alpha_S = 1$ for $\Omega > 0.75$; and $\beta_S(\Omega)$ such that $\alpha_S > 0.2$ and $\alpha_F = 0$ for $\Omega = 0.75$. The Low North's deviation set is still $\beta_S(\Omega)$ such that $\alpha_S = 1$ for $\Omega > 0.75$; and $\beta_S(\Omega)$ such that $\alpha_S > 0.5$ and $\alpha_F = 0$ for $\Omega = 0.75$. Since the High North's deviation set contains, but is not equal to, the Low North's deviation set, the South should again expect that deviations are more likely from the High North such that $\Omega > P = 0.5$. While this is sufficient to eliminate equilibria defined by (MPE') such that $\Omega \leq 0.5$, it does not eliminate equilibria defined by (MPE") where $0.5 < \Omega < 0.75$ because these beliefs will still encourage both the High and Low North to choose *Confront*. We use the universally divine refinement which adds the restriction that the South places no posterior probability weight on the Low North, $\Omega = 1$, because it is less likely to deviate. Given $\Omega = 1$, both the High and Low North prefer *Taunt*, $\sigma_H = 1$ and $\sigma_L = 1$, which implies $Q(1,1) = 0.5$, contradicting $\Omega = 1$ (Banks and Sobel, 1987). This additional restriction is strong enough to eliminate any of the remaining equilibria defined by (MPE") because it eliminates beliefs $0.5 < \Omega < 0.75$. The remaining unique equilibrium defined by (UPSE") is equivalent to a universally divine equilibrium.

Again the High North, a favourite, always signals with *Taunt*, while the Low North, an underdog, signals with *Taunt* only one-third of the time. Because the Low North's value is approaching the South's value, the Low North has an even stronger incentive to exploit the South's lack of information with *Taunt*. Although this incentive can increase the inefficiency of the conflict, losses can be minimized if they maintain all-High and 1/3-Low *Taunts*. The universal divinity restriction supports this result by stating that the South has to be almost certain that *Taunt* comes from the North favourite because it is more likely to deviate.

3. BEHAVIOUR

The theory of equilibrium refinements relies on a comparison of deviation sets that is increasingly subtle. A key question is whether players actually perceive these subtleties in real gaming experiments.[8] We focus our gaming experiment on scenario (ii) Weak North underdog ($\pi_H = 60$ and $\pi_L = 105$) to see whether the unique partially separating equilibrium [UPSE] or the multiple pooling equilibria [MPE] better organize actual behaviour.

Experimental Design

Fifteen subjects were recruited for each of two sessions.[9] As the subjects entered the room, the monitor assigned them randomly to one of three groups, A1 (High North), A2 (Low North), and B (South), each with five players. The three groups played the game in Figure 11.1 where the A1s and A2s chose between 'L' (*Confront*) and 'R' (*Taunt*); the Bs chose between 'D' (*Fight*), 'M' (*Clash*), and 'U' (*Scuffle*); and $\pi_H = 60$ and $\pi_L = 105$.

Each session had five periods – one practice and four binding. At the beginning of each period, a subject completed a strategy sheet with two sets of questions. The first set elicited a subject's beliefs about how he or she thought the three 'representative' players would play the game. The second set elicited the subject's choices of how he or she wanted to play five games against the representative player(s).[10] The representative players were constructed from the second set of questions by randomly selecting one of the five choices made by each of the five players for a given type. These five randomly selected choices were then used as the five strategy choices for the representative players.

After all subjects had completed their strategy sheets, the monitor determined the representative player's choices for each group, and calculated the results of each game. The resulting earnings – the sum of the earnings for the five games plus a reward for correctly guessing how the 'representative' player in each group played – were returned to the subjects on a round earnings sheet.[11] The round earnings sheet also revealed the strategy choices of the three 'representative' players. A subject's earnings equalled the sum of his or her earnings in the four binding periods multiplied by one cent plus a ten-dollar participation fee.[12]

We used four design features to test more accurately how well the refined equilibrium (UPSE) organized subject behaviour relative to the unrefined equilibrium (MPE): (i) each B subject played against both the representative A1 and A2 player to eliminate the risks from randomizing devices;[13] (ii) the three representative players created a common information set;[14] (iii) we collected multiple observations for each subject – they played five trials of the same game in each period;[15] and (iv) each subject reported his or her subjective beliefs regarding how he or she thought the representative player would play the game (see Banks, Camerer and Porter, 1994).[16]

Results and Discussion

We focus on three behavioural indicators: strategies employed; the actual and predicted proportions of refined and unrefined perfect Bayesian equilibria; and efficiency.

Strategies

Table 11.1 shows the frequency of subjects who employed a particular strategy by period and group. In the second column for the A1 and A2s, 'Strategy'

Table 11.1 Subject strategies by group and period

Player group	Strategy	Period 1[a]	Period 2	Period 3	Period 4	Period 5
A1	[LLLLL][b]	1 (60)	1 (70)	2 (65)	0	0
	[RLLLL]	1 (40)	0	1 (70)	2 (75)	3 (57)
	[RRLLL]	2 (69)	5 (60)	3 (57)	1 (70)	3 (60)
	[RRRLL]	5 (62)	3 (60)	3 (63)	4 (65)	2 (70)
	[RRRRL]	1 (60)	1 (67)	0	1 (70)	1 (80)
	[RRRRR][c]	0	0	1 (50)	2 (50)	1 (70)
A2	[RRRRR][b,c]	5	5	8	9	9
	[RLLLL]	1	2	0	0	0
	[RRLLL]	2	1	2	0	1
	[RRRLL]	0	2	0	1	0
	[RRRRL]	2	0	0	0	0
B	[DDDDD]	0	0	0	1 (0.60)	0
	[MMMDD]	0	0	1 (0.50)	0	0
	[MMMMD]	1 (0.43)	0	0	0	1 (1.00)
	[MMMMM]	3 (0.78)	3 (0.94)	3 (0.78)	5 (0.78)	3 (0.83)
	[UMMMD]	1 (1.00)	1 (0.75)	1 (0.67)	1 (0.75)	1 (0.75)
	[UMMMM]	0	1 (0.67)	0	0	0
	[UUMDD]	1 (0.40)	1 (0.43)	0	0	0
	[UUMMD]	1 (0.43)	0	1 (0.56)	0	0
	[UUUMD]	0	0	1 (0.50)	0	0
	[UUUMM]	1 (0.43)	2 (0.57)	0	0	0
	[UUUUD]	0	0	0	0	1 (0.75)
	[UUUUM]	0	1 (0.00)	0	0	0
	[UUUUU][c]	2 (1.00)	1 (1.00)	3 (0.58)	3 (0.68)	4 (0.79)

[a] Period 1 through Period 5 is the number of subjects that used the particular strategy in that period (A1s' expected payoffs given their average reported belief, or Bs' average reported belief that the A subject is an A1 given that he/she chooses R).
[b] Unrefined perfect Bayesian equilibrium strategy.
[c] Refined perfect Bayesian equilibrium strategy.

represents the number of games in which they chose R and L. For example, Strategy [LLLLL] says that an A1 (or A2) plays a pure strategy of 0 Rs and 5 Ls in the five games; Strategy [RRLLL] says that an A1 (or A2) plays a mixed strategy of 2 Rs and 3 Ls. For the Bs, the Strategy represents the number of games in which they chose U, M and D, for example, Strategy [UUMDD] implies that a B plays a strategy of 2 Us, 1 M and 2 Ds for the five games.

The small numbers in parentheses next to the frequency of A1 strategies (columns 3–7) are the expected payoffs from choosing R given these subjects' average reported beliefs. If this value exceeds 60, game theory predicts that a risk-neutral subject will choose R. For instance, one A1 subject played R in all five games of period 5 (Strategy [RRRRR]). And given this subject's reported beliefs, he or she expected to earn 70 in each game. The subject's beliefs are consistent with his or her actions.[17]

The number in parentheses beside the frequency of B strategies (columns 3–7) is the Bayesian updated belief, Q, given these subjects' average reported beliefs. Recall that if $Q > 0.75$, game theory predicts that a risk-neutral B will choose U; if $0.25 < Q < 0.75$, B will choose M; and if $Q < 0.25$, a B will choose D. For instance, two B subjects played [UUUUU] in period 1. Given these subjects' average reported beliefs, $Q = 1.00$, both subjects strongly believed that only A1 subjects would choose R. These Bs were consistent with their best response U.

Equilibria

Recall that an A1's unrefined perfect Bayesian equilibrium strategy (MPE) is to choose *Taunt* or [LLLLL]; their refined equilibrium (UPSE) is to choose *Confront* or [RRRRR]. Table 11.1 reveals that A1 did not develop a preference for any particular strategy. Only 20 per cent of the A1s chose any equilibrium strategy in the first periods 1–3; one subject played the refined strategy and four played the unrefined strategy. By periods 4 and 5 two subjects played the refined strategy. Behaviour is inconsistent with predictions based on risk neutrality. Some subjects appear risk-loving (for example, Strategy [RRRRR] in periods 3 and 4) as they choose a more risky action with a lower expected payoff; other subjects appear risk-averse (for example, Strategy [LLLLL] in periods 2 and 3), choosing a less risky action with a lower payoff.

In contrast, the A2s moved towards the equilibrium strategy exclusively, [LLLLL]. We see that 50 per cent play the equilibrium strategy in periods 1 and 2, increasing to 80 per cent by period 3 and 90 per cent by periods 4 and 5. Given that the A2s' strategy is much easier to deduce and is independent of any other subject's behaviour, we would be worried about the experimental design if we had not induced A2s' equilibrium behaviour accurately.

For the Bs, we observe a trend towards the refined equilibrium strategy and away from strategies with mixed actions. Recall that the Bs' refined equilibrium strategy (UPSE) is to believe $Q > 0.75$ and to play [UUUUU]. The Bs' unrefined equilibrium strategy (MPE) is $\Omega \leq 0.75$ and $\beta_S(\Omega) \neq Scuffle$, which is equivalent to not playing [UUUUU].[18] In period 1, 20 per cent of subjects play their refined equilibrium strategy, falling to 10 per cent in period 2 before increasing to 30 per cent in periods 3 and 4, and 40 per cent in period 5.

In many instances, the Bs' actions were inconsistent with their beliefs. For example, three subjects played strategy [MMMMM] in all but the fourth period. In all periods, however, the reported beliefs ($Q > 0.75$) suggest that they should have preferred U. Instead, these individuals hedged their bets by selecting M, an action most rewarding when both the A1s and A2s choose R. This suggests some degree of risk aversion. For those Bs who only chose U, beliefs supported their actions in periods 1, 2 and 5, but not in 3 and 4. For the Bs who mixed different actions, the average reported belief generally suggested that they should have preferred M or U exclusively.

Figure 11.2 presents the actual and predicted proportions of refined and unrefined perfect Bayesian equilibrium play.[19] Circles represent session 1, and squares session 2; solid markers (except for the diamond) indicate period 1, and

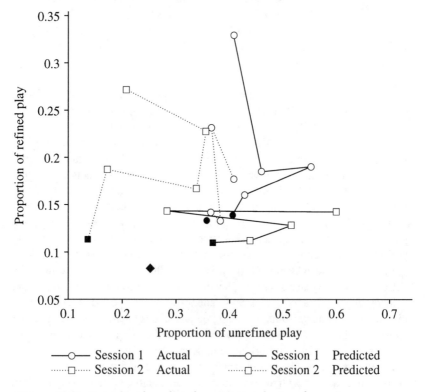

Figure 11.2 Actual and predicted experimental game dynamics

subsequent open markers attached by a solid or dotted line represent periods 2, 3, 4 and 5. The actual proportions are connected by a solid line, while the predicted proportions are connected by a dotted line. The solid diamond reflects a comparative benchmark of purely random play – the proportions of refined and unrefined play assuming all subjects choose randomly between actions with equal probability.

Note that both actual and predicted play tend to move away from random play and towards the refined and unrefined equilibria, although not uniformly. Session 1 play moves towards the refined equilibrium, while session 2 play moves towards the unrefined equilibrium. After five periods, predicted behaviour in session 2 also moves towards the more refined play, while predicted play in session 1 seems to move towards both refined and unrefined play.

For the first three periods, predicted play generally tracks actual play although it tends to underpredict the proportion of unrefined play. In period 4, subjects seemed to expect a significant increase in refined play that did not materialize – in session 1, there was a slight decrease in refined play and a large decrease in unrefined play; while in session 2, there was a slight increase in refined play combined with a large decrease in unrefined play. The period 5 predictions generally lagged towards the actual play in period 4.[20]

Overall, the behavioural patterns seem to be captured by Plott's (1996) discovered preference hypothesis. Plott argued that learning in the lab occurs in three stages. In stage 1, a subject's choices seem random or aimless as he or she tries to understand the nature of the experiment. In stage 2, a subject becomes purposeful as revealed by his or her preference for specific actions. In stage 3, a subject gains sophistication, and his or her actions reveal well-developed preferences for a particular action and an anticipation for other subjects' actions. (also see El-Gamal, McKelvey and Palfrey, 1993).

In the early periods of our gaming experiment, about 50 per cent of the A2s played in equilibrium, and all but one of the A2s moved to equilibrium play by period 5. This suggests that most A2s began in stage 3, and the others started in stage 1 and quickly moved to stage 3. Over half of the Bs played pure strategies, through all five periods, suggesting stage 2 – specific preferences over actions. On average, about 25 per cent of the Bs played an optimal equilibrium strategy given that the A2s chose their equilibrium strategy, a proportion that increased with experience. By period 5, most Bs in stage 2 made it to stage 3. Half of the remaining Bs seemed locked in stage 1, while the other half reached stage 2. The A1s generally played randomly or without an apparent purpose, suggesting stage 1. These results suggest that it is important to improve understanding of the interdependent nature of learning in gaming experiments. A2s learned quickly, some of the Bs figured out the A2s' strategy and acted accordingly, but other Bs did not. A1s could not follow the refinement strategy

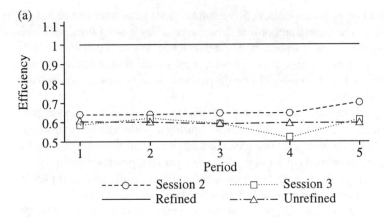
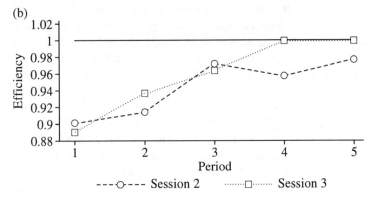
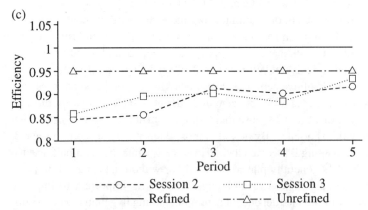

Figure 11.3 Proportions of the maximum obtainable rewards by session and period: (a) A1s, (b) A2, (c) Bs

if some of the Bs did not figure it out as well. This all suggests that more trials are needed to accommodate the interdependent learning needed to eliminate the unrefined equilibrium.

Efficiency

Finally, Figure 11.3 shows the average efficiency of the subjects' choices by group, session and period. We define efficiency as the proportion of the maximum obtainable rewards captured by the subjects. In Figure 11.3, 'Refined' and 'Unrefined' denote efficiency given that all the subjects play the refined [UPSE] and unrefined [MPE] equilibrium. Since the refined and unrefined equilibrium actions are the same for the A2s, a single line denotes efficiency for both refined and unrefined play, '(Un)Refined'. For all three subject groups, the maximum obtainable reward occurs when all subject types play the refined equilibrium.

There are three notable points taken from Figure 11.3. First, with a few exceptions, efficiency increased with experience. Second, efficiency for A2s converged rapidly towards 100 per cent. Third, although the A1s did not generally play either equilibrium strategy, their efficiency was about as great as if they had.

4. CONCLUDING COMMENTS

We conclude with two brief observations on policy. First, falling into a pooling equilibrium due to unrefined beliefs increases the inefficiency of an environmental conflict. But as the signalling game becomes more complex, the rationality required to eliminate inefficient pooling equilibria is not trivial. Refinements demand a player's full concentration to form reasonable beliefs about another player's actions. While our experimental results were not overwhelmingly supportive of such concentration, it remains an open question as to whether this low rationality translates into the wilds with higher stakes and more formidable institutions. Second, the inability to refine beliefs precisely suggests that policy makers might improve efficiency by removing or reducing the informational asymmetries through non-market valuation. But in doing so they also need to look more closely at how the bias and imprecision of non-market valuation affects the efficiency of an environmental conflict. Hurley and Shogren (1998) show that efficiency can suffer if non-market valuation exercises send biased and imprecise signals that make the conflict appear less lopsided. The policy maker who understands the link between effort expended and the nature of the estimated value distribution can affect the efficiency of the environmental conflict.

NOTES

1. Harsanyi (1967–68) first proposed this method of solving games with incomplete information.
2. The first number in parentheses in Figure 11.1 is the North's expected payoffs, the second the South's. We constructed the expected payoffs based on the equilibrium reward structure of the appropriate Stackelberg contest given the North's and South's relative values. We then normalized the payoffs to ease the experimental test of equilibrium refinements discussed in Section 3.
3. The South's incomplete information is indicated by the dotted line labelled South connecting the upper and lower half of the right-hand side of Figure 11.1.
4. A perfect Bayesian equilibrium is a strategy combination and set of beliefs such that: (i) the actions taken at each information set are sequentially rational given a player's beliefs, and (ii) beliefs are updated by Bayes rule on the equilibrium path and consistent with equilibrium behaviour off the equilibrium path. Condition (i) implies that a country's actions must be Nash best responses given its beliefs, while condition (ii) implies that Bayes rule must be used to update a player's beliefs where possible, and where Bayes rule does not apply, beliefs must not provide an incentive for any country to deviate from the equilibrium. See Rasmusen (1989, p. 110) or Fudenberg and Tirole (1991, pp. 324–6).
5. An equilibrium is referred to as 'pooling' when both the High and Low North choose the same initial behaviour: both choose *Confront* or both choose *Taunt*. Multiple equilibria are common when there are off-the-equilibrium-path beliefs in a pooling equilibrium because the perfect Bayesian equilibrium places only mild restrictions on what off-the-equilibrium-path beliefs are acceptable. Any belief satisfying these restrictions constitutes a new equilibrium even though equilibrium actions may be identical for a large set of alternative beliefs. From a practical standpoint, since the equilibrium set of actions on the equilibrium path are unique for this game, equilibrium behaviour is unique.
6. Banks, Camerer and Porter (1994) provides a good intuitive discussion and technical details of these and other refinements.
7. The Low North will choose both *Confront* and *Taunt* with positive probability if it is indifferent between the two actions, which is only the case when $\alpha_C = 0.5$ and $\alpha_S = 0.5$. The South will choose both *Fight* and *Scuffle* with positive probability if it is indifferent between the two actions, which is only the case when $Q = 0.75$. Since the High North prefers *Taunt* to *Confront* when $\alpha_C = 0.5$ and $\alpha_S = 0.5$, the Low North must choose *Taunt* 1/3 of the time so that $Q(1, 1/3) = 0.75$. If the Low North chose *Taunt* less than 1/3 of the time, the South would choose *Scuffle*, which would make the Low North want to deviate and strictly choose *Taunt*. If the Low North chose *Taunt* more than 1/3 of the time, the South would choose *Clash*, which would make both the High and Low North want to deviate and strictly choose *Confront*.
8. Also see Brandts and Holt (1992,1993) and Banks, Camerer and Porter (1994).
9. Additional detail can be found in Hurley (1995, pp. 73–111).
10. All A1 and A2 players played against the representative B; all B players played against the representative A1 and representative A2.
11. We paid subjects $0.25 for each correct prediction to encourage thoughtful revelation of beliefs.
12. A complete set of instructions is available from the authors on request or can be found in Hurley (1995, Appendix C, pp. 160–74).
13. Since the solution to the game relies on the assumption of risk-neutral players, it is important to eliminate as many sources of uncertainty as possible. By having the Bs play both an A1 and A2 in every game, the Bs' hypothesized objective function is conceptually the same, but no longer subject to the risk associated with traditional randomizing devices.
14. In previous experiments, players were randomly matched with a sequence of different opponents such that each player could have a vastly different experience depending on these matchings. Therefore, if two players behave differently, it is not clear whether the difference is due to different *a priori* beliefs, preferences or experiences. By forcing all players to have a common experience within a session, we can eliminate this confounding factor, and test for the importance of experience between sessions.

15. Previous experiments made only one observation per player per period. Therefore, it is unclear whether differences in play from one period to the next are the result of a change in preferences, or preferences for multiple actions, say, in a mixed strategy. By having subjects play multiple games under a common information set, we can better identify a player's preferences over actions, and whether those preferences are for a single action or for multiple actions.
16. This method supplies information on beliefs and whether deviations from equilibrium behaviour are related to out-of-equilibrium beliefs.
17. A similar number is not reported for the A2s because their equilibrium strategy should always be [LLLLL], regardless of their beliefs.
18. Note that without the strategy sheets we would never know the Bs' off-the-equilibrium-path actions or beliefs.
19. Since previous experiments did not collect sufficient information to determine whether off-the-equilibrium-path play supported equilibrium behaviour, we maintain consistency with these previous studies by ignoring the Bs' actions off the equilibrium path when calculating the proportion of refined and unrefined play in Figure 11.2. Predicted play is based on the subjects' predictions of the 'representative' players' actions.
20. We conducted Wilcoxon tests on both the aggregate and disaggregate data. At the aggregate level, enough statistical evidence exists to reject the hypothesis that subject behaviour was purely random. We also reject the hypothesis that subject behaviour was identical in sessions 1 and 2. Disaggregating by group, sufficient evidence exists to reject random play for the A2s in both sessions and the Bs in session 1. There is insufficient evidence, however, to reject purely random play by the A1s in both sessions and the Bs in session 2. For a detailed discussion of the statistical methods and results see Hurley (1995). This result supports Brandts and Holt's (1992) conclusion that the equilibrium may depend on the dynamics of the game and experience of the players. Also see the work of Camerer and Weigelt (1988) and McKelvey and Palfrey (1992).

REFERENCES

Askins, Robert (1995), 'Hostile Landscapes and the Decline of Migratory Songbirds', *Science*, **267**, 1956–7.

Baik, Kyung Hwan and Jason Shogren (1992), 'Strategic Behavior in Contests: Comment', *American Economic Review*, **82**, 359–62.

Baik, Kyung Hwan and Jason Shogren (1994), 'Environmental Conflicts with Reimbursement for Citizen Suits', *Journal of Environmental Economics and Management*, **27**, 1–20.

Banks, Jeffrey, Colin Camerer and David Porter (1994), 'An Experimental Analysis of Nash Refinements in Signaling Games', *Games and Economic Behavior*, **6**, 1–31.

Banks, Jeffrey and Joel Sobel (1987), 'Equilibrium Selection in Signaling Games', *Econometrica*, **55**, 647–61.

Brandts, Jordi and Charles A. Holt (1992), 'An Experimental Test of Equilibrium Dominance in Signaling Games', *American Economic Review*, **82**, 1350–65.

Brandts, Jordi and Charles A. Holt (1993), 'Adjustment Patterns and Equilibrium Selection in Experimental Signaling Games', *International Journal of Game Theory*, **22**, 279–302.

Camerer, Colin and Keith Weigelt (1988), 'Experimental Tests of a Sequential Equilibrium Reputation Model', *Econometrica*, **56**, 1–36.

Cho, I.-K. and David Kreps (1987), 'Signaling Games and Stable Equilibria', *Quarterly Journal of Economics*, **102**, 179–221.

Deacon, Robert (1995), 'Assessing the Relationship Between Government Policy and Deforestation', *Journal of Environmental Economics and Management*, **28**, 1–18.

Dixit, Avinash (1987), 'Strategic Behavior in Contests', *American Economic Review*, **77**, 891–8.
El-Gamal, Mahmoud A., Richard D. McKelvey and Thomas R. Palfrey (1993), 'A Bayesian Sequential Experimental Study of Learning in Games', *Journal of the American Statistical Association*, **88**, 428–35.
Fudenberg, Drew and Jean Tirole (1991), *Game Theory*, Cambridge, MA: MIT Press.
Harsanyi, J. (1967–68), 'Games with Incomplete Information Played by Bayesian Players', *Management Science*, **14**, 159–82, 320–34, 486–502.
Hurley, Terrance (1995), 'Private Participation in Public Policy: The Economics of Strategic Lawsuits Against Public Participation', dissertation, Iowa State University.
Hurley, Terrance and Jason Shogren (1997), 'Environmental Conflicts and the SLAPP', *Journal of Environmental Economics and Management*, **33**, 253–73.
Hurley, Terrance and Jason Shogren (1998), 'Environmental Conflicts and Non-Market Valuation', University of Wyoming, photocopy.
Lutz, Ernst and Herman Daly (1991), 'Incentives, Regulations, and Sustainable Land Use in Costa Rica', *Environmental and Resource Economics*, **1**, 179–94.
McKelvey, Richard D. and Thomas R. Palfrey (1992), 'An Experimental Study of the Centipede Game', *Econometrica*, **60**, 803–36.
Myers, Norman (1992), *The Primary Source*, New York: Norton.
Plott, Charles (1996), 'Rational Individual Behavior in Markets and Social Choice Processes', in *The Rational Foundations of Economic Behavior*, London: Macmillan and New York: St Martin's Press.
Rasmusen, Eric (1989), *Games and Information*, Cambridge: Blackwell.
Rhodes, Thomas and Paul Wilson (1995), 'Sky Islands, Squirrels, and Scopes: The Political Economy of an Environmental Conflict', *Land Economics*, **71**, 106–21.
Shogren, Jason, Kyung Hwan Baik and Thomas Crocker (1991), 'Environmental Conflicts and Strategic Commitment', in R. Pethig (ed.), *Conflicts and Cooperation in Managing Environmental Resources*, Berlin: Springer-Verlag, pp. 85–106.

12. International dynamic pollution control*

Aart de Zeeuw

1. INTRODUCTION

Any system of production and consumption creates pollution in the form of emissions and waste because, according to the laws of thermodynamics, 100 per cent recycling of materials is not possible. Our natural environment can assimilate part of this pollution, but nowadays many societies face the problem that pollution often exceeds natural assimilation capacity. This leads to a loss of well-being (amenity, health) and productivity (soil erosion), and may in the long run threaten the life support function of the natural environment. Societies are now confronted with a trade-off between the benefits of the current production and consumption system, on the one hand, and damages due to pollution, on the other hand. Economics provides tools to analyse this trade-off, and this chapter is mainly intended to describe some of these tools in a specific context.

Although some pollutants like noise are purely of the flow type, most damages are caused by accumulated pollutants such as the stock of greenhouse gases or the acidification level in soils and water bodies. This is one reason why the problem is essentially dynamic. Another reason is that adapting to sustainable pollution levels takes time. In fact a second trade-off occurs in the sense that a faster adaptation process is more costly but yields less damage on the side of pollution. The most suitable mathematical framework for this type of problem is optimal control analysis, because this can handle intertemporal objective functions with dynamic constraints.

Many important pollutants such as the greenhouse gases and the substances that cause acid rain also cross national borders. This can be seen as a transboundary externality because countries unintendedly harm other countries. For the countries as a group it will be best to internalize these externalities, but each individual country will in general have an incentive to deviate from the common policy. This phenomenon is known as the prisoners' dilemma. Another way to put it is to describe the problem as a game. Cooperative behaviour takes total social welfare of the countries together as the objective, whereas in non-

---
* The comments of the editors Henk Folmer and Nick Hanley are gratefully acknowledged.

cooperative behaviour each country only takes its own social welfare as its objective, implying that transboundary externalities are ignored. It is common to use the Cournot–Nash equilibrium concept to describe a solution in the case of non-cooperative behaviour. The cooperative outcome yields higher total social welfare but rational countries have incentives to deviate and in this way end up in the inferior Nash equilibrium. In the absence of a supranational government, no institution exists that can enforce cooperative behaviour. Much research in game theory has focused on the issue of whether non-cooperative equilibria can be designed that yield cooperative outcomes, and again dynamics plays an essential role. Most of the ideas boil down to a tit-for-tat strategy where players will be punished later if they deviate from the cooperative strategy now, so that the cooperative outcome becomes self-enforcing.

A final issue in this context is the availability of information. For example, tit-for-tat strategies are only possible if the players can observe (the effects of) the actions of the other players. However, this chapter will focus on another topic related to information. In general, a different Cournot–Nash equilibrium results if the players can observe the stock of pollutants and condition their strategies upon this information, because of the increased dynamic interaction with the other countries. It is also important whether the countries can commit themselves to their future strategies or not. This implies that the assumptions on information and commitment influence the equilibrium payoffs and thus the possible benefits of cooperation. Surprisingly enough, in the case where the players can observe the stock of pollutants but cannot commit themselves to their future strategies, the players become worse off in equilibrium so that the possible benefits of cooperation increase. The mechanism through which this occurs is as follows. Countries react to higher stocks with lower emissions. Each country reasons that more emissions will lead to higher stocks and thus to lower emissions by the other countries. Therefore, at the margin countries emit more, expecting that this will be partly offset by the other countries, which leads to higher stocks in equilibrium.

Because stock pollution matters and transboundary pollution matters, the structure of this type of problem is a combination of an optimal control problem and a game, for which a theory was developed called 'differential game theory' (Başar and Olsder, 1982). The literature provides quite a number of analyses of international pollution control problems on the basis of differential game theory (for example Hoel, 1992; van der Ploeg and de Zeeuw, 1992; Kaitala, Pohjola and Tahvonen, 1992; Dockner and van Long, 1993), Without some knowledge of the theory of differential games, this literature is not easily accessible. The main purpose of this chapter is to review some of the concepts and techniques of the theory of differential games.

The chapter is organized in the following way. Section 2 describes the basic structure of the international pollution control problem. Section 3 presents an introduction to some of the concepts and techniques of differential game theory. In Section 4 the basic results and some extensions are discussed. Section 5 is a conclusion.

2. THE INTERNATIONAL POLLUTION CONTROL PROBLEM

It is not the intention of this chapter to give a broad survey of all models and extensions in this area but to concentrate on the basic structure and the ways to solve it (see Cesar, 1994, for a survey on pollution control models). This section describes the most simple model that still captures the essential features of the problem.

Consider first the dynamics of pollution accumulation. The most general structure is

$$\dot{s}(t) = f(y(t), s(t)), \qquad (1)$$

where s denotes the stock of pollution and y the level of production. The function f both describes the addition to the stock, due to production, and the natural assimilation that can depend on the current level of the stock. In the literature one finds several constructs for the function f. Regarding natural assimilation it is common to use δs, mimicking the well-known capital depreciation term. It is understood that for many pollutants the assimilation rate δ depends on s but, in order not to lose the linear structure, δ is assumed constant. The term δs is not a bad description for the assimilation of greenhouse gases (Michaelis, 1994) but for the acidification process it is better to use a constant (Mäler and de Zeeuw, 1998), because nature assimilates a fixed amount of acid that depends on the kind of soil but not on the acidification level. This discussion is important because the outcomes of the pollution control analysis are very sensitive to the choice of assimilation function (Cesar and de Zeeuw, 1995).

Regarding the relationship between production and the flow of pollution, we follow Forster (1975) and Dasgupta (1982) by introducing a so-called emission–output ratio α. Of course, it is also possible to formulate a more general technology function indicating how much pollution is generated by a certain level of production, but the approach with an emission–output ratio is simple without losing the essence of the problem. If N countries, denoted by the subscripts $i = 1, ..., N$, all contribute to one stock of pollutants, which assimilates according to δs, and if these N countries all have the same emission–output ratio α, the dynamics of the concentration level of this stock of pollutants becomes

$$\dot{s}(t) = \frac{\alpha}{N}\sum_{i=1}^{N} y_i(t) - \delta s(t); \quad s(0) = s_0. \tag{2}$$

Equation (2) can be considered as the most simple description of the greenhouse effect. The one-to-one relationship between production and emission also allows us to formulate this equation directly in terms of emissions but with α we can also consider the possibility of investment in clean technology, in order to lower the emission–output ratio, by making α a function of clean technology capital (van der Ploeg and de Zeeuw, 1994).

The greenhouse effect is an example of a global pollution problem where each country contributes to one stock of pollution that affects all countries in a similar way. If damage is more local in nature we have to model a different stock for each country. It remains a game, however, when the emissions also cross borders. An example is the so-called 'acid rain game' in which countries emit sulphur and nitrogen oxides which are partly deposited in other countries, due to the winds. Because in this case the natural assimilation is best described with a constant, the pollution accumulation dynamics becomes

$$\dot{s}(t) = Ae(t) - c; \quad s(0) = s_0, \tag{3}$$

where s is now a vector of stocks, e is a vector of emissions, and A denotes the transport matrix describing the fractions of each emission that are transported to the other countries. The vector c is sometimes referred to as the vector of critical loads, because depositions below these levels will not result in increasing damage and may even give the soil room to recover.

Consider next the objective function. What is needed here is a social welfare function in which damage to the environment plays a role. Because this chapter is primarily meant to explain a specific technique of analysis, the modelling is kept as simple as possible. In fact damage to the environment has different aspects such as amenity effects, the depletion of resources, a threat to the life support system and production/consumption externalities. In this chapter it is simply assumed that damage is a function of the stock of pollutants which is subtracted from a function that denotes the benefits of consumption. Again in order to keep the model simple, it is further assumed that no capital investment and trade occurs, so that what each country produces is also consumed. A large part of the literature, starting with Keeler, Spence and Zeckhauser (1971), treats pollution control in combination with capital accumulation, but most of these articles are not concerned with the game-theoretic aspects of transboundary pollution. The social welfare of country i is therefore given as a discounted stream of benefits of production minus damages due to the stock of pollutants,

$$W_i = \int_0^\infty e^{-rt}\left[B(y_i(t)) - D(s(t))\right]dt, i = 1,\ldots,N, \qquad (4)$$

where r denotes the social rate of discount, and the functions B and D are assumed to be concave and convex in the relevant range of analysis and the same for all countries. Note that if there is no concern for the environment, the problem becomes static with optimality conditions $B'(y_i(t)) = 0$. Note also that if only flow pollution matters, with concentration level $s = (\alpha/N)\Sigma y_j$, the problem becomes again static but it remains a game. The Nash equilibrium conditions for this game are the reaction functions $B'(y_i) = (\alpha/N)D'((\alpha/N)\Sigma y_j)$ (marginal benefits equal to marginal costs). If the countries cooperate in this game, with the sum of the social welfare functions as the objective, the optimality conditions become $B'(y_i) = \alpha D'((\alpha/N)\Sigma y_j)$. The output levels are lower in the case of cooperation because the negative externalities due to transboundary pollution are internalized. It is easy now to see the so-called 'prisoners' dilemma'. Although the countries know that they are better off in the cooperative outcome, each country individually has an incentive to follow the reaction function corresponding to the Nash equilibrium above which mean that each country has an incentive to increase output. If all countries give in to these incentives they ultimately end up in the Nash equilibrium, which is Pareto-inferior to the cooperative outcome. The same type of results will be found later in the dynamic analysis with stock pollution.

If the problem is formulated with emissions as the control variable, the objective function is usually chosen to be a discounted stream of costs which have to be minimized. These costs are composed of the damage costs and the costs of emission reduction, which can include a loss of production but also abatement costs. The objectives become

$$W_i = \int_0^\infty e^{-rt}\left[C(e_i(t)) - D(s(t))\right]dt, i = 1,\ldots,N, \qquad (5)$$

where the function C denotes the costs of emission reduction.

Both the game given by the N objectives (4) with dynamic constraints (2) and the game given by the N objectives (5) with dynamic constraints (3) are called differential games with infinite horizons. The first one is simpler because it has only one state variable and is fully symmetric. This game will be analysed in Section 4. However, the other differential game has a vector of N state variables and is asymmetric, because the transport matrix A in (3) is not symmetric. The analysis of this game can be found in Mäler and de Zeeuw (1998) in connection with an analysis of the European acid rain problem.

The dynamic constraints are linear. In certain parts of the analysis it will be necessary to assume that the objective functions are quadratic, which turns the game into a so-called linear–quadratic differential game. In fact a second-order approximation is introduced. The following notation will be used in objective (4):

$$B(y) = \beta y - \tfrac{1}{2} y^2; \ D(s) = \tfrac{1}{2}\gamma s^2. \tag{6}$$

The rationale is that benefits B initially increase with the level of production as this means a higher level of consumption, but at high levels of production/consumption the marginal utility of consumption becomes lower than the marginal utility of leisure, so that benefits decrease with the level of production. Damage D and also marginal damage increase with the concentration level of pollutants.

As we have seen, in the case of flow pollution the game becomes static and the analysis is simple and clear. The differential game, however, is rather complex. Therefore, the next section will first provide a short introduction to differential game theory.

3. DIFFERENTIAL GAME THEORY

The basic issue in differential game theory was put forward in a seminal article by Starr and Ho as early as 1969. It might be useful to repeat an instructive example from that article. There are two time periods, two players and each player has two possible actions, labelled 0 and 1, in each time period. The game starts in a state x with label 1 and moves to one of three possible states x in the next period with labels 0, 1 and 2, depending on the actions taken by the players. Action pair (1,0) leads to state 0, action pairs (0,0) and (1,1) lead to state 1, and action pair (0,1) leads to state 2. An action pair denotes the respective actions of player 1 and player 2. In each time period each pair of actions incurs costs for the players. These costs are different and depend on the prevailing state.

One approach to the problem is to look first at the situation in the second period. In each of the three possible states in the second period $x = 0$, $x = 1$ and $x = 2$, the players play a bi-matrix game, whereby the action available to player 1 is listed in the column, and the action available to player 2 is listed in the row. These bi-matrix games are given in Table 12.1.

The Nash equilibria in these bi-matrix games are action pair (1,0) with costs (4,1), action pair (1,1) with costs (0,3), and action pair (0,0) with costs (2,2), respectively.

It makes sense to assume that in period 1 the players will expect the Nash equilibrium to be played in period 2. This implies that in period 1 the players will play a game where to each pair of costs of the bi-matrix of that period the

Nash equilibrium costs of the second period are added. Note that these Nash equilibrium costs are dependent on the state that will be reached with the action pair corresponding to the pair of costs under consideration. The change from the bi-matrix game of period 1 with the initial state with label 1 to the bi-matrix game including the expected Nash equilibrium costs of period 2 is given in Table 12.2.

Table 12.1   Bi-matrix games for three states in period 2

$x = 0$	0	1	$x = 1$	0	1	$x = 2$	0	1
0	(5,2)	(2,3)	0	(2,2)	(3,1)	0	(2,2)	(1,3)
1	(4,1)	(1,4)	1	(2,4)	(0,3)	1	(4,1)	(0,2)

Table 12.2   Bi-matrix game of periods without and with expected costs of period 2

$x = 1$	0	1	Total	0	1
0	(2,2)	(2,2)	0	(2,5)	(4,4)
1	(−1,1)	(5,0)	1	(3,2)	(5,3)

The Nash equilibrium of the resulting bi-matrix game is action pair (0,1) with total costs (4,4). This implies that in period 1 the actions 0 and 1 are played which lead to state 2 in period 2, and that in period 2 the actions 0 and 0 are played. The action pair (0,0) is a Nash equilibrium in period 2 for state 2, and the action pair (0,1) is a Nash equilibrium for the game that results from adding to the cost structure of period 1 the expected future equilibrium costs.

The problem has now been solved by backward induction or dynamic programming. The resulting bi-matrix game can be recognized as the value function, which adds up current costs and future equilibrium costs. In dynamic optimization problems with one decision maker this procedure yields the optimal solution because Bellman's principle of optimality holds. In a game, however, optimality is not the issue, but equilibria are looked for. The technique of dynamic programming yields a certain type of equilibria, if they exist, but other equilibria can be found from a different approach. The example above can also be described as follows. Each player can act twice, once in period 1 and once in period 2, and has two possibilities for each action, so that each player has four possible strategies: 00, 01, 10 and 11. This approach leads to one bi-matrix game in which the costs incurred in the two periods together are the sum of the costs incurred in the two periods separately (Table 12.3).

244   *Game theory and the environment*

Table 12.3 *Bi-matrix game for two periods at once*

$x = 1$	00	01	10	11
00	(4,4)	(5,3)	(4,4)	(3,5)
01	(4,6)	(2,5)	(6,3)	(2,4)
10	(4,3)	(1,4)	(7,2)	(8,1)
11	(3,2)	(0,5)	(7,4)	(5,3)

The Nash equilibrium of this bi-matrix game is (11,00) with total costs (3,2). This was a surprising result. Note that the total costs are for both players lower than in the dynamic programming outcome. Starr and Ho (1969) concluded in their article that this casts doubt on the applicability of Bellman's principle of optimality. It is better to say, however, that the use of dynamic programming leads to a different equilibrium concept. In the dynamic programming approach it is assumed that in each possible state in the second period the corresponding Nash equilibrium will be played, which eliminates all the other action pairs in that period. In this framework the outcome with total costs (3,2) cannot be a Nash equilibrium because player 1 has an incentive to choose action 0 instead of action 1 in the first period. The reason is that player 1 argues that the game will then move to state 1, where a Nash equilibrium will be played with costs (0,3), so that total costs for player 1 go down to 2. In the 4×4 bi-matrix game above player 1 does not have an incentive to choose action 0 in the first period. It is assumed here that player 2 has fixed its strategy 00 for the whole game, so that total costs for player 1 would go up to 4. It is important to note that the Nash equilibrium of the 4×4 bi-matrix game leads to state 0 in period 2 and prescribes action pair (1,0) here, which is not a Nash equilibrium for the 2×2 bi-matrix game for this state in this period only.

The discussion on this issue has dominated the literature for a long time. On the one hand it seems reasonable to assume that a Nash equilibrium will be played in the second period, because the players are not committed to actions chosen in the period before. This idea was also developed by Selten (1975) into the well-known subgame-perfectness concept for games in extensive form. On the other hand, Pareto-superior equilibrium costs are possible if the players can commit themselves in one way or another to future actions.

Another angle for this discussion is the role of information. If the players cannot observe the current state of the game, it reduces to a one-shot game represented by the 4×4 bi-matrix above. However, if the players can observe the current state, the outcome depends on the possibility of commitment. If the players cannot commit themselves, the dynamic programming outcome occurs. Since this outcome is worse for both players as compared to the outcome of the one-shot game, they were better off when they were not able to observe the state.

However, if the players, in addition to observing the state, can commit themselves to future actions, the Nash equilibrium with low costs becomes possible again. For example, the players can commit themselves to play action pair (1,0) in the second period irrespective of the state they will observe in that period. It is easy to see that now the total costs (3,2) can result from a Nash equilibrium again. In general, if the players can observe the state in period 2, each player has eight possible strategies, because the actions in period 2 can be conditioned on the state. For example, a strategy for player 1 is to play 0 in period 1, to play 0 if state 1 occurs, and to play 1 if state 2 occurs (note that state 0 cannot occur if player 1 plays 0 in period 1). The game can be represented by an 8 × 8 bi-matrix. It is somewhat tedious but straightforward to show that this game has three Nash equilibria, among which, of course, is the one with total costs (3,2).

It has become common to use the term 'open-loop' information structure for the case where the players cannot observe the state, so that the strategies are only a function of time and initial state, to use the term 'feedback' information structure for the case where the players can observe the current state but cannot be committed, and to use the term 'closed-loop' information structure for the case where the players can observe the current state and can be committed to their announced strategy.

The example above is a simple differential game with two discrete time steps and a finite horizon. To be able to solve a more general differential game, one has to resort to solution techniques developed for optimal control problems with only one decision maker. The two main solution techniques are Pontryagin's minimum (maximum) principle and Bellman's dynamic programming. For an optimal control problem these two methods yield the same solution because of the principle of optimality, but for a differential game the outcomes are generally different. In fact Pontryagin's minimum (maximum) principle assumes an open-loop information structure whereas Bellman's dynamic programming by construction leads to a feedback Nash equilibrium. Before we show in the next section what this implies for the game of international pollution control, the two techniques are first worked out for the simplest linear–quadratic differential game with a finite horizon, given by the objectives

$$\int_0^T \tfrac{1}{2}\left[x^2(t) + u_i^2(t)\right]dt + \tfrac{1}{2}x^2(T), \quad i = 1, 2, \tag{7}$$

which have to be minimized subject to

$$\dot{x}(t) = x(t) + u_1(t) + u_2(t); \; x(0) = x_0, \tag{8}$$

where x is the state variable and u_i is the control variable of player i. The linear–quadratic structure was motivated in Section 2 and the last term in the objectives (7) accounts for the costs after time T as a function of the state reached at time T.

The open-loop Nash equilibrium is found as follows. First, the optimal control problem for player 1 is solved by means of Pontryagin's minimum principle, given the control strategy of player 2 as a function of time, and similarly for player 2. In fact reaction functions are derived in the space of control strategies. Second, the open-loop Nash equilibrium requires consistency of these reaction functions, which means that the optimality conditions of the two optimal control problems have to hold simultaneously. The Hamiltonians are

$$H_i(x, u_i, t, p_i) = \tfrac{1}{2}(x^2 + u_i^2) + p_i(x + u_1 + u_2), \; i = 1, 2, \qquad (9)$$

where p_i denotes the co-state or adjoint variable for player i. The necessary and sufficient conditions for the two minima simultaneously are (8),

$$\dot{p}_i(t) = -H_{ix} = -x(t) - p_i(t); \; p_i(T) = x(T), \; i = 1, 2, \qquad (10)$$

and

$$H_{iu} = u_i(t) + p_i(t) = 0, \; i = 1, 2, \qquad (11)$$

where H_{ix} and H_{iu} denote the partial derivatives of the Hamiltonian H_i with respect to the state x and the control u_i, respectively.

Equation (11) gives an expression for u in terms of p so that, after substitution of Equation (11) into Equation (8), the set of Equations (8) and (10) forms a system of three differential equations with mixed boundary conditions that has to be solved. A way to achieve this is to postulate the linear relations $p_i(t) = k_i(t)x(t)$ between the co-states and the state. Then straightforward calculus shows (see the Appendix) that the functions $k_i(t)$ have to satisfy the coupled so-called Riccati differential equations

$$\dot{k}_i(t) = -1 - 2k_i(t) + k_i^2(t) + k_i(t)k_j(t); \; k_i(T) = 1. \qquad (12)$$

Furthermore, Equation (8) becomes

$$\dot{x}(t) = [1 - k_1(t) - k_2(t)]x(t); \; x(0) = x_0. \qquad (13)$$

The set of differential Equations (12) and (13) is much easier to solve. The only difficulty is the coupling between k_1 and k_2 in (12), but numerical packages exist that can solve this type of problem. The solution yields k_1 and k_2 and then

x as functions of time, so that p_1 and p_2 are also known. Using (11), the pair (u_1, u_2) as functions of time is found, which is the open-loop Nash equilibrium.

The feedback Nash equilibrium is found by dynamic programming or backward induction. In discrete time it is easy to describe what happens. First the Nash equilibrium in the last period is determined, which yields the equilibrium costs for that period as a function of the state. Then the penultimate stage is considered, where the objectives of the players are the sum of their current costs and the expected equilibrium costs of the last period. The Nash equilibrium of this game yields the costs-to-go for the last two periods as a function of the state in the penultimate period. Backwards, step by step, the feedback Nash equilibrium unravels.

The central concept in dynamic programming is the value function that denotes the costs-to-go for a player at time t starting in state x at time t, given that from time t onwards the equilibrium strategies will be played. It can be shown (for example, Davis, 1977, for the optimal control problem) that in continuous time the value functions have to satisfy the so-called Hamilton–Jacobi–Bellman equations, which for the problem (7) and (8) become

$$V_{it}(t, x) + \min[½(x^2 + u_i^2) + V_{ix}(t, x)(x + u_1 + u_2)] = 0 \qquad (14)$$

and

$$V_i(T, x) = ½x^2, i = 1, 2. \qquad (15)$$

The Nash equilibrium at time t in state x becomes

$$u_i(t, x) = -V_{ix}(t, x), i = 1, 2. \qquad (16)$$

The difficulty is how to solve the partial differential Equation (14)–(15) after substitution of (16). One solution is found by postulating quadratic value functions $V_i(t, x) = ½k_i(t)x^2$, so that Equation (14) becomes a quadratic equation in x. Since it has to hold for every x, the coefficient of x^2 has to be zero, which ultimately leads (see the Appendix) to the coupled Riccati differential equations

$$\dot{k}_i(t) = -1 - 2k_i(t) + k_i^2(t) + 2k_i(t)k_j(t); k_i(T) = 1. \qquad (17)$$

If (17) can be solved, a feedback Nash equilibrium consists of the pair of functions (u_1, u_2), which are now functions of time and state, given by $u_i(t, x) = -k_i(t)x$. It has been shown, however, in a model with one state variable and infinite horizon, that other feedback Nash equilibria exist which are not linear in the state with value functions that are not quadratic in the state (Tsutsui and

Mino, 1990). It goes beyond the scope of this chapter to give the derivation, but the consequences will be discussed in the next section.

Because the open-loop Nash equilibrium strategies can be represented as $u_i(t) = -k_i(t)x(t)$, it is immediately clear from comparing the respective Riccati equations (12) and (17) that the open-loop Nash equilibrium and the linear feedback Nash equilibrium differ. Note that if the players do not influence each other's state, so that the game aspects disappear, the Riccati equations (12) and (17) are the same, which means that the open-loop and feedback equilibria coincide, as is to be expected from Bellman's principle of optimality.

Most economic analyses within the framework of differential games are problems with an infinite horizon and a discount factor e^{-rt} in the integrand of the objective functions. It is then common to use in the open-loop case the Hamiltonians $e^{rt}H_i$ and in the feedback case the value functions $e^{rt}V_i$. It is easy to show that this leads in the open-loop case to

$$\dot{p}_i(t) - rp_i(t) = -H_{ix} = -x(t) - p_i(t), i = 1, 2, \qquad (18)$$

instead of (10), and in the feedback case to

$$V_{it}(t, x) - rV_i(t, x) + \min[\tfrac{1}{2}(x^2 + u_i^2) + V_{ix}(t, x)(x + u_1 + u_2)] = 0, i = 1, 2, \qquad (19)$$

instead of (14). The boundary condition in (10) changes into the so-called 'transversality condition', namely $\lim e^{-rt}p(t)x(t) = 0$ for $t \to \infty$, and the boundary condition (15) changes in a similar way.

This has been only a short introduction to one of the issues in differential game theory. The basic reference for this theory is Başar and Olsder (1982) but this book is difficult for non-specialists. However, without any background in this theory it is difficult to understand the typical analysis of international dynamic pollution control. This section was meant to provide some background to enable understanding of the following section.

4. THE GAME OF INTERNATIONAL POLLUTION CONTROL

In this section the insights of the preceding section are used to analyse the game given in Section 2 with objective functions (4) and dynamic constraints (2), where the quadratic benefit and damage functions are defined in (6). The analysis draws heavily on a paper by van der Ploeg and de Zeeuw (1992) but similar analyses can also be found elsewhere (for example Hoel, 1992; Kaitala, Pohjola and

Tahvonen, 1992). Note that in the preceding section the objective was to minimize a cost function, which is the dominant approach in differential game theory, whereas in this section the objective is to maximize a net benefit function, which is the dominant approach in economic analyses. The mathematical structure of the problems is, of course, equivalent.

Consider first the open-loop Nash equilibrium of this differential game. The subscript N will be used to denote the open-loop Nash equilibrium. The Hamiltonians are

$$H_i(s, y_i, t, p_i) = \beta y_i - \tfrac{1}{2} y_i^2 - \tfrac{1}{2}\gamma s^2 + p_i\left(\frac{\alpha}{N}\sum_{j=1}^{N} y_j - \delta s\right). \tag{20}$$

Because of symmetry the equilibrium can be characterized (see the Appendix) by the set of differential equations

$$\dot{s}_N(t) = \alpha[\beta + (\alpha/N)p_N(t)] - \delta s_N(t); \; s_N(0) = s_0 \tag{21}$$

and

$$\dot{p}_N(t) = \gamma s_N(t) + (r + \delta)p_N(t); \; \lim e^{-rt}p_N(t)s_N(t) = 0, \tag{22}$$

where $\beta + (\alpha/N)p_N(t)$ are the equilibrium output levels.

Because maximization of the benefits of production plus p_N times the addition of pollutants to the stock would give the same production levels, $-p_N$ can be interpreted as an emission charge that governments would have to levy on the private sector to realize the socially optimal production levels.

Consider next the feedback Nash equilibrium (which will be denoted by subscript F) of the differential game. The Hamilton–Jacobi–Bellman equations are

$$V_{it}(t, s) - rV_i(t, s) + \max\left[\beta y_i - \tfrac{1}{2}y_i^2 - \tfrac{1}{2}\gamma s^2 + V_{is}(t,s)\left(\frac{\alpha}{N}\sum_{j=1}^{N}y_j - \delta s\right)\right] = 0. \tag{23}$$

It can be shown (see van der Ploeg and de Zeeuw, 1992) that the only stable solution is the stationary solution where the value functions do not depend on time. This is a standard result in the case where the parameters of the problem are time-independent. Because of symmetry the value functions are equal for all countries. Postulating quadratic value functions of the form $V(s) = -\tfrac{1}{2}ks^2 - gs + c$, substituting this into (23) where $y_i = \beta + (\alpha/N)V'(s)$, and setting the coefficients of s^2 and s in the resulting equation equal to zero, finally leads to a quadratic equation in k and a linear equation in g with k as a parameter. Because k has to be positive to get a maximum, only one solution to this quadratic equation is relevant. It follows (see the Appendix) that

$$k = \left[-(r+2\delta) + \left((r+2\delta)^2 + 4\gamma\alpha^2\left(\frac{2N-1}{N^2}\right)\right)^{1/2}\right] \bigg/ \left[2\alpha^2\left(\frac{2N-1}{N^2}\right)\right] \quad (24)$$

and

$$g = \alpha\beta k \bigg/ \left[(r+\delta) + \alpha^2\left(\frac{2N-1}{N^2}\right)k\right]. \quad (25)$$

Apart from the constant c, value functions are found that characterize the linear feedback Nash equilibrium with production levels $\beta - (\alpha/N)(ks + g)$ and, after substitution of this, pollution accumulation

$$\dot{s}_F(t) = \alpha(\beta - \alpha g/N) - (\alpha^2 k/N + \delta)s_F(t); \; s_F(0) = s_0. \quad (26)$$

It is interesting to note that now $ks + g$ can be interpreted as an emission charge on the addition to the stock of pollution, because this levy would induce the private sector to choose the same output levels.

In the previous section it was shown that the open-loop Nash equilibrium and the linear feedback Nash equilibrium differ, but it remains to be seen what the consequences are for the game of international pollution control. An important question is which equilibrium in the long run will lead to higher pollution stocks and why?

It is easy to check that the system of differential equations (21) and (22) is saddlepoint-stable so that in equilibrium the stock of pollutants will converge to the steady state with

$$s_N = \alpha\beta \bigg/ \left(\frac{\alpha^2\gamma}{N(r+\delta)} + \delta\right). \quad (27)$$

Differential equation (26) is stable so that in feedback equilibrium the stock of pollutants will converge to the steady state

$$s_F = \alpha\left(\beta - \frac{\alpha}{N}g\right)\bigg/\left(\frac{\alpha^2}{N}k + \delta\right). \tag{28}$$

From proposition 6.1 in van der Ploeg and de Zeeuw (1992) it follows that $s_N < s_F$. The conclusion is that the (linear) feedback Nash equilibrium leads to a higher pollution stock than the open-loop Nash equilibrium. The intuition is as follows. Each country knows that in a feedback information structure the other countries observe the stock of pollutants and react to higher stocks with lower output and pollution. Therefore, each country knows that an increase in output and pollution will then be partly offset by a decrease in all the other countries. This implies that the feedback equilibrium will lead to higher levels of pollution than the open-loop equilibrium, where the countries do not observe the stock of pollutants.

This result aggravates the prisoners' dilemma, which was described in Section 2. First, it is easy to see what happens in the cooperative outcome (that will be denoted by subscript C), because the derivation is very similar to the derivation above of the open-loop Nash equilibrium but with the Hamiltonian

$$H(s, y_1, \ldots, y_N, t, p) = \sum_{i=1}^{N}\left(\beta y_i - \tfrac{1}{2} y_i^2 - \tfrac{1}{2}\gamma s^2\right) + p\left(\frac{\alpha}{N}\sum_{i=1}^{N} y_i - \delta s\right). \tag{29}$$

The optimal output levels are $\beta + (\alpha/N)p(t)$ and the outcome is characterized by the set of differential equations (21) and (22), where in (22) γ is replaced by γN, which leads to the steady-state stock of pollutants

$$s_C = \alpha\beta\bigg/\left(\frac{\alpha^2\gamma}{r+\delta} + \delta\right). \tag{30}$$

It is immediately clear that $s_C < s_N$, which means that the cooperative outcome yields less damage to the environment than the open-loop Nash equilibrium. However, the cooperative outcome is vulnerable to unilateral deviations, which poses the prisoners' dilemma again. It seems reasonable to assume that the countries can observe the stock of pollutants and can also not be committed to future actions. This implies that the feedback Nash equilibrium is more relevant, but that aggravates the prisoners' dilemma because $s_C < s_N < s_F$.

As has already been described in the Introduction, much research in game theory has focused on the question of whether, in a dynamic context, cooperative outcomes can be made self-enforcing, so that the prisoners' dilemma disappears.

The main result in repeated games is the well-known 'folk theorem' (Fudenberg and Maskin, 1986) but a similar result has not yet been developed for differential games. Some research has been done on closed-loop memory equilibria in which the players can condition their actions not only on the current state but also on the past states (see Başar and Olsder, 1982). In this framework equilibria exist which are a Pareto improvement over the linear feedback Nash equilibrium, but this line of research was not pursued any further. The most promising development has been the discovery of non-quadratic value functions that satisfy the Hamilton–Jacobi–Bellman equations of a symmetric linear–quadratic differential game with one state variable and an infinite horizon. These value functions lead to non-linear feedback Nash equilibria that can sustain the cooperative outcome (Tsutsui and Mino, 1990). This result has been applied to a game of international pollution control, similar to the one analysed above, showing that the cooperative outcome can be approximated by a non-linear feedback Nash equilibrium (Dockner and van Long, 1993). A drawback of this approach is that the equilibrium strategies become very complex.

5. CONCLUSION

International pollution control can be viewed as a game and if it is realized that the stock of pollutants matters, and not so much the flow, the game becomes a differential game. In the literature a number of contributions in this area can be found, but much of the material is not easily accessible for non-specialists. Therefore, this chapter provides an introduction to some of the basic concepts and techniques of differential games. The main part of this chapter, however, constructs and analyses a simple typical model of international dynamic pollution control. Transboundary pollution externalities yield a prisoners' dilemma. If the countries observe the stock of pollutants and if they cannot commit themselves to future strategies, the standard framework of analysis results in worsening the prisoners' dilemma. This strengthens the case for international policy coordination and the search for equilibria that sustain cooperative outcomes.

REFERENCES

Başar, Tamer and Geert-Jan Olsder (1982), *Dynamic Noncooperative Game Theory*, London: Academic Press.

Cesar, Herman S.J. (1994), 'Control and Game Models of the Greenhouse Effect', *Lecture Notes in Economics and Mathematical Systems*, 416, Berlin: Springer-Verlag.

Cesar, Herman and Aart de Zeeuw (1995), 'Sustainability and the greenhouse effect: robustness analysis of the assimilation function', in Carlo Carraro and Jerzy A. Filar (eds), *Control and Game-Theoretic Models of the Environment*, Boston: Birkhäuser, pp. 25–45.

Dasgupta, Partha (1982), *The Control of Resources*, Oxford: Basil Blackwell.
Davis, M.H.A. (1977), *Linear Estimation and Stochastic Control*, London: Chapman and Hall.
Dockner, Engelbert J. and Ngo van Long (1993), 'International pollution control: cooperative versus noncooperative strategies', *Journal of Environmental Economics and Management*, **24**, 13–29.
Forster, Bruce A. (1975), 'Optimal pollution control with a nonconstant exponential rate of decay', *Journal of Environmental Economics and Management*, **2**, 1–6.
Fudenberg, Drew and Eric Maskin (1986), 'The folk theorem in repeated games with discounting and with incomplete information', *Econometrica*, **54**, 533–54.
Hoel, Michael (1992), 'Emission taxes in a dynamic international game of CO_2 emissions', in Rüdiger Pethig (ed.), *Conflicts and Cooperation in Managing Environmental Resources*, Berlin: Springer-Verlag, pp. 39–68.
Kaitala, Veijo, Matti Pohjola and Olli Tahvonen (1992), 'Transboundary air pollution and soil acidification: a dynamic analysis of an acid rain game between Finland and the USSR', *Environmental and Resource Economics*, **2**(2), 161–81.
Keeler, Emmett, Michael Spence and Robert Zeckhauser (1971), 'The optimal control of pollution', *Journal of Economic Theory*, **4**, 19–34.
Mäler, Karl-Göran and Aart de Zeeuw (1998), 'The acid rain differential game', forthcoming in *Environmental and Resource Economics*.
Michaelis, Peter (1994), 'The cost of stabilizing the atmospheric concentration of greenhouse gases', paper presented to the workshop, Designing Economic Policy for Management of Natural Resources and the Environment, Rethymnon, Crete.
Selten, Reinhard (1975), 'Reexamination of the perfectness concept for equilibrium points in extensive games', *International Journal of Game Theory*, **4**, 25–55.
Starr, A.W. and Y.C. Ho (1969), 'Further properties of nonzero-sum differential games', *Journal of Optimization Theory and Applications*, **3**(4), 207–19.
Tsutsui, Shunichi and Kazuo Mino (1990), 'Nonlinear strategies in dynamic duopolistic competition with sticky prices', *Journal of Economic Theory*, **52**, 136–61.
Van der Ploeg, Frederick and Aart J. de Zeeuw (1992), 'International aspects of pollution control', *Environmental and Resource Economics*, **2**(2), 117–39.
Van der Ploeg, Frederick and Aart J. de Zeeuw (1994), 'Investment in clean technology and transboundary pollution control', in Carlo Carraro (ed.), *Trade, Innovation, Environment*, Dordrecht: Kluwer Academic Publishers, pp. 229–40.

APPENDIX

Derivation of Equations (12) and (13)

Linear relations are postulated between state and co-states in the form $p_i(t) = k_i(t)x(t)$. Equation (11) yields $u_i(t) = -k_i(t)x(t)$. Substitution into Equation (8) yields Equation (13). Equation (10) becomes

$$\dot{p}_i(t) = \dot{k}_i(t)x(t) + k_i(t)\dot{x}(t) = [-1 - k_i(t)]x(t);\ k_i(T)x(T) = x(T),\ i = 1, 2. \quad (A1)$$

Substitution of Equation (13) into Equation (A1), and the notion that the result has to hold for every x, leads to Equation (12).

Derivation of Equation (17)

Quadratic value functions are postulated in the form $V_i(t, x) = \frac{1}{2}k_i(t)x^2$. Equation (16) yields $u_i(t, x) = -k_i(t)x$. Substitution into Equation (14) yields

$$\tfrac{1}{2}\dot{k}_i(t)x^2 + \tfrac{1}{2}(x^2 + k_i^2(t)x^2) + k_i(t)x(x - k_1(t)x - k_2(t)x) = 0. \quad (A2)$$

Since this has to hold for every x, Equation (17) follows immediately. The boundary condition of (15) translates directly into the boundary condition of (17).

Derivation of equations (21) and (22)

The partial derivatives of the Hamiltonian H_i, given in Equation (18), with respect to the control y_i and the state s, are

$$H_{iy} = \beta - y_i + \frac{\alpha}{N}p_i; \quad H_{is} = -\gamma s - \delta p_i. \quad (A3)$$

Because of symmetry the equilibrium production levels and the co-states are the same for all countries. Subscript N will be used to denote this open-loop Nash equilibrium. Equilibrium production levels follow immediately from the first partial derivative and the dynamic equation for the co-state follows from substitution of the second partial derivative in Equation (18).

Derivation of Equations (24) and (25)

Quadratic value functions are postulated in the form $V(s) = -\frac{1}{2}ks^2 - gs + c$. The value functions are time-independent, so that the first term in Equation (23) is zero. The derivative of the value function with respect to the state s is $-(ks + g)$, so that the equilibrium production levels are given by $y = \beta - (\alpha/N)(ks + g)$.

Substitution of these expressions into Equation (23) leads to a quadratic equation in s. Since this has to hold for every s, the coefficients of s^2 and s have to be equal to zero, which yields a quadratic equation in k and a linear equation in g with k as a parameter. The quadratic equation in k has roots

$$k = \left[-(r+2\delta) \pm \left((r+2\delta)^2 + 4\gamma\alpha^2\left(\frac{2N-1}{N^2}\right)\right)^{1/2}\right] \Big/ \left[2\alpha^2\left(\frac{2N-1}{N^2}\right)\right]. \quad (A4)$$

Since the value function has to be concave, only the positive root is relevant. The calculation of g in Equation (25) is straightforward.

13. Learning about global warming

Alistair Ulph[*]

1. INTRODUCTION

Two of the central policy questions that arise in the climate change debate are how to secure international cooperation to reduce emissions of greenhouse gases, and how to respond to the considerable uncertainty about both the extent of any possible climate change and any resulting damages in different parts of the world. The possibility that better scientific information in the future will reduce uncertainty leads to the suggestion that action to curb greenhouse gas emissions be delayed, while concern about the possible irreversible accumulation of greenhouse gases leads to the suggestion that such delay could be costly.

To date much of the analysis of these two policy questions has proceeded independently. Thus there is a substantial literature[1] which uses dynamic game theory either to compare cooperative and noncooperative time paths for emissions of greenhouse gases, or to design international environmental agreements to which independent nation states would voluntarily subscribe. The results from this literature show that non-cooperative equilibria will have higher current emissions and long-run stocks of greenhouse gases than cooperative equilibria, and that there are gains to cooperation. Two noncooperative equilibria are used – feedback Nash equilibria and open-loop equilibria, with the former having higher current emissions and stocks of greenhouse gas than the latter. The literature has also shown that it is unlikely that many countries will voluntarily agree to collaborate in reducing their emissions, in the sense that the number of countries that are likely to form a stable coalition is small. But this literature has ignored issues of uncertainty or learning.

There is also a substantial literature on uncertainty, learning and irreversibility in relation to climate change[2] which has addressed questions such as whether the possibility of obtaining better information in the future should result in higher or lower current emissions of greenhouse gases (in the extreme case, should we do nothing to abate greenhouse gas emissions until we get better information

---

[*] The research for this chapter was funded in part by the CSERGE programme on Global Warming. I am grateful to Henk Folmer and Nick Hanley for comments on an earlier version of this chapter.

about likely damages?) and what is the value of better scientific information? This literature shows that the possibility of getting better information in the future about the damages from global warming may raise or lower current period emissions depending on the functional forms for damage and abatement costs, and this is true whether greenhouse gas emissions are irreversible or reversible. There is always a positive value to better information. However, this literature has assumed a single decision maker, and so ignores the issue of many nation states taking decisions on greenhouse gas emissions independently.

In this chapter I shall survey a small number of papers which have attempted to integrate these two literatures. There are two reasons for doing this. The first is to check whether the conclusions derived from models of dynamic games with no uncertainty still apply when uncertainty and learning are introduced, and similarly whether the conclusions from models of uncertainty and learning with a single decision maker apply when there are many non-cooperative decision makers. A second reason for integrating the two literatures is to allow issues to be addressed which simply cannot arise without such integration; for example, does the presence of uncertainty reduce the incentives for cooperation; and would countries agree on the benefits of better information?

On the first point, I shall show that the conclusions derived from the literature on dynamic games about the differences in emissions and stocks of pollution between cooperative and non-cooperative equilibrium largely carry over to a world of uncertainty and learning, as do the conclusions about the benefits from cooperation. Specifically, Ulph and Ulph (1996) showed that: (i) the ranking of current emissions and final stocks of emissions would be highest in a feedback Nash equilibrium, next highest in an open-loop Nash equilibrium and lowest in a cooperative equilibrium, and this was true both if there were no learning and if there were the possibility of learning in the future about true damage costs of global warming; (ii) there are always gains from cooperation with both learning and no learning. However, the conclusions from the literature on uncertainty, irreversibility and learning for a single decision maker do not generalize to a world of many countries acting non-cooperatively, for in a non-cooperative equilibrium better information could make all countries worse off.

As I shall show, an important factor driving this result is the degree of correlation between the damage experienced by different countries. The result can only arise when there is less than perfect correlation between damages in different countries, that is, some countries may benefit from global warming while others lose substantially; this seems to be a likely description of the effects of global warming. Better information will then reveal that one country faces less damage than it had expected, while another country learns that it faces greater damage than it had expected. The non-cooperative responses of these countries to this information is what gives information potentially negative value. This can also have important implications for policies for dealing with current emissions – suggesting that current emissions should be lower if there is the possibility of obtaining better information in the future than would be the case if there were no such possibility. These results also suggest that there is an important additional dimension to international environmental agreements – it is not just a need to secure a general reduction in emissions, but also a need to coordinate responses to new information.

In terms of the second reason for integrating the two literatures, I shall show that it may be easier to secure cooperation between countries before uncertainties about global warming are resolved, and, as indicated above, that countries may differ in the value they attach to better information, with some countries attaching a positive value to information and others a negative value.

In this chapter I shall concentrate on explaining the theoretical arguments, and in most of this theoretical work I shall employ a very simple example, drawing on the more general analysis I have done in other papers. This will allow me to illustrate the issues, and refer the reader to the source papers for the more general analysis. In the next section I shall introduce the simple model, and summarize the results from the two separate literatures – the analysis of learning for a single-country model, and the analysis of dynamic pollution games under certainty. In Section 3, I shall integrate the two problems and discuss the results that can be obtained. I shall also discuss briefly a related paper on the implications for reaching international agreements. I emphasize that I do not pretend that the very simple models used here capture the real complexity of global warming – what they are designed to do is to show why some of our standard intuitions may be wrong. In Section 4 I shall say a bit about empirical work relevant to this chapter; while this will bring the discussion somewhat closer to the reality of global warming, the models remain very simple.[3]

2. BACKGROUND ANALYSIS

In this section I shall introduce a very simple model of global warming and use it to analyse first how the possibility of obtaining better information in the future about the damages from global warming would affect the emissions policy of a single decision maker (taken to represent the world) and then, second, to analyse how several countries would determine their emissions policies when there is certainty about the extent of damages from global warming. The analysis in this section draws heavily on Ulph and Ulph (1996, 1997).

2.1 Single Decision Maker with Uncertainty and Learning

There are two periods, $t = 1, 2$ which we can think of as the present and the future. In each period emissions of greenhouse gases are e_t and the utility or total benefits[4] from emitting these gases is given by $U(e_t) \equiv -0.5(e^* - e_t)^2$. This simple utility function has the property that the *marginal benefit* of emitting greenhouse gases is a downward-sloping linear function, and in the absence of any concern about global warming, emissions in each period would be set equal to e^*, which I shall interpret as the business-as-usual (BAU) level of emissions. Any damages due to global warming are caused by the total stock of emissions of greenhouse gases at the end of period 2, denoted by $X = e_1 + e_2$, and the costs of any damages are given by the total damage cost function[5] $D(X) \equiv 0.5\theta X^2$. Again the simple quadratic total damage cost function implies that the *marginal damage* cost function is upward-sloping and linear. Note that it is implicitly assumed above that first-period emissions of greenhouse gases do not decay by the end of the second period.[6] So the only way to reduce the stock of greenhouse gases and hence any damage from global warming is to reduce emissions of greenhouse gases.

There is uncertainty about the true extent of damages from global warming, which I capture by assuming that the true value of the parameter θ in the total damage cost function is unknown.[7] There are only two possible value *states of the world*, denoted by $s = l, h$, where in the *low* state, l, the parameter θ takes the value 0 (that is, global warming is not a problem) while in the *high* state, h, it takes the value $2\bar{\theta} > 0$. The decision maker believes that each state is equally likely to occur, so that the *expected* value of the damage cost parameter is $\bar{\theta}$. At the start of period 1 the true value of θ is unknown, but there are two possibilities for period 2. If there is *no learning*, then the decision maker is as uncertain about the value of θ at the start of period 2 as at the start of period 1. If there is *learning*, then by the start of period 2 the decision maker has obtained *perfect information*, and so knows the true value of θ.[8] The importance of being able to obtain perfect information by the start of period 2 is that the decision maker can condition second-period emissions on what has been learned about θ, and I denote this by saying that the decision maker sets emission level e_{2s}, $s = l, h$ in period 2 if the decision maker has learned that the true state is s. If there is no learning, then the decision maker is constrained to set a single value for emissions in period 2, which can be written as $e_2 = e_{2l} = e_{2h}$.

To complete the description of the model, it is assumed that there is no discounting. Thus we have the simplest possible model of global warming, with only two periods, two states of the world, linear marginal benefit and marginal cost curves, no discounting or decay of the stock of emissions.[9]

The problems facing the decision maker can thus be written as follows:

No learning
Choose e_1, e_2 to maximize

$$W^N(e_1, e_2) \equiv -0.5(e^* - e_1)^2 - 0.5(e^* - e_2)^2 - 0.5\bar{\theta}(e_1 + e_2)^2.$$

Learning
Choose e_1, e_{2l}, e_{2h} to maximize

$$W^L(e_1, e_{2l}, e_{2h}) \equiv -0.5(e^* - e_1)^2 + 0.5[-0.5(e^* - e_{2l})^2] \\ + 0.5[-0.5(e^* - e_{2h})^2 - 0.5 \times 2\bar{\theta}(e_1 + e_{2h})^2].$$

The key point to note is that when there is no learning, because second-period emissions are independent of the state of the world, θ, and because of the simple multiplicative form of the damage cost function, expected damages with no learning are given by the total damage cost function with θ replaced by its expected value, so with no learning there is *certainty equivalence*, that is, uncertainty can simply be handled by replacing the random variable by its expected value and then treating the problem as if it is one with certainty. On the other hand, with learning, because second-period emissions do depend on the true value of θ, then even with the simple multiplicative form of the total damage cost function, expected damage costs do not display the certainty equivalence property.

A central question I wish to address is whether the possibility of learning more in the future about the true damages from global warming means that *current* emissions should be higher or lower than would be the case if there were no possibility of getting better information in the future. To understand how to determine first-period emissions, recall that if this is a one-period pollution problem under certainty, then the solution would require setting first-period emissions so that the marginal benefit of emissions equals the marginal damage cost of emissions. In a multi-period problem under uncertainty the solution has a fairly similar form, namely that first-period emissions should be set so that marginal benefit of first-period emissions equals the *expected present value* of marginal damage costs caused by first-period emissions. So we need to be able to calculate the appropriate present value expected marginal damage costs of first-period emissions under both learning and no learning.

To do this, I introduce the following *(net) total damage cost function* for first-period emissions:

$$C(e_1, \theta) \equiv \min_{e_2}[0.5(e^* - e_2)^2 + 0.5\theta(e_1 + e_2)^2].$$

This is just the minimum cost of damages caused by period one emissions net of the benefits of period two emissions, given that the damage cost parameter is known to be θ, and that period two emissions are chosen optimally. Carrying out the optimization of second-period emissions we get:

$$e_2 = \frac{e^* - \theta e_1}{1+\theta}; \quad C(e_1,\theta) = \frac{\theta(e^* + e_1)^2}{2(1+\theta)}.$$

So the net damage cost function is a strictly increasing quadratic function of first-period emissions (so marginal damage costs are an increasing linear function of first-period emissions), and the damage cost function is also an increasing function of θ.

I now calculate the corresponding *marginal damage cost function*:

$$C'(e_1,\theta) \equiv \frac{\partial C(e_1,\theta)}{\partial e_1} = \frac{\theta(e^* + e_1)}{(1+\theta)}.$$

Then the decision maker's problems can be reformulated as:

No learning: Choose e_1 to maximize

$$-0.5(e^* - e_1)^2 - C(e_1, \bar{\theta}).$$

Learning: Choose e_1 to maximize

$$-0.5(e^* - e_1)^2 - 0.5[C(e_1, 0) + C(e_1, 2\bar{\theta})].$$

Again, the certainty equivalence property of the no learning case means that the relevant value of the cost function is just the cost function under certainty with the value of θ replaced by its expected value. The first-order conditions are given by:

No learning:

$$e^* - e_1 = C'(e_1, \bar{\theta}) = \frac{\bar{\theta}(e^* + e_1)}{1+\bar{\theta}}. \tag{1}$$

Learning:

$$e^* - e_1 = 0.5[C'(e_1,0) + C'(e_1,2\bar{\theta})] \equiv \bar{C}'(e_1) = \frac{\bar{\theta}(e^* + e_1)}{1+2\bar{\theta}}. \tag{2}$$

In each case, the left-hand expression is just the marginal benefit of first-period emissions, the right-hand expression is the *expected present value* of marginal damage costs of first-period emissions.

It is easy to see from (1) and (2) that for any level of first-period emissions, the expected present value of marginal damage costs is lower with learning than with no learning. In turn this implies that the optimal choice of first-period emissions with learning, e_1^L, is higher than the level of first-period emissions with no learning, e_1^N. This is shown in Figure 13.1, which presents the marginal benefit curve and the expected present value marginal damage cost curves under learning and no learning. In other words, the possibility of getting better information in the future means that the decision maker need not cut current period emissions as much as would be the case with no learning. However, this does not support the extreme view that the decision maker should do nothing at all to cut emissions until better information is obtained.

It is important to understand what lies behind this result, and in particular that the result is not completely general. A general statement of the results that can be obtained is contained in the following set of sufficient conditions:

$$\text{If } C'(e_1, \theta) \text{ is concave in } \theta \text{ then } e_1^L \geq e_1^N;$$
$$\text{If } C'(e_1, \theta) \text{ is convex in } \theta \text{ then } e_1^L \leq e_1^N.$$

These conditions are shown by Ulph and Ulph (1997) to be equivalent to the sufficient conditions derived by Epstein (1980) for the particular model of global warming considered here. To see why these sufficient conditions apply, note that they are just a standard statistical result (Jensen's inequality) that the value of a concave (convex) function evaluated at the expected value of a random variable is no less (greater) than the expected value of the function (see Figure 13.2). Recall that it is Jensen's inequality that explains why a strictly concave utility function implies risk aversion, since it means that the expected utility of a risky asset is less than the utility of the expected value of the asset. In our context, Jensen's inequality means that if the marginal damage cost is strictly concave in θ, the expected marginal damage cost of first-period emissions with learning (the analogue of a risky asset) is less than the marginal damage cost with no learning (a certain payoff); since the expected marginal damage cost of first-period emissions with learning is lower than with no learning, it is optimal to carry out more first-period emissions with learning than with no learning. As Ulph and Ulph (1997) note, it is difficult to provide general restrictions on the decision-making problem which guarantee that the marginal cost function $C'(e_1, \theta)$ is either concave or convex in θ, but a sufficient condition for the marginal cost function to be concave in θ is that the total benefit and total damage cost functions are quadratic, which is what I have assumed.[10]

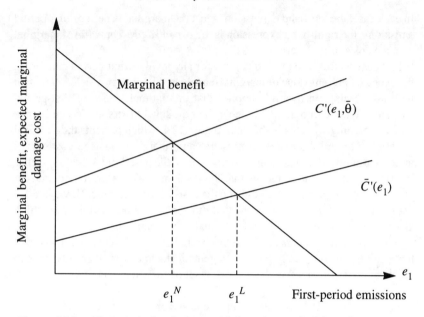

Figure 13.1   First-period emissions with learning and no learning

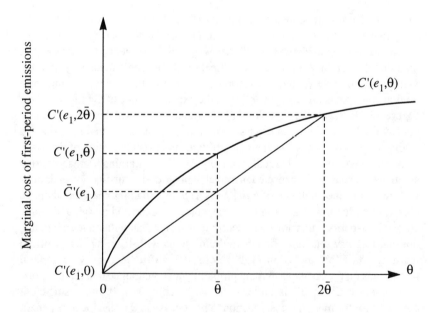

Figure 13.2   Why expected marginal cost with learning is less than with no learning

Learning about global warming

To complete the analysis of this subsection, it is useful to give explicit expressions for first-period emissions, the stock of emissions, and welfare under learning and no learning. These are derived by solving (1) and (2) to get first-period emissions with no learning and learning, substituting these values into the expression for second-period emissions, adding first- and second-period emissions to derive stocks, and substituting first- and second-period emissions into the welfare function. Note that under learning, there are two levels of stock of emission depending on whether the decision maker learns that θ takes a low or high value. These expressions are

$$e_1^N = \frac{e^*}{(1+2\bar{\theta})}; \quad e_1^L = \frac{(1+\bar{\theta})e^*}{(1+3\bar{\theta})} \quad e_1^N < e_1^L;$$

$$X^N = \frac{2e^*}{(1+2\bar{\theta})}; \quad X^{Ll} = \frac{2(1+2\bar{\theta})e^*}{(1+3\bar{\theta})}; \quad X^{Lh} = \frac{2e^*}{(1+3\bar{\theta})}; \quad X^{Lh} < X^N < X^{Ll};$$

$$W^N = \frac{-2\bar{\theta}e^{*2}}{(1+2\bar{\theta})}; \quad W^L = \frac{-2\bar{\theta}e^{*2}}{(1+3\bar{\theta})}; \quad W^L > W^N. \tag{3}$$

Note that the last result tells us that welfare is higher under learning than no learning. This result is perfectly general – a decision maker must always be able to do better by having better information than by not having better information, for the simple reason that if the decision maker was worse off with better information, the decision maker could just ignore that information. The difference in welfare between learning and no learning can be thought of as the *value of perfect information*.

To summarize, for the particular model of global warming set out here I have shown that the possibility of obtaining better information in the future about the extent of damages from global warming should lead a decision maker to choose higher current emissions than if there were no possibility of getting better information, and that having better information leads to higher welfare. While the last result is completely general, the former depends on the particular functional forms used for the benefit and damage cost functions.

2.2 Many Countries, Certainty about Damage Costs

I now assume that the damage cost parameter is known with certainty to take the value $\bar{\theta}$. The simplest extension from a single decision maker is to assume that there are two identical countries, and I suppose that each country has the benefit and damage cost functions set out in the previous section. The conclusions apply to many countries with asymmetries. The symmetry of the two countries means that most of the analysis can be done by considering just one country, whose emissions I denote by e_1, e_2; the emissions of the other country will be denoted by f_1, f_2. The main difference from the single decision maker model is to recognize that the global nature of global warming means that what causes damages in each country is the stock of emissions from both countries: $X = e_1 + e_2 + f_1 + f_2$.

The global nature of pollution means that the two countries are interdependent, and the main focus of interest in this section is how this interdependence is handled by the two countries, in particular the difference in emission policies depending on whether or not the two countries cooperate in setting their emissions. I shall consider two different equilibria to capture what happens when the two countries do not cooperate. The first is the open-loop Nash equilibrium (*OLN*); by this I mean that one country takes as given the emissions set by the other country in both periods and sets its emissions in both periods to maximize its own welfare. Implicit in this solution concept is the notion that each country can *commit* itself to a particular level of emissions in the future. Since it seems unlikely that governments can make such commitments, particularly over the time scales that are relevant for global warming, I also consider another non-cooperative equilibrium – the feedback Nash equilibrium (*FN*).[1] In this case, countries cannot commit to future emissions. So whatever emissions have been in the first period, when it comes to the second period there is a simple one-period Nash equilibrium in which each country takes as given the emissions of both countries in the first period and the emissions of the other country in the second period and chooses its second-period emissions to maximize its own welfare. The equilibrium second-period emissions will depend upon the emissions of the two countries in the first period, and in the first period there is again a one-period Nash equilibrium in which each country takes as given the first-period emissions of the other country and chooses its own first-period emissions to maximize its own welfare, but recognizing that the second-period emissions of both countries depend on the first-period emissions. Finally, I shall consider a cooperative equilibrium (*C*) where emissions of both countries in both periods are chosen to maximize world welfare, which in this symmetric case is just the sum of the welfares of the two countries.[12]

I first sketch the solutions for each of the equilibrium concepts – for further details for a more general version of this model see Ulph and Ulph (1996) – and then compare the three solutions.

Open-loop Nash

The country takes f_1, f_2 as given and chooses e_1, e_2 to maximize:

$$-0.5(e^* - e_1)^2 - 0.5(e^* - e_2)^2 - 0.5\bar{\theta}(e_1 + e_2 + f_1 + f_2)^2. \qquad (4)$$

The first-order condition, or *reaction function*, is

$$e^* - e_t = \bar{\theta}(e_1 + e_2 + f_1 + f_2) \quad t = 1, 2. \tag{5}$$

Equation (5) has the usual interpretation that the country sets emissions in each period so that marginal benefit equals present value marginal damage cost. Using symmetry, (5) is readily solved to yield the equilibrium emissions: $e_1 = e_2 = f_1 = f_2 = e^*/(1 + 4\bar{\theta})$. It is straightforward to solve for the equilibrium stock of emissions and welfare level, so that the open-loop Nash equilibrium can be summarized by:

$$e_1^{OLN} = \frac{e^*}{1+4\bar{\theta}}; \quad X^{OLN} = \frac{4e^*}{1+4\bar{\theta}}; \quad W^{OLN} = \frac{8\bar{\theta}(1+2\bar{\theta})e^{*2}}{(1+4\bar{\theta})^2} \tag{6}$$

Feedback Nash

Consider first the second period, and suppose that first-period emissions by the two countries have been e_1 and f_1. Then the country takes f_2 as given and chooses e_2 to maximize (4). The first-order condition, or reaction function, is again given by (5), and, using symmetry, this can be solved to yield the Nash equilibrium second-period emissions:

$$e_2 = f_2 = \frac{e^* - \bar{\theta}(e_1 + f_1)}{1+2\bar{\theta}}. \tag{7}$$

Turning to the first-period problem, we can substitute the equilibrium second-period emissions (7) into the welfare function (5), so that in the first period the country takes f_1 as given and chooses e_1 to maximize:

$$-0.5(e^* - e_1)^2 - 0.5\frac{\bar{\theta}(1+\bar{\theta})(2e^* + e_1 + f_1)^2}{(1+2\bar{\theta})^2}. \tag{8}$$

The first-order condition, or reaction function, is given by:

$$e^* - e_1 = \frac{\bar{\theta}(1+\bar{\theta})(2e^* + e_1 + f_1)}{(1+2\bar{\theta})^2}, \tag{9}$$

where again (9) has the interpretation that emissions are chosen so that marginal benefit equals present value marginal damage costs. Equation (9) can be solved using symmetry to yield the equilibrium first-period emissions:

$$e_1 = f_1 = \frac{(1+2\bar{\theta}+2\bar{\theta}^2)e^*}{(1+6\bar{\theta}+6\bar{\theta}^2)}. \tag{10}$$

Equation (10) can now be inserted in (7) to yield second-period emissions, and hence the stock of emissions, and into (8) to yield equilibrium welfare. Thus the feedback Nash equilibrium can be summarized by:

$$e_1^{FN} = \frac{(1+2\bar{\theta}+2\bar{\theta}^2)e^*}{(1+6\bar{\theta}+6\bar{\theta}^2)}; \quad X^{FN} = \frac{4(1+2\bar{\theta})e^*}{(1+6\bar{\theta}+6\bar{\theta}^2)};$$

$$W^{FN} = -\frac{8\bar{\theta}(1+\bar{\theta})(1+5\bar{\theta}+5\bar{\theta}^2)e^{*2}}{(1+6\bar{\theta}+6\bar{\theta}^2)}. \tag{11}$$

Cooperative equilibrium

e_1, e_2, f_1, f_2 are chosen to maximize:

$$-0.5\{(e^*-e_1)^2 + (e^*-e_2)^2 + (e^*-f_1)^2 + (e^*-f_2)^2 + 2\bar{\theta}(e_1+e_2+f_1+f_2)^2\}$$

for which a typical first-order condition is:

$$e^* - e_1 = 2\bar{\theta}(e_1 + e_2 + f_1 + f_2). \tag{12}$$

Again (12) has the interpretation that the marginal benefit from emissions should equal the present value marginal damage cost, where the relevant damage cost is the global damage cost, not the individual country damage cost. Equation (12) can be solved using symmetry to yield equilibrium emissions:

$$e_1 = e_2 = f_1 = f_2 = \frac{e^*}{(1+8\bar{\theta})},$$

from which it is straightforward to calculate the equilibrium stock of emissions and welfare level. The cooperative equilibrium can now be summarized as:

$$e_1^C = \frac{e^*}{(1+8\bar{\theta})}; \quad X^C = \frac{4e^*}{(1+8\bar{\theta})}; \quad W^C = -\frac{8\bar{\theta}e^{*2}}{(1+8\bar{\theta})^2} \quad (13)$$

From (6), (11) and (13) it is now straightforward to compare the three different equilibria and show that:

$$e_1^C < e_1^{OLN} < e_1^{FN} \quad (14a)$$

$$X^C < X^{OLN} < X^{FN} \quad (14b)$$

$$W^C > W^{OLN} > W^{FN} \quad (14c)$$

The intuition behind these results is straightforward. The non-cooperative equilibria result in higher current emissions and overall stock of emissions than the cooperative equilibria, because in the non-cooperative equilibria each country takes account only of the damage caused by its own emissions to its own environment, and ignores the impact on the environment of other countries, while in the cooperative equilibrium it is the global damage that is taken into account. Thus because the relevant marginal damage costs in the non-cooperative equilibrium are lower than in the cooperative equilibrium, countries are led to set higher emission levels and hence higher stocks of emissions in the non-cooperative equilibria than in the cooperative equilibrium. However, because all countries set higher emissions in the non-cooperative equilibria, this ends up making all countries worse off than in the cooperative equilibrium. The reason why the feedback Nash equilibrium involves higher current emissions than the open-loop Nash equilibrium follows from (7). In the open-loop equilibrium each country believes that an extra unit of current emissions will add to the total stock of emissions, since all other emission levels are being held fixed. By contrast, in the feedback Nash equilibrium from (7) each country realizes that an extra unit of current emissions will be partially offset by a reduction in second-period emissions by all countries, including itself. Thus the perceived present value marginal damage cost of first-period emissions is lower in the feedback Nash equilibrium than in the open-loop Nash equilibrium and so all countries set higher first-period emissions. This is not completely offset by lower second period emissions, and so the overall stock of emissions is higher in the feedback Nash equilibrium than the open-loop Nash equilibrium, and all countries are made worse off because of this. This ranking of emissions, stocks and welfare across the three different equilibria holds in much more general models than the one presented here.

The difference in welfare between the cooperative and non-cooperative equilibria is referred to as the *gains from cooperation*, and the analysis of international environmental agreements is concerned with designing mechanisms to realize these gains.

This completes this section which has presented the analysis of a single decision maker faced with uncertainty about the damages of global warming, but with the possibility of getting better information in the future about the extent of such damages, and the analysis of cooperative and non-cooperative approaches to setting emissions policies when there are several countries, but there is certainty about the extent of damages from global warming. In the next section I combine these two strands of analysis to consider how emissions will be set when there are several decision makers and there is uncertainty about damages from global warming, with the possibility of obtaining better information in the future. The question to be addressed is which of the results derived in this section will carry over to the more general model.

3. MANY COUNTRIES LEARNING ABOUT GLOBAL WARMING

In this section I begin by combining the two models of the previous section by assuming that we have the same two identical countries as in Section 2.2, but, as in Section 2.1, allowing for the fact that there is uncertainty about the extent of damages from global warming and that there may or may not be the possibility of obtaining perfect information about the extent of global warming damages by the start of the second period. I shall present the analysis of the cooperative and non-cooperative equilibria first under no learning then under learning (Subsections 3.1 and 3.2). I shall then compare the results of the four different cases – Subsection 3.3. The analysis reported in these sections constitutes special cases of the results reported in Ulph and Ulph (1996) and Ulph and Maddison (1997). Finally, in Subsection 3.4 I discuss a related paper on the implications for reaching international environmental agreements on global warming.

There is only one modification I need to make to the models of the previous section, and that is to allow for the very real possibility that global warming may have different impacts on the two countries; in particular what may be bad for one country may be good for the other. To capture this in the simplest way consistent with the models of the previous section, for country i the damage cost function is $0.5\theta_i X^2$. θ_i is a random variable which is equally likely to take the values 0 or $2\bar{\theta}$, and hence have expected value $\bar{\theta}$. I need to specify how the distributions of the two random variables θ_1 and θ_2 are related to each other, and I capture this by letting γ denote the degree of correlation (correlation coefficient) between the two variables. γ can take any value between -1 and $+1$. What this implies is that there are effectively four states of the world, $s = 1, \ldots, 4$, and Table 13.1 sets out for each of the four states the values of the two random variables, θ_{1s} and θ_{2s} and the probability of that state occurring, π_s.

Table 13.1 States of the world

State s	θ_{1s}	θ_{2s}	Probability π_s
1	$2\bar{\theta}$	$2\bar{\theta}$	$0.25(1 + \gamma)$
2	$2\bar{\theta}$	0	$0.25(1 - \gamma)$
3	0	$2\bar{\theta}$	$0.25(1 - \gamma)$
4	0	0	$0.25(1 + \gamma)$

Note two extreme cases. When there is perfect positive correlation between damages in the two countries, $\gamma = +1$, then only the two states 1 and 4 can occur, both with probability 0.5, that is, either both countries have positive damage from global warming or neither has. When there is perfect negative correlation between damages in the two countries, $\gamma = -1$, then only states 2 and 3 can occur, each with probability 0.5, so that with certainty one country has positive damage and the other does not, and the only thing which distinguishes states 2 and 3 is the identity of the country which experiences the damage.

Once again there will be two assumptions about information. At the start of period 1 neither country knows the true state of the world; under no learning, this is also true at the start of period 2, so each country sets its second-period emissions independent of the state of the world. Under learning both countries learn which of the four states of the world is the true state, and so can condition its second period emissions on the true state of the world. I shall analyse non-cooperative and cooperative equilibria under learning and no learning, and, for simplicity, I shall consider only one non-cooperative equilibrium, the open-loop Nash equilibrium (while the feedback Nash equilibrium is arguably more pertinent to global warming, it is somewhat more complicated to derive under uncertainty and learning; the results I want to derive hold also for the feedback Nash equilibrium; see Ulph and Ulph, 1996 for an analysis of the feedback Nash equilibrium with uncertainty and learning). To establish the notation for this section, there are four cases I shall consider: open-loop Nash with no learning, denoted (*ON*); open-loop Nash with learning (*OL*); cooperative equilibrium with no learning (*CN*); cooperative equilibrium with learning (*CL*). I shall derive the results for each of the four cases, and then compare them.

3.1 No learning

As with the single decision maker model of 2.1, with no learning the total damage cost functions of the two countries display a *certainty equivalence* property, that is, total damages can be treated as if they were known with certainty with the value of the random variables θ_1 and θ_2 replaced by their expected values $\bar{\theta}$. Thus the analyses of the open-loop Nash and cooperative equilibria under no learning are exactly the same as the analyses of these equilibria under certainty which I presented in 2.2. For completeness I repeat the summary of the results:

Open-loop Nash with no learning (*ON*)

$$e_1^{ON} = \frac{e^*}{1+4\bar{\theta}}; \quad X^{ON} = \frac{4e^*}{1+4\bar{\theta}}; \quad W^{ON} = \frac{8\bar{\theta}(1+2\bar{\theta})e^{*2}}{(1+4\bar{\theta})^2} \quad (15)$$

Cooperative equilibrium with no learning (*CN*)

$$e_1^{CN} = \frac{e^*}{1+8\bar{\theta}}; \quad X^{CN} = \frac{4e^*}{1+8\bar{\theta}}; \quad W^{CN} = \frac{8\bar{\theta}e^{*2}}{1+8\bar{\theta}} \quad (16)$$

3.2 Learning

Open-loop Nash equilibrium with learning (*OL*)
Country 1 takes as given f_1, f_{2s}, $s = 1, ..., 4$ and chooses e_1, e_{2s}, $s = 1, ..., 4$ to maximize:

$$-0.5(e^* - e_1)^2 - 0.5\left\{\sum_{s=1}^{s=4} \pi_s \left[(e^* - e_{2s})^2 + \theta_{1s}(e_1 + f_1 + e_{2s} + f_{2s})^2\right]\right\}$$

The first-order conditions are:

$$e^* - e_{2s} = \theta_{1s} X_s \quad s = 1, ..., 4$$
$$e^* - e_1 = \sum_{s=1}^{s=4} \pi_s \theta_{1s} X_s \quad (17)$$

where $X_s = e_1 + f_1 + e_{2s} + f_{2s}$. Equation (17) has the usual interpretation that emissions in each period and each state are chosen so that the marginal benefit of emissions equals the expected present value marginal damage cost of emissions. Using symmetry it is straightforward to solve (17) to yield:

$$X_1^{OL} = \frac{4e^*}{(1+\chi)(1+4\bar{\theta})}; X_2^{OL} = X_3^{OL} = \frac{4e^*}{(1+\chi)(1+2\bar{\theta})}; X_4^{OL} = \frac{4e^*}{(1+\chi)};$$

$$e_1^{OL} = f_1^{OL}\frac{(1-\chi)e^*}{(1+\chi)}; \quad e_{21}^{OL} = f_{21}^{OL} = e^* - 2\bar{\theta}X_1^{OL}; \quad e_{22}^{OL} = f_{23}^{OL} = e^* - 2\bar{\theta}X_2^{OL};$$

$$e_{23}^{OL} = f_{22}^{OL} = e_{24}^{OL} = f_{24}^{OL} = e^*;$$

$$W^{OL} = -\frac{2e^{*2}\left\{\chi^2 + 2\bar{\theta}(1+2\bar{\theta})\left[\frac{1+\gamma}{(1+4\bar{\theta})^2} + \frac{1-\gamma}{(1+2\bar{\theta})^2}\right]\right\}}{(1+\chi)^2}$$

where $\chi = \frac{2\bar{\theta}[1+(3-\gamma)\bar{\theta}]}{(1+2\bar{\theta})(1+4\bar{\theta})}$. (18)

Cooperative equilibrium with learning (CL)
e_1, f_1, e_{2s}, f_{2s}, $s = 1, ..., 4$ are chosen to maximize:

$$-0.5(e^* - e_1)^2 - 0.5(e^* - f_1)^2 - 0.5\left\{\sum_{s=1}^{s=4}\pi_s\left[(e^* - e_{2s})^2 + (e^* - f_{2s})^2 + (\theta_{1s} + \theta_{2s})(e_1 + f_1 + e_{2s} + f_{2s})^2\right]\right\}$$

The first-order conditions are:

$$e^* - e_{2s} = (\theta_{1s} + \theta_{2s})X_s \quad s = 1,...,4$$
$$e^* - f_{2s} = (\theta_{1s} + \theta_{2s})X_s \quad s = 1,...,4$$
$$e^* - e_1 = \sum_{s=1}^{s=4}\pi_s(\theta_{1s} + \theta_{2s})X_s$$
$$e^* - f_1 = \sum_{s=1}^{s=4}\pi_s(\theta_{1s} + \theta_{2s})X_s.$$
(19)

Again, these have the interpretation that marginal benefit of emissions equals expected present value marginal damage costs, where damage costs are now global damage costs, not just an individual country's damage costs. Equation (19) can be solved using symmetry to yield the following:

$$X_1^{CL} = \frac{4e^*}{(1+\xi)(1+8\bar{\theta})}; X_2^{CL} = X_3^{CL} = \frac{4e^*}{(1+\xi)(1+4\bar{\theta})}; X_4^{CL} = \frac{4e^*}{(1+\xi)};$$

$$e_1^{CL} = f_1^{CL}\frac{(1-\xi)e^*}{(1+\xi)}; \quad e_{21}^{CL} = f_{21}^{CL} = e^* - 4\bar{\theta}X_1^{CL};$$

$$e_{22}^{CL} = f_{22}^{CL} = e_{23}^{CL} = f_{23}^{CL} = e^* - 2\bar{\theta}X_2^{CL}; \quad e_{24}^{CL} = f_{24}^{CL} = e^*;$$

$$W^{CL} = -\frac{2\xi e^{*2}}{(1+\xi)};$$

$$\text{where } \xi = \frac{4\bar{\theta}[1+2\bar{\theta}(3-\gamma)]}{(1+4\bar{\theta})(1+8\bar{\theta})}. \tag{20}$$

3.3 Comparison of Cases

I now want to compare the outcomes of the four different cases in order to assess how far the results derived for the two separate models in Section 2 carry over when the two models are integrated. I begin by comparing the cooperative and non-cooperative outcomes and then the learning and no learning outcomes.

Non-cooperative and cooperative outcomes
We have seen that with no learning, the outcomes of the cooperative and non-cooperative equilibria are exactly the same as in the model of certainty in Section 2.2, so not surprisingly a comparison of (15) and (16) shows that all the results of that section carry over, namely:

$$e_1^{CN} < e_1^{ON}; X^{CN} < X^{ON}; W^{CN} > W^{ON}$$

that is, the cooperative outcome involves lower emissions, stocks of emissions and higher welfare than the non-cooperative equilibrium. For the case of learning, it is readily shown that $\xi > \chi$, so that from (19) and (20) it can be seen that

$$e_1^{CL} < e_1^{OL}; \quad X_s^{CL} < X_s^{OL}; \quad s = 1, \ldots, 4; \quad W^{CL} > W^{OL}.$$

Thus all the results derived in Section 2.2 for a comparison of the cooperative and non-cooperative outcomes carry over to a world of uncertainty about the extent of global warming, whether or not there is a possibility of obtaining better information in the future about the true level of damages.

Learning and no learning

For reasons discussed in Section 2.2, what I am interested in is the comparison of first-period emissions and welfare between the case of no learning and the case of learning. I begin by making this comparison for the cooperative equilibrium and then turn to the non-cooperative equilibrium.

Learning and no learning – cooperative equilibrium The first point to note is that $\partial \xi / \partial \gamma < 0$, from which it can be readily shown that $(\partial W^{CL})/\partial \gamma > 0$, $(\partial e_1^{CL})/\partial \gamma > 0$ so that in the cooperative equilibrium with learning welfare and first-period emissions are an increasing function of the correlation coefficient. It is also straightforward to calculate the values of welfare and first emissions when γ takes its extreme values of -1 and $+1$, which are:

$$\gamma = +1 \Rightarrow \xi = \frac{4\bar{\theta}}{1+8\bar{\theta}}; \quad e_1^{CL} = \frac{(1+4\bar{\theta})e^*}{(1+12\bar{\theta})}; \quad W^{CL} = -\frac{8\bar{\theta}e^{*2}}{1+12\bar{\theta}};$$

$$\gamma = -1 \Rightarrow \xi = \frac{4\bar{\theta}}{1+4\bar{\theta}}; \quad e_1^{CL} = \frac{e^*}{(1+8\bar{\theta})}; \quad W^{CL} = -\frac{8\bar{\theta}e^{*2}}{1+8\bar{\theta}}; \quad (21)$$

Comparing (21) with (16) we see that:

$$e_1^{CL} \geq e_1^{CN} \text{ and } W^{CL} \geq W^{CN} \text{ as } \gamma \geq -1$$

in other words, for the cooperative equilibrium first-period emissions and welfare with learning are strictly greater than with no learning except when there is perfect negative correlation, when they are equal. Moreover, in the case of perfect positive correlation, a comparison of (21) and (16) with (3) shows that the comparison between the outcomes with learning and no learning are the same for the multi-country case as for the single decision maker case except that the term $\bar{\theta}$ in the single decision maker case is scaled up by a factor of 4, which just represents the fact that with two countries damages are greater than in the single decision maker model.

The intuition behind these results is straightforward. The cooperative equilibrium involves the choice of emissions to maximize world welfare, and because of symmetry in each period and each state the two countries act identically; so the two-country case is really just like a single decision maker. Indeed, when there is perfect positive correlation between damages in the two countries, there are only effectively two states – either there is damage to the whole world or there is not – then the analogy with the single decision maker case is complete, apart from the scaling factor. On the other hand, when there is perfect negative correlation, there are only two states with positive probabilities – states 2 and 3 – where in both states one country suffers damages and the other does not. However, again because the cooperative equilibrium means that in each state both countries set the same levels of emissions, there is effectively no difference between these two states of the world; at the level of the individual countries it clearly matters which state occurs, but from a global perspective the only distinction between the two states is the name of the country which suffers the damages, and that has no real effect on any decision. So when there is perfect negative correlation there is no effective uncertainty, and so there is no difference, from a global perspective, between the no learning and learning cases, since there is nothing to learn; in particular the value of perfect information is zero.

Thus there are two extreme cases: when there is perfect positive correlation only states 1 and 4 matter, the multi-country case is just a scaled-up version of the single decision maker case, and first-period emissions and welfare are strictly greater with learning than no learning; when there is perfect negative correlation only states 2 and 3 matter, there is effectively no uncertainty and no difference between the no learning and learning cases. Any intermediate value of the correlation coefficient just produces a mixture of these two extremes, and as the correlation coefficient increases increasing probability weight is put on states 1 and 4.

In short, except for the case of perfect negative correlation, the results derived in Section 2.2 comparing the cases with learning and no learning for a single decision maker carry over to a multi-country case as long as the countries act cooperatively.

Learning and no learning – non-cooperative equilibrium I start by noting that $\partial \chi_1 / \partial \gamma < 0$ which implies that $(\partial e_1^{OL})/\partial \gamma > 0$, and $(\partial W^{OL})/\partial \gamma > 0$, so that, as with the cooperative equilibrium, first-period emissions and welfare are increasing functions of the correlation coefficient. Evaluating first-period emissions and welfare at the extreme values of $\gamma = +1$ and -1 yields:

$$\gamma = +1 \Rightarrow \chi = \frac{2\bar{\theta}}{1+4\bar{\theta}}; \quad e_1^{OL} = \frac{(1+2\bar{\theta})e^*}{1+6\bar{\theta}}; \quad W^{OL} = -\frac{8\bar{\theta}(1+3\bar{\theta})e^{*2}}{(1+6\bar{\theta})^2};$$

$$\gamma = -1 \Rightarrow \chi = \frac{2\bar{\theta}}{1+2\bar{\theta}}; \quad e_1^{OL} = \frac{e^*}{1+4\bar{\theta}}; \quad W^{OL} = -\frac{8\bar{\theta}(1+3\bar{\theta})e^{*2}}{(1+4\bar{\theta})^2}. \quad (22)$$

Comparing (22) with the outcome for the non-cooperative equilibrium with no learning (15) shows that

$e_1^{OL} \geq e_1^{ON}$ as $\gamma \geq -1$;

$\gamma = -1 \Rightarrow W^{OL} < W^{ON}$; $\gamma = +1 \Rightarrow W^{OL} > W^{ON}$.

In words, in the non-cooperative equilibrium, we again get the result that first-period emissions with learning are strictly greater than first-period emissions with no learning, except when there is perfect negative correlation, when they are equal. However, when there is perfect negative correlation, welfare is strictly lower with learning than no learning, while when there is perfect positive correlation welfare is strictly greater with learning than no learning. Since welfare with learning is a monotonically increasing function of the correlation coefficient, there will be a range of values for the correlation coefficient for which both countries are worse off with learning than with no learning; that is, for this range of values for the correlation coefficient perfect information has negative value. Figure 13.3 shows the welfare levels for the cooperative and non-cooperative equilibria under learning and no learning for all values of the correlation coefficient.

Thus, combining the analysis of learning and no learning with a non-cooperative game provides a rather striking reversal of a very general result with a single decision maker – that perfect information should have positive value.

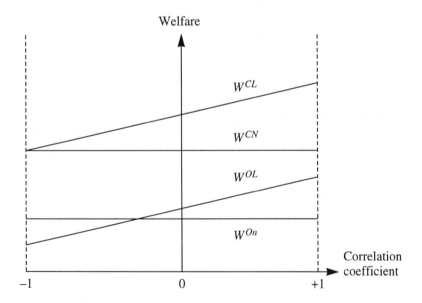

Figure 13.3 Welfare for ON, OL, CN, CL as functions of correlation coefficient

In fact, Ulph and Ulph (1996) also show that in a more general version of the current model it is also possible to show that when there is perfect negative correlation, then first-period emissions with learning can be less than first-period emissions with no learning, so that both of the results derived from the comparison between learning and no learning for a single decision maker do not carry over to the case of non-cooperative behaviour with several countries.

Again, the intuition behind these results is straightforward. Recall that when there is perfect positive correlation, only states of the world 1 and 4 are relevant, that is, both countries either experience global warming damage or they do not. Given the symmetry of the model, in both these states both countries set the same levels of emissions. So while in the non-cooperative equilibrium there is the usual distortion that the countries will set too high emissions compared to a cooperative equilibrium, both countries still benefit from being able to tailor their second-period emissions to the true state of the world, so the gains from perfect information that accrue to a single decision maker also accrue to the two countries acting non-cooperatively. Similarly the impact of learning on first-period emissions is the same as for a single-country case.

Now consider the case of perfect negative correlation, where only states 2 and 3 can occur. We saw that in the cooperative case there was effectively no uncertainty, because there was no effective difference between these two states. In the non-cooperative case there is crucial difference between the states, because if state 2 arises, say, country 1 will cut its emissions substantially while country 2 will set its emissions at the BAU level e^*, since it has learned that it faces no damages. The roles of the two countries are reversed in state 3. This has a crucial impact on welfare in the learning case compared to no learning. From (15), (18) and (22) it is readily shown that, for this special model, *total* second-period emissions are the same in states 2 and 3 as they would be under no learning.[13] But whereas in the no learning case each country would set the same level of emissions, or equivalently carry out the same level of abatement of emissions, in the case of learning, as I have just noted, the two countries set very different levels of emissions, that is, they carry out very different levels of abatement. But this just introduces an inefficiency, because from a global point of view whatever total level of abatement is to be carried out, the efficient solution, that is, the one which minimizes global total abatement costs, is to equalize the marginal costs of abatement across the two countries and, given symmetry, that means equalizing the levels of abatement across the two countries. Thus learning leads to the same total level of abatement as no learning, but the allocation across countries is inefficient and this reduces welfare in the learning case compared to no learning.

There is a second factor at work reducing welfare in the learning case. Again go back to state 2; country 1 learns that it faces damages, country 2 learns that it faces no damages. If they both set the same level of emissions, which, as I have argued above, is what efficiency requires, country 2 would clearly be better off than country 1; but country 2 can adjust to this information by increasing its emissions, forcing country 1 to adjust by cutting its emissions. This makes country 2 even better off and country 1 even worse off. So the *ex post* distribution of welfare across the two countries is widened under learning compared to no learning. This means that countries face greater risk under learning than no learning and, since the countries are risk-averse, this gives a second reason why learning makes countries worse off than they would be under no learning for the case of perfect negative correlation. Again, intermediate values of the correlation coefficient just produce a mixture of the outcomes with perfect positive and negative correlation.

Having explained why learning can have negative value in the non-cooperative equilibrium when there is perfect negative correlation, I now discuss briefly the results for first-period emissions. I have already noted that for this simple model, *total* second-period emissions in states 2 and 3 are the same with learning as they would be with no learning, and are also the same across both states. Since it is total emissions that determines damage costs, when each country compares the marginal benefit of first-period emissions with expected present value of marginal damage costs, this latter value is the same under learning as under no learning and so the level of first-period emissions is the same. I noted that this was a special result, and that in a more general model it is possible for first-period emissions with learning to be lower than with no learning. The reason, as noted by Ulph and Ulph (1996), is that total emissions in states 2 and 3 can be higher with learning than no learning, and to compensate for this countries set lower first-period emissions with learning than with no learning. The reason why total emissions in states 2 and 3 may be higher with learning than no learning are that, as I have already noted, the country that learns that it has low damage costs raises its emissions, while the country that learns that it has high damage costs cuts its emissions. In a more general model, these responses trigger further adjustments in emissions by the two countries, since the country with low damage costs will expand its emissions even further because the other country has cut its emissions, and vice versa. Since the increase in emissions by the low damage cost country outweighs the reduction in emissions by the high damage cost country (since it becomes increasingly costly to cut emissions), total emissions rise. These second-round effects trigger further responses until the Nash equilibrium is reached. In the simple model presented in this chapter, because low damage costs are zero, the low damage cost country sets emissions at e^* irrespective of what the other country does, and so the sequence of further adjustments outlined above does not arise in this simple model.

To summarize, I have shown that the comparisons between non-cooperative and cooperative equilibria derived for dynamic pollution games under certainty carry over to games with uncertainty with and without the possibility of learning more about the uncertain damages from global warming. Similarly the comparison between outcomes with learning and no learning in terms of welfare and first-period emissions that were derived for a single decision maker carry over to cooperative equilibria for many countries. However, these results may not carry over to non-cooperative equilibria. In particular, if, as seems likely, global warming may have very different impacts on different countries, with some benefiting and others losing significantly, then the value of better information may be negative,[14] and current emissions may need to be cut more severely because of future learning than would be the case without such learning.

3.4 Implications for International Environmental Agreements

The preceding analysis suggests two implications for the design of international environmental agreements. First, international agreements will need to consider more than just the usual question of how to get all countries to reduce their emissions – they will also need to consider what happens when better information becomes available, particularly if there is negative correlation among the damage costs to different countries. Second, and closely related to the previous point, while the analysis shows that there are always gains to cooperation, there may be much greater gains to cooperation when there is the possibility of learning better information than when there is not. This follows from a simple identity noted by Ulph and Maddison (1995):

$$\text{GfC (learning)} - \text{GfC (no learning)} = \text{VoI(coop)} - \text{VoI(non-coop)}.$$

GfC stands for gains from cooperation; VoI stands for value of information. Now we know that the value of information is always positive for cooperative equilibria. We also know that for sufficiently low values of the correlation coefficient the value of information will be negative for non-cooperative equilibria. Thus for these cases there are greater gains to be had from cooperation when learning is possible than when it is not.

However, the previous points are only suggestive of implications for international environmental agreements because the analysis to date does not explicitly analyse the question of how independent nations enter into such agreements, for it is one thing to show that there are gains from cooperation, quite another to show how they can be realized. A paper which explicitly examines the formation of international environmental agreements when there is uncertainty and the possibility of obtaining better information is Na and Shin (1995), and this has some strong links with the analysis reported here. To understand their paper I need to summarize very briefly the kind of analysis used to study international environmental agreements. A widely used approach for studying what kinds of international environmental agreements might be formed is to look for *stable coalitions* of countries.[15] A coalition of countries is simply a group of countries which act together to maximize the sum of the welfares of individual members, that is, to implement the cooperative solution among members, taking as given the emissions policies of non-members. Countries have to decide whether or not to join a coalition by comparing their welfare in the coalition with their welfare outside the coalition. There are three factors that will influence whether to join a coalition: by joining a coalition a country will have to increase its own abatement of emissions, and hence increase its costs; on the other hand other members of the coalition will also increase their abatement of emissions, which will benefit the country; but non-members of the coalition will respond to the higher abatement by the coalition members by reducing their abatement. The balance of these considerations will determine whether or not a country will join a coalition. A coalition is *stable* if no member country wishes to leave the coalition and no non-member country wishes to join the coalition. The question studied in this literature is what is the largest stable coalition that can be formed?

However, almost all of the literature on coalition formation assumes perfect information about the payoff functions of countries, in particular the damage cost functions of countries. An exception is the recent very elegant paper by Na and Shin (1995). They consider a three-country model, with a single period, where each country has a quadratic cost of abatement function and linear benefit of abatement function (in the terminology of this chapter this corresponds to a quadratic benefit of emissions function and a linear damage cost function). However, there is uncertainty about the benefits from abatement, equivalent to my assumption of uncertainty about the damage cost function. Specifically, it is known that one country will have high benefits from abatement, one country will have intermediate benefits from abatement and one will have low benefits from abatement, but the identity of these countries is not known, and *ex ante* each country has an equal chance of being the high-, intermediate- or low-benefit country. Of course this is exactly analogous to the case of perfect negative correlation for my two-country example. Countries have to decide whether or not to join a coalition, and there are two timing possibilities. In what I have called the no learning case, countries have to decide whether or not to join a coalition before the true state of the world is known, and of course they must then commit themselves to a level of abatement before the true state of the world is known. In the learning case, countries first of all learn the true state of the world and then have to decide whether or not to join a coalition. Na and Shin compare the expected benefits to countries in the no learning and learning case. What they show is that in the case of no learning, the only stable coalition is the 'grand coalition' of all three countries. In the case of learning it is much harder to form coalitions, in the sense that the grand coalition is unstable, and, depending on parameter values, either a coalition of the two countries with the highest benefits from abatement will be stable, or else there is no stable coalition – that is, the outcome is the non-cooperative outcome. What Na and Shin show is that whatever the parameter values, countries are always better off in the no learning case. The rationale is that it is easier to form coalitions the more similar countries are, and countries may be more similar before information is revealed, when they are faced with expected damage costs, than they are after information has been revealed.

It is clear that there are strong similarities between the Na and Shin (1995) analysis and that presented earlier in this section. The broad message is that if countries are likely to experience very different benefits and costs from global warming, then the strategic non-cooperative interactions between countries after information is revealed can offset the standard benefits decision makers have from being able to tailor their actions in the light of the better information provided to them, so that better information has negative value. The specific message from Na and Shin is that it may be better to try to reach international environmental agreements before too much information becomes available.

4. EMPIRICAL APPLICATIONS

In this section I shall very briefly summarize some empirical findings related to the theoretical analysis set out in the previous sections. Just as most of the theoretical analysis of the implications of learning about global warming has been conducted in the context of a single decision maker, taken to represent an agent seeking to maximize world welfare, so most of the empirical studies of the value of better information about global warming have been conducted in that framework. Manne and Richels (1992), Peck and Tiesberg (1993) and Nordhaus (1994) have all presented studies of the gains to be had from obtaining better information about global warming. Using a very simple model, Manne and Richels (1992) estimate the value of perfect information about global warming to be $81 billion, while Peck and Tiesberg (1993), using a rather richer model in which they allowed for a number of sources of uncertainty, calculated the value of perfect information at $273 billion. Nordhaus used a stochastic optimal growth model with climate change (the DICE model) where, like Peck and Tiesberg, there were many dimensions to the elements of uncertainty about global warming, and calculated that the benefit of bringing forward the resolution of uncertainty from 2020 to 1990 would be worth $1.176 trillion in 1989 prices. As the models of climate change have become more sophisticated, the estimates of the value of perfect information have risen substantially. It is also worth noting that as the date of resolution of uncertainty gets earlier in the

Nordhaus model, the level of abatement of emissions for the first period (1990–99) falls – from 15.7 per cent reduction for late resolution (that is, resolution in 2020) to 10.3 per cent for immediate resolution of uncertainty. This is consistent with the analysis presented in Section 2.2, showing that first-period emissions under learning would be higher than with no learning.

I am not aware of any studies of global warming which have used dynamic game models under certainty to assess the gains from cooperation. For example the MERGE model developed by Manne, Mendelsohn, and Richels (1993), which is a regional variant of the Manne and Richels (1992) Global 2200 model, analyses the costs and benefits of exogenously specified policies to tackle global warming for different regions, but this is not the same thing as conducting a strategic analysis of policies by different regions acting non-cooperatively.

The only empirical study I am aware of which compares the outcomes under learning and no learning in the strategic context set out in the last section is that by Ulph and Maddison (1995), which is an extension of an earlier single decision maker optimal control model developed by Maddison (1995). I do not have space to give the details of the model, for which readers are referred to Ulph and Maddison (1997). I shall simply sketch sufficient details so that the results can be understood. Underlying this model is a pair of econometrically estimated equations to capture climate change, one linking atmospheric concentrations of greenhouse gases to lagged emissions of greenhouse gases, the other relating changes in global mean temperature to lagged values of atmospheric concentrations of greenhouse gases. There are two country blocks – OECD and rest of the world (ROW) – and two time blocks – 1990–2020 and 2020–2150. There is uncertainty about the extent of damages from global warming; with low damages a 2.5°C increase in global mean temperature would cause damages amounting to 1.5 per cent of GNP; with high damages the same increase in temperature would cause damages amounting to either 15 per cent of GNP (Model I) or 5 per cent of GNP (Model II). A key parameter is the correlation coefficient linking the damages in the two country blocks. Finally, Model I uses a discount rate of 5 per cent, Model II a discount rate of 2 per cent.

Table 13.2 shows the value of information (the difference in welfare in $1990 trillion (tr.) between the equilibria with learning and no learning) for different values of the correlation coefficient for Models I and II and for open-loop Nash and cooperative equilibria. The values are given for OECD (a), ROW (b) and in total (Σ).

There are a number of points to be made. First, the aggregate value of information can be negative in the non-cooperative equilibrium when damages are significantly negatively correlated. Second, the value of information depends quite strikingly on the correlation coefficient between damages in the two country blocks. In Model I there is a difference of about $2 trillion between the value of information (in total across the two blocks) when the correlation coefficient is −1 and that when it is +1, while for Model II the difference is about $10 trillion, and this is true for both the cooperative and non-cooperative equilibria. Third, note that the value of information is always higher in the cooperative than the non-cooperative equilibrium. As Ulph and Ulph (1996) showed, this need not always be the case (the case where it was not was with a correlation coefficient of 1). A related result is that the difference in the value of information between the cooperative and non-cooperative outcomes falls as the correlation coefficient rises. The rationale for this is that in the non-cooperative equilibrium, in states 2 and 3 the responses of the two countries to each other's abatement policies creates inefficiencies which are not present in the cooperative case, and as the correlation coefficient rises this difference between the cooperative and non-cooperative cases carries less weight. Finally, the calculation of the value of perfect information for the cooperative equilibrium with perfect positive correlation is the closest analogue to the calculations for the single decision maker studies presented at the start of this section; as Table 13.2 shows, the values presented by Ulph and Maddison (1997) are significantly higher than those derived in those earlier studies, and the reader is referred to Ulph and Maddison (1997) for a discussion of why this discrepancy arises.

Table 13.2   Value of information

| | MODEL I | | | | | | MODEL II | | | | | |
| | Non-cooperative | | | Cooperative | | | Non-cooperative | | | Cooperative | | |
γ	a	b	Σ	a	b	Σ	a	b	Σ	a	b	Σ
−1.0	−0.61	0.28	−0.32	−0.45	0.60	0.15	−3.4	1.84	−1.5	−2.1	2.81	0.71
−0.75	−0.44	0.37	−0.07	−0.29	0.68	0.39	−2.5	2.17	−0.3	−1.3	3.14	1.86
−0.5	−0.27	0.45	0.18	−0.14	0.76	0.62	−1.5	2.51	0.94	−0.46	3.47	3.01
−0.25	−0.1	0.53	0.43	0.02	0.84	0.86	−0.66	2.84	2.18	0.36	3.81	4.17
0.0	0.07	0.61	0.68	0.17	0.91	1.09	0.25	3.17	3.42	1.18	4.14	5.32
0.25	0.24	0.69	0.93	0.33	0.99	1.32	1.16	3.5	4.66	2.0	4.47	6.47
0.5	0.41	0.77	1.18	0.48	1.07	1.55	2.07	3.83	5.9	2.82	4.8	7.62
0.75	0.58	0.85	1.43	0.64	1.15	1.79	2.98	4.16	7.15	3.64	5.14	8.78
1.0	0.75	0.93	1.68	0.79	1.22	2.02	3.89	4.5	8.39	4.47	5.47	9.93

Finally, I discuss briefly what the model of Ulph and Maddison (1997) says about the size of the gains from cooperation. The gain from cooperation in the no learning case is independent of the correlation coefficient, being $1 trillion in the case of Model I and $9.5 trillion in the case of Model II. The gain from cooperation for the learning case does depend on the correlation coefficient and declines as the correlation coefficient rises. In Model I it declines from $1.47 trillion to $1.34 trillion, while in Model II it declines from $11.8 trillion to $11.1

trillion.[16] The decline in the gain from cooperation under learning is explained by exactly the same factor that explains the narrowing of the gap in the value of information between cooperative and non-cooperative equilibria. This follows from the simple identity set out in Section 3.4:

$$VoI\ (Coop) - VoI(non\text{-}coop) = GfC\ (learning) - GfC\ (no\ learning).$$

To conclude, the empirical analysis of Ulph and Maddison (1995) shows that the question of a negative value for better information is more than just a theoretical curiosum, and the value of better information depends very sensitively on the degree of correlation between damages in different countries. This suggests that much more attention needs to be given to this aspect of global warming.

5. CONCLUSIONS

In this chapter I have argued that the economics of global pollution problems such as global warming have a number of features which make their analysis complex. While all these features have been analysed, very few studies fully integrate all these features. In particular, the analysis of uncertainty and learning about global warming has been conducted on the assumption of a single global decision maker, while the analysis of the strategic aspects of global warming, whether in terms of dynamic games or coalition formation, has ignored uncertainty and learning. I have surveyed a small literature which has sought to integrate these two strands. The striking new result to emerge from this exercise is that strategic non-cooperative interaction of countries in response to better information may make all countries worse off than if such information were not available. This is true both when countries are setting their emissions policies in response to better information or deciding whether or not to join a coalition. This possibility of information having negative value arises when global warming has very different implications in terms of costs and benefits for different countries, which seems to be a plausible feature of this phenomenon.

The models I have used in this survey have been kept as simple as possible since I have been more interested in explaining why some of our standard intuitions about the benefits of better information may not apply to global warming than in descriptive realism of the models. The limited empirical work that has been done to date suggests that the theoretical analysis may be quantitatively significant in practice. Clearly there is much more to do both in terms of developing the theory and, more importantly, the empirical analysis. Particular areas for further analysis are the implications for international environmental agreements, and, in terms of empirical work, more careful attention to the geographical differences in costs and benefits rather than aggregate world estimates.

NOTES

1. See Hoel (1992), van der Ploeg and de Zeeuw (1992), Barrett (1992, 1994), Black, Levi and de Meza (1993), Heal (1992, 1994), Carraro and Siniscalco (1993) among many others. The chapter by Art de Zeeuw in this book (Chapter 12) surveys the literature on dynamic pollution games while those by Tulkens (Chapter 2), Folmer and Gil (Chapter 8), and Botteon and Carraro (Chapter 9) consider different approaches to getting independent countries to cooperate in solving international pollution problems.
2. See Chichilnisky and Heal (1993), Kolstad (1993, 1996), Manne and Richels (1992), Nordhaus (1994), Peck and Tiesberg (1993), Ulph and Ulph (1997), among others.
3. For a discussion of the policy issues related to global warming which is up to date at the time of writing this chapter, the reader is referred to recent studies undertaken for the Intergovernmental Panel on Climate Change (Pillett and Gassman, 1994).
4. The total benefit function can be thought of as a very reduced-form equation for the rest of the economy, and comprises the consumer surplus from consuming all the products whose production generates greenhouse gases, plus the profits from producing these products. It is assumed that there are no other distortions in the rest of the economy, so that the total benefit function is really the maximum benefit which society can derive for a given level of emissions of greenhouse gases.
5. Again we can think of this as a very reduced-form equation which summarizes a number of very complex relationships linking emissions of greenhouse gases, their accumulation in the atmosphere, the subsequent impact on climate, and effect of any change in climate, crudely summarized by mean global temperature, on human society through impacts on agriculture, sea level rise, storm damage, loss of habitats and so on.
6. An important related question which, for simplicity, I shall not address, concerns the *irreversibility* of greenhouse gas emissions. By this I mean that there is no technology available for reducing the stock of greenhouse gases, at least on any significant scale. In practice this may be possible, for example, through reforestation which would 'lock up' carbon dioxide emissions. This irreversibility characteristic could be captured in this model by assuming that greenhouse gas emissions are non-negative, so that it is not possible to 'undo' the effects of emissions in the first period by having 'negative' emissions in the second period (see Ulph and Ulph, 1996, 1997). I shall not impose this constraint, so in principle first-period emissions could be reversed by having negative emissions in the second period, though at a cost which is captured implicitly by the utility function.
7. Recalling what I said in note 5 about what lies behind this total damage cost function, the uncertainty could relate to our understanding of how emissions of greenhouse gases might affect climate, or about the effect of climate change on society, or about how much society values any of these impacts.
8. Again, this is a very special assumption, and a more general treatment would allow the decision maker to obtain better information about the extent of global warming damages but not have all uncertainty resolved. Of course this raises the question of what is meant by 'better' information. For a model which incorporates this form of partial learning about global warming see Kolstad (1993, 1996).
9. The results presented below can be generalized to allow for more than two states of the world, with arbitrary prior probabilities, positive discounting and decay of the stock of emissions, an initial stock of emissions at the start of period 1, more general functional forms for the benefit and damage cost functions, damage costs arising in both periods. The key assumptions are that there are only two periods and that the unknown parameter in the damage cost function, θ,

enters the damage cost function in a simple multiplicative form, that is, $D(X) = \theta d(X)$ where $d(X)$ is a monotonically increasing, strictly convex function.

10. Recall that in note 6 I said that I would not impose the condition that emissions of greenhouse gases are *irreversible*. If I had imposed the assumption of irreversibility, then the same analysis would have applied, except that in the definition of the total cost function $C(e_1, \theta)$ the choice of second-period emissions would have been subject to the constraint that second-period emissions be non-negative. The same set of sufficient conditions could also be used. However, Ulph and Ulph (1997) showed that even with quadratic total benefit and total damage cost functions, the marginal cost function is neither concave nor convex in θ, so it is difficult to apply these sufficient conditions to even the simplest model of global warming with irreversibility. Ulph and Ulph (1997) derive an alternative sufficient condition for first-period emissions with learning to be less than first-period emissions with no learning.
11. This is also known as a subgame-perfect Markov equilibrium.
12. These three equilibrium concepts are standard in the literature on dynamic games – see van der Ploeg and de Zeeuw (1992) and Hoel (1992) for applications to dynamic pollution games.
13. For the case of perfect negative correlation, total second period emissions in states 2 and 3 under learning and no learning are $2e^*/(1 + 4\theta)$.
14. The result that information may have negative value in non-cooperative games is not a new result. See Basar and Ho (1974), Crawford and Sobel (1982) for general analysis, the literature on information transmission in oligopolies (Gal-Or (1985, 1986), Vives (1986) and Swierzbinski (1988) for an application to fisheries economics. A closely related argument, though not couched in terms of game theory, can be found in Hirshleifer (1971).
15. See Barrett (1994), Carraro and Siniscalco (1993), Chander and Tulkens (1992), Heal (1994), and the chapter by Tulkens in this book (Chapter 2).
16. We can derive the gains from cooperation under learning from knowledge of the gains from cooperation with no learning and the values for information in Table 13.2 using the identity shown in the text. For example, for Model 1 the gain from cooperation with no learning is $1 trillion; when the correlation coefficient is –1, the difference in the value of information in the cooperative equilibrium and the non-cooperative equilibrium is $0.47 trillion [that is, $0.15 trillion – (–$0.32 trillion)]; while when the correlation coefficient is +1 the difference in value of information between the cooperative and non-cooperative equilibria is $0.34 trillion ($2.02 trillion – $ 1.68 trillion). Thus the gain from cooperation in Model 1 declines from $1.47 trillion to $1.34 trillion.

REFERENCES

Barrett, S. (1992), 'International Environmental Agreements as Games', in R. Pethig (ed.), *Conflicts and Cooperation in Managing Environmental Resources*, Berlin: Springer-Verlag, pp. 11–36.

Barrett, S. (1994), 'Self-enforcing International Environmental Agreements', *Oxford Economic Papers*, **46**, 878–94.

Başar, T. and Y.C. Ho (1974), 'Informational Properties of the Nash Solution of Two Stochastic Non-zero-Sum Games', *Journal of Economic Theory*, **7**, 370–87.

Black, J., M.D. Levi and D. De Meza (1993), 'Creating a Good Climate: Minimum Participation for Tackling the Greenhouse Effect', *Economica*, **60**, 281–94.

Carraro, C. and D. Siniscalco (1993), 'Strategies for the International Protection of the Environment', *Journal of Public Economics*, **52**, 309–28.

Chander, P. and H. Tulkens (1992), 'Theoretical Foundations of Negotiations and Cost-Sharing in Transfrontier Pollution', *European Economic Review*, **36**, 388–98.

Chichilnisky, G. and G. Heal (1993), 'Global Environmental Risks', *Journal of Economic Perspectives*, **7**, 65–86.

Crawford, V. and J. Sobel (1982), 'Strategic Information Transmission', *Econometrica*, **50**, 1431–51.
Epstein, L. (1980), 'Decision Making and the Temporal Resolution of Uncertainty', *International Economic Review*, **21**, 269–83.
Gal-Or, E. (1985), 'Information Sharing in Oligopoly', *Econometrica*, **53**, 329–44.
Gal-Or, E. (1986), 'Information Transmission – Cournot and Bertrand Equilibria', *Review of Economic Studies*, **53**, 85–92.
Heal, G. (1992), 'International Agreements on Emission Control', *Structural Change and Economic Dynamics*, **3**, 223–40.
Heal, G. (1994), 'The Formation of Environmental Coalitions', in C. Carraro (ed.), *Trade, Innovation, Environment*, Dordrecht: Kluwer, pp. 301–22.
Hirshleifer, J. (1971), 'The Private and Social Value of Information and the Reward to Inventive Activity', *American Economic Review*, **61**, 561–74.
Hoel, M. (1992), 'Emission Taxes in a Dynamic International Game of CO_2 Emissions', in R. Pethig (ed.), *Conflicts and Cooperation in Managing Environmental Resources*, Berlin: Springer-Verlag, pp. 39–68.
Kolstad, C. (1993), 'Looking vs Leaping: The Timing of CO_2 Control in the Face of Uncertainty and Learning', in Y. Kaya, N. Nakicenovic, W. Nordhaus and F. Toth (eds), *Costs, Impacts and Benefits of CO_2 Mitigation*, IIASA, Austria 63–82.
Kolstad, C. (1996), 'Fundamental Irreversibilities in Stock Externalities', *Journal of Public Economics*, **60**, 221–33.
Maddison, D. (1995), 'A Cost-Benefit Analysis of Slowing Climate Change', *Energy Policy*, **25**, 337–46.
Manne, A., R. Mendelsohn and R. Richels (1993), 'MERGE – Model for Evaluating Regional and Global Effects of GHG Reduction Policies', mimeo, Stanford.
Manne, A. and R. Richels (1992), *Buying Greenhouse Gas Insurance: The Economic Costs of CO_2 Emission Limits*, Cambridge, MA: MIT Press.
Na, S. and H.S. Shin (1995), 'International Environmental Agreements under Uncertainty', mimeo, University of Southampton.
Nordhaus, W. (1994), *Managing the Global Commons: The Economics of Climate Change*, Cambridge, MA: MIT Press.
Peck, S. and T. Tiesberg (1993), 'Global Warming Uncertainties and the Value of Information: an Analysis Using CETA', *Resource and Energy Economics*, **15**, 71–97.
Pillett, G. and F. Gassmann (1994), *Steps Towards a Decision Making Framework to Address Climate Change*, Report from the Montreux IPCC WG III Writing Team II Meeting, Paul Scherrer Institute, Villigen.
Swierzbinski, J. (1988), 'When More Isn't Better: Information and Common-Property Resources', *Mathematical and Computer Modeling*, **11**, 899–902.
Ulph, A. and D. Maddison (1997), 'Uncertainty, Learning and International Environmental Policy Coordination', *Environmental and Resource Economics*, **9**, 451–66.
Ulph, A. and D. Ulph (1996), 'Who Gains from Learning About Global Warming?', in E. van Ierland and K. Gorka (eds), *The Economics of Atmospheric Pollution*, Heidelberg: Springer-Verlag, pp. 31–67.
Ulph, A. and D. Ulph (1997), 'Global Warming, Irreversibility and Learning', *The Economic Journal*, **107**.
Van der Ploeg, R. and A. de Zeeuw (1992), 'International Aspects of Pollution Control', *Environmental and Resource Economics*, **2**, 117–40.
Vives, X. (1986), 'Duopoly Information Equilibria: Cournot and Bertrand', *Journal of Economic Theory*, **34**, 71–94.

14. Migration and the environment

Markus Haavio

1. INTRODUCTION

Until the seventeenth century people believed that the Sun orbited the Earth. The long-lasting dominance of the Ptolemaean astronomy can no doubt be partly attributed to the intellectual authority of the Catholic Church and to the respect for the thinkers of antiquity. But perhaps a still more compelling reason is the fact that the geocentric world view seemed to be consistent with observations. Indeed, the Ptolemaean model with the Sun moving along its epicyclic orbit and the more modern Copernican universe where the Earth rotates around its own axis are two possible worlds where day follows night. For the alternation or light and dark the absolute velocity of the two celestial bodies is irrelevant. It is only the relative movement of the surface of the Earth with respect to the Sun that counts.

In this chapter, the interaction of household mobility and environmental policy is analysed by using the story about Ptolemy and Copernicus and the principle of relative movement as guidelines. The chapter develops a two-period game with accumulation of pollution and costly migration to suggest that the effects of household mobility on environmental policy are essentially equivalent to those of transboundary pollution.

By replacing the celestial objects figuring in the sketchy delineation of the two competing world views by concepts of environmental economics, the story can be retold. In a Ptolemaean economy people are immobile but pollution flows across national frontiers. In a Copernican world pollution is local but people can move from one country to another. In the astronomical context, both of these models give rise to the alternation of day and night. Now the claim is that the equivalence holds for international environmental economics as well: only relative mobility matters; just like mobile pollutants, mobile people create international externalities and distortions.

Demographic dynamics and environmental problems are known to be interlinked in a number of ways. A growing population increases the stress on the ecosystem. The state of the environment in turn influences death rates and people's incentives to have children.[1] In recent years, more attention has also been paid to the interaction between migration and the environment. The term 'environmental refugee' was coined in 1985 by the United Nations Environmental Programme.[2] Three years later a study by the Worldwatch Institute estimated that there were about 10 million people falling into this category in the late 1980s.[3] Most of them had escaped soil erosion or desertification depleting arable land in developing countries, especially in sub-Saharan Africa. On the other hand pollution also played its role. The number of environmental refugees and migrants is expected to increase in the future.

The degradation of the environment influences people's decisions to migrate. On the other hand there is some evidence suggesting that mobile people can in turn be harmful to the environment. A bulk of studies have established that shifting cultivation and nomadism may be partly responsible for deforestation in the tropics and for desertification in sub-Saharan Africa.[4] Shifting cultivators appropriate a piece of land by burning the forest. After a few harvests the field has to be abandoned and can be retaken into agricultural use, probably by others, only after a lengthy period of forest regeneration. Shifting cultivators move on and have no incentives to care for the ecological sustainability of the forest ecosystem.

Although population problems and the environment are acknowledged to be closely connected, economic research on international and interregional environmental issues has concentrated on studying transboundary pollution, trade and capital mobility.[5] Furthermore, and perhaps somewhat surprisingly, the existing small literature on migration and the environment doesn't see household mobility as a source of international or interregional environmental problems, but rather as a mechanism inducing implicit cooperation between selfish national governments. Indeed, the literature shows that under costless migration, all international externalities caused by, for example, transboundary pollution are internalized by national environmental policies, and the resulting outcome is socially optimal. Furthermore, the mechanism behind this result is found to be very strong:[6] an attempt to increase one's own welfare at the expense of others, by cutting back emission abatements and letting neighbours affected by transboundary pollution carry a part of the environmental costs, triggers immigration. As the population of the emitting country grows, the amount of fixed resources – for example, land or the carrying capacity of the environment – available per capita decreases, which in turn lowers welfare. Migration flows instantaneously cancel out all welfare differences: no country can be better off than any other country. As all countries can correctly anticipate the reactions of migrants and understand that a socially non-optimal policy is necessarily non-optimal from the national point of view, each country ends up maximizing the aggregate welfare of the economy. In other words, perfect household mobility renders the objective functions of individual countries identical to each other and equal to that of the social planner. As there are no conflicts of interest, the decentralized outcome is fully efficient.

In this chapter, our aim is to defend the opposite view, and to claim that the analogy between mobile pollutants and mobile people, and more generally models of the tragedy of the commons, constitutes a useful framework for the analysis of household mobility and the environment. When pollution flows across national boundaries, those who enjoy the fruits of production can avoid part of the environmental costs. National policies fail to recognize the damages occurring abroad: the inevitable consequence is overpollution. In the case of household mobility, the constellation is strikingly similar. People can produce, consume and pollute, and then escape the environmental consequences by moving away. Once again there's a discrepancy between costs and benefits.

A tragedy of the commons occurs when property rights over an asset are ill defined or cannot be enforced. Typically, the literature shows that common access leads to overconsumption and underinvestment.[7] When pollution flows across national boundaries, each country becomes a public dumping ground, and property rights over the environment are at best nominal. On the other hand, accumulation of pollution and household mobility together lead to the tragedy of the commons. A mobile household has incentives to consume now and to give a lower weight to future consumption and environmental amenities. If resources are saved, others will move in and appropriate them.

The nature of the migration–environment nexus may have several important policy implications. One of the objectives of the European Union is to reduce the obstacles to labour mobility between the member countries. Is an integrated European labour market a substitute for a common environmental policy or does it reinforce the need to delegate more power to Brussels? In the US environmental policy is conducted partly by states, partly by the federal government. The principle of subsidiarity adopted by the EU requires that all decisions be taken at the lowest possible level. What does the fact that Americans are more prone to move from state to state than Europeans from one country to another imply for the optimal division of power in the US and in the EU? How will the expected increase in the number of environmental refugees and migrants influence the relations between the North and the South?

In addition to the policy-oriented questions, there are more theoretical and methodological motivations for this study. Economic modelling always involves a trade-off between clarity and realism. In the literature on the local public sector it is standard to use static models and to assume that households are perfectly mobile.[8] Studies on economic integration often start with a model with an immobile labour force, which is then compared to an economy with perfect labour mobility.[9] For these ideal types to be relevant as stylized descriptions of the real world, the simplified settings should bear at least a qualitative resemblance to the more complex economic phenomena one wants to understand. One of the main results of this chapter is that in a dynamic model setting imperfect household mobility is qualitatively different from costless migration. Comparing immobile households to free mobility would give a misleading picture of the effects of economic integration.

The rest of the chapter is organized as follows. Section 2 presents two examples illustrating why household mobility can sometimes be harmful, sometimes beneficial for the environment. Section 3 develops a two-period game among selfish countries encompassing both the (partial) equalization of objective functions, resulting in implicit cooperation, and the tragedy of the commons as special cases. The model demonstrates that the effects of household mobility may depend crucially on governments' ability to make credible commitments. In addition we show that imperfect household mobility is qualitatively different from perfect mobility. Finally, Section 4 concludes.

2. TWO EXAMPLES

The case of perfect household mobility is particularly interesting. When people can move from one place to another without incurring any costs, the place where a person lives during a certain period doesn't affect his/her choice of location for the subsequent period: complete mixing of population is possible at each moment of time. If the tragedy of the commons is the right model for analysing the interaction between household mobility and environmental policy, the fact that people can escape the environmental consequences of their actions without incurring any costs should generate particularly strong distortions: indeed, perfect household mobility should be equivalent to global pollution. On the other hand the implicit cooperation argument, presented in the literature, tells us that costless migration implies social optimum.

In this section we develop two simple, and admittedly somewhat *ad hoc*, games to study environmental policy under perfect household mobility. We take seriously the claim that complete mixing of population is possible in each period, and assume that players are assigned to a country by a lottery. Although in a model, with the help of which one tries seriously to understand migration and the environment, the country where a person lives should depend on his/her own choice, not on pure chance, the simplistic approach we adopt in this section may give some useful insights. The following examples will illustrate that the effects of household mobility on environmental policy depend on at least two factors. (i) Does pollution accumulate to the environment? (ii) What is the exact sequence of events in the game? Does migration precede consumption and emissions or vice versa?

Tragedy of the Commons

The model is first presented as a cake-eating game. After that an environmental economic interpretation is given.

There are N players, N cakes and N chairs around a table. The game lasts for two periods. At the beginning of the first period each player takes a chair and finds a cake. The task of the players is to decide how big a share of the cake to eat in the first period and how much to save for the second period. The size of the cake is ω, the amount eaten in the first period is denoted by C, and the part saved for the second period is denoted by ε, $\varepsilon = \omega - C$. First- and second-period utilities are given by the functions $U(C)$ and $u(\varepsilon)$. Between the two periods the players change places. New chairs are determined by a lottery, giving each player a probability of $1/N$ for being assigned to each chair. In the second period the players eat the piece of cake remaining on the table next to their new seat.

As the players are assumed to be expected utility maximizers, the player sitting in chair i, $i = 1, ..., N$, in the first period chooses C^i so as to maximize

$$\max_{C^i} U(C^i) + \frac{1}{N} \sum_{j=1}^{N} u(\varepsilon^j). \qquad (1)$$

The corresponding first-order conditions are of the form

$$U'(C^i) = \frac{1}{N} u'(\varepsilon^i). \qquad (2)$$

The outcome of the game is clearly not Pareto-optimal. A social planner would divide the cakes so that the marginal utility of consumption would be equal in both periods, $U'(C^i) = u'(\varepsilon^i)$ The source of the inefficiency lies in the fact that players change places between the two periods. Each player can only decide how much cake is left in the place where s/he sits during the first period; the sizes of the cakes waiting next to all the other seats are beyond his/her control. Thus the probability of influencing one's own future is only $1/N$.

Next we give an environmental economic interpretation to the result. If C denotes consumption and ε is the quality of the environment in the second period, we can see that the model describes an economy with local stock pollution and mobile people. In $N-1$ cases out of N a player moves away from his/her original location and escapes the environmental consequences of his/her own actions. Thus the players don't have the appropriate incentives to take into account the environmental damages. Furthermore it's easy to see that the outcome of the game is equivalent to the result one gets when studying a model with global pollution, that is, an economy where only a share of 1/N of each player's emissions pollute his/her own environment.

One of the underlying themes in the game presented above is poorly specified property rights and the risk of expropriation. A person or a group of people is allowed to use a resource for a certain time, then the right may be taken away. The possibility of losing the resource makes people short-sighted and impatient.

Implicit Cooperation

Next we analyse a model where migration serves as a remedy to international externalities caused by transboundary pollution. As above, a cake-eating game will be followed by an environmental economic interpretation.

The basic set-up is identical to the one presented in the previous section: There are N players, N cakes and N chairs around a table. The game lasts for two periods.

At the beginning of the first period each player takes a chair and finds a cake. The players are given the task to divide the cake into two pieces: one of the pieces is left beside the chair, the other one is moved to the centre of the table. Once the cakes have been split, the players change places and new seats are determined by a lottery. In the second period each player eats the piece of cake s/he finds next to his/her new seat.

The size of each cake is ω, and the pieces eaten by the players are denoted by C^i, $i = 1, \ldots, N$; gastronomic pleasures are captured by subutility functions $U(C^i)$. In addition to eating, the players enjoy watching beautiful things, such as half-eaten cakes. If the piece of cake being removed at the centre of the table by the player having sat in seat i during the first period is denoted by ε^i, $\varepsilon^i = \omega - C^i$, the aggregate amount of cake not eaten is $E = \Sigma_{j=1}^{N} \varepsilon^j$. The utility each player derives when admiring the cakes is given by the function $V(E)$.

The player sitting in chair i, $i = 1, \ldots, N$ in the first period chooses C^i so as to maximize his/her expected utility

$$\max_{C^i} \frac{1}{N} \sum_{j=1}^{N} U(C^j) + V(E). \qquad (3)$$

The corresponding first-order conditions are of the form

$$U'(C^i) = NV'(E). \qquad (4)$$

Equation (4) is the Samuelson rule for the provision of public goods, and it can easily be checked that the outcome of the game is Pareto-optimal.

By relabelling C as consumption and E as the quality of the environment, an environmental economic interpretation of the game can be given. The model describes an economy with global flow pollution: the quality of the environment $E = \Omega - P$ depends on the aggregate level of emissions P, where $P = \Sigma^N_{j=1} C^j$ and $\Omega \equiv N\omega$. In a standard model of global pollution, players only take into account the domestic effects of their emissions: the level of environmental damages is determined by the set of equations $U'(C^i) = V'(E)$, and the pollution load is bigger than optimal. The fact that players move from one place to another, however, forces them to pay attention to each other. The utility of a player depends on where s/he sits during the second period. As places are changed between the periods, the players have to design the environmental policy while still ignorant of their future position; the constellation is to a great extent analogous to Rawlsian decision making behind the veil of ignorance.[10] Although environmental policy is nominally decentralized, Formula (3) shows that each player actually ends up maximizing the aggregate welfare of the economy. In other words, the objective functions of the players are identical to each other and to that of the social planner.

The simple games analysed above differed from each other in at least two respects. (i) While in the first model pollution accumulated to the environment, in the second model emissions were assumed to generate an instantaneous stream of disutility. Only if disutility from pollution occurs later than utility from consumption it is possible to escape the environmental consequences of one's actions by moving away. (ii) In the first model migration occurred between consumption and the degradation of the environment. In the second model people moved from one place to another after decision making but before consumption. As will become clear in the next section, household mobility induces countries to cooperate if migration falls between decision making and the implementation of the policy.

3. THE MODEL

In this section we develop a two-period game to show that the effects of household mobility on environmental policy are generated by an interplay between two conflicting incentives. (i) Strategic overpollution, resulting in a higher pollution stock, pre-empts *future* immigration and the appropriation of resources by foreigners. (ii) People can migrate to the country engaging in strategic environmental overpollution during the time that elapses between decision making and the implementation of environmental policy. This in turn lowers the payoffs of strategic environmental policy and induces implicit cooperation. Before proceeding to the technical analysis, we present an outline of the argument and briefly discuss the role of different assumptions.

The analysis of household mobility and environmental policy will centre around three intertemporal concepts: forward-looking and costly migration, the accumulation of pollution and governments' ability to make credible commitments.

When people moving from one country to another have to incur sunk costs, migration decisions become forward-looking: the momentary stream of utility at the point of time migration takes place is not essential. The whole discounted sum of future well-being must be higher in the new home country. Furthermore, shifting costs make migration a process taking place in real time: the regional distribution of population doesn't instantaneously react to changes in policy.

Environmental policy, on the other hand, can influence both future and past migration. The link to the future operates through the accumulation of pollution. If environmental damages occur only after consumption has taken place, people can first consume and then escape pollution by moving away. On the other hand strategic overconsumption, entailing a bigger pollution stock, is a way to pre-empt future immigration.

Environmental policy carried out at a certain point of time (t) influences migration taking place before that date, as well. If country 1 manages to increase its utility at the expense of its neighbours by overpolluting from date t onwards, there will be a difference in the discounted sum of utility in favour of country 1 at each moment before t. This in turn triggers migration flows in the direction of country 1 before the date (t) the strategic overpollution begins. Finally, immigration lowers the welfare in the country trying to exploit its neighbours. Thus the effects of environmental policy on past migration create a feedback mechanism making countries' objective functions more equal to each other and inducing them to cooperate.

The incentives to strategic overpollution in order to cut back future immigration always exist if pollution accumulates to the environment. The strength of the mechanism forcing countries to cooperate depends, however, on the time horizon of environmental policy. If governments can make credible commitments, the decisions concerning the environmental policy carried out at date t can be made at a date $t - h$ before t. It is evident that for the optimization happening at date $t - h$ only the events taking place after that date are relevant. Thus, of all the labour movements happening before t, only the share of migration occurring between $t - h$ and t is taken into account when designing the environmental policy. Now it is easy to see that the incentives to cooperation depend on the length of the period of commitment h. If the time horizon of environmental policy is long enough, incentives to cooperation outweigh incentives causing the tragedy of the commons. On the other hand, if commitment is impossible, only the incentives to overpollute remain: like mobile pollutants, mobile households create distortions.[11]

The assumption that migration is costly is especially important. Indeed, perfect household mobility is qualitatively different from costly migration. When households are perfectly mobile the distribution of population reacts instantaneously to policy changes. The strength of the mechanism inducing countries to cooperate doesn't depend on commitment technologies. As all welfare differentials are instantaneously cancelled out, a socially non-optimal policy is always necessarily harmful from the national point of view, as well. In other words, in the case of perfect household mobility, the decentralized outcome is fully efficient.

One possible way to formalize the argument presented above is to develop a differential game taking place in continuous time: consumers can react constantly to welfare differences and can migrate at each moment of time; the role of commitment is captured by altering the time over which governments can make credible plans over the environmental policy. Such a strategy is adopted in Haavio (1997). This study shows that the dynamic optimization problem faced by individual countries in the presence of migration boils down to the following basic structure: every time policy makers reoptimize, their decision entails a trade-off between present and future welfare. The present essentially means the present period, of length h, over which the countries can make credible commitments. The future is in turn captured by a value function, having the stock of pollution and the regional distribution of people as its arguments. The present affects the future through the accumulation of pollution. The pollution stock, together with the distribution of population, in turn determines the pattern of future migration. In addition to the links between the present and the future, the other important thing is what happens inside the present period. Here the essential aspect is the length of the period. How much migration can take place during the period; how strong is the feedback mechanism inducing implicit cooperation?

It is this basic structure that we are trying to capture in the simplest possible way in this chapter. To do so we shall develop a two-period model. The first period is the present, while the whole future is condensed into the second period. Through the accumulation of pollution, first-period emissions affect the second period: the quality of the environment and people's decisions to move from one country to another. The interaction between environmental policy and second-period migration leads to the tragedy of the commons. On the other hand, the fact that first-period migration also depends on the level of emissions results in the feedback effect inducing cooperation. Governments' ability to make credible commitments also enters the model. Decisions concerning environmental policy are taken at the beginning of the game; when the second period comes, governments reoptimize. By letting the length of the first period h vary, we can study how the effects of household mobility on environmental policy depend on the time of commitment.

Basic Assumptions

The economy consists of two countries, indexed by $i = 1, 2$, and lasts for two periods. The length of the first period is h, while the duration of the second period is fixed to unity. In what follows we shall refer to first-period variables by upper-case letters and to second-period variables by lower-case letters. The total population of the economy is unity and the number of consumers living in country i is denoted by N^i (n^i). Consumers are identical and derive utility out of consumption (C, c) and environmental amenities (E, ε). The representative consumption good is produced by using the environment as the sole input. The trade-off between first-period per capita consumption (C) and first-period emissions (X) is given by the equation[12]

$$X^i = N^i C^i. \qquad (5)$$

Not all emissions need to damage the environment in the country where production takes place. Transboundary pollution is captured by letting a fraction (q) of emissions, $0 \leq q \leq \frac{1}{2}$, be carried over by the wind. The bigger the value q takes, the bigger the share of transboundary pollution; if $q = \frac{1}{2}$ the pollutant is global.

In the literature, it is normal to make a distinction between flow and stock pollution. To allow for both alternatives, we assume that first-period emissions may, on the one hand, cause an instantaneous stream of disutility, and, on the other hand, the stock of environmental resources available for the second period may be depleted as well. The quality of the environment in country i in the first period is given by the formula

$$E^i = \Omega - v[(1-q)X^i + qX^j], \qquad (6)$$

where Ω is a constant describing the quality of the pristine environment and $v \geq 0$ tells how big a problem flow pollution is. Environmental resources left for the second period (ε^i) are in turn captured by the equation

$$\varepsilon^i = \Omega - s[(1-q)X^i + qX^j]h, \qquad (7)$$

where the parameter $s \geq 0$ indicates to what extent pollution accumulates to the environment. Note that the amount of resources depleted depends on the length of the period, h. For the sake of simplicity we assume that second-period consumption doesn't affect the quality of the environment. Thus in the second period it is optimal to consume all the resources left, and per capita consumption is given by the equation

$$c^i = \varepsilon^i / n^i. \qquad (8)$$

If the stream of utility during the first period is given by the function $U^i = U^i(C^i, E^i)$, with $U_C > 0$, $U_E > 0$, $U_{CC} < 0$, $U_{EE} < 0$, $U_{CE} > 0$, first-period utility can be expressed as a product of the utility stream and the length of the period, $U^i(C^i, E^i)h$. To keep the analysis as simple as possible, it is assumed that second-period utility can be described by a function having environmental resources per capita ε^i/n^i as its only argument, $u(\varepsilon/n) \equiv u(c)$, where the derivatives of the subutility function $u(c)$ have the signs $u'(c) > 0$, $u''(c) < 0$. Assuming a discount rate of ρ the intertemporal utility function (W^i) can now be written in the form

$$W^i = U(C^i, E^i)h + e^{-\rho h}u(c^i). \tag{9}$$

The sequence of moves in the environmental policy–migration game is the following:

0. At the outset of the game there's an equal number of consumers living in both countries: $N_0^1 = N_0^2 = \tfrac{1}{2}$

First period:

1. At the beginning of the first period the representative consumer of each country chooses the level of emissions X^i.
2. People can move from one country to the other. Those moving must incur a shifting cost $a(|K|)$, where $K \equiv (N^1 - N_0^1)/h$ is a measure of the migration stream, $a(\cdot)$ is an increasing, convex function and $a(0) = 0$.[13]
3. Each country emits as decided at stage 1. People get utility correspondingly.

Second period:

4. The representative consumer in each country decides how to allocate the resources left from the first period. As mentioned above the solution to this problem is trivial: it is optimal to consume all remaining resources.
5. People can move from one country to the other. Those moving must incur a shifting cost $a(|k|)$ where $k \equiv n^1 - N^1$ and $a(\cdot)$ is the increasing convex function defined above.
6. People consume and get utility.

Before solving the model, it is useful to mention two benchmark results. In the social optimum the marginal utility of first-period consumption equals the sum of the social marginal utility of environmental amenities and the marginal utility of second-period consumption:

$$U_{Ci}^i = vU_{Ei}^i N^i + e^{-\rho h} su_{ci}^i \qquad (10)$$

In the absence of household mobility, national policy leads to overconsumption in the first period: national authorities ignore the damages occurring abroad:

$$U_{Ci}^i = (1-q)\,[vU_{Ei}^i N^i + e^{-\rho h} su_{ci}^i] \qquad (11)$$

Solving the Game

In this section we shall analyse the symmetric equilibrium of the two-period game. Our primary aim is to demonstrate that the effect of imperfect household mobility on environmental policy is qualitatively different from that of costless migration. While perfect household mobility always forces countries to pay attention to each other and the resulting outcome is socially optimal, the effects of imperfect mobility on environmental policy depend on governments' ability to make credible commitments. If commitment is impossible, mobile people create new, dynamic externalities to the economy. Only if the time of commitment h is long enough can imperfect household mobility be beneficial.

As usual, the game is solved recursively, starting from the end. First we analyse people's incentive to migrate and then proceed to studying environmental policy.

Second stage: migration

Because of the symmetry of the model we can limit the analysis to the case where people migrate from country 2 to country 1. For migration to take place at the beginning of the second-period, the second period welfare differential between the countries has to be big enough to cover the shifting costs:

$$u(c^1) = u(c^2) + a(|k|). \qquad (12)$$

In the first period, potential migrants compare shifting costs to the difference in intertemporal utility

$$U(C^1, E^1) + e^{-\rho h} u(c^1) = U(C^2, E^2) + e^{-\rho h} u(c^2) + a(|K|). \qquad (13)$$

By totally differentiating (12) and (13), one can see that first-period emissions affect both past (K) and future (k) migration flows:

$$\frac{dK}{dX^1} = \frac{\left[U_{C1}^1 \frac{1}{N^1} - v(1-2q)U_{E1}^1 - e^{-\rho h}\frac{a'(|k|)}{2u_{c1}^1 \frac{c^1}{n^1} + a'(|k|)}\frac{s}{n^1}(1-2q)u_{c1}^1\right]h}{2\left[U_{C1}^1 \frac{C^1}{N^1}h + e^{-\rho h}\frac{a'|k|}{2u_{c1}^1 \frac{c^1}{n^1} + a'(|k|)}u_{c1}^1 \frac{c^1}{n^1}h + a'(|K|)\right]};$$

(14)

$$\frac{dk}{dX^1} = -\left[\frac{\frac{s}{n^1}(1-2q)u_{c1}^1}{2u_{c1}^1 \frac{c^1}{n^1} + a'(|k|)} + \frac{2u_{c1}^1 \frac{c^1}{n^1}}{2u_{c1}^1 \frac{c^1}{n^1} + a'(|k|)}\frac{dK}{dX^i}\right]h.$$

(15)

First stage: environmental policy

When decisions concerning environmental policy are made, the representative consumer takes into account that first-period emissions influence people's decisions to migrate. The maximization problem facing country 1 is of the form

$$\max_{X^1} U(C^1, E^1)h + e^{-\rho h}u(c^1)$$
s.t. (6),(7),(8),(12),(13)

The corresponding first-order condition is

$$U_{C1}^1 = N^1 \left\{ v(1-q)U_{E1}^1 + e^{-\rho h}u_{c1}^1 \frac{s}{n^1}(1-q) \right.$$
$$\left. + e^{-\rho h}u_{c1}^1 \frac{c^1}{n^1}\frac{dk}{dX^1}h^{-1} + e^{-\rho h}u_{c1}^1 \frac{c^1}{n^1}\frac{dK}{dX^1} + U_{C1}^1 \frac{C^1}{N^1}\frac{dK}{dX^1}h \right\} \quad (16)$$

The expression on the right-hand side of (16), inside the curly brackets, consists of five terms. The first term tells how first-period consumption affects the quality of the environment. The second term describes the trade-off between first- and second-period consumption. The third term captures the effects of environmental policy on second-period migration. The fourth term will vanish in all the cases we shall analyse, and is not of interest here. Finally, the last term reflects the feedback mechanism inducing cooperation. The feedback term will turn out to be crucial for many of the results that follow: will it disappear when the time of commitment h goes to zero?

Now we are all set to study the behaviour of the equilibrium under perfect and imperfect household mobility. For the sake of convenience we adopt the notation

$$\alpha \equiv a'(0).$$

The bigger the value α becomes the more costly migration is in the symmetric equilibrium. The two extreme values $\alpha = \infty$ and $\alpha = 0$ correspond to immobile households and perfect mobility.

Imperfect household mobility with no commitment

In this subsection and in the next one, we shall show that when migration is costly the effects of household mobility on environmental policy depend on governments' ability to make credible commitments. In this subsection we shall analyse the case of no commitment, $h \to 0$. First we demonstrate that imperfect household mobility creates a new dynamic externality to the economy: when pollution accumulates to the environment, the effects of household mobility on environmental policy are equivalent to those of transboundary pollution. After that we check that the externality is indeed dynamic; in the case of flow pollution new distortions are not generated.

As our primary aim is to find the dynamic externality created by the interplay between the accumulation of pollution and household mobility, the case of stock pollution is of special interest, and the parameter v describing flow pollution is set equal to zero. We begin the analysis by showing that the feedback term appearing in the first-order condition (16) vanishes as the period of commitment h goes to zero. From (14) and (16)

$$\lim_{h \to 0} U^1_{C1} \frac{C^1}{N^1} \frac{dK}{dX^1} h = \lim_{h \to 0} U^1_{C1} \frac{C^1}{N^1} \alpha^{-1} \left[U^1_{C1} \frac{1}{N^1} - \frac{\alpha}{2u^1_{c1} \frac{c^1}{n^1} + \alpha} s(1 - 2q) u^1_{c1} \right] h^2 = 0.$$

(17)

Shifting costs make migration a gradual process, demanding time. When the length of the period approaches zero, nobody has time to move between decision making and the implementation of the policy. Thus the feedback mechanism inducing cooperation is cut.

Migration and the environment

In contrast, the connection between environmental policy and future migration doesn't vanish when the time of commitment goes to zero. From (15) and (16)

$$\lim_{h \to 0} e^{-\rho h} u_{c1}^1 \frac{c^1}{n^1} \frac{dk}{dX^1} h^{-1} = -(1-2q) \frac{s}{n^1} \frac{u_{c1}^1 \frac{c^1}{n^1}}{2u_{c1}^1 \frac{c^1}{n^1} + \alpha} \neq 0 \qquad (18)$$

if $0 \leq q < \frac{1}{2}$.

Plugging (17) and (18) into (16), we get the first-order condition characterizing the economy as $h \to 0$:

$$U_{C1}^1 = u_{c1}^1 s[1 - q - Q], \qquad (19)$$

where

$$Q \equiv (1-2q) \frac{u_{c1}^1 \frac{c^1}{n^1}}{2u_{c1}^1 \frac{c^1}{n^1} + \alpha} \geq 0$$

A quick look at Equation (10) – note that $v = 0$ – tells us that the decentralized outcome is clearly not optimal. Furthermore, the comparison between (19) and (11) indicates that household mobility has brought one extra term to the equation characterizing national environmental policy. This term Q encapsulates the new dynamic externality. As Q is positive, the introduction of household mobility tends to increase first-period consumption. The result follows rather clearly the logic of the tragedy of the commons: early consumption is the optimal strategy. If resources were saved, others would move in and appropriate them.

Next we shall demonstrate that the effects of household mobility on environmental policy are equivalent to those of transboundary pollution. The bigger the share of pollutants that cross national borders, the worse. Similarly, the more mobile the households, the lower the quality of the environment. Moreover, when the derivative of the migration cost function $a'(0)$ approaches zero, the economy comes to resemble a world with global pollution.

Rearranging (19) shows that the symmetric equilibrium is characterized by the equation

$$\Phi(X^i, \alpha) = 0, \qquad (20)$$

where

$$\Phi(X^i, \alpha) \equiv \frac{U_{Ci}^i}{u_{ci}^i} - s\left[1 - q - (1-2q)\frac{u_{ci}^i \frac{c^i}{n^i}}{2u_{ci}^i \frac{c^i}{n^i} + \alpha}\right].$$

Now the total differentiation of (20) gives

$$\frac{dX^i}{d\alpha} = -\frac{\Phi_\alpha}{\Phi_{X^i}} < 0, \tag{21}$$

where

$$\Phi_{X^i} = \frac{U_{CC}^i \frac{1}{N^i} u_{ci}^i + u_{cc}^i \frac{s}{n^i} u_{ci}^i U_C^i}{(u_c^i)^2} - s(1-2q)\alpha \frac{u_{cc}^i \frac{s}{n^i} \frac{c^i}{n^i} + u_{ci}^i \frac{s}{(n^i)^2}}{\left(2u_c^i \frac{c^i}{n^i} + \alpha\right)^2}$$

$$= \frac{U_{CC}^i \frac{1}{N^i}}{u_c^i} - s(1-2q)\alpha \frac{u_{cc}^i \frac{s}{(n^i)^2}}{\left(2u_c^i \frac{c^i}{n^i} + \alpha\right)^2} + 2s\alpha \frac{u_{cc}^i \frac{s}{n^i} \frac{c^i}{n^i}}{\left(2u_c^i \frac{c^i}{n^i} + \alpha\right)^2}$$

$$+ 4s(1-q)\frac{u_{cc}^i u_c^i \frac{s}{n^i} \left(\frac{c^i}{n^i}\right)^2}{\left(2u_c^i \frac{c^i}{n^i} + \alpha\right)^2} + s(1-q)\alpha^2 \frac{s}{n^i} \frac{u_{cc}^i}{u_c^i \left(2u_c^i \frac{c^i}{n^i} + \alpha\right)^2}$$

$$< 0 \tag{22}$$

and

$$\Phi_\alpha = -s(1-2q)\frac{u_c^i \frac{c^i}{n^i}}{\left(2u_c^i \frac{c^i}{n^i} + \alpha\right)^2} \leq 0. \tag{23}$$

When deriving the last form of Expression (22), Equation (20) was exploited. An increase in household mobility – that is, a decrease in shifting costs α – implies more emissions in the first period. As the emission load is already bigger than optimal, welfare is lowered.

Next we note that $Q \to (\frac{1}{2} - q)$ as $\alpha \to 0$. Thus when moving costs approach zero, the first-order condition (19) takes the form

$$U_{Ci}^1 = u_{c1}^1 s \left[1 - \frac{1}{2} \right], \tag{24}$$

indicating that an economy with (almost) perfect household mobility behaves like an economy with global pollution.

To end this subsection, we check that the externality caused by household mobility is indeed dynamic. If s is set equal to zero and v equal to unity, the first-order condition (16) takes the form

$$U_{Ci}^1 = (1 - q) U_{Ei}^1 N^1, \tag{25}$$

identical to Equation (11) characterizing the economy with immobile households. In the case of flow pollution, household mobility doesn't generate new externalities. When the utility from consumption and disutility from pollution occur simultaneously, it is impossible to escape the environmental consequences of one's actions by moving away. On the other hand, there's no pollution stock to accumulate in order to pre-empt future immigration. Thus the preconditions for a tragedy of the commons to happen don't exist.

Imperfect household mobility with perfect commitment

In this subsection we shall study the case where governments' ability to make credible commitments is perfect. The aim of the section is twofold. First, it demonstrates the importance of commitment, by showing that when the period h is long enough, the feedback mechanism inducing cooperation comes to dominate, and imperfect household mobility can serve as a partial remedy to international externalities caused by transboundary pollution. Second, when the first period becomes infinitely long, the model virtually collapses into a static game. Thus comparing the results we shall derive here with those obtained in the previous subsection also serves to illuminate that a genuine dynamic model, for example our model when $h \to 0$, with local governments and mobile households, can lead to conclusions clearly at odds with those derived from a static model.

When the period of commitment h approaches infinity, the connection between environmental policy and second-period migration becomes insignificantly weak:

$$\lim_{h \to \infty} e^{-\rho h} u_{c1}^1 \frac{c^1}{n^1} \frac{dk}{dX^1} h^{-1} = 0. \tag{26}$$

The feedback effect, on the other hand, becomes increasingly strong as the period of commitment becomes longer:

$$\lim_{h \to \infty} U_{C1}^1 \frac{C^1}{N^1} \frac{dK}{dX^1} h = \lim_{h \to \infty} \left[U_{C1}^1 \frac{1}{N^1} - v(1-2q)U_{E1}^1 \right] \frac{U_{C1}^1 \frac{C^1}{N^1} h^2}{2 U_{C1}^1 \frac{C^1}{N^1} h^2 + \alpha} \tag{27}$$

Now the first-order condition (16) takes the form

$$U_{C1}^1 = U_{E1}^1 N^1 v [1 - q\theta], \tag{28}$$

where

$$\theta \equiv \frac{\alpha}{U_{C1}^1 \frac{C^1}{N^1} h^2 + \alpha}$$

$$0 \leq \theta \leq 1$$

From (28) it can be seen that household mobility doesn't introduce new distortions to the economy. On the contrary, comparing (28) and (11) shows that the fact that people can vote with their feet actually mitigates the existing distortions caused by transboundary pollution. Indeed, it is easy to see that if migration is costless, $\alpha = 0$, the decentralized outcome is socially optimal. Moreover, deepening integration, involving increasing household mobility, is good for the environment. Rearranging Equation (28) shows that the symmetric equilibrium is characterized by the equation

$$\Psi(X^i, \alpha) = 0, \tag{29}$$

where

$$\Psi(X^i, \alpha) \equiv \frac{U_{Ci}^i}{U_{Ei}^i} - N^i v \left(1 - \frac{q\alpha}{U_{Ci}^i \frac{C^i}{N^i} h^2 + \alpha} \right).$$

Totally differentiating (29) gives

$$\frac{dX^i}{d\alpha} = -\frac{\Psi_\alpha}{\Psi_{Xi}} > 0, \tag{30}$$

where

$$\Psi_{Xi} \equiv \frac{\left(U_{CC}\frac{1}{N^i} - vU^i_{CE}\right)U^i_E + \left(vU^i_{EE} - \frac{1}{N^i}U^i_{CE}\right)U^i_C}{\left(U^i_E\right)^2}$$

$$-N^i vq\alpha \frac{\left(U^i_{CC}\frac{1}{N^i} - vU^i_{CE}\right)\frac{C^i}{N^i} + U^i_C\left(\frac{1}{N^i}\right)h^2}{\left(U^i_C\frac{C^i}{N^i}h^2 + \alpha\right)^2}$$

$$= \frac{\left(vU^i_{EE} - \frac{1}{N^i}U^i_{CE}\right)U^i_C}{\left(U^i_E\right)^2}$$

$$+N^i v\alpha \frac{(1-2q)\left(U^i_{CC}\frac{1}{N^i} - vU^i_{CE}\right)\frac{C^i}{N^i}h^2 - qU^i_C\left(\frac{1}{N^i}\right)h^2}{\left(U^i_C\frac{C^i}{N^i}h^2 + \alpha\right)^2} \frac{C^i}{N^i}h^2$$

$$+N^i v \frac{\left(U^i_{CC}\frac{1}{N^i} - vU^i_{CE}\right)\left[\alpha\left(U^i_C\frac{C^i}{N^i}h^2 + (1-q)\alpha\right) + \left(U^i_C\frac{C^i}{N^i}h^2\right)^2\right]}{U^i_C\left(U^i_C\frac{C^i}{N^i}h^2 + \alpha\right)^2}$$

$$< 0 \tag{31}$$

and

$$\Psi_\alpha \equiv \frac{qU^i_C\frac{C^i}{N^i}h^2\alpha}{\left(U^i_C\frac{C^i}{N^i}h^2 + \alpha\right)^2} > 0. \tag{32}$$

When deriving the last form of Expression (32), Equation (29) was used. Increasing household mobility entails less first-period consumption and a higher quality of the environment. As the quality of the environment is lower than optimal, this increases welfare. The smaller the costs of migration, the stronger the feedback mechanism inducing cooperation. Mobile people migrate to countries trying to free-ride, which decreases the payoffs available from selfish environmental policy.

Perfect household mobility

In the two previous subsections we showed that under costly migration, the effects of household mobility on environmental policy depend on governments' ability to make credible commitments. In this subsection we shall demonstrate that perfect household mobility is qualitatively different from costly migration: independently of the time of commitment, perfect household mobility always implies social efficiency.

To derive the result, first note that the strength of the feedback effect forcing countries to pay attention to each other doesn't depend on the period of commitment. Using (14) we can see that when $\alpha = 0$,

$$U_{C1}^1 \frac{C^1}{N^1} \frac{dK}{dX^1} h = \frac{1}{2}\left[U_{C1}^1 \frac{1}{N^1} - v(1-2q)U_{E1}^1\right]. \quad (33)$$

When people can move from one country to another without incurring any costs, changes in the distribution of population can happen instantaneously. Thus the length of the period doesn't play any role. Now, plugging (14) and (15) into (16) shows that the first-order condition takes the form

$$U_{C1}^1 = vU_{E1}^1 N^1 + e^{-ph}su_{c1}^1, \quad (34)$$

clearly indicating that the decentralized outcome is socially efficient.

4. CONCLUDING REMARKS

The literature has shown that perfect household mobility can serve as a coordination mechanism inducing national policy makers to internalize international externalities caused by transboundary pollution. This chapter asked if the result can be extended to the more realistic case of imperfect household mobility, and presented an alternative hypothesis: the effects of household mobility on environmental policy were claimed to be equivalent to those of interregional pollution flows.

The motivation of the study was twofold: from the perspective of environmental policy it would be useful to know if imperfectly mobile households – possible operating in an integrated labour market – can be a substitute for explicit policy coordination, or if increasing household mobility, on the contrary, reinforces the need for centralized decision making. On the other hand, the standard framework for analysing the local public sector has been a static model with perfect household mobility. This chapter used the example of environmental policy to study if the qualitative features of such simplified models carry over to more complex dynamic settings.

The analysis, conducted with the help of a two-period game, indicated that the effects of household mobility on environmental policy are generated by an interplay between two conflicting incentives: (i) Strategic overpollution, resulting in a higher pollution stock, pre-empts *future* immigration and the appropriation of resources by foreigners. (ii) People can migrate to the country engaging in strategic environmental overpollution during the time that elapses between decision making and the implementation of environmental policy. This forward-looking behaviour by migrants lowers the payoffs of strategic environmental policy and induces implicit cooperation.

The findings of the chapter were rather surprising. While costless migration still implies the social optimum within the dynamic model framework, the effects of imperfect household mobility were found to depend crucially on governments' ability to make credible commitments. In particular, if commitment is impossible, imperfectly mobile households actually introduce new dynamic externalities to the economy, and welfare is lowered. Only if the period of commitment is long enough can costly migration be good for the environment. The qualitative difference between perfect and imperfect mobility suggests that the simplifying assumptions normally made in the literature may not be completely innocuous. On the other hand, as national governments can probably revise their environmental policy quite often, the analysis conducted in this chapter suggests that the combination of decentralized decision making and household mobility can actually be bad for the environment.

NOTES

1. See, for example, Dasgupta (1993, 1995).
2. El-Hinnawi (1985).
3. Jacobsen (1988).
4. See, for example, Cleaver and Schreiber (1994) or Peters and Neuenschwander (1988).
5. See, for example, Markusen, Morey and Olewiler (1994, 1993); Oates and Schwab (1988); Rauscher (1994); Mäler (1990).
6. Wellisch (1994, 1995); Mansoorian and Myers (1993).

7. Fisheries are analysed in the classic article by Gordon (1954) and in Levihari and Mirman (1980). Lancaster (1973) and Tornell and Velasco (1992) study the accumulation of capital and economic growth in an economy with ill-defined property rights.
8. The classic article in this literature is Tiebout (1956). Buchanan and Goetz (1972) and Flatters, Henderson and Mieszowski (1974) are often-cited earlier papers. More recent contributions include Boadway (1982), Wildasin (1980) and Myers (1990). Burbidge and Myers (1994) and Mansoorian and Myers (1993) are static models where the assumption that people derive utility from living in their native country introduces a form of imperfect household mobility. The dynamic modelling techniques applied in Hercowitz and Pines (1991) probably fall closest to the approach adopted in this chapter.
9. For example Bolton and Roland (1996) analyse the possibility of political integration under no labour mobility and perfect mobility.
10. Rawls (1972).
11. On the importance of the period of commitment see Karp and Perloff (1995); Reinganum and Stokey (1985).
12. A constant returns to scale technology using labour and environmental resources as inputs can be incorporated into the analysis without changing the structure of the model. Let $F(X, N) = Nf(X/N)$ be the production function and $u(C, E)$ be the utility function. Now $C = F(X, N)/N = f(X/N)$. Plugging into the utility function gives $u(f(X/N), E)$. But given the properties of the production function and the utility function, the relation between emissions X and utility can be captured by the production function (5) and a monotonic transformation of the utility function $U(C, E)$.
13. Although it is pretty standard in the literature to assume that shifting costs depend on the stream of migrants (see, for example, Baldwin and Venables, 1994; Karp and Paul, 1995; Krugman, 1991), some motivation may be useful. One possible way to justify frictional costs of the form presented here is to presume that the labour market in the new host country cannot immediately absorb an increase in the labour force. Migrants have to reckon with the possibility of an initial phase of unemployment.

REFERENCES

Baldwin, R. and A. Venables (1994), 'International Migration, Capital Mobility and Transitional Dynamics', *Economica*, **16**, 285–300.

Boadway, R. (1982), 'On the Method of Taxation and the Provision of Local Public Goods: Comment', *American Economic Review*, **72**, 846–51.

Bolton, P. and G. Roland (1996), 'Distributional Conflicts, Factor Mobility, and Political Integration', *American Economic Review*, **86**, 99–104.

Buchanan, J. and C. Goetz (1972), 'Efficiency Limits of Fiscal Mobility: an Assessment of the Tiebout Model', *Journal of Public Economics*, **1**, 25–43.

Burbidge, J. and G. Myers (1994), 'Population Mobility and Capital Tax Competition', *Regional Science and Urban Economics*, **24**, 441–59.

Cleaver, K. and G. Schreiber (1994), *Reversing the Spiral. The Population, Agriculture, and Environment Nexus in Sub-Saharan Africa*, Washington, DC: The World Bank.

Dasgupta, P. (1993), *An Inquiry into Well-being and Destitution*, Oxford: Oxford University Press.

Dasgupta, P. (1995), 'The Population Problem: Theory and Evidence', *Journal of Economic Literature*, **33**, 1879–902.

El-Hinnawi, E. (1985), *Environmental Refugees*, Nairobi, Kenya: United Nations Environmental Programme.

Flatters, F., V. Henderson and P. Mieszkowski (1974), 'Public Goods, Efficiency, and Regional Fiscal Equalization', *Journal of Public Economics*, **3**, 99–112.

Gordon, H. (1954), 'The Economic Theory of a Common Property Resource: The Fishery', *Journal of Political Economy*, **62**, 124–42.

Haavio, M. (1997), 'Migration and the Environment', Discussion Paper no. 430, Department of Economics, University of Helsinki.

Hercowitz, Z. and D. Pines (1991), 'Migration with Fiscal Externalities', *Journal of Public Economics*, **46**, 163–80.

Jacobson, J. (1988), 'Environmental Refugees: A Yardstick of Habitability', Worldwatch Paper 86.

Karp, L. and J. Perloff (1995), 'Why Industrial Policies Fail: Limited Commitment', *International Economic Review*, **36**, 887–905.

Karp, L. and T. Paul (1995), 'Labour Adjustment and Gradual Reform: Is Commitment Important?', CEPR Discussion Paper no. 1094.

Krugman, P. (1991), 'History Versus Expectations', *Quarterly Journal of Economics*, **106**, 651–67.

Lancaster, K. (1973), 'The Dynamic Inefficiency of Capitalism', *Journal of Political Economy*, **81**, 1092–109.

Levihari, D. and L. Mirman (1980), 'The Great Fish War', *Bell Journal of Economics*, **11**, 322–34.

Mäler, K.-G. (1990), 'International Environmental Problems', *Oxford Review of Economic Policy*, **6**, 80–107.

Mansoorian, A. and G. Myers (1993), 'Attachment to Home and Efficient Purchases of Population in a Fiscal Externality Economy', *Journal of Public Economics*, **52**, 117–32.

Markusen, J., E. Morey and N. Olewiler (1993), 'Environmental Policy when Market Structure and Plant Locations are Endogenous', *Journal of Environmental Economics and Management*, **24**, 69–86.

Markusen, J., E. Morey and N. Olewiler (1994), 'Competition in Regional Environmental Policies when Plant Locations are Endogenous', *Journal of Public Economics*, **56**, 55–78.

Myers, G. (1990), 'Optimality, Free Mobility, and the Regional Authority in a Federation', *Journal of Public Economics*, **44**, 107–21.

Oates, W. and R. Schwab (1988), 'Economic Competition among Jurisdictions: Efficiency Enhancing or Distortion Inducing?', *Journal of Public Economics*, **35**, 333–54.

Peters, W. and L. Neuenschwander (1988), *Slash and Burn*, Moscow, ID: University of Idaho Press.

Rauscher, M. (1994), 'On Ecological Dumping', *Oxford Economic Papers*, **46**, 822–40.

Rawls, J. (1972), *A Theory of Justice*, Oxford: Oxford University Press.

Reinganum, J. and N. Stokey (1985), 'Oligopoly Extraction of a Common Property Natural Resource: The Importance of the Period of Commitment in Dynamic Games', *International Economic Review*, **26**, 161–73.

Tiebout, C. (1956), 'A Pure Theory of Local Public Expenditures', *Journal of Political Economy*, **64**, 1208–31.

Tornell, A. and A. Velasco (1992), 'The Tragedy of the Commons and Economic Growth: Why does Capital Flow from Poor to Rich Countries?', *Journal of Political Economy*, **100**, 1208–31.

Wellisch, D. (1994), 'Interregional Spillovers in the Presence of Perfect and Imperfect Household Mobility', *Journal of Public Economics*, **55**, 167–84.

Wellisch, D. (1995), 'Can Household Mobility Solve Basic Environmental Problems?', *International Tax and Public Finance*, **2**, 245–60.

Wildasin, D. (1980), 'Locational Efficiency in a Federal System', *Regional Science and Urban Economics*, **10**, 453–71.

15. Strategic international trade and transboundary pollution: a dynamic model

Talitha Feenstra

1. INTRODUCTION

If domestic and foreign firms compete in an oligopolistic market, governments have a reason to introduce laxer environmental policy then they would apply otherwise. This is called 'environmental dumping'. When pollution is transboundary, countries may have an even stronger incentive for environmental dumping. Foreign emissions add to domestic pollution levels, and a strict environmental policy at home might increase the market share of foreign relatively dirty firms, or lead to home firms relocating to areas with laxer environmental policy. In this way the condition of the environment is made even worse.[1] Environmental dumping and related problems are discussed in a number of papers (among others Kennedy, 1994; Markusen, Morey and Olewiler, 1993, Conrad, 1993 and Rauscher, 1995; A.Ulph, 1994 provides an overview).

Most papers that discuss environmental dumping are static in their setting. They often use a multi-stage static game model to describe international competition. However, the problem has aspects that make an explicitly dynamic analysis interesting. First, a key role in the interaction between governments and between firms from different jurisdictions is played by the degree of 'commitment' to certain actions. The ability to commit to certain actions gives players a strategic advantage (see, for example, Tirole, 1988). Governments can improve the position of their domestic firms in the international market by providing such commitment. The government can do this more easily than the firm itself, since the government can impose a policy upon the firm, while the firm cannot credibly impose a policy upon itself.[2] Therefore governments have an incentive to distort environmental policies to provide such commitments. A full dynamic analysis is interesting because it allows for the analysis of strategies of firms and governments that differ in the degree of commitment, which is the key aspect of the effect on strategic interaction. A multi-stage static model results in an equilibrium comparable to just one of the different equilibria that are possible in a dynamic game structure. Furthermore, in a dynamic game model the behaviour of players at all points in time can be analysed, rather than just the steady state.

The aim of this chapter is to analyse why and in what direction governments would distort their environmental policies. Governments are assumed to have an interest in improving the position of their home firms, but also to desire a good environmental quality. They must strike a balance between these aims. The policy instruments of emission taxes and emission standards are compared in an explicit dynamic model.

Only pollution related to production processes is considered. Another type of pollution is related to products. If products pollute at their final disposal, they cause pollution in the country where they are consumed and disposed of, not in the country that produces them. This type of pollution is left out of consideration. Trade policies, for instance import restrictions for products that have been produced in a polluting way, are ignored too. This type of policies might conflict with free trade agreements. However, such agreements increasingly tend to take environmental concerns into account (see for instance the discussion on NAFTA by Esty, 1994).

The model below describes a firm that may invest in production with less pollution and thereby save production costs. By assumption, once the firm has invested in abatement, it has gained a competitive advantage. But the net present value of such an investment is negative, so without environmental policy, the firm would not invest in abatement.[3] These assumptions incorporate the idea that a reduction in emissions usually implies a more efficient production in the sense of fewer inputs per unit of output. Due to these assumptions the model differs from Kennedy's model (1994), where abatement is a pure cost to firms. A formulation comparable to ours is used in Kort (1994), Ulph and Ulph (1994) and D. Ulph (1994). But Ulph (and Ulph) use a multi-stage static game, while in a dynamic model Kort considers abatement investment as a flow rather than a stock variable. Ulph and Ulph (1994) speak of environmental R&D spending.

First a formalization of transboundary pollution is given in Section 2. Then, in Section 3, a list of motives follows that may lead regulators to distort environmental policy from its socially optimal level in a situation with transboundary pollution and international competition. A differential game model is formulated in Section 4 to describe the decision problems faced by firms and regulators. The next section, 5, discusses three scenarios, respectively a situation of full cooperation, a situation with a cooperative government that regulates competing firms and a situation where both firms and regulators compete on the international market. Section 6 concludes the chapter.

2. TRANSBOUNDARY POLLUTION

Transboundary pollution is an important aspect of the analysis in this chapter. The regulators in each country, i, have an environmental damage function, $D^i(\cdot)$ to value actual deposition in a given year. Countries that value pollution differently or that differ in natural characteristics have different damage functions. Marginal damage is assumed to be non-decreasing in depositions, $D^{i\prime\prime}(\cdot) \geq 0$. Desirable emission can be derived if one knows how emissions relate to depositions. A complication is that pollution is often transboundary and emissions in one country lead to depositions in other countries. The following linear equation is used to formalize the dispersion of emissions over the countries (see for example Mäler, 1989). Let depositions in country i be given by P^i and emissions from country i by e^i, then

$$P^i = \beta^{ii}e^i + \beta^{ij}e^j \tag{1}$$

where background pollution is ignored. β^{ij} is an element of a transportation matrix and denotes the percentage of emissions from one country that ends up in the other country. Given one unit of emissions in country j, β^{ij} of it ends up in country i and β^{jj} stays in country j. It is assumed that $\beta^{ij} + \beta^{jj} \leq 1$, since some of the pollution may go to a third country. This linear formulation contains a number of scenarios. For instance, in the absence of transboundary pollution, when pollution is purely local, $\beta^{ij} = \beta^{ji} = 0$. This case is briefly mentioned in Section 5, where it is compared with the case of transboundary pollution.

For many environmental problems, stocks of accumulated pollution rather than flows cause environmental damage.[4] In that case, ideally, policies should be derived from a careful consideration of biological processes. Here, the damage function directly links damage to flows of pollution.

3. REASONS TO DISTORT POLICY

Pigou concluded that it is optimal for regulators to set environmental policy such that marginal social costs are equated to marginal social benefits (Pigou, 1932). The standard analysis of environmental policy instruments is in a single-economy setting. In the context of more than one economy, several effects may cause distortions in environmental policy.

In the literature one can find effects that are entirely due to transboundary pollution and effects that have to do with trade and international competition. In the case of transboundary pollution a prisoners' dilemma type of game is played among governments, about who is going to take the responsibility to clean up.

Free-rider incentives cause governments to set laxer-than-optimal policies and to neglect their influence on depositions in the other country. International rivalry (in a situation of trade with imperfect competition) may lead countries to reduce the severity of their environmental policies as a substitute for tariffs and other trade policy.

The last effect may be relatively small in a case of local pollution, for the government that misuses its environmental policy for trade-strategic reasons has to pay for this with more environmental damage. In a case of transboundary pollution, however, the distorting effect is strengthened. The additional damage is partly deposited in foreign countries and hence is neglected by the home country, while a decrease in foreign output reduces home damage. So transboundary pollution and trade-strategic considerations are interdependent reasons to distort environmental policy from the level that is optimal from the point of view of all countries together.

These reasons for distortion will be elaborated in more detail below and given a number for later reference. First the reasons connected with transboundary pollution are listed: one distortion is due to countries taking only local damage into account. Damage abroad is a part of global social costs, but not reckoned as such by a national government. This leads to too lax an environmental policy (1). Another distortion occurs since countries want to shift costs of pollution reduction to other countries. If the state of the environment influences the decisions of the other country, a bad environment may stimulate foreign countries to more abatement. That may lead countries to set too lax a policy, with efforts of the others offsetting their own abuse (2).

Second, the reasons for distortion that are due to imperfect competition are listed. If domestic firms compete with foreign firms, there is reason for strategic distortion of environmental policy, since the choices of foreign firms can be indirectly influenced by domestic policy. Low levels of environmental policy in the home country stimulate domestic production, partially at the cost of foreign production. So some output is shifted from abroad (while total output increases). Three reasons can be distinguished. First, since governments want to shift rents from foreign to domestic firms, they distort their environmental policy (3). The type of distortion depends on the structure of the output market. In this chapter, we restrict our analysis to Cournot competition, and environmental policy is distorted downwards. An extension to Bertrand competition is straightforward (see Barrett, 1994). Second, countries want to reduce environmental damage from abroad, hence they want to discourage production abroad. This is another reason to set their own policy too lax (4). Finally, countries do not take into account that a decrease in their own firms' output (and profits) increases the profitability of foreign firms' production. This is the usual effect of oligopoly. If the firms were to form a cartel and cooperate, they could earn more profits. Given the objective function, that would be welfare-improving.[5] In short, governments overestimate the total (global) social marginal costs of emission reductions by their home firm and set policy too lax (5). These five reasons for distortion will be present in the analysis below. They all point in the direction of a laxer environmental policy than is socially optimal from the point of view of the two countries together.

When consumer surplus is explicitly taken into account, an additional distortion can be distinguished. In the case of oligopolistic competition, consumers favour increased output and hence lax environmental policies (6). Since the model below abstracts from consumer surplus, a good discussion of this effect is not possible. In the conclusions we come back to the implications of this.

Transboundary pollution (reasons 1 and 2) is, for instance, analysed by Conrad (1993), Katsoulacos, Ulph and Xepapadeas (1996), Kennedy (1994) and van der Ploeg and de Zeeuw (1992). Distortions due to trade policy objectives are the subject of a large number of papers (for example, Barrett, 1994, Conrad, 1993, Katsoulacos, Ulph and Xepapadeas, 1996, D. Ulph, 1994). A good overview is provided by A. Ulph (1994). Consumer surplus is included, for example, by Kennedy (1994) and Ulph (1996).

4. AN INTERNATIONAL DUOPOLY

In this section a differential game model is formulated to analyse the distortions mentioned above. The model describes two countries with home firms that compete with each other on a world market. Governments are assumed to maximize welfare. Welfare is determined by the level of firm profits and environmental damage. Consumer surplus is neglected for convenience. Firms are modelled as profit maximizers. The analysis below is only a partial analysis, since effects on other sectors of the economy (a decline in a polluting sector may go together with growth in other sectors) are left out, as well as adjustments in policies other than environmental policies (increases in environmental taxes may go together with decreases in other taxes). Governments set environmental policy instruments. Two instruments are discussed: a tax and an emission standard. Perfect foresight is assumed throughout the chapter.

A country's government by assumption acts as a Stackelberg leader *vis-à-vis* domestic firms. It is able to announce a credible policy because it can bind itself with the help of laws. On the other hand, firms act as followers. The length of the period of credible commitment for the government is an open question. It depends on the reality of law setting and the reputation of the government. If the government can commit for only a short period, a feedback Stackelberg equilibrium is the right equilibrium concept. This results in a solution that consists of strategies which vary with the situation at hand. These are time-consistent[6] and subgame-perfect. If the government can commit for a long period, it is better to apply an open-loop Stackelberg equilibrium. In such an equilibrium, the government sets a time path for its policy once and for all and cannot react to the situation at hand.

The interaction between governments of different countries is modelled as a Nash equilibrium. If countries can commit their policies for a long period, this is an open-loop Nash equilibrium. If not, a feedback Nash equilibrium is considered. For consistency, a government that uses open-loop strategies in the game with its own firm is also in open-loop equilibrium with the other country, and analogously for a government that is in feedback equilibrium. The interaction between firms is modelled as a Nash equilibrium. Firms compete in a Cournot–Nash fashion. Moreover, throughout the chapter it is assumed that firms set output according to a feedback strategy. They adjust their rate of output instantaneously without adjustment costs. This is an abstraction, but compared to investment decisions it seems reasonable to assume that it is easy to adjust output plans. If the investment decisions of firms are rigid and require long-term commitments, firms are modelled to compete in an open-loop equilibrium. If investment strategies can be changed without problems, firms are modelled to follow feedback investment strategies.

Several equilibria exist, depending on the type of strategies assumed to be relevant for the decision variables output, investment and environmental policy. As mentioned, output is always set according to a feedback strategy. For investment and environmental policy both open-loop and feedback strategies are considered. Three benchmark solutions are discussed, one where the two firms are a cartel and the governments cooperate, another where firms compete but governments cooperate, and a third where both firms and governments compete. In each case both countries apply the same environmental policy instrument. But countries may differ in the strictness of their policy. First the formal model of the firm and the regulator is presented.

4.1 A Duopoly Model

Consider a firm i that is maximizing profits from exports over an infinite time horizon. Let its production capacity be fixed to focus on the adjustment of technology to environmental requirements. For production of output, x^i, the firm uses a polluting input, e^i. The world market price per unit of this input is p^e. Environmental policy as faced by the firm is a tax, τ^i, on the use of the polluting input e^i. Alternatively, a standard on emissions, in the form of a maximum, $\bar{e}^i$, on the use of the polluting input is considered.

The environmental friendliness of the production process is summarized by a variable A^i, referred to as 'abatement capital'. If the firm owns a stock A^i of abatement capital and wants to produce x^i of output, it needs to use $e^i = E(A^i)x^i$ of the polluting input. Hence it is assumed that the firm needs a fixed amount of $E(\cdot)$ per unit of output, but that this amount can be reduced by investment in abatement technology: $E'(\cdot) < 0$. It follows that $\partial^2 e^i/(\partial A^i \partial x^i) < 0$: more abatement capital decreases the amount of emissions, e^i, per additional unit of output. Furthermore, consider the output that can be produced with a given level of polluting input, $x^i(e^i, A^i) = e^i/(E(A^i))$. The marginal productivity of abatement capital, $x^i_{A^i} = (-e^i E'(A^i))/(E(A^i)^2)$ is positive. It is assumed to be decreasing in A^i, so $x^i_{A^i A^i} < 0$.

Abatement capital can be accumulated by investment I^i at a current cost of $C^i(I^i)$. Investment costs are increasing and convex, $C^{i\prime\prime} > 0$ and $C^{i\prime\prime\prime} > 0$. Abatement capital grows according to a standard capital accumulation function:

$$\dot{A}^i = I^i - \delta A^i \qquad (2)$$

Revenues are denoted by $R^i(x^i, x^j)$. The firm sells output x^i on the world market where it has to compete with firm j's output x^j. Let subscripts denote partial derivatives. It is assumed that $R^i_j < 0$, $R^i_{ij} < 0$, $R^i_{ii} < 0$ and $R^i_{jj} = 0$:[7] revenues decrease if competing output increases, and marginal revenues decrease in own and foreign output, while the marginal effect of foreign output does not change with foreign output. The firm's profits in the case of taxes then read:[8]

$$\Pi^i = R^i(x^i, x^j) - (p^e + \tau^i)e^i - C^i(I^i) \qquad (3)$$

From revenues, the firm must subtract the costs of the polluting input e^i and costs of investment in abatement, $C^i(I^i)$. In the case of emission standards, profits are similarly defined except that the firm does not have to pay emission taxes.

The marginal change in profits due to an additional unit of abatement capital will be called MBA^i; this is the derivative of Π^i to A^i, $d\Pi^i/dA^i$, with output at its equilibrium level. The following regularity condition is assumed to hold for all scenarios that are discussed in Section 5:

$$MBA^i_{\ i}\, MBA^j_{\ j} > MBA^i_{\ j}\, MBA^j_{\ i}. \qquad (4)$$

This condition requires that own effects of abatement capital dominate cross effects. The optimization problem faced by the firm can be summarized as follows. It has to decide on strategies for its output and investment to maximize its discounted stream of profits, given the capital accumulation function (2) and environmental policy. In the case of taxes, this results in:

$$\max_{x^i, I^i} \int_0^\infty e^{-rt} \Pi^i dt$$

$$\text{s.t. } \Pi^i = R^i(x^i, x^j) - (p^e + \tau^i) E(A^i) x^i - C^i(I^i) \qquad (5)$$
$$\dot{A}^i = I^i - \delta A^i$$
$$I^i \geq 0; \ x^i \geq 0$$

In the case of standards, a similar optimization problem results, but subject to constraints on the use of the polluting input.

Whether environmental policy is required depends on the world market price for e^i. If this correctly internalizes the damage that results from the use of the input, then no environmental policy is needed. It is assumed here that prices are such that without government intervention, firms do not invest in abatement technology. A sufficient condition for this is:

$$C^{i\prime}(0) \geq \frac{1}{r+\delta}\left[-p^e E'(0) x_o^i + R_j^i x_{A^i}^j\right], \qquad (6)$$

which assures that $A^i = A^j = 0$ is an equilibrium steady state for the no-policy case. Here x_0^i denotes equilibrium output for $A^i = A^j = 0$. The condition is sufficient both when firms apply open-loop and when they apply feedback investment strategies. A proof is most easily given after the various equilibria have been derived and is therefore relegated to Appendix 2. Condition (6) means that investment costs must be higher than the properly[9] discounted marginal revenues of a marginal unit of abatement capital. These marginal revenues consist of reductions in factor costs, $-p^e E'(0) x_0^i$, and of a strategic advantage, $R_j^i x_{Ai}^j$. The last term, which has a positive sign, is due to commitment effects. A larger capital stock provides firm i with a strategic advantage. This results in less output for firm j and hence higher revenues for firm i. Given Condition (6), it is not optimal for a firm to invest in abatement when current levels of abatement capital are zero for both firms and no environmental policy is applied. It is assumed that this condition holds for all t for both firms and that at $t = 0$ both firms have no abatement capital installed due to lack of environmental policy until that time.

The regulator has to set taxes such that they balance firm objectives, Π^i, against environmental objectives as summarized by the damage function $D^i(P^i)$. The regulator's current welfare is then

$$G^i = R^i - p^e e^i - C^i(I^i) - D^i(P^i). \qquad (7)$$

Its intertemporal decision problem is given by:

$$\max_{\tau^i} \int_0^\infty e^{-rt} G^i \, dt \tag{8}$$

s.t. I^i, x^i, I^j, x^j from (5).

The government redistributes tax revenues in a lump-sum way. In contrast to the firm, it takes environmental damage into account. In the case of emission standards, the government optimizes its objective function with respect to the level of standards, $\bar{e}^i$.

Marginal social damage and marginal social benefits can now be defined. Both are defined per unit of emissions and for given levels of abatement capital. 'Social' here means from the point of view of the two countries together. Marginal social damage of one unit of polluting input used by firm i consists of marginal damage due to depositions $\beta^{ii}e^i$ in country i and marginal damage due to depositions $\beta^{ji}e^i$ in country j:

$$MD^i = \beta^{ii}D^{i\prime} + \beta^{ji}D^{j\prime}. \tag{9}$$

Marginal social (net) benefits of one unit of input used by firm i are determined by the amount of output, $1/E(A^i)$ that is produced with this unit. It consists of the marginal revenues to country i plus the (negative) marginal revenues to country j minus marginal production costs, that is, the price p^e of one unit:

$$MB^i = \frac{1}{E(A^i)}\left[R_i^i + R_i^j\right] - p^e. \tag{10}$$

From a static efficiency point of view, it is socially optimal if the government sets environmental policy such that the following condition holds:

$$MD^i = MB^i. \tag{11}$$

This level of policy, that equates marginal damage to marginal social benefits of emission, is referred to as the 'Pigouvian' level of environmental policy in this chapter. Similarly, the level of taxes that satisfies

$$\tau^i = MD^i \tag{12}$$

will be referred to as the 'Pigouvian' level of taxes.

5. EQUILIBRIUM POLICY FOR THREE SCENARIOS

5.1 The Case of Full Cooperation

Consider the 'full-cooperation' solution as a benchmark scenario. Assume that there is an overall government that wants the best for both countries together, while the two firms are owned by one overall manager. From the discussion in Section 3 it follows that in this case there are no reasons to disturb policy from its Pigouvian level. The motives 3 and 5 disappear since there is no competition between firms. The remaining motives, 1, 2 and 4 disappear since in the eyes of the overall government there is no transboundary pollution. Indeed, it turns out that social marginal damage (MD^i) equals social marginal benefits (MB^i) in equilibrium. The objective functions add the objectives of both firms and of both governments. In the case of taxes:

$$\max_{x^i, A^i, x^j, A^j} \int_0^\infty e^{-rt}\left(\Pi^i + \Pi^j\right)dt \quad \text{(cartel's objective function)} \quad (13)$$

$$\max_{\tau^i, \tau^j} \int_0^\infty e^{-rt}\left(G^i + G^j\right)dt \quad \text{(social objective function)} \quad (14)$$

with Π^i as defined in Equation (3) and G^i as defined in (7). The cooperative firms' manager divides production and investment in an optimal way over firm i and firm j, to maximize total profits. It takes environmental policy as given. The cooperative governments form a Stackelberg leader and set policy in country i and j to maximize welfare.

Analysis of feedback Stackelberg equilibrium conditions (see Appendix 1) shows that in equilibrium (11) must hold for both emission taxes and emission standards. It is understandable that it is optimal to set policy at its Pigouvian level, since none of the reasons to disturb policy from this level are present.

The first-order conditions for an open-loop Stackelberg equilibrium are also given in Appendix 1. The firms' manager chooses an optimal time path of investment, given a time path of policy levels. He/she balances adjustment costs against marginal revenues of additional abatement capital (reduced future payments for the use of e^i). The government takes firm behaviour as given and sets an optimal path of policy. In the case of taxes it can be shown (see Appendix 1) that a time-consistent policy path satisfies the first-order conditions and is an optimal path. This path is characterized by (11) or equivalently by (12). In the case of standards on emissions, manipulation of the first-order conditions for an open-loop Stackelberg equilibrium leads similarly to Condition (11). It can be proved that the solution is time-consistent.

So in the case of an open-loop Stackelberg equilibrium with one overall government and one overall manager the government chooses the Pigouvian level of environmental policy. Moreover the open-loop equilibrium equals the feedback equilibrium. In the case of full cooperation, the government optimally sets environmental policy at the Pigouvian level. This enables the government to reach the socially optimal path of investment in environmental improvement and of output. In the case of open-loop strategies, there is no time inconsistency, since the government achieves the social optimum. It does not need to try to improve on this result at a later time. It is not such a surprising result, if one realizes that the overall government possesses one instrument (either a tax or a standard) to reach one goal: to force the firms' manager to internalize environmental damage. Apart from this goal, there are no conflicts between the objectives of the government and the firms' manager.

5.2 Cooperative Government with Competition between Firms

As a second scenario, the case where cooperating governments regulate two firms that compete with each other in the output market is considered. The relevant objective functions are given in Equations (5) and (14). Since firms compete with each other, while governments cooperate, some of the effects mentioned in Section 3 work in a different direction in this scenario. For example, firms derive no utility from increases in profits of the foreign firm when they reduce their own output, while the common government values both firms' profits. Compared to the social optimum, firms produce too much output. Therefore effect 5 now induces the governments to set stricter policies to reduce output.

In the case of feedback Stackelberg equilibrium it can be proved (see Appendix 1) that Condition (11) must be satisfied by an optimal environmental policy. Governments cooperate, so they still equate full social marginal benefits to full social marginal damage, as in the first case. In the case of taxes, from the first-order conditions on a firm's choice of output, $R^i_j = (p^e + \tau^i)E(A^i)$, Condition (11) and Definition (10) it follows that: $\tau^i = MD^i - (R^j_i/E(A^i))$. The upward distortion ($-R^j_i > 0$) of taxes compared to the scenario in Section 5.1 is due to effect 5, as explained above.

In the case of an open-loop Stackelberg equilibrium the condition on optimal policy is

$$MB^i = MD^i + v^i \frac{B^i}{E(A^i)} + v^j \frac{B^j}{E(A^j)}. \tag{15}$$

The factors B^i and B^j are complex expressions (see Appendix 1) that denote the combined effect of marginal policy changes on the two firms' valuation of abatement capital. The v^i denote the shadow price of the cooperative government for the valuation by firm i ($i = 1, 2$) of its own abatement capital. These terms are due to time inconsistency that exists in the open-loop equilibrium in this case where firms compete. A rough explanation for this goes as follows. Due to firms' competition, the cooperative governments can at most reach a second-best solution. They apply open-loop strategies with commitment. Hence at a certain point in time, they decide on an optimal policy path for the whole future. After some time has elapsed, governments could steer firms to a better solution for the remaining future. So they would prefer to change their policy. But they have committed themselves to the chosen policy path. As noticed by Kennedy (1994), environmental policy can at most be a second-best instrument in this case, since there are two goals to be attained by one instrument (reduction of strategic behaviour, which is welfare-decreasing in this case, and reduction of environmental damage). So the first-best optimum is not obtainable. Since time inconsistency appears, the feedback solution, which by its definition is time-consistent, predicts a different time path of investment in abatement capital and environmental policy[10] than the open-loop solution.

If firms were in perfect competition, they would not be able to influence each other's revenues through output. Then taxes in a feedback equilibrium are not distorted from their Pigouvian level. There is no reason for cooperating governments to distort them, for there is no oligopolistic competition among firms which they can change. In open-loop equilibrium the distortions are absent as well, for the same reason that the government cannot influence competition if it is perfect. That can be seen from a consideration of the B^i-factors in Appendix 1. These factors equal zero in the case of perfect competition.

5.3 Competition between Firms and between Governments

In a situation of strategic international trade, when both governments and firms compete with each other, all the reasons for policy distortion mentioned in Section 3 are present and work the way they were presented there. The objective functions are given in (5) and (8). The feedback Stackelberg equilibrium with emission standards can be summarized by

$$MB^i = MD^i - D^{j\prime}\beta^{ji} + R_i^j \frac{1}{E(A^i)}. \tag{16}$$

Standards deviate from the Pigouvian level due to the distortionary effects 1, 2 and 5. Governments neglect foreign damage $D^{j\prime}\beta^{ji}$ and set standards which are too lax, so that marginal damage exceeds marginal benefits. In the feedback equilibrium, effect 2 works to reduce standards still further. Moreover, effect 5 leads governments to stimulate production by their own firms. This is represented by the term $R_j^i/E(A^i)$ in the formula above. In the case of emission taxes, the condition on optimal policy is

$$MB^i = MD^i - \beta^{ji}D^{j\prime} + R_i^j \frac{1}{E(A^i)} + \beta^{ij}D^{i\prime} \frac{E(A^j)}{E(A^i)} \frac{x_{\tau^i}^{jN}}{x_{\tau^i}^{iN}} - R_j^i \frac{1}{E(A^i)} \frac{x_{\tau^i}^{jN}}{x_{\tau^i}^{iN}}. \quad (17)$$

Compared to the case of standards, two more distortionary effects (3 and 4) are present, since firms have indirect influence on each other's output through the market price. They discourage foreign production to reduce damage from abroad (effect 4, represented by the term $D^{i\prime}\beta^{ij}(E(A^j)/E(A^i))(x_{\tau^i}^{jN}/x_{\tau^i}^{iN})$). And they discourage foreign production out of a rent-shifting motive (effect 3, represented by the term $-(R_j^i/E(A^i))(x_{\tau^i}^{jN}/x_{\tau^i}^{iN})$). Both terms are negative and lead to too lax policies. Using the condition on equilibrium output choice, $R_i^i = (p^e + \tau^i)E(A^i)$ and Definition (10), the condition on optimal taxes can be rewritten:

$$\tau^i = MD^i - \beta^{ji}D^{j\prime} + \beta^{ij}D^{i\prime} \frac{E(A^j)}{E(A^i)} \frac{x_{\tau^i}^{jN}}{x_{\tau^i}^{iN}} - R_j^i \frac{1}{E(A^i)} \frac{x_{\tau^i}^{jN}}{x_{\tau^i}^{iN}}. \quad (18)$$

Both in the case of taxes and in the case of standards, environmental policies are distorted and set too lax from a social point of view.

The open-loop Stackelberg equilibrium is characterized by the following condition on environmental policy in the case of emission standards:

$$MB^i = MD^i - D^{j\prime}\beta^{ji} + R_i^j \frac{1}{E(A^i)} - v^{ii}\left[R_i^i \frac{E'(A^i)}{E(A^i)^2} + R_{ii}^i \frac{E'(A^i)\bar{e}^i}{E(A^i)^3}\right] - v^{ij}R_{ij}^j\bar{e}^j \frac{1}{E(A^i)} \frac{E'(A^j)}{E(A^j)^2}. \quad (19)$$

In the case of taxes the condition is:

$$MB^i = MD^i - D^{j\prime}\beta^{ji} + R_i^j \frac{1}{E(A^i)} + D^{i\prime}\beta^{ij} \frac{E(A^j)}{E(A^i)} \frac{x_{\tau^i}^{jN}}{x_{\tau^i}^{iN}} - R_j^i \frac{1}{E(A^i)} \frac{x_{\tau^i}^{jN}}{x_{\tau^i}^{iN}}$$

$$+ \frac{1}{E(A^i)}\left[v^{ii} \frac{1}{x_{\tau^i}^{iN}} MBA_{\tau^i}^i + v^{ij} \frac{1}{x_{\tau^i}^{iN}} MBA_{\tau^i}^j\right] \quad (20)$$

As in the second benchmark case, the open-loop equilibrium solutions are not time-consistent. This can be seen from the presence of the non-zero terms with v^{ii} and v^{ij} representing the government's valuation of changes in the shadow price of capital as perceived by its home firm (v^{ii}) and the foreign firm (v^{ij}), respectively.

In general, the direction of distortions in the case of open-loop strategies (and in the case of comparable multi-stage static models) is inconclusive. This is due to the twofold effect of an increase in abatement capital: on the one hand it leads to fewer emissions per unit of output; on the other hand it may lead to increased output and hence emissions, since production costs per unit are lowered. For governments there is no general rule regarding in what direction to steer abatement investments. Hence it is inconclusive whether policies are distorted upward or downward. For feedback investment strategies that is not the case. Firms base their investment on their expectations about future policies. When current policies imply no commitments to future levels of environmental policy, as is the case in the feedback equilibrium, governments cannot directly influence investment in abatement technology with current policies. In this case the only distortions in policy levels are due to transboundary pollution and strategic trade effects.

Now compare the results above to a situation with only transboundary pollution. That can be done by considering (16) and (18) with $R^i_j = R^j_i = 0$. When firms do not try to influence each other's output, the terms with these derivatives and therefore also $x^i_{\tau j}$ and $x^j_{\tau i}$ disappear. Condition (16) then becomes

$$MB^i = MD^i - D^{i'}\beta^{ji}, \qquad (21)$$

while Condition (18) becomes:

$$\tau^i = MD^i - D^{i'}\beta^{ji}. \qquad (22)$$

The distortions numbered 3 and 4 disappear, since they are due to strategic interaction among firms. The resulting policies are closer to their Pigouvian levels. As a result, output as well as environmental damage is lower than in the equilibrium under scenario 5.3.

6. SUMMARY AND CONCLUSIONS

This chapter describes environmental policy setting by national governments that balance environmental targets with domestic firm competitiveness in a dynamic game model of an international duopoly. Three different scenarios were considered for two types of decision strategies on investment and environmental policy.

In the benchmark case, scenario 5.1, where governments and firms cooperate, no distortions from the Pigouvian policy occur and governments are able to reach the first-best solution. In this specific case open-loop and feedback strategies result in the same equilibrium.

If firms compete, while governments cooperate, scenario 5.2 applies. Then, governments have the double target to reduce environmental damage as well as competition among firms. Only a second-best solution can be reached with distortions in the environmental policy instruments. These distortions are the same with and without transboundary pollution, since the cooperating governments consider damage in both countries. Under perfect competition there would be no distortions at all. With oligopolistic firms, distortions exist and open-loop strategies are not time-consistent. It is undetermined whether policy instruments are distorted upward or downward. Feedback strategies are time-consistent and it can be seen that these are distorted upward.

The third scenario with competition between firms and between governments is characterized by distortions as well. Now, governments want to provide their domestic firms with a competitive advantage. Furthermore, each government only considers domestic damage. In open-loop equilibrium, distortions are undetermined of sign and the equilibrium strategies are not time-consistent. Feedback equilibrium strategies are time-consistent. These strategies are always distorted downwards, that is, environmental policy is laxer than the Pigouvian level.

With trade that is characterized by strategic interaction there are several additional reasons, compared to trade under perfect competition, for regulators to deviate from the Pigouvian level of environmental policy. Apart from the usual distortions due to transboundary pollution, governments may also distort policies to increase domestic firms' profits.

Compared to a multi-stage static model, a dynamic game model has the advantage that additional possible means of interaction between firms and governments may be analysed. With the most simple interaction possible, meaning a dynamic game model where all players use open-loop strategies, results are in general inconclusive and time-inconsistent. If feedback investment strategies are considered, though, the distortion of environmental policy is easier to characterize. Moreover, the formulas presented above characterize policy setting along equilibrium time paths, rather than providing a once-and-for-all equilibrium. Further research will try to use this to investigate the investment paths of firms in the model more carefully.

In this model, with perfect knowledge and no uncertainty, it seems logical that standards and taxes are equivalent instruments of environmental policy. However, consider the feedback equilibrium. As mentioned, the signs of the distortions in the case of feedback strategies can be determined. Both under taxes and under standards, environmental policy is set at laxer than socially optimal levels. But in the case of emission standards, firms' commitment to a certain output level is greater, because the standard is a binding constraint on output, for given abatement capital stocks. Therefore, it is more difficult to affect the output choices of the competitor with standards than with taxes. Some distortionary effects are absent under standards. It cannot be concluded that hence standards are always less distorted, because the remaining distortions may be stronger under standards. But it is clear that equilibrium output and emission levels differ under the two instruments, even in this model with complete knowledge and no uncertainty.

With feedback strategies, current policies do not influence the investment behaviour of firms since this is based on the future profitability of investments. This conclusion at the same time clarifies the circumstances under which the result holds. The analysis assumes perfect foresight, so that firms are indeed able to base their investment decisions on expectations about the future. In the absence of such foresight in reality, it may very well be the case that current taxes are the best estimate of future taxes. To compare what happens when firms are myopic and base their decisions on current tax levels is a possibility for further research.

An extension would be the inclusion of consumer surplus, as in Kennedy (1994) or Ulph (1996), so that two more aspects of distorted environmental policy, shifting of pollution to others and the benefits to consumers from increased production, could be analysed. The result of the inclusion of consumer surplus depends on how large a part of total production is consumed at home. If home consumers are only a small fraction of total demand, the results are not expected to change greatly.

NOTES

1. In the context of global warming, this is also referred to as 'carbon leakage'.
2. The strategic use of trade policy to provide commitment to home firms is analysed by Brander and Spencer (1983). In the following we assume that trade policy is not available to the government.
3. For an analysis of the possibility that this net present value is positive, see Gabel and Sinclair-Desgagne (1997).
4. See for example Van der Ploeg and de Zeeuw (1992) for a dynamic analysis with environmental damage from stocks.
5. Of course, consumer surplus is usually also included in welfare so that cartels are not better than oligopolies from a welfare point of view. In the current setting, however, this is the case, since the governments are solely considering environmental damage and firm profits.
6. An equilibrium path $x(t)$ for a decision variable x is time-consistent if it is an equilibrium path from the viewpoint of any arbitrary point in time t (see, for example, Brock and Malliaris, 1989).
7. For example, $R^i = p(x^i, x^j)x^i$, with p a linear decreasing function of x^i and x^j has this characteristic.
8. If environmental taxes are redistributed in a lump-sum way, this increases the level of profits, but it will not change the decisions taken by firms.

9. That is, taking depreciation into account.
10. Therefore, considering a dynamic model shows that the predictions of multi-stage static models, whose equilibria are comparable to our open-loop equilibrium, may be wrong if the players' interaction is better described by a feedback equilibrium.

REFERENCES

Barrett, S. (1994), 'Strategic environmental policy and international trade', *Journal of Public Economics*, **54**, 325–38.
Brander, J.A. and B.J. Spencer (1983), 'Strategic commitment with R&D: the symmetric case', *Bell Journal of Economics*, 225–35.
Brock, W.A. and A.G. Malliaris (1989), *Differential Equations, Stability and Chaos in Dynamic Economics*, Amsterdam: North-Holland.
Conrad, K. (1993), 'Taxes and subsidies for pollution-intensive industries as trade-policy', *Journal of Environmental Economics and Management*, **25**, 121–35.
Esty, D.C. (1994), 'Making trade and environmental policies work together: Lessons from NAFTA', *Aussenwirtschaft*, **49**, 59–79.
Gabel, L. and B. Sinclair-Desgagne (1997), 'The firm, its routines and the environment', in H. Folmer and T. Tietenberg (eds), *The International Yearbook of Environmental and Resource Economics: A Survey of Current Issues*, Cheltenham: Edward Elgar.
Katsoulacos, Y., D. Ulph and A. Xepapadeas (1996), 'Emission taxes in international asymmetric oligopolies', FEEM Nota di Lavoro, no. 63.96.
Kennedy, P.W. (1994), 'Equilibrium pollution taxes in open economies with imperfect competition', *Journal of Environmental Economics and Management*, **27**, 49–63.
Kort, P.M. (1994), 'Effects of pollution restrictions on dynamic investment policy of a firm', *Journal of Optimization Theory and Applications*, **83**(3), 489–509.
Mäler, K.G. (1989), 'The acid rain game', in H. Folmer and E. van Ierland (eds), *Valuation Methods and Policy Making in Environmental Economics*, Amsterdam: Elsevier, pp. 231–52.
Markusen, J.R., E.R. Morey and N.D. Olewiler (1993), 'Environmental policy when market structure and plant location are endogenous', *Journal of Environmental Economics and Management*, **24**, 69–86.
Pigou, A.C. (1932), *The Economics of Welfare*, 4th edition, London: Macmillan.
Rauscher, M. (1995), 'Strategic environmental policy in oligopolistic markets', Working Paper, Kiel.
Tirole, J. (1988), *The Theory of Industrial Organization*, Cambridge, MA: MIT Press.
Ulph, A. (1994), 'Environmental policy and international trade, a survey of recent economic analysis', Paper presented at the 1st HCM Workshop on 'Designing Economic Policy for the Management of Natural Resources and the Environment', Crete.
Ulph, D. (1994), 'Strategic innovation and strategic environmental policy', in C. Carraro (ed.), *Trade, Innovation, Environment*, Dordrecht: Kluwer, pp. 205–28.
Ulph, A. and D. Ulph (1994), 'Trade, strategic innovation and strategic environmental policy – a general analysis', Paper prepared for presentation at the conference 'Environment: Policy and Market Structure', Athens.
Ulph, A. (1996), 'Environmental policy instruments and imperfectly competitive international trade', *Environmental and Resource Economics*, **7**, 333–55.

Van der Ploeg, F. and A.J. de Zeeuw (1992), 'International aspects of pollution control', *Environmental and Resource Economics*, **2**, 117–39.

APPENDIX 1   THE SCENARIOS

Appendix 1 provides the details for Section 5. Each scenario has a separate subsection, where, after the conditions for equilibrium output, first details on the feedback equilibrium and then on the open-loop equilibrium are given. In this appendix, subscripts denote partial derivatives. A variable y in equilibrium is represented by $\hat{y}$. Furthermore, $\mathbf{A}$, $\boldsymbol{\tau}$, $\mathbf{x}$ and $\bar{\mathbf{e}}$ denote the vectors (A^i, A^j), (τ^i, τ^j), (x^i, x^j) and $(\bar{e}^i, \bar{e}^j)$ respectively. Remember that marginal benefits per unit of emission, MB^i, were defined by

$$MB^i = \frac{R_i^i + R_i^j}{E(A^i)} - p^e, \tag{A1}$$

and that marginal damage was defined by:

$$MD^i = D^{ii}\beta^{ii} + D^{ji}\beta^{ji}. \tag{A2}$$

Current welfare in country i was defined in (7) by

$$G^i = R^i - p^e e^i - C^i(I^i) - D^i(P^i). \tag{A3}$$

These definitions are used repeatedly in the rest of the appendix. Recall Definition (1) of pollution in country i, P^i. The derivative of P^i, to a tax τ^j is

$$P^i_{\tau^j} = \beta^{ii} E(A^i) x^i_{\tau^j} + \beta^{ij} E(A^j) x^j_{\tau^j}. \tag{A4}$$

The derivative of pollution in country i to a standard $\bar{e}^j$ is:

$$P^i_{\bar{e}^j} = \beta^{ij}. \tag{A5}$$

Scenario 1: Full Cooperation

The first-order conditions for optimal choice of output by an overall firm manager read in the case of taxes:

$$\begin{aligned} R_i^1 + R_i^2 &\le (p^e + \tau^i) E(A^i) \\ x^i &\ge 0 \\ x^i[R_i^1 + R_i^2 - (p^e + \tau^i) E(A^i)] &= 0. \end{aligned} \tag{A6}$$

All three conditions must hold for $i = 1, 2$. That results in optimal output choices $x^{1C}(\mathbf{A}, \boldsymbol{\tau})$ and $x^{2C}(\mathbf{A}, \boldsymbol{\tau})$. Assume that an interior solution with both outputs positive is reached. If these optimal output choices are inserted, the following differential game results:

Manager

$$\max_{I^1,I^2} \int_0^\infty e^{-rt}\left(\Pi^1 + \Pi^2\right)dt$$

$$\text{s.t. } \Pi^i = R^i(x^C) - (p^e + \tau^i)E(A^i)x^{iC} - C^i(I^i) \quad i = 1, 2 \quad \text{(A7)}$$
$$\dot{A}^i = I^i - \delta A^i \quad i = 1, 2$$
$$I^i \geq 0 \quad i = 1, 2;$$

Government

$$\max_{\tau^1,\tau^2} \int_0^\infty e^{-rt}\left(G^1 + G^2\right)dt \quad \text{(A8)}$$

s.t. firm behaviour.

The phrase 'firm behaviour' is a shorthand for the results of (A7). That is, the government, which is the Stackelberg leader, takes into account that the firm manager solves (A7).

In the case of an emissions standard for each firm the first-order conditions for optimal output choice read

$$\begin{aligned}
& R^1_i + R^2_i \leq (p^e + \phi^i) E(A^i) \\
& x^i \geq 0 \\
& x^i [R^1_i + R^2_i - (p^e + \phi^i) E(A^i)] = 0 \\
& \phi^i \geq 0 \\
& E(A^i) x^i \leq \bar{e}^i \\
& \phi^i[\bar{e}^i - E(A^i) x^i] = 0.
\end{aligned} \quad \text{(A9)}$$

Here $\phi^i + p^e$ is the shadow price for the polluting input. If $R^1_i(\mathbf{x}) + R^2_i(\mathbf{x}) \geq p^e E(A^i)$ for $x^i = \bar{e}^i/E(A^i)$, the standard is binding for a given output x^j. Assume that the case where both standards are binding is an equilibrium, that is, for $i = 1, 2$ it holds that

$$R^1_i\left(\frac{\bar{e}^1}{E(A^1)}, \frac{\bar{e}^2}{E(A^2)}\right) + R^2_i\left(\frac{\bar{e}^1}{E(A^1)}, \frac{\bar{e}^2}{E(A^2)}\right) \geq p^e E(A^i). \quad \text{(A10)}$$

In that case, $x^i = \bar{e}^i/E(A^i)$ is an equilibrium. The differential game reduces to:

Manager

$$\max_{I^1,I^2} \int_0^\infty e^{-rt}\left(\Pi^1 + \Pi^2\right)dt$$

s.t. $\Pi^i = R^i - p^e\bar{e}^i - C^i(I^i)$ $i = 1, 2$ (A11)
$\dot{A}^i = I^i - \delta A^i$ $i = 1, 2$
$I^i \geq 0$ $i = 1, 2;$

Government

$$\max_{\bar{e}^1,\bar{e}^2} \int_0^\infty e^{-rt}\left(G^1 + G^2\right)dt$$

s.t. firm behaviour.   (A12)

Feedback Stackelberg equilibrium

Under full cooperation, the Hamilton–Jacobi–Bellman equations are, in the case of taxes:

$$rU(A) = R^1 + R^2 - (p^e + \hat{\tau}^1)\,E(A^1)x^{1C} - (p^e + \hat{\tau}^2)\,E(A^2)x^{2C} - C^1(\hat{I}^1)$$
$$- C^2(\hat{I}^2) + U_{A^1}(\hat{I}^1 - \delta A^1) + U_{A^2}(\hat{I}^2 - \delta A^2)$$
$$rW(A) = R^1 + R^2 - p^eE(A^1)x^{1C} - p^eE(A^2)x^{2C} - C^1(\hat{I}^1) - C^2(\hat{I}^2) - D^1(P^1)$$
$$- D^2(P^2) + W_{A^1}(\hat{I}^1 - \delta A^1) + W_{A^2}(\hat{I}^2 - \delta A^2). \quad (A13)$$

Here U and W are the value functions of the cooperating firms and the cooperating governments, respectively, $\hat{I}^i$ is the equilibrium rate of investment in abatement and $\hat{\tau}^i$ the equilibrium rate of taxes. The equilibrium rate of investment must satisfy the following first-order conditions:

$$C^{i'}(\hat{I}^i) \geq U_{A^i}(A^1, A^2)$$
$$\hat{I}^i \geq 0 \quad\quad (A14)$$
$$\hat{I}^i\,[C^{i'}(\hat{I}^i) - U_{A^i}] = 0.$$

These result in $\hat{I}^i(A)$, so the firms' rate of investment is not directly influenced by environmental taxes. The equilibrium rates of taxes, $\hat{\tau}^i$, must satisfy the following first-order conditions:

$$\tau^1\,E(A^1)\,x^{1C}_{\tau^1} + \tau^2\,E(A^2)\,x^{2C}_{\tau^1} = D^{1'}P^1_{\tau^1} + D^{2'}P^2_{\tau^1}$$
$$\tau^1\,E(A^1)\,x^{1C}_{\tau^2} + \tau^2\,E(A^2)\,x^{2C}_{\tau^2} = D^{1'}P^1_{\tau^2} + D^{2'}P^2_{\tau^2}. \quad (A15)$$

These follow if the value function W is maximized over τ^i and (A6) is inserted. Use (A4) to rewrite (A15) to

$$E(A^1) x^{1C}_{\tau^i}[\tau^1 - D^{1\prime}\beta^{11} - D^{2\prime}\beta^{21}] = -E(A^2) x^{2C}_{\tau^i}[\tau^2 - D^{1\prime}\beta^{12} - D^{2\prime}\beta^{22}] \qquad \text{(A16)}$$

for $i = 1, 2$. It follows that

$$\hat{\tau}^i = D^{i\prime} \beta^{ii} + D^{j\prime} \beta^{ji} \qquad \text{(A17)}$$

or, with the help of Definition (A2),

$$\hat{\tau}^i = MD^i. \qquad \text{(A18)}$$

Use the first-order condition on output (A6), (A18) and Definition (A1) to find that, in equilibrium,

$$MB^i = MD^i \qquad \text{(A19)}$$

In the case of emission standards the Hamilton–Jacobi–Bellman equations read:

$$\begin{aligned}rU(A) &= R^1 + R^2 - p^e\bar{e}^1 - p^e\bar{e}^2 - C^1(\hat{I}^1) - C^2(\hat{I}^2) + U_{A^1}(\hat{I}^1 - \delta A^1) \\ &\quad + U_{A^2}(\hat{I}^2 - \delta A^2) \\ rW(A) &= R^1 + R^2 - p^e\bar{e}^1 - p^e\bar{e}^2 - C^1(\hat{I}^1) - C^2(\hat{I}^2) - D^1(P^1) - D^2(P^2) \\ &\quad + W_{A^1}(\hat{I}^1 - \delta A^1) + W_{A^2}(\hat{I}^2 - \delta A^2). \end{aligned} \qquad \text{(A20)}$$

Equation (A14) gives conditions for the equilibrium rate of investment. The equilibrium rates of standards, $\bar{e}^i$, follow from the first-order conditions for the maximization of W over $\bar{e}^i$:

$$\left(R^1_i + R^2_i\right)\frac{1}{E(A^i)} - p^e - D^{1\prime} P^1_{\bar{e}^i} - D^{2\prime} P^2_{\bar{e}^i} = 0 \quad \text{for } i = 1, 2. \qquad \text{(A21)}$$

Use (A5), (A1) and (A2) to rewrite this to:

$$MB^i = MD^i \qquad \text{(A22)}$$

Open-loop Stackelberg equilibrium

In the case of an open-loop Stackelberg equilibrium, the first-order conditions for cooperating firms read

$$\dot{A}^i = I^i - \delta A^i$$
$$C^{i'}(I^i) \geq \lambda^i \qquad \text{(A23)}$$
$$I^i \geq 0$$
$$I^i [C^{i'}(I^i) - \lambda^i] = 0$$
$$\dot{\lambda}^i = (r+\delta)\lambda^i - MBA^{iC}$$

all for $i = 1, 2$. Here MBA^{iC} denotes the marginal benefits per time unit of a unit of abatement capital in firm i, in case of cooperation. MBA^{iC} equals the reduction in payments for the polluting input. In case of taxes, $MBA^{iC} = -(p^e + \tau^i)x^{iC}E'(A^i)$. In the case of emission standards, $MBA^{iC} = -[R_i^1 + R_i^2]\bar{e}^i E'(A^i)/E(A^i)^2$.

The first-order conditions for cooperating governments read, in the case of taxes,

$$\left[R_1^1 + R_1^2 - p^e E(A^1)\right]x_{\tau^i}^{1C} + \left[R_2^1 + R_2^2 - p^e E(A^2)\right]x_{\tau^i}^{2C} - D^{1'}P_{\tau^i}^1 - D^{2'}P_{\tau^i}^2 - v^1\frac{\partial MBA^{1C}}{\partial \tau^i} - v^2\frac{\partial MBA^{2C}}{\partial \tau^i} = 0$$

$$\dot{\mu}^i = (r+\delta)\mu^i - \left[R_1^1 + R_1^2 - p^e E(A^1)\right]x_{A^i}^{1C} - \left[R_2^1 + R_2^2 - p^e E(A^2)\right]x_{A^i}^{2C}$$
$$+ p^e E'(A^i)x^{iC} + D^{1'}P_{A^i}^1 + D^{2'}P_{A^i}^2 + v^1\frac{\partial MBA^{1C}}{\partial A^i} + v^2\frac{\partial MBA^{2C}}{\partial A^i}$$

$$\dot{v}^i = -\delta v^i + \frac{C^{i'}(I^i) - \mu^i}{C^{i''}(I^i)}$$

$$v^i(0) = 0 \qquad \text{(A24)}$$

for $i = 1, 2$. Here μ is the shadow value for abatement capital and v the shadow value that the government as a Stackelberg leader attaches to λ. Insert the first-order condition on output, (A6), in (A23) and (A24) and try the solution $v^1(t) = v^2(t) = 0$. With this solution, all conditions in (A23) and (A24) are satisfied if taxes are set according to

$$\hat{\tau}^i = D^{i'}\beta^{ii} + D^{j'}\beta^{ji} \qquad \text{(A25)}$$

for $i = 1, 2$, for all t.

In the case of emission standards, the open-loop first-order conditions for cooperating governments read

$$\left[R_i^1 + R_i^2\right]\frac{1}{E(A^i)} - p^e - D^{1'}\beta^{1i} - D^{2'}\beta^{2i} - v^1\frac{\partial MBA^{1C}}{\partial \bar{e}^i} - v^2\frac{\partial MBA^{2C}}{\partial \bar{e}^i} = 0$$

$$\dot{\mu}^i = (r+\delta)\mu^i - \left[R_i^1 + R_i^2\right]x_{A^i}^{1C} + v^1\frac{\partial MBA^{1C}}{\partial A^i} + v^2\frac{\partial MBA^{2C}}{\partial A^i}$$

$$\dot{v}^i = -\delta v^i + \frac{(C^{i'} - \mu^i)}{C^{i''}}$$

$$v^i(0) = 0 \qquad \text{(A26)}$$

for $i = 1, 2$. The first-order conditions for the cooperating firms were given in (A23). Use $x^i = \bar{e}^i/E(A^i)$ and try the solution $v^1(t) = v^2(t) = 0$. It follows that all conditions in (A23) and (A26) are satisfied if standards are set such that

$$\frac{R_i^1 + R_i^2}{E(A^i)} - p^e = D^{1\prime}\beta^{1i} + D^{2\prime}\beta^{2i} \tag{A27}$$

or, equivalently,

$$MB^i = MD^i \tag{A28}$$

The latter condition follows immediately from (A1) and (A2).

So for both instruments a time-consistent open-loop equilibrium exists. This equilibrium is, moreover, the first-best solution. To see this, consider the social planning problem with objective function

$$\max_{I^1, I^2, x^1, x^2} \int_0^\infty e^{-rt}\left[R^1 + R^2 - p^e\left(e^1 + e^2\right) - C^1\left(I^1\right) - C^2\left(I^2\right) - D^1\left(P^1\right) - D^2\left(P^2\right)\right]dt$$

The first-order conditions for investment and output for the social planning problem equal (A23) and (A6) respectively (A9), with environmental policy (A25) or (A27) inserted. With these policies, the cooperating governments therefore reach the first-best solution. Furthermore, the optimality conditions are the same for feedback and open-loop strategies.

Scenario 2: Competition between Firms and Cooperative Governments

Assume that in the case of taxes an interior equilibrium results. Then the Nash equilibrium conditions for output are, in the case of taxes,

$$R_i^i = (p^e + \tau^i)\, E(A^i) \tag{A29}$$

for $i = 1, 2$. The Nash equilibrium output choices are denoted $x^{iN}(\mathbf{A}, \boldsymbol{\tau})$. If these output choices are inserted, the following differential game results:

Manager of firm i

$$\max_{I^i} \int_0^\infty e^{-rt}\left(\Pi^i\right)dt$$

$$\text{s.t. } \Pi^i = R^i(x^{1N}, x^{2N}) - (p^e + \tau^i)E(A^i)x^{iN} - C^i(I^i) \tag{A30}$$
$$\dot{A}^i = I^i - \delta A^i \quad i = 1, 2$$
$$I^i \geq 0$$

Cooperating governments

$$\max_{\tau^1,\tau^2} \int_0^\infty e^{-rt}\left(G^1 + G^2\right)dt \quad \text{(A31)}$$

s.t. firm behaviour.

Assume both standards are binding in equilibrium. Then in the case of standards $x^{iN} = \bar{e}^i/E(A^i)$. The assumption

$$R_i^i\left(\frac{\bar{e}^1}{E(A^1)}, \frac{\bar{e}^2}{E(A^2)}\right) \geq p^e E(A^i) \quad \text{(A32)}$$

for $i = 1, 2$, ensures that this is a Nash equilibrium indeed. The differential game reduces to:

Manager of firm i

$$\max_{I^i} \int_0^\infty e^{-rt}\left(\Pi^i\right)dt$$

$$\text{s.t. } \Pi^i = R^i - p^e \bar{e}^i - C^i(I^i) \quad \text{(A33)}$$
$$\dot{A}^i = I^i - \delta A^i \quad i = 1, 2$$
$$I^i \geq 0$$

Cooperating governments

$$\max_{\bar{e}^1,\bar{e}^2} \int_0^\infty e^{-rt}\left(G^1 + G^2\right)dt \quad \text{(A34)}$$

s.t. firm behaviour.

Feedback Stackelberg equilibrium

The Hamilton–Jacobi–Bellman equations for scenario 2 are, in the case of taxes,

$$rU^i(A) = R^i - (p^e + \hat{\tau}^i) E(A^i)x^{iN} - C^i(\hat{I}^i) + U_{A^i}^i (\hat{I}^i - \delta A^i) + U_{A^j}^i (\hat{I}^j - \delta A^j)$$
$$rW(A) = R^1 + R^2 - p^e E(A^1)x^{1N} - p^e E(A^2)x^{2N} - C^1(\hat{I}^1) - C^2(\hat{I}^2)$$
$$- D^1(P^1) - D^2(P^2) + W_{A^1}(\hat{I}^1 - \delta A^1) + W_{A^2}(\hat{I}^2 - \delta A^2). \quad \text{(A35)}$$

Here U^i is the value function of firm i and W is the value function for the cooperating governments. The first-order conditions for the equilibrium rate of investment, $\hat{I}^i$ are:

$$C^{i\prime}(\hat{I}^i) = U^i_{A^i}(A)$$
$$\hat{I}^i \geq 0 \qquad \qquad (A36)$$
$$\hat{I}^i[C^{i\prime}(\hat{I}^i) - U^i_{A^i}] = 0.$$

Note that this differs from (A14), since now each firm bases investments on its own value function.

The equilibrium rates of taxes, $\hat{\tau}^i$, follow from the first-order conditions:

$$\tau^1 E(A^1) x^{1N}_{\tau 1} + \tau^2 E(A^2) x^{2N}_{\tau 1} = D^{1\prime} P^1_{\tau 1} + D^{2\prime} P^2_{\tau 1} - R^1_2 x^{2N}_{\tau 1} - R^2_1 x^{1N}_{\tau 1}$$
$$\tau^1 E(A^1) x^{1N}_{\tau 2} + \tau^2 E(A^2) x^{2N}_{\tau 2} = D^{1\prime} P^1_{\tau 2} + D^{2\prime} P^2_{\tau 2} - R^1_2 x^{2N}_{\tau 2} - R^2_1 x^{1N}_{\tau 2}.$$
$$\qquad \qquad (A37)$$

Insert (A4) and solve for τ^i and τ^j:

$$\hat{\tau}^i = D^{i\prime} \beta^{ii} + D^{j\prime} \beta^{ji} - \frac{1}{E(A^i)} R^i_j. \qquad (A38)$$

Use (A29), (A1) and (A2) to rewrite this condition as

$$MB^i = MD^i. \qquad (A39)$$

In the case of emission standards the Hamilton–Jacobi–Bellman equations read

$$rU^i(A) = R^i - p^e \bar{e}^i - C^i(\hat{I}^i) + U^i_{A^i}(\hat{I}^i - \delta A^i) + U^i_{A^j}(\hat{I}^j - \delta A^j)$$
$$rW(A) = R^1 + R^2 - p^e \bar{e}^1 - p^e \bar{e}^2 - C^1(\hat{I}^1) - C^2(\hat{I}^2) - D^1 - D^2$$
$$+ W_{A^1}(\hat{I}^1 - \delta A^1) + W_{A^2}(\hat{I}^2 - \delta A^2). \qquad (A40)$$

For $\hat{I}^i$, the equilibrium rate of investment, the first-order conditions are given by (A36). For $\bar{e}^i$, the equilibrium standard, the first-order conditions are

$$\left(R^1_i + R^2_i\right)\frac{1}{E(A^i)} - p^e = D^{1\prime} P^1_{\bar{e}^i} + D^{2\prime} P^2_{\bar{e}^i} \qquad (A41)$$

Recall (A5) and use (A1) and (A2) to see that this is equal to

$$MB^i = MD^i. \qquad (A42)$$

Open-loop Stackelberg equilibrium

In the case of an open-loop Stackelberg equilibrium, the first-order conditions for competing firms are given by (A23), but with MBA^{iN} instead of MBA^{iC}. In the case of taxes, $MBA^{iN} = -(p^e + \tau^i)x^{iN}E'(A^i) + R^i_j x^{jN}_{A^i}$. The last term stands for the marginal decrease in competing output and the effect this has on own firm revenues. In the case of emission standards, $MBA^{iN} = -R^i_{\bar{e}^i}E'(A^i)/E(A^i)^2$.

The first-order conditions for the cooperating governments are, in the case of taxes, given by (A24) with x^{iN} instead of x^{iC} and MBA^{iN} instead of MBA^{iC}.

Insert (A29) in the adjusted versions of (A23) and (A24) and try the time-consistent solution $v^1(t) = v^2(t) = 0$. A contradiction is the result, namely:

$$\frac{R^j_i}{E(A^i)} x^{iN} + \frac{R^i_j(p^e + \tau^i)R^j_{ij}}{R^i_{ii}R^j_{jj} - R^i_{ij}R^j_{ij}} = 0. \tag{A43}$$

Therefore the open-loop equilibrium with taxes is not time-consistent. Insert (A29) in the first equation of (A24) for $i = 1, 2$. Rearrange the system of two equations that results to find

$$\tau^i = D^{i\prime}\beta^{ii} + D^{j\prime}\beta^{ji} - \frac{1}{E(A^i)}R^j_i + v^i\frac{B^i}{E(A^i)} + v^j\frac{B^j}{E(A^i)}, \tag{A44}$$

where B^i and B^j denote complex expressions:

$$B^i = \frac{MBA^{iN}_{\tau^i} x^{jN}_{\tau^j} - MBA^{iN}_{\tau^j} x^{jN}_{\tau^i}}{x^{iN}_{\tau^i} x^{jN}_{\tau^j} - x^{iN}_{\tau^j} x^{jN}_{\tau^i}}$$

and

$$B^j = \frac{MBA^{jN}_{\tau^i} x^{jN}_{\tau^j} - MBA^{jN}_{\tau^j} x^{jN}_{\tau^i}}{x^{iN}_{\tau^i} x^{jN}_{\tau^j} - x^{iN}_{\tau^j} x^{jN}_{\tau^i}}$$

Use (A1), (A2) and (A29) to rewrite (A44) as

$$MB^i = MD^i + v^i \frac{1}{E(A^i)} B^i + v^j \frac{1}{E(A^i)} B^j \tag{A45}$$

In the case of emission standards, the open-loop first-order conditions for the cooperating governments are given by (A26) with MBA^{iN} and x^{iN} instead of MBA^{iC} and x^{iC}. Try the solution $v^1(t) = v^2(t) = 0$ in the adjusted versions of (A23) and (A26). Some straightforward reordering gives

$$R_i^j \bar{e}^i \frac{E'(A^i)}{E(A^i)^2} = 0 \qquad (A46)$$

This is not true, so that there is no time-consistent solution to (A23) and (A26). Rearrange the first condition in (A26) and insert (A1) and (A2). The result is that in equilibrium standards should be set such that:

$$MB^i = MD^i + v^1 \frac{\partial MBA^{1N}}{\partial \bar{e}^i} + v^2 \frac{\partial MBA^{2N}}{\partial \bar{e}^i} \qquad (A47)$$

is satisfied.

Scenario 3: Nash Competition

In the case of taxes, the first-order conditions for Nash–Cournot equilibrium choice of output, $x^{iN}(\mathbf{A}, \boldsymbol{\tau})$, are given by (A29). Assume that an interior solution with both outputs positive is reached. If the Nash equilibrium output choices are inserted, the following differential game results:

Manager of firm i

$$\max_{I^i} \int_0^\infty e^{-rt} (\Pi^i) dt$$

$$\text{s.t. } \Pi^i = R^i(x^{1N}, x^{2N}) - (p^e + \tau^i) E(A^i) x^{iN} - C^i(I^i) \qquad (A48)$$
$$\dot{A}^i = I^i - \delta A^i \qquad i = 1, 2$$
$$I^i \geq 0;$$

Government of country i

$$\max_{\tau^i} \int_0^\infty e^{-rt} (G^i) dt \qquad (A49)$$

s.t. firm behaviour.

For standards on the polluting input, assume that both standards are binding in equilibrium, so that $x^{iN} = \bar{e}^i/E(A^i)$. The differential game is given by (A33) and (A49), except that the government optimizes over $\bar{e}^i$.

Feedback Stackelberg equilibrium

The Hamilton–Jacobi–Bellman conditions for the game above are, in the case of taxes,

$$rU^i(A) = R^i - (p^e + \hat{\tau}^i) E(A^i)x^{iN} - C^i(\hat{I}^i) + U^i_{A^i}(\hat{I}^i - \delta A^i) + U^i_{A^j}(\hat{I}^j - \delta A^j)$$
$$rW^i(A) = R^i - p^e E(A^i)x^{iN} - C^i(\hat{I}^i) - D^i(P^i) + W^i_{A^i}(\hat{I}^i - \delta A^i)$$
$$+ W^i_{A^j}(\hat{I}^j - \delta A^j). \quad (A50)$$

with $\hat{I}^i$, the equilibrium rate of investment, defined by (A36). The equilibrium rate of taxes, $\hat{\tau}^i$, must satisfy the following first-order conditions to maximize W^i:

$$[R^i_i - p^e E(A^i)]x^{i,N}_{\tau^i} = D^{i\prime} P^i_{\tau^i} - R^i_j x^{j,N}_{\tau^i} \quad (A51)$$

Insert (A29) and solve for τ^i to find:

$$\hat{\tau}^i = (D^{i\prime} P^i_{\tau^i} - R^i_j x^{j,N}_{\tau^i})/(E(A^i)x^{i,N}_{\tau^i}). \quad (A52)$$

Then use (A2) to rearrange this as

$$\hat{\tau}^i = MD^i - D^{j\prime}\beta^{ji} + D^{i\prime}\beta^{ij}\frac{E(A^j)}{E(A^i)}\frac{x^{jN}_{\tau^i}}{x^{iN}_{\tau^i}} - R^i_j \frac{1}{E(A^i)}\frac{x^{jN}_{\tau^i}}{x^{iN}_{\tau^i}} \quad (A53)$$

or, with (A1) also inserted,

$$MB^i = MD^i - R^i_j \frac{1}{E(A^i)}\frac{x^{jN}_{\tau^i}}{x^{iN}_{\tau^i}} + R^i_j \frac{1}{E(A^i)} - D^{j\prime}\beta^{ji} + D^{i\prime}\beta^{ij}\frac{E(A^j)}{E(A^i)}\frac{x^{jN}_{\tau^i}}{x^{iN}_{\tau^i}} \quad (A54)$$

In the case of standards, the conditions for a feedback equilibrium are

$$rU^i(A) = R^i - p^e\bar{e}^i - C^i(\hat{I}^i) + U^i_{A^i}(\hat{I}^i - \delta A^i) + U^i_{A^j}(\hat{I}^j - \delta A^j)$$
$$rW^i(A) = R^i - p^e\bar{e}^i - C^i(\hat{I}^i) - D^i(P^i) + W^i_{A^i}(\hat{I}^i - \delta A^i)$$
$$+ W^i_{A^j}(\hat{I}^j - \delta A^j). \quad (A55)$$

The first-order conditions for standards are

$$R_i^i \frac{1}{E(A^i)} = p^e + D^{i'} \beta^{ii}. \tag{A56}$$

Use (A1) and (A2) to rewrite this as

$$MB^i = MD^i + R_i^j \frac{1}{E(A^i)} - D^{j'} \beta^{ji}. \tag{A57}$$

Open-loop Stackelberg equilibrium

The first-order conditions for the firm manager are given by (A23) with MBA^{iN} instead of MBA^{iC}. For the government in country i, in the case of taxes the first-order conditions are

$$\left[R_i^i - p^e E(A^i)\right] x_{\tau^i}^{iN} + R_j^i x_{\tau^i}^{jN} - D^{i'} P_{\tau^i}^i - v^{i1} \frac{\partial MBA^{1N}}{\partial \tau^i} - v^{i2} \frac{\partial MBA^{2N}}{\partial \tau^i} = 0$$

$$\dot{\mu}^{ii} = (r+\delta)\mu^{ii} - \left[R_i^i - p^e E(A^i)\right] x_{A^i}^{iN} - R_j^i x_{A^i}^{jN} + p^e E'(A^i) x^{iN} + D^{i'} P_{A^i}^i + v^{i1} \frac{\partial MBA^{1N}}{\partial A^i} + v^{i2} \frac{\partial MBA^{2N}}{\partial A^i}$$

$$\dot{\mu}^{ij} = (r+\delta)\mu^{ij} - \left[R_i^i - p^e E(A^i)\right] x_{A^j}^{iN} - R_j^i x_{A^j}^{jN} + D^{i'} P_{A^j}^i + v^{i1} \frac{\partial MBA^{1N}}{\partial A^j} + v^{i2} \frac{\partial MBA^{2N}}{\partial A^j}$$

$$\dot{v}^{ii} = -\delta v^{ii} + \frac{C^{i'}(I^i) - \mu^{ii}}{C^{i''}(I^i)}$$

$$\dot{v}^{ij} = -\delta v^{ij} - \frac{\mu^{ij}}{C^{j''}(I^j)}$$

$$v^{ii}(0) = 0$$

$$v^{ij}(0) = 0, \tag{A58}$$

all for $i = 1, 2$. Insert the first-order condition on output, (A29), in the first line in (A58) and rearrange to find

$$\tau^i = D^{i'} \beta^{ii} + D^{j'} \beta^{ij} \frac{E(A^j)}{E(A^i)} \frac{x_{\tau^i}^{jN}}{x_{\tau^i}^{iN}} - R_j^i \frac{1}{E(A^i)} \frac{x_{\tau^i}^{jN}}{x_{\tau^i}^{iN}} + v^{ii} \frac{1}{E(A^i)} \frac{MBA_{\tau^i}^i}{x_{\tau^i}^{iN}} + v^{ij} \frac{1}{E(A^i)} \frac{MBA_{\tau^i}^j}{x_{\tau^i}^{iN}} \tag{A59}$$

Use the definitions of marginal benefits and marginal damage to rewrite this as

$$MB^i = MD^i - D^{j\prime}\beta^{ji} + R^j_i \frac{1}{E(A^i)} + D^{i\prime}\beta^{ij} \frac{E(A^j)}{E(A^i)} \frac{x^{jN}_{\tau^i}}{x^{iN}_{\tau^i}} - R^i_j \frac{1}{E(A^i)} \frac{x^{jN}_{\tau^i}}{x^{iN}_{\tau^i}} + v^{ii} \frac{1}{E(A^i)} \frac{MBA^i_{\tau^i}}{x^{iN}_{\tau^i}} + v^{ij} \frac{1}{E(A^i)} \frac{MBA^j_{\tau^i}}{x^{iN}_{\tau^i}}$$

(A60)

The solution $v^{11}(t) = v^{22}(t) = v^{12}(t) = v^{21}(t) = 0$ results in a contradiction if it is inserted in (A23) and (A58). Therefore the equilibrium is not time-consistent.

In the case of emission standards, the first-order conditions for the government of country i read

$$R^i_i \frac{1}{E(A^i)} - p^e - D^{i\prime}\beta^{ii} - v^{i1} \frac{\partial MBA^{1N}}{\partial \bar{e}^i} - v^{i2} \frac{\partial MBA^{2N}}{\partial \bar{e}^i} = 0$$

$$\dot{\mu}^{ii} = (r+\delta)\mu^{ii} - R^i_i x^{iN}_{A^i} + v^{i1} \frac{\partial MBA^{1N}}{\partial A^i} + v^{i2} \frac{\partial MBA^{2N}}{\partial A^i}$$

$$\dot{\mu}^{ij} = (r+\delta)\mu^{ij} - R^i_j x^{jN}_{A^j} + v^{i1} \frac{\partial MBA^{1N}}{\partial A^j} + v^{i2} \frac{\partial MBA^{2N}}{\partial A^j}$$

$$\dot{v}^{ii} = -\delta v^{ii} + \frac{C^{i\prime}(I^i) - \mu^{ii}}{C^{i\prime\prime}(I^i)}$$

$$\dot{v}^{ij} = -\delta v^{ij} - \frac{\mu^{ij}}{C^{j\prime\prime}(I^j)}$$

$$v^{ii}(0) = 0$$

$$v^{ij}(0) = 0 \qquad \text{(A61)}$$

for $i = 1, 2$. Rearrange the first condition in (A61) and insert (A1) and (A2). The result is that in equilibrium standards should be set such that

$$MB^i = MD^i - D^{j\prime}\beta^{ji} + R^j_i \frac{1}{E(A^i)} + v^{ii} \frac{\partial MBA^{iN}}{\partial \bar{e}^i} + v^{ij} \frac{\partial MBA^{jN}}{\partial \bar{e}^i} \qquad \text{(A62)}$$

is satisfied.

Try the solution $v^{ii}(t) = v^{ij}(t) = 0$ in (A23) and (A61). From the third and fifth equation in (A61) this requires that

$$R^i_j x^{jN}_{A^j} = 0.$$

This is not true, so there is no time-consistent equilibrium.

APPENDIX 2 NO-POLICY CASE

This appendix proves that Condition (6) in the main text,

$$C'(0) > \frac{1}{r+\delta}\left[-p^e E'(0)x_o^i + R_j^i x_{A^i}^{jN}\right], \tag{A63}$$

is sufficient to ensure that $A^i = A^j = 0$ is a steady-state equilibrium in the no-policy case, both for open-loop and feedback strategies. The proof is only given for the scenarios 2 and 3, with Nash competition between firms. For scenario 1, a slightly different condition is required.

Consider the Hamilton–Jacobi–Bellman conditions for the firm ((A35) and (A50), first equation) and assume that taxes are zero. These conditions are sufficient for an investment equilibrium in the no-policy case with feedback strategies. From (A36) it follows that, if $C'(0) > U_{A^i}^i(0, 0)$, then $I^i = 0$ is the equilibrium investment strategy given that $A^i = A^j = 0$. Moreover, since the inequality is strict, $\hat{I}_{A^i}^i = \hat{I}_{A^j}^i = 0$. Take the full derivatives of the Hamilton–Jacobi–Bellman conditions to A^i and A^j and evaluate them in $(0, 0)$:

$$(r + \delta)\, U_{A^i}^i = R_j^i x_{A^i}^j - p^e E'(A^i)x^i \tag{A64}$$
$$(r + \delta)\, U_{A^j}^i = R_j^i x_{A^j}^j$$

Here $I^i = 0$ has been inserted. If (A63) is satisfied, $\hat{I}^i = 0$ is the equilibrium choice of investment strategies indeed, as can be seen from $U_{A^i}^i$ in (A64).

For open-loop strategies, the first-order conditions for equilibrium investment in the no-policy case are given in (A23) with taxes equal to zero and $MBA^i = -p^e x^{iN} E'(A^i) + R_j^i x_{A^i}^{jN}$. If Condition (A63) holds, then $I^i = 0$ and $\lambda^i = MBA^i/(r + \delta)$ satisfies these first-order conditions for $A^i = A^j = 0$. This implies that $A^i = A^j = 0$ is an equilibrium steady state.

16. Going green or going abroad? Environmental policy, firm location and green consumerism

Michael Kuhn*

1. INTRODUCTION

In recent years politicians, business executives and economists have widely discussed the question whether firms would relocate from countries with relatively strict environmental regulation. Related to this issue is the fear of a 'race to the bottom', in which governments undercut each other's environmental standards or taxes in order to attract firms, thereby increasing environmental damage in all regions. Markusen, Morey and Olewiler (1993) and Motta and Thisse (1994) consider the location choices of duopolistic firms under environmental policies. Both studies conclude that, in order to avoid an increase in costs, firms tend to relocate in reaction to a unilateral tightening of environmental regulation. Motta and Thisse show that the existence of sunk costs or barriers to trade reduces the tendency to relocate. However, the loss of competitiveness for a producer not being able to relocate may force him out of business. Markusen, Morey and Olewiler (1995) and Rauscher (1997a) consider a monopolist whose location choice is dependent on the pollution tax rates, which are set by two welfare-maximizing countries in a non-cooperative game. A race to the bottom is the outcome unless governments have a second instrument at their disposal, say a subsidy, to influence firms' location choices (Rauscher) or unless disutility of pollution is sufficiently high (Markusen, Morey and Olewiler; and Rauscher).[1]

However, to my knowledge, all location models disregard a firm's option to use the installation of a – usually more costly – clean production technology as a selling argument. Suppose some consumers have a preference for goods that are produced in an environmentally harmless manner. Even without environmental regulation, a firm may then introduce a clean technology, because it gains a monopolistic profit by differentiating its product from those produced

---

* I wish to thank Henk Folmer and Thusnelda Tivig for their very helpful comments, while taking complete responsibility for any errors.

in a polluting way. Now, consider a producer who has not installed a clean technology, because the monopolistic rent to be gained from product differentiation does not fully compensate the higher cost. Yet, if faced by more stringent environmental regulation, s/he might install the clean technology rather than relocate if the overall decrease in profit for selling a 'green' good is smaller than a given cost of relocation. The producer of a *homogeneous* good in Motta and Thisse loses competitiveness if she cannot evade the cost increase by means of relocation. Yet, the producer of a *differentiated* green product may get around the loss of competitiveness without having to relocate. Hence, there are two forces counterbalancing the incentives for relocation: the cost of relocation and the option of product differentiation.

The reduced tendency of relocation implies that a country will not necessarily attract foreign firms by means of deregulation. The incentive for countries to engage in a race to the bottom is thus reduced once they take into account the green market potential. There even exists a potential for unilateral environmental policies now, a result which devaluates the popular claim that unilateral regulation is unsustainable in open economies.

To provide a more rigorous foundation of the argument above, I extend a discrete partial equilibrium model of vertical product differentiation by Ecchia and Mariotti (1994). It belongs to a class of models that apply the concept of vertical product differentiation to environmental economics (Motta and Thisse, 1993; Cremer and Thisse, 1994; Constantatos and Sartzetakis, 1995; Moraga-González and Padrón-Fumero, 1997).[2] When dealing with vertical product differentiation in the context of environmental economics we should address the motivation of green consumerism.[3] Suppose consumers are able to distinguish between non-green and green variants of a product, where the latter are characterized, say, by relatively low levels of negative externalities in any of the stages of production, transportation, consumption, recycling or disposal. Clearly, aggregate pollution would then be lower if consumption of the green variant took place. However, an individual consumer does not expect to influence the aggregate pollution level and thus does not account for the externalities associated with the variant s/he consumes. Owing to this social dilemma the green variant will not be demanded if offered at a higher price *vis-à-vis* the non-green unless it generates an additional private benefit. This benefit may be derived from a higher overall quality of the green product variant,[4] some intrinsic motivation to behave in what is perceived to be the morally correct way or from social rewards for conforming with a social norm.[5,6] In the presence of these physical or psychological benefits, environmental friendliness becomes an additive feature of a product's quality. Given that all other quality features of a product are fixed, consumers unambiguously rank the green variant higher. This gives rise to vertical product differentiation: if both variants were offered at the same price, only the green variant would be bought. However, if the green variant is offered at a higher price than the non-green variant, some consumers with a relatively low income or relatively low benefit from environmental friendliness will buy the latter.

The Ecchia and Mariotti model studies the demand and cost conditions under which clean technologies are introduced by duopolistic producers. The discrete character of the model captures the idea that technologies are usually not chosen from a continuous set of alternatives. It also provides for simple analytics, which is of some virtue, since I add a great deal of complexity, as will be seen below. For its discrete character the model is somewhat awkward compared to a continuous formulation. However, it allows for an analytical solution, where continuous duopoly models with endogenous location have to resort to numerical solutions even in a much simpler setting (for example, Markusen, Morey and Olewiler, 1993; Motta and Thisse, 1994).

The extensions are as follows. First, I allow for 'location' as a third choice variable for firms besides 'technology' and 'price'. Thereby, the cost of relocation is accounted for. Further, I explicitly incorporate the negative externalities generated by a polluting firm which gives rise to a disutility from pollution for consumers and a (potential) damage cost for other producers. Finally, I introduce a game between two regions choosing their environmental policies before the subgame of firm competition, where firms take the regions' policies as given.

In joining the issues of firm location and vertical product differentiation, Cordella and Grilo (1995) have followed a similar idea in the context of social dumping. However, they consider product quality levels as exogenously given, whereas I endogenize location *and* quality/technology choice. Moreover, they do not consider the strategic interaction between countries. Another related line of literature deals with the introduction of clean technologies in reaction to environmental regulation. Examples are Carraro and Topa (1994) and Ulph (1994). Whereas both analyse innovation towards clean technologies in a strategic competition context, neither incorporates the issue of product differentiation.

The chapter is organized as follows. Section 2 introduces the model. Section 3 solves the subgame of firm competition contingent on environmental policy choices and discusses the relocation issue. Section 4 solves the regions' game and comments on the implications for environmental policies in open economies. Section 5 concludes. Some of the proofs are relegated to an appendix.

2. THE MODEL[7]

Consider two identical regions (or countries) $j = A, B$. Each of two identical firms $i = 1, 2$ chooses its location of production in any one region exclusively.

Let $\phi_i \in \{A, B\}$ denote the location of firm i. The firms sell a single commodity on an integrated market consisting of the two regions, where in the absence of trading costs the law of one price holds. Each firm i produces with a technology $\theta_i \in \{G, N\}$, which is either green ($\theta = G$) or non-green ($\theta = N$). Technology N causes pollution as a local negative externality whereas G is a non-polluting technology. Pollution affects consumers and possibly other firms located in the same region.

Consumers

As in Ecchia and Mariotti (1994) consumers are differentiated in their willingness to pay (wtp) for environmental friendliness in the production of the good. In this sense, production technology is the only differentiation criterion, which takes on the role of 'quality' in the more common models of vertical differentiation. We thus distinguish the variants of the product by technology. Of a total of M consumers, there is a fraction $1 - m$ of non-green (type N) and a fraction m of green (type Γ) consumers. Let p_k^θ denote the reservation price of a consumer of type $k = \Gamma, N$ for a variant θ.[8] All consumers have a common reservation price for the non-green variant, which we normalize to $p_k^N \equiv 1$, with $k = \Gamma, N$. Non-green consumers have a wtp of zero for clean production of the good, and thus their reservation price is $p_N^\theta = 1$ regardless of technology.[9] They always buy the cheaper variant but weakly prefer G if offered at the same price as N. Green consumers have a marginal wtp of g for clean production of the good. Hence, their reservation price for the green variant is given by $p_\Gamma^G = 1 + g$ consisting of the reservation price for the standard version and the premium g. As argued above, the premium excludes the potential benefit from reduced pollution due to voluntary internalization, but rather reflects some extra moral, social or physical benefit the consumer derives from green consumption behaviour. Consumers are assumed to buy either one unit of their preferred variant or nothing at all. An individual consumer of type $k = \Gamma, N$, therefore has a demand of

$$q_k \in \{0, 1\}.$$

Let

$$CS_k^\theta = p_k^\theta - p(\theta) \tag{2.1}$$

denote the distance between reservation price p_k^θ of a consumer of type k and market price $p(\theta)$ for one unit of a variant θ. Consumer k's individual demand for a variant θ then is

$$q_k^G = \begin{cases} 1 & \text{for } CS_k^G \geq \text{argmax}\{0, CS_k^N\} \\ 0 & \text{for } CS_k^G < \text{argmax}\{0, CS_k^N\} \end{cases} \text{ and } q_k^N = \begin{cases} 1 & \text{for } CS_k^N \geq 0 \wedge CS_k^N > CS_k^G \\ 0 & \text{for } CS_k^N < 0 \vee CS_k^N \leq CS_k^G \end{cases}$$
(2.2)

A consumer demands one unit of a given variant θ if and only if the distance function takes on a non-negative value *and* exceeds the value of the distance function for the other variant, while weak preference for G is observed. The price of a variant θ not being offered is assumed to be $p(\theta) = \infty$.

Using the weights m and $1 - m$, respectively, we can derive the aggregate demand function for each variant $\theta = G, N$:

$$q^\theta(p(G), p(N)) = m q_\Gamma^\theta + (1-m) q_N^\theta. \tag{2.3}$$

Note that by (2.3) all quantities and thus all expressions containing quantities (consumer surplus, profit, welfare) are henceforth given in per capita terms, where 'per capita' always refers to total population M in both regions. Demand q_i for each firm's output depends on the technologies θ_i used by the two firms and the respective prices p_i, with $i = 1, 2$:

$$q_i = q_i(\theta_1, \theta_2, p_1, p_2). \tag{2.4}[10,11]$$

Using (2.1)–(2.4), we can explicitly determine the demand faced by firms for all possible combinations of technologies and prices. For $\theta = \theta_1 = \theta_2$ and $p = p_1 = p_2$ we assume that aggregate demand for variant θ is split evenly between firms so that

$$q_1^\theta = q_2^\theta = q^\theta(p)/2.$$

Since firms are symmetric, this assumption is well founded.

Aggregate consumer surplus is given by

$$CS(\theta_1, \theta_2, p_1, p_2) = m CS_\Gamma(\theta_1, \theta_2, p_1, p_2) + (1-m) CS_N(\theta_1, \theta_2, p_1, p_2), \tag{2.5}$$

where

$$CS_k = \begin{cases} CS_k^G q_k^G & \text{for } q_k^G > 0 \\ CS_k^N q_k^N & \text{for } q_k^N > 0 \\ 0 & \text{for } q_k^G = q_k^N = 0 \end{cases}$$

denotes the surplus of a consumer of type $k = \Gamma, N$. For a type k consumer and a variant θ, it is given by the product of the value of the distance function CS_k^θ, as given by (2.1), and individual demand for a variant q_k^θ, as given by (2.2).

Per capita disutility of local pollution in region j amounts to

$$D_j = d\left(\sum_{i=1}^{2} q_i(f_1, f_2)\Big|_{\theta_i = N \wedge \phi_i = j}\right)^2 \tag{2.6}$$

given by a damage function, which is quadratic in aggregate quantity of the non-green variant produced in region j, and a damage parameter d serving as a weight.[12]

The structure of demand, given by the weights m and $1 - m$, and the reservation prices p_Γ^θ and p_N^θ, as well as the damage parameter d are identical for both regions.

Firms

Production technology of each firm $i = 1, 2$ is characterized by the following cost function:

$$C_i(\theta_i, q_i) = q_i^2 + F(\theta_i), \tag{2.7}$$

where q_i^2 is a variable cost, assumed to be quadratic in quantity and independent of technology, and F is a technology-dependent fixed cost. Thereby, we assume $F(G) = \alpha > 0$ for production of G and $F(N) = 0$ for production of N. The fixed cost of green production may relate to some fixed end-of-pipe abatement capital or R&D in clean production processes. This cost is assumed not to be sunk at the outset.[13]

A firm may be harmed by pollution from a non-green producer located in the same region. Damage cost for a producer $i = 1, 2$ is given by

$$X_i(\theta_1, \theta_2, \phi_1, \phi_2, q_{-i}) = x(\theta_1, \theta_2, \phi_1, \phi_2)\, q_{-i}^2 = \tag{2.8a}[14]$$

where

$$x(\theta_1, \theta_2, \phi_1, \phi_2) = \begin{cases} x_{l_i}^{\theta_i} & \text{if } \theta_{-i} = N \wedge \phi_1 = \phi_2 \\ 0 & \text{otherwise,} \end{cases} \tag{2.8b}$$

where $l_i \in \{up, do\}$. By virtue of (2.8b) damages arise only if the other firm $-i$ produces with the non-green technology and both firms are located in the same region. The damage cost is quadratic in quantity of the non-green firm where a damage parameter $x_{l_i}^{\theta_i}$ is used as a weight. The damage parameter depends on the technology chosen by the pollution victim. We do not need to make any assumptions about the relative size of $x_{l_i}^{N}$ with regard to θ_i, while, in general, we expect a clean producer to be harmed more than a non-green producer. Finally, the impact of pollution may be determined by the location of the pollutee relative to the polluter within a region. Hence, the damage parameter $x_{l_i}^{\theta_i} \in \{\theta_{up}^i, \theta_{do}^i\}$ allows for a distinction between downstream (do) and upstream (up) pollutees. Usually the impact of pollution is stronger on victims located downstream, so that $\theta_{do}^i \geq \theta_{up}^i \geq 0$. The first relation holds as an equality in the case of symmetric externalities, while the second relation holds as an equality if the upstream firm is not affected by pollution at all.

Some degree of inter-firm pollution should be expected in all cases of firms sharing a common property resource such as a common body of air or water, or a limited stretch of land. Examples from industry are abundant. Inter-firm pollution occurs for any two food processing plants, paper mills or producers of chemicals using the same water body as a source for clean process water and a sink for effluents. Air pollution gradually destroys productive capital and reduces the productivity of a fixed stock of labour. Agriculture also provides a number of important examples, such as the deterioration of soil or common water resources or the spread of plant or animal diseases.[15] Note that in our model the externality gives rise to a damage cost which is separable from variable production cost. In this sense, we implicitly assume either that the externality reduces the productivity of the fixed factors of production, or that the firm undertakes a fixed investment in some sort of protection capital.[16-18]

Each firm is assumed to maintain production facilities in one region at the outset, where the historical locations are given by $\phi_1^0 = A$, $\phi_2^0 = B$. When relocating a firm incurs a set-up cost $s > 0$ at the new location. The set-up cost relates to all types of investment necessary for production excluding the investment in the green technology, α, which is assumed to be separable from general investment. The set-up cost at a new host region may only be interpreted as a cost of relocation it it is sunk for the location the firm holds at the outset such that $s|_{\phi_i=\phi_i^0} = 0$. This is not the case if, for example, siting decisions come along with an expansion of production or with the replacement of economically or technologically obsolete capital goods. In these cases the set-up cost would also be incurred at the former host region and thus may not be interpreted as a relocation cost. The cost of relocation accruing to firm $i = 1, 2$ can thus be written as

$$S_i(\phi_i) = \begin{cases} 0 & \text{if } \phi_i = \phi_i^0 \\ \tilde{s} & \text{if } \phi_i \neq \phi_i^0, \end{cases} \quad (2.9a)$$

where

$$\tilde{s} = s - s\big|_{\phi_i=\phi_i^0} = \begin{cases} 0 \text{ if } s\big|_{\phi_i=\phi_i^0} = s \\ s > 0 \text{ if } s\big|_{\phi_i=\phi_i^0} = 0. \end{cases} \quad (2.9b)$$

The cost takes on a positive value only if a firm switches location such that ϕ_i differs from ϕ_i^0, as by (2.9a), *and* the set-up cost is sunk for the historical location, as by (2.9b).[19]

For demand and cost, given by (2.4) and (2.7)–(2.9), the profit of firm $i = 1, 2$ is

$$\pi_i = p_i q_i(\theta_1, \theta_2, p_1, p_2) - C_i(\theta_i, q_i) - X(\theta_{-i}, \phi_1, \phi_2, q_{-i}) - S(\phi_i). \quad (2.10)$$

A firm's profit is thus dependent on its own and its competitor's choice of technology, location and price.[20] Each firm i chooses a strategy $f_i = \{\theta_i, \phi_i, p_i\}$ so as to maximize profit

$$\max_{f_i} \pi_i(f_1, f_2) \quad \text{for } i = 1, 2, \quad (2.11)$$

while taking as given its rival's strategy f_{-i}.

The structure of the game that determines the character of the strategies will be discussed below.

Regions

Welfare for each region $j = A, B$ is given by

$$W_j = \sum_{i=1}^{2} \pi_i(f_1, f_2)\big|_{\phi_i=j} + (1/2)CS(f_1, f_2) - d\left(\sum_{i=1}^{2} q_i(f_1, f_2)\big|_{\theta_i=N \wedge \phi_i=j}\right)^2, \quad (2.12)$$

consisting of the aggregate profit of firms located in region j plus regional consumer surplus less disutility of local pollution, as given by (2.6). According to symmetry, regional consumer surplus amounts to one half of aggregate consumer surplus, as given by (2.5).

Local governments in A and B have the jurisdictional power to impose environmental standards on production activity, for example, emission standards. The policy implemented in region j is captured in the variable $r_j \in \{0, 1\}$, which takes on a value of $r_j = 1$ if an environmental standard exists and $r_j = 0$ in the unregulated state. It is assumed that the polluting technology N can under no circumstances meet the standard. Then the existence of a standard effectively means a prohibition of technology N in the respective region. Hence, environmental policies affect firms' strategies and thereby welfare in each region. The government of each region j takes an environmental policy decision r_j so as to maximize local welfare

$$\max_{r_j} W_j(r_A, r_B) \quad \text{for} \quad j = A, B, \tag{2.13}$$

while taking as given the environmental policy r_{-j} of the other region.

Structure of the Game

Consider the following non-cooperative game under complete information and common knowledge.

Stage 1:
Governments in A and B play a simultaneous one-shot game, in which they maximize local welfare according to (2.13). Thereby, they take into account the expected reactions of the firms.

Stage 2:
Taking as given the regions' policy decisions, firms play a one-shot subgame, in which they maximize profit according to (2.11). It is important to observe that the existence of a standard in a region implies that for both firms any strategy involving non-green production in this region becomes infeasible. The firm subgame consists of two stages.

In stage 2.1 firms simultaneously decide on quality *and* location, $\delta_i = \{\theta_i, \phi_i\}$. By bundling the choice of quality and location into a single decision δ_i we can eliminate one stage of the game, thereby simplifying our analysis significantly. We are allowed to do so if the equilibria (strategies and payoffs) are unaffected by the order of decisions on quality and location. It is easily verified that for our model this is fulfilled as long as firms play subgame-perfect (SGP) equilibrium strategies. As SGP is our equilibrium concept, bundling will have no influence on equilibrium structure and is therefore a legitimate simplification.

In stage 2.2 firms engage in Bertrand competition. Each firm chooses a price p_i so as to maximize profit, taking as given the other firm's price p_{-i} as well as its own and its competitor's choice of technology and location, (δ_1, δ_2).

The game is solved by applying the SGP criterion and working by backward induction. Note that the game consists of three subgames: (1) price competition,

(2) the firm subgame – comprising technology/location choice and price competition – and (3) the game itself – comprising the policy game and the firm subgame. Accordingly, the game is solved in three steps. Step 1 gives the price equilibria (p_1^*, p_2^*) for the feasible sets (δ_1, δ_2) of technology and location. Then, firms' profits can be determined contingent on (δ_1, δ_2). Step 2 gives the SGP equilibrium decisions (δ_1^*, δ_2^*) in technology and location contingent on regions' strategies (r_A, r_B). Hence, $(f_1^* = \{\theta_1^*, \phi_1^*, p_1^*\}, f_2^* = \{\theta_2^*, \phi_2^*, p_2^*\})$ are the SGP equilibria of the firm subgame, where $(f_1^*(r_A, r_B), f_2^*(r_A, r_B))$. Using the equilibrium values $\theta_i^*, \phi_i^*, p_i^*$ for $i = 1, 2$ in (2.5) and (2.6), we can determine consumer surplus CS^* and disutility of pollution D^*. Inserting CS^*, D^* and equilibrium profits π_1^* and π_2^* into (2.12), we can calculate regional welfare levels, which are contingent on regions' strategies (r_A, r_B). Step 3 determines the SGP strategies (r_A^*, r_B^*). Then, $((r_A^*, r_B^*), (f_1^{**}, f_2^{**}))$ defines an SGP equilibrium of the game contingent on the parameters g, m, α, x and d. Thereby, f_i^{**} denotes firm i's SGP strategy given (r_A^*, r_B^*).[21]

3. THE FIRM SUBGAME

In this section we derive the equilibrium outcomes of the firm subgame. Proceeding in two steps, we first determine the Bertrand–Nash price equilibria contingent on the firms' technology and location choices (Section 3.1). In the second step (Section 3.2) we derive the equilibrium choices of technology and location contingent on regional environmental policies. Thereby, we concentrate on the case in which both firms' first-best strategy involves production with the polluting technology.

We cannot exclude *a priori* constellations of parameters and regions' strategies in which one or both firms realize a loss for any feasible strategy. Then, at least one firm would have to exit the market. Albeit not irrelevant, this case will be excluded, since it would complicate things while not adding insights to our analysis. Where necessary, equilibria with both firms being in the market will be guaranteed by the imposition of appropriate restrictions on the fixed cost of green production α, the externality parameter x, and the set-up cost s. The above notwithstanding, the model allows for the possibility of the market not being covered, in the sense that in equilibrium there may exist some consumers who do not buy the commodity.

3.1 The Price Equilibria

As usual in a framework of vertical differentiation, the equilibrium prices depend on the firms' quality – in our case, technology – choices. As (2.4) shows, this is owing to the mutual influence of the two firms' technologies on the demand schedules. However, in the presence of inter-firm externalities location may also have an effect on pricing behaviour. A firm located in the neighbourhood of a polluter may have an incentive to price the competitor out of the market so as to eliminate the externality. Hence, we have to allow for the external damage cost when deriving equilibrium prices. Yet, we may disregard the fixed cost of green technology α and the relocation cost S, which are given for the final stage of the game and have no effect on pricing behaviour. Hence, each firm $i = 1, 2$ maximizes

$$\Pi = p_i q_i(p_1, p_2, \theta_1, \theta_2) - q_i^2 - X(\theta_{-i}, \phi_1, \phi_2, q_{-i}) \quad (3.1)$$

by choosing p_i. Three constellations of technologies are possible: both firms employ the green technology G, one firm employs G and the other the polluting technology N, or both firms employ N. While the firms produce a homogeneous good in the first and last case, product differentiation takes place in the second case. In the following, we derive equilibrium prices for each of these cases.

Green price equilibrium: $\theta_1 = \theta_2 = G$

For both firms choosing the green technology we find the following payoff-dominant Bertrand–Nash equilibrium prices:

$$p_1^* = p_2^* = p^* = \begin{cases} 1 & \text{if } m \leq \sqrt{1/2} \\ 3m/2 & \text{if } m > \sqrt{1/2}, \end{cases} \quad \text{(PE3.1)}$$

where by assuming

$$\text{argmax } \{3m/2, 1\} \leq 1 + g \quad \text{(A3.1)}$$

we exclude the reservation price for the green variant, $1 + g$, as a third candidate equilibrium price. A green duopoly equilibrium exists for any value of m if $\alpha \leq 1/4$.

Proof 3.1: see Appendix.

Under use of (2.1)–(2.4) and (2.10) we derive the demand faced by each firm $i = 1, 2$ and the corresponding profit. Thereby, the profit is given net of the relocation cost S. For $p^* = 1$ we obtain

$$\pi_C^{GG} = 1/4 - \alpha, \quad (3.2a)$$

and for $p^* = 3m/2$

$$q_i = m/2,$$
$$\pi_{NC}^{GG} = m^2/2 - \alpha. \qquad (3.2b)[22]$$

For a relatively small fraction of green consumers, $m \leq \sqrt{1/2}$, the firms prefer to set a low price $p^* = 1$ and sell the product to green and non-green consumers such that the market is covered. For $m > \sqrt{1/2}$ serving the green market segment only at a high price becomes profitable, as the extra revenue from appropriating some of the green consumers' surplus is sufficiently large to offset the loss of scale economies.

Even though firms produce a homogeneous good and compete in Bertrand fashion, they gain positive operating profits, which may be explained as follows. For decreasing returns to scale, which are implied by a quadratic cost function, undercutting becomes unprofitable for some price greater than marginal cost, which in itself exceeds variable unit cost. The fact that Bertrand competition does not erode profits completely has an important implication: other than in the standard models of vertical differentiation, in our case, firms will not always have an incentive to differentiate products in order to gain some monopolistic rent.

Asymmetric price equilibrium: $\theta_i = G; \theta_{-i} = N$

If firms choose different technologies and thus differentiate products, the payoff-dominant Bertrand–Nash equilibrium prices are given by

$$p_i^* = 1 + g; p_{-i}^* = 1 \qquad (PE3.2)$$

if an equilibrium exists, irrespective of the presence of an externality. If the non-green producer does not impose a negative externality on the green producer, existence of an asymmetric price equilibrium requires $g \geq (m^2 - m + \alpha)m$. In the presence of a negative externality existence requires $g \geq [m^2 - m + \alpha + x_{l_i}^G (1 - m)^2]/m$, implying that the externality, as captured by $x_{l_i}^G$, must not be too strong.

Proof 3.2: see Appendix.

For the asymmetric equilibrium we obtain the following demand schedules and profits (net of S). A green producer faces a demand schedule

$$q_i = m,$$

and under observation of (2.8a) and (2.8b) realizes a profit of

$$\pi^{GN} = (1+g)m - m^2 - \alpha \qquad (3.3a)$$

if $\phi_1 \neq \phi_2$, and

$$\pi_i = \pi^{GN} - x^G_{l_i}(1-m)^2 = (1+g)m - m^2 - \alpha - x^G_{l_i}(1-m)^2 \qquad (3.3b)$$

if $\phi_1 = \phi_2$.

For the non-green producer demand schedule and profit is given by

$$q_{-i} = 1 - m,$$
$$\pi^{NG} = m - m^2. \qquad (3.4)$$

Due to differentiation both producers enjoy a monopolistic margin, which they use to skim off the total of consumers' surplus. Comparison of (3.3a) and (3.3b) shows that the externality lowers the green producer's equilibrium profit.

Non-green price equilibrium: $\theta_1 = \theta_2 = N$

If both firms chose the non-green technology the payoff-dominant Bertrand–Nash equilibrium price is given by

$$p_1^* = p_2^* = p^* = 1 \qquad (PE3.3)$$

irrespective of the presence of externalities. However, in the presence of inter-firm externalities a non-green duopoly equilibrium exists only if $x^N_{l_i} \leq 1$ for $i = 1, 2$, implying that the externalities must not be too strong.

Proof 3.3: see Appendix.

Demand faced by each firm $i = 1, 2$ is then given by

$$q_i - 1/2$$

and by (2.8a), (2.8b) and (2.10) profit net of S amounts to

$$\pi^{NN} = 1/4 \qquad (3.5a)$$

if $\phi_1 \neq \phi_2$, and

$$\pi_i = \pi^{NN} - x^N_{l_i}/4 = (1 - x^N_{l_i})/4 \qquad (3.5b)$$

if $\phi_1 = \phi_2$.

Again, for reasons of decreasing returns to scale, firms are able to charge an equilibrium price exceeding their average variable cost. Owing to their monopolistic margin, they appropriate consumer surplus completely. Inspection of (3.5a) and (3.5b) immediately shows that in the presence of an external damage equilibrium profit is lower.

3.2 Equilibrium Technology and Location Structure

We now derive the Nash equilibrium decision vectors (δ_1^*, δ_2^*) of technology and location. Together with the corresponding price equilibria, established in Section 3.1, they form the SGP equilibria (f_1^*, f_2^*) of the firm subgame. As the firms' technology and location choices depend on the regions' environmental policies, it is convenient to derive the equilibria for the three following cases separately: *laissez-faire*, where neither region imposes a standard; bilateral regulation, where both regions impose a standard; and unilateral regulation, where a single region imposes a standard. In the following we consider these cases in turn.

Laissez-faire $(r_A = r_B = 0)$

As neither region has introduced a standard, firms are unrestricted in their strategies. Using (2.8a)–(2.9a) and (3.2a)–(3.5b) for calculating the payoffs we can draw up the strategic form of the technology/location stage of the firm subgame starting at $(r_A = r_B = 0)$ which is depicted in Table 16.1.[23]

Under use of Table 16.1 and

$$\pi_C^{GG} \geq \pi^{NG} \Leftrightarrow \alpha \leq \bar{\alpha}_C := 1/4 + m^2 - m, \tag{3.6a}$$

$$\pi_{NC}^{GG} \geq \pi^{NG} \Leftrightarrow \alpha \leq \bar{\alpha}_{NC} := 3m^2/2 - m, \tag{3.6b}[24]$$

$$\pi^{GN} \geq \pi^{NN} \Leftrightarrow g \geq \bar{g} := \frac{\left(1/4 + m^2 - m + \alpha\right)}{m} \tag{3.7}$$

we are able to establish the following SGP equilibria.[25]

Green equilibrium:

$$(f_1^* = \{G, A, p^*\}, f_2^* = \{G, B, p^*\}) \tag{TLE3.1}$$

Table 16.1 Strategic form representation of technology/location stage for $(r_A = r_B = 0)$

	Firm 1			
Firm 2	$\{G, A\}$	$\{G, B\}$	$\{N, A\}$	$\{N, B\}$
$\{G, A\}$	$\pi_1 = \pi^{GG}$ $\pi_2 = \pi^{GG} - \tilde{s}$	$\pi_1 = \pi_2 = \pi^{GG} - \tilde{s}$	$\pi_1 = \pi^{NG}$ $\pi_2 = \pi^{GN} - x^G_{l_2}(1-m)^2 - \tilde{s}$	$\pi_1 = \pi^{NG} - \tilde{s}$ $\pi_2 = \pi^{GN} - \tilde{s}$
$\{G, B\}$	$\pi_1 = \pi_2 = \pi^{GG}$	$\pi_1 = \pi^{GG} - \tilde{s}$ $\pi_2 = \pi^{GG}$	$\pi_1 = \pi^{NG}$ $\pi_2 = \pi^{GN}$	$\pi_1 = \pi^{NG} - \tilde{s}$ $\pi_2 = \pi^{GN} - x^G_{l_2}(1-m)^2$
$\{N, A\}$	$\pi_1 = \pi^{GN} - x^G_{l_1}(1-m)^2$ $\pi_2 = \pi^{NG} - \tilde{s}$	$\pi_1 = \pi^{GN} - \tilde{s}$ $\pi_2 = \pi^{NG} - \tilde{s}$	$\pi_1 = \pi^{NN} - x^N_{l_1}/4$ $\pi_2 = \pi^{NN} - x^N_{l_2}/4 - \tilde{s}$	$\pi_1 = \pi_2 = \pi^{NN} - \tilde{s}$
$\{N, B\}$	$\pi_1 = \pi^{GN}$ $\pi_2 = \pi^{NG}$	$\pi_1 = \pi^{GN} - x^N_{l_1}(1-m)^2 - \tilde{s}$ $\pi_2 = \pi^{NG}$	$\pi_1 = \pi_2 = \pi^{NN}$	$\pi_1 = \pi^{NN} - x^N_{l_1}/4 - \tilde{s}$ $\pi_2 = \pi^{NN} - x^N_{l_2}/4$

Note: $\pi^{GG} = \begin{cases} \pi^{GG}_C & \text{if } m \leq \sqrt{1/2} \\ \pi^{GG}_{NC} & \text{if } m > \sqrt{1/2} \end{cases}$

exists as an SGP equilibrium if

$$\alpha \leq \text{argmax } \{\bar{\alpha}_C, \bar{\alpha}_{NC}\}$$

and is unique if

$$g \geq \bar{g}.$$

The equilibrium price p^* is determined according to (PE3.1). By inserting equilibrium profits, as given by (3.2a) or (3.2b), respectively, and consumer surplus, as given by (2.5) into (2.12), we can calculate welfare for each region $j = A, B$. For $m \leq \sqrt{1/2}$ and thus $p^* = 1$

$$W_C^{GG} = 1/4 + gm/2 - \alpha, \qquad (3.8a)^{26}$$

while for $m \geq \sqrt{1/2}$ and thus $p^* = 3m/2$

$$W_{NC}^G = (1 + g) m/2 - m^2/4 - \alpha. \qquad (3.8b)$$

Asymmetric equilibria:

$$(f_i^* = \{G, \phi_i^0, 1 + g\}, f_{-i}^* = \{N, \phi_{-i}^0, 1\})$$

exists as a twofold SGP equilibrium if

$$\alpha > \text{argmax } \{\bar{\alpha}_C, \bar{\alpha}_{NC}\}$$

and

$$g \geq \bar{g}.$$

For an asymmetric equilibrium, profits are given by (3.3a) and (3.4), respectively. Welfare for the region hosting the green producer then amounts to

$$W^{GN} = (1 + g) m - m^2 - \alpha. \qquad (3.9)$$

For the region hosting the non-green producer it amounts to

$$W^{NG} = m - m^2 - d (1 - m)^2, \qquad (3.10)$$

where disutility of pollution, as given by (2.6), has been taken into account.

Non-green equilibrium:

$$(f_1^* = \{N, A, 1\}, f_2^* = \{N, B, 1\}) \qquad \text{(TLE3.2)}$$

exists as a SGP equilibrium if

$$g < \bar{g}.$$

It is unique if

$$\alpha > \text{argmax } \{\bar{\alpha}_C, \bar{\alpha}_{NC}\}.$$

Proof 3.4: see Appendix.
Inspection of (3.7) shows that a non-green equilibrium is *ceteris paribus* the more likely the lower the wtp for environmental friendliness, g, and the higher the fixed cost of clean production, α. Clearly, for a decrease in g or an increase in α the profitability of green *vis-à-vis* non-green production declines. More surprisingly, the influence of the fraction of green consumers m is ambiguous. This can be explained as follows. Under product differentiation the quantity produced by the green producer is given by the share of green consumers m. As the equilibrium price is given by the green consumers' reservation price revenue is a linearly increasing function in m. The coexistence of a quadratic variable cost function with the fixed cost of green production gives rise to a U-shaped average cost curve. Together with the linear revenue function this implies the existence of an optimal scale of production. Profit, as given by (3.3a), is thus a concave function in m. By (3.5a) the profit of a competitive non-green producer is given as a constant. Then, the profitability of green *vis-à-vis* non-green production increases in m up to some optimum value and then decreases, thus giving rise to the ambiguity reflected in (3.7).[27]

For profits given by (3.5a), consumer surplus by (2.5) and disutility of pollution by (2.6), welfare in each region $j = A, B$ amounts to

$$W^{NN} = (1 - d)/4. \qquad (3.11)$$

Which of the equilibria is realized under *laissez-faire* depends on the structural properties of demand and technology as captured in the parameters g, m and α. Under *laissez-faire* firms are not restricted by standards in realizing their profit-maximizing strategies. Inspection of (3.4) and (3.5a) shows that choice of the non-green technology guarantees a non-negative profit, no matter what the structural properties of the economy and the competitor's strategy. Hence, a firm never has to leave the market and the existence of a duopolistic equilibrium is guaranteed under *laissez-faire* without any further assumption.[28]

Point of reference: the non-green regime
We intend to study the conditions under which unilateral environmental regulation induces a firm not to relocate but to introduce the clean technology. To make things interesting, it is thus reasonable to assume that demand and cost conditions are such that under *laissez-faire* neither producer has an incentive to introduce the clean technology. Labelling it a non-green regime we assume

$$g < \bar{g} \qquad (A3.2)$$

and

$$\alpha > \text{argmax } \{\bar{\alpha}_C, \bar{\alpha}_{NC}\} \qquad (A3.3)$$

to be satisfied. Obviously, firms' first-best strategies

$$(f_1^{fb} = \{N, A, 1\}, f_2^{fb} = \{N, B, 1\})$$

then involve production with the non-green technology in their historical location. The non-green regime will be our point of reference for the subsequent analysis of the interaction of environmental policies with firms' technology and location choices.

Bilateral regulation: $(r_A = r_B = 1)$
This case is trivial as the non-green technology is prohibited in both regions so that firms' technology/location choices are restricted to $(\delta_1 = \{G, \phi_1\}, \delta_2 = \{G, \phi_2\})$. Since $\pi^{GG} \geq \pi^{GG} - s$, relocation is never profitable for firms and a green equilibrium, as given by (TLE3.1) is enforced.

Obviously, the enforced green equilibrium is not first-best from the firm's point of view. Moreover, as shown in Proof 3.1, (TLE3.1) exists as a duopoly equilibrium only if $\alpha \leq 1/4$. However, this is not sufficient in the case in which the set-up cost is not sunk at the historical location so that $s|_{\phi_i = \phi_i^0} = s$. Allowing for this case, we assume henceforth

$$\alpha + s|_{\phi_i = \phi_i^0} \leq 1/4. \qquad (A3.4)$$

As only the green equilibrium is feasible under bilateral regulation, we need (A3.4) to exclude the case in which regulation forces one firm out of the market.

Unilateral regulation: $(r_j = 1, r_{-j} = 0)$
In order to make notation more accessible suppose that region A has imposed a standard unilaterally so that $(r_A = 1, r_B = 0)$. For the symmetry inolved the

analysis for region B is identical, where only the roles of regions and firms are exchanged. The standard in region A renders any strategy involving $\delta = \{N, A\}$ infeasible. Calculating payoffs by use of (2.8a)–(2.9a) and (3.2a)–(3.5b) we can draw up the strategic form of the technology/location stage of the firm subgame starting at $(r_A = 1, r_B = 0)$ as depicted in Table 16.2.

Table 16.2 Strategic form representation of technology/location stage for $(r_A = 1, r_B = 0)$

	Firm 1		
Firm 2	$\{G, A\}$	$\{G, B\}$	$\{N, B\}$
$\{G, A\}$ $\pi_1 = \pi^{GG}$ $\pi_2 = \pi^{GG} - \tilde{s}$		$\pi_1 = \pi_2 = \pi^{GG} - \tilde{s}$	$\pi_1 = \pi^{NG} - \tilde{s}$ $\pi_2 = \pi^{GN} - \tilde{s}$
$\{G, B\}$ $\pi_1 = \pi_2 = \pi^{GG}$		$\pi_1 = \pi^{GG} - \tilde{s}$ $\pi_2 = \pi^{GG}$	$\pi_1 = \pi^{NG} - \tilde{s}$ $\pi_2 = \pi^{GN} - x_{l_2}^G(1-m)^2$
$\{N, B\}$ $\pi_1 = \pi^{GN}$ $\pi_2 = \pi^{NG}$		$\pi_1 = \pi^{GN} - x_{l_1}^G(1-m)^2 - \tilde{s}$ $\pi_2 = \pi^{NG}$	$\pi_1 = \pi^{NN} - x_{l_1}^N/4 - \tilde{s}$ $\pi_2 = \pi^{NN} - x_{l_2}^N/4$

Note: $\pi^{GG} = \begin{cases} \pi_C^{GG} & \text{if } m \leq \sqrt{1/2} \\ \pi_{NC}^{GG} & \text{if } m > \sqrt{1/2} \end{cases}$

Under use of Table 16.2 and relationship

$$\pi^{GN} \geq \pi^{NN} - x/4 - s \Leftrightarrow g \geq \bar{\bar{g}} := \frac{\left(1 - x_{l_1}^N\right)/4 + m^2 - m + \alpha - \tilde{s}}{m} \qquad (3.12)^{29}$$

we are able to establish the following two SGP equilibria.

Enforced asymmetric equilibrium:

$$(f_1^* = \{G, A, 1+g\}, f_2^* = \{N, B, 1\}) \Leftrightarrow g \geq \bar{\bar{g}}, \qquad \text{(TLE3.3)}$$

where the boundary value $\bar{\bar{g}}$, as given by (3.12), is adjusted according to the specific assumptions about the externality (symmetric or unidirectional) and the set-up cost (sunk or not sunk). Profits and welfare are given by (3.3a), (3.4) and (3.9), (3.10), respectively.

Enforced non-green equilibrium:

$$(f_1^* = \{N, B, 1\}, f_2^* = \{N, B, 1\}) \Leftrightarrow g < \bar{\bar{g}}, \qquad \text{(TLE3.4)}$$

where the boundary value is adjusted according to the specific assumptions about the externality and set-up cost. Profit is given by

$$\pi_1 = \pi^{NN} - x_{l_1}^N/4 - \tilde{s} = (1 - x_{l_1}^N)/4 - \tilde{s}, \qquad (3.5c)$$

for firm 1 and by (3.5b) for firm 2. Note that (3.5c) is contingent on the specific assumptions with regard to the externality and set-up cost. The region that hosts both firms (region B) attains a welfare level,

$$W_B = W_2^{NN} = (2 - x_{l_1}^N - x_{l_2}^N)/4 - \tilde{s} - d, \qquad (3.13a)$$

which is also contingent on the assumptions with respect to externality and set-up cost. The region that does not host a firm (region A) realizes a welfare level of

$$W_A = W_0 = 0. \qquad (3.13b)$$

Proof 3.5: see Appendix.

Non-negativity of profit is not guaranteed for (TLE3.3) and (TLE3.4). The presence of damage and/or relocation cost in the case of enforced non-green equilibrium may imply that profit, as given by (3.5b) and (3.5c), becomes negative. In an asymmetric equilibrium, the green producer's profit, as given by (3.3a), may become negative for too low a level of wtp for environmental friendliness, g, relative to the fixed cost of green production α. If profits are negative in both the asymmetric and non-green equilibrium, at least one firm would have to leave the market. In order to ensure the existence of a duopolistic equilibrium under unilateral regulation, we assume that profit is always non-negative in the enforced non-green equilibrium. This is always guaranteed if

$$(1 - x^N)/4 - \tilde{s} \geq 0 \Leftrightarrow x^N/4 + \tilde{s} \leq 1/4, \qquad (A3.5)$$

which we assume to be satisfied.

We may summarize this result as follows.

Proposition 1: *Take as given (A3.1)–(A3.5) in general, and (A3.1A) for the case of $x_{up}^\theta = x_{do}^\theta = x^\theta > 0$; $\theta = G, N$ and $\tilde{s} = s$. For the case of symmetric inter-firm externalities, for the case of unidirectional externalities in which the* *relocating firm becomes the polluter and in the absence of externalities, regulation then induces*

(a) *both firms to produce with the non-green technology in the region without a standard if wtp for environmental friendliness is low, such that* $g < \bar{\bar{g}} < \bar{g}$ *(relocation case), and*
(b) *the firm which is located in the region with a standard to produce with the clean technology and the firm which is located in the region without a standard to produce with the polluting technology if wtp for environmental friendliness is high, such that* $\bar{\bar{g}} \leq g < \bar{g}$ *(non-relocation case), where the boundary values* $\bar{g}$ *and* $\bar{\bar{g}}$ *are given by (3.7) and (3.12), respectively.*

Comparison of firms' profits for (TLE3.2)–(TLE3.4) shows for the non-green regime that the presence of a unilateral standard usually induces a loss relative to the first-best profit for both firms. In the asymmetric equilibrium the additional fixed cost incurred by a green producer is only partially offset by the monopolistic margin, while the non-green producer suffers a (relative) loss from an uncompensated increase in variable cost. In the non-green equilibrium the relocating producer incurs a relative loss due to the cost of relocation and/or the damage cost, where the damage cost may also accrue to the non-relocating producer. When deciding whether to relocate or to introduce the clean technology the firm which is faced by a standard trades off the relocation and/or damage cost against the uncompensated increase in fixed cost for clean production. As easily derived, this trade-off is governed by (3.12), where $g \geq \bar{\bar{g}}$ implies that the cost increase for relocation exceeds the cost increase for introduction of the green technology.

Inspection of (3.12) shows that the non-relocation case is *ceteris paribus* the more likely, the greater the wtp for clean production, g, the greater the externality parameter x^N, the greater the cost of relocation s, and the lower *ceteris paribus* the fixed cost of clean production, α. Obviously, a greater g increases the monopolistic margin and the profit of a green producer, while α reduces profitability of green production. While set-up cost s is a direct relocation cost, the damage cost, as expressed by x^N, can be interpreted as an indirect cost of relocation. As for the *laissez-faire* case, the influence of the green market share m is ambiguous, where

$$\partial \bar{\bar{g}} / \partial m \gtreqless 0 \Leftrightarrow m \gtreqless \sqrt{(1-x^N)/4 + \alpha - \tilde{s}}.$$

Starting from a very low value of m, the boundary value $\bar{\bar{g}}$ decreases in m. Hence, the green market share bears a positive influence on the likeliness of non-relocation, given that it is not too large. This seems to be quite realistic in a world in which green markets are only emerging. Recalling the concave profit function, we would expect the green monopolist to produce below optimal scale so that a greater demand, as given by m, increases profit.

Consider $\tilde{s} = x^N = 0$. Then from (3.12) and under observance of (A3.2),

$$\bar{\bar{g}}\Big|_{\tilde{s}=x^N=0} = \frac{1/4 + m^2 - m + \alpha}{m} = \bar{g} > g,$$

so that relocation always occurs. Hence, $\tilde{s} = s \vee x^N > 0$ is a necessary condition for the non-relocation result. If there is no cost of relocation either as a set-up or as a damage cost, the producer faced with a standard is able to realize his/her first-best profit by relocating and employing the non-green technology, which s/he will always do. Note that the presence of transboundary inter-firm pollution is equivalent to the absence of inter-firm pollution. In the case of transboundary pollution firms are always harmed, no matter what their location, and thus the damage cost nets out of all payoff terms and becomes irrelevant.

Now, consider $m \to 0$. Then

$$\infty = \bar{\bar{g}}\Big|_{m \to 0} = \bar{g}\Big|_{m \to 0} > g,$$

so that relocation always occurs. Hence, $m > 0$ becomes a necessary condition for the non-relocation result. If there exist no green consumers, a monopolistic green producer has to compete with the non-green producer. However, as non-green consumers prefer the green variant if sold at the same price as the non-green variant and always buy the cheaper variant otherwise, there exists no equilibrium with both firms being in the market. It is easily verified that the green producer always incurs a loss of α, no matter whether s/he exits or captures the whole market. Clearly, a firm faced by a standard would always relocate then to become a non-green producer.

Finally, consider $g = 0$, which does not contradict (A3.1) for $m \le 2/3$. Then, the non-relocation result obtains for

$$0 \ge \bar{\bar{g}} = \frac{(1 - x^N)/4 + m^2 - m + \alpha - \tilde{s}}{m} \Leftrightarrow \alpha \le (x^N - 1)/4 + m - m^2 - \tilde{s}. \quad (3.14)[30]$$

For $m \le 2/3 < \sqrt{1/2}$ and under (A3.3), the satisfaction of (3.14) requires

$$1/4 - m^2 + m = \alpha_C < (x^N - 1)/4 + m - m^2 + \tilde{s}$$

as a necessary condition. As easily verified, the latter holds for

$$1/2 - \sqrt{(2x^N + 8\tilde{s})} < m < \mathrm{argmin}\,\{1/2 + \sqrt{(2x^N + 8\tilde{s})}, 2/3\}.$$

Hence, if the direct and/or indirect cost of relocation, as captured in s and x^N, are large relative to the fixed cost of clean production, α, and if m has an intermediate value so that (3.14) is satisfied, the firm facing a standard introduces the green technology and does not relocate even if the wtp for environmental friendliness approaches zero. In this case relocation is so costly that the firm is better off selling the green product even if it does not earn any monopolistic rent. In this case $g > 0$ is neither necessary nor sufficient for non-relocation. However, if α is sufficiently large relative to s and x^N, so that (3.14) is not satisfied, $g > 0$ becomes a necessary condition for the non-relocation result.

4. THE POLICY STAGE

In this section we determine the equilibria in regional strategies, which together with the corresponding equilibria of the firm subgame constitute the equilibria of the game. Thereby, we maintain our assumption of a non-green regime, as captured in (A3.2) and (A3.3), as well as the more technical assumptions (A3.1), (A3.4), (A3.5) and (A3.1A). In order to contain the number of subcases, we restrict analysis to the case of symmetric inter-firm externalities and the presence of a relocation cost so that $x^\theta_{up} = x^\theta_{do} = x^\theta > 0$; $\theta = G, N$ and $\tilde{s} = s$. It is convenient to separate analysis for the relocation case, as described by (TLE3.4), and for the non-relocation case, as described by (TLE3.3).

4.1 The Relocation Case

Suppose $g < \bar{\bar{g}} < \bar{g}$, so that a firm relocates if faced by a unilateral standard. Using regional welfare levels, as given by (3.8a), (3.8b), (3.11), (3.13a) and (3.13b), we derive the strategic form representation of the policy stage of the game as depicted in Table 16.3.

Under use of Table 16.3 and the relationships

$$W_C^{GG} \geq W_2^{NN} \Leftrightarrow d \geq \bar{d}_{NN2}^{GGC} := \left(1 - 2x^N\right)/4 - gm/2 + \alpha - s, \quad (4.1a)$$

Table 16.3 Strategic form representation of the policy stage of the game for the relocation case

	Region A	
Region B	$r_A = 1$	$r_A = 0$
$r_B = 1$	$W_A = W_B = \begin{cases} W_C^{GG} \text{ if } m \leq \sqrt{1/2} \\ W_{NC}^{GG} \text{ if } m > \sqrt{1/2} \end{cases}$	$W_A = W_2^{NN}$ $W_B = W_0$
$r_B = 0$	$W_A = W_0$ $W_B = W_2^{NN}$	$W_A = W_B = W^{NN}$

$$W_{NC}^{GG} \geq W_2^{NN} \Leftrightarrow d \geq \bar{d}_{NN2}^{GGNC} := (1-x^N)/2 - (1+g)m/2 + m^2/4 + \alpha - s, \quad (4.1b)$$

$$W_0 \geq W^{NN} \Leftrightarrow d \geq 1, \quad (4.2)$$

$$W_C^{GG} \geq W^{NN} \Leftrightarrow d \geq \bar{d}_{NN}^{GGC} := -2gm + 4\alpha, \quad (4.3a)$$

$$W_{NC}^{GG} \geq W^{NN} \Leftrightarrow d \geq \bar{d}_{NN}^{GGNC} := 1 - 2(1+g)m + m^2 + 4\alpha, \quad (4.3b)$$

we are able to establish the following.

Proposition 2.1:

(a) <u>Bilateral regulation</u>, as given by ($r_A = r_B = 1$) and the enforced green equilibrium (TLE3.1), is a unique and/or payoff-dominant SGP equilibrium if

- $d > 1$ (uniqueness (U) $\Rightarrow$ existence ($\exists$) + payoff dominance (PD)) or
- $1 > d \geq \bar{d}_{NN}^{GG}$ (PD $\Rightarrow \exists$) for $g \leq \tilde{g}$ and
- $1 > d \geq \bar{d}_{NN2}^{GG}$ ($\exists \Rightarrow$ PD) for $g > \tilde{g}$,

where

$$\tilde{g} = \begin{Bmatrix} \tilde{g}_C \\ \tilde{g}_{NC} \end{Bmatrix}, \bar{d}_{NN}^{GG} = \begin{Bmatrix} \bar{d}_{NN}^{GGC} \\ \bar{d}_{NN}^{GGNC} \end{Bmatrix}, \bar{d}_{NN2}^{GG} = \begin{Bmatrix} \bar{d}_{NN2}^{GGC} \\ \bar{d}_{NN2}^{GGNC} \end{Bmatrix} \Leftrightarrow m \begin{Bmatrix} \leq \\ > \end{Bmatrix} \sqrt{1/2}$$

and the boundary values are given by (4.1a), (4.1b), (4.3a), (4.3b) in the main text, and (4.1aA) and (4.1bA) in the Appendix.

(b) <u>Bilateral laissez-faire</u>, as given by $(r_A = r_B = 0)$ and the (first-best) non-green equilibrium (TLE3.2), is a unique and/or payoff-dominant SGP equilibrium if

- $d < \bar{d}_{NN}^{GG}$ $(PD \Rightarrow \exists)$ for $g \leq \tilde{g}$ and
- $d < \bar{d}_{NN2}^{GG}$ $(U \Rightarrow \exists)$ for $g > \tilde{g}$.

The bilateral laissez-faire equilibrium is Pareto-inefficient ('race to the bottom') if $g > \tilde{g}$ and $\bar{d}_{NN}^{GG} \leq d < \bar{d}_{NN2}^{GG}$.
(c) An equilibrium with unilateral regulation does not exist.

Proof: see Appendix.

The non-feasibility of unilateral regulation is not surprising. The firm always relocates from the region with a unilateral standard. As welfare falls to a zero level, a region has no incentive to set a standard unilaterally, unless hosting a non-green producer gives rise to a negative level of welfare. Inspection of (3.11) shows that this requires $d > 1$. However, for the high disutility from pollution implied, both regions have an incentive to introduce a standard. From the non-existence of asymmetric equilibria for the relocation case it follows that non-relocation of firms is, indeed, a necessary condition for the feasibility of unilateral regulation.

The conditions given in (4.1a), (4.1b), (4.3a) and (4.3b) imply that bilateral *laissez-faire* is the less likely, the greater disutility from pollution, as captured by d. This corresponds to the result found by Markusen, Morey and Olewiler (1995) and Rauscher (1997a), where in equilibrium higher pollution tax rates go with higher values of disutility from pollution. However, as their results are derived for the homogeneous-good case, the impact of the green-market potential, as given by the fraction of green consumers, m, and their wtp for clean production, g, on regulation is not considered. By observing the boundary values given in (4.1a), (4.1b), (4.3a) and (4.3b) we find that green-market potential, by both, g and m, has an unambiguously negative impact on the likeliness of bilateral *laissez-faire*. Hence, a government accounting for the private benefits from green consumerism, which are captured in green-market potential, is more inclined to introduce a standard. Thereby, it does not really matter how much of the private benefit increases consumer surplus and how much is skimmed off by the green producer and thus increases profit. The fixed cost of green production, α, has the expected positive impact on the likeliness of mutual *laissez-faire*, while the firm damage parameter x^N and the set-up cost s have a negative impact. As captured in (4.3a) and (4.3b), the policy decision is essentially determined by the trade-off between the social benefit from green production, consisting of the public benefit from eliminated pollution, and the green consumers' private benefit from green consumption, as opposed to the cost of clean production.

Using Conditions (4.1aA) and (4.1bA), as given in the Appendix, we are able to establish two sequences of equilibria depending on the interval in which the value of d lies. As before, 'U' stands for 'unique' and 'PD' stands for 'payoff-dominant'.

Case $g \leq \tilde{g}$:

$$
\begin{array}{r}
1- \\
\bar{d}_{NN}^{GG} - \\
\bar{d}_{NN2}^{GG} -
\end{array}
\left.\begin{array}{l}
\} \text{ U + PD bilateral regulation} \\
\} \text{ PD bilateral regulation} \\
\} \text{ PD bilateral } \textit{laissez-faire} \\
\} \text{ U + PD bilateral } \textit{laissez-faire}.
\end{array}\right. \quad (S4.1)^{31}
$$

Case $g > \tilde{g}$:

$$
\begin{array}{r}
1- \\
\bar{d}_{NN2}^{GG} - \\
\bar{d}_{NN}^{GG} -
\end{array}
\left.\begin{array}{l}
\} \text{ U + PD bilateral regulation} \\
\} \text{ PD bilateral regulation} \\
\} \text{ Pareto-inefficient bilateral } \textit{laissez-faire} \\
\} \text{ U + PD bilateral } \textit{laissez-faire}.
\end{array}\right. \quad (S4.2)
$$

Starting from $d > 1$, a lowering of d decreases the 'stability' of bilateral regulation stepwise until the equilibrium switches to bilateral *laissez-faire*. As d falls even further the 'stability' of a bilateral deregulation equilibrium increases stepwise.[32]

Inspection of (S4.1) shows that for $g \leq \tilde{g}$ all equilibria obtained along the sequence are optimal, in the sense of being payoff-dominant. Hence we have to be careful to distinguish cases of efficient *laissez-faire* from an inefficient race to the bottom. Obviously, for $g \leq \tilde{g}$ consumers do not care too much for the environment and disutility of pollution is sufficiently low so as to render bilateral *laissez-faire* always an efficient outcome. As (S4.2) shows, this is not always the case for $g > \tilde{g}$. Here, a Pareto-inefficient, that is, payoff-dominated, bilateral *laissez-faire* equilibrium exists for intermediate values of $d \in [\bar{d}_{NN}^{GG}, \bar{d}_{NN2}^{GG}]$. This may be interpreted as a race to the bottom: neither region sets a standard so as to attract the foreign firm or, at the least, to deter the domestic producer from relocating. However, each region would attain a higher welfare level in the case of bilateral regulation.

Notice that environmental regulation is not introduced because of the credibility of the firm's threat to relocate. In effect, the threat is never carried out. In this light, a race to the bottom, in which firms prevent the introduction of Pareto-efficient environmental policies by threatening to relocate, should only be expected if firms are actually able to carry out their threat, thus rendering it credible. *Ceteris paribus* we would then expect those industries to enjoy laxer regulation, which are characterized by a costly abatement technology, by a low set-up cost or the absence of sunk costs, by insensitivity to pollution and by operation in a market that does not exhibit a significant green potential.

4.2 The Non-relocation Case

Suppose $\bar{\bar{g}} < g < \bar{g}$ so that a firm does not relocate when faced by a unilateral standard. Using regional welfare levels, as given by (3.8a)–(3.11), we derive the strategic form representation of the policy stage of the game as depicted in Table 16.4.

Table 16.4 *Strategic form representation of the policy stage of the game for the non-relocation case*

	Region A	
Region B	$r_A = 1$	$r_A = 0$
$r_B = 1$	$W_A = W_B = \begin{cases} W_C^{GG} & \text{if } m \leq \sqrt{1/2} \\ W_{NC}^{GG} & \text{if } m \geq \sqrt{1/2} \end{cases}$	$W_A = W^{NG}$ $W_B = W^{GN}$
$r_B = 0$	$W_A = W^{GN}$ $W_B = W^{NG}$	$W_A = W_B = W^{NN}$

Under use of Table 16.4 as well as the relationships (4.3a), (4.3b) and

$$W_C^{GG} \geq W^{NG} \Leftrightarrow d \geq \bar{d}_{NG}^{GGC} := \frac{-1/4 + (2-g)m/2 - m^2 + \alpha}{(1-m)^2}, \quad (4.4a)$$

$$W_{NC}^{GG} \geq W^{NG} \Leftrightarrow d \geq \bar{d}_{NG}^{GGNC} := \frac{(1-g)m/2 - 3m^2/4 + \alpha}{(1-m)^2}, \quad (4.4b)$$

$$W^{GN} \geq W^{NN} \Leftrightarrow d \geq \bar{d}_{NN}^{GN} := 1 - 4[(1+g)m - m^2 - \alpha], \quad (4.5)$$

we are able to establish the following.

Proposition 2.2:

(a) <u>Bilateral regulation</u>, *as defined in Proposition 2.1(a), is a unique and/or payoff-dominant equilibrium*

  (i) *in the case of a small fraction of green consumers, $m \leq \sqrt{1/2}$, if*

$$d \geq \mathrm{argmax}\left\{\bar{d}_{NG}^{GGC}, \mathrm{argmin}\left\{\bar{d}_{NN}^{GN}, \bar{d}_{NN}^{GGC}\right\}\right\},$$

  where the boundary values are given by (4.3a), (4.4a) and (4.5), and

  (ii) *in the case of a large fraction of green consumers, $m > \sqrt{1/2}$, if*

- *for* $\alpha \leq \hat{\alpha}_{NC} : d \geq \bar{d}_{NN}^{GN}$ *(uniquenes $(U) \Rightarrow$ existence $(\exists)$), and*

- *for* $\alpha > \hat{\alpha}_{NC}$ *and* $\begin{cases} g \geq \check{g}_{NC} : d \geq \bar{d}_{NN}^{GN} & (U \Rightarrow \exists) \\ g < \check{g}_{NC} : d \geq \bar{d}_{NG}^{GGNC} & (\exists \Rightarrow U) \end{cases},$

where the boundary values are given by (4.3b), (4.4b) in the main text and (4.4aA), (4.5A) in the Appendix.
Bilateral regulation is Pareto-inefficient

  (i) *for $m \leq \sqrt{1/2}$ if $\bar{d}_{NN}^{GGC} > d \geq \mathrm{argmax}\ \{\bar{d}_{NG}^{GGC}, \bar{d}_{NN}^{GN}\}$, or*
  (ii) *for $m > \sqrt{1/2}$ if $\bar{d}_{NN}^{GGNC} > d \geq \mathrm{argmax}\ \{\bar{d}_{NG}^{GGNC}, \bar{d}_{NN}^{GN}\}$ where for $\alpha > \hat{\alpha}_{NC}$ the condition $g > \hat{g}_{NC}$ must hold also. $\hat{g}_{NC}$ is given by (4.2bA) in the Appendix.*

b) <u>Bilateral laissez-faire</u>, *as defined in Proposition 2.1(b), is a unique and/or payoff-dominant equilibrium*

  (i) *in the case of a small fraction of green consumers, $m \leq \sqrt{1/2}$ if*

$$d < \mathrm{argmin}\left\{\bar{d}_{NN}^{GN}, \mathrm{argmax}\left\{\bar{d}_{NG}^{GGC}, \bar{d}_{NN}^{GGC}\right\}\right\}, \text{ and}$$

  (ii) *in the case of a large fraction of green consumers, $m > \sqrt{1/2}$, if*

$$d < \bar{d}_{NN}^{GN} \ (\exists \Rightarrow PD).$$

Policy, firm location and green consumerism

Bilateral laissez-faire is Pareto-inefficient if

$$m \leq \sqrt{1/2} \text{ and } \overline{d}_{NN}^{GGC} \geq d > \text{argmin}\{\overline{d}_{NN}^{GN}, \overline{d}_{NG}^{GGC}\}.$$

(c) <u>Unilateral regulation</u> by either of the two regions, as defined by ($r_A = 1$, $r_B = 0$) or ($r_A = 0$, $r_B = 1$) in combination with the enforced asymmetric equilibrium (TLE3.3), is an equilibrium, which is unique vis-à-vis the symmetric equilibria

(i) in the case of a small fraction of green consumers, $m \leq \sqrt{1/2}$, if

$$\overline{d}_{NG}^{GGC} > d \geq \overline{d}_{NN}^{GN} \wedge \begin{cases} g \geq \breve{g}_c & \text{if} & m \leq 1 - \sqrt{1/8} \\ g < \breve{g}_c & \text{if} & 1 - \sqrt{1/8} < m \leq \sqrt{1/2} \end{cases}, \text{ and}$$

(ii) in the case of a large fraction of green consumers, $m > \sqrt{1/2}$, if

$$\overline{d}_{NN}^{GN} \leq d < \overline{d}_{NG}^{GGNC} \wedge \alpha > \hat{\alpha}_{NC} \wedge \breve{g}_{NC} > g(\exists \Leftrightarrow U).$$

Proof: see Appendix.

Remark: For expositional ease the neccessary and sufficient conditions have been given in a general form only in parts (a) (i) and (b) (i) of Proposition 2.2. The explicit conditions are easily derived under use of (4.8A) in combination with (4.2a), (4.3A) and (4.4aA), as given in the Appendix.

Corollary 2.2: The following equilibrium sequences may obtain for the non-relocation case. The constellations of parameters which give rise to each of the sequences is given in the Appendix.

$$\begin{matrix} \overline{d}_{NN}^{GG} - & \} \text{ U + PD bilateral regulation} \\ & \} \text{ Pareto-inefficient bilateral regulation} \\ \overline{d}_{NG}^{GG} - & \} \text{ unilateral regulation} \\ \overline{d}_{NN}^{GN} - & \} \text{ U + PD bilateral } \textit{laissez-faire} \end{matrix} \quad \text{(S4.3)}$$

$$\begin{matrix} \overline{d}_{NN}^{GG} - & \} \text{ U + PD bilateral regulation} \\ & \} \text{ Pareto-inefficient bilateral regulation} \\ \overline{d}_{NN}^{GN} - & \} \text{ PD bilateral } \textit{laissez-faire} \\ \overline{d}_{NG}^{GG} - & \} \text{ U + PD bilateral } \textit{laissez-faire} \end{matrix} \quad \text{(S4.4)}$$

$\bar{d}_{NN}^{GN}$ – } U + PD bilateral regulation
$\bar{d}_{NN}^{GG}$ – } PD bilateral regulation
$\bar{d}_{NG}^{GG}$ – } PD bilateral *laissez-faire*
} U + PD bilateral *laissez-faire* (S4.5)

$\bar{d}_{NN}^{GN}$ – } U + PD bilateral regulation
$\bar{d}_{NG}^{GG}$ – } PD bilateral regulation
} Pareto-inefficient bilateral *laissez-faire*
$\bar{d}_{NN}^{GG}$ – } U + PD bilateral *laissez-faire* (S4.6)

$\bar{d}_{NG}^{GG}$ – } U + PD bilateral regulation
$\bar{d}_{NN}^{GG}$ – } unilateral regulation
$\bar{d}_{NN}^{GN}$ – } unilateral regulation
} U + PD bilateral *laissez-faire* (S4.7)

$\bar{d}_{NG}^{GG}$ – } U + PD bilateral regulation
$\bar{d}_{NN}^{GN}$ – } unilateral regulation
$\bar{d}_{NN}^{GG}$ – } Pareto-inefficient bilateral *laissez-faire*
} U + PD bilateral *laissez-faire* (S4.8)

where

$$\bar{d}_{NN}^{GG} = \begin{cases} \bar{d}_{NN}^{GGC} \\ \bar{d}_{NN}^{GGNC} \end{cases}, \quad \bar{d}_{NG}^{GG} = \begin{cases} \bar{d}_{NG}^{GGC} \\ \bar{d}_{NG}^{GGNC} \end{cases} \Leftrightarrow m \begin{cases} \leq \\ > \end{cases} \sqrt{1/2}.$$

As for the relocation case, we find for all sequences that the equilibrium degree of regulation falls with the value of disutility from pollution, d, which is reflected in the equilibrium conditions given in Propositions 2.2.

According to Proposition 2.2 (c) and Sequences (S4.3), (S4.7) and (S4.8), an equilibrium with unilateral regulation is feasible for the non-relocation case. A general requirement is that disutility from pollution, as captured by d, is of some intermediate value. For a relatively small fraction of green consumers, $m \leq 1 - \sqrt{1/8}$, a sufficiently large wtp for clean production, $g \geq \tilde{g}_C$, is necessary to sustain unilateral regulation, a result we would expect. However, for larger fractions of green consumers, $1 - \sqrt{1/8} < m \leq \sqrt{1/2}$, wtp must be not too great, such that

$g < \tilde{g}_C$. For $m > \sqrt{1/2}$ an asymmetric equilibrium requires that the fixed cost of green production, α, is sufficiently high. Both results for the intermediate and large fractions of green consumers are not surprising as for too large a green-market potential relative to the fixed cost of green production both regions have an incentive to impose a standard. Hence, unilateral regulation requires that the green-market potential be sufficiently large but not too large. We should recall that the green-market potential, at the least, has to be developed so as to induce a producer faced by a standard not to relocate but to introduce the green technology. As unilateral regulation has been shown to be no equilibrium for the relocation case, the necessary conditions for non-relocation extend to the feasibility of unilateral regulation.

Unilateral regulation is not sustainable in the homogeneous-good case as considered by Markusen, Morey and Olewiler (1995) and Rauscher (1997a). In our model an equilibrium with asymmetric levels of regulation arises for regions which are identical with respect to all demand- and supply-side parameters, where usually the existence of asymmetric regulation is explained by regional asymmetries in the preference for environmental quality. The reason for this is that the concept of product differentiation extends from the firm level to the regional level. A region's option to specialize in the production of a green commodity, which is not only sold on a domestic but also exported to a foreign green market, renders unilateral regulation feasible. Hence, the popular claim that unilateral regulation is unsustainable in an open economy is reversed: by allowing for specialization trade becomes a necessary condition for unilateral regulation. This is easily proved. Suppose the two regions to be closed economies. As they are identical both regions would always choose the same environmental policy. The existence of asymmetric equilibria does not seem far-fetched. Developing countries usually introduce relatively lax environmental policies and trade in product variants which are produced in a polluting manner, while the industrialized countries with their stricter environmental regulation specialize on green variants of the same commodity.[33]

According to Proposition 2.2 (a) and Sequences (S4.3) and (S4.4), an equilibrium with Pareto-inefficient bilateral regulation may arise. Such an equilibrium may obtain if wtp for clean production, g, and disutility from pollution, d, are sufficiently, albeit not too large. Pareto-inefficient bilateral regulation corresponds to the 'not in my backyard' case found by Markusen, Morey and Olewiler (1995) and Rauscher (1997a), where each country imposes an excessive tax rate so as to keep out a polluting firm. In equilibrium the firm does not enter the market, which is an inefficient outcome for each region. In our case, each region introduces a standard so as to enforce clean production, even though each region would attain a higher welfare level if non-green production took place.

According to Proposition 2.2 (b) and Sequences (S4.6) and (S4.8), an equilibrium giving rise to Pareto-inefficient *laissez-faire* may materialize for $m \leq \sqrt{1/2}$ and relatively low values of d and g. In this case the race to the bottom does not result from the firms' threat to relocate, which would not be credible, but from each region's effort to establish its domestic firm as a non-green monopolist, and thereby realize a welfare gain that outweighs the increase in pollution.

5. CONCLUSIONS

A game has been developed and solved, in which two regions non-cooperatively decide on the introduction of environmental standards in the first stage and duopolists endogenously choose location and technology in the second stage. Production with a non-green technology causes local pollution which is a source of disutility for consumers and (possibly) a source of some external cost to other producers located in the same region. Consumers are heterogeneous with respect to their willingness to pay for clean methods of production. Our general conclusion with regard to the question as to whether firm relocation and the 'race to the bottom' are serious obstacles in the way towards effective environmental policies is that the answer can only be given in the light of supply *and* demand conditions. Specifically, we find that in the presence of a relocation cost and inter-firm pollution, firms are less prone to relocate in reaction to unilateral environmental regulation. The existence of a green-market potential, as given by the fraction of consumers with a willingness to pay for clean methods of production and the amount they are willing to pay, acts as a further counterbalance to a firm's tendency to relocate. Thus, existence of either a relocation cost or some inter-firm pollution and existence of a positive fraction of 'green' consumers are necessary conditions for relocation not to take place.

The alleviation of the relocation problem is paralleled by the finding that the existence of a green-market potential reduces governments' likelihood of engaging in bilateral *laissez-faire* policies. Unilateral regulation becomes feasible, given that relocation does not take place. Thus, the existence of equilibria with unilateral regulation is linked in two ways to the possibility of differentiating a green product variant. First, the existence of consumers buying a green product variant is a necessary condition for non-relocation, which by itself is a necessary condition for the sustainability of unilateral regulation. Second, the otherwise identical regions would always introduce the same environmental policies if there were not the possibility to specialize in trade of a green and non-green product. The existence of such asymmetric equilibria reverses the popular claim that unilateral regulation is unsustainable in an open economy. In our model, the very existence of trade becomes a necessary condition for unilateral regulation. Besides unilateral regulation and the (expected) cases of efficient bilateral regulation and bilateral *laissez-faire*, races to the bottom and inefficient introduction of standards may also occur under certain conditions.

Finally, we should pay heed to the fact that only the cases found for a small share of green consumers are of practical relevance. Even though empirical evidence on green markets is scarce and far from conclusive, any widespread occurrence of green consumerism seems to be far from realistic (as yet).[34] However, it is reassuring from an environmental point of view that the existence even of a small green-market potential may improve the feasibility of (unilateral) environmental policies in a global economy.

The main weakness of the approach used lies in the specific functional forms which have been chosen as to make the model tractable. Obviously, there is some potential for generalizations. Moreover, the introduction of trading costs, the case of variable costs of clean production and issues of asymmetric information provide some quite generous scope for extensions. Finally, some of the conclusions as to how the existence of a green-market potential influences firms' location decisions and environmental policies may provide some material for empirical analysis. I hope to address these issues in forthcoming work.

NOTES

1. For a more detailed discussion of the theoretical and empirical literature on the relocation issue see Kuhn and Tivig (1996). In particular, their overview includes models assuming perfect competition in the product market besides those of imperfect competition mentioned in this chapter, as well as a critical assessment of the misleading character of the term 'environmental capital flight' being widely used in the public debate.
2. These models are closely related to the somewhat more developed work on quality standards in vertically differentiated oligopolies (Ronnen, 1991; Boom, 1995; Crampes and Hollander, 1995).
3. For a more detailed overview of the following issues see Kuhn (1997).
4. For example, the use of pesticides in agricultural production leads to pollution, while the content of pesticides in the products also lowers their physical quality. Many handcrafted products may be acclaimed for being produced in a relatively environmentally friendly manner and at the same time be of a high overall quality.
5. See Rose-Ackerman (1996) for an overview on intrinsic motivation and Rauscher (1997b) for an application of the notion of social rewards to environmental economics.
6. Subsidization of green product variants may be interpreted as a monetary benefit from green consumption. Even though government incentives may play an important role in motivating green consumption, we exclude them. We wish to deal with a case where only some of the consumers reveal preferences for green products, whereas, in general, government policies create the same incentives for all consumers.
7. An informal discussion of the model is given in Kuhn (1997).
8. In the following, we use a superscript to denote technologies/variants ($\theta = G, N$), and a subscript to denote either consumer types ($k = \Gamma, N$), firms ($i = 1, 2$), or regions ($j = A, B$).

9. This does not imply that non-green consumers do not care about pollution. However, they do not derive an extra private benefit from green consumption and thus have no incentive to engage in it.
10. Because of the discrete quality choice between G and N, q_i is not a smooth but rather a step function in prices. Thereby, q_i is completely inelastic to price over certain intervals but may jump at threshold prices.
11. For ease of exposition, we shall use identical symbols for functions as well as functional values.
12. The specific functional form is chosen solely for ease of exposition. In general, the results derived hold for any damage function with positive marginal disutility of damage.
13. Clearly, green methods of production may also affect variable cost, for example when low pollution inputs are used in production.
14. A minus sign in front of an index indicates 'the other'.
15. I am indebted to Henk Peer for the second example.
16. Alternatively, the externality might raise the variable cost of production. Examples are a reduced productivity of a variable stock of labour, or the increase in variable fishing cost due to overfishing.
17. As an example not directly relating to pollution, consider two fisheries sharing a common stock of fish. The reduced catch due to overfishing induces each fishery to invest in more sophisticated catching equipment. A sustainable fishery undertakes an investment in the keeping of a 'private' stock of fish. Note that in this case green producers are not harmed by the negative externalities while disutility to consumers arises from the negative impact of conventional (over)fishing on amicable species such as dolphins or water birds.
18. For a more detailed discussion of the types of externalities and common property dilemmas we deal with, see Dasgupta and Heal (1977), Baumol and Oates (1988).
19. Note that the fixed cost α and the relocation cost s are given as per capita expressions, too.
20. Note that through the discrete nature of θ, ϕ and q the profit function is a step function in these variables.
21. An overview of the game in extensive form can be obtained from the author upon request.
22. With the superscript on profits we denote the corresponding quality choices of firms, where the first letter denotes the choice of the producer whose profit we look at and the second denotes the choice of his competitor. For the green equilibrium the subscript indicates whether the profit relates to a covered or non-covered market equilibrium.
23. We slightly misuse the strategic form representation as we leave out price as an element of firms' strategies. However, we are allowed to do so since we have shown in Section 3.1 that there exists a unique price equilibrium for every (δ_1, δ_2).
24. These conditions are expressed in terms of m in Ecchia and Mariotti (1994, 12–13). For our purpose expressing them in terms of α is more convenient. Note that $\bar{\alpha}_C \geq \bar{\alpha}_{NC} \Leftrightarrow m \leq \sqrt{1/2}$.
25. These equilibria correspond to those found by Ecchia and Mariotti (1994).
26. The indices read as suggested by note 22.
27. Note that a similar argument applies to the profitability of competitive production of the green good *vis-à-vis* monopolistic production of the non-green good which gives rise to an ambiguity in m of the boundary values in (3.6a) and (3.6b).
28. Note that we have omitted the case $\alpha \leq \text{argmax } \{\bar{\alpha}_C, \bar{\alpha}_{NC}\} \wedge g < \bar{g}$. This would give rise to the coexistence of a green and a non-green equilibrium. As it does not contribute any additional insights to our analysis, we exclude this case.
29. As comparison of (3.7) and (3.12) yields $\bar{g} \geq \bar{\bar{g}}$, (A3.2) does not exclude satisfaction of (3.12).
30. This implies that $p(G) = 1$ and $p(N) = 1 - \varepsilon$, where $\varepsilon \to 0$, such that demand for the green producer is $q^G = m$ and for the non-green producer $q^N = 1 - m$. Stability of this equilibrium is easily verified.
31. Note that $\bar{d}^{GG}_{NN2} > 0$ is not always satisfied. If $\bar{d}^{GG}_{NN2} \leq 0$, U + PD mutual *laissez-faire* does not exist as an equilibrium.
32. It should be quite clear that the sequences (S4.1) and (S4.2) as well as the sequences in Section 4.2 can only be interpreted in an ordinal way. This prohibits an assessment of the likelihood of an equilibrium.
33. Associated with this specialization in trade is an uneven distribution of environmental quality, which may be problematic from an ecological or distributional perspective.
34. See Kuhn (1997) for some references.

REFERENCES

Baumol, W.J. and W.E. Oates (1988), *The theory of environmental policy* (2nd edition), Cambridge: Cambridge University Press.
Boom, A. (1995), 'Asymmetric international minimum quality standards and vertical differentiation', *The Journal of Industrial Economics*, **43**, 101–19.
Carraro, C. and G. Topa (1994), 'Should Environmental Policy Be Internationally Coordinated?', in C. Carraro (ed.), *Trade, Innovation, Environment*, Dordrecht: Kluwer.
Constantatos, C. and E.S. Sartzetakis (1995), 'Environmental Taxation when Market Structure is Endogenous: the Case of Vertical Product Differentiation', Milan, FEEM Nota di Lavoro no. 76.95.
Cordella, T. and I. Grilo (1995), '"Social Dumping" and Delocalization: Is there a Case for Imposing a Social Clause?', Louvain; CORE Discussion Paper 9504.
Crampes, C. and A. Hollander (1995), 'Duopoly and quality standards', *European Economic Review*, **39**, 71–82.
Cremer, H. and J.-F. Thisse (1994), 'On the taxation of polluting products in a differentiated industry', Milan, FEEM Nota di Lavoro no. 31.94.
Dasgupta, P.S. and G.M. Heal (1977), *Economic Theory and Exhaustible Resources*, Cambridge: Cambridge University Press.
Ecchia, G. and M. Mariotti (1994), 'Market Competition and Adoption of "Green" Technologies in a Model with Heterogeneous Consumers', Milan, FEEM Nota di Lavoro no. 52.94.
Harsanyi, J.C. and R. Selten (1988), *A General Theory of Equilibrium Selection in Games*, Cambridge, MA and London: MIT Press.
Kuhn (1997), 'Environmental Policy, Firm Location and Green Consumption', in M. Accutt and P. Mason, *Environmental Valuation, Economic Policy and Sustainability*, Cheltenham, UK and Northampton, MA: Edward Elgar, forthcoming 1998.
Kuhn, M. and T. Tivig (1996), 'Ecological Dumping and Environmental Capital Flight: the Economics behind the Propaganda', Universität Konstanz: SFB 178 Working Paper, series II, no. 324.
Markusen, J., E.R. Morey and N. Olewiler (1993), 'Environmental Policy when Market Structure and Plant Locations are Endogenous', *Journal of Environmental Economics and Management*, **24**, 69–86.
Markusen, J., E.R. Morey and N. Olewiler (1995), 'Competition in regional environmental policies when plant locations are endogenous', *Journal of Public Economics*, **56**, 55–77.
Moraga-González, J.L. and N. Padrón-Fumero (1997), 'Pollution Linked to Consumption: A Study of Policy Instruments in an Environmentally Differentiated Oligopoly', Madrid: Universidad Carlos III de Madrid, Working Paper 97–06, Economics Series 02.
Motta, M. and J.-F. Thisse (1993), 'Minimum Standard as Environmental Policy: Domestic and International Effects', Milan, FEEM Nota di Lavoro no. 20.93.
Motta, M. and J.-F. Thisse (1994), 'Does environmental dumping lead to delocation?', *European Economic Review*, **38**, 563–76.
Rauscher, M. (1997a), *International Trade, Factor Movements, and the Environment*, Oxford: Clarendon Press.
Rauscher, M. (1997b), 'Voluntary Emission Reduction, Social Rewards, and Environmental Policy', University of Rostock: Thünen-Series of Applied Economic Theory, Working Paper no. 10.

Ronnen, U. (1991), 'Minimum quality standards, fixed costs, and competition', *RAND Journal of Economics*, **22**, 490–504.
Rose-Ackerman, S. (1996), 'Altruism, nonprofits, and Economic Theory', *Journal of Economic Literature*, **34**, 701–28.
Ulph, D. (1994), 'Strategic Innovation and Strategic Environmental Policy', in C. Carraro (ed.), *Trade, Innovation, Environment*, Dordrecht: Kluwer.

APPENDIX

Proof 3.1: Inspection of (2.8) shows that for $\theta_1 = \theta_2 = G$ there are no externalities involved. Thus firms' relative location is irrelevant, and the proof follows the lines of Ecchia and Mariotti (1994, 6–8).[1] To begin with, we have to distinguish between two potential equilibria, one with a covered, the other with a non-covered market.

Case 1: Covered Market Equilibrium

For any price $p \leq 1$ charged by either of the two firms, all consumers buy the product so that the market is covered and aggregate demand is $q^G = 1$. In this case, both firms will incur a non-negative profit only if they choose $p_1 = p_2 = p \in [(4\alpha + 1)/2, 1]$. Thereby, $(4\alpha + 1)/2$ is the zero-profit price, which is determined by solving $\pi_1(p)|_{\theta_1=\theta_2=G} = \pi_2(p)|_{\theta_1=\theta_2=G} = 0$ for p under use of (2.10), while we ignore a potential relocation cost S. A duopoly equilibrium exists only if $\alpha \leq 1/4$ so that $(4\alpha + 1)/2 \leq 1$ and the interval $[(4\alpha + 1)/2, 1]$ is non-empty. Assume that $\alpha \leq 1/4$ holds. Suppose both firms have chosen a price $p \in [(4\alpha + 1)/2, 1]$ so that each firm $i = 1, 2$ faces a demand of $q_i = q^G/2 = 1/2$. According to (3.1) firms then realize the operating profit $\Pi_i = p/2 - 1/4$. Suppose now that firm $-i$ undercuts its competitor's price by setting $p_{-i} = p - \varepsilon$. Thereby, it captures the whole market and realizes the operating profit $\Pi_u = p - \varepsilon - 1$. For $\varepsilon \to 0$ we have $\Pi_u > \Pi_i$ if and only if $p > 3/2$. Hence, for any price $p \in [(4\alpha + 1)/2, 1]$ undercutting is unprofitable, so that $p_1^* = p_2^* = p^* \in [(4\alpha + 1)/2, 1]$ defines a continuum of Nash equilibria.[2] To resolve the problem of multiplicity we apply the concept of payoff dominance (Harsanyi and Selten, 1988) as a selection criterion and obtain $p^* = 1$.

Case 2: Non-Covered Market Equilibrium

For any price $p \in \,]1, 1 + g]$ charged by either of the two firms, only the green consumers buy the product, so that the market is not covered and aggregate demand is $q^G = m$. In this case, both firms realize a non-negative profit only if they choose $p_1 = p_2 = p \in [m/2 + 2\alpha/m, 1 + g]$. Thereby, $m/2 + 2\alpha/m$ is the zero profit price, which may be greater or smaller than one. Suppose both firms have chosen $p \in $]min $\{1, m/2 + 2\alpha/m\}, 1 + g]$. In this case each firm $i = 1, 2$ faces a demand of $q_i = q^G/2 = m/2$ and by (3.1) realizes an operating profit $\Pi_i = pm/2 - m^2/4$. Suppose now that one firm undercuts its competitor's price by setting $p_u = p - \varepsilon$. Thereby, it captures all of the green consumers' demand and realizes $\Pi_u = (p - \varepsilon) m - m^2$. For $\varepsilon \to 0$ we have $\Pi_u > \Pi_i$ if and only if $p > 3m/2$. Alternatively, the undercutting firm may choose $p_u = 1$ so as to capture the whole market. This is always unprofitable since $\Pi_u = 1 - 1 = 0 < \Pi_i$. Hence, for any price $p \in $]min $\{1, m/2 + 2\alpha/m\}, 3m/2]$ undercutting is unprofitable, where we assume $3m/2 \leq 1 + g$ in order to avoid too great a number of equilibrium prices. Then, $p_1^* = p_2^* = p^* \in $]min$\{1, m/2 + 2\alpha/m\}, 3m/2]$ defines a continuum of Nash equilibria. Applying the concept of payoff dominance we select $p^* = 3m/2$.

Finally, we have to determine which of the two equilibria will be chosen. Comparison of profits for $p^* = 1$ and $p^* = 3m/2$ shows that

$$\pi(1) = 1/4 - \alpha \geq m^2/2 - \alpha = \pi(3m/2) \Leftrightarrow m \leq \sqrt{1/2}$$

Application of this condition and the payoff-dominance criterion allows for an unambiguous selection of $p^* \in \{1, 3m/2\}$. QED

Corollary 3.1: As easily verified, $\alpha \leq 1/4$ and $m > \sqrt{1/2}$ imply that the zero profit satisfies $m/2 + 2\alpha/m \leq 3m/2 \leq 1 + g$. Hence, existence of a non-covered market (duopoly) equilibrium is guaranteed for $\alpha \leq 1/4$ and $m > \sqrt{1/2}$.

Proof 3.2: As $\theta_i = G$, $\theta_{-i} = N$, firm $-i$ may impose a unidirectional externality on firm i if $\phi_1 = \phi_2$, so that the relative location of firms becomes relevant. We therefore establish equilibrium prices for the case in which externalities are present, while equilibrium prices for the case of no externalities follow as a corollary. The proof follows Ecchia and Mariotti (1994, 9–11), while the effect of the externalities is also considered. We proceed in two steps. First, we show that symmetric equilibrium prices never exist, then we establish under which condition the green and non-green consumers' reservation prices are the unique equilibrium prices for the green and non-green producer, respectively.

Non-Existence of Symmetric Equilibrium Prices

First suppose that both firms charge a price $p \in $] $1, 1 + g]$. In this case only green consumers will demand the green variant, while non-green consumers do not buy at all. Hence, $q_\Gamma = 1$, $q_N = 0$ and $q^G = q_i = m$. Firm $-i$, offering N, faces zero demand, $q^N = q_{-i} = 0$. By setting a price $p_{-i} = 1$, firm $-i$ could sell its product to non-green consumers, such that $q^N = q_{-i} = 1 - m$, and realize an operating profit

$\Pi_{-i} = m - m^2 \geq 0$. Hence, firm $-i$ always has an incentive to deviate and a symmetric price equilbrium with $p \in]1, 1 + g]$ does not exist.

Now, suppose that both firms charge a price $p \leq 1$. In this case all consumers buy the green variant, where the non-green consumers reveal weak preference for the green version. Hence, $q_\Gamma = 1$, $q_N = 1$ and $q^G = q_i = 1$. Again, firm $-i$, offering N, faces zero demand, $q^N = q_{-i} = 0$. By setting a price $p_{-i} = p - \varepsilon$, with $\varepsilon \leq g$, firm $-i$ captures the non-green market segment, such that $q^N = q_{-i} = 1 - m$. Its profit then is $\Pi_{-i} = (p - \varepsilon - 1 + m)(1 - m)$. For $\varepsilon \to 0$ we get $\Pi_{-i} \geq 0$ if $p \geq 1 - m$. Hence, a symmetric price equilibrium with $1 - m \leq p \leq 1$ is not stable. However, for $p < 1 - m$ the green producer's operating profit is $\Pi_i < 1 - m - 1 \leq 0$. Hence, $p < 1 - m$ is no symmetric equilibrium either.

Existence of a Unique Asymmetric Price Equilibrium with $p_i^* = 1 + g$; $p_{-i}^* = 1$

Suppose $p_i = 1 + g$; $p_{-i} = 1$. Then, $q_\Gamma = q_N = 1$, $q^G = q_i = m$, and $q^N = q_{-i} = 1 - m$. In the presence of externalities the green and non-green producers' profits are, according to (3.1), given by $\Pi_i = (1 + g) m - m^2 - x_{l_i}^G (1 - m)^2$ and $\Pi_{-i} = m - m^2$, respectively. Note that existence of this equilibrium requires $\pi_i = (1 + g) m - m^2 - \alpha - x_{l_i}^G (1 - m)^2 \geq 0$ and thus $g \geq [m^2 - m + \alpha + x_{l_i}^G (1 - m)^2]/m$, where $\pi_{-i} = m - m^2 \geq 0$ is always satisfied. By undercutting and setting a price $p_u = 1 - \varepsilon$, either of the producers would capture the whole market. Consider the non-green producer first. By undercutting s/he would realize a profit $\Pi_u (N) = (1 - \varepsilon) - 1$. It is easily verified that $\Pi_{-i} \geq \Pi_u (N)$ always holds. Thus, the non-green producer never has an incentive to undercut. Now consider the green producer. By undercutting s/he would realize a profit $\Pi_u (G) = (1 - \varepsilon) - 1$. As $\varepsilon \to 0$, we have $\Pi_u (G) = 0 < \Pi_i$ if $g \geq [m^2 - m + x_{l_i}^G (1 - m)^2]/m$. However, as existence requires $g \geq [m^2 - m + \alpha + x_{l_i}^G (1 - m)^2]/m \geq [m^2 - m + x_{l_i}^G (1 - m)^2]/m$, undercutting is not profitable for the green producer either. Thus, $p_i^* = 1 + g$; $p_{-i}^* = 1$ defines a stable Bertrand–Nash equilibrium. Due to the step shape of demand functions neither firm may increase the demand for its product by a lowering of price unless it causes the exit of the other firm. Hence, such reductions in price would only reduce profit. As $p_i^* = 1 + g$; $p_{-i}^* = 1$ corresponds to the reservation prices of the green and non-green consumers, respectively, an increase in prices is not feasible. Hence, the equilibrium is unique.   QED

Corollary 3.2: Suppose now that an externality does not exist, as, in particular, for $\phi_1 \neq \phi_2$. The proof of the non-existence of a symmetric equilibrium goes as above. For $p_i = 1 + g$; $p_{-i} = 1$ the green producer's operating profit is now given by $\Pi_i = (1 + g) m - m^2 \geq 0$. Hence, undercutting, which yields $\Pi_u (G) = 0 \leq \Pi_i$, is never profitable for the green producer. Hence, $p_i^* = 1 + g$; $p_{-i}^* = 1$ forms a stable Bertrand–Nash equilibrium. Uniqueness is proved as above. Note that, in this case, existence of an asymmetric equilibrium requires that $g \geq (m^2 - m + \alpha)/m$.

Proof 3.3: As $\theta_1 = \theta_2 = N$, negative inter-firm externalities may exist according to (2.8), whenever $\phi_1 = \phi_2$. Hence, the location of firms becomes relevant. We establish the equilibrium price for the case in which externalities are present. Except for our inclusion of the externality, the line of argument is close to Ecchia and Mariotti (1994, 9). The equilibrium price for the case of externalities not being existent follows as a corollary.

Suppose that $\theta_1 = \theta_2 = N$, and $\phi_1 = \phi_2$ such that $x = x_{l_i}^N \geq 0$. Then, both firms will only realize a non-negative profit for $p_1 = p_2 = p \in [(1 + x^N)/2, 1]$. Thereby, $(1 + x^N)/2$ is the zero-profit price for the producer that suffers the greater damage. It is given by $(1 + x^N)/2 = \text{argmax } \{(1 + x_{l_1}^N)/2, (1 + x_{l_2}^N)/2\}$, where $(1 + x_{l_i}^N)/2$ for $i = 1, 2$ is determined by solving $\pi_i(p)|_{\theta_1=\theta_2=N \wedge \phi_1=\phi_2} = 0$ for p under use of (2.8) and (2.10), where the relocation cost S is disregarded. In the presence of externalities an equilibrium in which both firms realize a positive profit exists only if $x^N \leq 1$, so that $(1 + x^N)/2 \leq 1$ and the interval $[(1 + x^N)/2, 1]$ is non-empty. Assume $x^N \leq 1$ to be satisfied. Suppose both firms choose a price $p \in [(1 + x^N)/2, 1]$. In this case, all consumers buy N, that is, $q_\Gamma = q_N = 1$, $q^N = 1$, and $q_i = 1/2$. By (3.1) each firm's profit is $\Pi_i = p/2 - (1 + x^N)/4$, $i = 1, 2$. If an undercutting firm sets $p_u = p - \varepsilon$ it captures the whole market and realizes a profit $\Pi_u = p - \varepsilon - 1$. Note that by driving its competitor from the market the undercutting firm has also eliminated the externality. For $\varepsilon \to 0$ we have $\Pi_u > \Pi_i$ if $p > (3 - x^N)/2$. However, existence of an equilibrium requires $x^N \leq 1$. In this case undercutting only occurs for prices $p > 1$ which lie outside the range of relevant prices $[(1 + x^N)/2, 1]$. Hence, $p_1^* = p_2^* = p^* \in [(1 + x^N)/2, 1]$ defines a continuum of Nash equilibria. Applying the concept of payoff dominance we select $p^* = 1$.
QED

Corollary 3.3: If inter-firm externalities are not present, in particular when $\phi_1 \neq \phi_2$, then $x^N = 0$. In this case undercutting does not occur for $p \leq 3/2$, which is always true for the range of relevant prices, where $p \in [1/2, 1]$. According to payoff dominance $p^* = 1$ is then selected as the equilibrium price.

Proof 3.4: From Table 16.1 we derive the best response $\tilde{\delta}_i(\delta_{-i})$ of each firm $i = 1, 2$ to a given strategy of firm $-i$ and obtain

$$\tilde{\delta}_1(\{G, \phi_2\}) = \begin{cases} \{G, A\} & \text{if } \text{argmax}\{\pi_C^{GG}, \pi_{NC}^{GG}\} \geq \pi^{NG} \Leftrightarrow \alpha \leq \text{argmax}\{\overline{\alpha}_C, \overline{\alpha}_{NC}\} \\ \{N, A\} & \text{if } \text{argmax}\{\pi_C^{GG}, \pi_{NC}^{GG}\} < \pi^{NG} \Leftrightarrow \alpha > \text{argmax}\{\overline{\alpha}_C, \overline{\alpha}_{NC}\} \end{cases}$$

$$\tilde{\delta}_1(\{N,A\}) = \begin{cases} \{G,A\} & \text{if } \pi^{GN} - x_{l_1}^G(1-m)^2 > \text{argmax}\{\pi^{GN} - \tilde{s}, \pi^{NN} - x_{l_1}^N/4, \pi^{NN} - \tilde{s}\} \\ \{G,B\} & \text{if } \pi^{GN} - \tilde{s} > \text{argmax}\{\pi^{GN} - x_{l_1}^G(1-m)^2, \pi^{NN} - x_{l_1}^N/4, \pi^{NN} - \tilde{s}\} \\ \{N,A\} & \text{if } \pi^{NN} - x_{l_1}^N/4 > \text{argmax}\{\pi^{GN} - x_{l_1}^G(1-m)^2, \pi^{GN} - \tilde{s}, \pi^{NN} - \tilde{s}\} \\ \{N,B\} & \text{if } \pi^{NN} - \tilde{s} > \text{argmax}\{\pi^{GN} - x_{l_1}^G(1-m)^2, \pi^{GN} - \tilde{s}, \pi^{NN} - x_{l_1}^N/4\} \end{cases}$$

$$\tilde{\delta}_1(\{N,B\}) = \begin{cases} \{G,A\} & \text{if } \pi^{GN} \geq \pi^{NN} \Leftrightarrow g \geq \bar{g} \\ \{N,A\} & \text{if } \pi^{GN} < \pi^{NN} \Leftrightarrow g < \bar{g} \end{cases}'$$

and

$$\tilde{\delta}_2(\{G,\phi_1\}) = \begin{cases} \{G,B\} & \text{if } \text{argmax}\{\pi_C^{GG}, \pi_{NC}^{GG}\} \geq \pi^{NG} \Leftrightarrow \alpha \leq \text{argmax}\{\bar{\alpha}_C, \bar{\alpha}_{NC}\} \\ \{N,B\} & \text{if } \text{argmax}\{\pi_C^{GG}, \pi_{NC}^{GG}\} < \pi^{NG} \Leftrightarrow \alpha > \text{argmax}\{\bar{\alpha}_C, \bar{\alpha}_{NC}\} \end{cases}$$

$$\tilde{\delta}_2(\{N,A\}) = \begin{cases} \{G,B\} & \text{if } \pi^{GN} \geq \pi^{NN} \Leftrightarrow g \geq \bar{g} \\ \{N,B\} & \text{if } \pi^{GN} < \pi^{NN} \Leftrightarrow g < \bar{g} \end{cases}'$$

$$\tilde{\delta}_2(\{N,B\}) = \begin{cases} \{G,A\} & \text{if } \pi^{GN} - \tilde{s} > \text{argmax}\{\pi^{GN} - x_{l_2}^G(1-m)^2, \pi^{NN} - \tilde{s}, \pi^{NN} - x_{l_2}^N/4\} \\ \{G,B\} & \text{if } \pi^{GN} - x_{l_2}^G(1-m)^2 > \text{argmax}\{\pi^{GN} - \tilde{s}, \pi^{NN} - \tilde{s}, \pi^{NN} - x_{l_2}^N/4\} \\ \{N,A\} & \text{if } \pi^{NN} - \tilde{s} > \text{argmax}\{\pi^{GN} - \tilde{s}, \pi^{GN} - x_{l_2}^G(1-m)^2, \pi^{NN} - x_{l_2}^N/4\} \\ \{N,B\} & \text{if } \pi^{NN} - x_{l_2}^N/4 > \text{argmax}\{\pi^{GN} - \tilde{s}, \pi^{GN} - x_{l_2}^G(1-m)^2, \pi^{NN} - \tilde{s}\} \end{cases}$$

where the boundary values are given by (3.6a), (3.6b) and (3.7). Combining the firms' best responses we obtain five Nash equilibria:

$$\left(\delta_1^* = \{G,A\}, \delta_2^* = \{G,B\}\right) \Leftrightarrow \alpha \leq \text{argmax}\{\bar{\alpha}_C, \bar{\alpha}_{NC}\} \quad \text{(E3.1A)}$$

$$\left.\begin{array}{l}\left(\delta_1^* = \{G,A\}, \delta_2^* = \{N,B\}\right) \\ \left(\delta_1^* = \{N,A\}, \delta_2^* = \{G,B\}\right)\end{array}\right\} \Leftrightarrow \alpha \leq \text{argmax}\{\bar{\alpha}_C, \bar{\alpha}_{NC}\} \land g \geq \bar{g} \quad \text{(E3.2a/bA)}$$

$$\left(\delta_1^* = \{N,A\}, \delta_2^* = \{N,B\}\right) \Leftrightarrow g < \bar{g} \quad \text{(E3.3A)}$$

$$\left(\delta_1^* = \{N,B\}, \delta_2^* = \{N,A\}\right) \Leftrightarrow$$
$$\pi^{NN} - \tilde{s} > \text{argmax}\{\pi^{GN} - x_{l_i}^G(1-m)^2, \pi^{GN} - \tilde{s}, \pi^{NN} - x_{l_i}^N/4\}; i = 1,2. \quad \text{(E3.4A)}$$

Note that there are two multiplicities of equilibrium involved. For (E3.2a/bA) with an asymmetric technology structure the assignment of technologies to firms and thus to regions is undetermined. However, we may ignore this problem as our reference case, yet to be defined (see below), will be an equilibrium, in which both firms use the non-green technology under *laissez-faire*. The second multiplicity arises between (E3.3A) and (E3.4A). Firms choose the non-green technology in both cases, where both firms maintain their location from the outset in (E3.3A) and both firms relocate in (E3.4A). A comparison of payoffs in Table 16.1 immediately shows that (E3.4A) is payoff-dominated by (E3.3A), and is thus excluded from further analysis. Note that the remaining types of equilibria (E3.1A) – the green structure, (E3.2aA) or (E3.2bA) – the asymmetric structure, and (E3.3A) – the non-green structure – are mutually exclusive. Joining (E3.1)–(E3.3) with the corresponding price equilibria (PE3.1)–(PE3.3), we establish the SGP equilibria given in the main text.

Proof 3.5: From Table 16.2 we can derive the firms' best response functions $\tilde{\delta}_i(\delta_{-i})$, $i = 1, 2$. Considering firm 1 first, we observe that $\delta_1 = \{G, A\}$ strictly dominates $\delta_1 = \{G, B\}$. This is immediately given by a comparison of the respective payoffs in Table 16.2. After elimination of $\delta_1 = \{G, B\}$ firm 1's best reactions are given by

$$\tilde{\delta}_1(\{G, \phi_2\}) = \begin{cases} \{G, A\} & \text{if } \operatorname{argmax}\{\pi_C^{GG}, \pi_{NC}^{GG}\} \geq \pi^{NG} - \tilde{s} \Leftrightarrow \alpha \leq \operatorname{argmax}\{\overline{\alpha}_C, \overline{\alpha}_{NC}\} + \tilde{s} \\ \{N, B\} & \text{if } \operatorname{argmax}\{\pi_C^{GG}, \pi_{NC}^{GG}\} < \pi^{NG} - \tilde{s} \Leftrightarrow \alpha > \operatorname{argmax}\{\overline{\alpha}_C, \overline{\alpha}_{NC}\} + \tilde{s} \end{cases}$$

$$\tilde{\delta}_1(\{N, B\}) = \begin{cases} \{G, A\} & \text{if } \pi^{GN} \geq \pi^{NN} - x_{l_1}^N/4 - \tilde{s} \Leftrightarrow g \geq \overline{\overline{g}} \\ \{N, B\} & \text{if } \pi^{GN} < \pi^{NN} - x_{l_1}^N/4 - \tilde{s} \Leftrightarrow g < \overline{\overline{g}} \end{cases}$$

where the boundary values are given by (3.6a), (3.6b) and (3.12). For firm 2 we obtain

$$\tilde{\delta}_1(\{G, \phi_2\}) = \{N, B\} \text{ by (A3.3)},$$

$$\tilde{\delta}_2(\{N, B\}) = \begin{cases} \{G, A\} & \text{if } \pi^{GN} - \tilde{s} > \operatorname{argmax}\{\pi^{GN} - x_{l_2}^G(1-m)^2, \pi^{NN} - x_{l_2}^N/4\} \\ \{G, B\} & \text{if } \pi^{GN} - x_{l_2}^G(1-m)^2 > \operatorname{argmax}\{\pi^{GN} - \tilde{s}, \pi^{NN} - x_{l_2}^N/4\} \\ \{N, B\} & \text{if } \pi^{NN} - x_{l_2}^N/4 > \operatorname{argmax}\{\pi^{GN} - \tilde{s}, \pi^{GN} - x_{l_2}^G(1-m)^2\} \end{cases}$$

From the reaction functions we derive the following Nash equilibria:

- $(\delta_1^* = \{G, A\}, \delta_2^* = \{N, B\}) \Leftrightarrow g \geq \overline{\overline{g}}$ (E3.5A)

- $\left(\delta_1^* = \{N, B\}, \delta_2^* = \{G, A\}\right) \Leftrightarrow$

$\alpha > \mathrm{argmax}\{\overline{\alpha}_C, \overline{\alpha}_{NC}\} + \tilde{s} \wedge \pi^{GN} - \tilde{s} > \mathrm{argmax}\{\pi^{GN} - x_{l_2}^G(1-m)^2, \pi^{NN} - x_{l_2}^N/4\}$

(E3.6aA)

- $\left(\delta_1^* = \{N, B\}, \delta_2^* = \{G, B\}\right) \Leftrightarrow$

$\alpha > \mathrm{argmax}\{\overline{\alpha}_C, \overline{\alpha}_{NC}\} + \tilde{s} \wedge \pi^{GN} - x_{l_2}^G(1-m)^2 > \mathrm{argmax}\{\pi^{GN} - \tilde{s}, \pi^{NN} - x_{l_2}^N/4\}$

(E3.6bA)

- $\left(\delta_1^* = \{N, B\}, \delta_2^* = \{N, B\}\right) \Leftrightarrow$

$g < \overline{\overline{g}} \wedge \pi^{NN} - x_{l_2}^N/4 > \mathrm{argmax}\{\pi^{GN} - \tilde{s}, \pi^{GN} - x_{l_2}^G(1-m)^2\}$

(E3.7A)

Thereby, each of the equilibria (E3.6aA) and (E3.6bA) is a multiple equilibrium to (E3.5A). However, neither of the equilibria is payoff-dominated. For the presence of a standard in region A, both (E3.6aA) and (E3.6bA) seem counter-intuitive. However, as analysis proceeds they can be eliminated under reasonable assumptions.

We now distinguish the cases of symmetric and unidirectional inter-firm externalities.

Case 1: Symmetric Inter-firm Externalities: $x_{up}^\theta = x_{do}^\theta = x^\theta > 0; \theta = G, N$

In this case the extent of damages does not depend on whether a firm locates up- or downstream from a polluter. Hence, we may write $x_{l_i}^\theta = x_{up}^\theta = x_{do}^\theta = x^\theta > 0$; $\theta = G, N$ for both firms $i = 1, 2$. In this case,

$$g < \overline{\overline{g}} \Leftrightarrow \pi^{NN} - x^N/4 \geq \pi^{NN} - x^N/4 - \tilde{s}, > \pi^{GN} \geq$$
$$\mathrm{argmax}\{\pi^{GN} - \tilde{s}, \pi^{GN} - x^G(1-m)^2\}$$

so that (E3.7A) simplifies to

$$(\delta_1^* = \{N, B\}, \delta_2^* = \{N, B\}) \Leftrightarrow g < \overline{\overline{g}} \qquad \text{(E3.7'A)}$$

We now use (2.9b) to distinguish between the existence and non-existence of a relocation cost.

Case 1.1: $s|_{\phi_i=\phi_i^0} = 0 \Leftrightarrow \tilde{s} = s$

Under the existence of a relocation cost we may eliminate the equilibria (E3.6aA) and (E3.6aB) in the following way. Note that existence of (E3.6aA) and (E3.6bA) requires

$$\alpha > \text{argmax } \{\bar{\alpha}_C, \bar{\alpha}_{NC}\} + s.$$

As easily proved under use of (3.7a) and (3.7b), this condition is never satisfied for

$$s \geq \alpha. \tag{A3.1A}$$

Hence, by assuming that (A3.1A) holds, we eliminate (E3.6aA) and (E3.6aB). Note that (A3.1A) requires that the set-up cost of production facilities never falls short of the fixed cost of green production. This seems quite realistic, while it may exclude some cases in which substantial amounts of R&D outlays are necessary in order to develop green production methods. Amending (E3.5A) and (E3.7'A) by the corresponding price equilibria (PE3.2) and (PE3.3), we obtain the SGP equilibria (TLE3.3) and (TLE3.4), as given in the main text, respectively.

Case 1.2: $s|_{\phi_i=\phi_i^0} = s \Leftrightarrow \tilde{s} = 0$

If there exists no cost of relocation, (E3.6bA) consitutes no equilibrium since

$$\pi^{GN} - x^G(1-m)^2 > \text{argmax } \{\pi^{GN}, \pi^{NN} - x^N/4\}$$

never holds. On the other hand, the existence condition for (E3.6aA) can be rewritten as

$$(\delta_1^* = \{N, B\}, \delta_2^* = \{G, A\})\} \Leftrightarrow \pi^{GN} > \pi^{NN} - x^N/4\} \; g \geq \bar{\bar{g}}|_{\tilde{s}=0} \tag{E3.6'A}$$

where the boundary value is given by setting $\tilde{s} = 0$ in (3.12). Having appended to (E3.5A), (E3.6'A) and (E3.7'A) the corresponding price equilibria (PE3.2) and (PE3.3), respectively, we obtain the SGP equilibria (TLE3.3.), (TLE3.4), as given in the main text, and a third asymmetric equilibrium

$$f_1^* = \{N, B, 1\}, f_2^* = \{G, A, 1+g\}) \Leftrightarrow g \geq \bar{\bar{g}}|_{\tilde{s}=0},$$

which is a multiple to (TLE3.3), where only the firms' roles have been reversed. As technology and location structure as well as regional welfare is given identical to (TLE3.3), we ignore this equilibrium henceforth.

Case 2: Unidirectional Inter-firm Externalities

In this case the extent of damage incurred by a firm depends on whether a firm locates up- or downstream from a polluter, where $x_{do}^{\theta_i} \geq x_{up}^{\theta_i} \geq 0$. While inter-firm externalities arise in (E3.6bA) and (E3.7A), it is not clear *a priori* which of the firms is the down- and upstream producer, respectively. It seems likely that a firm being historically sited in a region holds a locational advantage and becomes the upstream producer, while a firm that relocates becomes the downstream producer in its new host region. Hence, firm 1 is an upstream producer in region A and a downstream producer in region B, where the opposite applies to firm 2. For simplicity, assume that an upstream producer is not subjected to externalities at all, while a downstream producer incurs a damage according to (2.8a) and (2.8b). Hence,

$$x_{l_i}^{\theta} = \begin{cases} x_{up}^{\theta} = 0 & \text{if } \phi_i = \phi_i^0 \\ x_{do}^{\theta} = x^{\theta} & \text{if } \phi_i \neq \phi_i^0, \end{cases}$$

for each firm i = 1, 2 and $\theta \in \{G, N\}$.

Allowing for this, (E3.6aA) and (E3.6bA) fail to be equilibria since

$$\pi^{NN} > \text{argmax } \{\pi^{GN} - \tilde{s}, \pi^{GN}\}$$

always holds by virtue of (A3.2). Again, (E3.7A) simplifies to (E3.7'A). Joining (E3.5A) and (E3.7'A) with the corresponding price equilibria (PE3.2) and (PE3.3), respectively, we obtain (TLE3.3) and (TLE3.4), as given in the main text.

Alternatively, one might envisage that the relocating firm exploits a second-comer advantage by choosing its location relative to the incumbent firm so that it becomes the upstream firm. The incumbent firm is not able to react if its set-up cost is sunk. In this case the firms' exposure to externalities is exactly reversed. By a formal analysis, which is omitted, (TLE3.3) and (TLE3.4) can be established, albeit under somewhat more restrictive conditions.[3]

It is easily verified that the case in which externalities are absent, so that $x_{l_i}^N = x^N = 0$ for $i = 1, 2$, follows as a corollary of Case 2. However, note that $\tilde{s} = s$ now becomes a necessary condition for (TLE3.3). QED.

Proof of Proposition 2.1: From table 16.3 we derive the best responses $\tilde{r}_j(r_{-j})$ for region $j = A, B$, which by symmetry are

$$\tilde{r}_j(1) = \begin{cases} 1 & \text{if } W^{GG} \geq W_2^{NN} \Leftrightarrow d \geq \bar{d}_{NN2}^{GG} \\ 0 & \text{if } W^{GG} < W_2^{NN} \Leftrightarrow d < \bar{d}_{NN2}^{GG} \end{cases}, j = A, B,$$

$$\tilde{r}_j(0) = \begin{cases} 1 & \text{if } W_0 \geq W^{NN} \Leftrightarrow d \geq 1 \\ 0 & \text{if } W_0 < W^{NN} \Leftrightarrow d < 1 \end{cases}, j = A, B,$$

where

$$W^{GG} = \begin{cases} W_C^{GG} & \text{if } m \leq \sqrt{1/2} \\ W_{NC}^{GG} & \text{if } m > \sqrt{1/2} \end{cases}$$

and

$$\bar{d}_{NN2}^{GG} = \begin{cases} \bar{d}_{NN2}^{GGC} & \text{if } m \leq \sqrt{1/2} \\ \bar{d}_{NC}^{GGNC} & \text{if } m > \sqrt{1/2} \end{cases}.$$

The boundary values are given by (4.1a) and (4.1b). Observing $\bar{d}_{NN2}^{GG} < 1$ we obtain the two Nash equilibria:

$$(r_A = r_B = 1) \Leftrightarrow d \geq \bar{d}_{NN2}^{GG} \quad \text{(E4.1A)}$$

$$(r_A = r_B = 0) \Leftrightarrow d < 1. \quad \text{(E4.2A)}$$

For $1 > d \geq \bar{d}_{NN2}^{GG}$ both equilibria (E4.1) and (E4.2) may obtain. Relationship (4.3a) or (4.3b), respectively, establishes payoff dominance of (E4.1) over (E4.2) and can thus be used as a selection criterion. The relationship between the boundary values $\bar{d}_{NN2}^{GG}$ and

$$\bar{d}_{NN}^{GG} = \begin{cases} \bar{d}_{NN}^{GGC} & \text{if } m \leq \sqrt{1/2} \\ \bar{d}_{NN}^{GGNC} & \text{if } m > \sqrt{1/2} \end{cases},$$

as used in (4.3a) or (4.3b), respectively, is determined by

$$\bar{d}_{NN}^{GGC} \geq \bar{d}_{NN2}^{GGC} \Leftrightarrow g \leq \tilde{g}_C := \frac{(2x^N - 1)/6 + 2\alpha + 2s/3}{m} \quad (4.1aA)$$

$$\bar{d}_{NN}^{GGNC} \geq \bar{d}_{NN2}^{GGNC} \Leftrightarrow g \leq \tilde{g}_{NC} := \frac{(1 + x^N)/3 + m^2/2 - m + 2\alpha + 2s/3}{m}$$

$$(4.1bA)[4]$$

From combination of (E4.1A), (E4.2A), (4.3a), (4.3b), (4.1aA) and (4.1bA) Proposition 2.1 follows immediately. QED

Proof of Proposition 2.2: From Table 16.4 we obtain the best responses $\tilde{r}_j(r_{-j})$ for each region $j = A, B$, which by symmetry are given by

$$\tilde{r}_j(1) = \begin{cases} 1 & \text{if } W^{GG} \geq W^{NG} \Leftrightarrow d \geq \bar{d}_{NG}^{GG} \\ 0 & \text{if } W^{GG} < W^{NG} \Leftrightarrow d < \bar{d}_{NG}^{GG} \end{cases}, j = A, B,$$

$$\tilde{r}_j(0) = \begin{cases} 1 & \text{if } W^{GN} \geq W^{NN} \Leftrightarrow d \geq \bar{d}_{NN}^{GN} \\ 0 & \text{if } W^{GN} < W^{NN} \Leftrightarrow d < \bar{d}_{NN}^{GN} \end{cases}, j = A, B,$$

where

$$W^{GG} = \begin{cases} W_C^{GG} & \text{if } m \leq \sqrt{1/2} \\ W_{NC}^{GG} & \text{if } m > \sqrt{1/2} \end{cases}$$

and

$$\bar{d}_{NN}^{GG} = \begin{cases} \bar{d}_{NN}^{GGC} & \text{if } m \leq \sqrt{1/2} \\ \bar{d}_{NN}^{GGNC} & \text{if } m > \sqrt{1/2} \end{cases},$$

The boundary values are given by (4.4a)–(4.5). From the reaction functions we obtain four Nash equilibria:

$$(r_A = r_B = 1) \Leftrightarrow d \geq \bar{d}_{NG}^{GG} \quad (E4.3A)$$

$$(r_A = r_B = 0) \Leftrightarrow d < \overline{d}_{NN}^{GN} \qquad \text{(E4.4A)}$$

$$\left. \begin{array}{l} (r_A = 1, r_B = 0) \\ (r_A = 0, r_B = 1) \end{array} \right\} \Leftrightarrow \overline{d}_{NG}^{GG} > d \geq \overline{d}_{NN}^{GN}. \qquad \text{(E4.5A)}$$

Note that $\overline{d}_{NG}^{GG} < d < \overline{d}_{NN}^{GN}$ renders the asymmetric equilibria infeasible and gives rise to multiplicity of the symmetric equilibria. Payoff dominance, established by relationship (4.3a) or (4.3b), is then used as a selection criterion. From (E4.3A), (E4.4A) in combination with (4.3a) and (4.3b) follow parts (a) (i) and (b) (i) of Proposition 2.2.

In the next step we establish the ordering of the boundary values given in (4.3a)–(4.5). We shall proceed by analysing the case of $m \leq \sqrt{1/2}$ (small fraction of green consumers) and the case of $m > \sqrt{1/2}$ (large fraction of green consumers) separately.

The 'Small Fraction of Green Consumers' Case: $m \leq \sqrt{1/2}$

Comparison of the three boundary values given in (4.3a), (4.4a) and (4.5) yields:

$$\overline{d}_{NN}^{GGC} \geq \overline{d}_{NG}^{GGC} \Leftrightarrow \begin{cases} \text{always if } m \leq 1/2 \\ g \geq \hat{g}_C \text{ if } 1/2 < m \leq \sqrt{1/2} \end{cases}; \hat{g}_C := \frac{1/4 + m^2 - m + (3 + 4m^2 - 8m)\alpha}{(3/2 + 2m^2 - 4m)m}$$

(4.2aA)

$$\overline{d}_{NN}^{GGC} \geq \overline{d}_{NN}^{GN} \Leftrightarrow g \geq \widehat{g} := \frac{1/2 + 2m^2 - 2m}{m} \qquad \text{(4.3A)}$$

$$\overline{d}_{NG}^{GGC} \geq \overline{d}_{NN}^{GN} \Leftrightarrow \begin{cases} g \geq \breve{g}_C \text{ if } m \leq 1\sqrt{1/8} \\ g < \breve{g}_C \text{ if } 1 - \sqrt{1/8} < m \leq \sqrt{1/2} \end{cases}$$

$$\breve{g}_C := \frac{(5 + 4m^2 - 8m)(1/4 + m^2 - m) + (3 + 4m^2 - 8m)\alpha}{(7/2 + 4m^2 - 8m)m}. \qquad \text{(4.4aA)}$$

Note that the conditions in (4.2aA), (4.3A) and (4.4aA) are necessary and sufficient. However, for some constellations of α and m the boundary values given in (4.2aA) and (4.4aA) may not lie within the interval [argmax

{0, 3m/2 − 1}, $\bar{g}$], which is implied by (A3.1) and (A3.2).[5] In this case, the respective condition would be satisfied either always or never, depending on whether the boundary value exceeds the upper bound or falls short of the lower bound of the interval.[6] For both (4.2aA) and (4.4aA) it can be shown that under satisfaction of some necessary conditions the boundary value lies within the interval [argmax {0, 3m/2 − 1}, $\bar{g}$]. As tedious calculations are involved that do not offer any insights by themselves the derivation and presentation of the necessary conditions implied by (4.2aA) or (4.4aA) will not be given here.[7]

Comparison of the three boundary values given in (4.2aA), (4.3A) and (4.4aA) yields:

$$\hat{g}_C \geq \hat{g} \Leftrightarrow \begin{cases} \text{always} & \text{if } m \leq 1/2 \\ \alpha \geq \hat{\alpha}_C & \text{if } 1/2 < m \leq \sqrt{1/2} \end{cases}; \quad \hat{\alpha}_C := \frac{(1/4 + m^2 - m)(8m - 4m^2 - 2)}{(8m - 4m^2 - 3)} \quad (4.5A)$$

$$\breve{g}_C \geq \hat{g}_C \Leftrightarrow \begin{cases} \text{always} & \text{if } m \leq 1/2 \\ \alpha \leq \hat{\alpha}_C & \text{if } 1/2 < m \leq 1 - \sqrt{1/8} \\ \alpha \geq \hat{\alpha}_C & \text{if } 1 - \sqrt{1/8} < m \leq \sqrt{1/2} \end{cases} \quad (4.6A)$$

$$\hat{g}_C \geq \breve{g}_C \Leftrightarrow \begin{cases} \text{always} & \text{if } m \leq 1/2 \\ \alpha \geq \hat{\alpha}_C & \text{if } 1/2 < m \leq 1 - \sqrt{1/8} \\ \alpha \leq \hat{\alpha}_C & \text{if } 1 - \sqrt{1/8} < m \leq \sqrt{1/2} \end{cases} \quad (4.7A)$$

Combining (4.5A)–(4.7A) we obtain the ordering

- $m \leq 1/2$: $\quad \hat{g}_C \geq \breve{g} \geq \hat{g}$
- $1/2 < m \leq 1 - \sqrt{1/8}$: $\begin{cases} \alpha \leq \hat{\alpha}_C \Leftrightarrow \hat{g}_C \geq \hat{g} \geq \breve{g}_C \\ \alpha > \hat{\alpha}_C \Leftrightarrow \breve{g}_C > \hat{g} > \hat{g}_C \end{cases}$
- $1 - \sqrt{1/8} < m \leq \sqrt{1/2}$: $\begin{cases} \alpha \leq \hat{\alpha}_C \Leftrightarrow \hat{g} \geq \hat{g}_C \geq \breve{g}_C \\ \alpha > \hat{\alpha}_C \Leftrightarrow \breve{g}_C > \hat{g}_C > \hat{g} \end{cases}$ (4.8A)

Thereby, we observe that $m \leq 1/2$ implies $\hat{\alpha} \leq \bar{\alpha}_C$ and $\hat{g}_C \geq \bar{g}$ so that $\hat{g}_C > g$ is always satisfied by virtue of (A3.2). For $m > 1/2$ it can be shown that

$$\{\text{argmax}\{\hat{g}_C, \hat{g}, \breve{g}_C\}, \text{argmin}\{\hat{g}_C, \hat{g}, \breve{g}_C\}\} \in [\text{argmax}\{0, 3m/2 - 1\}, \bar{g}]$$

is feasible and thus $g < \text{argmin } [\hat{g}_C, \hat{g}, \breve{g}_C]$ or $g > \text{argmax } [\hat{g}_C, \hat{g}, \breve{g}_C]$ are not excluded by (A3.1) or (A3.2).[8]

From (4.8A) in combination with (4.2aA), (4.3A), (4.4aA) and (E4.3A)–(E4.5A) we can establish the equilibrium conditions for the 'small fraction of green consumers' case, $m \leq \sqrt{1/2}$. As the necessary conditions for bilateral regulation and bilateral *laissez-faire* are not very accessible they are explicitly stated only for unilateral regulation in part (c) (i) of Proposition 2.2.

The 'Large Fraction of Green Consumers' case: $m > \sqrt{1/2}$

Comparison of the three boundary values given in (4.3b), (4.4b) and (4.5) yields:

$$\overline{d}_{NN}^{GGNC} \geq \overline{d}_{NG}^{GGNC} \Leftrightarrow g \geq \hat{g}_{NC} := \frac{-3m^2/4 + m/2 - (1-m)^4 - (3+4m^2-8m)\alpha}{(4m-2m^2-3/2)m}$$

(4.2bA)

$\overline{d}_{NN}^{GGNC} \geq \overline{d}_{NN}^{GN}$ always satisfied by virtue of (A3.1),

$$\overline{d}_{NG}^{GGNC} \geq \overline{d}_{NN}^{GN} \Leftrightarrow$$
$$g \geq \breve{g}_{NC} := \frac{-3m^2/4 + m/2 - 4(1-m)^2(1/4+m^2-m)-(3+4m^2-8m)\alpha}{(8m-4m^2-7/2)m}.$$

(4.4bA)

Note that the conditions (4.2bA) and (4.4bA) are necessary and sufficient. For both it can be shown that under satisfaction of some necessary conditions the respective boundary value is included in the interval $[3m/2 - 1, \overline{g}]$.[9]

Comparison of the boundary values given in (4.2bA) and (4.4bA) yields:

$$\hat{g}_{NC} \geq \breve{g}_{NC} \Leftrightarrow \alpha \leq \hat{\alpha}_{NC} := \frac{-3m^2/2 - m + (1-m)^2(1-2m^2)}{(8m-4m^2-3)}. \quad (4.9A)$$

Furthermore, it can be established that

$$\alpha \leq \hat{\alpha}_{NC} \Leftrightarrow 3m/2 - 1 \geq \hat{g}_{NC} \geq \breve{g}_{NC} \quad (4.10A)$$

so that $g \geq \hat{g}_{NC} \geq \check{g}_{NC}$ by virtue of (A3.1). On the other hand, it can be shown for $\alpha > \hat{\alpha}_{NC}$ that

$$\left\{\mathrm{argmax}\{\hat{g}_{NC}, \check{g}_{NC}\}, \mathrm{argmin}\{\hat{g}_{NC}, \check{g}_{NC}\}\right\} \in [3m/2 - 1, \bar{g}]$$

so that $g < \mathrm{argmin}\{\hat{g}_{NC}, \check{g}_{NC}\}$ or $g > \mathrm{argmax}\{\hat{g}_{NC}, \check{g}_{NC}\}$ are not excluded by (A3.1) or (A3.2).[10]

From (4.9A) and (4.10A) in combination with (4.2bA), (4.4bA) and (E4.3A)–(E4.5A), follow parts (a) (ii), (b) (ii) and (c) (ii) of Proposition 2.2.
QED.

Corollary 2.2: In the following we establish the different constellations of parameters which give rise to the equilibrium sequences, as given by (S4.3)–(S4.8) in the main text.

The 'Small Fraction of Green Consumers' Case: $m \leq \sqrt{1/2}$

The equilibrium sequences are obtained from (4.8A) in combination with (4.2aA), (4.3A) and (4.4aA) and (E4.3A)–(E4.5A):

Case 1: $m \leq 1/2 \Leftrightarrow \hat{g}_C \geq \bar{g} \geq \check{g}_C \geq \hat{g}$

(i) $\bar{g} > g \geq \check{g}_C \Rightarrow$ (S4.3),
(ii) $\check{g}_C > g \geq \hat{g} \Rightarrow$ (S4.4),
(iii) $\hat{g} > g \Rightarrow$ (S4.5).

Case 2: $1/2 < m \leq 1 - \sqrt{1/8}$

(a) $\alpha \leq \hat{\alpha}_C \Leftrightarrow \check{g}_C > \hat{g} > \hat{g}_C$:

(i) $g \geq \check{g}_C \Rightarrow$ (S4.3),
(ii) $\check{g}_C > g \geq \hat{g} \Rightarrow$ (S4.4),
(iii) $\hat{g} > g \geq \hat{g}_C \Rightarrow$ (S4.5),
(iv) $\hat{g}_C > g \Rightarrow$ (S4.6).

(b) $\alpha > \hat{\alpha}_C \Leftrightarrow \hat{g}_C > \hat{g} > \check{g}_C$:

(i) $g \geq \hat{g}_C \Rightarrow$ (S4.3),
(ii) $\hat{g}_C > g \geq \hat{g} \Rightarrow$ (S4.7),
(iii) $\hat{g} > g \geq \check{g}_C \Rightarrow$ (S4.8),
(iv) $\check{g}_C > g \Rightarrow$ (S4.6).

Case 3: $1 - \sqrt{1/8} < m \leq \sqrt{1/2}$

(a) $\alpha \leq \hat{\alpha}_C \Leftrightarrow \hat{g} \geq \hat{g}_C \geq \check{g}_C$:

(i) $g \geq \hat{g} \Rightarrow$ (S4.4),
(ii) $\hat{g} > g \geq \hat{g}_C \Rightarrow$ (S4.5),
(iii) $\hat{g}_C > g \geq \check{g}_C \Rightarrow$ (S4.6),
(iv) $\check{g}_C > g \Rightarrow$ (S4.8).

(b) $\alpha > \hat{\alpha}_C \Leftrightarrow \hat{g}_C > \check{g}_C > \hat{g}$:

(i) $g \geq \check{g}_C \Rightarrow$ (S4.4),
(ii) $\check{g}_C > g \geq \hat{g}_C \Rightarrow$ (S4.3),
(iii) $\hat{g}_C > g \geq \hat{g} \Rightarrow$ (S4.7),
(iv) $\hat{g} > g \Rightarrow$ (S4.8).

The 'Large Fraction of Green Consumers' Case: $m > \sqrt{1/2}$

The equilibrium sequences are obtained from (4.9A) and (4.10A) in combination with (4.2bA), (4.4bA) and (E4.3A)–(E4.5A).

Case 1: $\alpha \leq \hat{\alpha}_{NC} \Leftrightarrow g > 3m/2 - 1 \geq \hat{g}_{NC} \geq \check{g}_{NC}: \Rightarrow$ (S4.4).

Case 2: $\alpha > \hat{\alpha}_{NC} \Leftrightarrow \check{g}_{NC} > \hat{g}_{NC}:$

(i) $g \geq \check{g}_{NC} \Rightarrow$ (S4.4),
(ii) $\check{g}_{NC} > g \geq \hat{g}_{NC} \Rightarrow$ (S4.3),
(iii) $\hat{g}_{NC} > g \Rightarrow$ (S4.7).

Notes

1. Ecchia and Mariotti do not use operating profit, but overall profit, including the fixed cost component α, for their proof. It is not quite clear why the fixed cost, α, which firms take as given at this stage of the game, should be taken into account. While this does not principally alter the results, some of the argument must be slightly different.
2. Multiple equilibria are due to the price elasticity of demand being zero at all points of the demand function except the discontinuities.
3. The formal analysis may be obtained from the author.
4. The conditions given in (4.1aA) and (4.1bA) are necessary and sufficient. For certain constellations of the parameters α, s, m and x^N the boundary values given in (4.1aA) and (4.1bA) may lie outside the interval [argmax $\{0, 3m/2 - 1\}, \bar{\bar{g}}$] implied by (A3.1) and (TLE3.4). If a boundary value lies to the left (right) of the interval, the respective condition (4.1aA) or (4.1bA) is never (always) satisfied. The satisfaction of some necessary conditions guarantees that the boundary values are enclosed in the interval. As tedious calculations are involved that do not offer any insights by themselves, the derivation and presentation of the necessary conditions implied by (4.1aA) or (4.1bA) is omitted here. It may be obtained from the author upon request.
5. Note that the boundary value in (4.3) always lies within the interval implied by (A3.1) and (A3.2).
6. The case of (4.2aA) for $m \leq 1/2$ can be explained that way: as easily shown, $\bar{d}_{NN}^{GGC} \geq \bar{d}_{NG}^{GG} \Leftrightarrow g < \hat{g}_C$ for $m \leq 1/2$. However, $\hat{g}_C > \bar{g} \Leftrightarrow \alpha > \bar{\alpha}_C \wedge m \leq 1/2$, which is always satisfied by virtue of (A3.3). Hence, by virtue of (A3.2), $\bar{d}_{NN}^{GGC} \geq \bar{d}_{NG}^{GG} \Leftrightarrow m \leq 1/2$.
7. The necessary conditions and their derivation may be obtained from the author upon request.
8. The proof will be supplied by the author upon request.
9. Again, the derivation and presentation of the necessary conditions implied by (4.2bA) or (4.4bA) will not be given here but may be obtained from the author upon request.
10. The proof will be supplied by the author upon request.

17. A game-theoretic approach to the roundwood market with capital stock determination

Erkki Koskela and Markku Ollikainen[*]

1. INTRODUCTION

Traditionally, price and quantity determination in the roundwood[1] market have been approached using the assumption of competitive roundwood markets. The equilibrium price is determined by assuming that the demand and the supply of timber are equal. This makes it possible to estimate demand and supply functions as well as the determinants of equilibrium prices in terms of exogenous demand and supply parameters. The demand for timber is postulated to result from the profit-maximizing behaviour of firms as an application of the theory of the demand for factors of production. As for the supply of timber, it is often described by using a simple two-period intertemporal model, in which the forest owners decide upon the time path of harvesting, that is, how much to harvest now and in the future.[2]

Price and quantity determination in the roundwood market have been empirically studied in the above mentioned framework, for example, in Johansson and Löfgren (1985, chap. 9), in Hultkrantz and Aronsson (1989), using Swedish data, and in Hetemäki and Kuuluvainen (1992), using Finnish data. Though the performance of the estimating equations has usually been relatively good in many respects, these models suffer from some weaknesses. First, the results are not always very plausible. For instance it is not very easy to accept the result that timber is a substitute for labour.[3] Second, the competitive model does not directly account for the possibility that investments in the forest industry affect

---

[*] We are indebted to Mr Markku Lanne for professional research assistance and Mr Kari Pihkala for collecting and organizing the data and the Research Unit on Economic Structures and Growth (RUESG) for financial support. An earlier version of the chapter was presented at the XVIII Symposium of Finnish Economists, in Vaasa, 11–12 February 1996, at the Department of Forestry in Virginia Polytechnic Institute and State University, 15 May 1996 and at the 7th Annual Conference of European Association of Environmental and Resource Economists (EAERE), in Lisbon, 26–29 June 1996. Helpful comments by participants as well as by Henk Folmer and Nick Hanley are gratefully acknowledged. The usual disclaimer applies.

roundwood markets and, vice versa, that the price of roundwood and its expected development may affect capital stock decisions of the firms in the forest industry. These interactions may be important. More specifically, investments in the forest industry increase production capacity, tending to increase demand for timber, which forest owners may take into account in the price negotiations. Finally, and importantly, one can criticize the assumption that prices are determined so as to equalize demand and supply. A better hypothesis might be that prices are subject to negotiations between firms and forest owners. For instance in Finland and Sweden both forest owners and the forest industry are well organized, and negotiations on timber prices have been an everyday practice since the 1960s.

The purpose of this chapter is to provide a framework which approaches price and quantity determination from this slightly new perspective. In the spirit of the trade union literature we formulate the model of timber price determination in accordance with the notion that the forest owners' association determines timber prices, after which firms in the forest industry decide upon the quantity of timber used in the production of the final good (for example, pulp). The novelty here is to incorporate investment decisions of firms into the model. The stress on investment decision reflects the fact that firms in the modern paper and pulp industry are big and capital-intensive. Both parties in the negotiation know well that new investments will have effects on the demand for timber and quite likely take this into account in their strategic behaviour.[4]

The game is assumed to be played in two stages. First, the forest owners' association and firms decide on timber prices and capital stock, respectively. In the second stage, firms determine the demand for timber conditional on timber price and capital stock. Thus the relevant equilibrium concept is the subgame-perfect Nash equilibrium, because in the first stage of the game both firms and the forest owners' association account for the fact that timber demand is determined by the profit maximization of the firms. Finally, we apply the resulting game-theoretic model of the determination of prices and quantities of timber and capital stock to annual data for the Finnish paper and pulp industry over the period 1960–92. We compare the resulting specifications concerning prices and quantities of timber and capital stock to the alternative, somewhat more traditional hypotheses. All in all, the empirical results are generally quite favourable for the hypotheses implied by the game-theoretic model, thus suggesting that the approach is promising. In particular, diagnostics and various test procedures indicate that both the timber price equation and the conditional demand for timber equation outperform specifications implied by the conventional theory of the demand for factors of production.

The chapter is organized as follows. In Section 2 the model is presented, the equilibrium is defined and various comparative static properties are developed. Section 3 is devoted to estimation results and to various testing procedures for the annual data from the Finnish paper and pulp industry over the period 1960–92. Finally, there is a brief conclusion.[5]

2. THEORETICAL MODEL: A TWO-STAGE GAME APPROACH

The model to be developed in this section tries to capture some crucial features of the annual timber price negotiation practice in Finland. The prevailing system can be described as follows. The representatives of the forest industry and forest owners (Central Union of Agricultural Producers and Forest Owners (MTK)) started to make voluntary timber price recommendations during the 1960s. The first real timber price agreement was signed for the cutting year 1978–79. During the 1980s both parties supplemented the timber price agreement by a voluntary recommendation regarding the timber quantity to be sold. Since then the negotiation system has worked in this way. As the evidence of timber price negotiations is so obvious, it is worth examining seriously how this hypothesis works empirically and to test it against alternative hypotheses of the roundwood market. In this section we formulate a model for timber price determination in accordance with the notion that the forest owners' association determines the timber price, while firms in the forest industry decide upon the amount of timber used.[6]

Structure of the Model

The firms in the forest industry are assumed to produce the final product (for example, pulp) by using two inputs, namely capital (k) and roundwood (x). To keep the analysis as simple and as clear as possible we assume that the production function is of the Cobb–Douglas form, with constant returns to scale according to (1).

$$Q = f(k, x) = k^a x^{1-a}, 0 < a < 1 \qquad (1)$$

The firms face a downward-sloping demand curve given in Equation (2):

$$ZD(p) = Zp^{-\varepsilon} \qquad (2)$$

The demand curve is given in a separable form (see, for example, Nickell, 1978), where the parameter Z describes the position of the demand curve, that is, the exogenous demand components other than price. Moreover, it is isoelastic, with elasticity of demand being given by the parameter ε. The firms produce what is demanded so that $Q = D(p)Z$. This makes it possible to express the price as a function of the quantity supplied, $p = p(zQ)$, where $z = Z^{-1}$. With the functional forms (1) and (2) one obtains $p = (zk^a x^{1-a})^{-1/\varepsilon}$. As a special case we have the situation of perfect competition when the price of the final product is exogenously given from the viewpoint of an individual firm.

The profit maximization problem of the firms in the forest industry can be expressed in a general form as maximizing

$$\pi = p[zf(k, x)] f(k, x) - rk - qx, \tag{3}$$

with respect to x and k, where p is the price of final output, r the real interest rate and q the price of timber.

Forest owners supply timber to the market provided that timber price is high enough. We assume that they are represented by a forest owners' association. The forest owners' association chooses a timber price so that the product of timber times the real timber price over a given reservation price is maximized. A rise in the price of the final good is assumed to reduce the utility of the forest owners' association so that

$$U = \left[\frac{q}{p} - e(r)\right] x, \tag{4}$$

where U represents the target function of the forest owners' association and $e(r)$ is the reservation price of timber, which is assumed to depend negatively on the real interest rate r, that is, $e'(r) < 0$.[7] According to formulation (4) the forest owners' association is not willing to sell timber if the real timber price falls below the reservation price.

The next task is to solve the Nash equilibrium of the model in the standard way of backward induction, starting with the last stage of the game and utilizing this solution in solving the first stage.

Nash Equilibrium

In the second stage, the firms in the forest industry decide how much timber to use, given the optimal choice of k and q during the first stage. This amounts to maximizing (3) by choosing x so as to maximize their profits. At the interior solution firms maximize their profits by equating the marginal revenue of timber use to its factor price as in (5):

$$MR(p) f_x = q, \tag{5}$$

where $MR(p) = p + p'z$.

The second-order condition is given by Equation (6):

$$\pi_{xx} = MR(p)f_{xx} + MR'(p)f_x z < 0, \qquad (6)$$

where $MR'(p) = p' + p''z$. Non-increasing marginal revenue is a sufficient, but not necessary condition for this to hold.

Utilizing the specified functional forms (1) and (2), we explicitly solve for the optimal demand for timber in terms of exogenous variables.[8] Derived demand for timber is given in a qualitative form in Equation (7). A rise in the capital stock (other input), a fall in the exogenous component of demand $z = Z^{-1}$ (via the inverse demand $p = p(zQ)$) and a rise in the price of final product p all boost the demand for timber, whereas a higher timber price decreases it (see Appendix for the details).

$$x^* = x^*\left(\underset{+\ -\ -\ +}{k, q, z, p}\right) \qquad (7)$$

We now move on to the first stage of the game, in which the firms in the forest industry and the forest owners' association decide on the capital stock and timber price, respectively, taking the other player's decision variable as given. Using (7) as a constraint in these optimizations provides the requirement for the subgame perfection of the equilibrium.

The firms in the forest industry decide the optimal capital stock by choosing k so as to maximize profits (8), taking (7) as a constraint and the timber price q as given.

$$\underset{\{k\}}{\text{Max}} \ \pi = p[zf(k, x^*(k, q, p, z))]f(k, x^*(k, q, p, z)) - rk - qx^*(k, q, p, z). \qquad (8)$$

This gives, using (5) as the envelope condition, Equation (9), which has a similar interpretation as earlier: the marginal revenue of capital use must be equal to its factor price at $\pi_k = 0$.

$$MR(p)f_k = r. \qquad (9)$$

The second-order condition is given in

$$\pi_{kk} = MR(p)f_{kk} + MR'(p)zf_k < 0 \qquad (10)$$

and it can be shown to hold under the specified functional forms (1) and (2).

The first-order condition (9) gives the optimal capital stock for a given timber price and is thus *the reaction function of firms in the forest industry*. Using the specified functional forms (1) and (2), the first-order condition (9) can be solved explicitly for the capital stock.[9] The partial equilibrium capital stock depends positively on the price of the final output and on the amount of timber x^*, and negatively on the real interest rate as well as on the exogenous inverse component of demand z due to its effect on the price of final good (see note 8). Thus we can write the capital stock equation qualitatively as

$$k^* = k^*\left(\underset{+\ -\ -\ +}{p, r, z, x^*}\right) \tag{11}$$

The forest owners' association optimizes (4) subject to (7), taking the capital stock exogenously given. This leads to the following first-order condition:

$$U_q = \left[\frac{q}{p} - e(r)\right]x_q + \frac{x}{p} = 0,$$

which can be rewritten as

$$U_q = \frac{1}{p} - \frac{1}{\eta}\left[\frac{q}{p} - e(r)\right] = 0, \tag{12}$$

where the association is assumed to account for the endogeneity of the price of final good p, and $\eta = -x_q\, q/x$ is the price elasticity of timber demand. According to (12), the timber price is set so as to equate the marginal benefit from increasing timber price $((1/p) > 0)$ to the marginal cost due to a resulting fall in timber demand when q increases

$$\left(-\frac{\eta}{q}\left[\frac{q}{p} - e(r)\right] < 0\right).$$

The second-order condition is given in

$$U_{qq} = -\frac{(\eta - 1)}{pq}(1 - \psi) < 0 \tag{13}$$

where $\eta > 1$ and $\psi = (\eta - 1)/(\eta + \varepsilon - 1) < 1$ so that the second-order condition holds (see Appendix for further details).

Equation (12) gives the optimal timber price for a given capital stock and thus defines *the reaction function of the forest owners' association*. It can be written as

$$q^* = pe\left(\frac{\eta}{\eta-1}\right), \text{ where } e = e(r). \tag{14}$$

Thus the partial equilibrium timber price depends positively on the reservation and output prices and the mark-up of real timber price over the reservation price $(\eta/(\eta - 1))$. Here the negative demand shift and the real interest rate affect timber price negatively. Thus we can write qualitatively

$$q^* = q^*\left(\underset{+\ +\ -\ -}{e, p, z, r}\right) \tag{15}$$

where the negative demand shift affects via the price of final product p (that is, $p_z < 0$, see note 8).

The optimal choices of the firms in the forest industry and of the forest owners' association in Equations (9) and (12) respectively define the Nash equilibrium of the capital stock – timber price game. They define the reaction functions of the forest industry, H, and the forest owners' association, G, that is, they give the best choice of k or q, given the other's choice of q or k.

$$H(k, x, q; r, z, e) \equiv \pi_k = 0 \tag{16a}$$

$$G(k, x, q; r, z, e) \equiv U_q = 0 \tag{16b}$$

Due to the second-order conditions for the choice of capital stock and timber price, one obtains for the reaction functions that $H_k = \pi_{kk} < 0$ and $G_q = U_{qq} < 0$. To determine the slopes of the reaction functions, one has still to analyse the signs of the cross-derivatives $H_q = \pi_{kq}$ and $G_k = U_{qk}$. As $H_q < 0$ and $G_k < 0$, both the industry's and the forest owners' association's reaction function is downward-sloping in the (q, k) space.[10]

Equations (16a) and (16b) describe the static, one-shot nature of our Nash equilibrium. In order to make comparative statics, we have to postulate a dynamic adjustment and to check whether it is stable. Following the literature in the field, we imagine that firms and the forest owners' association adjust their capital stock and timber price in the direction of increasing profits and utility, respectively. This leads to a dynamic system for which the stability conditions are (i) that the second-order conditions for the maximization of the target functions for firms and the forest owners' association hold, that is, $\pi_{kk} < 0$ and $U_{qq} < 0$, and (ii) that the determinant of the matrix of the second-order derivatives must be positive, so that $\pi_{kk}U_{qq} - \pi_{kq}U_{qk} > 0$. As we have $\pi_{kq}U_{qk} > 0$, the stability of the Nash equilibrium presupposes that the reaction function H must be steeper than the reaction function G. Under specifications (1) and (2), this condition can be shown to hold at the interior solution. Intuitively, the determinant condition means that the own effects dominate the interaction effects (for further details of stability analysis in the oligopoly context, see Dixit, 1986). Optimal capital stock and timber price (k^*, q^*) is determined at the point where the reaction functions intersect in the (q, k) space in Figure 17.1, which describes a stable Nash equilibrium.

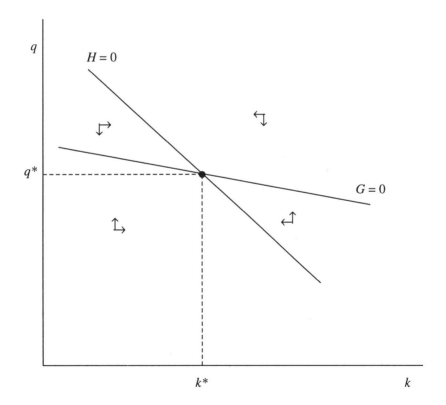

Figure 17.1   Stable Nash equilibrium

Comparative Statics of Capital Stock and Timber Price

The final step in the analysis of the model is the derivation of comparative static properties of the Nash equilibrium. This requires the determination of the dependence of H and G on the exogenous variables r, z and e. For the reaction function of the firms in the forest industry one obtains

$$H_r < 0, H_z < 0 \text{ and } H_e = 0. \tag{17}$$

The effects of exogenous variables on the forest owners' association's reaction function are, respectively,

$$G_r < 0, G_z < 0 \text{ and } G_e > 0. \tag{18}$$

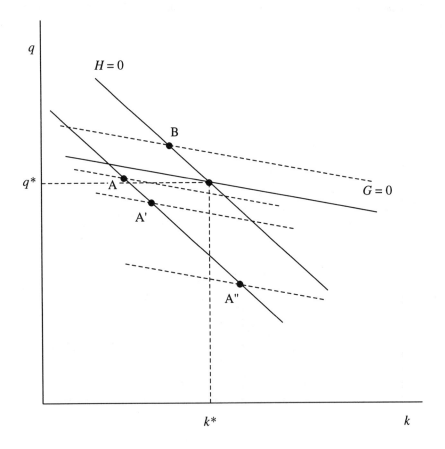

Figure 17.2 Comparative statics of the Nash equilibrium

The shifts of the reaction functions condensed in Equations (17) and (18) can be combined to offer a convenient graphical presentation of the comparative statics of the Nash equilibrium in Figure 17.2. The original Nash equilibrium is given by the intersection of the reaction functions (solid lines). The dashed lines represent the shifts of the reaction functions due to changes in exogenous variables. These changes produce various new equilibria, which are marked by capital letters from A, A' and A" to B. Table 17.1 shows the qualitative results of the comparative statics. The first column in Table 17.1 shows which exogenous variable is changing, the second indicates its effect on the reaction functions, the third identifies the new equilibrium point in Figure 17.2 and the fourth column gives the effects of exogenous variables on the capital stock, timber price and demand for timber, respectively.

Table 17.1 Comparative statics of the Nash equilibrium

Type of a shift in exogenous variable	Effect on reaction function	New equation point at	Effect on capital, timber price and demand for timber
$\Delta r > 0$	$H_r < 0, G_r < 0$	A	$\Delta k < 0, \Delta q > 0, \Delta x < 0$
		A'	$\Delta k < 0, \Delta q < 0, \Delta x = ?$
		A"	$\Delta k > 0, \Delta q < 0, \Delta x > 0$
$\Delta e > 0$	$H_e = 0, G_e > 0$	B	$\Delta k < 0, \Delta q > 0, \Delta x < 0$
$\Delta z > 0$	$H_z < 0, G_z < 0$	A	$\Delta k < 0, \Delta q > 0, \Delta x = ?$
		A'	$\Delta k < 0, \Delta q < 0, \Delta x = ?$
		A"	$\Delta k > 0, \Delta q < 0, \Delta x = ?$

According to the comparative statics, a rise in the real interest rate shifts both reaction functions to the left and we have three possible outcomes: both k and q decrease (A'), q increases and k decreases (A) or q decreases and k increases (A"). It is easy to show that the effect on the demand for timber is ambiguous (A'), negative (A) or positive (A"), respectively. For example, in the case A, a rise in the real interest rate increases timber price and reduces capital stock. For both these reasons demand for timber falls; and analogously for other cases (see Appendix for details). A rise in the reservation price of timber reduces capital stock and increases timber price. Via both channels the demand for timber decreases. The effect of a rise in the (inverse) demand shift parameter for final products has a negative effect on both reaction functions. Again we have three possible outcomes: both q and k decrease (A'), q increases and k decreases (A) or q decreases and k increases (A"). In all cases, however, the effect on the demand for timber remains ambiguous.

3. EMPIRICAL APPLICATION TO THE FINNISH PAPER AND PULP INDUSTRY

We now move on to the empirical part of the chapter where we test for various hypotheses suggested by our two-stage model. We start by postulating dynamics associated with the capital stock, timber price and timber demand equations. Then we specify the corresponding equilibrium equations and combine them with the dynamics to be estimated. Finally, the full information maximum likelihood (FIML) estimation results for the system of capital stock – timber price and the ordinary least squares (OLS) estimation results for timber demand are presented for the Finnish paper and pulp industry over the period 1960–92. In this context we test for the structure of decisions implied by the two-stage game, and we contrast our timber demand equation – conditional on timber prices and capital stock – with the determination of the quantity of timber suggested by the conventional theory of the demand for factors of production.

Dynamics and Specification of Equations

According to the time structure of the model, timber price q and capital stock k are determined simultaneously, and conditional on these, timber demand x is determined recursively. Hence, it is appropriate to discuss the dynamics of adjustment separately for timber price and capital stock on the one hand and for timber demand on the other.

For the adjustment process for timber price and capital stock, we follow a formulation now commonly used in the stability analysis of oligopoly equilibria (for details, see Dixit, 1986). According to this myopic rule, forest owners and firms in the paper and pulp industry increase the timber price and capital stock, respectively, when they perceive positive marginal utility and positive marginal profit from doing so. Using this standard oligopoly stability analysis and taking the linear approximation around the equilibrium ($\log k^*$, $\log q^*$), the following dynamic system is obtained:

$$D \log k = \lambda_{11}[\log(k_{-1}) - \log(k^*)] + \lambda_{12}[\log(q_{-1}) - \log(q^*)] \quad (19a)$$

$$D \log q = \lambda_{21}[\log(k_{-1}) - \log(k^*)] + \lambda_{22}[\log(q_{-1}) - \log(q^*)], \quad (19b)$$

where D is the difference operator and where we have used the log formulation for the Nash equilibrium. For the system (19a)–(19b) the stability conditions require that the eigenvalues of the expression

$$1 + \begin{bmatrix} \lambda_{11} & \lambda_{12} \\ \lambda_{21} & \lambda_{22} \end{bmatrix} = I + \Lambda \quad (20)$$

are inside the unit circle (here I is the unit matrix).

As for the determination of timber demand, we do not postulate any dynamics, but assume that it adjusts within a year to various shocks perturbing the equilibrium conditional timber demand. The theoretical framework in Section 2 suggests potentially relevant variables and their *a priori* signs in the determination of the equilibrium values for capital stock, timber prices and timber demand. Assuming the semi-log functional form we obtain the following equilibrium system of equations:

$$\log k^* = \alpha_1 + \alpha_2 \log\left[\frac{q^*}{p}\right] + \alpha_3 r + \alpha_4 \log Z \qquad (21a)$$
$${\scriptstyle (-)}\phantom{\log\left[\frac{q^*}{p}\right] + \alpha_3}{\scriptstyle (-)}{\scriptstyle (?)}$$

$$\log q^* = \beta_1 + \beta_2 \log p + \beta_3 \log k^* + \beta_4 r + \beta_5 \log Z \qquad (21b)$$
$${\scriptstyle (+)}{\scriptstyle (+)}{\scriptstyle (?)}{\scriptstyle (?)}$$

$$\log x^* = \gamma_1 + \gamma_2 \log\left[\frac{q^*}{p}\right] + \gamma_3 \log k^* + \gamma_4 \log Z \qquad (21c)$$
$${\scriptstyle (-)}\phantom{\log\left[\frac{q^*}{p}\right] + \gamma_3}{\scriptstyle (+)}{\scriptstyle (?)}$$

where the variables with asterisks refer to equilibrium values and the variables in parentheses refer to hypothesized signs. In what follows, we do not test for the restrictions implied by the specified functional forms (1) and (2) utilized in the derivation of comparative static results, so that the theoretical exercise should thus be seen here as suggesting qualitative hypotheses. Lack of appropriate data is the reason why Equation (21b) does not include the direct reservation price e of the forest owners' association.

According to Equation (21a (21b)), the firms' (the forest owners') actions depend on the forest owners' (the firms') reaction function. This kind of interdependence is problematic in the sense that if Equations (21a) and (21b) describe the simultaneous move game, then the capital stock and timber price equations cannot be identified in the dynamic system (21a)–(21b). In order to avoid this identification problem, the variables $\log(q^*)$ and $\log(k^*)$ in the dynamic system (19a)–(19b) are replaced by forecasts $\log(q^f)$ and $\log(k^f)$, which are made at time $t - 1$ for the Nash equilibrium prevailing at time t.[11] Instead, in the simultaneous equilibrium system of Equations (21a)–(21b) the actual values of q and k are used for q^* and k^*.

Equations are estimated for the Finnish paper and pulp industry using annual data over the period 1960–92. Data sources and construction of some variables are explained in Koskela and Ollikainen (1996). The sum of real sales volumes to Germany and the United Kingdom were used as a proxy for Z, describing the position of demand curve. We also experimented with some other proxies and the results were rather similar so that they are not reported here (but are available from the authors upon request). The real interest rate was measured by the difference between the nominal yield of government bonds and the inflation rate. The basic set of dynamic equations (19a)–(19b) jointly with the equilibrium equations (21a)–(21c) provide the dynamic equations to be estimated. For convenience these are expressed below in a semi-log form.

$$\log k = \alpha_1 + \alpha_2 \log(k_{-1}) + \alpha_3 \log(q/p) + \alpha_4 r + \alpha_5 [\log (q_{-1}) - \log (q^f)] + \alpha_6 \log Z + \varepsilon \quad (22a)$$

$$\log q = \beta_1 + \beta_2 \log(q_{-1}) + \beta_3 \log p + \beta_4 \log k + \beta_5 r + \beta_6 [\log(k_{-1}) - \log(k^f)] + \beta_7 \log Z + \omega \quad (22b)$$

$$\log x^* = \gamma_1 + \gamma_2 \log(q/p) + \gamma_3 \log kk + \gamma_4 \log Z + \nu \quad (22c)$$

where ε, ω and ν refer to the error terms of the equations. Note that q in the capital stock equation (4a) and k in the nominal timber price equation (4b) are endogenous, while q and k in the timber demand equation (9) are exogenous according to the hypotheses given in Section 2. After some experimentation we decided to substitute log kk – the capital stock adjusted by its utilization rate – for log k in (22c).

According to the time structure of the model, timber prices and capital stock are determined simultaneously, and timber demand is determined recursively, conditional on the timber price–capital stock game. This structure was tested by carrying out Hausman's exogeneity test for the system (22a)–(22b) on an equation-by-equation basis (for details, see, for example, Davidson and MacKinnon 1993, pp. 237–42). Contrary to our theoretical reasoning, we could not reject at the 1 per cent significance level the hypothesis that the capital stock is an exogenous variable in the demand for timber equation, but the hypothesis that timber price is an exogenous variable in the capital stock equation was rejected. Despite this slightly mixed evidence we proceeded to system estimation of the capital stock and timber price.[12]

The FIML estimation results of the system of Equations (22a) and (22b), together with some diagnostics, are presented in Table 17.2. The estimation results can be briefly summarized as follows.[13]

First we look at the stability of Nash equilibrium associated with the dynamic structure of the system (19a)–(19b). Because the system has been estimated in the level form, we have to check whether the eigenvalues of $I + \Lambda$ are inside the unit circle. The eigenvalues of $I + \Lambda$ from Table 17.2 are given after calculation in

$$\cong \frac{.69 \pm \sqrt{.35}}{2}, \tag{23}$$

which are clearly less than one in absolute value. Hence, the capital stock–timber price system is stable and the adjustment coefficients lie in conformity with the oligopoly stability requirements.

Table 17.2 FIML estimation results of the capital stock–timber price system

Variable	log k		log q	
Constant	3.86	(4.00)	−18.88	(−3.10)
$\log(k_{-1})$	0.59	(5.12)		
$\log(q/p)$	−0.13	(−4.55)		
r	0.30	(2.54)	−2.19	(−4.28)
$\log(q_{-1}) - \log(q^f)$	−0.11	(−1.95)		
log Z	0.17	(3.78)	−1.06	(−3.96)
$\log(q_{-1})$			0.10	(1.16)
log p			0.80	(6.55)
log k			2.18	(3.35)
$\log(\delta k_{-1}) - \log(I^f)$			−0.25	(−4.33)
Diagnostics for single equations				
χ^2_{nd}	1.33	(0.52)	0.86	(0.65)
F_{ar}	$F(2, 19) = 4.66$	(0.02)	$F(2, 19) = 0.21$	(0.73)
F_{arch}	$F(1, 19) = 0.15$	(0.70)	$F(1, 19) = 0.01$	(0.91)
F_{het}	$F(15, 5) = 0.34$	(0.95)	$F(15, 5) = 0.58$	(0.81)
Diagnostics for the whole system				
χ^{2v}_{nd} 3.27 (0.51)				
F^v_{ar} $F(8, 36) = 1.63$ (0.35)				

Notes: χ^2_{nd} refers to the Jarque–Bera normality test statistics, F_{ar} to the second-order autocorrelation test statistics, and F_{arch} and F_{het} describe the ARCH and WHITE heteroscedasticity test statistics, respectively. Finally χ^{2v}_{nd} is a test for normality for the whole system (see Doornik and Hansen, 1994) and F^v_{ar} is a test for the vector autocorrelation. The numbers in parentheses for parameter estimates are t-values and those for the diagnostics are the marginal significance levels (see Doornik and Hendry, 1991 for details).

Second, the diagnostic performance of the system of equations is good. The single-equation evaluation statistics for no heteroscedasticity (F_{arch} against first-order heteroscedasticity and F_{het}) and for no non-normality (χ^2_{nd}) show good performance. Instead there is some slight evidence for serial autocorrelation (F_{ar} against second-order autocorrelation) at the 5 per cent but not at the 1 per cent significance level in the case of the capital stock equation. But as for the system (vector) tests, neither normality nor lack of autocorrelation can be rejected at the standard significance levels (χ^{2v}_{nd}, F^v_{ar}).

Third, the parameter estimates are rather precise and of expected sign from the viewpoint of our theoretical reasoning. The capital stock equation adjusts sluggishly; the real timber price ($\log(q/p)$) affects it negatively and the variable describing the position of the demand curve ($\log Z$) positively. Moreover, a rise in the forecast made at time $t-1$ for the Nash equilibrium q^* prevailing at time t, which was calculated by using an AR forecast, reduces the capital stock, although the parameter estimate is small and statistically significant only at the 6 per cent level. Finally, the real interest rate has a positive coefficient estimate, which is significant at the 2 per cent level. This lies in conformity with the theoretical model; while the partial equilibrium effect of the real interest rate on capital stock is negative, the 'total' effect in the Nash equilibrium can be of any sign. As for the timber price equation, the timber price adjusts sluggishly, and is positively and significantly affected by the price of the final good. The investment plans which are included in the term $\log(\delta k_{-1}) - \log(I^f)$ will have a significantly positive effect on the timber price. This is natural; when firms plan to invest more, forest owners tend to increase timber price. The demand and capital stock variables are statistically significant at the 1 per cent level. The effect of the former is negative while that of the latter is positive. Both coefficient estimates lie in conformity with the hypothesis presented earlier.[14] Finally and importantly, the real interest rate affects the timber price negatively and statistically very significantly.

Testing for Alternative Specifications of the Demand for Timber

Next, we move on to look at the specification of the demand for timber which, according to our hypothesis, is determined recursively, conditional on the timber price–capital stock Nash equilibrium. Therefore we estimate specifications of timber demand by OLS and do not include them in the system to be handled by FIML. We contrast this specification (model A in what follows) with two alternative hypotheses. According to one hypothesis the demand for timber is affected by the relative prices of factors of production as well as by the output. This cost-minimization hypothesis is presented as specification B. According to another hypothesis the demand for timber is affected by its real price and the real interest rate as well as the variable describing the position of the demand curve in the output market. This imperfect competition hypothesis – according to which firms face a downward-sloping demand curve – is presented as specification C. Specifications B and C can be derived from the theory of the demand for factors of production, when firms in the paper and pulp industry face the excess supply of goods (model B) or the downward-sloping demand in the goods market (model C), respectively.

The OLS estimation results are presented in Table 17.3, where we have used the lagged real timber price in the model specifications in order to capture overlapping cutting periods. In what follows we start by discussing the properties of our proposed specification A. Estimation results can be briefly characterized as follows. First, the performance of the equation is relatively good; there are no signs of misspecifications in terms of the diagnostics of the error term. Normality, autocorrelation, heteroscedasticity and functional form test statistics indicate that the error term does not suffer from these diagnostic problems. Second, with the exception of the demand variable, which can be of any sign according to our theoretical model, the explanatory variables are significant and behave according to the hypothesis suggested by the theoretical model. The capital stock adjusted by its utilization rate has a positive sign, while the (lagged) real timber price has a negative effect on the demand for timber, and both coefficient estimates are statistically significant at the standard levels.

Table 17.3 OLS estimation results of alternative timber demand equations

Variable	Model A		Model B		Model C	
Constant	−1.13	(−4.72)	−4.33	(−1.78)	−1.63	(−1.68)
$[\log(q/p)_{-1}]/r$			−0.01	(−2.51)		
r					1.23	(1.57)
$\log(q/p)_{-1}$	−0.79	(−4.70)			−0.84	(−4.05)
$\log Q$			0.38	(2.74)		
$\log kk$	1.16	(4.34)				
$\log Z$	−0.21	(−1.68)			0.27	(3.06)
Diagnostics						
R^2	0.62		0.24		0.41	
χ^2_{nd}	0.83	(0.66)	2.57	(0.28)	1.53	(0.46)
DW	1.74		1.56		1.15	
F_{ar}	$F(2, 26) = 0.91$	(0.42)	$F(2, 27) = 0.63$	(0.54)	$F(2, 27) = 2.95$	(0.07)
F_{arch}	$F(1, 26) = 0.03$	(0.87)	$F(1, 27) = 0.52$	(0.48)	$F(1, 26) = 0.01$	(0.93)
F_{het}	$F(6, 21) = 0.90$	(0.52)	$F(5, 23) = 0.79$	(0.57)	$F(9, 18) = 2.43$	(0.05)
F_{reset}	$F(1, 27) = 2.29$	(0.14)	$F(1, 28) = 0.44$	(0.51)	$F(1, 27) = 11.07$	(0.00)

Notes: R^2 is the goodness-of-fit statistic, χ^2_{nd} is the normality test statistics, DW is the Durbin–Watson statistic for the first-order autocorrelation, F_{ar} is the test statistic for the second-order autocorrelation, F_{arch} and F_{het} are heteroscedasticity test statistics, and F_{reset} describes the test statistics for the functional form. Numbers in parentheses for the coefficient estimates are t-values, while those for the diagnostics are marginal significance levels.

We also made some further checks. First, we tested for the parameter constancy of model specification A by replacing a standard assumption that there is a single structural break in the sample by a more general one stating that the parameters of the model may change continuously over time.[15] The idea was to present the smooth transition regression model (STR) as an alternative to the parameter constancy model, in which the transition from 'one regime to another' was determined by the hth degree polynomial of the time trend. There is no economic theory available for choosing h, so that we used a statistical selection technique based on a short sequence of nested tests as in Granger and Teräsvirta (1993, chap. 7). The test statistics for values $h = 1, 2, 3$ can be called LM1, LM2 and LM3, respectively.[16] The following F-tests were obtained for the specification A: LM1: $F(4, 24) = 3.38$ (0.025); LM2: $F(8, 20) = 1.83$ (0.129) and LM3: $F(12, 16) = 2.09$ (0.085), where the numbers in parentheses are marginal significance levels. Thus, only the simplest LM1-test rejected the null hypothesis of parameters constancy at the 5 per cent, but not at the 1 per cent significance level. Hence, these analyses give some support to the notion that the conditional demand for timber displays parameter stability.

Second, we compared the conditional demand for timber with two alternative specifications B and C (Table 17.3). These are dominated by our proposed hypothesis in terms of the overall performance of the equations; the goodness of fit statistics and diagnostics of the error term show worse performance for B and C than for A. The goodness-of-fit is significantly worse for B. For the specification C, there are signs of heteroscedasticity and the functional form misspecification.[17]

4. CONCLUDING REMARKS

The purpose of the chapter has been to provide a framework which approaches price and quantity determination in the roundwood market from a slightly new perspective. In the spirit of the trade union literature, a model of timber price determination was formulated in which the forest owners' association determines timber prices, after which forest firms unilaterally decide upon timber used. The game was played in two stages. First, the forest owners' association and the firms in the forest industry decide on timber prices and capital stock, respectively. In the second stage, the firms determine timber demand conditional on the timber price–capital stock game, so that the equilibrium concept was a subgame–perfect Nash equilibrium. The model was applied to annual data from the Finnish paper and pulp industry over the period 1960–92. Estimation and testing results concerning the price and quantity determination of timber as well as capital stock determination turned out to be generally favourable for our hypotheses.

More specifically, the FIML estimation results of the capital stock–timber price system can be briefly summarized as follows. Their diagnostic performance is good, and the parameter estimates are rather precise and of the expected sign. As for the capital stock equation, the demand variable has a significantly positive effect, while the real timber price has a negative and the real interest rate a positive effect. This lies in conformity with the theoretical model: while the partial equilibrium effect of the real interest rate on capital stock is negative, the 'total' effect in the Nash equilibrium can be of any sign. Timber price is positively and significantly affected by the price of the final good, by the investment plans of the firms in the paper and pulp industry, and by the capital stock. Estimation results for the equation of the demand for timber suggests that the capital stock adjusted by its utilization rate has a positive and significant effect, while the (lagged) real timber price has a negative and significant effect on the demand for timber. Finally, the conditional demand for timber specification, as proposed by our game-theoretic model, dominates some common alternative specifications both in terms of diagnostics and various test procedures.

NOTES

1. The term 'roundwood' refers to unmanufactured timber which is used as an input in the production process of forest industry.
2. See for example, Koskela (1989) and Ollikainen (1993) for applications of two-period harvesting models to various issues of forest taxation.
3. See for example, Hetemäki and Kuuluvainen (1992) in which the demand for timber is positively affected by the costs of labour so that, according to their estimation results, timber and labour are substitutes in the production of final output.
4. There is little research about the functioning of the roundwood market under imperfect competition. Notable exceptions are the studies by Johansson and Löfgren. They modelled roundwood markets as a monopsonistic market, where the local industry gets a spatial monopsony due to transportation costs differences, and they also analysed the price determination subject to bargaining between forest owners and forest industry, when the forest owners' association maximizes utility of harvest revenue over the competitive timber price level and the forest industry maximizes its profits (see Johansson and Löfgren, 1985, chap. 8). They, however, neither allowed for the capital stock determination nor evaluated the bargaining hypothesis empirically.
5. Some of the technical material as well as the description of the data have been presented in Koskela and Ollikainen (1996) and are available from the authors upon request.
6. Here we draw on the literature on trade unions. See Anderson and Devereux (1988) and Holm, Honkapohja and Koskela (1994) in particular. One may criticize the assumption that the forest owners' union sets the timber price. A more realistic assumption might be that the timber price is determined in a bargain between the forest owners' union and firms. This 'right-to-manage' approach – according to which timber prices are negotiated, while the amount of timber is unilaterally determined by the firms – does, however, yield qualitative results similar to those achieved when the forest owners' union unilaterally determines timber price.
7. It is easy to show by using an intertemporal model of harvesting behaviour that the willingness to sell timber – the reservation price – depends negatively on the real interest rate. An intuitive explanation goes as follows. A rise in the real interest rate increases the opportunity cost of holding money in timber. Thereby forest owners become willing to sell timber at a lower price, that is, the reservation price falls. (A proof is available from the authors upon request.) Reservation price could also depend on the price in the international roundwood markets to which the forest owners supply timber if they don't get a higher price in the domestic markets. Alternatively, e could reflect forest owners' trade-off between harvest income and valuation

8. Using (1) and (2) makes it possible to write the demand for timber as $x^* = \alpha k p^\eta q^{-\eta}$, where $\alpha \equiv (1-a)^\eta (1-1/\varepsilon)^\eta > 0$ and $\eta = -(qx_q)/(x) = 1/a > 1$ denotes the price elasticity of timber demand. Substituting this for x in $p = (z k^a x^{1-a})^{-1/\varepsilon}$ and rearranging yields $p = c(zk)^{-\psi/(\eta-1)} q^\psi$, where $c = \alpha^{-\psi/\eta}$ and $\psi = (\eta-1)/(\eta + \varepsilon - 1)$, so that $0 < \psi < 1$. One should thus notice that changes in z, k and q also change the price of the final good, which must be taken into account when solving for the comparative statics of z, k and q.
9. This yields the following expression for k: $k^* = nx^* p^\beta r^{-\beta}$, where $n = ((1-1/\varepsilon)a)^\beta$ and $\beta = (1-a)^{-1}$.
10. It can be shown that

$$H_q = \pi_{kq} = \frac{r}{q}\left(\frac{(\eta-1)(1-\varepsilon)}{\eta+\varepsilon-1}\right) < 0 \text{ and}$$

$$G_k = U_{qk} = -\frac{(1-\eta)}{pk}\left(\frac{1}{\eta+\varepsilon-1}\right) < 0.$$

11. The forecasts for $\log(q^f)$ were obtained by modelling timber prices as an AR process. The capital stock forecasts ($\log(k^f)$) were obtained as follows. According to the capital depreciation formula, capital stock forecast is a function of investment forecast I^f such that $k^f - k_{-1} = I^f - \delta k_{-1}$, where δ is the capital depreciation coefficient. Firms' investment plans made in the previous spring were used as a proxy for I^f. For an evaluation of δ, see Koskela and Ollikainen (1996).
12. A complete set of results from the exogeneity tests is available from the authors upon request.
13. The system of equations was also estimated by the two-stage least squares (2SLS) method. Results turned out to be very similar to those of FIML. Hence they are not reported here, but are available from the authors upon request.
14. In note 8 we presented an explicit form for the equation of the price of the final good. In logarithmic form it is given by $\log(p) = const + \beta_0(\log k - \log z) + \beta_1 \log q + u$, where u is an error term. OLS estimation results supported this specification. The coefficient restriction for ($\log k - \log z$) could not be rejected; coefficient estimates were of expected sign ($0 > \beta_0 > -1$ and $0 < \beta_1 < 1$) and highly significant. This gives further support for the approach. (A complete set of results is available from the authors upon request.)
15. See Lin and Teräsvirta (1994) for how this can be done.
16. If $h = 1$, there is only one break and the change is monotonic. If $h = 2$, the change can be symmetric around the break point, while for $h = 3$, one can have several breaks and the change need not be monotonic. See Lin and Teräsvirta (1994) for details.
17. Finally, we made some further comparisons by doing two types of non-nested tests, namely the J-test suggested by Davidson and MacKinnon (1981) and the encompassing test suggested by Mizon and Richard (1986). According to these tests, our proposed specification A performed best. A complete set of results is available from the authors upon request.

REFERENCES

Amacher, G.S. and R.J. Brazee (1997), 'Designing Forest Taxes with Budget Constraints', *Journal of Environmental Economics and Management*, **32**, 323–40.

Anderson, S. and M. Devereux (1988), 'Trade Unions and the Choice of the Capital Stock', *Scandinavian Journal of Economics*, **90,** 27–44.

Davidson, R. and J.G. MacKinnon (1981), 'Several Tests for Model Specification in the Presence of Alternative Hypotheses', *Econometrica*, **49,** 781–93.

Davidson, R. and J.G. MacKinnon (1993), *Estimation and Inference in Econometrics*, New York: Oxford University Press.

Dixit, A. (1986), 'Comparative Statics for Oligopoly', *International Economic Review*, **27,** 107–22.

Doornik, J.A. and H. Hansen (1994), 'A practical test for univariate and multivariate normality', Discussion Paper, Nuffield College.

Doornik, J.A. and D.F. Hendry (1991), *PcFiml 80: Interactive Econometric Modelling of Dynamic Systems*, London: International Thomson Publishing.

Granger, C.W.J. and T. Teräsvirta (1993), *Modelling Nonlinear Economic Relationships*, Oxford: Oxford University Press.

Hetemäki, L. and J. Kuuluvainen (1992), 'Incorporating Data and Theory in Roundwood Supply and Demand Estimation', *American Journal of Agricultural Economics*, **74,** 1010–18.

Holm, P., S. Honkapohja and E. Koskela (1994), 'A Monopoly Union Model of Wage Determination with Capital and Taxes: An Empirical Application to the Finnish Manufacturing', *European Economic Review*, **38,** 285–303.

Johansson, P.-O. and K.-G. Löfgren (1985), *The Economics of Forestry & Natural Resources*, Oxford: Basil Blackwell.

Koskela, E. (1989), 'Forest Taxation and Timber Supply under Price Uncertainty and Perfect Capital Markets', *Forest Science*, **35,** 137–59.

Koskela, E. and M. Ollikainen (1996), 'A Game-Theoretic Model of Timber Prices with Capital Stock: An Empirical Application to the Finnish Forest Industry', mimeo.

Koskela, E. and M. Ollikainen (1997), 'Optimal Design of Forest Taxation with Multiple-Use Characteristics of Forest Stands', *Environmental and Resource Economics*, **10,** 41–62.

Lin, C-F.J. and T. Teräsvirta (1994), 'Testing the Constancy of Regression Parameters Against Continuous Structural Change', *Journal of Econometrics*, **62,** 211–28.

Mizon, G.E. and J.-F. Richard (1986), 'The Encompassing Principle and Its Application to Testing Nonnested Hypotheses', *Econometrica*, **54,** 657–77.

Nickell, S.J. (1978), *The Investment Decisions of Firms*, Cambridge: Cambridge University Press.

Ollikainen, M. (1993), 'A Mean-Variance Approach to Short-Term Timber Selling and Forest Taxation Under Multiple Sources of Uncertainty', *Canadian Journal of Forest Research*, **23,** 573–81.

APPENDIX: NASH EQUILIBRIUM AND COMPARATIVE STATICS

This appendix presents all the results given in the chapter with Cobb–Douglas production function and separable, isoelastic demand.

The Conditional Demand for Timber: (the Second Stage of the Game)

$$\underset{\{x\}}{\text{Max}}\ \pi = \left(zk^a x^{1-a}\right)^{-1/\varepsilon}\left(k^a x^{1-a}\right) - rk - qx, \quad (A1)$$

where $p = (zk^a x^{1-a})^{-1/\varepsilon}$ is the separable, isoelastic demand.

The first-order condition defines the conditional demand for timber

$$\pi_x = \frac{1-a}{x}\left(k^a x^{1-a}\right)p\left(1-\frac{1}{\varepsilon}\right) - q = 0 \Rightarrow x^* = \alpha k p^\eta q^{-\eta}, \quad (A2)$$

where

$$\eta \equiv -\frac{qx_q}{x} = \frac{1}{a} > 1$$

is the price elasticity of timber demand and

$$\alpha \equiv (1-a)^\eta \left(1-\frac{1}{\varepsilon}\right)^\eta > 0, \varepsilon > 1.$$

Nash Equilibrium of Capital Stock and Timber Price: (the First Stage of the Game)

In the first stage of the game firms decide on k and the forest owners' association on q, given the conditional demand for timber $x^* = \alpha k p^\eta q^{-\eta}$.

$$\underset{\{k\}}{\text{Max}}\ \pi = \left(zk^a x(k,q,p,z)^{1-a}\right)^{-\frac{1}{\varepsilon}} k^a x(k,q,p,z)^{1-a} - rk - qx \quad (A3a)$$

$$\underset{\{q\}}{\text{Max}}\ U = \left(\frac{q}{p} - e(r)\right)x \quad (A3b)$$

The first-order conditions define optimal k and q as follows:

$$\pi_k = \frac{a}{k}\left(k^a x^{1-a}\right)p\left(1-\frac{1}{\varepsilon}\right) - r = 0 \Rightarrow k^* = nxp^\beta r^{-\beta} \quad (A4a)$$

$$U_q = \frac{1}{p} - \frac{\eta}{p}\left(\frac{q}{p} - e(r)\right) = 0 \Rightarrow q^* = pe(r)\left(\frac{\eta}{\eta-1}\right) \quad \text{(A4b)}$$

where

$$n = \left(\left(1-\frac{1}{\epsilon}\right)a\right)^\beta \text{ and } \beta \equiv (1-a)^{-1}.$$

The second-order conditions are

$$\pi_{kk} = -\frac{r}{k}\left[-\left(1-\frac{1}{\eta}\right) - \frac{1}{\eta+\epsilon-1}\right] < 0 \quad \text{(A5a)}$$

$$U_{qq} = -\frac{(\eta-1)}{pq}(1-\psi) < 0. \quad \text{(A5b)}$$

Moreover, we have

$$\pi_{kq} = \frac{r}{q}\left(\frac{(\eta-1)(1-\epsilon)}{\eta+\epsilon-1}\right) < 0 \text{ and } U_{qk} = \frac{(1-\eta)}{pk}\frac{1}{\eta+\epsilon-1} < 0.$$

The stability of Nash equilibrium requires that

$$\Delta = \begin{vmatrix} \pi_{kk} & \pi_{kq} \\ U_{qk} & U_{qq} \end{vmatrix} > 0, \quad \text{(A6)}$$

which holds as

$$\Delta = \frac{(\eta-1)r}{pqk(\eta+\epsilon-1)}[\epsilon\eta + (\eta-1)(\epsilon+\eta-1)] > 0.$$

Comparative statics of the Nash equilibrium can be calculated by Cramer's rule from

$$(\Delta)\begin{bmatrix} k_\theta^* \\ q_\theta^* \end{bmatrix} = \begin{bmatrix} -\pi_{k\theta} \\ -U_{q\theta} \end{bmatrix}, \qquad (A7)$$

where θ refers to exogenous variables.

Total Comparative Statics of the Demand for Timber

The change in the demand for timber due to changes in exogenous variables is obtained as follows:

$$\frac{dx}{dr} = x_q q_r + x_k k_r < 0 \qquad (A8a)$$

$$\frac{dx}{de} = x_q q_e + x_k k_e < 0 \qquad (A8b)$$

$$\frac{dx}{dz} = x_z + x_q q_z + x_k k_z = ? \qquad (A8c)$$

Index

abatement benefit 72
abatement capital 60, 346
  strategic trade and transboundary pollution 315–16, 318, 319, 321, 323, 325, 331
abatement constraint 11
abatement costs 11, 69–70
  global warming 279
  international dynamic pollution control 241
  nuclear power games 99, 102, 104, 111, 119
  renegotiation-proof equilibria 137, 153
  see also marginal
abatement levels 73, 187, 188, 189
abatement policy 166
Abreu, D. 46, 59
acid rain 3, 6, 13, 237, 239
  Europe 4, 241
  game 2, 102, 240
  Great Britain and Ireland 14
  interconnected games 165
  nuclear power games 98
acid rain and international environmental aid: Finland, Russia and Estonia 84–96
  data and model 85–92
  optimal cooperation 92–5
actions, non-binding and binding 212, 213
adjustment reactions 150–51
Agenda XXI 182
agriculture 347
air pollution 347
  see also transboundary pollution
Amann, M. 89
Ames, R. 75
Andersen, M.K. 72
Andersen, P. 21–2, 65–83
Anderson, D. 165

Aronsson 392
Askins, R. 219
Aspremont, C.A. d' 33, 186, 195
assimilation functions 13, 239
asymmetric emissions, enforced 359
asymmetric equilibrium 352–3, 356, 378–82
asymmetric information 3
asymmetry 9, 264
  environmental policy, firm location and green consumerism 345, 360, 372
  issue linkage 182, 183, 184, 186, 194, 197
  see also conflicts
Axelrod, R. 18, 117

Bac, M. 60
backward induction 243
Baik, K.H. 219
Banks, J. 224, 225–6, 227
bargaining 98
  see also Nash
bargaining game *see* renegotiation-proof equilibria
bargaining power 99, 108, 109, 110, 111
Barrett, S. 7, 8, 10, 12, 17, 18, 19, 20, 33, 46, 98, 103, 142, 313, 314
  on commitment and fairness 67–8, 68–72, 77, 78–80, 81
  on issue linkage 182, 183, 184, 186, 190, 193, 198
Bartsch, E. 8
Basar, T. 61, 238, 248, 252
base case 9–11
base saturation 14
battle of the sexes game 80, 215
Bayes rule 223
Bayesian equilibrium 24, 223, 224, 228, 229, 230
Bayesian updated belief 229

Becker, R.A. 60
Bellmans' dynamic programming 245
Bellman's principle of optimality 243–4, 248
benefits 71, 73, 312
　abatement 72
　curves, marginal 113
　function 75, 115, 249
　social marginal 319
　strategic trade and transboundary pollution 318
　via risk abatement 102–4
Benhabib, J. 61
Bernheim, B.D. 142, 153, 179
Bertrand competition 313, 349, 352
Bertrand-Nash equilibrium 350, 351, 352, 353, 378–9
bi-matrix games 242–5
Bierman, H.S. 1
bilateral externalities 52–5
bilateral *laissez-faire* 365, 366, 368–9, 372, 373, 389
bilateral regulation 358, 364, 368, 371, 373, 389
Binmore, K. 1
Blackhurst, R. 165
Bloch, F. 199
Boes, D.C. 210
Botteon, M. 7, 23, 33, 40, 41, 181–200, 202–3
burden-sharing rules 23, 183, 184, 192–8
business as usual 10, 11, 12, 258, 276
buy one – get one free 150
buy one – get two free 140, 150
buy two – get one free 140, 150

Camerer, C. 227
Canada 24, 179, 184, 190, 191
capital 16
　accumulation 14, 16
　human 14
　mobility 288
　stock *see* roundwood market
　see also abatement
carbon dioxide 1, 13, 15, 16, 137
　agreement 11–12
　commitment and fairness 66
　emissions 80, 181
　emissions reduction 185–92

joint bargaining 18
tax 16
Carraro, C. 7, 23, 33, 37, 40, 41, 142, 181–200, 202–3, 343
　on commitment and fairness 67, 68, 72, 75, 80
carrot and stick 46, 56, 59, 60
Cason, T.N. 212, 214
Central and Eastern Europe 98, 99, 100, 101, 109, 112, 184, 190, 191, 192, 196
certainty 257, 259, 263–8, 269, 272, 277
　equivalence 259, 260, 270
Cesar, H.S.J. 9, 13, 15, 16, 17, 67, 182, 183, 198, 204, 239
Chander, P. 8, 34, 37, 40, 182, 184, 186, 190
Chander-Tulkens rule 9
cheap talk 23, 205, 207, 208, 210–15, 216
Chernobyl 98, 105, 106, 115
Chew, M.S. 199
chicken game 80
China 72, 184, 190, 192, 196
chi-squared variate 210, 211
chlorofluorocarbons 66, 181
Cho, I.-K. 224, 225
clash 222, 223, 224, 225, 227
clean production technology 341–2, 343
climate change 12, 15, 255
　see also global warming; greenhouse gases
climate change conference (Kyoto) 216
Climate Change Convention 7, 8, 18, 20, 181, 182
closed-loop memory equilibria 252
closed-loop Nash equilibrium dynamic resolution of inefficiency 60
coalition-proof equilibrium strategies 153
coalitions 4–9, 41, 185, 186, 196, 198, 280
　optimal 194
　stable 7, 194, 196, 279
　see also grand; small stable
Cobb-Douglas form 394
Cobb-Douglas production function 411
Colorado River Treaty 179
Columbia River Treaty 179

commitment 22, 72–5
  migration 298, 300, 304, 307
  perfect 303–6
  strategic trade and transboundary pollution 310, 321, 325
common knowledge 349
competition 3
  Bertrand 313, 349, 352
  between firms 320–21
  between firms and government 321–3, 332–6
  Cournot 313
  imperfect 313, 407
  Nash 336–9, 340
  perfect 324
  price 349, 350
  strategic trade and transboundary pollution 315, 324
concession exchange 206
conflicts with asymmetric information 219–35
  behaviour 227–33
    efficiency 223
    equilibria 229–33
    experimental design 227
    strategies 228–9
  theory 220–26
    analytical framework 221–3
    equilibria and refinements 223–6
conflicts and interconnected games: institutional design 204–17
  cheap talk 210–15
  example 205–7
  experimental design 207–8
  parallel versus joint institutions 208–10
confront 221, 223, 224, 225, 226, 227, 229
Conrad, K. 310, 314
Constantatos, C. 342
constrained social optimum *see* Pareto-dominance
consumer surplus 325
consumers 344–6
contract curve 108, 127
control 45
  variables 13
Cooper, R. 215

cooperation 4–9, 16, 20, 21, 22, 23, 24, 25
  bilateral 84
  commitment and fairness 69, 75, 79
  conflicts and interconnected games 205, 215
  dynamic resolution of inefficiency 46
  efficient 22
  firms 320–21
  free-riding 17, 19
  global emission abatement 82–3
  global warming 255–7, 266–9, 270–83 *passim*
  governments 320–21, 332–6
  implicit 290, 292–3, 307
  interconnected games 166, 167, 179
  international dynamic pollution control 237, 238, 241, 251, 252
  issue linkage 182, 187, 188, 193, 194, 195, 196, 198
  migration 294, 295, 300
  nuclear power games 98–9, 114, 118, 119, 130–31, 132–4
  optimal 92–5
  possible gains 9–11
  renegotiation-proof equilibria 136, 142
  in research and development and carbon dioxide emission reduction 185–92
  strategic trade and transboundary pollution 313, 315, 324, 330, 331, 332, 335, 336
  transboundary air pollution 93, 94, 95
  trilateral environmental 85
  see also cooperation versus free-riding; full cooperation
cooperation versus free-riding 30–43
  differences and similarities 36–41
    characteristic functions 38–40
    coalitions and coalition formation 36–7
    free-riding and threats 37–8
    transfers and side payments 40–41
  economic-ecological model 30–32
  'grand stable coalitions' thesis 34–6
  'small stable coalitions' thesis 33–4
Copernicus 287
Cordella, T. 343
core meltdown 101

costs
    air pollution 88
    -benefit analysis 11
    commitment and fairness 71
    -effectiveness analysis 11–12
    function 11, 75, 193, 249, 301
    joint 92, 93
    marginal 96, 262
    -minimization hypothesis 406
    production 347
    relocation 342, 360, 361, 372
    set-up 347–8, 359, 360, 362, 367
    -sharing rule 8, 12
    social 312
    sunk 341, 367
    trade 373
    transaction 20, 118, 205
    see also abatement; damage
Cournot competition 313
Cournot oligopoly 196
Cournot-Nash equilibrium 238, 315, 336
covered market equilibrium 376
credibility 18, 45, 118, 142
Cremer, H. 342
Crocker, T. 219
Cronshaw, M.B. 21, 45–64
Czech Republic 109

Daly, H. 219
damage
    environmental policy, firm location
        and green consumerism 341, 360
    global warming 256, 257, 258, 268,
        269, 273–4, 278, 281
    international dynamic pollution
        control 240, 242
    issue linkage 191
    linear marginal 11
    strategic trade and transboundary
        pollution 313, 314, 318, 319,
        320, 322
    see also damage cost
damage cost 12
    certainty 263–8
    conditions 121–2
    environmental policy, firm location
        and green consumerism 346,
        347, 361, 362
    global warming 258–61, 265–8, 270,
        277, 280

issue linkage 189, 190
marginal 93, 139, 271
nuclear power games 102–4, 106, 107
renegotiation-proof equilibria 137
strategic trade and transboundary
    pollution 312, 317
transboundary air pollution 91, 92
D'Arge, R.C. 95
Dasgupta, P. 65–6, 239
Davidson, R. 404
Davis, D.D. 214
Davis, M.H.A. 247
Deacon, R. 220
deforestation 288
demand function 190, 345
Denmark 66
depositions 86, 312
desertification 288
deviation set 224–5, 226, 227
DICE model 280
differential/difference game 13, 15–16,
    24, 25, 249, 252
    dynamic resolution of inefficiency
        60
    international dynamic pollution
        control 241
    linear-quadratic 242
    migration 295
    strategic trade and transboundary
        pollution 314
    theory 238, 242–8
differentiated green product 342
direct-sum game 19, 168, 169, 170
discount rate 206, 281, 297
distance function 345, 346
divine and universally divine equilibria
    224
Dixit, A. 219, 221, 399, 402
Dockner, E.J. 16, 61, 238, 252
Donsimoni, M.P. 186
Doornik, J.A. 405
Driffill, J. 143
duopoly, international 314–18
dynamic externality 300, 301, 303
dynamic games 3, 12–16, 25, 60, 256
dynamic programming 243, 244, 245
dynamic resolution of inefficiency 45–64
    bilateral externalities 52–5
    patience and worst punishment 55–60
    unidirectional externality 47–52

Eastern Europe *see* Central and Eastern Europe
Ecchia, G. 199, 342, 343, 344, 377, 379
eco-taxes 67
Economides, N.S. 186
efficiency 233
effluent taxes 22, 135
El-Gamal, M.A. 231
emissions 86
  abatement 75, 82–3
  aggregate 148, 150, 151, 152
  asymmetric 359
  bilateral externality 52, 53
  dynamic resolution of inefficiency 47
  global aggregate 65–6
  nuclear power games 100, 101, 115
  -output ratio 239, 240
  permits 52, 136, 147, 162–3
    renegotiation-proof equilibria 140, 148, 149, 150, 151, 152, 153
  reduction quotas 22, 135
  reductions *see* renegotiation-proof equilibria
  standards 67, 348
    environmental policy, firm location and green consumerism 341, 371, 373
    strategic trade and transboundary pollution 311, 314, 318–22, 324–5, 328, 331, 335–7, 339
  stock 263
  targets 67
  taxes 153, 311, 322
end-of-pipe technology 14
Endres, A. 17, 22, 135–56, 158–64
enforcement deficit 20–21
envelope theorem 54
environmental
  agreements 195
    see also international
  asset 219
  conflicts 24
  dumping 310
  games 23, 205–6
  organization 204
  policy 25, 299–300
    migration 294, 298, 301, 303, 307
    public and private 3
  strategic trade and transboundary pollution 310, 312–13, 315, 317–18, 321–2, 324–5, 332
  unilateral 342
  see also environmental policy, firm location and green consumerism
refugee 288
research and development 311
standards 349, 372
environmental policy, firm location and green consumerism 341–74, 376–91
  firm subgame 350–63
    equilibrium technology and location structure 354–63
    price equilibria 350–54
  model 343–50
    consumers 344–6
    firms 346–8
    game structure 349–50
    regions 348–9
Epstein, L. 261
equilibrium 229–33
  asymmetric price 352–3, 378–82
  Bayesian 24, 223, 224, 228, 229, 230
  Bertrand-Nash 350, 351, 352, 353, 378–9
  closed-loop memory 252
  coalition-proof strategies 153
  divine and universally divine 224
  green price 351–2
  intuitive 224, 225
  multiple pooling 224, 225, 226, 227, 229, 230, 233
  price 352–3, 378–82
  quality 26
  strongly symmetric 56–9
  unique partially separating 224, 225, 226, 227, 229, 233
  see also equilibrium technology and location structure; feedback; subgame-perfect
equilibrium technology and location structure 354–63
  asymmetric equilibria 356
  bilateral regulation 358
  covered market equilibrium 376
  enforced asymmetric equilibrium 359
  enforced non-green equilibrium 360

green equilibrium 354–6
laissez-faire 354
'large fraction of green consumers' case 389–90, 391
non-covered market equilibrium 376–7
non-existence of symmetric equilibrium prices 377–8
non-green equilibrium 353–4, 357, 358, 360
policy stage 363–72
  non-relocation case 367–72
  relocation case 363–7
'small fraction of green consumers' case 387–9, 390
symmetric inter-firm externalities 382–4
unidirectional inter-firm externalities 384–7
unilateral regulation 358–9
unique asymmetric price equilibrium 378–82
Escapa, M. 8–9
Estonia 11, 22
  see also acid rain
Esty, D.C. 204, 205, 311
Europe 99, 105, 196, 241
  see also Central and Eastern Europe; European Union
European Bank for Reconstruction and Development 112
European Monitoring and Evaluation Programme 22
European Union 12, 109, 118, 184, 190, 191
  carbon dioxide emissions 181
  global warming 72
  issue linkage 195
  migration 289
evolutionary models 61
expropriation 292
externality 359, 360
  bilateral 52–5
  dynamic 300, 301, 303
  inter-firm 382–7
  unidirectional 47–52, 377

face-to-face communication 215
fairness 21–2, 75–80
Fankhauser, S. 10

Farrell, J. 46, 142, 144
feedback 248
feedback equilibrium 320, 323
feedback investment strategies 317
feedback Nash equilibrium 14–15, 247, 249, 255–6, 264–7, 269, 315
feedback solution 321
feedback Stackelberg equilibrium 314, 321, 329–30, 333–4, 337–8
feedback strategies 61, 315, 324, 325, 340
Feenstra, T. 25, 310–40
Fernandez, L. 1
Fershtman, C. 60
fight 222, 223, 224, 225, 227
Finland 11, 13, 22, 392, 393, 394, 408
  Finnish Integrated Acidification Assessment project 89
  Finnish-Russian sulphur dioxide agreement 11
  Finnish-Soviet Commission for Environmental Protection 85
  paper and pulp industry 402–8
  Technical Research Centre 89
  see also acid rain and international environmental aid
Finus, M. 17, 22, 135–56, 158–64
firms 346–8
  international trade and transboundary pollution 310, 311, 313, 315, 318, 320–25, 329, 332–6
  issue linkage 186–7, 190, 192
  location *see* environmental policy, firm location and green consumerism
  subgame 350
first-order conditions 112–13, 127
first-order derivative 126
first-period emissions/variable 262, 263, 278, 296, 297, 298, 299, 301
fishery conflicts 24
flow pollution 296, 300, 312
Folk theorem 15–16
  bilateral externality 55
  conflicts and interconnected games 206
  dynamic resolution of inefficiency 45, 46, 47
  free-riding 17

international dynamic pollution
    control 252
  renegotiation-proof equilibria 152,
    153
  unidirectional externality 48, 51
Folmer, H. 1–27, 67, 96, 165–80, 182,
    183, 198, 204, 205, 215
former Soviet Union 11, 13, 22, 184,
    190, 191, 192
  nuclear power games 98, 99, 100,
    101, 105, 112
  see also acid rain
Forster, B.A. 239
Fox, A.B. 205
free-riding 4, 6, 12, 15, 17–20, 22, 37–8
  coalition 21, 38
  commitment and fairness 66–7, 69,
    70, 75
  individual 37, 40
  interconnected games 166
  issue linkage 182, 183, 184, 192, 195,
    197, 198
  migration 306
  nuclear power games 116, 117, 118,
    119
  reduction 13
  renegotiation-proof equilibria 139,
    142, 148
  strategic trade and transboundary
    pollution 313
  see also cooperation versus
    free-riding
Friedman, J. 45, 169, 170–71, 173
Fudenberg, D. 2, 46, 142, 252
full cooperation 4, 9, 10, 11, 12, 14, 22
  commitment and fairness 70, 75, 78,
    80, 81
  free-riding 18
  nuclear power games 99, 107–12,
    115, 116, 117, 118, 126–7
  renegotiation-proof equilibria 138,
    147, 148, 149, 152
  risk abatement 128–9
  strategic trade and transboundary
    pollution 319–20, 327–32, 329
  transboundary air pollution 92
full information maximum likelihood
  estimation 402, 404, 405, 406, 408

G7 summit 112

G-24 database 112
Gabszewicz, J.J. 33, 186
gains, sharing of 4–9
Gardner, R. 79, 214
General Agreement on Tariffs and Trade
  18, 182, 204
Germany 98, 109, 112, 403
Gibbons, R. 1
Global 2200 model 281
global warming 1, 3, 24, 25, 255–85
  background analysis 257–68
    many countries, certainty about
      damage costs 263–8
    single decision maker with
      uncertainty and learning
      257–63
  commitment and fairness 66
  empirical applications 280–83
  European Union 72
  interconnected games 165, 166
  international dynamic pollution
    control 240
  international environmental
    agreements 278–80
  issue linkage 192
  learning and no learning 273–8
  many countries and learning 268–80
    learning 270–72
    no learning 270
    non-cooperation and cooperation 272
  nuclear power games 98
governments 348
  competition with firms 320–23
  full cooperation 320
  international duopoly 314, 315, 318
  international trade and transboundary
    pollution 310, 324, 329, 331,
    335, 336
  issue linkage 186–7, 188, 189, 190
  policy distortion 312–13, 314
grand coalition 7, 21, 197, 279
grand stable coalition 32, 34–41 passim
Granger, C.W.J. 408
Graybill, F.A. 210
green consumerism 342, 365
  see also environmental policy
green equilibrium 354–6
green price equilibrium 351–2
greenhouse gases 1, 13, 22, 24, 118, 119,
  255

international dynamic pollution
control 237, 239
renegotiation-proof equilibria 148
Grilo, I. 343
Gutierrez, M.J. 8–9
Guttman, J.M. 19

Haavio, M. 25, 287–308
Hackett, S. 214, 215
Hamilton-Jacobi-Bellman
equations/conditions 247, 249, 252,
329, 330, 333, 334, 337, 340
Hamiltonians 246, 248, 249, 251, 254
Hanley, N. 1–27
Hansen, H. 405
Harsanyi, J. 9, 99
Haurie, A. 61
Hausman's exogeneity test 404
Heal, G. 182
heavy metals 85
Heister, J. 9, 18, 110
Hendry, D.F. 405
Hessian 54
Hetemäki, L. 392
Ho, Y.C. 242, 244
Hoel, M. 8, 15, 16, 17, 19, 107, 116, 182,
186, 238, 248
commitment and fairness 67, 68, 72,
81
homogeneous good 342
House of Commons Environment
Committee 78
household mobility 290
imperfect 306, 307
imperfect with no commitment
300–303
imperfect with perfect commitment
303–6
perfect 306
Howe, C. 169
Hultkrantz 392
human capital accumulation 14
Hurley, T. 24, 219–35

imperfect competition 313, 407
implicit cooperation 290, 293, 307
import restrictions 205, 206
incentives 67
incomplete information game 136
India 72, 184, 190, 192, 196

indifference curves 49–50
inefficiency *see* dynamic resolution
information 20–21, 261, 263, 280
asymmetric 3, 24
complete 349
exchange parameter 188
global warming 256–7, 268, 269, 272,
281
imperfect 221
incomplete 136, 221
international dynamic pollution
control 244
perfect 258, 263, 276, 279, 280, 282
private 60
structure 245
value 278, 282, 283
see also conflicts
instability 182, 193, 195, 279
institutional constraints 148
institutional design *see* conflicts and
interconnected games
institutional inertia 205
inter-firm externalities 382–7
inter-firm pollution 347, 372
interconnected games 19, 165–80
characteristic function form 171–8
cooperation 23
non-cooperation 168–71
see also conflicts
International Atomic Energy Agency
100, 112
International Convention on Nuclear
Safety 112
international desertification convention
18
international dynamic pollution control
237–54
differential game theory 242–8
game 248–52
international environmental agencies 81,
143, 280, 283–4
commitment and fairness 77, 79, 80
global warming 255, 257, 268
international environmental agreements
71, 72, 73–4, 278–80
commitment and fairness 67, 68, 69
renegotiation-proof equilibria 135,
136
international environmental aid 95
see also acid rain

international environmental policies 21–2
international environmental problems 2–3
International Labour Organization 204
international trade 25, 165
  see also strategic
intuitive equilibrium 224, 225
Ireland 14
irreversibility 25, 255, 256
issue linkage 18, 23, 81, 181–200, 202–3
  economic model of cooperation in research and development and carbon dioxide emission reduction 185–92
  under different burden-sharing rules 192–8

Jacquemin, A. 195
Japan 98, 184, 190, 191, 192, 196
Jensen's inequality 261
Jeppesen, T. 21–2, 65–83
Johansson, M. 89
Johansson, P.-O. 392
joint commission 84–5
joint costs 92, 93
joint implementation 12, 20
joint institutions 206, 207, 208–10, 213, 214, 215–16

Kaitala, V. 11, 13, 15, 16, 22, 60, 61, 84–96, 238, 248–9
Kalai-Smorodinsky solution 9
Kandori, M. 52
Kangas, L. 86–7
Katsoulacos, Y. 314
Keeler, E. 240
Kennedy, P.W. 310, 311, 314, 321, 325
Konoplyanik, A. 112
Kort, P.M. 311
Koskela, E. 26, 392–414
Kreps, D. 224, 225
Kroeze-Gil, J. 19, 23, 67, 165–80
Kroll, S. 23, 204–17
Krueger, A. 205
Kuhl, H. 9
Kuhn, M. 26, 341–74, 376–91
Kuuluvainen, J. 392
Kverndokk, S. 10, 11–12, 148

labour mobility 289
Lagrange multiplier 53
laissez-faire 354, 357, 358, 361, 372
  bilateral 365, 366, 368–9, 372, 373, 389
learning 255, 256, 257–63, 268, 269, 276, 277, 278
  with cooperative equilibrium 271–2, 273–4
  empirical applications 281, 282, 283
  international environmental agreements 279
  non-cooperative equilibrium 274–5
  with open-loop Nash equilibrium 270–71
legislation 19
Leitmann, G. 61
linear feedback Nash equilibrium 248, 250, 251, 252
linear marginal damage 11
linkage 18, 19, 166–7, 168, 179, 205
  see also issue-linkage
location 25, 26, 343, 348, 349, 372, 384
Lochard, J. 104
Löfgren, K.-G. 392
Luce, D. 2
Luenberger, D.G. 56–9
Lutz, E. 219

McKelvey, R.D. 231
MacKinnon, J.G. 404
McMillan, J. 46
Madagascar forest 220
Maddison, D. 268, 278, 281, 282, 283
Mäler, K.-G. 2, 4, 6, 10, 14, 46, 68, 98, 102, 166, 239, 242, 312
  and transboundary pollution 85, 88, 89–91, 95
Manne, A. 280, 281
MapleV-3 115
marginal abatement cost 90, 91, 93, 110
  issue linkage 191, 192
  nuclear power games 113, 115
  renegotiation-proof equilibria 139, 140, 141, 149, 151
marginal benefit curves 113
marginal cost 96, 262
marginal damage cost 93, 139, 271
marginal utility 297

Mariotti, M. 199, 342, 343, 344, 377, 379
Markov Nash equilibrium 61
Markov-perfect strategies 61
Markusen, J. 310, 341, 343, 365, 371
Martin, W.E. 16, 60
Marwell, G. 75
Maskin, E. 46, 142, 144, 252
Mason, C. 23, 204–17
matching mechanism 19
maximax payoffs computation 164
Mendelsohn, R. 281
MERGE model 281
methane 1
Mexico 179, 206
Mißfeldt, F.K. 1–27, 98–134
Michaelis, P. 239
migration 25, 287–308
   implicit cooperation 292–3
   model 293–306
      basic assumptions 295–8
      first stage: environmental policy 299–300
      imperfect household moblilty with no commitment 300–303
      imperfect household moblilty with perfect commitment 303–6
      perfect household mobility 306
      second stage: migration 298–9
   tragedy of the commons 291–2
minimax 55, 60, 206
   payoff 143, 144, 163–4, 171
minimum game 174
Mino, K. 247–8, 252
monetary transfers 48–52
Montreal Protocol 7, 12, 18, 47, 67, 181, 182, 204
Mood, A.M. 210
Moraga-González, J.L. 342
morality 77
Moreno, D. 153
Morey, E.R. 310, 341, 343, 365, 371
mortality rates 191, 192, 287
motion equation 13
motivation 20
Motta, M. 341, 342, 343
multiple pooling equilibrium 224, 225, 226, 227, 229, 230, 233
Musgrave, P. 184, 190–92
Musu, I. 6

mutual issue linkage 18
Myers, N. 219

Na, S. 278–80
Nash 21, 105–7
   competition 336–9, 340
   conflicts and interconnected games 210
   contest 221
   cooperation versus free-riding 35, 38, 41
   dynamic resolution of inefficiency 46
   inefficient static 51
   nuclear power games 115
   renegotiation-proof equilibria 144
   reversion 21
   see also Nash bargaining; Nash equilibrium
Nash bargaining 8–9, 23, 72
   issue linkage 183–4, 192–8, 202–3
   nuclear power games 99, 109, 110, 111
Nash equilibrium 6, 10, 11, 16, 19, 22, 23, 26
   bilateral externality 55
   commitment and fairness 75, 81
   conflicts and interconnected games 209, 211
   cooperation versus free-riding 39
   dynamic resolution of inefficiency 45
   environmental policy, firm location and green consumerism 354, 376, 377, 380, 381, 385, 386
   global warming 277
   globally optimal solution 137–8
   interconnected games 166, 170, 171
   international dynamic pollution control 241, 242–3, 244, 245
   issue linkage 186
   nuclear power games 99, 108, 110, 113, 116–19, 123–5, 130–34
   Partial Agreement 35, 37, 38, 39
   renegotiation-proof equilibria 136, 139, 142, 148, 153
   risk abatement 128–9
   roundwood market and capital stock determination 395–404 *passim*, 406, 409, 411–14
   static 46, 47, 53, 56, 59

strategic trade and transboundary pollution 315, 332, 333
sub-game perfect 15
transboundary air pollution 91, 95
unidirectional externality 49
see also closed-loop; Cournot-Nash; feedback; linear feedback; non-linear feedback; open-loop
Nechaev, V. 112
Newbery, D. 95
Nickell, S.J. 394
nitrogen 85
   dioxide 78
   oxide 240
Nitzan, S. 60
no learning 258, 260–63, 268–9, 270, 273
   empirical applications 281, 282
   international environmental agreements 279, 280
   non-cooperative equilibrium 274–8
noise 237
non-cooperation 4, 12, 15, 25, 26
   commitment and fairness 67, 69, 70, 74, 78, 79
   conflicts and interconnected games 204
   environmental policy, firm location and green consumerism 341, 349, 372
   free-riding 17, 18, 19
   global emission abatement 83
   global warming 255–6, 264, 267–9, 272, 274–8, 280–83
   interconnected games 166, 168–71, 179
   international dynamic pollution control 237–8
   issue linkage 183, 186, 187, 192
   nuclear power games 116
   renegotiation-proof equilibria 136, 138, 142
   transboundary air pollution 95
   see also Nash; Stackelberg
non-covered market equilibrium 376–7
non-governmental organizations 220
non-green equilibrium 353–4, 357, 360
non-green regime 358
non-linear feedback Nash equilibrium 16, 252

non-linear Markov-perfect strategies 61
Nordhaus, W. 148, 280–81
Nordlund, G. 86–7
North America 192, 196
   see also Canada; United States
North American Free Trading Area 206, 311
North underdog 225–6
North-South conflict 220
Norway 20
'not in my backyard' 371
nuclear accidents 3, 22
Nuclear Energy Agency 112
nuclear policy 165
nuclear power games 98–134
   abatement cost function 104
   damage function: benefit via risk abatement 102–4
   damage function conditions 121–2
   first-order conditions under different solution 127
   full cooperation 107–12, 126–7
   general solution for values of PE and PW along contract curve 127
   non-cooperation: Nash and Stackelberg 105–7
   nuclear risk PE and PW in Nash equilibrium 123–5
   reaction function 122, 123
   risk abatement under different solution concepts 112–14
   second-order condition for non-cooperation 123
   simulation 114–18, 126, 128–34
   Stackelberg, derivation of 125–6
Nuclear Safety Account 112
Nuclear Safety Assistance Coordination 112
nuclear testing 77
null hypothesis 210, 211, 212

objective function 240, 241, 242, 313
Olewiler, N. 310, 341, 343, 365, 371
oligopoly 196, 324
Ollikainen, M. 26, 392–414
Olsder, G.-J. 61, 238, 248, 252
open-loop 248
   equilibrium 321, 323
   investment strategies 317

Nash equilibrium 14–15, 264–5, 270–71
  dynamic resolution of inefficiency 60
  global warming 255, 256, 267, 269, 281
  international dynamic pollution control 246, 247, 248, 249, 250, 251, 254
  strategic trade and transboundary pollution 315
  Stackelberg equilibrium 315, 319, 320, 322, 330–32, 335–6, 338–9
  strategies 61, 324, 340
optimal coalitions 194
optimal taxes 322
optimality see Bellman's
ordinary least squares regression 402, 406, 407
Organization for Economic Cooperation and Development 9, 18, 112, 281
Ostrom, E. 79, 214
overlapping generations models 61
ozone layer depletion 3, 66, 67

Padrón-Fumero, N. 342
Pages, P. 104
Palfrey, T.R. 214, 231
parallel frame 206
parallel institutions 207, 208–10, 211, 212–13, 215–16
Pareto 61
Pareto-dominance 6
Pareto-efficiency 10, 12
  bilateral externalities 53–5
  conflicts and interconnected games 209, 210, 211, 213, 215
  dynamic resolution of inefficiency 46, 60
  free-riding 19
  nuclear power games 109
  unidirectional externality 48, 50, 52
Pareto-frontier 16, 54, 55
Pareto-improvement 19, 252
Pareto-inefficiency 366, 368, 369, 371, 372
Pareto-inferiority 119, 241
Pareto-optimality 6, 7, 8, 9, 14, 15, 16, 22
  migration 292
  nuclear power games 99
  transboundary air pollution 95

Pareto-superiority 50, 244
patience 55–60
Patrick, R.H. 16, 60
payoffs
  commitment and fairness 76–7, 78
  conflict with asymmetric information 221, 222, 223, 224, 225, 229
  conflicts and interconnected games 204, 205, 206, 207, 209, 216
  environmental policy, firm location and green consumerism 351, 353, 354, 359, 362, 365, 366, 368, 381, 387
  global warming 261, 279
  individually rational 143–4
  interconnected games 169, 170, 172–3, 175–6, 178
  international dynamic pollution control 238
  issue linkage 184, 186, 190, 192, 195, 196
  maximax 164
  migration 293, 306, 307
  minimax 143, 144, 163–4, 171
  non-cooperative 185
  nuclear power games 117
  rational 146
  renegotiation-proof equilibria 142, 145, 147, 148
  see also safety
PE and PW values along contract curve 127
Pearce, D. 46
Peck, S. 280
Peleg, B. 153
permits see emissions; tradable
Petersmann, E.-U. 205
Pethig, R. 20–21
Petrakis, E. 8
Pigou, A.C. 310
Pigouvian level 318, 319, 320, 321, 323
Pigouvian policy 324
Pigouvian tax 50
Plott, C. 231
Pohjola, M. 11, 13, 16, 22, 60, 61, 85, 238, 248–9
Poland 95
Polemarchakis, H.M. 186
policy
  distortion 312–13, 314

game 350
see also environmental
political constraints 148
see also governments
polluter pays principle 9, 50
pollution 2, 13, 16
   abatement 11, 46
   accumulation 239
   aggregate 342
   conflicts and interconnected games 206
   dynamic resolution of inefficiency 45, 60
   efficiency 47, 56
   emissions 205
   flow 296, 300, 312
   game 206
   inter-firm 347, 372
   migration 288, 289
   permits 66
   reduction measures 14
   river and marine 3
   stock 238, 296, 300, 312
   strategic overpollution 294, 307
   see also international dynamic pollution control; transboundary pollution
Pontryagin's minimum (maximum) principle 245, 246
population growth 14
Porter, D. 227
preservation value 221, 223
price 26, 343, 348
   competition 349, 350
   equilibrium, asymmetric 352–3, 378–82
principal-agent theory 3, 20
prisoner's dilemma 19, 46, 167, 312
   commitment and fairness 66, 67, 68, 76, 80
   international dynamic pollution control 237, 241, 251, 252
   nuclear power games 117, 118
probabilistic safety assessment 101
product differentiation 26, 342, 343, 351, 357
production cost 347
production function 394
production technology 344
   see also clean

profitability 77, 182–3, 185, 190, 198
property rights 289, 292
Ptolemy 287
punishment 45, 46, 55–60, 142, 145, 146, 204

quality 349
quotas 22, 135, 136, 138–9, 147, 148–53 *passim*, 161

Rabin, M. 21, 68, 75–7, 79, 80–81
'race to the bottom' 341, 342, 366, 372, 373
radioactive fallout 103, 105
Radner, R. 61
Ragland, S. 8, 9, 17, 19, 23, 96
   conflicts and interconnected games 204, 205, 215
   interconnected games 166, 168, 170–71
   issue linkage 182, 183, 198
Raiffa, H. 2
random end-game procedure 207
Rasmussen, E. 9
rationality 6
Rauscher, M. 310, 341, 365, 371
Rawlsian decision 293
Ray, D. 142
reaction function 75
   condition from slope of 123
   derivation 122
   environmental policy, firm location and green consumerism 381, 386
   global warming 265
   international dynamic pollution control 241, 246
   issue linkage 190, 199
   nuclear power games 105, 106, 107, 125, 126
   roundwood market and capital stock determination 397, 398, 399, 400, 401, 403
recycling 14
regulation, bilateral 358, 364, 368, 371, 373, 389
regulation, unilateral 358–9, 369–70, 371, 372, 373
relocation cost 342, 360, 361, 372
renegotiation 56

renegotiation-proof equilibria in
    bargaining game over global
    emission reductions 135–56,
    158–64
  maximax payoffs computation 164
  minimax payoff computation 163–4
  negotiation of emission reductions
    137–41
    globally optimal solution and Nash
      equilibrium 137–8
    quota scheme 138–9
    tax scheme 139–40
    transferable discharge permit
      scheme 140–41
  permit scheme 162–3
  policy instruments evaluation 148–53
  quota schemes 161
  stability analysis of emission
    equilibria 141–8
    checking 147–8
    conditions 144–7
    payoff space, individually rational
      143–4
    preliminaries 141–3
  tax scheme 162
renegotiation-proof strategies 15
renegotiation-proofness 18, 23, 46
rent-seeking 205
repeated games 13, 15
research and development 16, 142,
  183–92 *passim*, 194, 195, 196, 198
reservation price 344, 346, 357, 377
resource conflicts 24
Rhodes, T. 219
Riccati differential equations 246, 247,
  248
Richels, R. 280, 281
Rio conference 18, 204
Rio summit 216
risk 229
  aversion 230, 261, 277
  ranking 109
  see also risk abatement
risk abatement 102–4, 111
  nuclear power games 115, 116
  under different solution concepts
    112–14
  under Nash, Stackelberg and full
    cooperation 128–9
Rosenthal, H. 214

roundwood market and capital stock
    determination 392–414
  capital stock 396, 397, 399, 401–9
  Central Union of Agricultural
    Producers and Forest Owners
    394
  empirical application to Finnish paper
    and pulp industry 402–8
    alternative specifications, testing
      for and demand for timber
      406–8
    equations, dynamics and
      specification of 402–6
  firms 393
  forest owners' association 393, 395,
    396, 397, 398, 400, 408, 412
  Nash equilibrium and comparative
    statics 411–14
  profit maximization 393
  quantity determination 392, 393
  timber demand 394, 401–4, 406–9,
    412, 414
  timber price 26, 392–6, 398–9, 401–9,
    412–14
  two-stage game approach 394–401
    comparative statics of capital stock
      and timber price 400–401
    model structure 394–5
    Nash equilibrium 395–9
Rundshagen, B. 148, 154

safety
  equipment 99, 100
  function 108, 116
  optimization 99
  payoff 99, 101, 105, 110, 116, 119,
    121, 125
  variable 99, 100, 101
Samuelson, P.A. 4
Samuelson rule 292
sanctions 18
Sartzetakis, E.S. 342
Schelling, T. 2
Schlager, E. 214, 215
Schneider, K. 8, 17, 19
Schultz, C. 143
Scott, A.D. 95
scuffle 222, 223, 224, 225, 226, 227, 230
second-period variables 296, 297, 298,
  299, 303

self-enforcing agreements 182
Selten, R. 142, 244
sensitivity analysis 94, 95
set-up cost 347–8, 359, 360, 362, 367
Sethi, R. 61, 79
Shapley value 8, 9, 23
   issue linkage 183, 184, 192–8 *passim*, 202
shifting cultivators 288
Shin, H.S. 199, 278–80
Shogren, J.F. 23, 24, 204–17, 219–35
side payments 9, 11, 16, 23, 40–41
   free-riding 17, 18
   interconnected games 166, 167
   nuclear power games 108, 110, 111–12, 116, 118, 119
   transboundary air pollution 94, 95, 96
simulation 114–18, 126, 128–34
single-agent problem 60
Siniscalco, D. 7, 142
   commitment and fairness 67, 72, 75, 80
   cooperation versus free-riding 33, 37, 40, 41
   issue linkage 182, 183, 184, 186, 190, 193, 198
Slovak Republic 98, 109
small stable coalition 32, 33–4, 36, 37, 38, 39, 40, 41
smooth transition regression model 408
Sobel, J. 224, 225–6
social dumping 343
social marginal benefits 319
social norms 19–20
soil erosion 288
Somanathan, E. 61, 79
South America 12
sovereignty 220
Spain 24
Spence, M. 240
spillovers 98, 99, 105, 106, 110, 116, 117, 118, 119, 142
   issue linkage 187, 188, 195
   research and development 194
   valuation 104
stability 136
   active 41
   analysis *see* renegotiation-proof equilibria
   global warming 280

issue linkage 182, 183, 185, 186, 193, 195, 198, 199
   passive 41
   tests 153
stable coalitions 7, 194, 196, 279
Stackelberg 22, 105–7
   contest 221, 222
   equilibrium 319
     see also feedback; open-loop
   game 74
   leader 73, 314, 319
   nuclear power games 113, 115, 116, 118, 119, 125–6, 130–31
   risk abatement 128–9
   solution 99
   strategic trade and transboundary pollution 328
stage game 169, 170
Stähler, F. 103
standards
   environmental 349, 372
   unilateral 365
   see also emission
Starr, A.W. 242, 244
static games 3, 22, 68, 106, 132–4
Stein, A. 166
Stein, O. 18
stochastic optimal growth model with climate change (DICE model) 280
stock pollution 238, 296, 300, 312
strategic international trade and transboundary pollution 310–40
   competition between firms and government 320–23, 332–6
   full cooperation 319–20, 327–32
   international duopoly 314–18
   Nash competition 336–9
   no policy case 340
   policy distortion 312–14
   transboundary pollution 312
strategic overpollution 294, 307
strategies 228–9
   strictly dominated 117
strong North underdog 226
strongly symmetric equilibrium 56–9
sub-Saharan Africa 288
subgame-perfect equilibrium 349, 350, 354, 356, 357, 359, 364, 365, 381, 383

subgame-perfect Nash equilibrium 393, 408
subsidies 341
sulphur 85, 86, 87
   abatement 90, 92, 95
   damage cost 94
   deposition 91
   dioxide 13, 78, 84, 119
   emissions 84, 85, 93, 95
   oxide 240
   transportation model 87–8
sunk costs 341, 367
supranational institution, absence of 66
Sweden 95, 392, 393
symmetric equilibrium prices, non-existence of 377–8
symmetric inter-firm externalities 382–4
symmetry 8, 9
   environmental policy, firm location and green consumerism 348, 358
   global warming 264, 265, 266, 273, 276
   issue linkage 184, 186, 193–4
   nuclear power games 99

Tähtinen, M. 89
Tahvonen, O. 11, 13, 60, 85, 238, 248–9
taunt 221, 222, 223, 224, 226, 227, 229
taxes 16, 45, 136, 139–40, 162
   carbon dioxide 16, 66
   eco-taxes 67
   effluent 22, 135
   emission 153, 311, 322
   environmental 66
   environmental policy, firm location and green consumerism 341, 365, 371
   international 9, 16
   optimal 322
   Pigouvian 50
   renegotiation-proof equilibria 136, 147, 148, 149–50, 152
   strategic trade and transboundary pollution 314, 318, 320–21, 324–5, 329, 332–3, 335, 340
   unidirectional externality 52
   see also emission
technology 26, 343, 348, 350, 372, 384
   cooperation 182, 187, 188, 189, 196
   end-of-pipe 14

leakage parameter 188
transfers 9
tensor games 19, 168, 169–70, 171
Teräsvirta, T. 408
Thaler, R.H. 75
Thirty Per Cent Club 78
Thisse, J.-F. 341, 342, 343
threat 37–8
   -point 117
   see also Nash equilibrium strategy 142
Three-Mile Island accident 101
three-stage game 22
Tiesberg, T. 280
timber industry *see* roundwood market
time consistency *see* cost-sharing
Tirole, J. 2, 310
tit-for-tat strategy 18, 117, 238
Tolwinski, B. 16, 60, 61
Topa, G. 343
tradable emission permits 9, 12, 16, 22, 45, 135
trade 179, 182
   barriers 341
   costs 373
   games 23, 205–6
   migration 288
   sanctions 142
   see also strategic
trade-offs 237
tragedy of the commons 66, 79, 215, 291–2
   migration 289, 290, 294, 295, 301, 303
transaction costs 20, 118, 205
transboundary externalities 238
transboundary pollution 3, 4, 6, 8, 10, 12, 20, 21, 24
   cooperation versus free-riding 30, 41
   Finland, Russia and Estonia 22
   free-riding 18, 19
   inter-firm 362
   international dynamic pollution control 238
   migration 287, 288, 296, 303, 304
   nuclear power games 98, 100, 101
   see also acid rain; strategic international trade
transfer function 31
transfer payments 94, 96, 136

transferable discharge permit scheme 140–41
transfers 40–41
transportation model 92
transversality condition 248
trigger strategies 15, 16, 17–18, 170–71
tropical rainforests 24
Tsutsui, S. 247–8, 252
Tulkens, H. 7, 8, 21, 30–43, 85, 182, 184, 186, 190
Tuovinen, J.-P. 86–7
two-period game 307
two-period model 295
two-player fishery game 61

Ulph, A. 24–5, 255–85, 310, 311, 314, 325
Ulph, D. 256–7, 261, 264, 268, 269, 276, 277, 282, 311, 314, 343
uncertainty 24–5, 199, 255, 256
   cooperative equilibrium 268
   empirical applications 280, 281
   global warming 269, 283
   and learning 257–63
   non-cooperative and cooperative outcomes 272
   non-cooperative equilibrium 277
unidirectional externality 47–52, 377
   inter-firm 384–7
   with monetary transfers 48–52
   without monetary transfers 48
unilateral action 19
unilateral environmental policies 342
unilateral regulation 358–9, 369–70, 371, 372, 373
unilateral standard 365
unique partially separating equilibrium 224, 225, 226, 227, 229, 233
United Kingdom 14, 166–7, 403
   Thirty Per Cent Club 78
United Nations Conference on the Environment and Development 181
United Nations Environmental Programme 288
United States 20, 72, 166–7, 184, 190, 191, 206
   Agency for International Development 220
   Colorado River Treaty 179
   Columbia River Treaty 179
   migration 289
   power companies 12

value functions 249–50, 252, 254
Van der Ploeg, F. 15, 60, 238, 240, 248, 249, 251, 314
van Long, N. 16, 61, 238, 252
van Mouche, P.H.M. 8, 9, 17, 19, 23, 96
   conflicts and interconnected games 204, 205, 215
   interconnected games 166, 168, 170–71
   issue linkage 182, 183, 198
Varian, H. 108
vertical differentiation 350, 352
victim pays principle 9, 23, 166
Victor, D.G. 19
voting game 195, 197, 198

Walker, J. 79, 214, 215
Walley, J. 165
Walter, I. 95
weak North 223–4, 227
   underdog 224–5
welfare
   environmental policy, firm location and green consumerism 349, 350, 356, 363, 365, 366, 371, 372, 384
   global warming 263, 265–8, 273–9 *passim*, 281
   international dynamic pollution control 237–8, 240, 241
   issue linkage 185, 186, 189, 190
   migration 288, 293, 294, 295, 298, 303, 306
   renegotiation-proof equilibria 143, 151–2
   strategic trade and transboundary pollution 313–14, 317, 319
Welsch, H. 149
Western Meteorological Centre of the European Monitoring and Evaluation Programme 86
Whalley, J. 17, 18
Wheeler, D. 98
Whinston, M.D. 153, 179

willingness to pay 26, 31, 166
   environmental policy, firm location
      and green consumerism 344,
      361, 363, 365, 370, 371, 372
Wilson, P. 219
Wooders, J. 153
World Association of Nuclear Operators 112
World Intellectual Property Organization 204
World Trade Organization 204

Worldwatch Institute 288

Xepapadeas, A. 8, 15, 16, 314

Yi, S. 199

Zaccour, G. 18
Zeckhauser, R. 240
Zeeuw, A.J. de 13, 14, 15, 24, 60, 67, 182, 183, 198, 237–54, 314
Zeuthen 9, 99